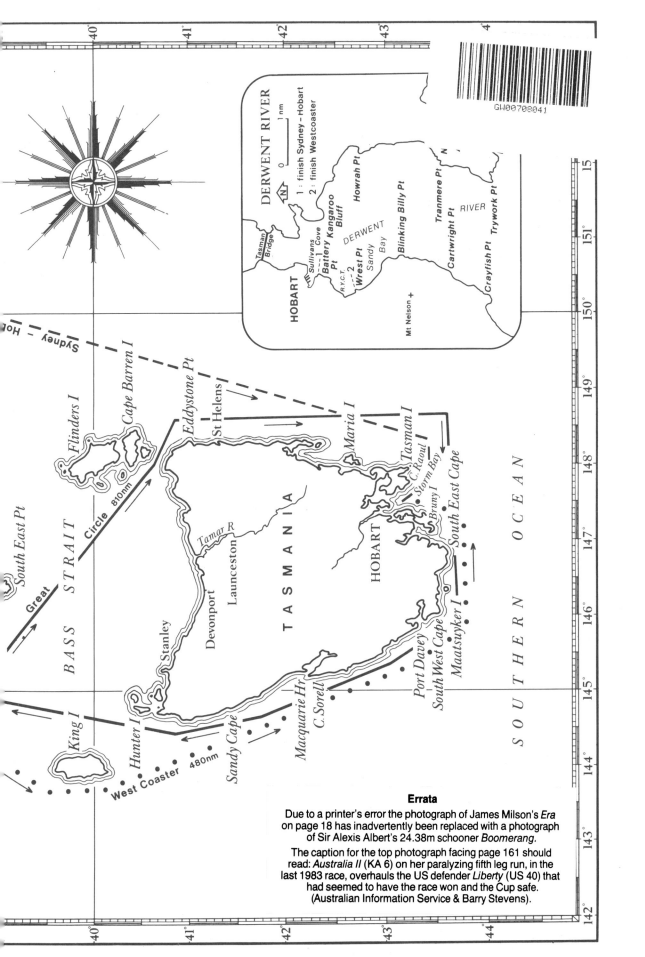

DERWENT RIVER

0 ___ 1 nm

1 : finish Sydney – Hobart
2 : finish Westcoaster

HOBART

Tasman Bridge

Sullivans Cove
R.Y.C.T.
Battery Kangaroo Bluff
Wrest Pt
Sandy Bay

DERWENT

Howrah Pt
Blinking Billy Pt

Tranmere Pt
Cartwright Pt
RIVER
Crayfish Pt
Trywork Pt

Mt Nelson +

GW00708041

Errata

Due to a printer's error the photograph of James Milson's *Era*
on page 18 has inadvertently been replaced with a photograph
of Sir Alexis Albert's 24.38m schooner *Boomerang*.

The caption for the top photograph facing page 161 should
read: *Australia II* (KA 6) on her paralyzing fifth leg run, in the
last 1983 race, overhauls the US defender *Liberty* (US 40) that
had seemed to have the race won and the Cup safe.
(Australian Information Service & Barry Stevens).

YACHTING IN AUSTRALIA

YACHTING IN AUSTRALIA

From Colonial Skiffs to America's Cup Defence

LOU d'ALPUGET

Collins

Other books by Lou d'Alpuget
Successful Sailing
Let's Go Sailing
Sydney's Beaches
Boating for Beginners (with Bob Ross)

© Lou d'Alpuget 1986

First published in 1980 by the Hutchinson Group
(Australia) Pty Ltd

This edition published in 1986 by William Collins
Pty Ltd, Sydney

Typeset by Midland Typesetters, Maryborough, Victoria
Printed and bound by Dai Nippon Printing Co., Hong Kong

d'Alpuget, Lou.
   Yachting in Australia.

   2nd ed.
   Includes index.
   ISBN 0 00 217544 4.

   1. Yacht racing. 2. Yachts and yachting — Australia.
   I. Mooney, Tony. II. Title.

797.1′4′0994

Contents

To Tess van Sommers

Foreword

I WAS HONOURED to be asked to read this wonderful book. It is a work of enormous scope and covers the spectrum of sailboating past and present in this lucky country.

I know of no one better qualified than the author, Lou d'Alpuget, to tackle such a huge task. Lou, a lifelong yachtsman and boat owner, has for many years been a journalist and broadcaster whose authoritative reports and comments and instructional textbooks on yachting at every level have enjoyed a wide audience in Australia and overseas. Lou's research assistant, Tony Mooney, is a yachting administrator of distinction whose work is increasingly respected in all States and internationally.

In this book Lou has intertwined tremendous detail with fascinating anecdotes that range from grim to hilarious. One aspect I really enjoyed was his even-handed approach to the various classes of sailboats. I agree with him, nevertheless, that we in Australia have erred in our gigantic proliferation· of classes, diluting our talent. Some years ago I tried, unsuccessfully I fear, with Lloyd Burgess (one of our leading officials) and with the late Colin Ryrie (a distinguished Olympian and publisher) to introduce into Australia a competition similar to America's Mallory Cup. In this series of races the best sailors in many classes sail off against each other in a different type of boat each year. The aim is to produce a champion of champions and so help to lift the overall quality of yachtsmen and yachtswomen. I still feel that such contests, held regularly, could achieve a similar result in this country and ultimately help to concentrate our resources, so that we would have better chances in hard-fought international events. In a modest way in recent years we have started an annual Hardy Challenge series with NSW competitions in centreboard dinghies and in small keelboats that, I hope, with a little more encouragement from class and State associations, could develop along the lines of the American championship events.

Our isolation in Australia from the great centres of world championship sailing and therefore our need for regular government assistance in transporting overseas the crews and yachts that have earned the right to represent our nation in their various classes is another theme in this book with which I heartily concur. Other countries use their national airlines and shipping lines for such a purpose. I see no valid reason why we should not do the same.

Yachting in Australia also presents penetrating and exclusive analyses of Australia's efforts in the Olympic Games, the America's Cup and the Admiral's Cup. Its examination of ocean racing in this country and, where relevant, overseas, demonstrates how much effort yachtsmen must make to campaign offshore craft, and the total physical and mental dedication necessary when we aim to reach the winners' circle.

The chapter on the epic Trans-Tasman races is a self-contained thriller; and the accurately detailed report of Australia's part in the 1979 Fastnet race is an imperishable record of that tragic event. Overall, here is a book that will become the benchmark of yachting publications for many decades.

Sir James Hardy

Acknowledgements

IT IS OFTEN SAID that salt water is thicker than blood and, indeed, when a yachtsman asks a yachtsman for help it usually comes spontaneously, as from a brother. There were non-sailors interested in the project, too. Thanks are due to:

Joe Adams, John Anderson, Rob Antill, Hal Barnes, Barbara Beashel, Ken Beashel, John Bennett, Ken Black, Graham Blackwood, Frank Bonnitcha, Ken Bradley, Doug Brooker, John Brooks, Alan Brown, Hedley Calvert, Alan Campbell, Bruce Campbell, Peter Campbell, Dick Cawse, Ron Chapman, Ian Cherry, Shirley Cherry, Phil Coles, Pat Collis, Geoff Comfort, Ken Cook, Peter Cowie, John Crosbie, Lock Crowther, Bob Cumming, Colin Dingle.

Ron Elliott, Simon Feeley, Ian Finlay, Mike Fletcher, Tom Flint, Andrew Forbes, David Forbes, Geoff Foster, Bob Francis, Charlie Frazer, Geoff Gale, Jack Gale, Bob Gear, Bert Gietz, Gary Gietz, David Goode, Trevor Gowland, Syd Grange, Peter Green, Paul Gregg, Dave Griffiths, David Hales, Richard Hammond, Sir James Hardy, Phil Harrison, Magnus Halvorsen, Noreen Halvorsen, Trygve Halvorsen, Ron Hayden, John Haynes, Stan Higgins, Warwick Hoban, Alf Hutton, Greg Hyde, Frank Ikin, Ivan Irwin, Malcolm Jones, Peter Kurts.

Graeme Lambert, Brian Lees, Ben Lexcen, David Linacre, Bob Lundie, Tony Manford, Frank Martin, John Martin, Gordon Marshall, Frank McNulty, Barry Miflin, Bill Miller, Sue Monkhouse, Bruce Morrissey, Jim Murrant, Iain Murray, Sir William Northam, John Notley, Peter O'Donnell, John Parrington, Richard Parsons, Alan Payne, Jack Pollard, Ken Rainey, David Rayment, Gordon Reynolds, Arthur Robb, Brian Robertson, George Robinson, Jack Rooklyn, Bob Ross, Peter Rysdyk, Dick Sargeant, Jack Savage, John Shaw, Campbell Scott, Jim Robson-Scott, Peter Shipway, Bill Solomons, Barry Stevens, Keith Storey, Bruce Taylor, John Taylor, John Tavener, Hugh Treharne, Jim Turner, Harold Vaughan, Martin Visser, Hedley Watson, Grahame Watt, Cedric Williams, David Woods, John Yeomans.

Introduction

THIS BOOK is not, as might be assumed by some, a complete history of the sport in this country. No one volume could do justice to the breadth of the topic; it deserves a shelf-full. The aim is to put certain events and developments in Australian yachting into historical perspective, and, where necessary, in some detail. The warmly human, anecdotal side is kept in sight as sailing is a sport that is rich in exciting incidents and tends to bring out individuality in its followers.

Overall, what has been attempted is a picture of where Australia stands as a yachting nation, by world standards, this being the only reasonable criterion by which to judge any country's sporting prowess in any field. In general terms, Australia has almost ideal conditions for sailing—a superb climate most of the year, marvellous waterways, more open sea space than anyone knows what to do with, and the high level of individual prosperity needed to pursue what is a relatively expensive pastime. Given all these advantages, do we stand where we should in the hierarchy of world yachting, not only competitively but also at all levels of competence? And if not, why not? Yachting can be looked at from two angles—as a delightful, healthy, strenuous way of having fun by messing about in boats, or as a delightful, healthy, strenuous sport that is brought to peaks of perfection by competition. It is competition that improves yachts and yachting techniques, though that is not for a moment to denigrate the joys and rewards of cruising.

If this book seems therefore to concentrate rather heavily on ocean racing, the Olympic classes, the America's Cup, Six Metre classics and the strenuously campaigned open boats like our unique 18-footers and 16 ft and 12 ft skiffs, and on those remarkable waterspiders, the C class catamarans, it is because in these arenas Australians come near to getting out of yachting what the best of the rest of the world's yachtsmen in many kinds of boats strive to achieve— high performance.

If such areas of sailing in Australia as the flotillas of dinghies of various kinds, the club handicappers, miscellaneous fun boats of keel, centreboard and multihull types are passed over somewhat more lightly, it is because of a belief that some (if by no means all) of what goes on in these numerous classes cannot be taken as seriously, in the world view, as the efforts of the others.

Part of the trouble is that Australia supports far too many small-boat classes. The well-known Australian tendency to want to do things the easy way finds an outlet in setting up dozens of minor leagues, each with its proud little court of champions, instead of concentrating on a relatively few classes and making the competitions so hot that titles are hard-won and richly deserved.

With some notable exceptions, Australian yachtsmen and yachting authorities are not good at documenting the achievements and history of the sport. In some cases, even so-called official records differ at the source, and it is not uncommon to come across widely varying accounts of the same happening. Every effort has been made in this book to check all the data given. In some instances, the facts related are collated for the first time ever in one text.

As is the international custom, sea distances have been expressed in nautical miles (nm) and speeds in knots (k) since metrication as yet has no valid application to these measurements of arc over the earth's surface.

Winning and losing margins are given in abbreviated form, as is the international custom when detailing results of yacht races. Thus 1.10 equals one minute and ten seconds. A win by fifty-five seconds is shown simply as 55s. A series of winning margins is shown as 1.10, 1.56, 34 (for seconds, without the following letter s), 3.51. In ocean racing, when margins are usually much larger, winning times, when applicable, are given with the letters: h (hours), m (minutes), s (seconds) after each figure.

Long series of placings are given, as is customary, as 9, 15, 34, 27, 1, 1, 9 instead of spelling out ninth, fifteenth, thirty-fourth, twenty-seventh, first, first, ninth. Disqualification is expressed as dsq; did not finish course as dnf; retired as rtd; premature start as pms; did not start as dns.

The lineal measurements of boats in some cases are given in feet and inches besides metres, since these are the scales by which many are still identified. In Australia ocean racing yachts are measured in metres but ratings are shown in feet and decimal parts of feet because the international formula by which these craft are rated has not yet been converted to metrication. Of course, some boats must be called by their metric names both overseas and in Australia — 12s, 8s, 6s and 5.5s among the keelboats and the 420s, 470s and 505s among the dinghies — because of the formulae under which they are designed. For landlubbers it sometimes lends an air of glorious confusion to the nautical scene. Yachtsmen, however, find their way around it with a certain degree of relish, just as they do with the esoteric and generally unique names of the equipment aboard their boats.

Lou d'Alpuget

1

Historical Background and Development in All States

LET A YACHTSMAN praise our ancient, sun-blessed Australia. . .Most of us are favoured with a kind climate; vast, easily navigated stretches of a bold, 12,500 nm coastline; moderate rises and falls of tide; steady, predictable winds; and some of the finest harbours and cruising grounds in the world. While millions of people in the northern hemisphere shudder away from the sea for four months or more of the year under a blanket of ice and snow, our sailors, even in the southernmost State of Tasmania, can spend much of their winters, like their summers, comfortably afloat if they have a mind for it, with few concessions to the change of season.

So the noble pastime of boat sailing is possible all the year around our island continent and those who pursue perfection in boats need never be out of practice. It should therefore be no wonder that we Australians, in spite of our small population, are when we race our boats seriously among the most accomplished yachtsmen in the world. We have won scores of international championships and world titles in dozens of different classes of boats (see tables on pages 64–70) from dinghies to the largest ocean racers, and since 1962, when we first entered the lists, have performed better than any other nation with the temerity to try in the most demanding competition of all — the challenges for the America's Cup, which we won in 1983.

Of course, yachting is not all racing. There is simple joy in communion with the sea on leisurely cruises for a day, a week or a month. More than half the 500,000 or so people of all ages of both sexes who man boats in Australia in the open sea, on our hundreds of harbour bays, gulfs, rivers, lakes and dams, are content with that alone as an escape from the pressures of urban living. But it is in the nature of humans to be competitive and it is a rare sailor indeed, however philosophically he may resist the idea, who has not or will not want to match his skill and his boat in some modest way against another.

The history and progress of yachting is inseparably mixed with racing. The passion to make one vessel faster, more sea-kindly than another, has developed naval architecture from a primitive form of guesswork into a sort of art-science, still far from exact, but at least a much happier combination of engineering and physics and their offshoots, hydrodynamics and aerodynamics, than in the days when a shipwright carved out of a block of wood a shape that pleased his eye and hoped that the lines transferred full scale from it and built into a yacht would be faster than his last attempt. It is true, however, that some inspired guesses in the past by men of genius who combined experience with a basic understanding of physics had by the end of the nineteenth century produced hull forms that were at least as fast and often more easily handled than many modern craft. Some yachts designed since the 1960s, especially ocean racers hemmed in by measurement rules that encourage disproportionate ratios between heeled waterlines and beams, have little directional stability and are wild-headed in a seaway. (See Chapter 16: Level Rating and the Ton Classes.) Lighter, better engineered construction, better sails, spars and equipment are often all they have in their favour.

Designing a yacht of specific performance, even with the help of a computer, is still a complex exercise, an attempt to harmonize imponderables. Every curve or angle in a yacht's hull form makes it behave differently as it heels and presents a different shape to the water through which it is moving. Since every angle of heel is dependent on the strength of the wind, which is rarely constant, neither is the performance of the hull constant. The yacht also changes the shape it presents to the water as it pitches up and down, slides sideways and moves across an ever-changing surface — the sea. And, as if that were not enough, one must add other sets of variables: the distribution of weight throughout the structure and the subtle differences in the interaction of forces that are exerted on the hull and the rig as the sails change their shape and their angles of attack while the wind fluctuates in direction and strength. It is a mathematical labyrinth that has taxed man's ingenuity during thousands of years. But racing of yachts — the concept of sliding over the water rather than battering a way through it — in the last 100 years has done more to solve the realities of the problems than all the experience of seafaring in the preceding ages. And Australians have contributed significantly towards that solution.

Yachting in Australia might be said to have begun soon after Captain Arthur Phillip had given his often misquoted opinion of Port Jackson as 'one of the finest harbours in the world, in which a thousand sail of the line might ride in perfect security'. He landed his wretched human cargoes and had cutters sent to explore the mysterious bays and inlets. According to contemporary accounts, the first participants in sailing in Australia seemed to have got little enjoyment from it. The first privately organized offshore cruise and serious effort to escape the tedium of life ashore could perhaps be credited to the convict William Bryant who, with his wife Mary and seven other absconders, stole a fishing boat in 1791 and sailed it northwards more than 3,000 nm to Timor. For daring and endurance this trip rivalled much more celebrated sea adventures, but it hardly fits into the category of a pleasure voyage. There were, however, occasional rowing and sailing races between the crews of ships visiting NSW and, as the colony began to thrive by the late 1820s, a few privately owned craft belonging to successful settlers were afloat on Sydney Harbour. In 1827 the merchant Robert Campbell had an open three-ton cutter in which he regularly took his ease on the waters and, in the same year, on 28 April, a regatta was organized by the captains and officers of two warships in port, HMS *Success* (Captain Stirling) and HMS *Rainbow* (Captain H.J. Rous).

The *Sydney Gazette* generously described it as the first Australian regatta which, in fact, it was not, since naval officers in Hobart Town, in the sub-colony of Tasmania, then known as Van Diemen's Land, had held a similar function on the Derwent River on 5 January the same year. The *Hobart Town Gazette* also mentions a regatta of some kind as early as 1824. Pleasure sailing continued in both places, with, according to Royal Sydney Yacht Squadron's official history *Sydney Sails*, Sydney's annual Anniversary Day regatta being held on 26 January, or as near as possible to it, to celebrate the landing of the first unwilling settlers. It would appear, however, that the regatta for 1837 may indeed have been held on 31 December 1836. According to author Ralph P. Neale, in his excellent *Jolly Dogs Are We, The History of Yachting in Victoria*, there is no positive record of an official Sydney Anniversary Day regatta being held on 26 January until 1838. In any case, either on 26 January 1837 or 31 December 1836 the regatta included a sailing race for first class boats in which nine vessels competed. James Milson junior, in his twelve-tonner *Sophia*, a gift from his influential father, a North Shore farmer, won the main prize. A conscientious newspaper reporter, however, noted that Harry Sawyer's *North Star* would have been the first home had she not gone the wrong side of the judge's boat and been obliged to recross the line. Perhaps Sawyer's crew, like others in races of later years, was distracted by the behaviour of spectator craft. A Hobart packet, which carried a brass band and a large party of ladies and was beguilingly named the *Francis Feeling*, ran aground near Milson's Point during the regatta and remained there until the next day. Another sightseeing vessel, the paddle steamer *Australian*, cruised about the course with ladies and gentlemen who 'kept up dancing' throughout the regatta.

By 1838, a Jubilee year, things were better organized and a newspaper was able to report that 'there was not so much drunkenness and riot as we have been in the habit of seeing'. On 1 December 1838, Hobart's new governor, Sir John Franklin, announced that city's regatta 'to commemorate the discovery of Van Diemen's Land by Abel Tasman in 1642', gave £100 to the funds and urged 'rich and poor, young and old to come to Pavilion Point in anticipation of a carefree day'. The regatta committee provided 'good colonial ale, biscuits, and cheese, free of charge of any sort'. This gesture quelled a series of sour jibes at the regatta by the *True Colonist*, whose editor had stigmatized it as a 'show got up at short notice for the mushroom aristocracy'. The day was a great success; a flotilla of sixty boats of various kinds took part, there were sailing races for first and second class yachts (those above and below 7.92 m on the keel) and at the end of the day, according to the *Hobart Town Gazette*, 'there was ample evidence left on the ground that the populace had right royally enjoyed themselves'.

Sydney's and Hobart's anniversary regattas, now distinguished with the prefix Royal, have been held annually ever since. Many thousands of craft in dozens of categories and classes have sailed thousands of races in the intervening 149 years. But while Hobart's regatta has held the interest of local yachtsmen and the public there has been a steady decline in the size and quality of the fleets competing at the Sydney gala.

Many of the Sydney regatta's races in recent years have been held under the control of officials of individual clubs, over courses of their own choosing, and

Racing on Sydney Habour in the 1880s. Prominent yachts of the day: *Sao, Assegai,* and *Lotus.* (RSYS Archives)

incorporated in club point score competitions with token regatta prizes added. One of the reasons for the unwillingness of yacht owners and crews to support the regatta directly has been the claim that races in the recent past were too often poorly organized and controlled and that officials spent too much time in self-congratulatory luncheons aboard flagships. These owners have preferred their own club races on courses in their own areas away from crowded regatta starting and finishing lines on the main harbour. This attitude has angered and saddened many people with a sense of history but in fact it would now be an embarrassment for regatta organizers if all the thousands of keel yachts and centreboard boats that race in the sprawling Sydney metropolitan area, on Pittwater, the Harbour and Botany Bay, and elsewhere like Port Hacking, entered for the Anniversary regatta and gathered in a central area. They would create such a traffic jam on the water that serious racing would be impossible.

Parochialism, reluctance to leave one's own area, and a preference for club racing, mainly on performance handicaps, in various classes of open boats and in mixed divisions and groups of keelboats of nondescript design, have been for many years remarkable features of both the strength and weakness of yachting in Australia — depending upon one's point of view. Some clubs' Spring–Summer pointscore handicap competitions, over a series of thirty or more weekend races are contested as fiercely as international championships.

Other are sailed in a spirit of tolerant camaraderie, with give-and-take rather than strict observance of the racing rules, and good-natured joshing at the club bar later. The standards of helmsmanship and crew-work in many of these weekly club events is uneven, ranging from incompetent to brilliant. This suits those who want only a Saturday afternoon's airing with a spice of friendly but lighthearted rivalry. It infuriates those who try hard, because they find themselves tangled with those who don't — and in situations in which it is dangerous to assert legitimate right-of-way advantages without risks of collisions and damage, personal and material. Since World War II, and particularly in the last twenty years, those with a desire for better standards of racing have strongly supported the trend to so-called one-design boats, especially of small keel yachts, mass-produced dinghies and, to a lesser degree, trailerable yachts. A total of sixty-eight different classes of centreboard dinghies, thirty-two classes of monohull yachts, thirty-four different classes of catamarans and thirty-seven classes of trailerable yachts plus two classes of sailboards, each holding its own club, state and in many cases national title events, have gained varying degrees of support.

These title races have produced hundreds of moderately sized frogs in small ponds, with each skipper and crew able to display a championship trophy of their own and to croak with pride at their achievements. However, the multiplicity of classes, each with some real or fancied virtue to suit individual whims or local weather patterns, has greatly diluted the talent available for top-quality racing in internationally recognized classes.

Setting aside the thousands of one-off, cruiser-racer keel yachts that sail only in performance-handicap divisions around harbour buoys, and the hundreds of individually designed ocean racers, there would be tremendous improvement in the overall standard of Australian racing if we concentrated on only twenty classes of one-design dinghies instead of sixty-eight and on a dozen catamaran classes. Most champion foreign yachtsmen in international classes have to fight their way up through hundreds and sometimes thousands of high-performance boats of the same design in their own countries and in others within easy travelling distance. In world title events they are constantly astonished at the excellence of Australian sailors who have had only a twentieth of the opposition. 'If only you had fewer classes and were forced to try harder, if you stopped sailing for amusement and took it seriously, you would be supreme', it has been said. But far from weeding out the classes in Australia we add to them annually. Moreover, fewer than one in ten of those who do sail in the recognized international classes are willing to spend the time and trouble to bring their boats and themselves to world standards.

Some of those who try hard are motivated by their commercial interest in sailing — as sailmakers, shipchandlers, riggers, and boatbuilders — and the indirect advertising advantages that success may bring. They can therefore justify the cost of extended training campaigns and the best of equipment. This arguable degree of semi-professionalism, once openly condemned, is now internationally accepted. A yachtsman is an amateur, even in the Olympics, so long as he does not directly advertise and is not actually paid for racing.

And the practice of semi-professionalism is not, of course, peculiar to Australia — at least 10 per cent of overseas champions have business connections with the sport, and in some eastern European countries yachting representatives are State-supported. But it does discourage many true blue amateurs, who feel that they will have little chance against such competitors. So although Australia has a tremendous pool of potential title winners, our world and Olympic champions and near champions come from fewer than a thirtieth of those who take part in racing. They are men and women of extraordinary ability.

In 1986 there were 358 yacht and sailing clubs in Australia, with 105,173 members and 28,887 craft registered. There were 8,832 fixed-keel yachts; 16,211 dinghies, skiffs and trailerable monohull yachts (these latter mostly centreboarders); and 3,854 multihulls. Official estimates of crew members sailing in registered boats but not members of clubs totalled 150,000. There were also about 200,000 people sailing casually but not racing, in at least the same number of unregistered boats of numerous types and classes including 70,000 sailboards. The number of unregistered multihulls was estimated at 6,000. So overall, in 1986 more than half a million Australians were taking part in sailing in some form.

The following table shows the distribution of affiliated clubs and associations and the various types of craft registered in each State. (K: fixed-keel yachts; CDST: centreboard dinghies, skiffs and monohull trailerable yachts; M: multihulls.)

State	Clubs	Assns	K	CDST	M
NSW	115	105	3088	4195	555
Vic.	87	99	1778	6029	1473
WA	31	55	730	1797	490
Qld	65	44	1500	2184	682
SA	33	55	474	1101	484
Tas.	25	30	1145	794	151
NT	2	7	117	111	19

Club yachting, as has been shown, is now the great strength of the sport in Australia. But it was slow to begin. Tasmanians had a Tamar Yacht Club, with eight boats on the register for racing, near the charming town of Launceston, as early as 1837. It lapsed after a brief success, and shortly afterwards attempts to form enduring clubs among the robust citizens of Hobart were unsuccessful because arguments arose among rival factions. It took them until 1874 to form the Derwent Sailing Boat Club, and they had three name changes before they settled in 1887 on Derwent Yacht Club (which in 1910 became the present Royal Yacht Club of Tasmania). Meanwhile on Port Jackson, our first and largest centre of settlement, by the late 1840s there were dozens of privately owned sailing craft of various sizes whose owners and crews used them mainly for picnic cruises around the majestic waterway and for exploratory trips to the bays and beaches that reached almost continuously from the upper reaches of Middle Harbour to the Parramatta River. The more adventurous made short journeys north, 20 nm up the coast to Broken Bay and Pittwater, backed by the superb Hawkesbury River, navigable for 80 nm inland.

While the Tasmanians at first seemed ready to race in any sort of boat at the drop of a hat, in Sydney racing of yachts was considered the most heroic and dashing manifestation of the sailor's art. It was the sort of public endeavour one made occasionally in the presence of admiring spectators at annual regattas — on the main harbour on Anniversary Day, at the Balmain Regatta (founded 1849 and held every 30 November until the outbreak of World War I in 1914), or in answer to direct challenges from individuals or groups of other owners for two-boat match races, or for special engagements between mixed fleets. Inevitably, though, as Sydney's population grew and prospered, the number of yachts increased and interest in regular racing intensified. By the early 1850s in Sydney there was need for some form of organization or at least for a generally accepted system by which racing could be conducted.

And in the infant city of Melbourne, too, some of the new rich who were rolling in money as a result of the gold rushes and who were extravagantly confident of the future, were acquiring yachts and disporting themselves on the shallow and at times treacherous waters of Port Phillip Bay. Seven of these Melbourne yacht owners and 132 'other interested persons' in 1856 founded Victoria Yacht Club. It was the first such body, of which there are positive records, formed on the Australian mainland. But its members were mainly interested in cruising and organized only one regatta before losing interest. This club, like Geelong Sailing Club (later Geelong Yacht Club) which seems from equivocal reports to have been formed in 1859 and later amalgamated with VYC, apparently lapsed and died. The resuscitation of these two clubs, VYC in 1872 and GYC in 1880, and their survival today as Royal Yacht Club of Victoria (Royal Warrant granted 1887) and as Royal Geelong Yacht Club (Royal Warrant 1924) were later to lead to one of the most extraordinary legal battles in Australia's sporting history (see page 35).

NEW SOUTH WALES

Meanwhile, on Port Jackson, yachting was well established and consolidating. Sydney's first club had a short but much more spectactular early career than its Victorian contemporaries. It was called the Sydney Yacht Club and was founded in 1856 with the magistrate Hutchinson Brown as its commodore. While keenly supporting and sponsoring special events at the regattas and laying down the law about their conduct, the Sydney Yacht Club did not at first seem to be much interested in the arranging and on-the-spot control of these races. Finally

James Milson's *Era* racing on Sydney Harbour in 1861. (RSYS Archives)

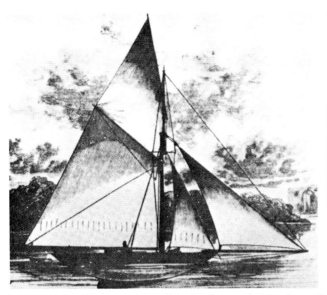

Left Diagram shows 'mackerel' hull of remarkable *Australian*, built in Sydney 1858, that revolutionized many concepts of yacht design. (RSYS Archives)
Right *Australian* still under sail in the 1880s. (RSYS Archives)

it set about drawing up rules for races, defining classes in which craft of different sizes and types should compete, and working out fair methods of handicapping them. Like many officials who were to follow him, Magistrate Brown in his private capacity as an amateur sailor had been called on so often to adjudicate on arguments arising from catch-as-catch-can races between high-spirited rivals that he and his associates felt it would be a good idea if there were definite standards for all to follow.

Sydney Yacht Club members, alive to the need for 'happy intercourse of opinion between comrades afloat', also promoted goodwill by social niceties. They launched their club with a Grand Foundation Ball at the Prince of Wales Theatre in Sydney in 1856. It was held, according to one observer, in an atmosphere 'the extravagances of which fairly paralyzed Sydney society and the finances of the club'.

The club's other most notable achievement in the ensuing five years was its sponsorship of an 'outside race' of 28 nm from Sydney Harbour to Botany Bay and back, held at the same time as the Anniversary Regatta of 1861. The Sydney Yacht Club put up as first prize the staggering sum for those days, when a tradesman's wages were £2 a week, of £300, with a second prize of £75, worth enormously more in today's currency. When handicaps were adjusted at the end of the race the prosperous dock master Captain J.S. Rountree, a former master mariner, was the winner over the six other starters in his 15 tonne *Annie Ogle* (named after his daughter). Captain Rountree was equal to the occasion. He spoke modestly of his good luck in winning, divided £100 of his prize money among his crew, and gave the other £200 to charities.

The Irish-born Richard Harnett, second in his *Australian*, a radical 10.97 m 10 tonne double-ender, which had led most of the way and was beaten only in a fading breeze, spent his prize on new equipment for his remarkable yacht. Harnett was then widely considered Sydney's most skilful gentleman yachtsman.

Sydney 8 July 1862.

We the undersigned Yacht Owners hereby constitute ourselves into a Club to be termed the "~~Royal~~ Australian Yacht Squadron."

Names	Yacht

Foundation document of 1862 with signatures of the nineteen yacht owners who formed what a year later became Royal Sydney Yacht Squadron. (RSYS Archives)

He had learned small boat sailing as a boy in Cork, Ireland, where the world's first yacht club, now Royal Cork, had been founded in 1720. He had designed *Australian* himself. He claimed to have based her hull form on the underbelly sections of a fish, a mackerel, that he had caught in Sydney Harbour. She was 9.15 m on the waterline, 1.98 m beam, with a tumblehome in her topsides. Some of her features, such as her fine entrance, overhanging bow exactly the same shape as her stern, and short, arced, cutaway keel, were many years ahead of her time and a startling departure from the long, straight keels and deep forefeet of most yachts of the day. *Australian* raced with distinction for more than a quarter of a century and influenced concepts of design in Australia and overseas.

But the Sydney Yacht Club's grandiloquent gesture at the regatta of 1861 was its finale and it disbanded soon afterwards. This left the field clear for the formation in 1862 of the Australian Yacht Squadron. The founders of the Squadron were nineteen leading merchants, businessmen, lawyers, a doctor, all, including Captain Rountree and Richard Harnett, yacht owners keen on racing and cruising. They soon gathered around them as fellow members many other men of means. Unlike the free spenders of the Sydney Yacht Club they made sure that their club had a sound financial basis, and they set uncompromising rules of behaviour for members afloat and ashore. Happily, their standards hold good to this day.

Within eight months of its founding the Squadron had asked for and been given an Admiralty Warrant and Royal patronage. At the same time it changed its name from Australian to (Royal) Sydney Yacht Squadron. This was a shrewd political move stage-managed by the Duke of Newcastle, then Secretary of State for the Colonies. Knowing that the Sydney club's influence did not spread beyond the NSW border, Newcastle did not wish it to carry the broad title of 'Australian', which might offend rival yachtsmen in Victoria. Eventually, he hinted, they also would like a Royal charter for their club. So today, although Victorians may claim that the Royal Yacht Club of Victoria is the oldest surviving yacht club in Australia (which they may do if they choose to ignore its early demise and resurrection in 1872) there is no question that the Royal Sydney Yacht Squadron was the first outside the British Isles given the designation Royal. There are now thirteen other Royal clubs in Australia. Port Phillip Bay has four. Some people are inclined to look coolly on such honours, claiming that it is what a club does, not what it is called, that matters. But there are few yacht clubs in Australia whose committees would not be flattered and eager if they thought they might qualify for the prefix Royal, with the cachet it brings worldwide.

Sydney got its second enduring club in 1867 when a group of ardent sailors, with Richard Harnett as their first commodore, formed Prince Alfred Yacht Club (Royal in 1911). Earlier it was called The Mosquito Fleet because many of its boats were smaller than those that the Squadron, with growing sense of its own importance, considered suitable to its dignity. In 1872 a third club, Sydney Amateur Sailing Club, catering for even more modest types of racing craft, was formed. 'The Alfreds' as the RPAYC is known, now has yachts of all sizes. It has enjoyed from its beginnings the warm approval of succeeding Dukes of Edinburgh, beginning with the son of Queen Victoria after whom the club is named. This Prince Alfred, shot at and painfully wounded in the back by a would-be assassin during a harbour picnic at Clontarf, Sydney, in 1868, was pleased to lend the club his name and patronage in celebration of his escape from death. For sixty years at one time and another there was an edge of asperity in dealings

Richard Harnett, designer of *Australian*, foundation member of Royal Sydney Yacht Squadron in 1862 and foundation commodore of Royal Prince Alfred Yacht Club, 1867.

From its earliest days Royal Prince Alfred Yacht Club has been blessed with a succession of officials dedicated to its progress and is now one of the wealthiest aquatic clubs in the world. But who, among this stern committee of 1897, gave vice commodore P. H. Sullivan permission to remove his cap? (RPAYC Archives)

between the Squadron and The Alfreds about racing and social affairs, but in recent times under the guidance of enlightened committees this has given way to friendship and co-operation. Dozens of yachtsmen and yachtswomen are members of both clubs. The Squadron, with 2,290 members and 243 yachts and boats on its register, preserves its headquarters in a handsome if not over-large residential clubhouse at Kirribilli, on the north shore of Sydney Harbour. Its landmark from the water is an enormous pair of whale's jawbones arching the path to the sea front. The Alfreds, with 1,784 members and 655 yachts and boats, spreads itself across a multimillion-dollar modern complex on the shores of Green Point and Crystal Bay, Pittwater. It also has membership privileges of The Sydney Club in the business centre of the city. The Sydney Amateur Sailing Club, with 456 members and 96 boats, in spite of its long life and excellent record of keen racing, failed to make the best of chances that might have raised it to the same physical status as other senior clubs. For many years it suffered from committees who lacked foresight and were over-timid about money matters. While many more recent clubs, such as Sydney's Middle Harbour Yacht Club, with 2,052 members, 739 yachts and boats, a regular racing fleet of 200 craft, winter and summer, and a large clubhouse at The Spit, have bounded to success, The Amateurs today is quartered in a modest building in Mosman Bay. Members sometimes recall that in 1883, the only time in its first eighty years that the club had the courage to build a clubhouse, NSW government authorities brutally dispossessed it. The site that members had chosen was right on Bennelong Point, where Sydney's Opera House now stands.

Until the turn of the century a dozen or so other sailing clubs were formed around Port Jackson, mainly to cater for the special classes of craft, dinghies and skiffs that their members favoured. Some of the boats they developed were unique and bizarre. These included open 22-footers and 18-footers that carried more sail and crew than keel yachts three times their size (see Chapter 7); spoon-shaped 6-footers and 10-footers buried under ridiculous clouds of sail that made a mockery of hydrodynamics but nevertheless required remarkable feats of balance and judgement to keep them afloat; sleek, skittish 16-footers the dimensions of which were to change little in eighty years. Sydney's suburban sprawl between the two World Wars produced other groups of sailors cut off from easy access to the main harbour and led to the formation of forty or more clubs on the waterways nearest to them — along the Parramatta River and around Botany Bay, Port Hacking and Pittwater.

But the spread of boating under sail did not really begin in earnest, State and nation wide, until the early 1950s. Then the development and marketing of waterproof sheet plywood, reliable marine glues and simplified plans began to make building easy for the home handyman or boy with a few tools and space to spread his elbows. Thousands of small boats of different designs were built as family projects, sometimes with the kitchen table as the main workbench. Clubs were formed throughout NSW wherever there was water to float boats. The established clubs also adopted fleets of these small craft and set up training schools for youngsters which were and are eagerly attended. (It is reliably estimated that by the 1960s more than 2,000 of the 3.43 m Heron class dinghies and a similar number of the 3.31 m Mirror class dinghies had been home-built in Australia.)

The advent of strong, man-made, rot-proof fibres for sails, halyards and sheets, of aluminium alloy for spars, of stainless steel wire for shrouds and stays and

Top Few yachtsmen in any country enjoy such magnificent private facilities as those provided for members of Sydney's Royal Prince Alfred Yacht Club at Pittwater. (RPAYC Archives)
Bottom In the late 1890s Sydney Flying Squadron's 22-footers, not yet supplanted by the 18-footers, still raced on the Harbour under enormous spreads of sail, including ringtails of 35 sq m down their mainsail leeches and crews of sixteen. (Roy Stevens)

an excellent variety of ready-made alloy and stainless steel yacht chandlery, and, in more recent years, the development and mass-marketing of ready-made fibreglass hulls of more than eighty different designs, has almost swamped NSW waterways with small boats and yachts. There is hardly a stretch of sheltered water along the coast, or a river — salt or fresh — lake or dam in any corner of the State without a sailing club. Few of these clubs have any of the traditional shedding for boats once thought essential, or any need to go to the expense of building it. Road trailers allow owners and crews to keep their boats at home and to tow them behind cars to launching points. In 1985, as well as the 115 clubs (each holding races for at least one and some for up to ten different classes of boats) affiliated with the Yachting Association of NSW, there were also 105 registered class associations. And they are growing every year.

VICTORIA

The story is somewhat the same in the State of Victoria. Pleasure boating there, according to Ralph P. Neale, in his well-documented history of early yachting in Victoria, *Jolly Dogs Are We*, began with some sort of regatta arranged by Captain Stephen Addison of the barque *Eudoria* in Hobson's Bay (off Williamstown) in 1838. But since there were then no newspapers in Melbourne no details of the affair can be traced. In the same year there were some match races in small boats. It seems that the first properly organized regatta of which we have any records was held on Port Phillip by the exclusive Melbourne Club in 1840. A flotilla of thirteen barques, three brigs and a ship, all dressed in flags, was anchored off Williamstown near the starting and finishing lines.

On New Year's Day, 1842, another regatta was arranged for Williamstown by William Dawson, proprietor of the Albion Hotel not, it seems, because of any special interest in water sports, but mainly to drum up trade. There were three aquatic events, one for four-oared rowing gigs and two for sailing boats. In the race for whaleboats two locally built craft beat an imported English boat *Paddy From Cork*.

In 1843 and 1844 two so-called regattas at Port Melbourne each featured only one water event, in one case a whaleboat rowing contest and in the other a short sailing race.

The depression of 1845 to 1851 reduced interest in pleasure boating in Victoria and attempts to hold regattas at Williamstown met with little success. But at Geelong, where there had been a pioneer regatta in 1844, sailing carnivals were held on Corio Bay in the summers of 1848 and 1849. In spite of the accidental drowning shortly before the 1849 regatta of a member of the organizing committee and three companions, and widespread damage caused by storms a fortnight earlier, there was a crowd of several thousand and the events were judged the best ever held. There were seven boating races, including one for amateurs pulling whaleboats.

In 1850, Geelong, under some pressure from the authorities to separate heavy drinkers among the spectators from the respectable townsfolk, held what was described as 'a tame affair'. Historian Neale notes that criticism arose about the administration of the regatta funds which the 'nobs' were alleged to have spent on champagne lunches for themselves, an accusation that was to recur often in later years about regatta committees in other States.

Regattas were held sporadically off Geelong and Williamstown with varying degrees of success during the next ten years but there remained a long period before regular sailing races were organized on the wide-open 725 sq nm, shallow, often turbulent and wind-swept waters of Port Phillip. In 1856 Victoria Yacht Club was formed and adopted rules for measurement so that yachts could race equitably. It also laid down elaborate rules for dress and undress uniforms, all plastered with gold braid, by which to measure the status of its officers, sailing committee, and yacht owners. The club held a regatta of sorts on Easter Monday, 1856, but a year later went into decline and either disbanded or lapsed.

In 1858 some attempt was made to establish a club at Williamstown under the name of the Royal Yacht Club of Victoria but this too, after one regatta, disappeared from view. Meanwhile at Geelong in 1857, a vigorous committee organized that town's twelfth regatta, which attracted a crowd of 3,000. Geelong held another highly successful annual regatta in 1858 in which John Cosgrove, one of Victoria's founding fathers of serious yacht racing, in his 9.1 m *Paddy From Cork*, won the main prize, a massive silver cup worth £25 and £15 added cash. Geelong Yacht Club was formed in 1859 and seems to have flourished for a while then declined and disappeared in 1871. It was reformed in 1880 as Geelong Sailing Club, renamed Geelong Yacht Club and ultimately became today's Royal Geelong Yacht Club.

When the gold rushes of the 1850s had subsided and the slumps of the 1860s set in only occasional regattas kept the sport of sailing alive. It wasn't until the early 1870s that Victorian yachting began to look up with the re-formation in 1872 of the Victoria Yacht Club, later the Royal Yacht Club of Victoria, and the foundation in 1875 and 1876 of Brighton Sailing Club (later Royal Brighton Yacht Club) and St Kilda Sailing Club (later Royal St Kilda Yacht Club and then, since 1961, Royal Melbourne Yacht Squadron).

The first sailing establishments around the now populous eastern shores of Port Phillip Bay were modest indeed. Some of the founding boatsheds of what were to become august clubs started off as little better than shanties. Today's Royal Melbourne, at St Kilda, had rather fewer early ups and downs than some others, but was not trouble free. Unsympathetic municipal authorities and local residents tended to object to the club's yachts being towed to the water through the streets on horse-drawn and man-drawn drays. This had to be done because for many years there were no proper places on the shore for the yachts. Lack of amenities was not the only hazard to Port Phillip sailors in the early days. For many years boats making the passage between St Kilda and Brighton ran the risk of being holed, or their crews hurt, by stray bullets from the Elsternwick rifle range ashore.

During the nineteenth century, centreboard yachts and boats predominated — as indeed they still do today — although there were then, as now, some magnificent fixed-keel craft where they could be safely moored. Along the 31 nm length and 20 nm breadth of Port Phillip there are no sheltering bays or headlands, apart from Corio Bay, near Geelong in the south-west, and Hobson's Bay, near Williamstown in the north. In the early days there were none of the man-made breakwaters that have since been built at great expense. So centreboarders were forced on those who did not have the time or means to travel to Geelong or Williamstown. Centreboarders offered the best chance of avoiding trouble in heavy weather. When forced to run to a lee shore to escape from storms the boats' boards could be lifted and they could be dragged up the

Humble beginnings on the beach: A century of enthusiasm and dedication by members of Royal Brighton Yacht Club has replaced this shanty with spacious modern premises. (RBYC Archives)

sand, well above the high waterline and out of reach of the short, breaking seas that pounded in from the south and west.

The Victorians were at first discouraged from ocean racing (see Chapter 13) by notoriously rough seas outside the port, in Bass Strait, where there were few places to shelter, and by the difficulties and dangers of coping with the seven knot eddies at The Rip (between Point Lonsdale and Point Nepean) in order to get out into blue water. As a result, minds turned inward upon round-the-buoys bay races, at which Victorians soon excelled. The testing conditions on their enclosed waters, studded with shifting sandbanks, tidal swirls and tricky wind shifts, developed a brand of tactical sharpness and seamanship sometimes lacking among Sydney Harbour sailors, who were used to less choppy, deeper water and steadier breezes.

Before the days of built-in buoyancy tanks and buoyancy vests that allowed crews freedom of movement, the short, steep seas that quickly rose when winds were fresh also made Port Phillip dangerous for boats without generous sidedecks. These conditions discouraged attempts to introduce craft like Sydney's completely open 16 ft skiffs and 18-footers that depended largely on leecloths to keep them free of water.

In the late nineteenth century Victorians mounted interstate (then called intercolonial) regattas on their home waters against visitors from Sydney, Tasmania, South Australia and occasionally New Zealand. In 1861 Melbourne's pride, *Paddy From Cork*, then owned and sailed by George Robbins, was taken to Sydney to compete for the £300 first prize at the Anniversary Regatta. She finished a distant sixth, 36.30 behind the winner *Annie Ogle*.

NSW first competed in Victoria in 1883 when the energetic Dr F. Milford, commodore of Sydney's RPAYC, sent his English-designed five tonner, *Doris*, to Melbourne. The Sydney crew was somewhat surprised to find that Victorians still started from fixed moorings and turned all marks on the port hand. Nevertheless *Doris* won first prize of £50 and the doctor and his friends were 'overwhelmed with hospitality'. The affluent 1880s and early 1890s were the golden years for these intercolonial contests and one of their keenest promoters was Sir William Clarke, a Tasmanian-born millionaire grazier, commodore of Victoria Yacht Club and a member of the Victorian Legislative Council. Sir William was rightly proud of his 33 tonne cutter *Janet*. She was locally built, 18.3 m overall with a load waterline of 16.6 m, a beam of 3.96 m and a draft of 2.79 m. One of the smartest craft of her day, she was, if one can believe what was said of her, remarkably fast in all conditions, even by modern standards. In 1881, *Janet*, hard driven under a great spread of sail by her helmsman Dick Banner, outclassed four other yachts in a special 33 nm match around Port Phillip. Her rivals were *Taniwha*, 33 tonnes, from New Zealand, brought across the Tasman for the contest; *Edith*, 43 tonnes, from Glenelg Yacht Club, South Australia; *Zephyr*, 23 tonnes, from South Australian Yacht Club; and *The Corio*, 12 tonnes, from Geelong Yacht Club. *Janet* beat *Taniwha* by 5m 59s — the other three retired — in the officially recorded time of 3h 20m 46s for the 33 nm, at the almost unbelievable average speed of 9.8 k.

An overjoyed Sir William arranged a rematch, with the first prize of £700. As the historian of Royal Brighton Yacht Club remarks, it is hard to equate that figure to modern values but a contemporary newspaper had just advertised an eight-room, brick family house built on land 19.5 m by 54.86 m near the Yarra River for £750. So Sir William's purse was probably worth at least $60,000 by today's standards. In any case, *Janet* won again and her victory, combined with Sir William's enthusiasm, encouraged other wealthy men to buy and build large yachts for the Victoria and Geelong Clubs fleets. The largest craft registered at that time were the *Cushie Doo*, a 44.19 m, 245 tonne, three-masted schooner built in Scotland for gold miner-pastoralist William Henty Osmond (she could cruise at 8.5 k under her auxiliary steam engine, which drove an adjustable two-bladed propeller), and Charles Millar's *Red Gauntlet*, a 30.78 m, 135 tonner that in 1882 'with several gentlemen aboard, left Port Phillip Heads for a leisurely three-week cruise to Hobart and back'.

In 1887 Sir William Clarke sent *Janet* to Sydney 'to establish annual contests and foster intercolonial rivalry' in a best-of-three series of races. He put up £100 for a cup, and members of Royal Sydney Yacht Squadron added £100 stake money and nominated their two best boats to meet him. These were Alfred Milson's 15.11 m waterline *Waitangi* and James Fairfax's 14.02 m waterline *Magic*. Under the handicapping rules both had time allowances from Sir William's bigger boat but they hardly needed it. *Janet* was disabled in a southerly squall off Sydney Heads in the first race over 28 nm from Farm Cove in Sydney Harbour to a flag mark off Botany Bay, and back. She was forced to retire. *Waitangi* won. In the second race, sailed entirely in Sydney Harbour in a fresh breeze, *Waitangi* finished only 29s behind *Janet* and, with her time allowance, beat her easily.

Top right Alfred Milson's 20.42 m cutter *Era*, winner of the Centennial Exhibition regatta on Port Phillip in 1888, on her return to Sydney. (RSYS Archives)

Bottom right Hardly an object of beauty but an air of solid worth about it nevertheless. The Sayonara Cup, symbol of yachting excellence. (RSYS Archives)

Top Victorian champion *Sayonara*, winner of the first Sayonara Cup match in 1904. (RSYS Archives)

Bottom New South Wales representative *Bona*, narrowly beaten in the first challenge match for the Sayonara Cup in 1904. (RSYS Archives)

With two wins, *Waitangi* had won for Alfred Milson the first organized intercolonial contest held in Sydney, if we accept Royal Sydney Yacht Squadron's history, just fifty years after his father had won the first organized Anniversary Day regatta in 1837. Although there was no need for further races, a special match was arranged for *Janet* and *Magic* over a 40 nm course from Sydney Harbour to Barranjoey, north of Sydney, and back. The Victorian boat won, and Sir William, whose sportsmanship and good humour had also won him many friends, returned to Melbourne, happy with the result of his voyage, to receive with delight the news that the club of which he was commodore had just been raised to Royal status.

A year later, on Port Phillip, *Janet* met two new Sydney champions in the main intercolonial race at the Centennial Exhibition regatta. The visitors were both recent creations of the Sydney naval architect Walter Reeks: Alfred Milson's 20.42 m cutter *Era*, with a waterline length of 17.67 m and a sail area of 389.35 sq m; and W.P. Smairl's *Volunteer*, 19.81 m with 343.73 sq m sail area. *Era* finished first and won the main prizes, a £400 cup and a £100 gold anchor that the Victorian Government and Sir William Clarke had given for the race. *Volunteer* was second. A third entry from Sydney, NSW parliamentarian Jack Want's 40 tonne centreboard yawl *Miranda*, had also been expected to beat *Janet* but she had been caught in a south-easterly gale on the way to Melbourne, had burst her water tanks, sprung a leak and had failed to reach the starting line. Her ship's company, most of them teetotallers, had only whisky and some soda to drink for three days. (But they were better off than the three-man crew of one of Want's earlier yachts, *Mignonette*, who, cast adrift in a dinghy when

Sir Alexis Albert's 24.38 m Sydney schooner *Boomerang*, once a centreboarder, built for Melbourne owner in 1903 as *Bona*, often confused with 15.24 m Sayonara Cup racer *Bona*, a cutter.

Walter Marks's Sydney 10-metre *Culwulla III*, which in 1910 won the Sayonara Cup on Port Phillip from the Victorian holders. The trophy remained in Sydney for 22 years. (RPAYC Archives)

the vessel sank off South Africa on a delivery voyage from England to Australia, starved for two weeks then ate their fifteen-year-old cabin boy. They were picked up by a passing vessel, confessed their crime and were gaoled for it but pardoned six months later. *Mignonette's* skipper, Captain Dudley, migrated to Sydney, set up business as a sailmaker, and raced in the crews of several yachts until 1900, when he was the first victim of an outbreak of bubonic plague.)

Interstate racing lapsed after the Melbourne Centennial Regatta of 1888 and was not resumed until 1904 when Victorian Alfred Gollin sailed his handsome clipper-bowed *Sayonara*, a 17.67 m, 3.27 m beam cutter, to Sydney from Melbourne and challenged anyone to race him for a £100 cup. Royal Sydney Yacht Squadron and Prince Alfred Yacht Club mounted a joint effort and nominated *Bona*, a lively NZ-built 15.24 metre yacht with a formidable record. But *Sayonara*, superbly built (in 1898 in Adelaide) to a design of the famous Scottish naval architect William Fife, and newly rigged with hollow, lightweight US-made spars and English sails, was just a shade too good. She won two out of three races off Sydney Heads and laid the foundation of the Sayonara Cup interstate challenge series that for the next fifty-eight years remained the symbol of pre-eminence in big boat, round-the-buoys racing in Australia and, at times, led to a high degree of acrimony.

Victoria defended the Cup successfully on Port Phillip in 1907 and 1909 with *Sayonara* against Sydney challengers but lost it in 1910 to Walter Marks' well-tuned and expertly crewed 10-metre class *Culwulla III* (formerly *Awanui*). England's Yacht Racing Association ruled that the Sydney yacht, being smaller than the defender *Sayonara* (rated 12 m under the then-existing measurement rules) was entitled to time allowances. The races had been sailed in Port Phillip off-the-mark with both parties agreeing to submit the finishing times to an independent authority for decision. There was therefore a delay of six months after the three-race contest before the winner was known. Victoria did not challenge for eighteen years, then made four unsuccessful bids with different boats in 1928-29-30-31. All were beaten off by 8-metre class boats representing RSYS, and all with Charles Trebeck at the helm. Victoria regained the Sayonara Cup in 1932 when the Melbourne helmsman James Linacre bought the Sydney title-holder *Vanessa* and challenged with her. He beat the Sydney defender *Norn* in a closely fought five-heat series off Sydney Heads.

Except for one spell of a year (1953) when Tasmania's Ted Domeney, in *Erica J*, wrestled the Sayonara Cup free, it remained in Victoria until 1955 during three other jousts with Tasmania's *Erica J* (in 1951-52-54) while NSW yachtsmen brooded because they had no suitable challenger. In 1955 the ebullient Bill Northam (see Chapter 4) put an end to this thirty-three year mortgage with his imported British champion *Saskia*, representing Royal Sydney Yacht Squadron against Victoria and Tasmania.

In 1956, with Northam again at the helm against Victoria and Tasmania, and in 1962 with Bill Solomons at the helm for a new owner, against Victoria, *Saskia* won easily. For more than twenty years there were no more challenges for the Sayonara Cup and the trophy remained, gleaming defiance, in a glass cabinet at the Royal Sydney Yacht Squadron, a relic of past glories. Then in 1983, with no more 8-metre class challengers built and none likely to be in the immediate future, officials of Royal Sydney Yacht Squadron agreed to accept interstate challenges for the Sayonara Cup in international Dragon class sloops. These weatherly 8.9 m long boats, with three-man crews including the helmsmen, had been designed by Norwegian Johann Anker in 1928 and used in Olympic regattas from 1948 to 1972, when Queenslander John Cuneo won the gold medal. Their displacement by the Soling class for Olympic competition had not greatly reduced the popularity of the Dragons, especially in Australia, where they were raced in NSW, Victoria, Tasmania, South Australia, and Western Australia. Changes in the class rules to allow construction in fibreglass as well as wood, aluminium spars and high tech equipment had also considerably improved the boats' performance, especially in light weather. So, in 1984, after State selection races in Tasmania and Victoria and an elimination series, Royal Sydney Yacht Squadron's defender *Kirribilli*, skippered by Rob Porter, met Tasmanian challenger *Tahune*, skippered by Stephen Shield, in a best-of-five series on Sydney Harbour. It was an uneven match. Porter, a former world title holder in *Kirribilli*, won 3-0. In 1985, Ted Albert, son of Sir Alexis Albert, whose 8 metre *Norn* had won the Sayonara Cup against Victoria in 1928 and lost it in 1932, defended the trophy for RSYS in his Dragon, *Rawhiti*. The name was an echo of a famous NZ-designed 16.4 m racing machine that Albert's grandfather, Frank Albert,

Saskia defending the Sayonara Cup off Sydney in 1962. The yacht, refitted, handsomely maintained and occasionally raced, is now owned by veteran Sydney helmsman Joe Palmer. (*SMH*)

had restored and sailed with distinction in Sydney fifty-eight years earlier.

Twenty years before that, *Rawhiti*, owned by Charles Brockhoff, had been twice beaten for the Cup by *Sayonara* herself. But the modern *Rawhiti* was a superlative boat of her class. Albert and his crew, after months of careful tuning and training under the direction of Olympic and America's Cup coach Mike Fletcher, were fit to sail for any title. They demolished the challenger *Anastasia*, sailed by Guyan Wilson of Royal Geelong Yacht Club, who had earlier eliminated the Tasmanian contender, in three straight races. In 1986, Albert, in *Rawhiti*, again defeated Wilson in *Anastasia*, 4-1 in a best-of-seven series. Although the Sayonara Cup is no longer a symbol of big boat supremacy, after a lapse of many years it has served to re-establish high class interstate match racing. And that is just what Alfred Gollin had intended it to do when he put up the trophy so long ago.

Victorians have fought hard and with great success in other interstate challenge battles for historic trophies, most notably the Northcote Cup for the international 6-metre class (of which more elsewhere). But as interest in yachting has spread and dozens of clubs have been formed around Port Phillip Bay and throughout Victoria, catering for a bewildering variety of boats of all sizes and classes, championships have lost much of the flavour of individual rivalry that existed when there were two or three-sided matches settled on a sudden death basis when one boat had scored two or three wins. All championships now for interstate, or as they are called, national titles, in 100 or more different classes are diffused affairs — decided on fractions of decimal points scored over seven races, with the worst performance discarded — between fleets that often total sixty, representing all States. Victoria, for a long time pre-eminent in round-the-buoys racing, especially in Olympic class boats, and for many years the administrative centre of yachting in Australia, has in recent times been forced to share much of its authority with other States. But Victorians have kept an admirable sense of tradition. They honour their past champions in classes discarded and forgotten elsewhere and treasure fine old trophies that their great-grandfathers encouraged titled persons, among them State Governors and Governors-General, to give for the encouragement of the sport. Many such dignitaries were valued members of the clubs. But crestolatry did not blind Victorian yachtsmen to the realities and responsibilities of club membership. In 1901 when Lord Brassey, a former State Governor of Victoria, failed to pay his annual subscription of 10s and 6d, Brighton Yacht Club expelled him.

Questions of club seniority and precedence reached a state of crisis soon after the turn of the century and threatened to split the Victorian Yacht Racing Association. The rows culminated in a court ruling without precedent in the history of yachting. It was based on rivalry that had smouldered for years between Geelong Yacht Club and Brighton Yacht Club on the issue of which had been first founded. The argument burst into legal flames when both parties took the matter before Sir John Madden, Chief Justice of Victoria. His Honour, after five years of deliberation and the examination of a vast conglomeration of documents and club records, in 1911 ruled that the senior club was Brighton, formed in 1875. Although Geelong had preceded Brighton by at least sixteen years, the former had lapsed as a club in the 1870s, lost its identity and ceased to function until re-formed in 1880. Sir John, in the course of his summary, also cast some doubt on the age of the State's most venerable club, the Royal Yacht Club of Victoria. Until then RYCV had been unchallenged as the oldest continuously surviving yacht club in Australia, having been first formed in 1856 as the Victoria Yacht Club. He found evidence to suggest that it, too, had ceased to function and had been re-formed under its original name in 1872. Few members of the RYCV felt inclined to thank him for his opinion. And members of South Melbourne's Albert Park Lake Yacht Club, who traced its continued existence on the now-enclosed swamp from 1871, must have smiled slyly. But Brighton and Geelong shook hands and both were granted Royal warrants in 1924.

Victorian yachting suffered a disastrous reverse in 1933 when heavy seas, driven by near-hurricane force winds, destroyed sheltering breakwaters, tore dozens of craft from their moorings and scattered them along the eastern shoreline of Port Phillip. Some boats, drawn up ashore on slipways, were blown over and damaged. The worst sufferers were members of Royal Brighton Yacht Club who lost three-quarters of their club fleet, among them many famous vessels, when the Brighton Pier broke up under the pounding of the seas, and heavy baulks of timber from which much of it was built drifted among yachts moored nearby, battering them to pieces. In a way the storm did much to change the course of yachting in the State. A fleet of strictly one-design craft, stout 5.49 m Jubilee class centreboarders, was built to replace boats lost and these enabled many people who had despaired for the future of the sport in that area to get afloat again. The Jubilees, ostensibly as alike as peas in a pod, and with restrictions on rig that taxed the ingenuity of the most ardent rule benders, provided excellent racing. The attraction of competing in craft that were, in theory at least, exactly the same shape and rig and therefore depended for success only on the skill of the men aboard, greatly appealed to yachtsmen, not only in Victoria, but also in all other States. Until then, strict one-design racing had been almost entirely confined to youngsters' boats — 3.66 m cadet dinghies and the nationally popular 3.50 m Vaucluse Junior (VJ) and 4.57 m Vaucluse Senior (VS) dinghies. Earlier attempts to sustain interest in one-design racing in yachts suitable for grown men, especially in 21 ft (6.40 m) restricted waterline class centreboard sloops that seemed ideal, had failed because the measurement rules permitted too much latitude in hull shapes and rigs. Hotly contested interstate championships for the Forster Cup in the 21-footers had subsided before the onslaught of those with the money and will to take advantage of the rules and build boats that were inherently faster than their rivals.

So the Jubilee class, the brilliant creation of Charles Peel, a Melbourne boatbuilder, gave one-design idealists new hope. It also helped to put Victorians, like the rest of Australians, in the properly receptive frame of mind for the flood of other so-called one-design boats of all types and sizes that began in the early 1950s and continues today. Yachtsmen worldwide have now, of course, lost their innocence about this pattern of perfection and have learned that without ironbound measurement controls, strict supervision of construction, and restrictions on equipment that admit no argument, it is almost impossible to produce two boats exactly the same, of wood, metal or fibreglass, even out of the same mould. But they had to keep on trying.

In 1985 Victoria had registered fleets of 104 different so-called one-design classes. Of these classes 4862 were centreboard dinghies; 1167 trailerable yachts; 1473 multihull; and 1778 fixed-keel yachts, making a grand total of 9280 registered sailing craft. And, with the growth of the centreboard classes, the exposed, sweeping sandy shorelines around Port Phillip, once cursed because they provided no shelter, have become a boon for off-the-beach sailors who can tow their boats on trailers to natural launching sites.

Victoria's inland waters, rivers, lakes and dams have big fleets of boats of all kinds, too, wherever there is room to sail them. The annual Marlay Point overnight marathon race of 60 nm, a joyous handicap for all comers, through the Gippsland Lake system — across Lake Wellington, along the winding canal of McLennan's Strait into Lake Victoria, to Metung, around Raymond Is. to Paynesville, in Lake King — is one of the biggest races (if one judges size on the number of competitors) in the world. In 1980, a total of 607 boats, forty-five of them from outside Victoria, ranging in length from 4.88 m to 8.53 m, started in the Marlay Point race and created a state of happy chaos that took a day to untangle.

WESTERN AUSTRALIA

Western Australia, ironically for a State that presents its yachtsmen with the most wind-swept, brutally exposed, havenless coastlines in the Commonwealth, failed in its first serious attempts at competitive sailing because of a lack of breeze. Sailing races started up on the Swan River at Perth with a regatta, billed for 1 June 1841, and were designed as part of the colony's celebrations of its Foundation Day. Because of calms, however, no races were held until 3 June, and even then the light airs were so uninviting that some owners withdrew, leaving the largest boat (competing in the over 18 ft class) to win the top sailing prize of £5 by completing the course alone. In the following twenty years further efforts were made to stir up sailing interest on Foundation Days, but in the face of fiascos such as that of 1861, when such a day-long calm prevailed that it took eleven hours to drift five miles, enthusiasm was understandably lacking.

In the early 1870s a novel and daring notion was presented: why not abandon the fluky months of May and June and hold regattas at windy Easter-time? Or even in blustery November? This innovation did the trick, and one or more regattas became almost an annual event on the Swan. The sailing fraternity tried hard to ignore the fact that the most popular events with the public remained the rowing or 'pulling' events that took up a large slice of each water carnival programme.

As with most nascent competitive sailing in the nineteenth century, many competitors tried to insist that the sport was one that ought to be reserved for gentlemen. Captain Croke, the harbour master at Fremantle, lost an appeal to the regatta committee against the ban on government boats competing, even when he told them poignantly that he personally bore all the expenses of his boat, *Little Stranger*, and 'knowing her good qualities. . .treated her like a child'.

Moves to form a yacht club coalesced and dissolved like fog until 13 November 1876, when twelve 'interested gentlemen' held the first general meeting of the club that was the forerunner of the Perth (later Royal Perth) Yacht Club. This body held its first regatta on the Swan two years later, bowing to popular prejudice by including races for oarsmen and a walking-the-greasy-pole event. And it went on holding an annual carnival, in spite of members' grumbles that the organizing costs and prize money ought more properly to be spent on a boathouse and a jetty — the latter chiefly to help prevent members' feet being cut on broken glass as they waded through the shallows near Barrack Street, where many moored their yachts.

A grant of land from the City Council and an overdraft made up for the financial havoc caused by low membership fees (a guinea a year) and regatta prizes, and by 1882 Perth Yacht Club had its own shed and slipway. Emboldened by this, the Club introduced WA's first season of summer handicap racing, and the first class-races, apart from regattas. Soon afterwards, the club president officially became a commodore (P.A. Gugeri), his opening broadside under that rank being a command to members to keep the boathouse tidy by putting away their own gear. There was more worry attached to this pioneer boathouse than a mess of untended gear, however. People were breaking into the shed at night. A watch was kept, and high embarrassment followed when it was found that the intruder was a prominent man who used the shed as a place in which to sleep off his hangovers. The committee moved that members would have to pay 2s 6d a time to borrow the boathouse keys from the night-watchman.

By 1889 the Club had decided its commodore ought to wear a uniform with sleeve stripes and a wealth of cap buttons, and that even ordinary members must sail in white trousers, blue serge coat and cap, and insignia. (One member, at least, stubbornly stuck to his favourite sailing headgear — a bowler hat.) The glory of this fancy dress — which was similar to that long affected by prosperous amateur sailors in all Australian yachting centres — was a little dimmed when the Press, covering the Club's ritual procession of yachts from Perth water to Crawley and back, reported that '. . .as the crew of each yacht saluted their Commode [sic] the sight was one that will not easily be forgotten'. More important than the sumptuary laws of 1888 was the Club's decision in that year to adopt the new rule of handicapping by sail area, though this was to lead to endless protests and wrangling.

Money troubles plagued the Perth Yacht Club up to the post-World War II boom. In the late 1880s, the treasurer reported that he had paid no accounts because the bank would give no more credit. Still, enough promise of money was raised to introduce the Swan River Championship Gold Cup, in 1889. The inaugural race was marked by a strong outburst by the veteran member William Mumme, who protested against the use of outriggers. These were at once banned by the club. Mumme won the second Championship Cup in *Nautilus* but the cup itself was not forthcoming for some time, as many of its so-called sponsors had not paid up. Not long after this, the winner of a minor race, on stepping up to collect the prize of £5 was handed only £1 5s, it being pointed out that he owed the club the balance in dues. Perhaps in financial desperation, soon after this it was decided to admit ladies to the club premises on the payment of 5s annual subscription.

There was, however, a compensation in sight for this penury. In 1890 Queen Victoria gave the club a charter, and it became the first of the WA clubs to become 'Royal'. No dampening of euphoria was felt by members when one published comment referred to 'absolutely sickening nonsense. . .asking permission to dub a potty little Yacht Club in a fourth-rate colonial city that hasn't a ten-tonner in its fleet, a "Royal Yacht Club. . ."' WA's other Royal club is Royal Freshwater Bay Yacht Club, formed as Freshwater Bay Boating Club in 1896 and granted its warrant in 1934, when no one considered it more than its due.

During the 1890s Royal Perth's keenness and competitiveness, and its social prestige, triggered a widespread interest in organized sailing, and other clubs began to proliferate, always encouraged by Royal Perth, even when it meant loss of members to itself. The list of growth is remarkable: Perth Sailing Club, 1894; Perth Flying Squadron, 1896; Freshwater Bay Boating Club, 1896; Mounts Bay Sailing Club, 1899. The Mounts Bay Club in 1905 made WA history by sending the 4.27 m *Rene* to compete in the January–February interstate sailing carnival on Sydney Harbour. In the new century further clubs appeared: West Australian Yacht Club, 1902 (a fusion of Fremantle Sailing Club, originally formed in 1876, and Fremantle Yacht Club), which went in for deep sea outings; Perth Dinghy Club, 1903, which attracted at once, at a 5s a year fee, forty young members, owners of 14 ft dinghies, and was later prominent for a time in promoting Sydney's queer, over-canvased 10-footers. (In 1909 Perth won its first 14-footer national title when *Elma*, skippered by Andy Roche of Perth, alone sailed the Sydney Harbour course in a blow. In later years, in modernized 14-footers, WA sailors were to establish an extraordinary record in national title events. They won the title in 1931 and from 1947 to 1985 won twenty-four of the thirty-five annual championship series of races sailed in Perth, Adelaide, Sydney, Melbourne and Brisbane.)

Nearly all Perth's early clubs had a shed in the colony of clubhouses at the foot of Barrack Street, where Royal Perth also remained until 1953, when it moved to Crawley. In the twentieth century outlying clubs began to hive: Claremont and The Swan Yacht Club, 1904–05; South Perth Yacht Club 1906–07 (called South of Perth Yacht Club since 1960, when it was forced to move its premises); Fremantle Sailing Club (re-establishing its separate identity and continuity from 1876 after five years from 1902 as part of the ailing West Australian Yacht Club), 1907; 18 Foot Yacht Club, 1908. So-called rated boats — of the 14 ft, 16 ft, and 18 ft class — had been active on the Swan since the early 1890s, though the 16-footers had for a time dwindled. (Subsequently, though, the 16s revived, and WA boats won ten national titles. Jack Cassidy, of Perth, in his string of *Evelyns*, won six of the eleven series sailed between 1953 and 1964.)

The 18 Foot Yacht Club's first race, in 1908, was for lady skippers. Two of the four who entered capsized in a fresh easterly before the start, to the considerable satisfaction of some gentlemen who believed that sailing should be an entirely male preserve. A combination club for rated boats, the Rater's Yacht Club, was established in 1909. The Edwardian decade ended with an upsurge of even more new clubs, the Princess Royal (at Albany), the Victoria Park, and the Waverley — the last-named distinguished by stipulating that all boats registered with it had to carry the name of a character in one of the novels of Sir Walter Scott. Some of the old clubs disbanded but new ones have appeared in WA in the past seventy years, and in 1985 there were thirty-one registered with the Yachting Association of Western Australia. They now spread from as far as Lake Argyle (formed by the Ord River dam) in the Kimberleys, to the north-west coast at Port Hedland, to Esperance on the south-east coast and then inland again to Lake Dumbleyung. There is even some sailing on Lake Lefroy, near Widgiemooltha, south of Kalgoorlie, when it rains and provides enough water for boats to float. When the lake is dry, which is most of the time, the local Kambalda Sailing Club conducts races for lands yachts, 'kept afloat' by motorbike wheels. State-wide in 1985, WA clubs had a total of 10,791 members, sailing 730 miscellaneous types of fixed-keel yachts, 1,381 centreboard dinghies, 490 catamarans and 416 trailerable yachts. It is officially estimated that there were also another 1,500 catamarans, not registered with any club, scattered throughout the State. There are also 180 sailboards registered and, according to marketing authorities, the astonishing total of at least 12,000 sold in WA but not registered with clubs.

The Royal Perth, meanwhile, went on its own way, outwardly serene, senior and superior, inwardly torn with anxieties such as unpaid bar accounts, the quality of the club whisky, the complaint of a member that another had stolen his cap, the fact that the club caretaker wanted to get married (the committee, after long discussion, decided to allow him to do so). In 1904 and 1905 a cloud gathered over all WA yachting. In the first year, twelve yachtsmen were drowned in three separate tragedies, and in the following year five men, women and children, passengers in a hired yacht, were lost. Just before World War II, Royal Perth was at such a low ebb that the clubhouse piano had to be sold. But the club hung on grimly and was mindful not only of its small band of ageing members but also of its duty to the new generation of yachtsmen. It was due to Royal Perth that Cadet dinghies were established as a class on the Swan River, in 1930. Six years later the club took in Sharpie members, and later still it encouraged the Pelican class.

It was the Perth Flying Squadron and the Mounts Bay Sailing Club, however, that markedly helped to pioneer interstate competition in WA waters and return venues. Back in 1907 Ted Tomlinson, in *Aeolus*, won the Australian 18-footer championship for WA on the Swan, beating Chris Webb, of Sydney, in *Australian II*, which ran on to a sandbank. And in 1912 WA won the same championship on the Swan when Chris Garland, in *Westana*, outsailed three local rivals and the NSW representative, *Nimrod*, whose skipper, Charlie Hayes, could not drive his boat hard when she cracked her mast in the final stages. Garland took *Westana* to Sydney for another title race in 1913 but was narrowly beaten by the NSW boat *Kismet* (Billy Dunn). A week later, however, on Sydney Harbour, Garland and his crew made amends in an interstate handicap against NSW and Queensland when they sailed *Westana* through a full gale that flattened all the other twenty boats competing. The blow burst after a period of light winds, caught the fleet under big sails and did great damage around the harbour. It was named the Westana Gale to commemorate the Perth boat's performance. Perth Flying Squadron elected Garland a life member. Nine years later, on the Swan, Garland won WA's third national 18-footer title in *Mele Bilo*.

Between the World Wars, Royal Perth also began to take an active interest in interstate competition in several classes and soon had an impressive list of national champions to its credit. Other WA clubs have also added to their State's gallant tries and wins in top class competition in Australia and abroad. By 1986 West Australians had won dozens of national titles in a wide range of fixed-keel and centreboard classes and had competed with honour at the Olympic Games and in many of the world's major ocean races (see later chapters). They had also won twelve world titles in high performance dinghy classes: Flying Dutchman (Rolly Tasker, helmsman); Cherub (Russell Bowler); Hornet (Syd Lodge); Moth (Rob O'Sullivan twice, Greg Hilton); Fireball (John Cassidy, son of 16 ft skiff champion, Jack Cassidy); B class catamarans (Rolly Tasker); Nacra class catamarans (Kevin Allen); in Flying 15 class keelboats (John Cassidy, Graham Lillingston); and in Two Ton Cup class keelboats (Peter Briggs with Noel Robins skipper). In 1985, Allen, of Jervoise Bay Sailing Club near Fremantle, and his crew, Kim Stephens, used four different boats to win the world Nacra class catamaran title on Lake Fort Gibson, in Oklahoma, USA. Three of the boats supplied by the host club so badly de-laminated during the seven-race series that officials agreed to replace them.

In recent years, young WA helmsmen and crews have consistently outsailed youngsters from other States for the right to represent Australia in world youth championships. In 1974 Rodney Beurteaux and Jim Whitton (420 dinghies) and Mark Edwards (Moth) raced at Barcelona, Spain; in 1975 Willie Packer and John Ryan (420) raced at Largs, near Glasgow, Scotland. In those series all finished in the middle of the top quality international fleets against which they raced, greatly improving their own techniques, and dutifully passing on their knowledge to local rivals. In 1978, on the Swan, Beurteaux and Geoff Backshall finished second in the world youth championships for 420 dinghies, and Packer finished second in the Laser class. In 1979, in Poland, Backshall and Brett Matich, representing Australia as 'foreign' entrants, outclassed all comers in the European youth championship series for 420 class dinghies. In 1982, Denis Jones and

Anthony Dean finished second in the world youth championships in 420 class dinghies on Lake Como, Italy. 'Our tradition in the West is to foster young sailors, and we expect to produce many more world champions,' says Ken Cook, former commodore of Fremantle Sailing Club and former president of the Yachting Association of WA.

In 1974 Royal Perth Yacht Club had the honour of nominating *Southern Cross* (campaigned by Alan Bond) for the America's Cup challenge, although this distinction lost some of its gloss when Sun City Yacht Club, housed only in a shed at Yanchep, 45 kilometres from Perth, nominated Bond's *Australia*, in 1977. Royal Perth was again the challenging club with *Australia* in 1980 and with the victorious *Australia II* in 1983 (see Chapter 5), although both boats, while in WA, made Fremantle Sailing Club and its marina their training headquarters.

By 1979 Perth's main sailing area, Melville Water, on the Swan, had become so restricted with massed fleets of boats of every kind that officials had been forced to seek out-of-town courses for special smooth-water regattas. Sixty kilometres south of Perth the developing Cockburn Sound, where the Cruising Yacht Club of WA fostered catamarans and dinghies, was one of the alternatives; so was the remote harbour at Geraldton 626 kilometres north. But after 1979 the development on the coast at the city of Fremantle, adjoining Perth, of Fremantle Sailing Club's superb Success Harbour marina brought dramatic relief. Soon yachts and boats that had been bottled for so long in the Swan had good shelter on the edge of the sea and unlimited room to sail, although conditions on the coast were bouncier than on the Swan. By 1985, at the cost of $10 million, Fremantle Sailing Club's marina had 750 berths for medium to large yachts, permanent hard standing areas for 250 small keel craft, sheds for dinghies, four launching ramps, slipways, a 200 m beach and lawn for rigging small boats, maintenance facilities, a fine clubhouse and 2,500 members. Most of the boats had come out of the Swan's Melville Waters. Now, with easy access from the new marina, they could have courses laid directly off the clubhouse. By 1985 there were also two other marina developments, as part of the WA government's preparation for the 1987 defence of the America's Cup. These were the HMS *Challenger* boat harbour, with 86 berths for big boats and special shore facilities to the immediate north of Fremantle Sailing Club's marina, and a $4.5 million artificial harbour with shelter and moorings for up to 1,000 medium-sized boats at Sorrento, 24 kilometres north of Fremantle. Because a shallow reef from Rottnest Island (11 nm off the coast west of Fremantle) stretches almost continuously south-south-east back to the coast at Garden Island, there is a dampening barrier to the full force of the south-west seas sweeping up from the southern Indian Ocean towards Fremantle. Therefore, although under the pressure of the prevailing strong summer south-west winds, a punishing chop can develop inside this 'bay' formed to the north-east of the reef, boats are spared from big ocean swells. Elsewhere they beat the WA coast for many hundreds of miles. West Australians are apt to be apologetic about these boisterous seas, and for the hard winds from the Indian Ocean and the treacherous currents that bedevil most other places where they sail. But during a century and more of the State's devotion to sailing in these conditions a tenacious breed of amateur mariners has been produced, aggressive on the race-course but ashore perhaps a little more conservative in their manners and at times their dress than those from other States, though always courteous and fair-minded.

41

QUEENSLAND

Queensland is a yachtsman's extravaganza. It has a total coastline of 3,236 nm, a climate that ranges from temperate to fully tropical, and moderate to fresh winds for the most part, with a hurricane or two each season to add spice to life. There is a splendid procession of sandy beaches, a hundred sheltering headlands, bays and harbours from one end of its vast coast to the other, and waters that swarm with exotic life. And, as if that weren't enough, it has also at hand the marvellous 1,200 nm chain of islands of the Great Barrier Reef. Boating tourists from all over Australia rave about the joys of cruising the Queensland coast and its Barrier Reef, and thousands annually fly halfway across the world for the privilege of doing so.

So Queenslanders, who can sail almost the year round in their shirtsleeves, have opportunities denied most other Australians, and no one would find it odd if all of them lazed away their time afloat, basking in the sun, without a thought for the starter's gun. On the contrary, behind their easy-going manner and welcoming smiles a large number of Queensland yachtsmen are quite ruthlessly competitive and devoted to racing. They have won more than 100 national championships in boats of every kind, have produced internationally renowned helmsmen and crews, some of Australia's greatest Olympic sailors and (as detailed elsewhere) revolutionized the design and performance of the world's fastest monohull boats — Australia's 18-footers.

Queenslanders began sailing on the Brisbane River and around the enormous stretches of Moreton Bay soon after the colony's separation from NSW in 1859, and the State's oldest club, Royal Queensland Yacht Squadron, was formed in 1885. Today there are sixty-five clubs, stretching all down the east coast at the main centres of population (and some inland), registered with the Queensland Yachting Association. They have 11,222 members who sail 1,987 dinghies, 682 multihulls and 197 trailerable yachts. There are also 1,500 registered keel yachts of miscellaneous design and, it is officially estimated, at least the same number of keelboats used exclusively for cruising, not registered with any club.

Queensland's successes in major open boat racing began in 1895 when the Brisbane 18-footer *Britannia* won the national title. They continued unabated in this class until 1961 when Bob Miller (who in 1977 changed his name by deed poll to Ben Lexcen) won the world championship in his radical, self-designed, plywood skimmer *Venom*. In between those years Queensland helmsmen and crews won twenty-three national 18-footer titles, scoring four in a row with Vic Vaughan at the helm of the sensational *Aberdare*, and four more between 1951 and 1957 with the burly Norm Wright's *Jenny IV, V* and *VI*.

In the even more hotly contested 16 ft skiff class Queenslanders have scored twenty-one national title wins, five over a period of ten years between 1921 and 1931 by the crafty Alf Whereat, and four, one after another, between 1936 and 1940 by Ron Hendry, whose skill and aggressive spirit at close quarters was enough to rattle many of his rivals.

But Queensland's most celebrated sailor in modern times is John Cuneo, dual Olympian and gold medal winner at Munich in the Dragon class in 1970; America's Cup deputy skipper and tactician in *Southern Cross* in 1974 (see Chapters 4 and 5); four times national champion in Lightweight Sharpies, twice in Dragons and once in 505 dinghies. Cuneo, a Brisbane optometrist, and now, in middle age, a much respected yachting administrator and Australia's former

Olympic coach, was often thought, even at the height of his competitive career, the antithesis of an aggressive sailor. To some he seemed fussy, too cerebral and concerned with minor details, excessively modest, mild-mannered and without the fire of a great champion. But Cuneo was a masterly tactician with an almost obsessive will to win. He designed and made much of his own equipment because he abhorred gear failures, and he drove his boats, his crews and himself to the limit of physical endurance.

Similarly dedicated was Queensland's great single-handed sailor Ron Jenyns, often forced to train by himself because he had no worthy pacemakers. He was a dual Olympian in Finn dinghies and ten times national titleholder of the class between 1958 and 1970.

Another Queensland star is Peter Hollis, twice world champion in 4.87 m Contender dinghies (another Miller-Lexcen design) and three times national champion in that demanding class and once in Star boats. Hollis has also proved himself as much at home offshore, as crewman or helmsman, as in smooth water and is in great demand for important ocean races.

Queensland has a comparatively small but growing fleet of quality ocean racers among its keelboat fleets and has sent few serious competitors to major offshore events in southern States. But they compete vigorously in local ocean races and offer generous prizes and lavish hospitality to induce the best of interstate competitors to sail north and join them. 'Make the trip worthwhile with a cruise through the Barrier Reef after the races', they say, in effect, 'and we'll show you what paradise is like.' Every year the fleets that answer invitations such as this are increasing.

SOUTH AUSTRALIA

No yachtsman would have blamed South Australians if they had rejected Adelaide as a place for settlement and established their city on the south-western shores of Spencer Gulf, with the wonderful harbour of Port Lincoln and adjoining Boston Bay at its doorstep. Indeed, there were many who favoured the idea when the foundation of the province of South Australia was first proposed. Port Lincoln is one of the finest stretches of clear, protected water in the continent, 13 nm long and 4 nm wide, up to 18.3 m deep with a tidal range of only 1.42 m, and ideal for ships and sailing of every kind. Matthew Flinders, who discovered Port Lincoln in 1802, admired it so much that he named it in honour of 'my native province'. But that many-talented, firm-minded surveyor, Colonel William Light, rejected Port Lincoln, partly because of the absence of fresh water near at hand, partly because of the barren nature of the land, and settled on Port Adelaide. Most yachtsmen near that largest centre of the State's population have been stuck with the exposed, often savage waters of Gulf St Vincent ever since. The long fetch of the prevailing south-westerly summer winds that build up to about 18 k and sometimes reach 30 k, and the gales from the north-west that sweep up and down the Gulf, make the sandy eastern coastline a dead lee shore with one-and-a-half metre seas breaking on the edge for at least 80 nm. When the 'Gully' winds blow hard from the east, any craft caught offshore has to fight her way back or run 35 nm across open water to shelter that is far from comfortable.

Surprisingly, however, South Australians started pleasure sailing soon after foundation in 1836, and held their first regatta at Glenelg, on the occasion of the Prince of Wales' birthday, 9 November 1855 'in unpropitious weather that cleared up in the afternoon'. There were four races for vessels of from more than 20 tonnes to lifeboats, and prize money totalled £160. A crowd of some 5,000 members of the public came to watch. In the next few years a total of fifteen yachts of various sizes were reported to be sailing in and out of Port Adelaide, but there are scanty records of their activities until the South Australian Yacht Club, now Royal South Australian Yacht Squadron (Royal warrant, 1890) was formed in 1869 with 'some of the foremost men of the time' as members. At first they were able to use the cramped inner harbour and the narrow Port River for racing but inevitably, as the needs of commercial shipping grew, this was denied to all but small craft. Most boats were of modest size in the early days, sailing off time allowances of half a minute for each foot of waterline length, although there were some fine seagoing yachts, too. These latter cruised extensively in the open waters up and down the Gulf, rejoicing in excellent fishing when they anchored, as they do today, but soon became wary of the packs of ferocious sharks that haunt some of the bays around Kangaroo Island.

By 1873 Mr Justice Bundey (later Sir Henry), vice commodore and commodore of the club for fourteen years, was racing his 20 tonner *Zephyr* and by 1883 his 19.51 m 50 tonne (Thames measurement) *Wanderer* with her topmast truck towering 24.4 m above the deck.

Sir James Ferguson, governor of the province and patron of the club, sailed *Edith*, a 43 tonner. She raced against the redoubtable Victorian yacht *Janet* in the Melbourne intercolonial regatta of 1881. By 1893 A.P. Wyley had the superb *Alexa*, a William Fife-designed 14.02 m cutter, named gratefully after the skilful Adelaide builder Alex McFarlane. She remained the fastest yacht in SA for at least ten years, and so impressed Victorians that they had Fife design 'a bigger version of the same boat' for McFarlane to build. She was christened *Sayonara*, beat the best racing vessels in Australia for many years and established the interstate challenge series for the Sayonara Cup.

During the 1890s and early 1900s wealthy SA owners built and bought many big vessels, sail and power driven. One was a steamship, *Adele*, of 44.2 m, built in Scotland. The firm who built her, apparently under the impression that a number of members of the Royal South Australian Yacht Squadron had private goldmines, wrote to the club recommending *Adele* for their inspection and offering to build as many more as they would like to order. Matters of cost apart, the number of sizeable yachts in the Squadron's fleet was always restricted because it was dangerous to leave any craft moored in the open Gulf (several had been driven ashore and wrecked) and there were no sheltered waters, apart from the Squadron's Birkenhead quarters, and some minor club's sheds, in the inner harbour. The big boats finally lost this accommodation in 1924 after a long and at times bitter struggle with the Marine Board, and were forced to move to the artificial Outer Harbour. Only a few small craft of other clubs have clung to their inshore sites. After half a century of dredging and extension of shoreline facilities, the Squadron now has room in its Outer Harbour basin, called The Pool, with clubrooms nearby, for about 200 moderately sized yachts — far fewer than the thousands of sailing enthusiasts among Adelaide's population of 1,000,000 would support if there were more room.

But between 1978 and the early 1980s, a new era began for Adelaide's yachtsmen. The Cruising Yacht Club of South Australia, primarily interested in ocean racing, cast aside gloomy predictions of financial ruin for all who backed it and built its North Haven marina in a man-made harbour at Gulf Point, just south of the Outer Harbour. Initially it had berths for 200 craft, but these places were so much in demand that there was expansion to accommodate 500. The Australian Yachting Federation conducted team selection trials for the 1984 Olympic Games in Gulf St Vincent with the CYCSA as host club and North Haven as headquarters for craft of all seven Olympic classes. By 1985, the complex, with modern slipping and maintenance facilities, was expected eventually to be developed to accommodate 1,000 yachts floating in berths and on hard-standing ashore, with launching ramps for trailerable craft. For the first time in more than a century Adelaide's yachtsmen had room to breathe.

In the meantime, especially after the post-World War II upsurge of sailing and its recognition as a sport for the people and not just a pastime for the privileged, and the use of trailers to transport boats to launching sites, SA had become predominantly a small-boat State. In 1986 it had 1,101 registered centreboard craft, 484 catamarans, 417 trailerable yachts, and 474 keel yachts in thirteen affiliated metropolitan clubs near Adelaide (the biggest number in the Brighton and Seacliff Yacht Club, which races 380 boats) and in 20 country clubs scattered along the coastline of the State in ports and bays from Ceduna in the west to Port McDonnell, near Mount Gambier, on the Victorian border, and inland to Broken Hill in NSW. One is the Royal Port Pirie Yacht Club catering for small craft and a few fixed-keel vessels and surely the least likely of any aquatic body in the British Commonwealth to carry the designation, Royal. Members are fiercely proud of it, needless to say. Further down Spencer Gulf skippers and crews of the growing Port Lincoln Yacht Club fleet, owned by the surrounding population of only about 10,000 people, luxuriate in their fine harbour, tending to smile indulgently on their less fortunate compatriots. Port Lincoln, although remote, has in recent years become recognized as one of the best areas in Australia for serious class-boat racing, so much so that in 1979 it was chosen as the venue for the Soling class national titles.

But Adelaide sailors have learned to live with the Gulf St Vincent, watching the weather and the seas during the seven-month warm season of racing. In the semi-surf that rises quickly when the winds are onshore and fresh, their boat-launching techniques leave visiting competitors floundering. The adversities under which Adelaide yachtsmen so often have to sail also have inspired them to rise to standards of excellence in general seamanship and boat handling that have won the State many national and international honours in a wide range of craft.

Among SA's outstanding sailors in recent times have been: Jim Hardy (Max Whitnall crew), world 505 class dinghy champion, dual Olympian and three times an America's Cup skipper; Brian Farren-Price (Chris Hough crew), and John Parrington (Chris Hough crew), world 505 class dinghy champions; John Gilder (Doug Giles crew), twice, and Anders Wangel (Doug Giles crew), world 420 dinghy class champions; Chris Tillett (David Tillett crew) world International Cadet class dinghy champion; Chris Tillett (Mike Rogers crew) world Fireball class dinghy champion. They won their titles in all conditions of wind and sea in the USA, Ireland, Israel, France and Australia, in some cases against crews chosen from overseas fleets totalling 20,000. Whenever it blew really hard, they staggered their opponents with their rough-water skills. Hardy went to the Olympics of 1964 and 1968, and in 1984 South Australians Chris Pratt (Finn) and Chris Tillett with Richard Lumb (470 class dinghy) were chosen for the Los Angeles Games (see Chapter 4: Olympics).

TASMANIA

Surprisingly, Tasmanians are not the ace small-boat sailors one might expect them to be, although, as detailed earlier, they took to pleasure boating on their magnificent waterways from the early days of settlement, held some of Australia's first regattas, formed one of the first clubs, and quickly developed a reputation for offshore seamanship of a high order.

But, in spite of this background, in recent years they have won comparatively fewer national and international championships in small centreboard boats than one might have expected. In 1985 the respectable total of 709 dinghies, 151 multihulls and eighty-five trailerable yachts were registered with the State Yachting Association. It is true, of course, that water and air temperatures in Tasmania are usually much lower than in other States and are therefore not conducive to year-round sailing in exposed open boats; but there are still eight months of the year when the climate is reasonably mild and when waterproof wet suits can insulate sailors from sudden cold spells. Their real trouble, Tasmanian yachting administrators explain, is their isolation. Tasmania's small-boat fleets are split into twenty-three different classes, racing with twenty-five clubs, some widely separated from the others. Also, apart from this isolation at home, few boat owners and their crews can afford the sacrifices in time and money necessary to ship their boats to the mainland for tuning and battle-practice against the best competitors from other States. So, with their class fleets spread thinly, even in the two main centres of population of Hobart and Launceston, and only occasionally able to combine for massed races, crews generally lack intense competitive experience, their boats are not always highly tuned, and they fail to reach the peaks of excellence critical for success in open company. In the same way that all Australian sailors, in comparison with the rest of the world, suffer through a dilution of talent among too many classes, so do Tasmanians suffer in our national title series. Tasmanian Yachting Association officials, well aware of this weakness, have recently organized Youthsail Seminars and, with the aid of commercial sponsors, have brought prominent small-boat sailors from mainland States to lecture promising young Tasmanians. Only when an outstandingly brilliant individual boat and crew emerges or when a class is concentrated in a group and their efforts organized, as they once were in the 3.66 m Cadet dinghy and the 3.66 m Rainbow dinghy classes, and are now in the International Cadet 3.22 m dinghy class, have Tasmanians met their mainland rivals on equal terms. They had many successes in the 3.66 m Cadet dinghies for the Stonehaven Cup national championships and won ten national Rainbow class titles between 1957 and 1971, decisively out-sailing other State representatives.

In early 1979 three well-trained, two-boy crews from Tasmania were the most consistent State team in the Australian and the world International Cadet championships at Adelaide. They raced against a fleet that included eight overseas boats. Tasmanian David Rees who, with Grant Maddock as crew, won the world title, demonstrated the value of consistent experience in open competition. He'd been aboard the runner-up in the world title series in Bombay in 1976 and the winner of the Australian title in the Melbourne series of 1977. Another pair of Tasmanian youngsters, Rodney Behrens and Justin Keating, won the world Cadet title in England in 1979. Individual Tasmanians of great natural ability have also had sporadic national successes in Sharpie and Status 19 (for women) classes and in Cherub, Finn, Enterprise and Heron dinghies. Again, in the hotly contested International Fireball class in 1983, Tasmanians Stewart Hamilton and David Connor (crew) won the national title at Lake Cootharaba (Queensland) and the right to represent Australia in the world championships in Switzerland, where they also won. In the following year, Gary Smith, with Nick Connor as crew, repeated the performance, winning the nationals in Hobart and the world championship in the USA, demonstrating the inherent talent in the State when Tasmanians concentrate on a class.

As a corollary, Tasmania's bigger boats, whose crews have been able to combine skill and consistent training at home with the means to transport their boats to the mainland for regular interstate campaigns, have lifted their game enormously. In the once popular 21 ft Restricted Waterline (7.62 m overall) class centreboarders Tasmanians were almost unbeatable in the Forster Cup series for the national title. The late brothers 'Skipper' (W.P.) Batt and Harry (H.C.L.) Batt won the Cup in their *Tassie, Tassie Too* and *Tassie III* ten times in the thirteen title series they contested up to 1938. Other Tasmanian crews, one with Neil Batt as the helmsman, later won another string of 21-footer titles. More recently Tasmanian Dragon and Diamond class keelboats have scored in national championship series. In ocean racing (see Chapters 10–13) Tasmanians have had fair successes in major interstate events, mainly because of their qualities of seamanship in heavy weather, though their boats have often been out-gunned by changing measurement rules. In 1985 Don Calvert's One Ton Cup class ocean racer *Intrigue*, designed by UK-based Portuguese naval architect Tony Castro, won the right to represent Australia in the Admiral's Cup and was top scorer of the national team of three yachts in that five-race series. *Intrigue* also finished tenth overall on points in the fifty-four boat fleet (see Chapter 14). Earlier, however, in the world One Ton Cup class series (also sailed off the south coast of England), Calvert, a former Australian champion Dragon class keelboat helmsman, found his boat out-paced in a fleet of thirty-eight ultralight, high-tech performers and finished twenty-seventh.

Overall, though, most of the skippers and crews of the 1,145 miscellaneous keelboats registered with Tasmania's twenty-five clubs (with 5,006 members) are content, when they race at all, with low-key contests on their own club courses, as are so many other yachtsmen throughout Australia. In addition, a large proportion of Tasmanians are passionately devoted to husky, sea-going cruising yachts that never raise a sail in anger. With such a superb diversity of unspoilt places to go, from the robust spread of Storm Bay, in the south, all along the east coast, through the Bass Strait Islands to Stanley on the north-west corner of the jewel-like State, who can blame them?

NORTHERN TERRITORY

Visitors to the remote, high-tidal ports of the Northern Territory once used to joke that the best way to go boating from its humid, tropical shores was in a steamer southward bound. In the last thirty years, though, there has been a steady surge of interest in sailing among Darwin's permanent residents. By 1986 there was an enthusiastic core of amateur sailors racing and cruising a fleet of 180 craft with the Darwin Sailing Club. They included forty centreboard dinghies, ten catamarans, ninety keelboats and forty trailerable yachts competing mainly on the expansive Fanny Bay. And the Bay certainly does expand and contract. When the 7.3 m Spring tide is out yachtsmen have quite a walk over exposed sand banks to reach their moorings. Only when the tide is in can they load their gear into a dinghy and row. A dozen or so of Darwin's larger seagoing craft sail a restricted season of ocean races with the main event the NT Cruising Yacht Association's 530 nm Arafura–Banda Sea handicap to Ambon Island in the Moluccas. The NTCYA, with its tongue somewhat in its cheek, formally invites entries in the race from all other Australian and foreign clubs. Some yachts cruising in the area have joined the local fleet but there has not yet been any concerted rush by yachtsmen from southern States to navigate half the continent for that purpose. Nevertheless in 1985 a fleet of twenty-four local and visiting boats competed, representing Britain, Canada, France, Indonesia, and New Zealand, besides Australia. The cruising NZ family, Frank and Janet Hall (with sons Greg and Michael), won the race narrowly in their 12.8 m *Sirocco*. Second was Bill Gibson's *Evergreen* (the rebuilt former Sydney 16.45 m *Even*, first home in the 1955 Sydney–Hobart race). With admirable diplomatic skill the Territorians persuaded the Indonesian Government to provide a naval patrol boat and a helicopter to guard the fleet. Senior Indonesian officials from Djakarta also attended the presentation party.

Darwin has twice been host to Australia's Catamaran Week national championship regatta that annually circulates in all States. In 1978 more than 100 cat owners from southern States trailered boats many thousands of miles to compete, and some sent their boats by air freight. At Gove Yacht Club, in the Gulf of Carpentaria, there is a thriving fleet of twenty-seven keel yachts, thirteen trailerable yachts, eighteen centreboarders, and nine multihulls. Northern Territory sailors are deservedly proud that three of Australia's popular catamaran classes originated there. These are the 3.66 m Arafura Cadet, an ideal training boat for youngsters which can be easily home-built and car-topped; the low cost 4.27 m Arrow cat, and the 4.88 m Mosquito. All were designed by Neil Fowler of Darwin, the Arrow in collaboration with Melbourne engineer Roy Martin, designer of the former world C-class champion catamaran *Miss Nylex*.

Top Anniversary Day regatta in 1856. James Milson's *Mischief* is leading *Enchantress* (left) and *Challenger* (right). An artist's impression from the Archives of Royal Sydney Yacht Squadron.

Bottom By 1986 sailboards, with 1,000,000 sold, were the world's most popular boats. Australian exponents in the Windsurfer class were equally adept in rough and smooth water. (Neva Griggs)

Right Former JOG Australian champion *Mullberry,* 7.93 m, skippered by Jim Voyzey, of Sydney's RPAYC, is a trailerable Sonata 8, popular but not yet officially registered registered as a class. (Bob Ross) (Bob Ross)

Bottom left 1979 Laser champion Peter Conde, of Queensland, is hard pressed to keep his boat on her feet. (Bob Ross)

Bottom right 505 dinghy masters: Boat-building brothers Terry and Geoff Kyrwood (shown here), father Bob and crewman Reg Crick have been close to four world title wins and, in different pairings, have won six consecutive national championships. Terry and Crick won the 1983 world title. (Bob Ross)

2

Classes in Australia, Centreboard and Keel, their Status and Distribution

IN PREPARING the following lists of classes of craft and their distribution in Australia the only accurate source of information has been the class association membership of the various State yachting authorities. The detailed lists include only those classes that are registered in more than one State, with those classes registered in one State only being grouped together alphabetically at the end of each yacht type.

It is known that there are some classes of boats other than those listed, the owners of which have not formed a class association in any State. Their numbers, however, are so few that they have little significance except, as mentioned earlier, further to dilute the talent available for serious class racing. There may also be some classes shown in the lists that are sailed in States other than those listed but which are not recorded here as such because they have no class association in those States. For example, the popular Tasar class is not shown as having an association in WA although Tasars are known to be sailing in that State.

Between 1978 and 1985, most notable in the category of Australia's part-registered but generally unregistered classes was the stunning total of 70,000 craft of a completely new type. This was generically called the Sailboard, a single-hulled, featherweight, rudderless cross between a surfboard and a sailing boat, with a pivoting centreboard. Several mass-produced types of different sizes (between 3.92 m and 2.45 m in length), styles and brand names were on the market in many countries, but the most popular in Australia (about 44 per cent) was a brand called Windsurfer, of which approximately 30,000 had been sold in eight years. All depended on a flexible, swivelling mast, jointed at the deck, and a single sail (from 6.5 sq m to 3.8 sq m in area) rigged inside a wishbone and controlled by the operator standing and balancing his or her weight against the pressure of the wind. Speeds of more than 28 k had been recorded in fresh winds and smooth water. Most sailboards were used as fun boats for casual sailing

49

in smooth water, but a few craft of special construction and without centreboards were also used for wave riding in the surf. Novelty sailboards for two, three and four rider-sailors were being built in several countries. Australians were among major place-getters in overseas and Australian championship regattas and between 1980 and 1984 won twelve world titles in medium to heavyweight divisions against professional and semi-professional riders. Internationally the staggering total of 800,000 sailboards had been sold by mid-1983 (one million in 1985) and because of this worldwide popularity the International Yacht Racing Union, after agreeing to class the craft as boats, decided to include races for them in future Olympic Games. The type of sailboard chosen for the 1984 Los Angeles Games was the European-made Windglider, a so-called displacement type board, considered most suitable for sailors of varying physique but not then available in Australia because of a patent dispute later settled in the courts (see Chapter 4: Olympics). But competitive sailors were in the minority. Of the Australian total of 70,000 sailboards sold by 1985, fewer than 3,000 had been registered with the Class Association and only 1,500 of these ever raced in organized club, State or interstate competitions. A solid core of 500 sailboard riders competed regularly, and the best of these qualified for competition in sponsored regattas for rich prizes, sometimes worth $15,000 to the winner. In 1984 the Windsurfer world championships, held at Nedlands Yacht Club, near Perth, WA, attracted more than 400 sailboarders, representing fifteen countries. Australians won five of the eight titles contested.

Definition of Class Types

I — International

A class recognized by the International Yacht Racing Union as an International Class. It must be actively sailed in a representative number of countries and have sufficient distribution around the world to indicate popularity.

Na — National

A class recognized by the Australian Yachting Federation as a National Class. It must be actively sailed in and be an affiliated member of at least five State/Territory yachting authorities. It must hold an annual national championship.

Tr — Training

A class which is considered to be or was designed to be suitable to introduce newcomers into the sport and in which they can participate competitively.

H — High Performance

A class which is designed to perform well and which is normally sailed by skilled crews with previous sailing experience.

O — Olympic

A class which is selected by the International Yacht Racing Union from among its International Classes. The IYRU policy was to change at least one class but not more than two classes each Olympiad — since 1980 it has not done so.

Note: Many excellent craft of sound performance do not fit into any type, as required by IYRU and AYF definitions.

Definition of Where Sailed

N — New South Wales
V — Victoria
Q — Queensland
S — South Australia

W — Western Australia
T — Tasmania
NT — Northern Territory

Note: For the purpose of yachting administration in Australia, the Australian Capital Territory is considered to be part of New South Wales.

Class Name	Length (M)	Type	Where Sailed					

Centreboard Dinghies

Class Name	Length (M)	Type	N	V	Q	S	W	T
Banshee	3.9	Tr	N			S		
Cadet Dinghy	3.66	Tr		V		S		T
Cadet International	3.22	I Tr		V		S		T
Cherub	3.66	Na H	N	V	Q	S	W	T
Contender	4.87	I H	N	V	Q			
Corsair	4.95		N	V	Q		W	
18-Footer	5.49	H	N		Q	S	W	
Finn	4.5	I O	N	V	Q	S		
Fireball	4.93	I H	N	V	Q	S	W	T
505	5.05	I H	N	V		S		
Flying Ant	3.20	H Tr	N	V			W	
Flying Dutchman	6.05	I O H	N	V	Q	S		
Flying Eleven	3.43	Tr	N		Q	S		
14 ft Dinghy	4.26	Na H	N	V	Q	S	W	
470	4.70	I O H	N	V	Q	S	W	T
420	4.20	I	N	V	Q	S	W	
Gwen 12	3.66	H	N	V		S	W	
Heron	3.43	Na Tr	N	V	Q	S	W	T
Impulse	4.0		N	V				
Javelin	4.27	H		V			W	
Laser	4.23	I H	N	V	Q	S	W	T
Laser II	4.39	I	N	V				
Lightweight Sharpie	5.90	Na H	N	V	Q	S	W	T
Manly Junior	2.63	Tr	N				W	T
Minnow	2.74	Tr		V	Q			
Mirror	3.31	Tr	N	V	Q	S	W	T
Moth	3.35	I H	N	V	Q	S	W	T
National E	4.50	Na	N	V	Q	S	W	T
NS14	4.27	H	N	V	Q	S		T
OK	4.0	I H	N	V		S		T
125	3.81	Na Tr	N	V	Q	S	W	T
145	4.42		N	V	Q			
Pacer	3.83		N	V				
Rainbow	3.66	Na	N	V		S	W	T

Top left South Australians have won three 'worlds' in 505 dinghies. (J. D. Macpherson)

Top right 505 (foreground) hurtles into uncontrollable capsize.(*Modern Boating*)

Centre left Flying Ants are a challenge for agile youngsters. (WA Newspapers)

Centre right Cherubs race in all States. Perth's Russell Bowler, Peter Walker won 1969–70 national and world titles in *Jennifer Julian*. (WA Newspapers)

Bottom left WA's intense training programme helped Perth youngsters Geoff Backshall, Brett Matich win national youth championship in 420 dinghy class. (Fico)

Bottom right English-designed Heron, 3.43 m, can be home-built from sheet plywood and has introduced many Australians to sailing. It is roomy and stable in boisterous weather. (Mary Clarke)

Class Name	Length (M)	Type	Where Sailed						
Sabre	3.77	H	N	V	Q	S			
Sabot	2.44	Tr	N	V	Q			T	
Sailfish	3.50	Tr	N	V					
Skate	4.27	H	N				W		
16 ft Skiff	4.87	H	N		Q		W		
Solo	3.78		N	V					
Tasar	4.52	Na H	N	V	Q	S			NT
12 ft Skiff	3.66	H	N		Q				
Vee Jay	3.50	H Tr	N				W		

Centreboard Dinghies (one State only)

Enterprise (T), Fairy Penguin (V), Flying Junior (V), Frisco (V), GP14 (V), Holdfast (S), Hornet (W), JB18 (Jollyboat) (V), Leader (N), Manly Graduate (N), Miracle (V), Mudlark (W), Northbridge Junior (N), Optimist (T), Payne Mortlock Canoe (S), Pelican (W), Seafly (N), Seamate (S), Signet (W), Sparrow (V), Spiral 3.8 (N), Swinger (N), Thorpe (Q), 303 (S), Vee Ess (N).

Keel Yachts

Class Name	Length (M)	Type	Where Sailed					
Bluebird	6.70		N	V				
Diamond	9.14	Na	N	V	Q		W	T
Dragon	8.90	I	N	V		S	W	T
Endeavour 24	7.41		N	V			W	
Etchells 22	9.29	I	N	V	Q	S	W	
Flying Fifteen	6.10	I	N	V	Q		W	
Half Ton	9.14 app.					S		T
JOG	Varies		N	V	Q	S	W	T
J24	7.32	I	N	V				
S80	8.00		N	V			W	
Soling	8.15	I O	N	V		S	W	
Thunderbird	7.92		N	V	Q		W	

Top left Four times national champion Darryl Anderson with crewman Rob Sublet rocket along on a tight reach in their unrestricted 14 ft dinghy *Valiant III*. West Australians have won 27 national and one world title in this extremely high-performance class. (*Modern Boating*)

Top right Strict design rules have made the 4.23 m Laser one of the world's most popular single-handers. (Bob Ross)

Centre Originally a modest training class, the Manly Junior, 2.63 m, is now more sophisticated and ideal for youngsters with a zest for competitive sailing. (WA Newspapers)

Bottom left International Moth, 3.35 m single-handed scow, an open developmental class with few restrictions. Former national champion Rick Le Plastrier demonstrates experimental forerunner of moulded fibreglass versions (*SMH*)

Bottom right Hotly contested club, State and national title races in modern Moths have lifted Australian exponents to a high pitch of excellence. (*SMH*)

Class Name	Length (M)	Type	Where Sailed					

Keel Yachts (one State only)

Adams 8 (N), Adams 10 (N), Bonbridge 215 (N), Cavalier 28 (N), Endeavour 26 (N), 5.5-Metre (N), Folkboat (N), Hood 23 (N), M27 (W), S. & S. 34 (W), Santana 22 (N), Spacesailer 22 (W), Spacesailer 24 (V), Star (N), Stella (N), Traditional 30 (N), Triton 24 (N), Tumlaren (V), Viking 30 (W), Yngling (N).

Trailerable Yachts

Class Name	Length (M)	Type	N	V	Q	S	W	T
Austral 20	6.10			V		S		
Bonito 22	6.71			V		S		
Boomerang 20	6.29		N	V				
Hartley 16	4.97	Na	N	V		S	W	T
Jubilee	5.49		N	V				
Noelex 25	7.75		N			S		
RL24	7.31		N	V		S		
Sunmaid 20	6.10			V				
Timpenny 670	6.70		N	V				
Tramp	5.64		N	V		S		

Trailerable Yachts (one State only)

B25 (S), Boomaroo 22 (N), Careel 18 & 22 (N), Castle (V), Cherry 16 (N), Clifton (V), Cole 19 & 23 (V), Court 650 & 750 (W), 845 (T), Explorer (V), Farr 3.8 (N), Hartley 18 & 20 (V), Investigator (N), Kestrel (V), Matilda (V), MB (W), Princess (N), Red Jacket (V), Red Witch (W), Seaway 25 (V), Solo 16 (V), Sonata (V), Sorcerer (W), Status 580 (V), Ultimate 16, 18 & 23 (V), Usual 6 (S).

Multihull Yachts

Class Name	Length (M)	Type	N	V	Q	S	W	T
A Class	5.48	I H	N	V	Q			
Arafura Cadet	3.35	Tr	N	V	Q	S		
Arrow	4.27		N	V	Q	S		
Calypso 14	4.27				Q	S		
Calypso 16	5.05				Q	S		
Cobra	4.95	H	N	V	Q			T
Dolphin	4.88			V		S		

Top left NS14, high-stepping two-man dinghy popular in all States except WA. (Bob Ross)

Top right Demanding OK dinghy, trainer for Olympic Finn class. (*Modern Boating*)

Centre left Cat-rigged, pram-bowed, Sabot class, 2.44 m, are excellent trainers for small children. Many hundreds are registered for racing in eastern States. (Bob Ross)

Centre right Many yachting champions graduated from home-built plywood VJs, designed 1931. Modern versions in fibreglass are still popular. (*SMH*)

Bottom left The 4.27 m Skate, another home-grown Australian design, developed from the VJ, is a robust, high-performance craft, especially in fresh winds. Skipper and crewman gain tremendous leverage from long sliding planks but special techniques are needed to manage them. (WA Newspapers)

Class Name	Length (M)	Type	Where Sailed					
Hobie 14	4.27		N	V	Q	S	W	
Hobie 16	5.05		N	V	Q	S	W	
Hobie 18	5.49		N	V	Q	S	W	
Hydra	5.0		N	V	Q			
Kitty	3.66			V			W	
Maricat	4.27		N	V		S		
Mosquito	4.88		N	V	Q	S		T
Nacra	5.20		N	V		S	W	
Paper Tiger	4.27	Na H	N	V		S	W	T
Prindle 15	4.57		N	V				
Prindle 16	5.05		N	V				
Prindle 18	5.49		N	V				
Stingray	5.48	H	N		Q	S		
Sundance	4.30		N			S		
Tornado	6.10	I O H	N	V	Q	S	W	
Windrush 12	3.84		N	V		S	W	
Windrush 14	4.33		N	V		S	W	
Yvonne 20	6.10			V			W	

Catamarans (one State only)

Blackwitch (S), C Class Cat (V), Caper Cat (Q), Elwood Junior (V), Gemini (N), Hawke (W), Maricat 4, 4.3 & 4.8 (N), Miniquest (V), Quest B2 (V).

Sailboards

Open Division II	3.92	I	N	V	Q	S	W	
Windsurfer	3.65		N	V	Q	S	W	T

Top left Another Australian original. Lively Bluebird class, 6.7 m, introduced in 1947 as build-it-yourself plywood boats, are now available in fibreglass and hold their popularity in the face of opposition from many craft of more modern design.

Top right Sailing for Australian yachtsmen comes in all degrees of effort: relaxed cruising in the sunshine or exhilarating battles around the buoys. Etchells 22s in action. (RPAYC Archives)

Centre left Highly competitive fleets of Flying Fifteen class keelboats, designed by Englishman Uffa Fox, race in four States. (David Wicks)

Centre right Sacrificing sleek lines for roomy cabin accommodation, the West Australian Kim Swarbrick-designed 7.31 m Spacesailer, a stockboat, is nevertheless astonishingly fast in light weather. (*SMH*)

Bottom left International Olympic class Soling, 8.15 m overall, enjoyed a surge of popularity in Australian club racing until middle-aged yachtsmen realized it was a craft that demanded a high degree of athleticism. Here, former world 18-footer skipper Ken Beashel, fresh from open-boat triumphs, is hard on a wind in the Soling *Silver Mist*, with NSW title rivals yet to reach the leeward mark. (*SMH*)

In general, the number of States where boats are sailed gives some indication of their total registration but they are often unequally spread. The single-handed Laser dinghy, for instance, with representatives in all States, in 1986 had a total official registration in Australia of 840, with 270 in NSW, while the Lightweight Sharpie registration totalled 700, with only forty-five in NSW. A complete analysis of the numbers and distribution of all registered classes would serve little purpose because some officials are slack and fail to keep proper records but some examples of the numbers of better known monohull classes, centreboard and keel, that are officially registered are:

Sabot 800 in Australia, 164 in NSW; Heron 788 (355); Mirror 549 (97); NS14 dinghy 1,700 (1,000); National E 154 (33); Moth 350 (92); Vee Jay 147 (137); Flying 15 keelboat 100 (24); Fireball 150 (16); Cherub 150 (84); Corsair 130 (35); Flying Ant 150 (90); 505 dinghy 100 (55); Dragon keelboat 100 (42); E 22 keelboat 170 (94); Soling keelboat 110 (47); Flying Dutchman dinghy 40 (10).

The numbers and distribution of most multihulls (see Chapter 9) are almost impossible to trace with any degree of accuracy. While thousands of these craft sail in organized and casual races in dozens of clubs, many are not registered with class associations or clubs. Typical of this is the Paper Tiger catamaran of which more than 2,000 are believed to be sailing in Australia although only 500 are officially registered, 66 in NSW.

The quality of the performance of the boats and the standards of racing in them, whether they are competing in club, State or national title events can usually be gauged from the accepted definition of their types (see preceding tables). Thus races in boats recognized as both of international class and high performance, like the two-man 505 dinghy and the scow-bowed 4.93 m Fireball, in which Australian exponents have for years been among the best in the world, are certain to be superbly contested by athletes of rare skill. From these and other dinghy classes have come some of our outstanding champion skippers and crewmen in Olympic, America's Cup and ocean racing craft. But many yachtsmen, devoted to the high performance and lesser classes, have chosen to remain with them until well into middle age. Some boats, however, put such demands on physical fitness that usually only young men can sail them efficiently. A good example is the very demanding three-man Lightweight Sharpie that has few equals in performance to windward, is sailed in most university clubs in Australia and truly deserves its definition – high performance and national.

Of course, as we have said earlier, the intensity of effort that yachtsmen and yachtswomen put into their sport depends on the inclination of the individuals. A family trainer like a two-handed Heron dinghy, which more than any other two classes has served to introduce people of all ages to sailing, may be as competently handled and as fiercely competitive in its minor league as a 505.

In any case, at every level there is a tremendous amount of fun, excitement and hard sailing in scores of classes of small boats many of which, like the Moth, Vee Jay (Vaucluse, Sydney, Junior), Vee Ess (Vaucluse Senior), Manly Junior, Manly Graduate, Contender, Swinger, Flying Eleven, Frisco, NS14, Gwen 12 and Tasar, originated in Australia. They have been indispensable and still are as the training ground for those yachtsmen who have given us world status.

3

World Beaters: Our Champions in All Classes

To be the world champion in any type of competitive endeavour, from eating pies to playing chess, implies that one has achieved a degree of supreme excellence unequalled by the representatives of all other nations.

But what is the status of a world title won in a field so esoteric that no one else has heard of it, or is so remote from foreign interest that no one outside one's own country contests it? Australians have to ask themselves those questions when they consider their world champions in sailing. Superficially, up to 1985 we can list a magnificent total of 151 of what were called world championships won by Australians in forty-one different types of craft. They include sixteen classes of centreboard dinghies, seven classes of smooth-water keel yachts, ten classes of multihulls, five classes of ocean racing keel yachts and three classes of sailboards. Some of those title races were fiercely contested by sixty boats of the same class, culled from thousands after months of elimination heats in a dozen countries. The Australians who emerged as winners could quite reasonably be called the best in the world. In other title races only a dozen boats competed, with one or two foreigners, or none at all, and, in some cases the so-called world champion scored a victory in what was little more than an interdominion series between Australia and New Zealand. Others were interstate or, at worst, interclub contests. Most of the total of twenty-eight world 18-footer championships have fallen into one or the other of these latter two categories.

But this is not to detract from the performances of the winners. In all of the modern 18-footer races, there is no question that the winners were sailors of such an extraordinarily high standard that no one else in the world would have had much chance of beating them, even if the representatives of fifty countries had practised for a year before they tried. The 18-footer champions have been in somewhat the same category as the heavyweight boxer Mohammad Ali at the peak of his career. Their titles were open to challenge from all, but they were so good that hardly anyone except local exponents seriously believed they

61

could aspire to be 'The Greatest'.

So how do we grade world sailing titles that Australians have won? Perhaps the most satisfactory method is to list in order of preference those wins in craft that are designated 'International', because they are recognized by the International Yacht Racing Union as those that are 'actively sailed in a representative number of countries and have sufficient distribution around the world to indicate popularity'. On this basis Australians have won sixty-nine world titles in the following classes: single-handed Moth class dinghies, nine times; 5.5 metre keel yachts, eight times; 505 dinghies, six times; International Cadets, five times; 420 dinghies, four times; Contender dinghies, four times; Etchells 22 keel yachts, four times; Fireball dinghies, four times; Tornado catamarans, three times; OK dinghies, three times; Flying Fifteen keel yachts, three times, Dragon keel yachts, once; Flying Dutchman dinghies, once; C class catamarans, once; Soling keel yachts, once; J24 keel yachts, once; and, in special events, women's single-handed Laser dinghies, twice; youth Lasers, once; youth sailboard (Mistral class), once; Laser masters, twice; Laser grand masters, five times. As in some other classes, Australians have also on a number of occasions been runners-up or among the high point scorers in the world title competitions for the class designated 'International', which these days are usually decided on the basis of a boat's best placings in six of seven races. The skilful Sydney helmsman Norman Booth was three times runner-up in world title series, twice in Dragons, once in 5.5-metres, before he won the 5.5-metres title in 1974.

Popularity of a class and its international status do not, nevertheless, necessarily define the standards of sailing one is likely to see in it. The two-handed 3.22 m International Cadet dinghy, for instance, is a training class for youngsters while the two-handed 6.05 m international Flying Dutchman dinghy and the two-handed 5.05 m international 505 dinghy are high performance craft that demand extreme skill, physical endurance and split-second co-ordination between helmsman and crew. Further, while the 3.35 m Moth class dinghy and the 4.87 m Contender class dinghy are both designated 'International' and 'High Performance', the bigger boat demands a greater degree of gymnastic agility, besides sailing skill, from the man operating it from a trapeze, than does the smaller.

Again, in the case of the modern 18-footer class, these, as we have said, are among the most demanding of all boats to sail but they do not enjoy the designation 'International' although in recent years they have gained some small acceptance in countries outside Australia and New Zealand. Indeed, 18-footers do not even qualify for the status of 'National' in this, their country of origin, because they are not 'actively sailed in five States' as required by the Australian Yachting Federation.

So Australia's world champions come in all shapes, sizes, and degrees of performance and although the competition abroad becomes keener every year, their numbers grow, as the chronological sequences of the following table show.

Apart from officially recognized world championships, Australian helmsmen have also won some of the world's most coveted trophy series against strong overseas competition. The most notable of these are: the Scandanavian Gold Cup, a golden shell encrusted with precious stones, currently for 5.5-metre class yachts (Gordon Ingate, once, and Frank Tolhurst, four times); King Olaf Cup for 5.5-metres (Frank Tolhurst); the Coupe de France for 5.5-metres (Norman Booth); the English Speaking Union Cup for Dragon class yachts (Jack Linacre).

Top left Savage close-quarter battles typify international title races in 5.5-metre class. Australians (Frank Tolhurst three times) have won eight world championships in 5.5 m. (*SMH*)

Bottom left South Australians John Gilder (helm), Doug Giles (crew), in their 420 dinghy *Flying Kangaroo*, won world title of the class against strong opposition in Israel in 1970, and successfully defended it in France in 1971. (Malcolm Gray)

Right Olympic gold medallist in Star class, David Forbes, drives 5.5-metre *Carabella* through a lumpy sea off Broken Bay, Sydney, to win world title. His crew: Kevin McCann, Jim Gannon. (*SMH*)

Year Helmsman & Crew (if applicable)   Place Sailed

International Classes
Moth Dinghy (single-handed)

Year	Helmsman & Crew	Place Sailed
1969	David McKay	USA
1970	David McKay	Victoria
1972	Ian Brown	NZ
1974	Rob O'Sullivan	Sweden
1975	Peter Moor	Japan
1975	Miss Vanessa Dudley (junior title)	Japan
1978	Rob O'Sullivan	Queensland
1978	Michael Dudley (junior title)	Queensland
1982	Greg Hilton	NSW

5.5-Metre Keel Yacht

Year	Helmsman & Crew	Place Sailed
1964	Bill Northam, Peter O'Donnell, Dick Sargeant	Tokyo
1970	David Forbes, Kevin McCann, Jim Gannon	NSW
1974	Norman Booth, Peter O'Donnell, Carl Ryves	NSW
1976	Frank Tolhurst, Mark Tolhurst, Norman Hyett	Norway
1977	Harold Vaughan, Ron McLaine, Phil Smidmore	France
1978	Frank Tolhurst, Jon Mitchell, Steve Gosling	Sweden
1979	Frank Tolhurst, Jon Mitchell, Keith Ravell	Norway
1981	Roy Tutty, Phil Smidmore, Colin Beashel	Nassau

International Cadet Dinghy

Year	Helmsman & Crew	Place Sailed
1970	Chris Tillett, David Tillett	Tasmania
1974	Frank Bucek, Miss Addy Bucek	Portugal
1979	David Rees, Grant Maddock	S. Australia
1979	Rodney Behrens, Justin Keating	England

420 Dinghy

Year	Helmsman & Crew	Place Sailed
1970	John Gilder, Doug Giles	Israel
1971	John Gilder, Doug Giles	France
1973	Anders Wangel, Doug Giles	S.Australia
1981	Craig Ferris, Bryan McKay	S.Australia

505 Dinghy

Year	Helmsman & Crew	Place Sailed
1963	Brian Farren-Price, Chris Hough	USA
1964	John Parrington, Chris Hough	Ireland
1966	Jim Hardy, Max Whitnall	S. Australia
1983	Terry Kyrwood, Reg Crick	S. Australia
1984	Dean Blatchford, Tom Woods	Germany
1985	Gary Bruniges, Greg Gardiner	Japan

Contender Dinghy (single-handed)

Year	Helmsman & Crew	Place Sailed
1972	Peter Hollis	Holland
1973	Peter Hollis	Italy
1984	Barry Watson	Italy
1985	Barry Watson	Denmark

International Fireball, 4.93 m scow, only narrowly missed selection for Olympic regattas. With one man on trapeze it planes easily, and is ideal for fresh Australian breezes. All States have fleets. (Photomarine, Perth)

Lightweight Sharpie, a fast, close-winded 5.90 m dinghy that also flies off a wind. It was developed in Australia from the old-fashioned heavyweight 12 sq m (of sail) Sharpie that was used at Melbourne's 1956 Olympic regatta. LW Sharpies race in all States and are used in inter-university competitions. (Photomarine, Perth)

Queenslander Peter Hollis at full stretch on
the trapeze wire of Australian Ben Lexcen-
designed 4.87 m Contender dinghy. Hollis
won two world titles in the class, the hardest
single-hander to manage. (*SMH*)

Darwin physician Lyndall Coxon, a member
of a Sydney family of accomplished sailors,
twice world woman champion in Laser class.
(*SMH*)

65

Year	Helmsman & Crew (if applicable)	Place Sailed

Etchells 22 Keel Yacht

1978	Frank Tolhurst, Norman Hyett, John Stanley	NSW
1979	John Savage, Stephen Wheeler, Andrew Buckland	Canada
1980	Peter O'Donnell, Richard Coxon, Dick Lawson	Victoria
1984	Iain Murray, Peter Gilmour, Paul Westlake	NSW

Dragon Keel Yacht

| 1979 | Rob Porter, Ian Porter, Rob Antill | Victoria |

Fireball Dinghy

1974	John Cassidy, Warwick Crisp	S. Australia
1981	Chris Tillett, Mike Rogers	S. Australia
1983	Stewart Hamilton, David Connor	Switzerland
1984	Gary Smith, Nick Connor	USA

Flying Dutchman Dinghy

| 1958 | Rolly Tasker, Ian Palmer | Austria |

OK (single-handed)

1983	Peter Gale	England
1983	Anthony Reynolds (junior title)	England
1984	Glen Collings	Denmark

Soling

| 1982 | Mark Bethwaite | W. Australia |

24

| 1982 | Mark Bethwaite | NSW |

Flying 15

1979	John Cassidy, Don Russell	W. Australia
1982	Peter Gale, Mark Remington	NZ
1984	Graham Lillingston, Mike McKenzie	Ireland

Tornado Catamaran

1969	Maurie Davies, Ian Ramsay	Victoria
1983	Chris Cairns, Scott Anderson	Germany
1984	Chris Cairns, Scott Anderson	Victoria

C Class Catamaran

| 1966 | Lindsay Cunningham | Victoria |

Year	Helmsman & Crew (if applicable)	Place Sailed

Women's Championships

| 1977 | Lyndall Coxon (single-handed Laser class) | England |
| 1978 | Lyndall Coxon (single-handed Laser class) | Holland |

Youth Championships

| 1980 | Larry Kleist (single-handed Laser class) | USA |
| 1985 | Keill Price (sailboard, Mistral class) | Switzerland |

Laser Masters

| 1982 | Paul Millsom | Sardinia |
| 1984 | Richard Vercoe | Thailand |

Laser Grandmasters

1981	Alan Clarke	France
1982	Alan Clarke	Sardinia
1983	Alan Clarke	USA
1984	Alex McClure	Thailand
1985	Alex McClure	Canada

Other Classes

Cherub Dinghy
1969	Russell Bowler, Peter Walker	W. Australia
1974	Miss A. (Mandy) Wilmot, Andrew Buckland	England
1976	Miss Nicky Bethwaite, Julian Bethwaite	S. Australia
1985	Greg Hartnett, James Synge	NZ

National E Dinghy

| 1979 | Rod James, Ray Cole; dead heat with Canadians Egon and Kevin Frech | Canada |

Tasar

| 1985 | Norman Rydge III, Oliver Shtein | NSW |

14 ft Dinghy (unrestricted)

| 1979 | Bill Devine, Peter Bryson | USA |

Hornet Dinghy

| 1969 | Syd Lodge, John Bolton | England |

Jollyboat Dinghy

| 1968 | Roger Byrne, Bill Binks | USA |

Year	Helmsman & Crew (if applicable)	Place Sailed

Thunderbird Keel Yacht

| 1968 | Tony Redstone (USA crew) | USA |
| 1970 | Tony Parkes, Mike Fletcher, Walter Sullivan, John Laurie | NSW |

18-Footers

Year	Yacht	Helmsman	Place Sailed
1938	*Taree*	Bert Swinbourne NSW	Sydney
1948	*Crow's Nest*	Bill Hayward NSW	NZ
1949	*Marjorie Too*	Tony Russell NSW	Sydney
1951	*Myra Too*	Bill Barnett NSW	Sydney
1956	*Jenny VI*	Norm Wright Qld	Brisbane
1958	*Jantzen Girl*	Len Heffernan NSW	Sydney
1961	*Venom*	Bob Miller Qld	Brisbane
1963	*Schemer*	Ken Beashel NSW	NZ
1964	*Toogara*	Cliff Monkhouse NSW	Sydney
1965	*Travelodge*	Bob Holmes NSW	NZ
1966	*Travelodge*	Bob Holmes NSW	Brisbane
1967	*Assoc Motor Club*	Don Barnett NSW	Sydney
1968	*Daily Telegraph*	Ken Beashel NSW	NZ
1969	*Travelodge*	Bob Holmes NSW	Brisbane
1970	*Thomas Cameron*	Hugh Treharne NSW	Sydney
1971	*Travelodge*	Bob Holmes NSW	NZ
1973	*Travelodge*	Bob Holmes NSW	Sydney
1975	*KB*	Dave Porter NSW	Brisbane
1976	*Miles Furniture*	Steve Kulmar NSW	Sydney
1977	*7 Color*	Iain Murray NSW	NZ
1978	*Color 7*	Iain Murray NSW	Brisbane
1979	*Color 7*	Iain Murray NSW	Sydney
1980	*Color 7*	Iain Murray NSW	NZ
1981	*Color 7*	Iain Murray NSW	Brisbane
1982	*Color 7*	Iain Murray NSW	Sydney
1983	*Tia Maria*	Peter Sorensen NSW	NZ
1984	*Tia Maria*	Peter Sorensen NSW	Sydney
1985	*Bradmill*	Rob Brown NSW	Brisbane

Note: In 1978 *Color 7* (Iain Murray) won an Open International 'World Series' in Plymouth, England (see Chapter 7) but this was not listed as an official world championship by Australian and NZ 18-footer authorities.

Ocean Racing

Quarter Ton Cup Class

| 1982 | *Quartermaster* | Graham Jones | Victoria |

Half Ton Cup Class

| 1976 | *Foxy Lady* | Tom Stephenson | USA |

Year	Helmsman & Crew (if applicable)	Place Sailed

One Ton Cup Class

| 1971 | *Stormy Petrel* | Syd Fischer | NZ |

Two Ton Cup Class

| 1981 | *Hitchhiker* | Peter Briggs | Italy |

Admiral's Cup (teams championship)

1967	*Balandra*	Bob Crichton-Brown	England
	Caprice of Huon	Gordon Reynolds	
	Mercedes III	Ted Kaufman	
1979	*Impetuous*	Graeme Lambert, John Crisp	England
	Police Car	Peter Cantwell	
	Ragamuffin	Syd Fischer	

Catamarans

A Class Catamaran

1966	John Smallman		1971	Brian Leverton
1967	Graham Johnston		1979	Kerry Holmes
1968	Philip Stevenson		1980	Bill Anderson
1969	John Goodier		1984	Alan Goodall
1970	Philip Stevenson		1985	Alan Goodall

B Class Catamaran

1966	Rolly Tasker		1969	Bruce Proctor
1967	Peter Blaxland		1970	John Henry
1968	Peter Blaxland		1971	Paul Swinnerton
	(dead-heat with Reg White, of England)			

Australis Class Catamaran

| 1971 | Graham Johnston |

Paper Tiger

| 1980 | David Hart |
| 1984 | Gary Williams |

Hydra

| 1979 | Colin Metcher, Ann Metcher |

Hobie 16

| 1981 | Brett Dryland |
| 1984 | Garry Metcalfe |

Nacra 5.2

| 1982 | Mitch Booth |
| 1985 | Kevin Allen |

Hobie 18

| 1981 | Ian Bashford, Steve Whelon |
| 1984 | Gary Metcalfe, Michael Meirs |

Year	Helmsman & Crew (if applicable)	Place Sailed

Sailboards

Windsurfer Class
1980	Grant Long (heavyweight)	
1982	Peter Lynch (medium heavyweight)	
	Greg Johns (heavyweight)	
1983	Teams Event (Greg Butchardt, Stuart Gilbert, Melanie Braun)	
1983	Tom Luedecke (heavyweight)	
	Bob Wilmot (light heavyweight)	
	Greg Hyde (medium weight)	
1984	Tom Luedecke (heavyweight)	
	Bruce Wylie (pentathlon and light heavyweight)	
	Greg Hyde (medium weight)	
	Bob Wilmot (marathon)	

Dufor Class

1983	John Buick	

4

Olympics: All the Races Australians have Sailed

AUSTRALIA'S FIRST and most startling victory in Olympic class yachting was Bill Northam's gold medal at the Tokyo Games in 1964. It came about through an incident that seemed at the time almost trivial.

Northam, then the dynamic Australian chairman of Johnson and Johnson, was amusing himself on a balmy summer afternoon on Long Island Sound by playing jester to his millionaire boss, US General Robert Wood Johnson, the Band Aid emperor. They were aboard the General's 35.97 m ketch, *Argosy*, cruising majestically from New York to Newport RI to see the 1962 America's Cup and Johnson, almost as an aside to one of Northam's tall tales, suddenly turned to him and said, 'You know, Bill, you should get another yacht now you've sold that ocean racer. Can't let yourself get stale; bad for the company image.'

'You're right, General,' said Northam, a master of the conversational blockbuster, 'I was thinking of getting one of those 5.5 metre boats and having a crack at the Olympic Games.'

A moment later he could have bitten his tongue. 'It was a throwaway line,' he said that night in private. 'I knew the Old Man liked a bit of a swagger, but I forgot for a second that he often took me seriously. What the hell would I be doing with an Olympic class boat?'

But by then the General *had* taken him seriously, and in two days Northam found himself, in company with Johnson, whisked by private plane to the office of Bill Luders, America's foremost 5.5 metre boat designer, and signing a document that was to change the course of his life. The yacht Luders designed became *Barranjoey*, a sleek, 9.75 m mahogany-hulled racing machine which, with its equipment, set Northam back £10,000 that he had never intended to spend. It also set him on a road to glory that brought him world renown as a yachting phenomenon who broke all the rules of the game, established him at sixty years of age as the oldest man ever to win an Olympic medal in any sport, and contributed to his knighthood and other honours. It also lent a new dimension to Australia's status in international class boat racing.

Wisecracking grandpa who astonished the critics: Australia's first Olympic yachting champion Bill Northam and his crew, Dick Sargeant and Peter O'Donnell. (*SMH*)

LONDON 1948

Australia's first entry into Olympic yachting — at the London Games of 1948 — was almost apologetic, as far as the local governing body, the Australian Olympic Federation, was concerned. Some members of its executive made it clear that they, along with many members of the public, considered yachting as no sport at all but a pastime for silvertails, and that the idea of providing money to ship boats half way across the world for a regatta at Torbay was abhorrent to them. One celebrated official became almost apoplectic with distaste when he heard the proposal.

But the Victorians were already germinating a plan to seek the Games for Melbourne in 1956 and they were justly proud of the pre-eminent skill of their Port Phillip sailors in restricted class boat racing. They brushed aside the AOF's opposition and extracted guarantees that yachtsmen would be permitted to go to the Games if they paid their own way (repercussions in high places were promised if the AOF did not fall into line). Then they went on to raise all the money they needed on the Old Boy Circuit. One of the celebrated Victorians they approached was world billiards champion Walter Lindrum, who agreed to give an exhibition at Brighton Town Hall to a 'special audience'. Lindrum, who got seasick at the sight of a boat, found himself playing trick shots while yachtsmen from all over the State, many of them prominent businessmen, bet on the results. They raised £1,000 in four hours.

Soon it was announced that Australia's champion Star class boat *Moorina*, a 6.93 m sloop, and her skipper Alexander Stuart Sturrock (called 'Jock' to distinguish him from his similarly named father), who dominated the class and had a long string of titles in other types of boats, and his crewman Len Fenton, would sail at Torbay. And, as an aside, the Victorians also nominated a strapping young Victorian dinghy sailor, Bob French, so that he could compete in the single-handed 3.66 m Firefly class. That was indeed folly because at that stage French had never even seen such a boat, since there was none in Australia. So it was somewhat defiantly that the three-man yachting team put on their Australian blazers and joined the rest of the Olympic squad.

French, as might have been expected, was outclassed in the series of seven Firefly races at Torbay, finishing eighteenth in the fleet of twenty-one and scoring only tenth place in the one truly heavy weather race, the last, that was expected to favour him. (That last race, in winds of 30 k, and the series, was won by a muscular Danish youth called Paul Elvstrom, who stowed his jib before the start, reefed his mainsail and romped around the course while his rivals floundered. It was the first of four successive Olympic gold medals in yachting and a score or more of world titles in many classes of boats that Elvstrom was to win.) French's placings in the seven races were 18, 11, 19, 16, 9, 12, 10.

Sturrock and Fenton, hampered by a heavy boat that they soon realized was years out of date by international standards in the highly competitive Star class (with thousands registered for racing in many countries) and by sails suitable only for fresh winds, had little chance in the generally light and fluky Torbay breezes. But they finished a creditable seventh in the fleet of seventeen over the series, beating many fancied competitors in faster boats with their natural skill. On the two days when the winds were honest they outsailed everyone. Their placings were dnf, 4, 15, 6, 10, 4, 1. *Moorina* led almost from the start of the first race until her mainsail touched the American entry, *Hilarious* (the ultimate winner), as she heeled at the last rounding mark, forcing Sturrock to retire; and in the near-gale-force last race *Moorina* won by a handsome margin.

Sturrock came home advising yachtsmen that to have a voice in world affairs they must properly organize their State associations and appoint delegates to a central Australian Yachting Federation that could affiliate with the world governing body, the International Yacht Racing Union, and that to have a chance in future Olympics and to lift the standard of Australian yachting generally, they must plan to send sailors overseas regularly for experience in class boat regattas. It was a song sung with interminable encores in subsequent years to largely apathetic audiences — torn by parochial club interests and bitter interstate rivalries. The Australian Yachting Federation was formed in 1950 but it was not until 1967 that it severed its administrative apron string from Britain's Royal Yachting Association, to which it first clung, and affiliated directly with the IYRU; and it was not until 1969 that a full-time professional official was appointed to run the affairs of a State (NSW) association. By 1976 the States had at last come to recognize that only by truly co-operative effort and forward planning could they hope to administer a sport that had more than half a million adherents, and that they must agree to find the money to discard part-time honorary muddling and pay a national executive officer. By 1979, yachting, like all other sports, had gained allocations of State and Federal Government monies, with grants from the AOF, and commercial sponsorship of Olympic training programmes and regattas was openly permitted by the International Olympic

Committee without the stain of professionalism.

But, in the meantime, Australia's Olympic endeavours in yachting, failures and successes, continued mainly through the herculean efforts of small groups of dedicated individuals and class officials, hammering on the doors of all they thought likely to help them.

HELSINKI 1952

We got to Helsinki (Finland) in 1952 only by shaking begging bowls for funds, and fists for approvals under the noses of AOF officials who still regarded yachtsmen as dressed-up fishermen. And Helsinki was a disaster. The Finns had refused to learn anything from the well-organized British regatta at Torbay four years earlier and ran the races off Harmaja Islands — a five-mile tow from the moorings — with all the finesse of a Viking orgy. Facilities for the yachts were crude, courses were tangled, few of the officials knew their jobs, and many of the races were farcical. Sturrock was again Australia's main hope, this time in the 8.90 m Dragon class. But he and his Victorian crew, Bevan Worcester and Doug ('Puffy') Buxton, could not afford to ship their own boat to Helsinki, and the old heavyweight they chartered, *Vinha*, was a clunker. They scrambled in twelfth overall out of seventeen and their best placing was fifth in the only race (the third) sailed in a fresh breeze. Their other placings were 10, 14, 10, 12, 14, 14. Victoria's Bart Harvey and Kevin Wilson, who sailed the Star *Hornet*, finished eighteenth out of twenty-one, placing 14, 20, 8, 18, 19, 12, 20. In the 4.5 m cat-rigged Finn dinghy class, introduced for the first time, Peter Attrill, of Tasmania, after two disqualifications, limped in twenty-second out of twenty-eight. His other scores were 11, 18, 10, 18, 15. Once again Elvstrom, who had spent two years of rigorous training in the single-handed class, made the rest of them look like beginners.

Sturrock nevertheless returned afire with enthusiasm for the 5.5-metre class that had been designed only two years earlier and had raced in the Olympics for the first time at Helsinki, where the gold medal had gone to *Complex II*, helmed by the eminent US bio-physicist Britton Chance, whose lanky young son, Britton Chance jnr, was later to become the world's foremost designer of these elegant sloops. Chance had put into practice what others, including Sturrock, had been preaching — a three months' campaign before the Games, racing his boat all over Europe against the best in the country. Sturrock urged Australian owners to build 5.5 metre boats for the Melbourne Games in 1956. They would be ideal, he said, for the lively waters of Port Phillip where the Olympic regatta would be held. He also advised Australian officials and yachtsmen in general to pull up their nautical socks and to train seriously if they hoped to have a show on their home ground in four years time.

MELBOURNE 1956

Officials certainly took Sturrock seriously, and the organization, control of races and facilities for the yachts and their crews at the Melbourne Olympics were superb. The layout of the courses on the northern end of vast Port Phillip Bay ensured that there was none of the over-lapping tangles between classes that had hampered and infuriated competitors at Helsinki, and, although Sydneysiders were inclined by habit to describe the place as a deep marsh, even they found little reason for criticism. The 148 competitors from twenty-eight nations sailing seventy-one boats in five classes praised the regatta as the best at any Olympics. Many, used to mud banks, tidal rips, reefs and tricky shifts of winds during races at home, were delighted with the clear, open, if somewhat shallow, waters of the Bay and its golden, sandy shorelines. They accepted the range of predictable breezes that varied from day to day between light, moderate and fresh, and were even philosophic about a well-forecast gale of 40 k on the fourth day. It dismasted some, capsized many, and forced cancellation of the Finn dinghy single-handed race.

Australia for the first time was represented in all classes: 5.5-metre, Dragon, Star, 12 sq metre Sharpie (then an awkward, heavyweight, 6.0 m gunter-rigged hardchiner – an anachronism of a boat that had changed little since its design in 1928, and chosen in 1956 for the first and last time in the Olympics), and the Finn single-handers. (Australians were later to re-design the heavily planked Sharpie into a lightweight plywood version, give it a modern bermudan rig and trapezes, and convert it into one of the fastest, most exciting craft of its length in the world.)

Although Australian yachtsmen still lacked overseas experience against the world's best they had trained harder than at any time previously, and the trials for places in the national team had been more hotly contested. Sturrock, with crewmen Dexter ('Dev') Mytton and Doug Buxton, in the 5.5-metre *Buraddoo*, after narrowly beating Sydney's Pat Taylor in *Kirribilli* in the trials, remained our number one hope. Victorians, indeed, believed that none of the other competitors – Britain, France, Germany, Italy, Norway, Russia, South Africa, Sweden, and the USA – would stand a chance against the Master of Port Phillip, who had won hundreds of races there in all classes of craft since he was a small boy. But Sturrock's boat lacked an edge of speed and his crew's work lacked a little of the polish of some of their rivals. *Buraddoo's* placings – 4, 4, 2, 4, 1, 3, 4 – gave her third in the series, for a bronze medal, following Sweden and Britain. The sensation of the regatta, for Australia, was the performance of a young Western Australian accountant, Rolly Tasker, with his husky crewman, Malcolm ('Huck') Scott, in the Sharpie class centreboarder *Falcon IV*. Such was the fragmentation of yachting in Australia in those days that few Sydney sailors had heard of Tasker before the Games' trials. But in the West and in SA where the Sharpie class was strongest, officials for years had rated Tasker's opponents on the distances they finished behind him. He had graduated from Vee Jay dinghies to 16 ft skiffs, then to the Sharpies in which he had set an overall record of 180 wins, thirty-three of them in national title series. He was later to become a world champion Flying Dutchman dinghy helmsman and an ocean racing skipper and to make a fortune as a sailmaker with branches in many countries.

Tasker could have won Australia's first gold medal at Melbourne but he was beaten into second place in the fleet of thirteen and awarded the silver medal in very peculiar circumstances. Until the last race Tasker had scored 6,086 points with placings of 1, 2, 2, 1, 2, 2. His only serious rival among the twelve other nations competing was New Zealand's *Jest*, skippered by the dashing Peter Mander, a dual world champion 18-footer helmsman (whose loss of the sight of one eye as a boy made little difference to his skill and judgement), with Jack Cropp as crew. Mander had scored placings of 2, 1, 5, 4, 1, 1 for a total of

5,688 points. With the mandatory drop of points at this stage for each boat's worst performance — 914 for one of *Falcon IV's* seconds, and 516 for *Jest's* fifth — they were level on 5,172 points. So long as Mander finished third (worth 738 points) or worse in the last race it really didn't matter where Tasker finished. He would still win the gold medal. But if the New Zealand boat finished second then the Australian had to win to clinch the gold medal. Tasker therefore set out to match-race Mander in the final, aiming to pin him back in the fleet. In the middle stages of the race there was little between them when the skipper of the French Sharpie, *Kannibaltje,* on starboard tack, called Tasker, on port tack, to give right of way. The Australian, anxious to respond, called upon the skipper of the Canadian boat, *Beaver,* that was also on port tack, slightly astern of him, but close to windward, to tack to starboard so that Tasker might give the Frenchman his rights. Instead, the Canadian held course, pinning Tasker, and the latter, instead of tacking on to starboard and protesting the Canadian for failing to obey his call, sailed on, on port tack, and attempted to screw away under the French boat's stern. His bow clipped *Kannibaltje* and the Frenchman therefore caught him in a classic port and starboard breach.

During the subsequent protest hearing, with Australian Yachting Federation secretary Lloyd Burgess arguing vehemently on the Western Australian's behalf, Tasker, waiting outside the committee room, wept openly. 'They made me the ham in the sandwich,' he said. 'I believe that if I had tacked on to the Canadian he was ready to protest me for not giving him room and would have called the French as witnesses.'

The international jury refused to listen to Tasker's pleas and he was disqualified. The race went to the British boat *Chuckles,* with Mander, in *Jest,* placed second, adding 914 points to his tally. When Mander had dropped his worst race he had a score of 6,086 points. Tasker, dropping his disqualification, also had 6,086 but, on the count back, the New Zealander, with three wins to Tasker's two, was awarded the gold medal.

The other Australians who had not been blooded in international competition learned just what a test of excellence the Olympics were. Graham Drane, at the helm of the Dragon, *Paula,* with Brian Carolan and James Carolane in his crew, scored fifth place out of sixteen, with placings 2, 10, 14, 4, 4, 4, 9. Bob French with Jack Downey in the Star *Naiad,* scored ninth in the fleet of twelve with 8, 9, 12, 6, 11, 9, 11. And the former national champion 12 ft skiff skipper, Colin Ryrie, got tenth out of twenty in the Finn class, placing 4, 13, 11, dnf, 7, 14, 5. In one race the self-bailer in Ryrie's Finn jammed, but he determinedly completed the course with the boat full of water. It won him praise, that blossomed into friendship and later into a business partnership, from the mighty Elvstrom, who had taken five of the races.

ROME 1960

The yachting regatta at the Rome Games of 1960 was sailed on the often glassy smooth waters of the Bay of Naples and clearly revealed weaknesses from which many Australian sailors, nationwide, suffered — and still do: boats rigged for fresh winds, and a lack of concentration, patience and skill to keep them moving well in very light airs. The reasons, of course, are that Australians get little practice in light conditions at home, and that our boats are rarely turned or our sails cut to suit them. Wind strengths on most of Australia's major sailing centres, unlike those of overseas, are steady in direction and rarely below 8 k during mid-mornings and early afternoons when races are held, and even among the top echelons of our most dedicated class boat sailors we seem to have a stubborn resistance to organizing and holding serious competitions at other times, when winds are light and variable. For almost twenty years our yachtsmen in all classes of craft have returned home after overseas failures, cursing the dead airs on the courses on which they raced but in which Europeans and Americans have excelled.

Rome was a perfect example. Four of the seven heats in each of the five classes were sailed in fickle airs that would have been considered unsuitable for racing in Australia. On two days the breeze reached 10 k and on another the highest gust was 14 k. Our best placing was fourth out of thirty-five in the fiercely competitive Finn dinghies, achieved by a young Queenslander Ron Jenyns, who had trained in Brisbane, often alone, for hundreds of hours, many in light airs. Since all the Finns were supposedly identical, and their hulls, masts and sails were supplied, as was traditional, by the host nation, he was at no disadvantage on the score of boat speed. Jenyns' placings were 6, 6, rtd, 6, 2, 3, 10. He survived protests from France and Canada in the first race for 'pumping' his sail, when the international jury at twenty minutes past midnight decided this was legal when there was any wind at all but illegal when there was none. At the time Jenyns had pumped there had been some movement in the air!

Sturrock, with crewmen Ernest Wagstaff and Dave Bingham, finished tenth out of nineteen in the 5.5-metre *Buraddoo,* now clearly outdated in this development class that allows designers to exploit marginal but significant differences in hull forms within the measurement formula. *Buraddoo* lacked pace even when the breeze did fill, and Sturrock could not read the shifts. His placings were 4, 12, 2, 13, 14, 12, 18. There was some consolation for Sturrock, though, and for Australian yachting in general. As an Olympic representative for the fourth consecutive time he was chosen to carry the flag for the whole Australian team at the opening ceremony. Although our sailors had not won the honours that had been showered on our swimmers, they were at least recognized now as genuine Olympic competitors.

Tasker, by now in the Flying Dutchman class, with Ian Palmer as crew, scored an unbelievably poor eighteenth out of thirty-one. In Australia he had been one of the favourites for a medal in the class, having transferred to the FD immediately after the Melbourne Games and having won the world title on Lake Attersee in Austria in 1958, where he had beaten forty-eight boats from twenty-seven countries. And Tasker, too, was well aware that conditions on the Bay of Naples would be light. After easily winning the Australian Olympic trials in moderate to fresh breezes with heavyweight Andy White as crew, he had resisted considerable criticism by insisting that he should take the lighter Palmer with him to the Games. But by 1960 the FDs had been much refined, with modern go-fast gear and flexible aluminium alloy spars. In the fleet of thirty-one FDs at Rome only two boats, one of them Tasker's *Falcon VI,* carried wooden spars. Furthermore, many competitors had spent the preceding four months training on the Naples course and tuning their boats to the conditions. Tasker's boat was just too slow in the light airs. She placed 17, 11, 19, 9, 8, 20, 23. (Two years later Tasker, with White as crew and a better rig, and in fresher winds, sailed a close second to the Danes, Hans Fogh and Paul Elvstrom, in the 1962 FD world title series at Florida.)

In the Star class at Naples, Bob French and his crewman Jack Downey in *Pakaria* scored eighteenth out of twenty-six with placings 13, 21, 20, 21, 10, 20. Neither they nor their boat were equal to the hot competition they faced.

The only Australian crew who seemed to have a genuine excuse for failure was the one that Australian yachting officials had least expected to shine. They were the Victorians Harold ('Mick') Brooke, Alan Cain and John Coon, in the Dragon class. Brooke, in spite of the handicap of a withered arm which he had suffered from childhood, had a remarkably subtle touch on the helm, especially in light weather, although he had won the right to represent in his boat *Ghost III* in a series of moderate to fresh winds. In pre-Games tune-up trials on the Bay of Naples, Brooke and his crew and *Ghost III* seemed to be in their element. They had the boat tuned like a harp and they outpaced several of their overseas rivals in these early brushes. It was their undoing. Twenty hours before the first Olympic race *Ghost III* was barred from competing on the grounds that her transom measurement was too small. Brooke, normally a mild-mannered man, who at sixty years of age had achieved his life's ambition by winning a place in Australia's Olympic team, was furious. His boat had a valid measurement certificate in Australia, which allegedly qualified her to sail as a certified Dragon anywhere in the world. Moreover, Brooke claimed that when she had been check-measured on arrival in Naples, Olympic officials had passed her as eligible. The turnabout had come only after certain of her rivals had seen *Ghost III* in action. Here, it seemed, was a fine example in reverse of the noble principles of Baron Pierre de Courbertin, founder of the modern Olympics, who had proclaimed so proudly that the important thing about the Games was the honour of competing, not winning. Certain of Brooke's opponents had nobbled *Ghost III*'s chances as effectively as if they had sunk her at the moorings. The stern measurement of the boat could in no way have made *Ghost III* go faster, but the measurement committee, once a complaint was made, could not ignore it. Their delay in announcing their decision until the eve of the first race was, however inexcusable. There was no appeal, and the best that Lloyd Burgess, the Australian yachting team manager, could do at that late hour was to charter an Italian boat for Brooke and his crew to sail. She was called *Gabbiano* and was shockingly out of tune and much heavier than the Australian boat, and Brooke and his crew had to work desperately during the regatta to make her competitive. They did a remarkable job to get eleventh place on the point score after sailing 8, 10, 8, 6, 15, 19, 5 in the seven races in the fleet of twenty-seven.

Brooke was still turbulent with indignation when he returned to Melbourne, especially when he heard that someone had spread a rumour that only *Ghost III*'s so-called illegal stern had enabled him to win her place in the Australian team. With a committee of measurers carefully checking every detail, Brooke had *Ghost III* altered exactly according to the rulings laid down by the Olympic officials at Rome, took her to Hobart for the 1961 national championships and outsailed all of those he had beaten in the Olympic trials.

But overall the Australian Olympic score for yachting at Rome was poor. No one wanted to hear the details of failure. To the fickle public, even to most members of yacht clubs now paying a compulsory annual levy of $2 a head to an Olympic Fund, the only good news was how we won.

TOKYO 1964

Well, they got the good news at Tokyo in 1964, when Grandpa Bill Northam performed the impossible and brought home the gold. Northam was the Australian public's ideal of a sportsman hero — at every level. He had style. He was rich, robust and respected for his intelligence and business acumen; he gave service to the community as a Sydney City Council alderman; he was informal and friendly, at ease in any company; governors-general and garbos called him 'Bill'; bar-rooms and board meetings rocked with laughter at his off-beat wisecracks, and only a brave man would follow him as an after-dinner speaker. But the hierarchy of yachting found it hard to take Northam seriously as an Olympic-class sailor. Certainly he had won and successfully defended the Sayonara Cup, the historic challenge trophy for Australian interstate big class racing, but *Saskia*, the 15.24 m former champion 8-metre class boat he had imported from England for that purpose, had been so superior to her rivals, and his crew had been so good, that it was felt his role as helmsman had been only incidental.

Northam had also owned and skippered the ocean racer *Caprice of Huon* with some success and had finished fourth in the Sydney–Hobart race. But he had sold that boat and given up offshore sailing, remarking succinctly that it was an 'uncomfortable way to spend the Christmas holidays'. What, the know-alls asked each other, did this eccentric with a wall-to-wall grin and a Rolls Royce, who hadn't even been aboard a sailing boat until he was forty-eight years of age, think he was doing at the helm of a new 5.5-metre, nominating for the Australian championships and the Olympic trials? They were to eat a lot of words.

Northam brought to his Olympic campaign all the drive and organizing ability that had lifted him from toothbrush salesman to chairman of a big company, the competitive spirit and concentration that had made him a champion speedcar driver and a four-handicap golfer. He outfitted *Barranjoey* with superlative equipment, imported American sails, and persuaded Peter ('Pod') O'Donnell and Dick Sargeant, two young for'ard hands he had admired aboard *Gretel* in her 1962 America's Cup challenge, to crew for him. Like most things Northam touched, they turned to gold. They had been recognized as good hands previously but neither had been given full credit for his expertise. In fact, Sargeant and O'Donnell were complete yachtsmen in every sense, superbly efficient in all departments, who had been sailing since they were small boys. They had the balance and sense of timing of cats; they knew the tactics of racing and the rules inside out; they could rig and tune a boat to suit any conditions; they could set and trim sails together without exchanging a word. At first, though, Northam bewildered them.

'He was so damned off-hand ashore, so full of clowning and jokes, sometimes pretending to be drunk or lame, and he seemed to know so little about the technical details of sailing that you wondered what was going to happen next,' says Sargeant. 'But afloat, steering, he was incredibly good. He got the ultimate out of the boat. His concentration was so complete that he was oblivious of everything else. You had to tell him when to tack and when we got to a rounding mark you had to tell him whether to turn left or right.'

They swept all before them. Northam confessed later that in the national championships on Lake Macquarie (NSW) that preceded the Olympic selection

Olympic and world 5.5-metre champion *Barranjoey* on one of her few tuning trials before Northam won the national title, the Olympic selection trials and took her to Tokyo for the 1964 Games. (Fotomarine)

trials he taught himself how to sail *Barranjoey*. 'I'd had no practice; she'd been launched only a few weeks earlier,' he said. 'But I had a speedo in the hull — the first, I believe, ever used in an Olympic-class boat — and I used to check it against a strange vibration, a sort of rumble, I felt when we got her going at her fastest. I used to ask the boys to trim the gear either on or off until she got those rumbles. They thought at first I was off my rocker but then they'd take a look at the speedo and see for themselves.'

That was the only demand Northam made of his crew. He was too wise a man to question the way O'Donnell and Sargeant set up the boat, or to argue with them about tactics. 'Nobody ever had the privilege of sailing with anyone better than that pair,' he says. 'They knew every detail of every bit of equipment and they serviced everything themselves. Nobody else was allowed to touch anything. In all our sailing together I picked only one good windshift — in the final Olympic trials on Lake Macquarie — that they missed. Normally, if I offered any comment Pod would just grunt, but Dick, who was like an angry tomcat, would snarl, "Shut up, and just steer".'

The system they used on *Barranjoey* — of the helmsman concentrating on that job alone — was, and continued to be, one of the secrets of the USA's constant successes in America's Cup races in modern times. Bus Mosbacher, Bob Bavier, Bill Ficker, Ted Hood and Ted Turner played practically no part in the mechanical operation of the yachts they raced. Regardless of their own tremendous skills, these helmsmen merely steered the courses their navigators set for them and obeyed without question the tactics called.

To that, Northam added his organizing genius ashore. The personal comforts and facilities for his crew, and the range and quality of equipment for the boat, from split pins in the rigging to the motor tender that carried spares and towed them to and from the race courses, set new standards. Still, Northam had to fight all the way to beat his two main rivals — Jock Sturrock in *Pam*, and the highly competent Norman Booth, a former champion Dragon skipper, in *Southern Cross* — in the national championships and the Olympic trials. Both boats were new designs. *Barranjoey* scored two wins, a second, a third and a disqualification to *Pam*'s two wins, two thirds and a disqualification, in the nationals. The Olympic trials were even closer. Northam needed to finish first or second in the last of the seven heats to beat Sturrock or Booth in the compulsory six-race point score. It was in that race that he picked the windshift that his crew missed and climbed from third to second place on the final work to the finishing line. When Northam dropped his worst placing, a seventh, his six-race points total was 5,126. When Sturrock, who had scored the greatest overall number of points in the seven races, dropped his worst placing, a fourth, his total was 4,950; Booth was a close third, with 4,598. Even then, when Northam had the points on the board and had clearly won the two series, there was still some resistance to his selection in the Olympic team. Victorians, especially, reminded the Australian Yachting Federation that it did not necessarily have to choose the winner of the trials. Other yachtsmen who had spent a lifetime racing with only minor successes could not bring themselves to accept this irreverent newcomer who jested that he had outsailed Australia's proven champions between drinks.

The AYF, to its credit, stood firm against this prejudice and chose *Barranjoey* and her skipper and crew along with all the other winners of the Olympic trials. So Northam went to Tokyo and on Sagami Bay outsailed the champions of fourteen nations in his first and only international series. With O'Donnell calling the shots, he steered through bewilderingly unpredictable wind changes that varied in strength from light to moderate and only once blew really hard. But there was always a breeze. Northam's placings — 1, 6, 2, 1, dnf (foul against Italy), 1 and 4 — gave him the gold medal by a wide points margin from the Swede, Lars Thorn, a former Olympic champion, sailing *Rush VII*, and, like Northam, sixty years of age. A close third was the USA's John ('Don') McNamara junr, a widely experienced helmsman who had been the hot favourite. McNamara's boat, *Bingo*, also a Luders design, and *Barranjoey* were unquestionably the fastest in the series, but Northam's crew were superior. That, and the Australian skipper's clowning ashore and afloat on the way to the starting lines, needled the American into some nervous tension. Still, in the last race, with earlier placings of 10, 1, 1, 6, 2, 3, the American could have got the gold medal with a win, provided *Barranjoey* placed fourth or worse; or with a second, provided *Barranjoey* placed seventh or worse. After trailing in fourth place, with *Barranjoey* sixth, at the first three marks, McNamara got to the front from Thorn, with Northam back in fifth place, in a wind shift on the last beat 100 m from the finishing line. In the fluctuating breeze the American was just unable to lay the line, and in a daring bid to clinch it he tacked on to port and attempted to sail clear across the Swede's bows. Thorn, on the starboard tack, had to alter course to avoid hitting him. McNamara's foul was irrefutable and he retired, leaving Thorn the winner of the race and Northam fourth and therefore clear ahead in the overall point-score. McNamara got the bronze medal but he was so chagrined about the whole affair that he later wrote a long chapter in a book to explain why he had thrown away his positive chance of a silver medal. The celebrations in the Australian camp for Northam's victory were ecstatic. Even Japanese admirals came to pay their respects to the venerable *Ogesan* (Old Man). Northam could not bring himself to point out that there was one flaw to the gold medal the Japanese had struck for him: they had misspelt the name of the sport as Yotching.

The best of the other Australian yachtsmen at Tokyo was Colin Ryrie, of Sydney, who finished sixth out of thirty-three in the Finn single-handers, with placings 3, 22, 1, 15, 11, 4, 14. Ryrie had narrowly beaten Queenslander Ron Jenyns for the right to represent after a hard series of trials on Moreton Bay, near Brisbane. Jenyns had finished first five times in those seven races on his home waters but had been disqualified in one race and had had to include a seventh and a tenth in his points score, while Ryrie had a win, four seconds and a third to count. But at Tokyo the competition was keener still and although Ryrie was at all times close and seemed until the last race a hope for the bronze medal, he just lacked the edge of polish, and the luck, needed to pick his way through the fluky wind changes.

In the Star class, the burly Martin Visser, of Sydney, a former Dutch Olympic reserve and later to feature in the 1970 America's Cup as co-helmsmen with Jim Hardy of *Gretel II*, finished tenth, with Tim Owens as crew. Their placings in the old-fashioned *Maryke*, which nobody gave a ghost of a chance against the sixteen featherweights they met, were a creditable 8, 16, dnf, 10, 5, 7, 12. Visser got *Maryke*, 150 kg heavier than any of her opponents, within striking distance of the leaders on the first windward beats, but his boat could not pace them downwind.

Australia's Dragon, *Cambria*, skippered by Graham Drane with John Coon and Ian Quartermain as crew (all Victorians) finished a disappointing twelfth in the fleet of twenty-three, with placings 9, 12, 6, dnf, 11, 12, 4.

In the Flying Dutchman class, two more Victorians, John Dawe and Ian Winter, who were favourites before the regatta in *Diablo*, scored fourteenth out of a fleet of twenty-one after a series of mishaps that forced them to retire from three races. In one, Winter was left swimming after a capsize in a 25 k wind and was picked up by the Swedes, who were awarded a special Tokyo medal for their sportsmanship. Australia's FD placings were 13, 4, dnf, 7, dnf, dnf, 9.

MEXICO 1968

In 1968 the Melbourne-based Australian Olympic Federation announced that it would send a total team of 170 'of quality' to the Mexico Games. This followed performances that were judged well below international standards by many of the 302 competitors and officials in all sports whom it had sent to Japan four years earlier, and reports of misbehaviour by some of them. No criticism could be made, however, of the yachtsmen at Tokyo who, on overall scores, had finished second only to the USA, and whose conduct had been exemplary. But yachting, like other sports, was to be pruned, and only eight sailors, with a manager, would be sent, whatever boats they sailed, the AOF said. One Olympic official revealed the depth of his lack of knowledge about sailing when he asserted that he saw no reason why some crews could not double-up in different boats so that Australia could be represented economically in each of the five classes that were listed to compete. He was unabashed when it was explained that in Olympic yachting there were no eliminations and that the races in all classes were sailed on the same days, at the same times and on three different courses. So the trials on Botany Bay, near Sydney, to decide the best boats and men to send to the Acapulco regatta, were held somewhat under a cloud. But they were the most searching and the best organized of any to date. With the preceding national championships in each of five classes, a total of 163 boats — fifteen 5.5-metres, forty-seven Dragons, fifteen Stars, forty-seven Flying Dutchmen and thirty-nine Finns — took part in sixty-nine races during twenty-nine days. The quality of the sailing was higher than ever before because many new boats, built and rigged to the latest international standards, were engaged, and a sprinkling of the skippers and crews had improved their techniques in overseas championships five months previously. They had done this mostly at their own expense, meagerly supplemented by hard-earned class association funds.

Federal and State Goverments and the AOF had not then learned that only by subsidizing our sportsmen into regular international competitions, as other nations did, could we hope to keep our heads high at the Games. Nor had commercial sponsors yet been allowed to 'taint' the hallowed amateur scene with their money. Overseas, of course, no one any longer pretended to believe that these quadrennial festivals were just friendly athletic gatherings of dedicated lily-white amateurs doing their natural best in a spirit of loving camaraderie. The Olympics were at least in part a substitute for war, with many of its political overtones. The armies had to be trained, conditioned, provided with the best of equipment and given real battle practice if they were not to be driven from the field.

So Australian Yachting Federation officials, anxious at least to broaden the experience of our sailors, and in spite of a threat of the AOF axe, selected for the regatta at Acapulco a team of eleven men, a reserve and a manager, not the total of eight men and a manager that had been specified. In fact, the AYF's selection was really only a basic minimum team for five boats, and they defied anyone to cut it. Then they hedged their bets to some degree by naming the team in order of preference. The balding, tigerishly competitive Brisbane optometrist, John Cuneo, with a lifetime of success in dinghy racing and a reputation for unremitting effort, was, with his crew John Ferguson and Tom Anderson, listed number one in their Dragon *Jock Robbie* after easily winning the national title and the Olympic trials. Queenslander Ron Jenyns, in the Finns, was number two. The Sydney sailors Carl Ryves and Dick Sargeant, in the FD *Sidewinder*, were third. Dave Forbes and Dick Williamson, of Sydney, in the Star *Ginger*, were fourth. And in last place were the Sydney group Bill Solomons with Scott Kaufman and Mick York, in the 5.5-metre class. West Australian Tony Manford, an outstanding Dragon helmsman, was nominated as manager.

Reserve was Jim Hardy, formerly of SA but now of Sydney, who had been a reserve at Tokyo and who, as former world champion in 505 dinghies and a skilled crewman, was of a quality that could not be denied.

The grading of the 5.5-metre as last on the list put the AOF properly on the spot. The boat that Solomons — a member of *Gretel*'s 1962 America's Cup squad and successful helmsman of the 8-metre *Saskia* in the Sayonara Cup (after Northam had sold her) — and his crew were to sail was none other than *Barranjoey*, which they had chartered from Northam. Although yachting officials privately knew that *Barranjoey* was outdated by new 5.5-metre designs and had been lucky to win the Botany Bay trials (on a countback of wins against Norm Booth's ultramodern *Southern Cross III*), they also knew it would test the courage of the AOF's selection committee to drop the boat that had won a gold medal at Tokyo. They also launched a shrewd public relations and lobbying campaign designed to influence the AOF in their favour.

Yachting, it was emphasized, next to swimming and athletics, was Australia's biggest Olympic sport, with about 200,000 participating in races nationwide; it had strong public support and interest; Australian standards were high and we were held in world esteem because of our America's Cup and Admiral's Cup challenges; a heavy investment had been made in boats and equipment. But probably the most telling point was one made behind the scenes by Bill Northam himself. As chairman of the Olympic fund-raising appeal committee which had extracted promises of more than $200,000 from the public to support representatives of all sports, Northam let it be known that many of his friends and the boards of companies who had promised large contributions would not be enthusiastic about signing cheques if *Barranjoey* and her crew were dropped from the Games. To explain the mechanism of this little hand grenade, he and two other influential men took Sir Harry Alderson, veteran NSW member of the AOF, to lunch on the day of a decisive AOF meeting. Then they escorted him to Sydney airport so that he could fly to the Melbourne headquarters with their explosive message fresh in his mind.

The AOF caught on quickly, and *Barranjoey* and her crew and all the others were officially endorsed as members of the Olympic yachting team. Sweetness and light continued to prevail when Mick York, because of a business commitment, withdrew from *Barranjoey*'s crew, Jim Hardy replaced him and Bob Miller was unofficially added to the squad as sailmaker, maintenance man and reserve.

And the choice of the full team was justified. Although no Australian boat won a medal, none of them finished worse than seventh in the final points tally in any class and on overall performances they did better than any other nation in the most competitive Games regatta ever held. They did it under great difficulties, too. Many nations sent not only full teams but also back-up teams and boats to pace and tune their champions in pre-Games training; and, as well, coaches, trainers, sailmakers, riggers, engineers, shipwrights, meteorologists, mobile land-based and floating workshops, and towboats. By comparison, the Australian shoestring support was pitiful. While Manford went to sea in an outboard-powered rubber duck to advise his team, other managers operated from massive, airconditioned mother ships. Our crews sweltered in 32 degree temperatures and 85 per cent humidity as they steered their own boats on the hour-long tows to the offshore courses, while scores of their rivals travelled in comfort aboard cruisers, leaving reserves to handle the racing craft until they were ready to take over.

We also lacked hard race-training. Although our team, after a slack winter season, arrived on the course three weeks before the regatta started in mid-October, they had no craft of quality to train against, whereas northern hemisphere competitors were fresh from recent international championships in which our men had not had the resources to compete; and we suffered to some extent because conditions in Acapulco were vastly different from what our sailors had been led to expect.

These conditions were forecast positively to be light to moderate winds on smooth sea swells. They were exactly that for three weeks before the Games regatta. Then, under the influence of a hurricane in the area, the winds for two days reached 14 k to 10 k before they dropped to 8 k and 6 k, and the swells changed to rolling hillocks of water with 200 m between 4 m crests that persisted throughout the series. These were equally unfair to everyone except that those nations with strong ancillary forces could much more quickly adjust their boats and tactics to suit.

The strange seas particularly baffled Cuneo. But he did well to finish fifth in the strong twenty-three boat fleet with placings of 8, 4, 9, 2, 5, 11, 9. He admitted that he could not adapt to the conditions, and he also found that his habit of twitching at the mainsheet trim, instead of leaving it to his crew and concentrating on steering his rather full-bowed boat through the uneven seas, cost him speed and distance.

In the Finns our No 2 team selection, Ron Jenyns, scored a good fourth out of thirty-six with placings of 4, 1, dnf, 7, 15, 16, 2. He was points leader after the first two races but seemed to lose concentration when the winds died, and in one race mistook the five-minute gun for the ten and was badly left at the start. Still, he clearly outsailed the 1964 gold medallist, Willi Kuhweide, of West Germany, who was fifteenth; bronze medallist Henning Wind, of Denmark, eighteenth; and world Finn champion, Jurgen Mier, of East Germany, fourteenth.

In the sophisticated Star class, the most demanding of any, in which fine tuning and trim are so critical, Forbes and Williamson did well to finish sixth in the fleet of twenty that included three former gold medal winners. Their score was 4, 7, 5, 12, dnf, (hit mark when in fifth place), 6, 4. Forbes added his voice to the Australian theme song: 'At home we are spoiled by steady breezes and smooth water. We should try to get more experience in light airs and difficult seas.'

Solomons and his crew probably had the greatest struggle. They found *Barranjoey* completely outgunned by a new breed of American Britton Chance-designed 5.5-metres — narrow, vee-shaped, short-keeled, mid-ruddered hulls, ideal for the peculiar sea conditions, especially when the winds in the late stages of the series fell to 6 k or less. But with impeccable tactical sailing the Australians got seventh out of fourteen with placings 5, 4, 6, 6, 12, 12, 5. *Barranjoey*'s last three races were a nightmare. On the morning of the fifth race a 30 tonne Mexican tugboat ran amok near the 5.5-metre docks where the delicate sloops were moored, alternatively bow and stern, broke four of their light mooring lines and, before her reverse gear engaged, pressed the stern of the British boat underwater to deck level. When the pressure was suddenly released the British boat reared up with tremendous force and smashed her angular transom into *Barranjoey*'s varnished mahogany topsides for'ard of the port chain plates. The impact did no serious structural damage to the British boat but it stove in a section of *Barranjoey*'s shoulder almost 2 m long and 0.5 m wide, just above the waterline.

Carl Ryves and Dick Sargeant in the FD *Sidewinder* (271) were often well placed and just missed a bronze medal in the Acapulco regatta at the Mexico Games in 1968. (Jim Ryves)

The horrified Australians, with the help of a Canadian shipwright and some Mexicans, slipped the boat, pushed the shattered section back into place, shored it inside with baulks of timber, and laid a plaster of fibreglass and quick-drying lacquer over the outside. 'The weight of the shoring gave her a queer unbalanced feeling but miraculously it all held together and didn't leak,' says Solomons. He subsequently refused an offer by the Mexican government to repair the boat at the host nation's expense and had *Barranjoey* restored to new condition by shipwright Bill Barnett when she had been shipped back to Sydney.

Australia's FD team, Ryves and Sargeant, in *Sidewinder*, placed fourth in the fleet of thirty with 3, 5, 3, 20, 8, 4, 3, missed the bronze medal by only .7 of a point, and were only 5.4 points from the silver medal winner, sailed by Ulrich Libor, of West Germany. Ryves said, 'Like the rest of the Australians, we missed out because we were not quite as sharp as we could have been with more experience in hot competition. We made little mistakes, like standing on a few seconds too long on a wind shift, that we could get away with at home in weaker fleets but not when we were up against so many good boats and crews all ready to profit by any error of a rival. It is critical that Australians get overseas for regular international regattas against big fleets of high quality.'

And, as if to underscore that point, the FD gold medal skipper, Rodney Pattisson of Britain, who counted five wins and a second in his score, had spent six months before the Games (on full pay from the Royal Navy in which he was a lieutenant) honing his boat *Superdocious* and his technique in European regattas. Pattisson's win was Britain's first gold medal in twenty years and it ended what had long been accepted as a tradition of English yachting — that trying too hard was unsporting. All the British team had trained hard and had magnificent support in personnel and equipment, and the fact that the Australian boats finished ahead of them in the Dragons, Finns and Stars, mainly through sheer skill and determination, showed what the Australians might have done if they had had the same sort of intense preparation. That was the message of the Mexico Games that Australian Olympians in a score of sports brought back, and to which officialdom at last began to listen.

MUNICH 1972

The world stood up and cheered Australia's yachtsmen after the Munich Olympics of 1972 when they won two gold medals in conditions that broke the spirit of some famous sailors and wrecked the hopes of many. The Kiel regatta on the Baltic was supposed to produce hard, constant winds — the place was noted for them — but no day brought a temporary gust above 21 k, two days were lost to calms, and, on three days, with the breeze never above 6 k, no one in the trapeze classes ever got out on the wire. The windshifts were also dramatic and unpredictable. In these conditions two crews of Australians, of the breed usually at a loss in light, fluky airs, had their greatest successes. It was significant that our two gold medals went to men who had been battle-hardened in previous Games and who had spent months in European campaigns sharpening their techniques against the world's best — Queenslander John Cuneo, with Tom Anderson and John Shaw, in their meticulously reconditioned Dragon *Wyuna*; and Dave Forbes, of Sydney, with John Anderson (Tom Anderson's twin brother) in the chartered Swiss Star *Simba V*.

And in the Finn dinghies, Victorian John Bertrand scored fourth, beaten for a certain silver medal by a few metres — not in distance behind another competitor, but from the finishing line. There he lay, completely becalmed, when the time limit ran out in the sixth race, and so suffered a dnf penalty, since the four boats that had crept in before the breeze died validated the event. We got an eighth in the Flying Dutchman dinghies (Mark Bethwaite, with Tim Alexander), a sixteenth in the new Olympic 8.15 m Soling class (Bob Miller, with Ken Berkeley and Denis O'Neil), and a nineteenth in the new Olympic 6.70 m Tempest class (Gordon Ingate, with Bob Thornton), all competitors from Sydney. Our representatives in those boats, although generally of high standard in hard breezes, just could not adjust to light airs, could not read the devastating changes in wind direction and, to a lesser degree, suffered some bad luck.

The successes were rightly seen as a direct result of four years of concentrated campaigning in Australia and overseas and of the Australian Yachting Federation's determination, with the blessing of the Australian Olympic Federation, to send the crews to Europe for special, last-minute, pre-Olympic training. This time the team was also better organized than ever before and excellently managed by Victorian David Linacre. We had some strong support troops, too, including, as one of the team reserves, the brilliant Sydney sailmaker Mike Fletcher, a champion helmsman in many classes and unquestionably one of the world's best boat tuners. Fletcher analyzed Cuneo's mediocre fourteenth place in the world Dragon series that preceded the Olympics, showed him how to re-set his rig, altered some of his sails, and persuaded him to concentrate entirely on steering his boat and to leave all sail-handling and sheet trimming to Anderson and Shaw.

In final tune-up trials on the Kiel course Cuneo and his crew suddenly found that *Wyuna* was the go-boat of the fleet in light to moderate winds and choppy water. They began the Games races with three paralyzing wins in the fleet of twenty-three, picking windshifts perfectly but at no time taking tactical risks. Then they crashed to nineteenth in the fourth race, in which the breeze was 21 k at the start and 10 k at the finish, with a lively sea, conditions which normally they would have relished. But the breeze veered and oscillated wildly and *Wyuna* was always in the wrong position to take advantage of the variations. After two lay days she came back with a third in the fifth race in a moderate but steadier breeze and, with her nineteenth as a discard, was still in a commanding points position. The sixth race started in 10 k but died to a calm and none of the Dragons (or the Solings) was able to complete the course in the four-and-a-half hour time limit, although enough boats finished in the other four classes to make those events count.

The calms and baffling windshifts were beginning to get on everyone's nerves and at the start of the Solings' sixth (and later aborted) race, the Dane, Paul Elvstrom (four times consecutive winner in single-handers in previous Olympics), while attempting to start on the favoured port end of the line, hit the French boat and the flagmark buoy. He re-rounded, crossed the line, sailed on for a minute, then retired, packed up his boat, abandoned the regatta and drove home to Copenhagen, although he would still have had a chance of a medal. He was later reported ill.

John Cuneo in the Dragon *Wyuna* (131) won the trials on Port Phillip for the 1972 Munich Games and the gold medal. (*Herald and Weekly Times*)

That evening the news of the murders of the Israeli Olympians in Munich brought everything to a halt for twenty-four sombre hours of mourning. Calms and fogs made racing in all classes impossible the next day. When the regatta resumed there were no more spare days, so the Dragon and Soling series were reduced to six races, with five to count. Only one boat, skippered by American Donald Cohan, could now beat Cuneo's *Wyuna* for the gold medal, and it had to finish first in the last heat, with the Australians worse than sixteenth. Cuneo and his crew sailed a wary, conservative race, avoiding all close-quarter duels in the fluctuating breeze, that varied between 15 k, 9 k and 6 k, while Cohan, desperately changing headsails to suit different wind strengths, could do nothing right. He finished twelfth, for the bronze medal, giving Cuneo the gold with an overall score of 1, 1, 1, 19, 3, 4, for a total of 13.7 penalty points, a crushing margin of 28 over the East German silver medallist, Paul Borowski.

In the Stars, Forbes, a gentle bear of a man, and his stalwart crew, John Anderson, won their gold medal not only because of their great sailing skills but also because of their intense knowledge of the behaviour of the hull forms and rigs of their class of boat in different conditions of wind and sea. Moreover, no two yachtsmen ever had more capacity for critical self-analysis. They were faced with a dilemma that would have demoralized anyone less resourceful after a month of pre-Olympic European campaigning in their Australian champion, *Scallywag*. She was a beautiful craft, in mint condition, with excellent equipment of the highest quality, and she had waltzed away with the Australian national titles and the Olympic selection trials, and had won scores of other local races. But, repeatedly, in the open Kiel Week regatta, it was clear that she lacked the speed of a new crop of Olympic hopefuls, specially built and rigged for variable European conditions.

In spite of what seemed to be near-perfect helmsmanship by Forbes and flawless crew work by Anderson, *Scallywag* limped in a miserable twenty-eighth. Were Forbes and Anderson failing in the techniques of setting up and adjusting the twitchy rig, or was the fault inherent in the hull, spars and sails? The next series, in the European championships, in Sweden, in which *Scallywag* finished tenth, convinced the Australians that the flaw was in their boat, that *Scallywag* would not be competitive in the Olympics and that, if they were to have a serious chance, they must discard her completely and seek a better Star with a more suitable rig. Forbes studied those available for charter and chose *Simba V*, which the Swiss sailor Heinz Maurer agreed to lend to him. The hull had less spring than the Australian boat and thus marginally more waterline; it had a stiffer bottom; the rudder stock was slightly more vertical, giving an improved angle of entry; and the bulb keel was fractionally more streamlined. *Simba V* also had an American mast and a stiffer boom than *Scallywag*.

Forbes and Anderson spent the last three weeks before the Olympics systematically making *Simba V* mechanically perfect, fitting extra pumps, strengthening the boom vang system, altering a new mainsail and remorselessly tuning up against *Scallywag*, sailed by reserves. When the Games regatta began they were confident that in 8 k to 14 k of wind there would be no craft faster than theirs. But they also knew that they were up against one of the hottest Star fleets ever assembled, seventeen highly refined champions sailed by crews with a string of international titles, all willing and able to capitalize on each other's slightest errors. So the Australians set out to sail a cool, carefully calculated series, always resisting any temptation to make radical breakaways in search

Ruthless self-analysis by David Forbes of his techniques and his boat's performances persuaded him to discard Australian champion Star *Scallywag* and charter the Swiss boat *Simba V* (5687) in which he won the Munich gold medal. (Warren Clarke)

of a better breeze, and using the rest of the fleet as a guide to windshifts. They never led around the weather mark on the first leg in any race but were always among the first six. Then they used boatspeed and pointing ability to hold and improve their position, and avoided all situations that might involve them in technical rules breaches.

They played the game throughout like a chess match and placed 3, 8, 2, 3, 4, 1, 3 in the seven races. In the sixth heat, the only race *Simba V* won, Forbes patiently burnt off his main rivals and took the lead in the last 100 m. After discards, the Australians began the last race clear on points but were still threatened by Sweden's former world Starboat champion, Pelle Petterson, who had begun the series strong favourite and even halfway through had seemed the likely winner. Steady as ever, Forbes and Anderson set out to match-race the Swede, established a narrow lead, and did not relax their cover until they had crossed the line in third place, with Petterson two places behind them. It was a classical demonstration of how to win against a fleet of champions with only hairline differences of speed and skill between them.

Australia's fourth in the Finn dinghy single-handed class was the hard luck story of those yachting Olympics. Bertrand, a tall, handsome sailmaker with a Master's degree in engineering and naval architecture, was undoubtedly the best all-round sailor in the fleet of thirty-five, and everyone's favourite to win the gold medal. He had campaigned extensively in America and Europe, had been runner-up in the world Finn title, and was in superb physical and psychological shape for the demanding contest. He quickly tuned the boat, mast and sail issued to him, and proved in final pre-regatta trials that it had the speed and high-windedness to outsail any of his rivals. Then the light, shifty Baltic breezes took charge and turned the whole series into a gamble. Bertrand just could not go the right way. In the first two races, with the maximum gust 5 k, the Australian's body weight of 83 kg put him at a positive disadvantage against the much lighter competitors, but his skill when the breeze was constant kept him within range—until they oozed away in zephyrs, leaving him to suffer massive windshifts. He finished eleventh in the first race and a humiliating seventeenth in the second. In the third race, with gusts sometimes reaching 16 k, but dropping, Bertrand confidently sailed to the layline and suffered instant disaster in a wind change of 25 degrees. He finished ninth but significantly ahead of his lighter rivals. Bertrand changed his tactics in the next two heats when the gusts at times touched 21 k but were often below 10 k. He tried to weave short rhumbline courses to the marks rather than sail direct to what were theoretically layline positions fraught with windshifts. He scored a third and a seventh while the best of the lightweights struggled home in the mid-twenties. Then, after holding the leaders early, came his agonizing dnf in the sixth heat when the 10 k breeze collapsed and died, with Bertrand in fifth place, almost at arm's length of the line when the time limit ran out. He did much better in the more constant 11 k breeze in the final race and finished second to Sweden's Tom Lundquist. But, with his overall placings of 11, 17, 9, 3, 7, dnf, 2, Bertrand had to count his 17 (23 penalty points) in his six-race score, giving him 76.7 points, two behind bronze medal winner Victor Potapov, of Russia. So, if Bertrand had made the line for fifth place in the critical sixth heat, and therefore had been able to discard his seventeenth placing, his score would have been 61.7, only 3.7 behind France's gold medal winner Serge Maury (16 kg under the Australian's weight) and 9.3 ahead of silver medallist Ilias Hatzipavlis, of Greece.

Bethwaite and Alexander, in the FD *Verve*, like the rest of the fleet of twenty-eight, were completely outclassed by Britain's Rodney Pattisson (with Chris Davies), who won his second consecutive gold medal without starting in the last race. The Australians made good starts and had a chance of a bronze after five heats with placings of 14, 6, 4, 4, 4. Then, in the last two light-weather heats, they ran into calms and windshifts and crashed with 14 and 22, for eighth place.

Australia's Soling skipper, Bob Miller, in *Alexia*, said with disarming frankness that he seemed to need 'two years of practice in light weather, and a seeing-eye dolphin' to find his way through the maze of windshifts. He placed 15, 15, 13, 12, 11, 13 in the six races sailed by the fleet of twenty-six. His sixteenth put him in close company with many other famous helmsmen, equally rueful.

Gordon Ingate, with Bob Thornton on the trapeze, in Australia's Tempest *Sou' Wester,* might have done better if they had followed Forbes' example and got themselves another boat. On the overall score they beat only two of the fleet of twenty-one in this fibreglass half dinghy-half keelboat class, with placings of 14, 15, 17, 17, 12, dnf, 17.

MONTREAL 1976

Everyone had the formula for success at the Montreal Games of 1976 — hard international racing against quality opposition, constant training in local class regattas, scientific tuning of boats and equipment. The trouble for Australians was that yachtsmen in other countries not only knew all about it, too, but also that hundreds of them, with lavish support from their governments, spent four years and millions of dollars preparing for the seven races to be sailed in each of six classes at the Kingston regatta on Lake Ontario, and the standards of excellence those efforts produced in all classes were higher than ever before. Australia won two bronze medals, in the Finn and 470 dinghy classes, and scored a fourth placing (Tornado catamaran), a ninth (FD), a tenth (Tempest), and an eleventh (Soling) in a regatta of predominantly light to moderate winds.

On different days the winds ranged in strength from 14 k to 6 k to 10 k to 20 k, with periods of calm in between, and shifts of direction from 30 to 180 degrees. The variations bamboozled many expert weather forecasters, and in at least one race the windshifts turned losers into winners. But in all classes luck played little part in the ultimate placings, and the best prepared, most consistent sailors won the prizes.

The results were far below the expectations of the Australian public, of Australian Yachting Federation officials, of the Australian Olympic Federation and of the Australian competitors themselves. But overall they were better than our achievements in any of the other sports in which our representatives at the Montreal Games competed — no other section won two medals — and they brought into focus our strengths and weaknesses in comparison with the rest of the world. The uninformed, though popular, jingoistic image of bronzed Australians lording it over lesser breeds through sheer natural ability was finally expunged.

Australian Federal Governments and some State Governments during the four years before the Games had made what seemed to many politicians to be generous gifts of money to our amateur sporting bodies. These sums were ceremoniously handed out and gratefully received in the belief that among other things they would lessen the burden of administrative duties that traditionally had been performed by over-worked and often inefficient honorary officials. The public at large was encouraged to believe that the money would help to promote community health as well as sporting talent. The paltry nature of these handouts alongside the support given to sport by governments of other nations (nine cents a head of population in Australia, eighty cents in Britain, $1.80 in Canada) was put into perspective only after the Games, during the public outcry that followed the failure of the Australian contingent as a whole. Much more money was provided to prepare potential teams for the highly controversial Moscow Games of 1980. The total, however, was still only a fraction of the aid that overseas nations provided for their sports men and women at the Montreal Games.

Groups of our best yachtsmen certainly were encouraged to compete overseas in the years before the Montreal Olympics and most of those selected for the Games were sent to major regattas in Europe in the spring and early summer of 1976 before they went to Canada for final tune-up training. They also had stronger back-up support than in previous Olympics, although much of the money for that came from fellow yachtsmen and from commercial sponsorship. Foreign yachtsmen of almost every European nation, East and West, whatever its shade of political opinion, received ten times as much aid compared with the costs of sending our boats and men overseas as we did — financially, physically and philosophically. As a matter of course, groups of British, Dutch, East and West German, Russian and Canadian yachtsmen of promise in all classes were sent, with all expenses paid, to at least four and up to six international regattas each year for four years as part of their Olympic training. Australians got to one or two regattas each year. Some crews paid out years of personal savings for the privilege because the official subsidies barely covered the cost of transport. Many men mortgaged two years of annual leave. East and West Germans and the Russians training for the Games had their boats and all equipment supplied and most of them had no need to worry about losing time and money during the months they were away from work since they were on their governments' payrolls. At Montreal, the Germans and the Russians were also provided with full squads of back-up troops in each class, from coaches to riggers to meteorologists, and in most cases their nation's next-best boat and crew on which to sharpen their techniques. Against this avalanche of opposition Australia's sailors stood up remarkably well, although it was significant that all six gold medals, four of the six silver medals, and one of the six bronze medals went to European competitors. The only other nations, out of the forty competing in yachting, to win medals were Australia, the USA, and Brazil.

Two of the classes were new to the Olympics — the 470 (4.70 m) two-man trapeze dinghy and the Tornado (6.10 m) two-man trapeze catamaran — included after years of clamour for recognition by open boat supporters, whose argument, that worldwide there were more than twenty times as many high-performance centreboarders as keel boats, had at last been heard.

The two classes in which Australians had won gold medals at Munich four years earlier — the Dragon and the Star — had been dropped to make way for the newcomers, and it was in one of the new boats, the 470, that we won a bronze medal for third place. A stainless steel shackle that broke under pressure cost us a certain silver medal in the Tornado class. Our second bronze medal score was in the Finn dinghies. Even our strongest rivals expected Australians to be among the front runners in the 470, Tornado and Finn series. Our boats in these classes had been consistently prominent in the European and international championships in which they had managed to compete during the preceding two years, and in special pre-Olympic CORK (Canadian Olympic Regatta, Kingston) regattas held on Lake Ontario courses as full-dress rehearsals for the Games. And almost everyone was prepared to believe that Australia's Soling, with Dave Forbes, the Munich Star class champion, at the helm would win a gold medal. Forbes seemed the natural benchmark for the class.

He had transferred easily to the helm of the longer, three-man boat from the Star, and with his Munich partner, John Anderson, and Denis O'Neil, who had sailed with Miller in the Solings at Munich, as crew had beaten down strong opposition in the class in Australia in his locally built *Pocohontas*. Forbes had

Left In 1967 Forbes won the right to represent Australia in the Soling *Pocohontas* at the Montreal Games but preferred a new US-built boat. He fought hard to finish eleventh in the series. (*SMH*)

Right Victorian John Bertrand missed a silver medal by only a few metres in the Finn class in the Munich Games regatta at Kiel, but sailed a safe series to win the bronze at Montreal (Bob Ross)

also sailed second to Paul Elvstrom in a hotly contested world Soling championships off the Sydney coast in early 1974, and his win at the second CORK regatta during the northern summer of 1975 had given him top seeding. The flaw in this expectation was that later that year and almost throughout the Australian summer of 1975 Forbes, at the behest of fellow-members of Sydney's Royal Prince Alfred Yacht Club, had spent most of his time in a frustrating and unsuccessful Australian–American Six Metre challenge match race series (see Chapter 6) at the helm of a radical, bulbous-bowed boat called *Prince Alfred*, the brainchild — many described it otherwise — of Paul Elvstrom. The expense of spirit and effort in the Six Metre seemed to have jaded Forbes and put him out of touch with close-quarters, fleet racing when he returned to the Soling class for the national selection trials. Indeed, he had to fight hard to win his way to Montreal. Then, after a couple of short US campaigns in borrowed boats, he became convinced that *Pocohontas* would not be competitive in the Games, and bought a new boat, *Matilda*, in Canada, leaving himself precious little time to tune it against real opposition before the racing began.

Forbes started the series shakily and did not get his boat or himself into true championship form until the last couple of heats. His placings, 19, 6, 14, 9, dsq, 7, 4, put him eleventh in the fleet of twenty-four and was the worst score of any of the Australian representatives. Forbes' nineteenth in the first race was the result of a momentary flick by the edge of his spinnaker against the wing mark buoy as the boat gybed, well up with the leaders. The touch was so light that neither Forbes nor his crew noticed it, and they sailed on downwind until a following rival yelled to them. When Forbes' for'ard hand, Denis O'Neil, told him that it was possible the sail could have flicked the mark, Forbes ordered the spinnaker down and beat back 300 m through the fleet to perform the mandatory 360 degree re-rounding. He was in last place when he resumed racing and did well to overhaul five boats before the finish. Forbes suffered from windshifts in other races when in good positions but his ultimate injury came after a fifth heat drifting match when the international jury, following a two-hour protest meeting that lasted until 3 am, disqualified him for a windward-leeward breach against the boat that represented the Virgin Islands.

John Bertrand, who had so narrowly missed a medal at Munich in the Finns, clinched his bronze in the class at Montreal with placings of 2, 6, 1, 22, 5, 5, 6 in the fleet of twenty-eight. He led on the final windward beat in the first race until a 15 degrees windshift put the Canadian boat seven seconds ahead of him. He started last in the second race after a recall when he was forced over the line early, then fought his way through the pack to get sixth. He took the third race and the point score lead in a light-weather tactical battle. The breeze in the fourth race was again light but full of holes, and Bertrand sailed into most of them, finishing twenty-second. Nevertheless, with this as his discard, he still held a narrow points lead from the Russian, Andrei Balashov. The fifth heat put the Russian ahead when the breeze on the final beat completely reversed direction and brought the Russian from twenty-second to third at the line, with the Australian fifth. Bertrand's only lapse from copy-book sailing throughout the regatta came in the sixth heat in a 20 k breeze, the hardest of the series, when he attempted to shoot inside a rival at a rounding mark, with his centreboard raised, and failed to balance his boat as a sea hit him. He capsized, turned turtle, and lost almost three minutes and many placings. Somehow, working every shift, he overhauled a dozen boats to finish fifth. As the points stood, Bertrand could still have won the gold medal in the final race if he had finished first with both the East German champion, Jochen Schumann, and the Russian, Balashov, third or worse. But if he abandoned that ambition and concentrated only on beating the Brazilian, Claudio Biekarch, he was certain of the bronze medal. This Bertrand decided to do. He ignored the others, grimly match-raced the Brazilian from the start, at one stage pinning him back into fifteenth place, and did not release his cover until there were four boats between them on the final beat to the finish. Then Bertrand went into overdrive and clinched his bronze medal with a sixth placing to Biekarch's eleventh.

Australia's 470 was *Hocus Pocus*, with Sydney shipwright Ian Brown, a former Moth class world champion, as helmsman and the boat's owner, Ian Ruff, a Taree (NSW) businessman who had won many national Vee Ess titles, as crew. They had teamed together only ten months earlier and had won their way to the Games after a bitterly fought selection series on Melbourne's Port Phillip Bay. In Montreal they got the bronze medal not only through sound, consistent sailing but also through the unselfish devotion to the Australian cause of their main rivals for Games selection, Gary Gietz and Greg Johns. Gietz, a Sydney sailmaker, the former 470 national champion, who as a boy had also won titles in Flying Ant and Cherub class dinghies, and Johns, in their *Pyrotechnist* had earlier seemed a natural choice for the Games. They had campaigned in Europe and over seven races in the 1975 CORK regatta on the Lake Ontario courses, in fresh winds and bouncy seas, and sailed an impressive third against a fleet of fifty-nine international rivals. However, in similar conditions in the Melbourne trials, in early 1976, the heavier combination of Brown and Ruff had the edge on them. Brown and Ruff spent five weeks sharpening themselves in European regattas and arrived in Kingston for final tune-up training in the fluky light to moderate weather that then prevailed and continued almost throughout the Games. Immediately, they were dismayed to find that their boat was hopelessly outclassed by a hired 470, sailed by Gietz and Johns, who had been sent over to act as their sparring partners.

On the face of it, to dispassionate observers, it appeared that the No 2 crew, in the boat they had, would have been a better pair to race for Australia. But that never seemed to enter their minds. The four of them pooled their knowledge and skills in a fortnight of experimental tuning of the Australian boat. They fitted a new centreboard, adjusted *Hocus Pocus'* rig, altered her sails and devised a new jib-sheeting technique. On the eve of the Games regatta they had *Hocus Pocus* sailing as fast as the hired 470 and a match for any of her twenty-seven rivals.

Brown and Ruff placed 14, 4, 4, 17, 9, 1, 4 in the seven races. Their two worst performances were not as bad as they seemed. In the first race they made two minor tactical errors but finished within 200 m of the winner; in the fourth race, like a dozen others, they were caught in calms and windshifts. Their all-the-way win in the sixth race was scored in the only full-blooded breeze of the regatta, gusts of 18 k to 20 k with a boisterous metre-high sea. Their fourth in the last race gave them 57 points, equal to the Russian boat helmed by Victor Potapov, and it was their delighted team-mate, Gietz, waiting on the dock, who told them that they had won the bronze medal on a countback.

No potential Olympians made a more concentrated effort to prepare for the Montreal Games than the West Australians, Brian Lewis and Warren Rock, business partners in a chain of pharmacies. They spent hundreds of hours in training and, apart from the cost of their Tornado catamaran *Daring,* and her expensive equipment, paid out $13,000 of their own money to bolster AYF and AOF subsidies they received for their 1975 and 1976 overseas campaigns. A flaw in a $3 shackle cost them a certain silver medal. Their placings—rtd, 6, 2, 12, 1, 6, 1—gave them fourth out of fourteen.

Lewis and Rock won the right to represent Australia after placing second in the world championship of the class on Botany Bay, Sydney, and shortly afterwards by winning six whirlwind heats in combined national titles and Olympic trials on Port Phillip Bay. Two of their vanquished rivals were fellow West Australians Jim Dachtler and his crew, Phillip Snook, former Australian champions who had once seemed invincible. Lewis and Rock arrived early in Kingston to tune their boat, and although *Daring* was overshadowed somewhat by the British Tornado, skippered by the dashing 1976 world title holder, Reg White, none of the other twelve contestants in the class seemed likely to beat the Australians.

Top Hood 23 keelboat named after designer Warwick Hood, of Sydney, is an able and popular class for cruising, club racing and low key interstate competition. (Bob Ross)

Bottom left Young Sydney helmsman John Savage in Etchells 22 class keelboat, *Gull II*, fought off strong American opposition to win world title in Canada in 1979. (Bob Ross)

Bottom right Fierce competition kept Australian standards high in the Olympic 470 dinghy class, with Gary Gietz and crewman Greg Johns always among the front runners. (Bob Ross)

Olympic flyer: Australia's champion Tornado class catamaran *Daring* (Brian Lewis and Warren Rock) of Perth, WA, unlucky at Montreal Games. (Bob Ross)

Lewis started the first race in the 14 k breeze with superior upwind speed and duelled with White, narrowly in the lead, all around the course. There was little between them as they turned for the final beat to the finish. Then a quarter-inch shackle, attaching the port shroud to the Australian boat's mast at the hounds, snapped, and the rig collapsed over the side. Lewis and Rock had no way of juryrigging the spar to make the finishing line and were forced to retire. The damage, however, was not severe and *Daring* was re-rigged well in time for the second race. But she was clearly not back into high tune, and her crew, knowing that their retirement must count as a discard, and that they could afford no more mishaps, sailed a tentative race. They started poorly and finished sixth. They had *Daring* in better tune for the light-weather third race, and led most of the way. Near the finish the American skipper, David McFaull, broke clear of spectator craft through which the Australians were dodging, and beat them to the gun by eleven seconds. There was hardly enough wind to start the fourth race, but Lewis and Rock managed to hold a safe sixth place in the fluky air until the last leeward mark. Then they went for a flier off the main track, drifted into a calm patch and struggled home twelfth. That sealed their fate, in spite of brilliant wins in the at first abandoned and then resailed fifth race, and in the seventh.

Mark Bethwaite and Tim Alexander, representing Australia for the second time in the FDs, did not begin to get their boat *Verve* into proper tune until the regatta was half over. They placed 10, 15, 13, 9, 5, 6, 2 and scored ninth out of twenty in a scrambling series. The gold medal winner, Joerg Diesch, of West Germany, did not win a race, and the Spaniard, Jandro Abascal, the only skipper to win two races, finished seventh on the point score. The pre-race top favourite, skippered by Frenchman Yves Pajot, finished eighth, only 2.7 points ahead of the Australian boat.

Australia's Tempest representative, *The Sting*, with Joern Hellner, a former Dragon crewman as helmsman, and James Byrne as crew, finished tenth out of a fleet of sixteen. Their placings were 14, 13, 10, 14, 4, 8, 9. They had been surprise winners of the Australian selection trials in a small fleet in this unpopular class and suffered from lack of experience and final training on the Lake Ontario course, although their German-built boat had reasonable speed. She was forced over the line and recalled in the first race, and collided with another boat in the second race.

The Tempest, included in the Games as a sop to a British lobby within the IYRU, had never gained the wide international support expected of a class chosen for the Olympics, and after Montreal it was dropped from the schedule for the Moscow Games of 1980. An inflammatory comment on the class was provided after the final Games race by the British Tempest competitors Alan Warren and his crewman David Hunt, whose best placing in their aged *Gift Horse* was an eighth. They set fire to the boat with kerosene and flares and recited a Viking funeral oration as it dissolved and sank into Lake Ontario.

In place of the Tempest the IYRU's Olympic Committee chose the Star, that had been used in every Games regatta from 1932 to 1972. Although originally designed in 1911 in the USA (by William Gardner), the boat had been constantly modernized in hull construction and rig and had remained one of the most popular, most demanding and most able fixed-keel craft of its size. During its four-year Olympic eclipse since the Munich Games, the Star had been again rejuvenated and had maintained its popularity as a boat for sailing aficionados.

Although there were no victory flags flying when the Australian team returned home from Montreal, the yachtsmen had every reason to feel that they had performed with honour against odds more powerful than those any previous team had faced. Yacht racing was no longer the province of privileged dilettantes with a romantic love of the sea, and Olympic yachting had become a highly organized test for skilled athletes, using all the technological advances that science could devise. There could be no more illusions about Australia's chances of success unless we met the rest of the world on equal terms. Even to compete with dignity at future Games we would need detailed and expensive programmes of systematic training to encourage our champions and to develop new talent, and these would have to be heavily backed with government and private finance. A group of AYF officials dedicated to that purpose as early as 1973 had formed the Australian Olympic Planning Committee. Now, with much more impetus and with government, AOF and commercial sponsorship they helped to send squads of Olympic class sailors to European regattas in 1977-78-79, and in 1978-79 to pre-Olympic trials at Tallinn, in Estonia, on the Gulf of Finland, the site for the Moscow Games regatta of 1980.

MOSCOW 1980

In early 1980, Australian trials for the six Olympic classes were fought out between 252 dedicated sailors in 125 boats for the right to represent Australia. The AYF chose courses in NSW on Lake Macquarie (Soling, Star), on Botany Bay (Tornado, Flying Dutchman, 470) and in Victoria on Corio Bay, Port Phillip (Finn). But the races were held under the shadow of international political protests against Russia's invasion of Afghanistan and an American-led campaign for a general boycott of the Moscow Games. The Australian Federal Government was one of the first of many to support the boycott and, although it did not order the Australian Olympic Federation not to send a team, it strongly urged it not to do so. In response to this the AYF, although it had submitted a proposed yachting team for Tallinn to the AOF, unilaterally announced that it would support any AOF boycott. When the AOF executive later decided by a vote 6-5 that it would not support a boycott, the AYF, along with some other sporting organizations, withdrew the yachting team from the Australian Olympic Squad.

There was bitter disappointment among some of the yachtsmen chosen in the team who said that they had not been individually consulted and that their Federal body was out of touch with their wishes. They claimed that Australia's team would have had strong chances of gold medal wins in at least three classes, Tornado, Soling and Flying Dutchman, particularly in the absence of many outstanding rivals whose countries had boycotted the Tallinn regatta, if not the Games entirely.

But the AYF decision was irreversible. For the record, the team chosen was, in Soling class: John Bertrand, Gary Sheard, Tim Dorning (all Vic.); Flying Dutchman: Ian Brown, Glen Bourke (NSW); Tornado: Brian Lewis, Barry Robson (WA); Star: Peter O'Donnell, Richard Coxon (NSW); 470: Gary Gietz, Greg Johns (NSW); Finn: Geoff Davidson (NSW). Substitutes: Mark Bethwaite (Vic.), Jonathon Holmes, Ian MacDiarmid (NSW). Manager: John Parrington (SA); coach: John Cuneo (Qld); meteorologist: Tim Alexander (NSW).

LOS ANGELES 1984

During the next four years, Australian yachtsmen were gradually encouraged to rekindle the Olympic flame on the ashes of the 1980 disappointment. The AYF got a new executive, including Tony Mooney (formerly of the NSW Association) as executive director, generous financial support (a total of $174,244 from State Associations, the AOF and the Federal Government) and a more liberal interpretation of amateurism from the IYRU and the IOC. Individuals were now to be allowed, with some limitations, to seek personal sponsorship from commercial organisations to cover extra expenses in travelling overseas and shipping their boats and equipment for international competition and, so long as they were not directly paid, could be identified with commercial products. They could even appear in advertisements endorsing various goods and services provided the money so earned was held in trust for them by the AYF. At last, after the best part of a century of lilywhite posturing, it was a sign that the IOC realised that the days of dilettante Corinthian sportsmen were over, that now it not only cost a city hundreds of millions of dollars to stage the Olympic Games but also that it cost the competitors an equal amount to prepare and compete in them. In any case, Soviet bloc countries had for twenty years been lending only lip service to the so called principles of amateurism and had completely supported their squads of competitors in all sports throughout their Olympic careers.

Selection trials for Australia's Olympic yachting team to sail at the Los Angeles Games of 1984 were held in Gulf St Vincent, off Adelaide, with the splendid new artificial harbour at North Haven as regatta headquarters. The races were hard fought and well conducted with only minor disagreements about those finally chosen for the seven classes to be sailed: Soling — Gary Sheard, Tim Dorning, Dean Gordon (all Vic.); Star — Colin Beashel, Richard Coxon (NSW); Flying Dutchman — Jamie Wilmot, James Cook (NSW); Tornado catamaran — Chris Cairns, Scott Anderson (NSW); 470 — Chris Tillett, Richard Lumb (SA); Finn — Chris Pratt (SA); Windglider sailboard (new Olympic class chosen because of the tremendous worldwide growth of sailboards of various types) — Greg Hyde (NSW). The manager was John Ferguson (Qld), with coaches Mike Fletcher (chief, NSW), Lex Bertrand (Vic.) and Warren Rock (WA). The meteorologist was Willie Packer (WA). Official reserves were Geoff Davidson (NSW), Ian Brown (NSW), Peter Gale (Vic.) and Stuart Gilbert (NSW). The back-up squad included Denis Jones (WA), Anthony Dean (WA), 470; Brian Lewis (WA), Barry Robson (WA), Tornado; Nick Patterson (SA), FD: Geoff Gadsen (Vic.), Star; Loch Simpson (WA), Colin Carnachan (WA), Soling.

No longer could anyone complain that Australia was going cap-in-hand to the Games without proper tune-up boats and crews, and training support. The sailors were hailed as the best we had ever sent to an Olympic regatta. All had years of competitive experience, many had won State, national and international titles, and six had won world titles. Two for the last two years had been the world champions in the class in which they were to compete. Manager Ferguson was inspired to report on the eve of their departure that he was 'excited with our prospect for medals'. Alas, for such confident predictions. In point of fact, our 'best team ever', sailing off Long Beach, California, in consistent and predictable fresh to light to moderate to fresh conditions of wind and sea, (to which they should have been well adjusted), performed well below what had seemed their potential.

Cairns and Anderson, current holders of the world title in the Tornado class and hot favourites to win the gold medal, only just scraped in third for the bronze medal by 0.7 of a point. And that was achieved when they won the last race. At first they had seemed confused by the conditions, unsure about the new pre-bent rig that Cairns, a clever, innovative sailmaker, had devised for their boat. He had originally developed that type of rig and had used it to dominate the world for two years. And so confident was he that he could duplicate it or improve on it that he had sold the rig. It had now been widely copied. Against nineteen rivals Cairns and Anderson had previously outsailed, they placed 4, 16, 3, rtd, 2, 6, 1. In the first race, in a 16 k breeze, after being pinned at the start and forced away from the favoured right hand side of the course in the early stages, they never recovered. They badly misjudged light windshifts in the second race. For the third they adjusted their rig for the 5–10 k breeze and improved dramatically. Then, in the fourth, sailed in 5–14 k, they were again off the pace, finished eighth but retired when they learned that they had fouled the Swedes at the start. Cairns desperately recut his mainsail during the two following lay days 'softening' the head of the sail for the light air starts, and finished the regatta with much more boat speed. His last race win gained him and Anderson a point score of 50.40, just ahead of Denmark's veteran Paul Elvstrom, four times a gold medal winner in single-handed dinghies and now aged fifty-six, competing in a summertime whimsy with his handsome daughter Trine as crew.

The only other Australians that at any stage seemed possible medal winners were Chris Pratt, sixth among twenty-eight hot rivals in Finns with placings of 7, 4, 12, 9, 1, 9, 11 for 68 points, and Greg Hyde, sixth among thirty-eight in Windgliders with placings of 8, 12, 8, 2, 7, 6, 1 for 56.70 points. Pratt, a muscular 24-year-old civil engineer, had trained hard and travelled extensively overseas seeking race experience because, as the only Finn dinghy sailor in SA, he had been unable to get competition at home. But he still lacked the fine edge of race tuning critical for success in the Olympics. Hyde suffered because he was comparatively new to the Windglider class, a heavier displacement type of craft than the Windsurfer class in which he was world champion. He had been unable to train on the Olympic board because the Windglider class could not be imported into Australia until October 1983, when the courts overturned a long-running and bitterly fought patent ruling. Additionally, Hyde made bad starts in two races and, because he lacked heft, could not match bigger rivals early. But under the stimulus of competition he finally developed a technique for fresh weather and led all the way in the last race in 20 k, the hardest wind of the regatta.

In the Soling class, Sheard, Dorning, and Gordon placed 5, 3, 5, 15, 4, 11, 7 for seventh overall against twenty-one rivals. Although their boat was fast and they did well in the first three races, they were pushed over the line early in the fourth, returned to re-cross and were left behind. All the starts were savagely contested and split-second timing was critical to get clear of the pack. After an encouraging fourth in the next race, they experimented with a heavy weather mainsail in the sixth and slipped out of serious contention.

Beashel and Coxon only rarely seemed to be able to get their Star class boat tuned to the pitch of their highly refined rivals for various conditions. They certainly lacked speed downwind in light air. This could have been partly because after a pre-Games European race-training campaign they lost faith in the boat in which they had earlier done so well, and bought a new one for Los Angeles. They clipped the stern of a rival in the first race and scored rtd, 3, 5, 12, 9, 8, 13 for eleventh position in the fleet of twenty-one. In the Flying Dutchman class Wilmot and Cook were hopelessly off the pace and at no stage a threat to the leaders. They had an excellent new German-built hull, but their rig did not match the heavily raked style that the Americans and Europeans favoured. They placed 12, 14, 12, 14, 6, 10, 10 for fifteenth in the fleet of seventeen. Tillett and Lumb slumped badly in the underpowered 470 class, placing dsq (hit rival), 11, 18, 10, pms, 12, dnf for twenty-first out of twenty-eight competitors. Although they had beaten twenty rivals in trials for the right to represent Australia at the Games, they were comparative newcomers to the 470 class. Tillett and Lumb had established their techniques in much flightier dinghies, Tillet as world champion in Fireballs, and Lumb as national champion in the 505 class. They tried hard under the guidance of the Australian coaches to suit their sailing styles to the 470 but were outclassed.

Overall it was a salutary lesson for a new generation of Australian Olympic sailors that their fellow-countrymen in bigger classes of boats racing for the America's Cup, Admiral's Cup, Clipper Cup, and other major international events had learned a long time before. That was never to underrate the opposition.

Everyone who had studied the intense three-year American training programme on the Long Beach, California, Olympic course and the depth of talent in the host country's team selection trials would have expected the US sailors to do well at the Games. But few were prepared for the clean sweep they made of the regatta — three gold medals and four silver. In 1964 US crews had won a medal in each of the five classes but no country ever since yachting was first included in the Olympics in 1900 had ever won more than two gold medals in one regatta. At Los Angeles, the Americans who won gold medals were Robbie Haines, Rod Davis and Ed Trevelyan (Soling) with placings 1, 9, 3, 5, 1, 2, dns; Bill Buchan and Steve Erickson (Star), 1, 9, rtd, 2, 6, 1, 1; Jonathan McKee and Carl Buchan, son of Star class helmsman, Bill Buchan (Flying Dutchman), 2, 1, 2, 3, 1, 4, 6. The Americans who won silver medals were Randy Smyth and Jay Glaser (Tornado); Steve Benjamin and Chris Steinfeld (470); John Bertrand, no relation of Australian America's Cup helmsman (Finn); and Scott Steele (Windglider).

New Zealanders, always highly competitive, won two gold medals, one in the Tornado class — Rex Sellers and Chris Timms with placings 3, 2, 1, 2, 1, 1, dns — the other in the Finn class — Russell Coutts placing 1, 7, 2, 2, 21, 3, 5. The other gold medals went to Spain in the 470 class (Luis Doreste, Roberto Molina) with placings of 3, 1, 5, 2, 1, 9, dns; and Holland in the Windglider class (Stephan Van den Berg) 4, 2, 1, 11, 4, 2, 3.

Among other features of the regatta was the absence of Russia and other eastern bloc countries — in retaliation for the US ban on the Moscow Olympics of 1980. This was generally considered to have made no significant difference to the results, since very few of the Soviet countries had competed in world regattas in the Olympic classes in the preceding four years, and those that did showed no form. There were, nevertheless, 300 competitors from sixty nations. Also, for the first time in an Olympic regatta, there was a woman skipper. She was Cathy Foster, representing Britain in the 470 class. She sailed with former New Zealander Peter Newlands as crew, won the boisterous last race and placed seventh overall in the fleet of twenty-eight.

5

America's Cup Challenges in Detail: Why We Failed and Ultimately Triumphed

THE WIND was gusting at 28 k, driving a lace of spray off the tops of the seas, and the 21.03 m, 29.5 tonne Australian yacht was scudding after them with 279 sq m of sail set. Then, as the first of a series of waves steeper than the rest welled around her quarters, she performed a feat never before achieved by a heavy, deep-keeled vessel of her 12-metre class. Instead of dipping her head and pitching forward for a short distance down the face of the first wave, she lifted bodily, held the same pace as the water tumbling round her, and surfed with it. Then she caught another wave, and another, and another . . . Her speed on each increased from 11 k to 13 k, and she ranged up alongside, then past, her American rival, to win the race.

It was a spectacle that astonished and delighted thousands of people on that wind-driven stretch of the Atlantic Ocean off Newport, Rhode Island, USA. Millions more saw it on television. It was to inspire a cascade of words of praise in a dozen languages for the men who had created and sailed the boat that almost flew downwind. It was also to establish Australia firmly as one of the world's greatest yachting nations and as the USA's major rival in a field of sophisticated sailing to which even countries with a dozen times our technical, scientific and industrial resources had never dared to aspire — challenging for the America's Cup.

The Australian yacht was Royal Sydney Yacht Squadron's *Gretel*; the occasion was the second race of the eighteenth challenge series for the historic trophy on 18 September 1962; the win was the only one to that date by a challenger in twenty-eight years, and only the sixth by any challenger in 111 years since the invincible *America* had first won the Cup in 1851.

Gretel took that race by 47s. Four days later she almost won again, in the fourth race. But the American defender, *Weatherly*, through a stratagem, held her off by 26 seconds before going on to take the best-of-seven match 4–1. In any other sport or any other branch of sailing a 1–4 defeat would seem a good

Top Artist's montage of *Gretel* surfing through a steep following sea in the 28 k wind as she approaches the finishing line. (Based on a copyright photograph by Stanley Rosenfeld)

Bottom Historic moment that sent spectators wild with excitement. *Gretel* (white spinnaker) surges up to and past American defender *Weatherly* in second race of 1962 series. (Warren Clarke) reason for despair by the loser and rapture by the winner. But racing for the America's Cup is not just a sporting event. It is a unique and deadly serious international struggle. At that time, representatives of the New York Yacht Club, who had always won, had grown to believe that they defended the honour and glory of their nation, and that any shade of weakness was a disgrace. A challenger that won even one race was a threat to the core of their ideals, and such was the surprise of *Gretel's* and the Australians' performance that the Americans' reaction was one of extreme alarm. As will be detailed later, they devised some drastic remedies.

Australian yacht clubs have since 1962 challenged six more times for the America's Cup – in 1967 with *Dame Pattie*; in 1970 (*Gretel II*); 1974 (*Southern Cross*); in 1977 (*Australia*); in 1980 with a refitted *Australia*; and in 1983 with the victorious *Australia II*. But until the extravaganza of 1983, which set new records for almost everything, no race, however close, in any of the matches in between, could compare with the original *Gretel's* runaway, for drama and excitement. That magic day when people at a boat race jumped up and down, yelling themselves hoarse, and strangers wrapped their arms around each other weeping with pleasure, owed its beginnings three years earlier to an almost casual gesture of defiance by one man. He was the late Sir Frank Packer, the Sydney publishing and television tycoon, who said at a luncheon, 'The Poms always fail; why don't *we* challenge for the America's Cup?'

In a more reflective mood some time later he said, 'I was inflated by liquor and visions of grandeur. That's the only way you could let yourself become involved in such a venture.' But it was too late then to withdraw gracefully, and, anyway, once committed Packer was no man to back down. He brushed aside an attempt by Britain's Royal Thames Yacht Club to conjoin with the challenge made on his behalf by Royal Sydney Yacht Squadron (the America's Cup contest is always between yachts representing clubs, not individuals or nations), firmly telling the English through his friend Bill (later Sir William) Northam, who went to London for the purpose, that the joint Comonwealth effort the English proposed was unthinkable. Without offending the influential British Red Duster committee, which included a group of aristocratic gentlemen used to getting their own way about almost everything, Northam had the task of saying that, while the British might fancy they had prior right to a 1962 challenge (Royal Thames' commodore, Captain John Illingworth, RN, had been sent to New York in an effort to get RSYS's bid set aside), the unshakable Australian view was that Britain during a century of tilts at the America's Cup had notched up enough failures. This time the Wild Colonial Boys would go it alone.

Northam was fond of describing himself as a salesman, and he said afterwards, 'I had to try to sell them the idea that we'd soften up the Yanks so that when the Poms had another go they might have a chance – and I got out alive.' Packer and Northam also persuaded the NYYC that it would be something of an amusement to have a Kangaroo boat try for the Cup, after fifteen unsuccessful challenges from Britain and two from Canada, and that the Australians were interested more in cementing good international relations than making a serious attempt to win. The Americans bought that package, too, and since a 12-metre class yacht had never been seen in Australia, let alone raced, they agreed to help the newcomers with advice in designing, building, equipping and sailing their contender, so that their challenge would not look too ridiculous. And such was the Americans' confidence that they were to mount one of their most casual defences in history.

With the preliminary formalities over, Packer, Northam, RSYS vice-commodore Richard Dickson, and the committee they had gathered, faced the realities of preparing their challenge champion. They imported the old American 12-metre class boat, *Vim*, for crew training and as a trial horse for the challenger, yet to be built. During the next eighteen months, a total of eighty-seven yachtsmen from all classes of craft from four States vied for places in the squad of twenty-six that was ultimately sent to the USA for final trials on the Newport race course. The final crew included sailmakers, riggers, engineers, shipwrights, company directors, salesmen, journalists, an advertising executive, and a truck driver.

Eight of Australia's leading amateur helmsmen were invited to try for the position of captain of the challenger. They were: Archie Robertson, formerly a champion skipper of dinghies, 6-metres and ocean racers, from Sydney; Alexander 'Jock' Sturrock (dinghies, Stars, Dragons, 5.5-metres and ocean racers), from Melbourne; Trygve Halvorsen (ocean racers), Sydney; Bill Solomons (8-metres, 30 sq metres and skiffs), Sydney; and Bill Barnett, Len Heffernan, Vic Robinson and Frank McNulty (18-footers and 12 ft skiffs), all from Sydney. The first three soon proved themselves outstanding.

Robertson, fifty-three, an executive of a car agency, was famed for his skill in tuning the rigs of yachts, for his subtle tactics and his shrewd touch in light weather. Sturrock, forty-eight, a director of a family firm of marine timber merchants and wharf builders was noted for his hard-driving, aggressive manoeuvres in racing starts, his intense concentration and physical strength. Halvorsen, forty-one, shipwright, engineer and yacht designer, was a director and partner of Lars Halvorsen and Sons (Australia's biggest builders of pleasure craft), and a magnificent seaman, renowned for his organizing ability and with few equals on the helm offshore in rough weather.

But apart from demonstrating or acquiring physical and tactical skills in steering a craft of international 12-metre class size, it was then considered essential that the potential helmsman of a challenger should prove his ability to direct and co-ordinate the work of the ten specialist crewmen handling the yacht's equipment. He would also need diplomatic skill in moulding them into a harmonious team ashore as well as afloat so that their enthusiasm would not wane during the final three months in camp away from home. And he had to imbue in them a sense of complete loyalty and trust in his decisions. In subsequent matches it has been shown that such paragons are not essential for the business end of 12-metre challengers (or defenders) so long as they can steer with unshakable concentration and delegate authority to efficient back-up men. But no one would have believed that in 1962.

Moreover, during Australia's first attempt, the captain would have the not-inconsiderable task of handling Sir Frank Packer who, as head of the challenging syndicate, was footing most of the bills (they ultimately ran to about $800,000 — a tenth of most challengers' 1986 costs), helped by contributions from Ampol Petroleum and W. D. & H. O. Wills, the tobacco company, and other commercial firms. Sir Frank was noted for his shrewdness, his warm generosity of spirit, an imperious manner that made sensitive souls cringe, and what seemed to many who had to carry out his orders, capricious changes of mind. He had some small experience as a racing yachtsman in his younger days and was inclined at times to be persuaded by those anxious to please him that he knew it all. Through this furnace, designed to test the temper of any man, Sturrock emerged, singed in places, as the Australian challenger's skipper. Robertson, who had organized most of the early crew training, was named as his deputy. Trygve Halvorsen was number three helmsman and also captain in charge of maintenance of the Australian challenge fleet (which included two motor tenders) and house manager of the team. Solomons was retained for crew work and as a possible emergency helmsman, and McNulty, because of his all-round skill and physical fitness, as a specialist crewman.

Robertson and Halvorsen, and later Sturrock and a steady stream of crewmen, spent almost a year of weekends aboard *Vim* learning how to handle the heavy and complicated equipment. The flexible steel wire sheets and braces that control the sails on a 12-metre yacht are always a danger to the clumsy and careless, and on tacks, gybes, spinnaker sets and drops perfect co-ordination and timing are essential between the helmsman and the afterguard beside him in the cockpit, the three for'ard hands, the two sheet-tailer-trimmers, and the two winchmen winding the back-breaking pedestal coffee grinders. A momentary error, a foul turn around a winch drum, can cost a minute, worth 200 m in distance; an unsecured running backstay can bring the mast down. From a distance a racing 12-metre is a picture of lean elegance, slicing effortlessly through the water. Aboard it is a scene of noisy, violent physical effort. Even in light weather no human muscle power can directly handle the many tonnes of force transmitted through the sails to the deck leads; only skilful use of the manually operated machinery (no stored power is permitted) is effective.

Those months of preliminary training aboard *Vim* eliminated the starry-eyed romantics from among the scores of original candidates for a place aboard the challenger. The squad was whittled down to thirty dedicated realists, all with a lifetime of sailing experience in various types of craft, and all as fit as prize fighters. And up to that stage they had learned only how to sail a 12-metre. No one had had any experience of the cut-throat split-second match racing that they were to face when they met the American defender of the trophy.

They began to get some inkling of it when *Gretel* was launched at the end of February 1962. She was a handsome boat, designed by the forty-year-old English-born Sydney naval architect Alan Newbury Payne (a diplomate of Sydney Technical College), slim, earnest, softly spoken, with a hesitant manner that belied a tigerish sense of purpose. Payne had had success designing small boats and a string of ocean racers. He had a sound engineering background and an understanding of the hydrodynamic and aerodynamic theories that make a yacht sail. But he had no experience of the 12-metre class, or of any craft of such high-stepping calibre, when he began. Yachts of the 12-metre class must be designed within a complex formula that takes into account length, girths, sail area, and freeboard, all hemmed in by limitations that make these boats usually between 19.81 m and 21.34 m in length, 3.66 m in beam, with about 176.5 sq m of measured sail area, and weigh between 23.4 and 30 tonnes.

Payne spent months studying *Vim* and the 12-metre class rules and tried twenty variations of seven small-scale models that by agreement with the New York Yacht Club he was allowed to test in the towing tank of the Stevens Institute of Technology at Hoboken, New Jersey, USA. He admitted later that he had worked largely in the dark, and was unsure if the theoretical information he gained from tank tests on models would work full scale in practice. Ratios of drag at various speeds and angles of heel seemed conclusive enough to indicate

Designer Payne had innate modesty and a capacity for critical examination of every part of the great racing machine he had created. Many of his innovations were adopted world wide. (Warren Clarke)

In 1961 New York Yacht Club officials allowed Australian designer Alan Payne to test models of *Gretel* in US Stevens Institute towing tank, a privilege not repeated. (Graphic House Inc.)

a desirable hull shape but there was no real way (at that stage) of measuring the likely behaviour of the yacht in a seaway — ahead, abeam or astern. It was largely a matter of guesswork. So was the exact position in the yacht at which to step the 28 m aluminium mast to balance the rig. Payne's initial guesses about the rig needed considerable adjustment in the light of experience. In America the mast had to be moved almost half a metre forward to make the yacht controllable, the steering wheel had to be moved aft, complicated backstay winches and a massive single-wire mainsheet reel winch had to be discarded. But many other fittings, notably linked coffee-grinder sheet winches and quick-release spinnaker halyard clips (known worldwide as *Gretel* clips until manufacturers adopted the unpatented design) broke new ground. And, for a first attempt, Payne's concept of the hull shape was a stroke of genius. *Gretel* had an easy entrance, although with a shade too much fullness behind the shoulders, that gave her reasonable pace to windward, and a long, flat run in

Left Powerful after sections gave *Gretel* tremendous speed downwind in fresh weather. But later 12s had shorter keels, finer entrances, and weighed much less. (Warren Clarke)

Right Even in early crew training trials *Gretel* gave glimpses of her remarkable potential but many refinements of equipment were needed. (Warren Clarke)

the afterbody, with a hard turn around the quarters, that made her probably the fastest yacht of her class on reaches and runs in fresh winds ever built.

Until 1974 the international class required all 12-metres to be built of wood. By today's standards of aluminium construction, *Gretel* was about two tonnes too heavy above the waterline, and she had too much weight in her ends to prevent her pitching through short head seas. But she was beautifully built, by Lars Halvorsen and Sons, of Ryde, Sydney, of three skins of mahogany with a laminated spine and frames of Queensland maple, and she was finished to a degree of perfection usually reserved for fine furniture. American and British shipwrights were later to pronounce her the strongest and best built 12-metre ever known.

When she was launched and christened *Gretel* (after Sir Frank Packer's late wife) by Dame Pattie Menzies, wife of Australia's Prime Minister, only seven months remained before the yacht was due to be racing in America. That left barely three months for tuning and testing all her sails and equipment in trials against *Vim* in Sydney, two months for shipping both yachts to America, and two months for final trials on the Cup course. With Sturrock in charge of *Gretel*, Robertson in *Vim*, and a few interchanges, they engaged in mock battles three days a week, sometimes for ten hours a day, that left everyone ready to drop from exhaustion. Four days a week maintenance gangs swarmed over the yachts to fit them for their next trials.

And with admirable persistence Sir Frank spent many weekends at sea observing the trials from a motor tender with other syndicate members, direction operations by two-way radio and offering advice — much of it pungent, but some of it leaving the sweating sailors bewildered.

'Pull harder, hoist quicker, change the jib, change the mainsail, change your personality, you dopey bastard,' they'd mutter in mock alarm to each other. 'Can't you see Big Daddy is watching — and Little Daddy (Trygve Halvorsen) has got his eye on you, too?'

By May 1962, when the yachts were cradled for their passage as deck cargo on a freighter to America, the raw beginners in 12-metres of eighteen months earlier had been shaped into twenty superbly conditioned deck hands, burly, tough-handed, sure-footed, averaging twenty-eight years of age and 79 kg body weight, with the strength and stamina of an international football team. Their navigator was the brilliant former New Zealander, Terry Hammond, a graduate engineer, who, although not normally called upon to work on deck, was as able a hand as any his size, and a fine seaman as well. The crew continued daily gymnasium exercises and weekend sailing in small yachts until they flew to America with the afterguard to help unload the 12-metres and to tow them to the scene of the battle.

The Australians were received like visiting princelings when they reached the USA and set up their camp at the luxurious Castle Hill Hotel on the shores of Newport Harbour. Gifts and privileges of all kinds were lavished on them. Newporters, accustomed to the rather stiff-necked reserve of NYYC representatives, who traditionally had been drawn from among the scions of the most influential families, were delighted with the informality of the Australians, with their strange accents and their democratic attitude as they laboured side by side on the slipways and rollicked in harbourside bars. Big Daddy and Little Daddy refused many invitations to parties on behalf of the squad. They feared such cavortings would destroy discipline and wreck the hard-

'Big Daddy' takes the helm. One of the rare occasions that Sir Frank Packer sailed aboard *Gretel* in her pre-race trials. Cumbersome single-wire mainsheet system and runner winches were later discarded. (Warren Clarke)

won condition they had achieved. But the delights of the town, rapidly filling with about 30,000 roistering visitors, were a temptation, and many of the freer spirits in the Australian camp defied the curfew, risking the threat of expulsion and ignominious return home. The trials in America had shown that only twelve men were now likely to be considered for the eight working places on *Gretel*'s deck, apart from the three in the afterguard who would bring the total crew to eleven. The other members of the Australian squad were being retained mainly as maintenance labourers and to handle *Vim* as a punching bag for the challenger. However, all were kept guessing right up to the last minute.

It was not until the eve of the first Cup race that Big Daddy, strolling ashore from a tender after observing the last workout, named the crew almost nonchalantly to a group of pressmen waiting on the wharf of the Port O'Call marina. Soon a score of Australian sailors had gathered, asking the reporters if they were in or out. They were not told officially until they sat down for dinner at the Australian HQ that night. US newspapers made great play of what they considered Sir Frank's dictatorial attitudes. One of the most astonishing omissions from the crew for the first race was Terry Hammond, the navigator from Queensland, who had been dropped apparently because of Sir Frank's conviction that pinpoint position-fixing up and down a six-mile track was not necessary. He had said earlier that anyone competent ought to be able to see their way over such a short distance. It was a measure of Australia's ignorance of the nature of match racing, in which 50 m sailed too long on one tack can mean the difference between success and failure, and of the changeable conditions on the Rhode Island course where fogs, brewed on the edge of the adjacent Gulf Stream current, can swirl and blot out a rounding mark only 200 m away.

In the afterguard for the first race Sir Frank had placed two men to whom he could not fail to feel great obligation — Robertson, who had laboured incessantly for two years to train the crews, and Trygve Halvorsen without whose meticulous organization the challenger would probably not have got to the starting line in racing condition. The others largely chose themselves through specialized excellence at their jobs. They were: Mick York, Peter O'Donnell and Dick Sargeant (for'ard hands); Bruce Anderson and Frank McNulty (winchmen); Brian Northam and Trevor Gowland (sheet trimmers); and Magnus Halvorsen, Trygve's 114 kg brother, (mainsheet hand). All of them had sailed boats from childhood and had raced craft of many different types under pressure in countless championships. But none was prepared for the scene that met them when they were towed out into the Atlantic Ocean to the start, nine miles off the coast of Rhode Island, on that sparkling morning of 15 September.

The sea for miles was packed with an armada of spectator craft that ranged from Navy destroyers to rowing dinghies, from 61 m coastguard cutters to cabin cruisers, from schooners to sailing skiffs. Dirigibles and helicopters hovered overhead, and a dozen aeroplanes buzzed a little above mast height. That maritime traffic jam has been conservatively estimated at 2,200 craft with 35,000 people aboard, and the behaviour and standard of seamanship of those in charge of half of the vessels varied between bad and appalling. For two hours the rubberneckers churned the sea around the challenger and defender into a froth and refused to keep clear enough to allow the racing yachts to manoeuvre. It

Sir Frank Packer expected unswerving loyalty from his crew and offered many privileges in return. Part of *Gretel*'s 1962 squad at a farewell dinner: (L to R) Barry Russell, Peter O'Donnell, Doug Fairfax, Richard Dickson, Sir Frank, Alan Belyea, Joe Pearce, Brian Northam (obscured), Terry Hammond, Bob Thornton, Norm Wright, Bill Solomons, Mick York, Peter Cole. (*SMH*)

Helmsman Jock Sturrock (left) discusses last-minute alterations to equipment with shipwright-crewmen Norm Wright and Trevor Gowland. Changes cost many days of valuable training on the race course. (Warren Clarke)

took a score of picket boats of the coastguard service more than an hour to drive them far enough off the track to make a race possible. The next day, President John Kennedy, a spectator with his family and a White House entourage aboard a destroyer, was one of those who apologized to the Royal Sydney Yacht Squadron for the unruliness of the spectator fleet, and an Admiral of the coastguard announced that arbitrary $500 fines would be imposed on skippers of all craft who in future failed to obey instructions to keep the course clear.

Although *Gretel* suffered more from interference by the spectator fleet than the American defender, *Weatherly*, it made little difference to the result of the first race. Sturrock had been persuaded to use a new, comparatively untried and full-cut light-weather mainsail for the 12 k WNW breeze and smooth sea (except where the propellers of the spectators had churned it into a wild bobble). It was soon apparent that *Weatherly*, with a better shaped mainsail and skippered by the wily Emil 'Bus' Mosbacher, a man of consummate skill in getting the best out of any boat, had the edge on the challenger when beating to windward. Moreover, the course for the first race, 6 nm direct to windward and return, twice round, meant that *Gretel* would need to be markedly superior over the two downwind legs to remain in contention.

The pressure of the occasion, the spectator wall and Mosbacher's tactical manoeuvres (in the classical match race fashion he tried to force the Australian boat into a technical breach of the rules and thus disqualify herself before the race began) cost Sturrock several lengths at the start. Within fifteen minutes *Weatherly* was clearly in charge — to windward and well ahead. When *Gretel*,

Top Olympic Finn dinghies demand physical endurance and special techniques. Geoff Davidson, of Sydney, winning 1979 national title. (Sean Harrison)

Bottom When they transferred from Olympic class dinghies to Solings, Victorian helmsmen Mark Bethwaite (*Terror*, KA 144) and John Bertrand (*Odds 'n Ends*, KA 150) fought many close battles. Bertrand scored in the 1980 trials for the Moscow Games. (Bob Ross)

Top No quarter given in this 1983 contest. *Australia II* (KA 6), ahead at second mark in the first race, failed to protect her flank on the following reach and defender *Liberty* (US 40), with staysail set under her spinnaker, here dashes through to windward. (Paul Darling)

Bottom A fight to the finish on the final leg of the first 1983 race with the rudder-crippled *Australia II* (KA 6) unable to catch the defender *Liberty*. Launch at left is judges' *Black Knight*; right is guardian coastguard cutter. (Paul Darling)

Left Seaman extraordinary: Trygve Halvorsen, 'Little Daddy', whose organizing genius got *Gretel* to the starting line in racing condition. (Warren Clarke)

Right A small segment of the thousands of spectator craft that jammed the Cup course for the first race in 1962. President Kennedy, who watched from a Navy destroyer, apologized for the unruly public behaviour. (Warren Clarke)

without Hammond as navigator to call the layline to the first mark, sailed 100 m too far, the race was virtually over. *Gretel* rounded 1 m 28s behind the defender when they began their first run downwind, and gained 23s over the next six miles. But she was still 1m 5s behind when they started their second beat upwind, with no hope of catching the American. On this leg the wind freshened to 20 k in gusts, and the fullness of *Gretel*'s mainsail further contributed to her leeward sag. At the top *Weatherly* was another 2.5 ahead, turning with 3.10 in hand. After *Gretel* rounded, the pack of spectator craft closed in behind her, robbed her of breeze, and she lost another 33s on the final run, finishing 3.43 behind.

There was a soul-searching in the Australian camp and, after a break on Sunday and a lay day on Monday for experiments with new gear, Big Daddy announced two crew changes. For the second race Hammond would replace Trygve Halvorsen, so that the challenger would have a specialist navigator. Norm Wright, of Queensland, would replace Robertson to work the running backstays. The Australians came out with new heart on 18 September to sail the alternative 24 nm triangular course, each of 8 nm legs, in a whistling 22–28 k wind that backed WxS. This time, with only one upwind leg, *Weatherly*, even if she proved superior in that style of sailing, would not have such a built-in advantage. As well, *Gretel*'s crew this time had set her well-tried, flatter-cut, entirely American-made mainsail. It made a tremendous difference to the challenger's performance, although *Weatherly* was still slightly closer winded, probably due to Mosbacher's greater experience in racing this class of boat. After an even start the Australian crew initiated a close-tacking duel on the long beat to windward, forcing the defender to cover tack to keep between them and the next mark. The vigour and strength of the Australians and the power of their double-linked pedestal sheet winches, which allowed four men to wind instead of the two operating *Weatherly*'s individual pedestals, almost exhausted the Americans, who finally broke off the engagement. At the first mark *Weatherly* was only 12s (two-and-a-half lengths) ahead. After the following tight reach without spinnakers (the wind had backed almost 20 degrees) the margin was the same. And then, on the square spinnaker run to the finish, *Gretel* surfed into the lead as described earlier. Mosbacher drove up across the challenger's wake in an attempt to blanket her, but the US boat's spinnaker pole hit her own forestay and broke, and the kite collapsed. The shocked US crew took six minutes to replace the pole but their delay made little difference. *Gretel* was by far the faster boat downwind in fresh conditions, and the defender had no chance of catching her.

The Australians called for another lay day, unwisely, it proved, since the next day there was another good, hard breeze, which would have suited them. The crew, with an army of wellwishers including Big Daddy himself, spent much of the night celebrating their surprise victory, starting in the 'Royal Cameo Yacht Squadron', a raffish harbourside bar they had adopted. As a result, many of them needed the lay day and more to recover. But the tensions of the last two years were dissipated in that roaring, rumbustious booze-up, with a topless lady dancing on the bar. The morale of the crew, if not the physical condition, was never higher.

The realities of racing for the America's Cup returned, however, when they lined up for race three. It started in a fluky 6–7 k NxE breeze, with changes forecast, over the 6 nm windward and return course, twice round. *Gretel* won the start by 30s when Sturrock, who had learned rapidly that it paid to be aggressive in match racing, outmanoeuvred Mosbacher. But *Weatherly*, better rigged for the conditions, gradually squeezed to windward and took the lead, which she held during twelve short tacks. At the first mark *Weatherly* was only 150 m ahead although in the fading air it represented 58s of time, and *Gretel* was still a serious threat. Then, on the square run, with the breeze only 4 k, Sturrock made an unaccountable decision. Instead of sailing directly astern on the same course as his opponent, with a chance of blanketing her or of bringing up a new breeze, he went searching for a private draught of air, and headed high to windward into a dead calm, right under the lee of a phalanx of spectator craft. The Australians desperately made three spinnaker changes to try to get their boat moving again, while *Weatherly* drifted into a lead of 2 nm. When *Gretel* crawled clear and turned for the second windward beat the defender was 23.17 ahead. The faint breeze then backed to the west, eventually swung north at 8 k, turning the beat into a fetch, and *Gretel* came to life, carrying the new wind with her and gaining rapidly. At the turn *Weatherly* was 15.16 ahead, having lost 8.1 of her lead. The wind came in suddenly at 15 k from the NW, providing a spinnaker reach to the finish, and *Gretel* came romping along with it, gaining another 6.36 on that leg. But she was still 8.40 behind, and a mile in distance, at the finish.

It was a race of lost opportunities. American 12-metre buffs came ashore shaking their heads about Sturrock's tactics at the first mark. Dr Norris Hoyt, one of the USA's leading authorities, and the ace America's Cup broadcaster,

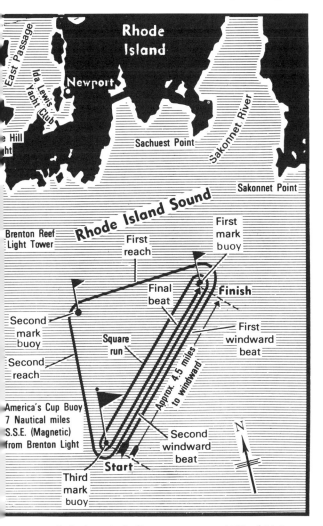

Left America's Cup course up to 1983 of 24.3 nm, with three beats to windward of 4.5 nm split by two reaches of 3.15 nm and a square run of 4.5 nm. It reduced the chances of downwind flyers. (*SMH*)

Right Although *Gretel* (KA1) was later judged to be the faster boat, the all-round match racing skills of American helmsman Emil 'Bus' Mosbacher gave Cup defender *Weatherly* an edge on beats upwind. (Warren Clarke)

pronounced *Gretel* by far the better boat. 'With Mosbacher and his afterguard aboard her and the Australian huskies on deck she'd beat *Weatherly* every race,' he said.

Gretel's HQ called for another lay day and missed another NW wind. The fourth race produced more frustrations for *Gretel*'s supporters. It was sailed over another 24 nm triangular course, with each leg 8 nm in a 5–6 k SxE wind that freshened to 12 k and settled between 9–11 k. After an even start *Weatherly* again proved herself closer winded on the first leg, or at least Mosbacher was able to read the windshifts better. He gradually squeezed his boat up from leeward until he could force the challenger to tack to clear her wind, then tacked a few lengths ahead and to windward to keep her in his wind shadow. It was the classic match-race pattern of covering one's opponent and keeping between her and

Top American designed-and-made dacron sails gave *Gretel* advantages, especially on windward legs, that no later challenger was to enjoy. (Warren Clarke)

Bottom The downwind speed of the Australian challenger stunned many American experts. At the finish of the second race she was 47s ahead of *Weatherly*. (Warren Clarke)

the next mark.

The Australians tried determinedly to break out of it by tacking on to the alternate leg, aiming to get free from the defender's wind shadow, force her into an error or, hopefully, exhaust her crew as they worked to cover tack. After a duel of twenty tacks Mosbacher admitted later, the Australians did almost bring the Americans to their knees. But at that stage the American helmsman broke off the engagement, stood on for a windshift that lifted his boat and knocked the Australians, and gained a lead of 1.31 at the mark. There were now two 8 nm spinnaker reaches, *Gretel*'s best point of sailing, and she soon began to overhaul *Weatherly*. She had gained 36s when they gybed for the final leg with *Weatherly* still 55s ahead and 8 nm to go. The breeze had lightened and changed direction slightly, slowing both boats. Gradually it came in fresh again.

There was at first a hush from the spectator fleet, then excited yells as it became clear that *Gretel* was soaring in the quartering breeze, travelling faster than *Weatherly* and gaining rapidly. Halfway down the track she had ranged up almost level and 150 m to leeward. For three minutes it was a neck-and-neck battle, with the finishing line a little to windward of their track. All *Gretel* had to do was go for it and harden up to a shy reach in the last mile. It looked like a carbon copy of the second race. A win would square the match two-all. Then Mosbacher took the gamble of his sailing career. He had his crew hoist a genoa jib, drop their spinnaker and harden on the sheets as he deliberately sailed his boat to windward. Although he was heading above his required course for the finish, then 2.5 miles away, his move suggested that he could not lay the line unless he got higher to windward. Astonishingly, Sturrock, in *Gretel*, took the bait, against the advice of his navigator that he was already on the lay line. Sturrock ordered his crew to hoist a genoa and drop their spinnaker, too, and then he followed the defender up to windward. The dramatic change of direction meant that *Gretel*, previously leeward boat, was now trailing behind *Weatherly* instead of running level with her. The manoeuvre amazed knowledgeable spectators (and some members of *Gretel*'s crew), who angrily insisted that the Australian boat had been on course for the finishing line and could not have failed to win if she had gone straight for it. But somehow Mosbacher had got away with his stratagem.

He timed his next move just as adroitly. With 1,200 m to go, *Weatherly*'s crew, with skill developed during hundreds of hours of practice, squared away downwind, whipped up their spinnaker and dropped their genoa. It took them ten seconds. The line was now in sight. *Gretel*'s crew, who had gained nothing

Joyous celebrations at the Newport harbourside bar, nicknamed Royal Cameo Yacht Squadron, with 'Big Daddy' in the thick of it. (Warren Clarke)

Critical fourth race of the 1962 series: *Gretel* gaining on final downwind leg. A few seconds later Mosbacher had his crew replace the spinnaker staysail with a genoa and drop the kite so that he could entice Sturrock to follow him. (Warren Clarke)

by chasing the Americans upwind, hoisted their spinnaker and followed them. Square before the wind *Gretel* again began to close the gap, but with the line so close she had no chance of bridging it. *Weatherly* crossed six lengths (120 m) ahead. In time the margin was 26s. There was chagrin and anger afloat and ashore. Few yachts in the history of the America's Cup contest had neglected to seize such a glorious opportunity. Hoyt wrote later, 'It is hard to believe that a well-coached schoolboy would have let Mosbacher get away with that downwind shuffle, or that an Olympic medallist, which Sturrock was, would have bought it'. But Sir Frank Packer took the defeat philosophically. 'We gave them a great race,' he said. 'Don't forget it's only a game.'

The race was the closest on record on official margins but not the closest in actual time. In 1902 the challenger, *Shamrock II*, in the third and deciding race, crossed the finishing line 2s ahead of *Columbia*, but the defender, given 43s time allowance, won by 41s. In 1920, in the third race, the challenger, *Shamrock IV* finished 19s ahead, after starting 19s ahead of the defender, *Resolute*. Yachts were then timed when they crossed the starting line, not when the starting gun went. Both yachts thus sailed the 30 nm course in exactly the same time (4h 3m 6s) but, with her time allowance of 7.1, *Resolute* officially won by 7.1.

After the fourth race *Gretel* called for another lay day and missed the chance of a heavy-weather race, though it is doubtful if officials would have allowed it, since at times the wind was recorded at 30 k, considered dangerous for 12-metre class racing machines. They lined up for the fifth race on 25 September over a 6 nm windward and return course, twice round. It was a cold, hazy day with the wind WSW 6–8 k, at times 12 k, backing to the south. With *Weatherly* now leading three races to one interest had dwindled and the spectator fleet had dribbled away to fewer than 100 boats. After an even start, Sturrock, in *Gretel*, tried enticing tacks in an effort to draw his rival into a duel, but Mosbacher, after an early cover, ignored him and sailed purposefully for the mark, gaining steadily. *Gretel* lost all chance in a windshift as she approached the first mark, overlaid it by more than a minute, and turned 2.4 behind. The spinnaker handling on board the Australian boat was uninspired, too, and on the first run she dropped another 24s. *Weatherly* turned the bottom marker 2.28 ahead, gained another 1.11 on the second beat, and added one second to that on the final run. She came in 3.40 clear, clinching the match 4–1. Australia's first challenge for the America's Cup was over.

It was said at the time that some members of the Australian crew, disheartened by what they believed had been poor tactics by their afterguard in the close fourth race, and because of the overlaying of the mark on the first beat in the final race, did not over-exert themselves. In fact, while the Australians had improved in technique, there was no question but that Mosbacher and his crew, thoroughly alarmed by the prospect of losing the Cup to the maverick Australian boat into which Payne had designed such extraordinary free-sheet speed, sailed like supermen and squeezed the last ounce out of *Weatherly* in the last race. Overall, of the seven true windward beats in the series, *Weatherly* was at all times faster, probably because of Mosbacher's skill on the helm. *Weatherly* also had the advantage in three of the five square runs; *Gretel* clearly was faster on the reaches, winning four, with two even.

The series, above all else, established Australia in future Cup contests as a most dangerous challenger to whom no quarter should be given. The New York Yacht Club, as sole arbiters of Cup racing, set about closing loopholes. No future challengers were to be given such concessions as American sails or sailcloth, they decided. Other equipment and services would be denied them, too, unless these were absolutely unobtainable in the challengers' country of origin or elsewhere. And in case anyone might remain in doubt about the NYYC's intentions and begin to fancy that challenges for the Cup were to be merely sporting contests, the Club issued a special memorandum instructing the world that the races were to be a test of the technology of the competing countries as well as their sailing skill.

Nevertheless, in spite of the new rules yachtsmen throughout the world looked forward to an even stronger contender than *Gretel* when Royal Sydney Yacht Squadron next sent a 12-metre to America to race for the Cup. This was in 1967, after the Americans in 1964 had demolished an ill-mounted bungling bid by Britain's *Sovereign* in four straight races by humiliating margins of 5.34, 20.24, 6.33, and 15.40. It was Britain's sixteenth challenge since 1870, and it seemed that British yacht designers, sailmakers and crewmen of big boats, although their fellow-countrymen were among the world's best in small craft, had learned nothing from their previous defeats; had, in fact, regressed. There was no suspense, no tactical manoeuvring at the starts, no hope. The most notable feature of the contest was that for the first time the yachts raced over what was to become the standard six-legged course for six future Cup challenges. This was an Olympic-style triangle with three windward legs of 4.5 nm, one square run of 4.5 nm, and two reaching legs of 3.15 nm. The accent was definitely on windward work, with 13.5 nm of the 24.3 nm total, including the starting and finishing legs,

Left Amused or ready to bite? Masterly Mosbacher, dual defender of the America's Cup, in the inferior *Weatherly* against *Gretel* and in the vastly superior *Intrepid* against *Dame Pattie*. (Warren Clarke)

Right Gentleman Jim Hardy, skipper of *Gretel II* (1970), *Southern Cross* (1974) and *Australia* (1980) carried his country's flag with dignity and honour throughout a series of controversies and emerged as popular with Americans as with Australians. (Anne Hardy)

devoted to that aspect of sailing. The Americans did not want any more downhill gallopers bringing up the breeze and scaring hell out of their defenders.

They needn't have worried about Australia's second challenger, *Dame Pattie*, named after the wife of Prime Minister Sir Robert Menzies, heavily supported by commercial sponsors and extravagantly promoted as a likely winner by public relations staff who felt their duty was to market the product as 'the best' with the same enthusiasm as they might have sold mouth-wash. When *Dame Pattie* arrived in Newport in mid-1967 she had a cheer squad unequalled in size and enthusiasm by any previous Cup contender. She also had container loads of equipment contributed by her generous sponsors, and enough refrigerated Australian food to stock a supermarket — tinned goods of all kinds, barrels of ice cream, tonnes of steak of the choicest cut, hundreds of cases of beer, wine and spirits — even frozen bread and butter. Cynics suggested that if the NYYC could be persuaded to engage in an eating competition instead of sailing, the Australians would be certain winners. The bookmakers quoted *Dame Pattie* a 10–1 underdog as soon as they had seen her under sail, and offered odds of 4–1 that she would not win a race. They were right.

Dame Pattie was built by Bill Barnett, of Sydney, to the design of Warwick Hood, formerly an assistant to *Gretel*'s designer, Alan Payne, and in series of trial races in Sydney she had clearly outpaced *Gretel*. Keen analysts of those trials, however, thought them inconclusive because *Gretel*, in an attempt to improve her light-weather performance, had been twice altered and extensively rebuilt. She had also been skippered and crewed in the trials by a new batch of Australian sailors, competent but with little match racing or 12-metre experience. So *Gretel* could not really be considered the same 1962 yardstick against which one could measure *Dame Pattie*'s quality. Moreover, Sturrock, with the experience of the 1962 challenge, was now skippering *Dame Pattie* with a crew he had chosen from more than 100 applicants. Last-minute alterations which some critics claimed took the life out of the boat had been made to *Dame Pattie*'s underbody to provide her with a bustle, or skeg, like the latest of the US boats. And, worst of all, since she was denied American dacron for her sails, she had to depend on Australian-made terylene fabric. However, at Newport RI statements about *Dame Pattie*'s potential speed and strong chance of winning the Cup were issued daily, and a minor argument about the measurement of the challenger and the new US defender, *Intrepid*, was blown up out of all proportion to its real importance. A diplomatic reconciliation between Sturrock and Mosbacher (again his rival helmsman) was engineered by a newspaperman and held, to the amusement of some observers, in an icecream bar.

Finally, all the misgivings of the insiders were realized. Within the first ten minutes of the first race it was clear that *Dame Pattie* was no boat to cheer. She heeled excessively, the camber of her headsails — despite all the desperate efforts her skilled sailmaker, Joe Pearce, had made to correct them — stretched like balloons, and her mainsail bucketed inside out. Her crew work at times was sloppy, too. And she hobby-horsed in the notorious Newport slop almost as badly as the two British 12-metre challengers, *Sceptre*, of 1958, and *Sovereign*, of 1964, had done. Before the first beat to windward had finished, the Press corps had renamed the challenger *Damn Pity*. And so it was. This clearly was no worthy successor to Australia's *Gretel*, the boat from Down Under with the rollicking gang of hard-drinking guys who, in two races at least, had given the 1962 defender one of the toughest matches in Cup history. Yet analysis of *Dame Pattie*'s shape suggests that in very light air, with sails of US quality, even equal to those *Gretel* had carried five years earlier, the *Dame Pattie* might have done much better. As it was, against the hawk-bowed *Intrepid* she had the misfortune to meet one of the most efficient machines ever designed for the America's Cup, with unbelievable speed to windward in moderate to fresh winds. And that's what they were most of the time. Mosbacher, *Intrepid*'s helmsman, had also developed his match-racing authority to a standard of excellence that inspired awe, and his highly organized crew handled their complicated equipment with an ease that was almost derisive.

Dame Pattie did not do as badly as *Sceptre* or *Sovereign*, but she was beaten around every one of the twenty marks she rounded in four races straight (of the best-of-seven series), with finishing margins of 5.58, 3.36, 4.41 and 3.35. In all, the total time *Dame Pattie* lost was 1,070s over 97.2 nm of racing on the now-standard Olympic-type course (triangle, windward, leeward, windward) of 24.3 nm — or an average of 11s every mile. On three legs only of the twenty-four they sailed did *Dame Pattie* gain any time — 7s on the second 4.5 nm beat of the second race when Mosbacher, a comfortable 2.03 in front, took a couple of extra tacks to make sure of his loose cover; then 1s on the first reach in the third race when the 16 k breeze eased temporarily; and 1.29 on the run in the final race when the 12 k breeze faded to 8 k.

Designer Hood painfully regretted during the series that he had gambled too heavily on light weather, which meteorological surveys over a century had shown prevailed 75 per cent of the time in the early autumn off Newport RI. He should,

Moderate to fresh winds, short steep seas and *Dame Pattie*'s stretching sails and tendency to hobby-horse put *Intrepid* (right) ahead of the challenger at every one of the 20 marks they rounded. (Douglass Baglin)

he saw in retrospect, perhaps have tried for an all-rounder. The insiders, however, saw it differently. They cited *Intrepid*'s trim-tab rudder just behind her keel, coupled with her second rudder hung on a skeg aft, as prime factors in her windward ability and tight turning circle. They admired her concentration of weight amidships, and especially her short lead keel, chopped-off overhangs, and winches mounted well below deck level. One knowledgeable US critic, Bob Bavier, who had skippered *Constellation* during her wipeout of Britain's second 12-metre challenger, *Sovereign*, three years earlier, said he thought *Dame Pattie* an excellent boat. But she seemed to him, he said, too much like the 1964 defender, *Constellation*, and therefore lacking original thought and failing to take into account the fact that the 1967 defender would have made design advances. It would have been interesting, nevertheless, to have seen *Dame Pattie* under a truly good suit of US sails racing in a breeze between 6–9 k and with a crew as well-disciplined as those eleven sparklers who sailed aboard *Intrepid*. Then the hundreds of Australians who had spent a lot of money going to Newport to cheer *Dame Pattie*, and the millions back in Australia who had believed the propaganda about her great potential, might not have felt so badly let down by her failure.

Australia came back in 1970 with a boat that the Americans and, indeed, yachtsmen throughout the world will find difficult to forget. She was *Gretel II*, Alan Payne's second concept of a 12-metre, again sponsored almost entirely by Sir Frank Packer, and Royal Sydney Yacht Squadron's third challenger. *Gretel II* was the result of Payne's nine years close observation of 12-metre boats and three years of intense research, one year of it on models in the refurbished towing tank of Sydney University's School of Mechanical Engineering. Payne, unlike some designers before and after him, cleverly interpreted the towing tank data and created a distinctive hull that moved smoothly through the chop-over-groundswell sea conditions off Newport that have been the downfall of so many test tank champions. There is no question but that in light to moderate weather *Gretel II* was faster than *Intrepid*, the boat that had defeated *Dame Pattie* so easily and which the Americans again put up as their defender, after she had won a series of trials against other contenders. *Intrepid*'s helmsman this time was the former world champion Starboat sailor and match race expert, Bill Ficker, of California, tall, muscular, with a bald, sun-bronzed head, and a gentle manner and charming smile that camouflaged a savage determination to win. But the 1970 *Intrepid* he sailed was considerably different, especially in the afterbody and keel, from the 1967 boat that Olin J. Stephens, of New York, had designed. She had now been re-designed by the young US naval architect, Britton Chance, famous for a string of 5.5-metre class boats and ocean racers. He had personally supervised her reconstruction. There were and still are members of the New York Yacht Club who believed that the changes did nothing to improve *Intrepid* but in fact on some points of sailing made her slower. To 12-metre observers and to some who had previously sailed in the boat, she now seemed to lack the extraordinary acceleration out of tacks, the instant response to her helm and the ability to turn almost within her own length, that had been so evident three years earlier. She also lacked the artful Mosbacher on her helm.

On the other hand, *Gretel II*, although a great advance on *Dame Pattie* in performance, with a beautifully engineered and riveted mast (designed by Payne and built by aircraft fabricators Fred and Bert Byron, of Sydney) that permitted adjustments to suit her mainsail to a range of winds, had one special flaw. The shape and size of her main rudder (she also had a trim tab) made her skittish to steer and she needed absolute concentration from a very skilled helmsman. Royal Sydney Yacht Squadron found the right man for the job. He was handsome dual-Olympian Jim Hardy, of Sydney, a former world champion 505 class dinghy skipper who had graduated during a lifetime of sailing into championship competition in round-the-buoys keel boats and in ocean racers. Hardy also had other distinguishing qualities — he came from a leading Australian wine-producing family and was well educated and at ease in any company. What one did not see behind the social charm and the well-bred smile was the same killer-winner instinct that moved Ficker.

The Americans recognized Hardy immediately as a fine ambassador for his country, and within days of his arrival with *Gretel II* at Newport for the final training and for the elimination series against the French contender for the Cup, *France*, for the right to challenge, he was known as Gentleman Jim. Hardy needed all his poise to emerge with his reputation unmarked from the troublesome events that followed within the next month. In the early stages he had a comparatively easy time. The French, making their first try for the Cup in a boat a lot better than it appeared were (unfortunately for Australia) extremely disorganized. Their syndicate head, Baron Marcel Bich, the ballpoint pen millionaire, swapped his skippers and crews around when they did not win, sacked two of his world-class helmsmen, and, for the final race, took the wheel himself. He got lost in a fog and failed to finish. Australia won the elimination series 4–0. It was a rather comic prelude to the real Cup races, but it would have been better for *Gretel II* and her crew if the French had given them closer competition; a seven-race series could have honed them to a fine edge of match race sharpness, which is what they lacked.

By contrast, *Intrepid's* team had won their right to the defence of the Cup in twenty-seven hard trial races. They knew almost automatically the right move at the right time; no tactic Hardy tried with *Gretel II* could surprise them. The Cup defender's excellence of conditioning in real racing was once again to prove Australia's undoing, as it was to do in later challenges. The *Gretel II-Intrepid* series was also to prove again one of the essential principles of match racing — a slower boat can win if her crew is superior. But the winning margins were small.

The races for the twenty-first defence of the America's Cup started on 15 September in driving rain and a lumpy sea. They lasted until the autumn twilight of 28 September, and into those fourteen days there were packed more sensations, controversies and exciting sailing than in all the preceding 119 years of Cup racing. *Intrepid* won the series — in the record books — by a score of 4–1. There were some present, however, who believe even today that *Gretel II* should have been credited with two of the wins scored to *Intrepid*, thereby reducing the defender's tally to two and increasing the challenger's to three. Martin Visser, vice-captain of the Australian team and Hardy's deputy helmsman, said in 1979, nine years after the contest, that morally he considered the series had never been sailed to a proper best-of-seven conclusion.

'We won one race without argument and finished first in another, but we were robbed of the credit; and we should have got another when we were fouled before the start,' declared Visser. Whatever the rights and wrongs of the protests and controversies that surrounded the events, no one after that series could suggest that match racing in yachts is always dull. The new media coverage, both the knowledgeable and the hysterically ignorant, was the heaviest in Cup history. This incited hot discussions about yachting in some strange places: in parliaments, company board meetings, university lecture halls, bars, taxis, dining rooms, and TV parlours that had never before heard a word of nautical argument. Unfortunately, it all left a false impression among many people that the New York Yacht Club would do almost anything, short of dropping an atom bomb, to save the America's Cup. This greatly disturbed the proud members of that body, who, for their part, believed that they had many times strained to the limit to make sure that the Cup challengers had a fair chance. As holders of the Cup they were determined to defend the trophy with the best boat, best helmsman, and best crew that their enormous scientific, technical and money resources could muster. And after the scare they got from *Gretel* in 1962 they could not be expected to give anything away. But how, they asked, aghast at the brouhaha that surrounded the 1970 challenge, could anyone accuse them of foul play?

The answer was, of course, that New York Yacht Club officials had always set the conditions for the challenge, always measured the yachts and interpreted the international 12-metre rule, always controlled the races, always heard and decided protests. In short, they had always sat in judgement on themselves, and had rarely found themselves anything but innocent.

But there was no hint of the bitterness that was to follow that raw day of 15 September when the first race started, in a 20 k easterly wind. A fleet of about

600 spectator boats, with most of their occupants wearing foul weather gear, gathered around the base of the huge diamond encompassing the 24.3 nm Olympic-type course, consisting of the now-standardized triangle, followed by a beat, run, and beat. There was a flurry about seven minutes to go to the starting gun when *Intrepid*, on port tack, and *Gretel II*, on starboard, converged and suddenly changed headings; then consternation when protest flags broke out on each boat. (Later it was revealed that Hardy claimed a clear breach of the port and starboard right-of-way rule. Ficker in *Intrepid*, insisted Hardy, by changing course, had prevented him keeping clear. Both protests were later dismissed, much to the surprise of Australian supporters. At the core of the International Rules of racing, the Australians believed, was the law that gave a starboard tack boat, close-hauled or free and settled on her course in clear water, the right to expect a port tack boat, close-hauled or free, to keep clear. The NYYC's protest committee, however found that *Gretel II*, contrary to Hardy's claim that he had sailed his boat on a steady close-hauled course according to wind direction, had hunted upwind for *Intrepid* and so had not allowed the American boat to keep clear. The NYYC announced that because 'no contact' had been made, no action would be taken.) Then both boats veered back from the line on broad reaches, with Hardy to leeward overlapping and locked on to the advantageous tailing position hard on *Intrepid*'s stern and driving her away.

The Australian boat was positively in charge until Hardy, with 38s to go to the starting gun, tacked and headed back to the line, and Ficker, suddenly released, followed. It was not until the last 50 m that Hardy realized that he had made his move 10s too soon. To prevent *Gretel II* breaking the start, he had to drive off to leeward, while Ficker was able to charge up close-hauled and hit the line an instant after the gun. It gave the defender a paralyzing 75 m advantage to windward.

Intrepid just marched up that first 4.5 nm windward leg, and rounded the mark 1.3 ahead. *Gretel II*'s inherent speed had kept her within striking distance, but her crew still seemed shaken by the clanger of a start they had made. Their lack of match racing under pressure showed on their first attempt to set a spinnaker for the reach to the wing mark, 3.15 nm away. The kite rose from the deck then flipped across a slack sheet in a tangled mess. Desperate winching on the brace, sheet and halyard failed to clear it, and it hung there accusingly for six minutes, until some spectators began to jeer. *Intrepid*'s kite had been up and set in 10s.

'Are these clowning kangaroos trying to show how *not* to do it?' growled one rain-soaked critic.

Finally the twisted sail was dropped and another set in its place. *Gretel II* gathered pace. At the wing mark, astonishingly, she rounded only 1.8 behind *Intrepid*, having lost only 5s. The wind by then had hitched slightly, making the next leg a tight reach, not really suitable for spinnakers. *Gretel II*'s crew dropped her kite and continued the chase under main and genoa – and then crewman Paul Salmon was swept overboard from her foredeck by a steep sea. The race became an academic exercise; how long would it take for *Gretel II* to pick him up? And how far ahead would *Intrepid* be at the next mark? In fact, despite the 3.0 it took to rescue Salmon, *Intrepid* rounded the next buoy for the second beat upwind only 3.27 ahead. Theoretically, *Gretel II*, allowing for the lost time, had travelled down the 3.15 nm leg 41s faster than the defender. But there was still an impossible margin between them that nothing but serious damage to *Intrepid* could close. *Intrepid* stretched her advantage out to 4.11, a gain of 44s; widened it to 6.15 on the run and, as the breeze eased to 12–15 k, cruised in 5.52 in front. Spectators squelched ashore irritated at the sloppiness of the Australian effort. The race had been a demonstration of what a competent crew in a good boat could do to a group of brilliant individuals who lacked drill in a superb boat. Norris Hoyt summed it up, 'Don't give them up,' he said. 'They've got talent and a hell of a fine ship under them, and if they can pull it together we'll see a boat race yet.'

But it took five days to get *Gretel II*'s crew properly back at it. First they sought a lay day; then, the following day, they waited for two hours in bright sunshine but not enough wind to start. On the third day both boats covered only 6 nm before fog closed in and the race was abandoned. But an interesting aspect of that aborted race, in which the breeze never got above 12 k, was that *Gretel II* (with Martin Visser as starting helmsman before Hardy took over) no longer had aboard a disorganized tentative group of sailors. They had spent hours discussing their errors and planning drills, and for the first time they looked like a well co-ordinated, aggressive unit. To encourage them was the fact that *Gretel II* had led by more than a minute to the first mark and had lost the lead only narrowly when she had gone hunting in the fog for the second.

The Australians then exercised their right to declare another lay day. When they again lined up for the second race it was Sunday 20 September, the first Sabbath in America's Cup history on which a race was sailed (although one between *Dame Pattie* and *Intrepid* in 1967 had been listed for a Sunday but had to be abandoned because of fog). The weather this Sunday was delightful, with bright sunshine and a slight SW breeze 6–8 k. More than 1,000 spectator boats trekked out to sea to the start. Then the sensations began. First, on the tow to the starting line a Yellow Jacket wasp stung *Intrepid*'s navigator, Steve Van Dyck, on the lip, and he had to be airlifted by a rescue helicopter for emergency hospital treatment. A replacement for him had to be found. Next, what was at first identified as a floating wartime mine drifted through the spectator fleet until a naval expert identified it as a huge fishnet float. Then, seconds after the start at 2 pm, when the breeze was between 6–8 k, came the famous collision that broke off a false nose piece attached to *Gretel II*'s stem, resulted in her disqualification (after she had completely outsailed *Intrepid* in the race that followed), and caused a storm of criticism against the New York Yacht Club.

The collision in no way disabled either boat. After preliminary manoeuvres, *Gretel II*, again with Visser at the helm, approached the windward end of the starting line, close-hauled on starboard tack ahead of *Intrepid*, which was 50 m to windward of her and above the committee boat. As *Intrepid*, moving faster than her opponent, swept down for the start with sheets well sprung on starboard tack, her helmsman, Ficker, in the windward boat, had been obliged under the rules to keep clear. The moment the gun went, however, *Gretel II* was obliged not to sail above a close-hauled course to prevent *Intrepid* from passing between her and the committee boat. It was claimed by the Australians, and many of their supporters, that they had given the 3.66 m-wide *Intrepid* a good 9.14 m of clear water between *Gretel II* and the committee boat; that *Intrepid* was not properly steered on a close-hauled course according to the wind direction at the moment of the start; that Ficker, in the windward boat, had failed to keep clear and, in fact, had smashed his boat diagonally across *Gretel II*'s bows and should be disqualified.

Left Sensational collision at start of second race between *Gretel II* (left) and *Intrepid* that led to challenger's disqualification. Rules exponents argued whether challenger had illegally deprived US defender of room to pass between her and starter's boat, *Incredible*. (Copyright John T. Hopf)

Right Seconds after the collision *Intrepid*'s helmsman Bill Ficker, now on course for first mark, lifts clear of floundering rival. *Gretel II*'s crew rallied, passed the defender in the final stages, finished 1.7 ahead, then lost the race on protest. (Copyright John T. Hopf)

Hardy protested against *Intrepid* for violation of the international racing rules numbers 37.1, 37.2 and 40. Ficker protested *Gretel II* for violation of Rule 42.1 (e). The protest committee, appointed by the New York Yacht Club, found, however, as facts:

> Prior to the starting signal both yachts were approaching the starting line on starboard tack. *Intrepid* was to windward and rapidly overtaking *Gretel* from astern. *Intrepid* was on a close-hauled course to pass astern of the committee boat. *Gretel II* was slowly luffing. After the starting signal and before the yachts had

cleared the starting line, *Gretel II* continued her slow luff until she was above a close-hauled course. During this manoeuvre the yachts became overlapped, and converged. *Gretel's* bow struck *Intrepid* just abaft of the chainplates on the port side.

The committee then announced its decision:

Both yachts were approaching the starting line to start within the intent of Rule 42.1 (e). Prior to the starting signal *Gretel II* was under no obligation to give *Intrepid* room to pass to leeward of the committee boat. After the starting signal however, *Gretel II* acquired an obligation, as soon as the yachts were overlapped, not to deprive *Intrepid* of room to pass on the required side of the committee boat by sailing above close-hauled. Had *Gretel II* fulfilled her obligation to fall off to a close-hauled course under Rule 42.1 (e) *Intrepid* would have had room to pass between *Gretel II* and the committee boat. Therefore *Gretel II* is disqualified for infringement of Rule 42.1 (e). Since the above rule is part of Section 1 — rules for Exception and Special Application, it overrides any conflicting rules of Part IV, which precedes it, except the rules of Section A, rules which always apply. Rules 37.1, 37.2 and 40, under which *Gretel II* protested, are part of Section C, which precedes Section E, and are therefore overridden. *Gretel II's* protest is disallowed.

Then the storm broke. The New York Yacht Club, in some newspapers and on radio and television, was accused of a home-town decison, made by itself on its own behalf. It was claimed that some pictures taken from the air — not those examined by the committee — proved that *Intrepid* was not properly close-hauled, as the protest committee had found as a fact. Some critics also insisted that *Intrepid* had at least 9.14 m of room between *Gretel II's* stem and the committee boat and that she could have been sailed through that gap without collision if helmsman Ficker had made a serious attempt to do so. There were countless arguments about the fine points of the rules, many of them ridiculous. Attempts by Sir Frank Packer to have the New York Yacht Club re-open the protest hearing or, if not, to have an appeal heard by the International Yacht Racing Union, were rejected. So were pleas to have the event declared no race, to be re-sailed. This disqualification was discussed in the Australian Federal Parliament, one politician suggesting that Australian troops should be withdrawn from Vietnam, where they were fighting alongside Americans; and the US Ambassador to Australia apologized for the New York Yacht Club's action.

Sir Frank Packer summed it up, 'Appealing to the New York Yacht Club is like complaining to your mother-in-law about your wife!'

The controversy raged worldwide among yachtsmen and non-yachtsmen, with the body of opinion growing that the New York Yacht Club, whatever the rights and wrongs of the case, certainly had no moral right to sit in judgement on itself. On this point the NYYC, although adamant that its protest committee had acted correctly and honourably in all respects, subsequently made an important concession. It agreed that in future all protests entered by Cup challengers and defenders would not be heard by a committee appointed by the NYYC but would come before an independently appointed international jury; and also that an international panel would measure the yachts. The IYRU also re-phrased the controversial Rule 42 that some critics claimed the protest committee had conveniently misinterpreted.

What many people who argue over the collision forget about that controversial race is that the Australian crew sailed in it like men possessed. They recovered remarkably from the nerve-shattering swipe that *Intrepid* gave them as she zoomed across the line, and they held her to a dogged tacking duel right up the first windward leg. At one stage it seemed certain that *Gretel II* would break through the defender's tight cover, but Ficker broke off at a critical moment, picked up a fresh puff, and rounded 42s ahead. *Intrepid*'s flawless spinnaker drill gave her another 27s on the first reach and 33s on the next. She rounded with 1.42 in hand for the second beat but nothing she could do as the breeze lightened could quell *Gretel II*. At the top of the leg the challenger was only 100 m, in time 1.12, astern, and on the following run, with her flexible, riveted mast slackened forward and her spinnaker asleep, she ghosted through to lead by 50s. Ficker and his crew tried to pull *Gretel II* into a series of spoiling tacks on the final beat in the light air but came to realize that the challenger gained and the defender fell back on each tack. All Ficker could hope for over the last mile was a windshift. There was none. *Gretel II* came home 1.7 ahead to the cheers, yells, whistles, sirens and rockets of a gallery of spectators wild with delight. But the joy turned to anger the next day (a lay day to allow for repairs to *Gretel II*'s false nose piece) when the NYYC announced that the challenger had been disqualified and that *Intrepid* was the winner.

There was a much sobered atmosphere at the start of the third race, with a fresh sou'wester blowing at 12 k and a promise of much more to come — perfect weather for *Intrepid*. Ficker drove Visser, again *Gretel II*'s starting helmsman, well over the wrong side of the line, dipped back at the right moment, and crossed 9s late but 5s ahead and 50 m to windward. Then *Intrepid* held off a savage tacking duel up that first leg, gained steadily, and rounded 46s ahead. She gained nothing on the first reach, added 10s on the second, lost 3s on the second beat, added 23s on the run, 2s more on the final beat, and won by 1.18. She was at all times under threat and could have lost with one bad move. The race was what everyone had hoped for — a real dog fight. No one grudged Ficker that fine win, and no one had any doubt now about the quality of the Australian boat or her crew. Still, with three wins to none officially on the board, *Intrepid* was in a commanding position.

They shaped up two days later, after Hardy had called his fourth lay day, in a 10–12 k easterly breeze. The pattern of the start was almost a carbon copy of race three. Ficker again forced Visser to tack away to port, though behind the line this time; *Intrepid* continued on starboard tack to the favoured buoy end, flipped to port, and crossed the line to windward 8s ahead. Almost automatically, when Hardy took over the challenger's helm, the tacking routine began. Ficker at first answered with the traditional covering tacks, never letting his opponent get out of his wind range. Then suddenly he abandoned this machine-like persistence, ignored the challenges and sailed his own race. His admirers were aghast. Had Ficker cracked under pressure? Did he concede now that *Gretel II* accelerated so fast out of tacks that she would cut him down if he responded to her duelling? Had the Australian crew gained enough battle practice in three races to get on top? (Later, Ficker, faced with this barrage of questions at a Press conference, politely dodged the issue. 'Oh, I hope not,' he said.) Ficker clung to his lead all the way up the first beat and rounded the top mark 29s ahead. *Gretel II* cut this down to 24s on the first reach but on the second, when the wind shifted slightly and *Intrepid* carried a ballooner while the Australians clung to their spinnaker, she dropped 16s, and turned for the second beat 40s astern.

The Cup seemed won at the next mark when the defender turned 56s ahead, and also at the end of the run when she hardened up for the final leg with 1.2 to spare. But the breeze was shifty and easing. It started with almost a fetch straight up the track to the finishing line. Then the breeze veered again, and both boats sagged off on starboard tack. The canny Martin Visser aboard *Gretel II* was the first to see the next windshift, a riffle of new breeze well up to windward, and Hardy immediately tacked to get it before it reached *Intrepid*. By the time the afterguard in the defender realized the significance of the move, *Gretel II* was well up on her opponent's starboard quarter, lifting 20 degrees and gaining every second. When *Intrepid* tacked, desperate now to cover and put herself between *Gretel II* and the finishing line, it was too late. She had to sail into a header, fell away, tacked on the challenger's lee bow and was pinned, wallowing in the lightening air. *Gretel II* came away from her inexorably, made a short hitch near the line, and crossed with 75 m to spare. Her winning time of 1.2 was exactly the same as *Intrepid*'s leading margin at the last mark, so the Australian boat had gained 2.4 on the final beat.

It was an amazing comeback, and a perfect example of what could happen in a match race when the leader failed to cover. There was pandemonium aboard the spectator fleet. Many Australian supporters, still emotionally involved because they believed *Gretel II* had been robbed of her win in the second race, and that the series should now be squared two-all, wept.

This time *Intrepid*'s crew called for a lay day. It took three more days to get them back to the race course. Fog forced the cancellation on 26 September, and vicious squalls that swept through Newport the next day kept everyone in port. On 28 September, the fourteenth day of the long-drawn-out contest, there was a shifty but fading 12 k northerly under cool, grey skies. Only a small group of spectators went out to see what turned into one of the finest Cup matches ever sailed. It was a cliff-hanger throughout. Hardy, who steered *Gretel II* at the start (and won it well, crossing clear to windward, and one second ahead), made one error. He hesitated in covering *Intrepid* during a series of short tacks soon after the start, and let her get within striking distance. Soon afterwards, with *Intrepid* on starboard, Hardy tacked under her bow when it seemed certain to many educated observers (although Hardy, in a better position than most people, said later it was doubtful) that he could have crossed, and *Intrepid*, with the advantage of a lift, managed to squeeze through into command. They were still within biscuit-throwing distance at the mark but *Gretel II*, caught on the wrong tack as they approached, was forced to make two extra hitches to get round; *Intrepid* had 44s to spare but only 50 m in distance in the lightening air. They seemed roped together on the reaches, with *Gretel II* gaining 4s on the first and another 1s on the second.

The second beat produced another great tacking battle. Ficker was at first content with a loose cover, but when it became clear that *Gretel II* was edging out, looking for a shift in the breeze, he answered every tack at the instant the challenger changed course. Still *Gretel II* came on. At seventeen tacks she was almost alongside. They were still at it when they reached the mark, and there Ficker pulled his master stroke. When he was on the lay line for the mark, with both on port tack and *Gretel II* close under his bow, the American carried on, pinning his rival so that she could not turn for the mark until he chose to let her. Then Ficker, riding a puff, came about, while *Gretel II*, held on port for a few seconds before she could follow, lost precious distance. *Intrepid* drove

Fourth race brought another sensation when *Gretel II* caught *Intrepid* on the last windward leg and, as shown here, crossed ahead of her. The challenger went on to win by 1.2. (Bob Ross)

off for the mark with started sheets, and was round 51s ahead in the dying breeze. Both boats' spinnakers were barely full for much of the hour-long run that followed, with the Australians often running by-the-lee in an effort to get right on the Americans' wind, to blanket and slow them. Ficker gybed repeatedly to keep clear. *Gretel II* had cut down the margin to 20s, only half a boat length, at the bottom mark when they turned for the last 4.5 nm leg to the finish.

The breeze then shifted considerably to the east, making it a fetch rather than a beat, and *Intrepid* immediately tacked to starboard, almost on to the lay line for the finish. *Gretel II*'s crew, however, still clearing their decks after their spinnaker drop at the buoy, were forced to stand on port for wasted distance while *Intrepid* romped away for home. With 2 nm to go she had twelve lengths ahead. Ficker, his sheets just free, could now afford to ignore Hardy's invitations to a tacking duel. He just kept between him and the line, and, when *Gretel II* sailed into an airless void, built his lead to 1.44 at the gun. It had been a masterly exhibition. Every fair-minded witness agreed that, despite all the earlier argument, *Intrepid*, on that performance, if on no other, deserved to win the Cup. So in the record book it stands: *Intrepid* 4–1.

When Australia challenged again for the Cup in 1974, the NYYC, after such a close call with *Gretel II* four years earlier, was prepared to expect a very powerful opponent. The Americans knew that the 4–1 victory to *Intrepid* in the 1970 record book did not represent the true difference between the boats, and that the series could just as easily have gone the other way but for the disputed fouls before and at the starts of the first and second races, and a couple of chancy windshifts and good tactical decisions in the fifth. So when faced with a full-scale Australian publicity campaign of an intensity and dimension never before known in yachting (the boosting of *Dame Pattie* in 1967 was mild by comparison), the Americans came to believe that *Southern Cross*, the new Bob Miller-designed, aluminium-hulled 12-metre, representing Royal Perth Yacht Club, and backed by Perth real estate developer and commercial entrepreneur, Alan Bond, could be the strongest threat to the Cup ever to arrive in the USA. Derisive comments, captious criticism of the NYYC, personal insults to American yachtsmen in general and in particular interspersed with details of *Southern Cross*'s vast superiority over *Gretel II* in trials (Bond had bought both *Gretel* and *Gretel II* from Sir Frank Packer) flowed almost daily from the challenger's headquarters and from obedient reporters who rushed to put them in print. The boat was to be sailed by 'the best helmsman in the world', John Cuneo, from Queensland, 1972 Olympic Dragon class gold medallist, with Jim Hardy as adviser, and by a galaxy of supermen in the crew, so the stories ran.

The reason for this extravagant build-up sprang apparently from the naive idea that it would demoralize the Americans, force them into errors, and so give the West Australian boat an advantage. It did just the opposite. NYYC members are made of sterner stuff. In the face of the early threats they closed ranks and encouraged syndicates to raise enough money to build two new aluminium boats, to rebuild the wooden *Intrepid* to her original and supposedly faster 1967 shape, and to alter a previously discarded fourth boat, *Valiant*. Then the Americans mounted the toughest and most searching programme of defence trials in the 104 years since *Cambria* made the first challenge in 1870. It lasted three punishing months. When the new Olin Stephens-designed, aluminium *Courageous* finally emerged as narrow victor over *Intrepid* she was without question the most efficient sailing machine in the world, tuned like a harp, with a crew hardened in thirty nautical dog fights, thirsting for battle. They had not long to wait.

Earlier, *Southern Cross* had demolished the re-vamped *France*, again Baron Bich's contender, 4–0 in a pat-a-cake elimination series. With Jim Hardy at the helm (he had been preferred to Cuneo on the eve of the series) *Southern Cross* won by 7.32, 3.37, 6.59, and 4.22. And so *France* was again out of the Cup with hardly a whimper, and the Australians, as in 1970, had failed to get the close match race practice they so badly needed. None of the challenger's practice sessions against her trial horse, *Gretel II*, now skippered by Cuneo, could be taken seriously as races because both boats were in the same camp, and they were never really rivals. Observers had also detected other weaknesses in *Southern Cross* – a peculiar, double-jointed 'articulated' rudder, of which Olin Stephens said, 'I hope they keep it on her' (they didn't); a rather deliberate gait through tacks in the lighter range of breezes, and a marked slowness to accelerate.

And that became the story of the 1974 challenge. In a series of predominantly light winds, sometimes below 7 k, never above 16 k, *Courageous*, more than 1,000 kg lighter than *Southern Cross* (some hundreds fewer than her waterline dimensions under the 12-metre formula allowed, it was later revealed – which theoretically should have disqualified her!), glided away with four straight wins to nil. *Courageous*, skippered by Ted Hood, won 4.54, 1.11, 5.27, and 7.19.

Afterwards there was a mixture of relief and indignation among the boffins of American yachting at what they regarded as a gross mismatch; relief that the Cup was safe; indignation that the *Stone Banana*, as the Press had nicknamed the heavyweight yellow-hulled challenger, had been so extravagantly promoted by the publicity machine behind her. One elder of the New York Yacht Club said publicly, 'It was like watching a slow leak in a hot-air balloon'. The spectator fleet mirrored this opinion. More than 1,000 boats gathered for the first race but there were only about 100 when it became clear that nothing like the close races or dramas of the 1970 match between *Intrepid* and *Gretel II* were likely.

The starts, nevertheless, when the boats were at close quarters, were spectacular, and Hardy gave as good as he got from *Courageous*' fiery starting helmsman, Dennis Conner. Often they stood side by side, head-to-wind in a holding luff for minutes, daring each other to make a move. One swooping, pre-start snarl as they sparred almost alongside the international jury boat for the second race, with *Courageous* on starboard tack and *Southern Cross* on port, ended with a double protest. The jury dismissed both protests, much to the surprise of many Americans, who were sure that in the good old days the NYYC would have ruled against the challenger. At the post-race conference that evening, Bond complained about the way the crew of the *Courageous* had shouted at *Southern Cross*'s men during the pre-start manoeuvres. Conner replied with the perfect squelch: the Americans, he said, had merely been calling out the numbers of the rules that the Australians were breaking.

In one way it was probably just as well for the defenders of the Cup that they had taken the boastful West Australians seriously and had spent so much time, effort and money (a total of US $5 million was one considered estimate) on the four potential defenders. In light weather *Southern Cross* might have fallen far short of everyone's expectations, and her crew, though individually brilliant, may have lacked finesse as a team; but in hard winds she was unquestionably a very good boat. For a few moments in the series, when the breeze got to 16 k, the *Cross* came to life. Once, when it was 12 k in the first race she managed to take the lead, but lost it through poor navigation. Alan Payne, a detached observer, said later he believed that if there had been four days of racing in fresh winds, similar to those of the 1967 *Intrepid–Dame Pattie* series, the 1974 story might have been different.

Much later a new factor entered the postmortems on this challenge. This was the question of the underweight of the defender for her measured waterline length under the rules, a fact that was not made public until 1977. At that late date it was also revealed that senior officials of the NYYC had known about *Courageous*' shortcomings in the matter of weight before the Cup contests but had loftily dismissed the information as of no consequence.

In early 1977 when Alan Bond learned of *Courageous*' failure to weigh-in in 1974, he claimed, with some justification, that the defender had competed illegally as a 12-metre class yacht, and added, hopefully, that she should be disqualified in retrospect and that the America's Cup awarded to *Southern Cross*. NYYC officials, taking the view that it was the international measurers' duty to check by calculation, or accept designers' certificates of compliance with the rules about weight for waterline lengths, shrugged off the complaints. But they agreed that special scales would be used physically to weigh future challengers and defenders. It was also stated that until 1977 no scales were available that could have weighed a yacht of 25 tonnes to less than 1 per cent of accuracy either way, and thus

Courageous and *Southern Cross* could each have been 250 kg under or over the stated weights for their measured waterline lengths, if attempts had been made to weigh them in 1974. 'When it comes to interpreting any rule concerning the America's Cup, first apply Catch 22', wrote one critic.

But there was no question about *Courageous'* weight for the 1977 match. Her former skipper, Ted Hood, also a designer-sailmaker, remodelled her underwater shape, reducing her waterline 17.7 cm, bow and stern, to bring her down to a length that tallied with her displacement of 25.45 tonnes, and giving her a new run that removed the waterline crease she had previously carried around her quarters. Hood also trimmed lead out of *Courageous'* ballast to compensate for the extra weight of enclosed cockpits that by then were required under the latest changes in the 12-metre rules. It all improved *Courageous* greatly. She was put in the charge of the dynamic 38-year-old millionaire, Ted Turner, of Atlanta, Georgia, widely known as the Mouth of the South, famous for his drolleries and for his world championship wins in many classes of boat, from dinghies to ocean racers.

This brilliant helmsman chose and trained a crew who handled their jobs with the same breathtaking perfection as he steered the boat, and during three months of preliminary, observation and final trials, they overwhelmed the stiff opposition from two new boats for the right to defend the Cup. One of these new boats was *Independence*, designed and skippered by Ted Hood; the other was *Enterprise*, designed by Olin Stephens and skippered by former world Starboat champions, Lowell North and Malin Burnham. *Independence* never seemed to get completely into tune, but *Enterprise* was considered to be the last word in scientific refinement, after a year of tank tests on 6.70 m models and computer assessment of her equipment, and theoretically she was supposed to be the fastest 12-metre ever launched. Nevertheless *Courageous* gave her a series of narrow but positive whippings. During the final weeks of the US defence trials, Turner publicly seemed relaxed, whimsical and at times uproariously unconventional, apparently revelling in his role as the People's Choice against the New York Establishment. It was a popularly held opinion among insiders that the hierarchy of the NYYC found Turner too fluorescent for their tastes, although some Newporters said that the Club would choose Beelzebub himself as its skipper rather than risk the Cup. In any case, Turner and his crew and *Courageous* put the issue beyond doubt with six final victories over *Enterprise*, and five over *Independence*, and only one loss.

The defenders had little time to study the form of the four foreign candidates who had sailed a series of eliminations at the same time as the US trials on nearby Rhode Island Sound courses for the right to meet *Courageous* in the Cup challenge proper. This time Australia had two candidates. *Australia*, jointly designed for Alan Bond by the former Bob Miller (*Southern Cross's* designer, who had changed his name to Ben Lexcen) and Dutch-born Johan Valentijn, challenged for Sun City Yacht Club, WA; and the rebuilt *Gretel II* (redesigned by Alan Payne), represented Royal Sydney Yacht Squadron. Yacht Club d'Hyeres, France, for the third time fielded Baron Bich's *France*, which her owner skippered with Pierre Delfour. (Earlier private trials had eliminated the chances of another possible French contender, the Baron's new, handsome but heavyweight *France II*.) Royal Gothenburg Yacht Club, Sweden, competing for the first time, put up *Sverige*, designed and skippered by the former world Starboat champion, Pelle Petterson, with tremendous financial backing from the Volvo car company and other

Swedish firms.

After a round-robin series of grading trials, *Gretel II*, with Gordon Ingate and Graham Newland as helmsmen, was matched against Sweden's *Sverige* in one best-of-seven, semi-final series, and *Australia* was matched against *France* in another. *Gretel II* had shown herself outstandingly superior in very light airs but of questionable performance in fresh winds. She got a mixed bag of weather and lost a hard-fought series 3–4. One of *Gretel II*'s semi-final wins was a walkover, recorded in a blow of 27–30 k with higher gusts and steep seas, in which *Sverige*, leading 2.30 after only 10.8 nm of the 24.3 nm course had been sailed, was dismasted. Petterson, steering with a tiller, which he preferred to a wheel, was flung across the cockpit but not seriously hurt. The Swedes protested the race committee on the grounds that the race should have been called off in such high winds. The committee dismissed the protest on the basis that the official sailing instructions contained no wind limit. It added that a statement had been made at a pre-race skippers' meeting that no race would start in a southerly wind exceeding 23 k, but that the wind at the start of the race in question had, in fact, been recorded officially at only 16 k. It had freshened sharply afterwards.

Australia, skippered by Perth Soling class sailor, Noel Robins, with Olympic gold medallist, David Forbes, of Sydney, as relief helmsman, beat *France* 4–0 by margins of 5.53, 19s (after a wind change), 8.54, and 10.16. The fourth race started with an imbroglio and a double protest. Both yachts were close-hauled on port tack, with *Australia* a length to windward and almost a length astern,

Ben Lexcen (Bob Miller), brilliant Sydney designer of dinghies, 18-footers, ocean racers, and of the heavyweight America's Cup 12-metre *Southern Cross* in 1974. He was also co-designer of *Australia*, America's Cup challenger in 1977, redesigned her for 1980, designed *Australia II*, the winner in 1983, and *Australia III* and *Australia IV*, defence contenders for 1987. (Greg McBean)

In moderate conditions the rebuilt *Gretel II* of 1977 was no match for the latest Cup contenders. But she was highly competitive in very light airs. (Warren Clarke)

when *France* broke away, gybed and came hard up on a wind until she rammed *Australia* a metre forward of the port shrouds. The collision left a jagged gash in *France's* stem and a dent in *Australia's* topsides but it did not stop them sailing on. *Australia* crossed the starting line 15s late, and France 3.15 later, after her crew had lowered her headsail to examine the hull damage and found it mainly cosmetic. The protest committee disqualified *France* under Rule 41.2 because 'she had gybed (on to starboard tack) without allowing *Australia* sufficient opportunity to keep clear'.

So *Australia* went into the elimination final against *Sverige*, while *Gretel II's* captain, Ingate, endeared himself to the Newport crowd by praising his Swedish vanquishers. 'Ingate is so ecstatic about losing you'd think he had won', wrote one US reporter. Others, assessing the game by different standards, pointed out that if *Gretel II's* captains had sought a lay day instead of agreeing to race when the match was squared three-all, they would have beaten the Swedes on a countback of wins because, as forecast, there was a gale that would have prevented any sailing on the last day listed for sailing. That would have ensured an all-Australian final between the challenge contenders. Still, the match between *Australia* and *Sverige* seemed certain to provide close and exciting racing.

Educated observers noted that *Sverige's* hull was strangely similar to that of *Courageous*, with only superficial differences. *Australia's* designers, on the other hand, freely proclaimed her hull to be an improvement on the 1974 version of *Courageous* which had been conceived during the time that Valentijn had been employed in the New York office of Sparkman and Stephens, the American yacht's original creators. Somehow, since the costly designs of Cup boats are never public property, it seemed that Valentijn had kept the lines of the US yacht in his mind's eye so that he was able exactly to re-create her in model form for tests in the Delft (Holland) tank against models of his and Lexcen's proposed new design. Ultimately *Australia*, the yacht they produced from these tests was, at a declared weight of 24.86 tonnes, considerably lighter than *Courageous* and necessarily under the rules, shorter on the waterline. She also had 17.7 cm less freeboard, slightly less sail area, and was finer aft, with firmer midship sections. Lexcen and Valentijn proudly announced that they had saved so much wetted surface in their hull design that they had been able to give *Australia* a keel 762 mm longer aft than the keel on *Courageous*, with a much lower centre of gravity and more stability. Every fitting was also scientifically engineered for lightness and efficiency. Theoretically, when *Australia* lined up against *Sverige* the stage was set for a classic battle.

Three of the races were close — won by *Australia* with margins of 51s, 25s, and 50s. The finale, in fickle winds, was *Australia's* by a runaway 13.19. But even in the close races the Swedes managed to look like losers most of the time. Their crew work lacked an edge of polish; their sails were never quite right for the prevailing breeze; their mast hung off to leeward; and their helmsman, Petterson, and his tacticians and navigators, seemed to have a genius for tacking into unfavourable windshifts and failing to cover their opponent. Only in the first race, after *Sverige* won the start by 3s in the 12 k breeze, and gained a colossal 3.13 on the first beat (when *Australia* sailed into dead air a mile from the mark) did the Swedes seem like winners. They were 3.54 in front after the first reach in that first race but lost 2.07 on the second reach and another 2.0 on the following beat, when they threw the race away by failing to cover in the shifty breeze. That put them 13s behind *Australia* when they turned for the square run.

The Australians led them around every mark on the eighteen other legs sailed in the series, to clinch the match 4–0. *Sverige's* unequivocal defeat bewildered many of the Swedish squad, who stubbornly believed that, in theory at least, they had sailed the correct courses to benefit from windshifts and had suffered because the changes had been contrary to the normal pattern. The computers they carried aboard confirmed this, they claimed. Knowledgeable Newport yachtsmen shrugged: 'The Swedes were given all the right information but they insisted on reading the wind charts back to front.'

Australia's performances in the seeding trials, and her hollow victories over *Sverige* and *France* imbued in Bond, his skipper Robins and his crew an air of confidence that no other challenger had dared to assume in the twenty years since the Cup races had been sailed in 12-metre class yachts. It didn't last long. Although the challenger, by virtue of the four-boat elimination series, had had more serious racing than any that had previously sailed for the Cup, that competition could not be compared with the cut-throat duels that had sharpened the defender, her equipment, and her skipper and crew to the perfection that they brought to the race course. All of *Courageous'* sails, designed and made by her crewman, Robbie Doyle, of the US Hood loft, were sculptured exactly to suit whatever weight of wind the boat had to face; her rig was tuned to harmonize with every angle of trim, upwind and down; her crew's sail-handling was deft and unerring; and the tactics of her afterguard were as precise as those of a chess master. Combined with Turner's instinctive touch on the helm, these factors made *Courageous* probably the most powerful defender of any class ever to sail for the Cup. She beat *Australia* in a light to moderate weather series by 1.48, 1.03, 2.32, and 2.25, and in the first attempt to sail the second race was about 15.30 in front 300 m from the finish when the five-and-a-half hour time-limit expired.

Australia suffered mainly because her headsails, made by the Sydney brothers, Rob and Peter Antill, of the North (Aust.) loft, from cloth imported from Europe (a dispensation granted by the NYYC since Australia had no locally made fabric that was suitable for 12-metres) did not allow her to point quite as high to windward as *Courageous*; because her crew lacked the expertise of the Americans and made an accumulation of minor errors; and, to a lesser extent, because of tactical mistakes. Lexcen, her co-designer, a former sailmaker and dual Olympic team man, said before and after the series that *Australia's* headsails generally were too flat up high and too full down low, and that he argued with Robins, Forbes and Rob Antill before the races, in an effort to have changes made.

At the best our headsails had a draught of 10 per cent, where *Courageous'* headsails were much fuller up high, with a minimum of 13 per cent draught, and were sheeted in with the leech only 150 mm away from the spreaders. *Australia's* leeches hung 610 mm away from the spreaders. Our mast was not in tune. It sagged 380 mm to leeward at the top, robbing the mainsail of power and making the boat stand up straight and look tremendously stiff which, in fact, she is not. Robbie Doyle and Ted Hood told me after the series that they had known as soon as they had seen *Australia's* headsails that she'd never be able to point with the defender. They'd been worried earlier because they believed our hull form was at least the equal of *Courageous'*, possibly faster, as our tank tests told us. Turner could squeeze up from the leeward of *Australia* whenever she got within range in the same weight and direction of wind. I know we made other mistakes, too, minor ones of tactics and helmsmanship and handling, whereas the Americans were just about perfect

137

after months of hard match racing and tuning. Perhaps on that account alone they'd have beaten us, even if we'd had facsimiles of *Courageous'* sails. But we robbed ourselves of a chance because of our sails, our mast (a new mast made specially for *Australia* was never tried), and because we went into the finals after we'd beaten the French and the Swedes with the wrong frame of mind — starry-eyed and over-confident.

Australia's co-helmsman, David Forbes, later agreed with Lexcen that some of the headsails that the challenger carried were the wrong shape. The harsh facts of the racing were that *Courageous* led around every one of the twenty-nine marks they rounded, including the five in the race she failed to finish in the time limit, and gained time on twenty of the twenty-nine legs. *Australia* gained time on eight legs — on four beats, three runs and one reach, mainly through wind shifts or when Turner was manoeuvring defensively to protect his advantage. The closest *Australia* got to *Courageous* at any mark in the four races sailed to a conclusion was 40s, although at stages on the first windward beats of two races Robins had advantages on which he failed to capitalize.

In capsulated form, the races were sailed thus:

Race 1: 13 Sept., wind 225 degrees, 12.5 k at start; 205 degrees, 17 k at finish. *Australia* won start by 12s. *Courageous* led at first mark by 1.08, then 1.16, 1.23, 1.12, 1.18, 1.48 (at finish).

Race 2 (Aborted): 15 Sept., wind 050, 10 k at start; 125; 3 k when time limit expired. *Australia* won start by 1s. *Courageous* led at first mark by 48s, then 20s, 44s, 10.45, 5.37, 15.30 (estimated when within 300 m of finishing line).

Race 2: 16 Sept., wind 195, 11 k at start; 160, 15 k at finish. *Courageous* won start by 1s, led at first mark by 2.0, then 2.0, 2.38, 2.08, 1.06, 1.03 (at finish).

Race 3: 17 Sept., wind 238, 8 k at start; 310, 8 k at finish. (Second weather leg course changed to 275, wind 9–10 k.) *Courageous* won start by 12s, led at first mark by 1.50, then 2.31, 3.04, 3.27, 1.57, 2.32 (at finish).

Race 4: 18 Sept., wind 265, 14 k at start; 260, 9 k at finish. Even start. *Courageous* led at first mark by 44s, then 48s, 56s, 2.11, 2.35, 2.25 (at finish).

Courageous won match 4–0.

No one, least of all Australians, loves a loser, and a bald 4–0 defeat on the record books looks convincing. However, during the 15h 7m 10s that *Courageous* and *Australia* raced to decisions over 97.2 nm, the defender gained a total of only 7m 48s, or 4.8s a mile — 0.859 per cent of her time. Of course, there are no prizes for second place in the America's Cup, and a win by only one second in any race counts equally with a win by an hour. But by any reckoning the twenty-third challenge in 1977 showed that the technological gaps between the competing nations had closed dramatically, and that if challengers would recognize the need for consistent crew training, careful tuning of rigs, objective assessments of sails, and the sort of battle practice that the US defenders had shown to be critical to success, then the historic silver ewer bolted to a table in NYYC's West 44th Street premises, the trophy that so many had pronounced unwinnable, was not entirely safe.

Refitted, refined with new sails and a new team aboard, *Australia* returns in 1980 for her second tilt at the 'unwinnable' Cup. (*SMH*)

WHY WE FAILED IN 1980

The twenty-fourth challenge for the America's Cup in September 1980, the sixth heroic try by an Australian boat, was a major triumph for the underdog, *Australia*. She won one race that was among the most exciting in the total history of the contest, led by half a mile in another when the time limit of five and a quarter hours expired and, on the record books, equalled the achievements of *Gretel* in 1962 and *Gretel II* in 1970. However, *Freedom*, the awesomely efficient machine that the New York Yacht Club produced as defender of the trophy, took the series 4–1 and reinforced the legend of American invincibility.

Australia this time represented Royal Perth Yacht Club of WA, still with Alan Bond as head of the challenging syndicate and the privilege of meeting most of the enormously inflated costs. In 1978–79 Lexcen, no longer in partnership with Valentijn, who earlier had independently signed a contract with Baron Bich to design a new French boat, devised a number of important alterations to *Australia*'s underwater form. He shortened and sharpened the leading edge of the boat's keel, enlarged the trim tab and rudder, deepened and refined the shape of the bustle, moved the rig forward 30 cm and designed a new mast. Bond gave Lexcen almost a free hand in the choice of sails and sailmakers and the refitting of the boat. He also appointed him tactician and put beside him, as helmsman, Jim Hardy, now forty-eight and since the 1974 challenge toughened during six continuous years of international ocean racing. Hardy was the ideal choice. He was still a match-racing gladiator of rare skill, had the steadying experience of two earlier challenges and burning in his belly were the embers of frustration that had accompanied his defeats in *Gretel II* and *Southern Cross*. If he could win his way through to the final he knew he would be the first helmsman in history to have commanded three challengers. The crew came almost equally from Perth and Sydney and were magnificently fit athletes who blended happily together. On the foredeck were John Longley (34), Scott McAllister (27) and Peter Shipway (30); on the winches Phil Smidmore (26) and Peter Costello (33); trimming sheets John Bertrand (33) and Michael Lissiman (23); on the mainsheet Rob Brown (25). The navigator was Jack Baxter (40). Reserves were Joe Cooper (24) and John Stanley (40). Shore-based maintenance specialists were John Rosser (42) and Jock Barker (35), assisted by John Fitzhardinge (69). Warren Jones (43), a management consultant, who had so ably organized the innumerable details of the 1977 effort, for the second time accepted that unenviable task.

Once again we had a boat of high potential with a good crew that lacked match race practice against a serious rival and $150,000 of sails, made and on order that although incomparably better than those of 1977, had not been evaluated in a complete range of winds. They were from the rival Australian lofts of North and Hood and included many genoa jibs and spinnakers of the latest low-stretch mylar-dacron laminate and two North mainsails of superstrong, lightweight kevlar-mylar-dacron laminate.

On paper the foreign opposition for the right to challenge was formidable. Royal Gothenburg Yacht Club had sent the rebuilt *Sverige*, now with a snout-like fin beneath her for'ard waterline, and Pelle Petterson again at the helm. France's Yacht Club d'Hyeres sent Bich's *France 3* designed by Valentijn. At her helm was former dinghy and small keelboat champion Bruno Troublé, thirty-five, with owner Bich relieving him occasionally. And for the first time in sixteen years Britain had sent a challenge contender, from Royal Southern Yacht Club.

She was *Lionheart*, a black-hulled heavyweight designed by Ian Howlett, a little-known English naval architect with a touch of innovative genius. In early training trials the boat was sluggish in light weather under a normal rig, but then, with a radical 'walking stick' mast, the reinforced fibreglass top of which could be bent back to an extreme angle, she was suddenly transformed. The spar enabled her to carry an extra 14.86 sq m of untaxed area in her mainsail. *Lionheart* at first had as her helmsman John Oakeley, forty-six, sailmaker and former champion dinghy, small keelboat and ocean racing skipper. Lawrie Smith, twenty-four, world champion dinghy sailor, later replaced him. *Lionheart* and *Sverige* had been sailing for almost a year in their home waters and *France 3* had spent more than a year in America sparring with other 12s in the Baron's growing fleet, which now included the former Cup defender, *Intrepid*.

But Hardy and his crew in *Australia*, by a combination of brilliant helming, generally sound tactics, excellent crew work and sails of superior shape, beat them all. There were, however, dramatic moments of aberration in *Australia*'s performances that brought her supporters' hearts to their mouths. She waltzed away with the short-course round-robin seeding trials with a total of six wins and three losses, two of them to *France 3* (one on a protest after a collision) and one to Sweden. In the semi-final series against *Sverige*, lowest scorer in the round robin with three wins and six losses, *Australia* had wins of 5.20, 2.59, and 8.18 but in between lost two races by 3.28 and 1.25. *Sverige* would have had another win to her credit, in the second engagement of their series, when *Australia* was dismasted after a rigger spreader collapsed, so leaving the Swedes to finish the course unopposed, but Hardy successfully protested Petterson for a rules breach at the start and the race was not counted. They lined up on the last listed day for the semi-finals with a score two-all in a sudden-death match that would eliminate one of them. The breeze varied between 6 k at the start and 11 k at the finish, and *Australia* paraded around the course with *Sverige* trailing astern by demoralizingly bigger margins at every mark (8.18 at the finish).

Meanwhile *France 3* (5–4 in the round-robin trials) was battling *Lionheart* (4–5) in the other semi-final. The British won the first race by 2.26 and finished first by 2.29 in the second, but lost on a protest. *France 3* came back with wins of 1.36 and 9.40 (when *Lionheart* stopped racing to rescue forward hand Richard Clampett who had fallen over the side). In their fifth race *Lionheart*'s crew, with their boom goose-neck broken and cobbled up with rope, gave their opponents the race of their lives. *France 3* was 52s ahead at the last mark but Smith engaged *Troublé* in a vicious tacking duel all the way up the track to the finishing line. At one stage *Lionheart* drew almost level and banged her shoulder into *France 3*'s topsides when the French helmsman tacked too close to her. *Troublé* still had a narrow lead as they approached the finish. As they converged with 100 m to sail, with *France 3* on right-of-way starboard tack and *Lionheart* on port, Smith performed a classic manoeuvre that brought spectator fleet crews to their feet yelling with delight. The young English helmsman ducked behind the French stern with only an arm's length to spare and shot his boat head to wind at the line. *Lionheart* won by a metre, officially less than a second. *France 3* was also disqualified for her rules breach on the last windward beat. But the French took the series 4–2 in the next race when they sailed the course 54s faster and *Lionheart* was disqualified, unfairly many thought, for a collision at the start.

The elimination final was a dull match, sailed in predominantly light to moderate weather (7 k to 12 k to 18 k at times) in which *Australia*, with her equipment carefully checked for weaknesses and her crew, chastened after their scare against *Sverige*, sailed with copybook precision to a 4–1 victory. The margins were 2.04, 47s, 3.24 and 4.13. *France 3* took one race by 1.17 after trailing by 8.02 at the fourth mark when she came out of a downwind drift with a new breeze wide off the track while *Australia*, which had failed to cover her flank, floundered in dead air.

So the Australians qualified for the challenge final and now faced *Freedom*, the culmination of veteran Olin Stephens' lifetime of designing 12-metres. Dennis Conner, thirty-eight, *Freedom*'s helmsman, his tactician Dennis Durgan, twenty-seven, and their crew, chosen from 200 champion US sailors, had trained together for two years, match-racing much of that time against the unsuccessful but carefully refitted 1977 defence contender, *Enterprise*. The boats had interchangeable rigs, $350,000 worth of superlative computer-assessed sails, including mains of the new kevlar-mylar-dacron mix, and were tuned to the pitch of perfection regardless of effort or cost. Either could have defended the Cup. Conner chose *Freedom* because he judged her a shade better in the upper range of winds. In the US defence trials *Freedom* won forty-two of forty-seven races, seventeen against Ted Turner's 1977 champion *Courageous* and twenty-five against *Clipper*, rebuilt from the keel up from the 1977 discard, *Independence*, and helmed by Russell Long, twenty-four, and Tom Blackaller, forty.

The Americans were almost supercilious with confidence that they would overwhelm the challenger in all conditions. They were due for a great surprise. On the eve of the Cup races *Australia* was rigged with a new 'walking stick' mast with a 5.18 m fibreglass top, designed by Lexcen, built in Newport and similar to *Lionheart*'s. It could carry an enormously roached mainsail of combined kevlar-mylar-dacron, 16.26 sq m in area bigger than the defender's and, in very light air, below 10 k, it brought magic to *Australia*'s performance. But in the first race this big mainsail, hurriedly made by Rob Antill, of North Sails (Aust.) in Newport, still needed adjustment and *Australia* carried a smaller dacron alternative. *Freedom*, pointing higher, footing faster, led all the way in a 10–12 k breeze. *Australia* crossed the starting line 5s ahead but 300 m to leeward. *Freedom* led at the first mark by 52s, then by 1.33, 1.48, 2.14, 2.17, 1.52 (at finish). Conner revealed next day that he had steered the final leg with only the trim tab rudder when the linkage of the main rudder broke.

In light, fluky air in the second race *Australia*, still with her dacron main, trailed *Freedom* by 10s at the start, and by 42, 50s 1.09, 1.42 (fourth mark), then, hunting for air on a downwind drift, gained a tremendous advantage while *Freedom* lay becalmed. *Australia* got to the fifth mark 0.5 nm ahead with 4.5 nm to go when the time limit expired. *Australia* evened the score one-all in a sensational resailed second race. *Freedom* took the start by 5s but the challenger, carrying her big, beige-coloured mainsail for the first time, had more power in the fickle 6–8 k breeze, climbed clear and led by 28s at the first mark, then by 15s and 47s. Shocked American barrackers at first stood gaping at the Australian boat, then generously began to cheer her on. At the turn, however, the Australian foredeck trio performed a spinnaker drop of which nightmares are made. They lost control of the halyard, the sheet and the brace and soon the sail was streaming astern like a giant kite to the full extent of its lines, dragging the boat backwards and sideways – until the halyard came free and the sail, a drogue now, collapsed into the water. As they desperately winched it back over the starboard quarter, Hardy drove on grimly upwind with *Freedom* closing rapidly. 'I felt very

In the second race of the 1980 series *Australia*, with the aid of a radical bendy mast and a huge untaxed mainsail, outsailed the defending *Freedom* (US 30) but lost the series 1–4. (Paul Darling)

ordinary,' he said later.

But *Australia* still had a narrow lead and was so superior on the second beat that she turned 46s ahead. On the square run, though, with only zephyrs moving them, *Freedom* gybed away into a better draught of air, broke through and turned for the final beat 21s in the lead. It was 18s past 6.06 pm, with only forty-three minutes of daylight remaining and 4.5 nm to sail in 1 h 18m 42s in 3 k of breeze before the time limit expired. For the first forty minutes they crawled to windward with Conner, a few lengths clear, purposefully blocking Hardy's attempt to tack out of his wind shadow. Then, for two minutes, he let him go as the breeze shifted and rose to 8 k. *Freedom* sailed into a header and suddenly *Australia*, with a lift, was in command. Hardy held off Conner in a tense tacking duel as the sun set, the gloom settled and the moon rose. They were in semi-darkness, ringed by lights of a flotilla of spectator craft, when *Australia* crossed the line 28s ahead, and 8m 18s inside the time limit. She got a delirious welcome. A protest by Conner that *Australia* had not carried proper navigation lights was rejected by the jury.

After that everything was anti-climactic although in the third finished race, in a lumpy sea and a 12–16 k wind, *Freedom* blew out a spinnaker, ripped a jib and for a while her normally immaculate crew drill fell apart. But *Australia* was over-powered by her big mainsail on the final beat and the defender led all the way, by 3s at the start, then by 45s, 26s, 20s, 51s, by only 8s (during a spinnaker foul up) and by 53s at the finish. Dual protests for technical breaches of spinnaker setting rules were dismissed.

Australia virtually lost the fourth completed race before the start when forecasts of very hard winds persuaded Hardy to use an ordinary dacron mainsail in winds of 12–8–12 k. Conner, under a fuller rig, outmanoeuvred him by 13s at the start. *Freedom* then led by 1.48, 2.51, 3.08, 2.41, 2.21 and 3.48 (finish). After a lay day, which Conner called to dodge expected light winds, *Freedom* administered the *coup de grâce* in light rain and cold winds of 17–14 k, the hardest of the series. She took the start by 7s, then led by 52s, 1.04, 44s, 1.20, 3.10 and won by 3.38, thus clinching the series 4–1. Both crews congratulated each other and, after ritual dunkings in the murky dockside waters of Newport Harbour, Conner reiterated an earlier statement that *Australia*, in winds of 7–8 k, under her biggest rig, was the faster boat. But no one could seriously expect favours from the chancy Newport climate; only all-rounders could be expected to win.

Bond, like other defeated generals, said he would return, and intended challenges from new French and British syndicates were announced. Later two more Australian challengers and one each from Canada and Italy entered the lists. Perhaps in 1983 the Cup would be in real jeopardy. The NYYC said before the finals that it would probably lift embargoes on challengers using US-made sails, fittings, equipment, even sophisticated American testing tanks. Yachts would merely have to be built in their own countries, designed and sailed by their own citizens. Part of the rationale for these concessions was that the manufacture of yachting equipment had become international and no purpose would be served if prohibitions continued on goods that had originated in America. 'What it really means,' said one Newport cynic, 'is that after 110 years of challenges they don't want the Cup races to die and have decided to give the suckers an even break.' But had they? At the IYRU's next meeting US delegates persuaded the class rules committee to impose restrictions for the first time on the girth (fore and aft) measurements of 12-metre boats' mainsails. Bendy 'walking stick' masts were, therefore, nullified.

THE TRIUMPH OF 1983

The 1983 challenge was a never-to-be-repeated summer-long epic that wiped wars, politics, and economics from the front pages of newspapers and brought the subject of boat racing into such unlikely places as the Oval Office of the White House. It commanded TV and radio audiences of around 500 million. It engendered a campaign of contumacious argument and personal vilification unequalled in a sport once considered the province of gentlemen. It broke a world's record sequence of sporting successes that had begun 132 years earlier. It brought the people of Australia together as one nation with a common interest as had no other event since the end of World War II.

And, in the end, the members of the New York Yacht Club, always the most implacable opponents in all of the twenty-five challenges for the America's Cup, proved themselves dignified and gracious losers. In a ceremony in the sunshine on the piazza of the Marble House, Newport, Rhode Island, in the presence of political and civic dignitaries and distinguished fellow yachtsmen, the NYYC's Commodore, Robert G. Stone junr, surrendered the trophy. Royal Perth Yacht Club's Commodore, Peter Dalziell, received it — a glistening 76 cm (2 ft 6 in) high, bottomless silver ewer insured for $1 million — on behalf of his club and promised to guard it with all the resources that money and sincerity could muster. Then, temporarily, he released the precious object for a half hour of good-

Ben Lexcen's magic winged keel that reversed the tide of America's Cup racing. (Paul Darling)

John Bertrand, skipper of victorious *Australia II*, flourishes the America's Cup that the USA had held against all comers for 132 years. (Australian Information Service & Barry Stevens)

Left Warren Jones, executive director of the Western Australian syndicate, who out-thought and out-fought the New York Yacht Club. (Sally Samins)

Right Dennis Conner, superb match-race gladiator, who defended the ancient trophy to the last gasp in an inferior boat. (Sally Samins)

Top *Australia II* (KA 6) bursts across the starting line in the opening race of the 1983 drama with defender *Liberty* (US 40) snarling at her heels. Right is judges' launch *Black Knight*. (Paul Darling)

Bottom Euphoria in the grounds of Newport's fabulous Marble House with the legendary trophy many had thought unwinnable. Alan Bond and John Bertrand are in the centre of *Australia II*'s squad. (Australian Information Service & Barry Stevens)

Australia II romps along under shy spinnaker with the crew stowing the kite that they have just peeled in race three of the 1983 series. She won by the paralyzing margin of 3.14s. (Australian Information Service & Barry Stevens)

tempered buffoonery between Alan Bond, principal backer of the successful *Australia II* syndicate; Ben Lexcen, designer of the wing-keeled boat that had achieved the seemingly impossible; and helmsman John Bertrand and the crew who had sailed so well. As they passed the Cup overhead from hand to hand, nursed it like a baby, kissed its bottom, pretended to pour drinks from it, there was a ripple of disapproval from one small section of the large crowd gathered on the Marble House lawns.

An American voice said: 'You show no respect for tradition. That is a sacred object.' Few people who had followed the progress of the 1983 campaign and *Australia II*'s desperate last leg win 4–3 in the best-of-seven series could have agreed with such a pious sentiment. To my mind, competition for it has been dishonoured. It can never be the same.

Since James Ashbury's first challenge in 1870 the international battles for this most ancient sporting trophy have been studded with controversy and bickering. But never before have accusations and allegations of foul play, cheating, illegality, coercion, conspiracy, character assassination, defamation, and insult matched those that preceded the contest of 1983 – the year of the keel. Lifelong friendships were shattered, business associations severed, men young and old humiliated. The central controversy hinged on the invention of the Australian genius of yacht design, Ben Lexcen – his revolutionary winged keel for the Royal Perth Yacht Club's challenger *Australia II* and the unsuccessful attempts to have it banned.

This keel, moulded as an integral part of the central underbody of the yacht and weighing about 18 tonnes of her overall total of 23.6 tonnes, was claimed to give *Australia II* extraordinary lift to windward, the ability to turn in her own length and incredible acceleration out of tacks. The boat's stability was certainly obvious. Even in a stiff breeze she heeled much less than other boats of her class because of the counter-balancing effect of outward jutting wings on her keel. This had also enabled the craft to be built at least one and a half tonnes lighter, and consequently faster downwind, than any of the other six potential challengers (except the Royal Yacht Club of Victoria's *Challenge 12*, also designed by Lexcen) and the three potential defenders of the Cup. Rumours of the keel's strange shape and efficiency preceded the arrival of the boat in Newport, Rhode Island, but American gurus of yachting in the early stages of training before the elimination trials generally dismissed it as a useless gimmick. One was quoted as saying that it would not only slow the boat but also, in fresh conditions on Rhode Island Sound, threaten to suck the boat down in the sloppy seas and sink it. But although everyone had an opinion about the keel, very few people outside the syndicate had seen it, either in Australia or in the USA.

The yacht had been shipped to America with the keel covered by a solid wooden box 9 m long, 3 m wide, and 2.4 m high moulded to the shape of the bottom of the hull and built as an integral part of the shipping cradle. In Newport the hull had been constantly shrouded by heavy fabric screens whenever the boat was hoisted from the water. Security around the docks, and at the gantry lifts that held the yacht suspended after each training trial or race, prevented inspection of the keel by anyone unconnected with the *Australia II* camp. At first this had merely amused the Americans and some of those connected with the rival foreign challenge syndicates. They considered it a piece of gamesmanship of no consequence. Later it infuriated them. A Canadian underwater photographer, allegedly spying for US teams, was arrested and charged with trespass. At the official measuring of *Australia II* by an international committee in early

June none of the representatives of other challenge contenders troubled to go along to inspect the boat as they were specifically entitled to do under the rules; nor did any representatives of the New York Yacht Club's defending syndicates seek to attend the measuring as they had done of past challengers. The keel was not then an issue. Then, as *Australia II* went on consistently to outsail her rivals for the right to challenge, critics gradually began to change their views. As the summer proceeded and *Australia II* continued to demolish her rivals in elimination series A and B and started to chew them up in the eighteen-race series C, a certain disquiet began to spread among those who would rather have lost their wives than see the America's Cup leave its place in the glass case at the entrance to the model room in the New York Yacht Club's West 44th Street premises.

Then, on July 29, the first rocket was launched. A memorandum which was signed by Robert W. McCullough, chairman of the New York Yacht Club's America's Cup committee, and addressed to Mark Vinbury, US representative on the three-man international measurement committee which had measured all candidates for the Cup, was widely circulated. The memorandum sought support for the proposal that *Australia II* was not really a *bona fide* 12-metre. It claimed that because the boat's 'keel appendages' constituted a 'peculiarity' in build under Rating Rule 27 and Measurement Instruction 7, this must put the measurer(s) in doubt as to whether the rules, as written, rated the yacht fairly. Furthermore, the measurer(s) if in doubt were obliged to refer the matter to a national authority and it, if it thought fit, should refer the matter to the IYRU for a ruling.

The memorandum went on to say that NYYC America's Cup committee had no doubt that the keel appendages were a peculiarity, and that they gave *Australia II* a benefit or advantage that was not contemplated by the rules or instructions and was not therefore rated. Enclosed also with the memorandum was a sectional diagram purporting to be a scale outline of the winged keel and the hull showing that when *Australia II* heeled she got extra draft from her leeward wing digging down into the water and that if this draft was considered when the boat was heeling at 13 degrees, *Australia II* would have to be rated at 12.476 m. Although everyone believed that the measurers were sworn to secrecy about the precise dimensions of the yachts, the memorandum confidently stated that *Australia II*'s draft, measured as the vertical distance from the lowest of the wingtips to the load waterline plane with the yacht in normal upright position, to be 2.645 m and therefore the draft to the lowest wingtip when heeled at 13 degrees to be increased by 0.067 m to 2.712 m. Where this precise information came from the memorandum did not disclose.

Another memo, dated July 25, written by measurer Mark Vinbury and addressed to Tony Watts (chief measurer of the IYRU and chairman of the committee who with Vinbury and Jack Savage, of Australia, had, between May 29 and June 18, measured the America's Cup candidates for the challenge and the defence) was circulated on July 30. It was presented to all syndicates and circulated to the world's Press through the official America's Cup Press headquarters in Newport as Exhibit One of a four-part manifesto. Other sections proposed that *Australia II* should not be considered a proper 12-metre yacht under the rules and should be re-rated and penalized obviously by an enormous reduction in sail area for the excessive draft gained from her wings when heeled, or disqualified because her wings came into the same category as centreboards, which were banned under the rule.

In his letter to Watts, Vinbury said he had 'no question that our committee measured *Australia II*'s keel according to the rule'. He added:

> I am concerned, however, that the rule as it is currently written is not able to assess the unusual shape of this keel and thereby fairly rate the yacht. Enclosed is a brief from the America's Cup Committee expressing their concern. Also enclosed is an article stating the theoretical advantages of this design which appear to be verified by her performance record (*Australia II* had by then won thirty-six of her forty challenger elimination trials). Rating Rule 27 and Measurement Instruction 7 outline a course for the measurer and National Authority to follow to obtain 'a fair and equitable rating'. I feel the designer should have informed the measurer of the theoretical advantages of this keel, advantages which are apparently not being assessed by the rule, and thereby have obtained a ruling from the IYRU. Since I understand there has been no ruling, I feel it would be appropriate for our committee to ask the KBTC (Keelboat Technical Committee) to review these theoretical advantages of *Australia II*'s keel, together with her performance record, and request that they rule on whether the yacht is rating fairly and equitably as required. If you agree with this, I suggest we proceed immediately by contacting the Chairman of the KBTC.

Exhibit Two of the manifesto was a learned seven-page dissertation on and analysis of the winged keel by Halsey C. Herreshoff, naval architect and marine engineer, of Bristol, a descendant of the famous Herreshoff family whose designs had revolutionised world yachting for more than half a century and whose name was synonymous with America's Cup victories. Halsey Herreshoff opened his analysis with the chilling statement (to the New York Yacht Club's America's Cup committee): 'If the closely guarded peculiar keel design of *Australia II* is allowed to remain in competition or is allowed to continue to be rated without penalty, the yacht will likely win the foreign trials and will likely win the America's Cup in September 1983.'

Then, after examining theoretical aspects of the keel and its function, Herreshoff concluded with the proposal that the NYYC and foreign contestants should promptly develop a position of protest in the matter of *Australia II*'s keel. He added:

> The shroud should come off to enable competitors to fairly observe and assess that against which they are asked to race. *Australia II* should be presented with the following options: a. Withdraw from competition; b. Take a logical rating penalty for the keel wings; c. Remove, or diminish the wings such that there is no increase in draft compared to a conventional keel at large heel angle. The appropriate procedures and a hearing before measurers and the Keelboat Committee should be conducted with alacrity. The matter should be resolved before commencement of final foreign trials to select the challenger.

Unfortunately, respected as the man was (and is) as a yachtsman, designer, and scientist, some observers could not accept Herreshoff's arguments or regard them as entirely objective. He was, after all, an advisory co-designer with Johan Valentijn of *Liberty*, the yacht that then seemed most likely to carry (and ultimately did carry) the NYYC flag as defender of the Cup, and he was also the navigator of that vessel. One felt, morever, that supplementary enclosures by Valentijn and by the veteran US naval architect Bill Luders condemning the keel could hardly be seen as less than enlightened self-interest. Also, other

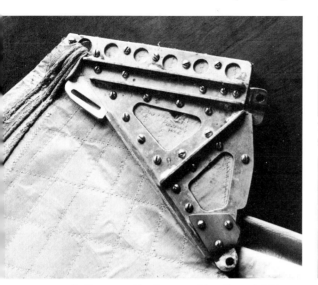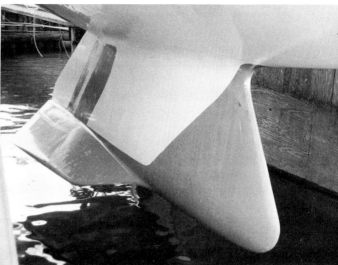

Left Close up of broken metal headboard (330 mm across) showing bolt hole through which holding pin sheered, causing leech of the sail to collapse. (Bob Ross)

Right The winged keel that gave *Australia II* such a technological advantage over US defender *Liberty*. Note forward jutting nose of fin and camouflaging that deceived aerial spies when the yacht heeled in clear water. (Paul Darling)

knowledgeable analysts of yacht design argued that if increases (and decreases) in measurements of draft and other proportions, such as length and beam, when yachts heeled were to be taken as criteria of rating, most vessels, including the American contenders, would be ineligible. These points were already being made around the Newport waterfront when the New York Yacht Club's America's Cup Committee made its next move. It dispatched Vinbury's letter to Watts, Herreshoff's analysis and opinions and Valentijn's and Luders' arguments and other documents echoing their sentiments to George Andreadis, Acting Chairman (since the recent death of Sir Gordon Smith) of the International Yacht Racing Union's Keelboat Technical Committee.

The NYYC *requested*, in such stentorian tones that it sounded more like a demand, that the KBTC, made up of fourteen members spread over half the world, who normally with due notice met once a year, should gather in urgent session and disqualify *Australia II*. The reaction must have startled the NYYC committee, composed of influential men not accustomed to opposition. First Tony Watts, who had gone from Newport to the pre-Olympics at Los Angeles, said that as far as he was concerned *Australia II* had been measured and rated fairly under the current 12-metre rules as he and Jack Savage interpreted them and that was that. Their decision was final. Then Dr Beppe Croce, an Italian and president of the IYRU, came to Newport and, at a Press conference called by the Aga Khan, principal supporter of the Italian challenge contender, *Azzurra*, announced that the NYYC was quite out of order in approaching the Keelboat Committee directly. The proper administrative procedure was for the US Yacht Racing Union, the national authority, first to approach the IYRU and request that it *might consider* convening a meeting of a quorum of the Keelboat Committee.

Then Olin Stephens, veteran yacht designer and for half a century darling of the NYYC, declared the keel legal. ('It's like a blessing from God,' commented Lexcen). Then all the challenging syndicates of the clubs from Italy, Britain, Canada, France and Australia met in Newport and re-affirmed an earlier decision to accept the original rating by the measurers of *Australia II* as a 12-metre. Bill Fesq, as the representative of Royal Sydney Yacht Squadron, Challenger of Record with the responsibility of conducting the elimination races, announced that the races would go on, in spite of demands to the contrary by certain people, and that *Australia II*'s rating by the measurement committee as a 12-metre was accepted unequivocally. The US YRU took over from the NYYC America's Cup Committee and formally applied to the IYRU in exactly the same terms as previously for a consideration of *Australia II*'s rating. As an aside, the US YRU claimed that a meeting months earlier in Australia between officials of the Australian Yachting Federation had failed to seek an IYRU ruling about *Australia II*'s keel because it feared this would disqualify the yacht.

Up to this stage Warren Jones, executive director of the *Australia II* syndicate, a master strategist, had answered equably and calmly all the charges made about the boat. He defended the secrecy about the keel, because, as he said, he feared (and how right he was subsequently proved to be) that the Americans might try to copy it and improve on it if it were revealed for them to study. But now, after the charge that the AYF had been coerced into not seeking IYRU consideration of the keel, Jones called a Press conference. He produced documents refuting the charge against the AYF and the yacht's original Australian measurer, Ken McAlpine, naval architect and surveyor, of Sydney. Then Jones dropped a bomb. He produced telegrams sent to him from Holland stating that a senior member of one of the US defence syndicates had tried to negotiate confidentially with the Netherlands Ship Model Basin at Wageningen, Holland, where designer Lexcen had conducted his researches on the yacht, to buy the design of *Australia II*'s keel. Copies of these telegrams and those of the Dutch rejections of the US offers were distributed to the world's news media.

'We came here in the same spirit of friendly competition as we have before,' said Jones evenly. 'We find the actions and attitudes of some of these people quite difficult to understand.'

While American officials of the defending syndicate, after admitting they had tried to buy details of the keel, were trying to explain that they had not really wanted to use the winged keel on one of their defence candidates but only on one of their discarded trial horses so that they could tune up against it, the IYRU announced that a sub-committee would meet in London in late August, during the final challenger elimination trials. The sub-committee would decide if it was necessary to ask the Keelboat Technical Committee to consider the US YRU's request about *Australia II*.

Then Peter de Savary, head of Britain's *Victory 83* syndicate, dropped his bomb. First he showed US measurer Vinbury wings on *Victory 83*'s keel, then he announced that his boat's designer, Ian Howlett, in July 1982, more than a year earlier, had submitted a series of questions about winged keels to the IYRU for official but confidential ruling, as he was entitled to do. These rulings, given by a sub-committee that normally acted on behalf of the Keelboat Committee between its annual meetings, had approved winged keels provided that they did not extend below the static draft of the boat (in other words did not exceed the permitted, measured draft of the boat, when it was stationary and upright) and provided the wings were fixed and not retractable under way.

'In fact,' announced de Savary, with undisguised relish at the affect he was having on the Press, 'we have been experimenting with winged keels for some time, first on our trial horse, *Australia* (the 1980 challenger bought from Bond) and currently on *Victory 83*. We'll be carrying the wings on *Victory 83* in our semi-final match tomorrow. That's why we have had screens around *Victory 83* in recent weeks similar to those around *Australia II*. Our wings are removable. Since they don't alter our rating in any way we can put them on to suit one set of conditions or remove them. Not only are our wings legal under IYRU ruling; so of course also are those of *Australia II*.'

A direct query by the Americans to the IYRU confirmed de Savary's statement. 'Yes,' came back the cable, 'the same ruling given on *Victory 83*'s keel applies to *Australia II*.'

The NYYC America's Cup committee had been outmanoeuvred and out-politicked. But there was more to come. Two days later Warren Jones alleged that an unsuccessful attempt had been made in Holland to prove that designer Lexcen had not been responsible for the design of *Australia II*'s keel. He produced a long telex from Dr Peter Van Oossanen, director of the Netherlands Ship Model Basin. The telex revealed that alleged agents of the NYYC had sought to induce Dr Van Oossanen to sign an affidavit swearing that *Australia II* was not designed by Ben Lexcen of Australia. If it could be shown that an Australian was not the designer then the boat could be disqualified from the America's Cup. Jones pointed out that the Netherlands Ship Model Basin at Wageningen did tank testing for Lexcen under Lexcen's direction and with the full approval of the NYYC. He produced a letter from the NYYC America's Cup committee secretary, Vic Romagna, to prove the latter point.

And Dr Van Oossanen certainly stood up for Lexcen. He said that Richard S. Latham, a member of the New York Yacht Club America's Cup Committee, and Will Valentijn, a close relation of the designer for the US *Liberty/Freedom* syndicate, presented him with an affidavit for his signature which attempted to suggest that Ben Lexcen was not solely responsible for the design of *Australia II*. Dr Van Oossanen said he was disturbed by the fact because he had informed NYYC representatives on a previous occasion that Ben Lexcen was, in fact, the sole designer of *Australia II*, yet they persisted in presenting him with a draft affidavit repeatedly contradicting this fact. (On a previous occasion, while admitting that Lexcen was not a trained scientist, Dr Van Oossanen had described Lexcen as 'a natural genius'.)

'It is unfortunate,' said Jones 'that the NYYC America's Cup Committee, which is an arm of the prestigious NYYC, has chosen to conduct this reprehensible campaign of harassment and false claims stemming from statements or claims from unknown persons or perhaps just dockside scuttle. It has now been necessary for Ben Lexcen to seek legal advice on his position, which he does so with our agreement, as statements made are defaming his reputation.' Jones added that the NYYC had failed to provide information as to where it obtained specific details about *Australia II*'s keel, which had never been released and which had been strenuously protected by shrouding the keel. He said, 'They can only have obtained such details through persons who gained the information illegally.'

The next day the New York Yacht Club issued a statement that it was 'pleased to announce that questions relating to the keels of *Australia 11* and *Victory 83* and the design thereof had been resolved'. It had accepted the IYRU ruling that the keels were legal. 'For reasons unknown to us, neither the British challengers nor the IYRU saw fit to advise the US YRU or us of this fact (until they were asked, as required by the rules) and regrettably this omission has resulted in unnecessary controversy.' The letter added that the NYYC would, through the US YRU, seek further clarification of rating for winged keels for future America's Cup matches but not for the current series. (Four months later at a meeting in London the IYRU's Keelboat Technical Committee rejected a lengthy submission from the US YRU that winged keels should be banned and endorsed the earlier confidential ruling made to British designer Ian Howlett that they were legal.)

On the issue of the design of *Australia II* the NYYC letter said the question arose from reports and newspaper articles in the Dutch Press intimating that the keel design was the product, if not the invention, of Dutch experts:

> Having been put on notice, the NYYC was obligated to investigate the matter and for this purpose interviewed such Dutch experts regarding their participation in the testing and development of the keel. Having completed such investigation as we felt necessary and proper we have concluded that the evidence available to us to date is insufficient to press that matter further at this time. With these matters resolved we can now all focus on the match itself to be settled on the water and may the better yacht win.

Later that day Robert G. Stone junr (Commodore of the NYYC) and Bob McCullough (chairman of the club's America's Cup Committee) spent an uncomfortable forty minutes in Newport before a packed news media conference, most sections of which were far from respectful, some derisive. McCullough said he accepted the IYRU decision on winged keels although he thought the ruling 'bizarre'. When Stone said the NYYC had felt obliged to follow up Dutch Press reports that *Australia II's* design might not be entirely Lexcen's work a pressman stated that the Dutch reports had been traced back to a certain interested party in America.

'It was a plant,' the pressman said, boldly.

On 11 September, two days before the first challenge race was due to be sailed, Commodore McCullough presented to Alan Bond for signature by Bond, Lexcen, Jones and Dalziell, a three page 'certificate of compliance' affidavit that spelled out in legal detail a declaration, to be made, under penalty of perjury, that the Australian design complied with ten points that the Americans now saw as 'conditions of the race'. Bond and the others refused to sign it. McCullough then went to Bill Fesq of Royal Sydney Yacht Squadron and reportedly said: 'Find another challenger.' Fesq refused to consider any challenger other than *Australia II*. The next day Bond agreed to sign a plain statement that his syndicate had complied with the conditions for the America's Cup as stated in the 'blue book' that governs the races. This says that yachts shall comply in every respect with the requirements regarding construction, sails and equipment contained in the Deed of Gift and Interpretive Resolutions applying to national origin of design and construction, in that 'design in a country' means that 'the designers of a yacht's hull, rig, and sails shall be nationals of that country'.

Later it was reported that a majority of the nine members of the NYYC's America's Cup Committee, led by Vic Romagna, on the eve of the Cup races, wanted to cancel the regatta and withdraw the trophy from competition. It was claimed one of the reasons they decided to let the competition proceed was the possibility of enormous claims for damages from challenging syndicates, from

Left *Australia II*'s skipper John Bertrand, under tremendous pressure throughout, struggled hard to stay cool and perform at top level, even though down 3–1 in the final challenge series. (Paul Darling)

Right Grant Simmer (left), unshakeable navigator who kept *Australia II* precisely on track during four months of racing, and Tom Schnackenberg, who designed most of the boat's superlative sails.

news media and travel organisations and from members of the public (in class actions) who had spent millions of dollars in expectation of the Cup contest.

Overall, in my own view, after seven visits to Newport from 1962 to report the Cup races, it was a lamentable affair, far removed from the original concept of the challenge 'to encourage friendly competition between nations'. Of course, as guardians of the America's Cup, the committee of the NYYC could reasonably claim that regardless of accusations of bias in the past they must see that rules for its competition were observed. It was the extraordinary manner in which they went about their task that dismayed so many people. But the Australians, mainly through the diplomatic skill, restraint, and timing of Warren Jones, came out of it all with dignity. Letters of congratulations, cables, and overseas and local telephone calls showered into the *Australia II* camp.

And then, a week later, while *Australia II* and *Victory 83* were battling it out on Rhode Island Sound to decide which would be the challenger, and *Liberty* and *Courageous* were fighting for the honour of defending the Cup, the high drama turned to low farce. Both American camps were fitting experimental wings of aluminium, plywood, and fibreglass on their trial horses, *Freedom* and *Defender*, with a view to using them on a boat in the challenge final. They turned out to be useless appendages and were quickly discarded because, unlike *Australia II*'s keel, they were merely additions to each yacht's normal keel.

As was revealed when she had won the Cup, *Australia II*'s 18-tonne all-lead keel was built as an integral part of the hull, with the top of the thick central fin moulded into a basin of lead to fit the canoe body of the yacht. The controversial wings, each extending out and down from the chunky, 3.9 m long bottom of the central fin, are scientifically designed to interact with the shape of the boat. To distribute the weight in harmony with the designed centre of buoyancy of the hull and to control the waterflow over the wings, the leading

Italy's *Azzurra* (14), dark hull, always fast downwind, zooming up to catch and pass *Canada I* in one of their semi-final engagements. (Lou d'Alpuget)

edge of the central fin keel slopes forward instead of aft like most other yacht's keels. Because of the heavy wings, each 1.8 m long and up to 0.8 m wide, on the bottom of the keel, the vertical centre of gravity is lower than on normal boats and therefore *Australia II* has much more stability than a yacht with a normal keel. Also, because of the effectiveness of this lower centre of gravity, less overall ballast is needed and the boat is only 23.636 tonnes in overall weight (just enough under the rules for her waterline length of 13.47 m) and at least 2,041 kg (4,500 lb) lighter than the defender, *Liberty*. After the Cup series, Lexcen explained the keel's value thus: 'With so much weight so low and so concentrated the boat is very stiff and can turn in its own length. When the boat is heeled, the wings and the forward-jutting central keel combine to keep the waterflow 'straight' so that it runs horizontally, almost parallel to the waterline, instead of diagonally down the keel as usually occurs with orthodox keels. The horizontal flow, directed straight on to the trim tab makes it work most efficiently and combines with other things to give the boat 'lift', most evident when *Australia II* climbs to windward away from her rivals. Actually she makes less leeway than the other 12s. In addition, and most important, there is reduced drag because the angled-down wings, particularly on the leeward side, where this is the area of greatest pressure, prevent turbulence flowing across the bottom of the keel and direct it aft, clear of the keel, greatly reducing the usual "tip vortex" effect. So there is much less drag.'

What Lexcen also admitted to a few knowledgeable observers who had closely studied the boat's performances was that *Australia II* had some weaknesses. One was that initially, she was not fast on broad reaches or on runs downwind in light to moderate weather. This was because, despite her lightness, her winged keel gave her slightly more wetted surface and hence more frictional drag than

154

well-designed, orthodox-keeled boats. Another weakness was that she was difficult to steer downwind because she had no form of skeg in her afterbody ahead of her rudder and therefore lacked directional stability. Bertrand and, in the early elimination races his deputy, Sir James Hardy, through intense concentration had learnt how to steer the boat downwind. *Australia II* then benefited from a careful programme of spinnaker development by North's Australian loft scientist Tom Schnackenberg and his sailmaking team. They produced running and reaching sails that were probably the most efficient ever seen on a 12-metre and almost completely masked *Australia II*'s weaknesses — indeed earned her a reputation as a downwind flyer. Of course, her crew had to bring their spinnaker drills to a pitch of flawless timing and coordination to realize the potential of the sails. But there was no question about *Australia II*'s ability upwind, especially in light to moderate conditions. She always had the edge on any boat. Her winged keel ensured her of that.

Lexcen, who first began experiments with such 'end plate' wings on the centreboard and the rudder of his world champion 18-footer *Venom* in 1961 and on 5.5 m keel boats, had devised the wings on *Australia II* after years of study, and in 1982, after four months of experiment with his concepts in the Dutch Wageningen tank. The last moment attempts by rival designers to match *Australia II*'s remarkable performance merely by adding pairs of oval or oblong side fins to their boat's keel showed that at that stage they had no real understanding of Lexcen's invention. By 1986, three years after *Australia II* had won the Cup and Lexcen had assigned his copyright gratis to the IYRU, American and other designers had enthusiastically endorsed the wing keel principle and had spent millions of dollars trying to improve on the original.

Australia II got to the starting line as the twenty-fifth challenger, representing Royal Perth Yacht Club, after an awesome display of superiority. She won forty-eight of fifty-four matches against six rival contenders. They were *Victory 83*, representing Royal Burnham Yacht Club, England; *Azzurra*, Yacht Club Costa Smeralda, Italy; *Canada I*, Secret Cove Yacht Club, Canada; *France 3*, Yacht Club de France, France; *Challenge 12*, Royal Yacht Club of Victoria, Australia; and *Advance*, Royal Sydney Yacht Squadron, Australia.

Over a series of short and full length (12–24.3 nm) courses, in light, moderate and occasionally fresh winds, *Australia II* won thirty-six of forty races in round-robin A, B and C eliminations. When Bertrand pinched a nerve in his neck during a volley ball exercise session Sir James Hardy, syndicate director, sailing adviser and deputy helmsman, skippered the boat. He won ten of eleven B series races. Overall *Australia II* beat *Victory 83* seven times; *Canada I*, *Azzurra*, *France 3* and *Advance* six times each and *Challenge 12* five times. Although *Advance*, an ungainly, full-ended, high-sided boat designed by Alan Payne, and the out-dated *France 3* never looked to have a chance, *Challenge 12*, helmed by John Savage, of Melbourne, in the early stages at least seemed the best of the others. She had been designed by Lexcen for Bond with an orthodox keel as an insurance against the possible failure of the radical-keeled *Australia II*, and in their first trials off Fremantle and in Port Phillip, Victoria, after Bond had sold her to industralist Richard Pratt, heading a hastily re-assembled Melbourne syndicate, was always a threat in light weather. In the early stages she was faster downwind than *Australia II*. In America *Challenge 12* was an immediate success, winning ten of her first twelve races and once beating *Australia II* convincingly by 51s. But without the experience of *Australia II*'s team afloat or ashore, she failed to improve and gradually her game began to fade. In the higher point-scoring second and third series of the eliminations her win-loss records fell to 7–5, then 7–9. While Savage, his tactician Graeme Freeman, and team coach Mike Fletcher experimented with a new mast, new mainsail and new genoas, not knowing which was helping or hindering the boat, *Challenge 12* slid by a few decimal points out of the score that would have given her a place in the semi-final rounds. She was eliminated, many felt without ever having achieved her full potential, with *France 3* and *Advance*. *Australia II* romped through the nine semi-final races with eight wins, three each over *Azzurra* and *Canada I* and two over *Victory 83*. The only real injury the Australian challenger had suffered at that stage was to her crew when the much admired bowman, Scotty McAllister, broke his arm in a horrifying accident 27 m above the deck. *Australia II* was off the coast in a bumpy sea preparing to race *Canada I* in a C series elimination final and McAllister had gone aloft to the masthead in a bo'sun's chair to lock off the carriage that carried the mainsail headboard so that, as usual, the main halyard could be used as the backstay. But, under pressure, the heavy metal masthead crane through which the main halyard was being winched tight collapsed and crushed his forearm, pinning him against the top of the spar. Mainsheet trimmer Colin Beashel went aloft in the next highest halyard, 19 m up to the headstay hounds, to bring his semi-conscious crewmate down. *Australia II* forfeited the race, *Canada I* got into the semi-finals, McAllister missed his life's ambition to sail in the crew that won the Cup, and Damien Fewster, a 21-year-old Melbourne carpenter, seconded from the foredeck of the eliminated *Challenge 12*, won a place in history.

The English boat beat *Canada I* three times, *Azzurra* twice and *Australia II* once and so qualified for the final best-of-seven contest to decide which boat would challenge the Americans. *Azzurra*, with four wins and five losses, was next with *Canada I* last, having failed to win a race. *Victory 83* had her one win over *Australia II* in a fickle breeze while the Australians were testing a new mainsail. In the last of the semi-finals, *Victory 83* carried a pair of wings on her keel, fitted overnight, for the first and only time. *Australia II* led her around the course by 46s, 49s, 53s, 35s, 32s and won by 1.21 in a breeze of 7 k that freshened to 14 k. Then, in the elimination finals, *Australia II* demolished *Victory 83* 4–1 in a predominantly light weather series that dragged on for eight days in sweltering heat and fickle airs. The British won the first race sailed to a conclusion in a sloppy sea and west south westerly breeze that held at 15 k most of the way, leading to suggestions that *Australia II* was vulnerable in fresh conditions. Bertrand said airily, 'I had an off day', but it was later revealed that he had carried an experimental light air mainsail to suit the official forecast that was a day early. (In most races the boat's sails suited her superbly, the best ever seen on a challenger. With few exceptions the sails *Australia II* used were from North's Australian loft and were designed by Tom Schnackenberg from a mixture of kevlar, mylar and dacron fabrics. One of the most successful spinnakers had been designed and built by tactician Hugh Treharne in his Sydney Sobstad sail loft. Schnackenberg greatly admired it and probably improved it when he rebuilt the middle sections. Another of *Australia II*'s highly prized spinnakers came from the Melbourne Hood sail loft.) In the next four races of the elimination finals *Australia II* beat *Victory* by 4.53, 3.07, 2.20 and 3.19.

Nobody had any doubt then that the Americans were in for the greatest challenge in the Cup's history. The burgundy-hulled *Liberty* was chosen to defend the trophy in preference to the new and twice altered *Defender* (Tom Blackaller) and finally in preference to the re-conditioned 1974 and 1977 champion *Courageous* (John Kolius). *Liberty's* selection in the view of many was pre-ordained because of Conner's record. He had skippered *Freedom* in her successful 1980 bid and had been twice relief helmsman of defence contenders. During preliminary, observation, and final US trials, *Liberty* amassed a score of thirty-four races or part races won, to seventeen lost, against *Courageous* and *Defender.* *Courageous'* score was nineteen wins against thirty-two losses and the score for *Defender* (eliminated a week earlier) was fourteen races won and twenty-eight lost.

Australia II's triumph, 4–3 in the best-of-seven grand finale of races against *Liberty*, was an achievement without parallel in competitive sport. Never before had there been such a contest with such an audience between two such skilled and dedicated crews of big boat gladiators. The NYYC's defeat, the first since the America's Cup had been put up for international competition in 1870, had the elements of a Hollywood scenario. An extraordinary yacht, backed by a rags-to-riches enthusiast, conceived by a maverick genuis of design, built in secret, is opposed and reviled by powerful forces behind the rival camp. The challenger, although under a cloud, easily overwhelms opponent after opponent in the elimination rounds. Then, plagued by bad luck in the main contest, she fights her way back from an almost impossible position and squares the match three-all. So they line up for a final struggle in the race of the century. With the world watching, the challenger seems well beaten after 19 nm of the 24.3 nm course has been sailed. Then she comes from behind in a miraculous fashion and fights off her opponent to score a glorious victory. No sports promoter, determined to hold a crowd's interest, could have stage-managed a more dramatic sequence of events.

Race 1: The first try

After months of high anticipation, the final series between *Australia II* and *Liberty* began on Tuesday, 13 September, with a sensational anticlimax. By 11 am, a fleet of 2,000 spectator vessels of all sizes, from Navy destroyers to inflatable runabouts, had gathered 10 nm off the coast of Newport ready for the official start at 12.10 pm. It was a warm and sunny day with a slight sea and light, fluky winds. A whirl of sixty helicopters and a blimp hovered overhead. Precisely at 11.50 am, when there was an 8 k breeze from 030 degrees, NYYC officials hoisted the course signals. Then at noon they fired the ten minute warning gun, and at 12.05 the five minute preparatory gun. The yachts, after entering from opposite ends, upwind from the starting line, were locked in combat, fighting for advantage, with neither gaining it, for eight minutes. Then, with only two minutes to go to the starting gun, the red and white striped postponement flag broke out on the starting boat *Black Knight*. The race was aborted.

Officials explained that they had recorded a 40 degree wind shift to the east. If they had started the race it would have converted the initial 4.5 nm windward beat into a close reach and ruined the integrity of the following two reaching legs before a new course could have been set for a second beat. So with the coastguard vessels herding spectator craft clear for a new track they tried again, with course signals set at 090 degrees at 1.50 pm for a 2 pm countdown. Once

Liberty (left) and *Australia II* in a 'standing hold', each crew daring the other to break away as they manoeuvre before the start of the deciding seventh 'Race of the Century'. (Australian Information Service & Barry Stevens)

more the contestants squared off, circling and blocking each other through a series of gybes and tacks and 'standing holds' while spectators gasped at the skill and daring of their crews. *Australia II*, spinning inside little more than her own length, definitely had the upper hand this time. Then, at 2.08 pm the postponement flag was hoisted once again. This time the blue and white 'A' flag was hoisted with it. There had been another windshift, this time of 35 degrees to ESE; it was too late for another try and racing was abandoned for the day. Some disappointed Australian supporters, suspicious of the NYYC's motives, grumbled that the races had been cancelled because the light airs would have favoured the Perth challenger and not the defender. Such an argument was unreasonable. The race committee, although appointed by the NYYC, was an independent body of experienced men of good judgement. One of them who concurred with the others was John Fitzhardinge, representing Royal Perth Yacht Club. While the spectator fleet headed back to port accompanied by *Liberty* in tow, *Australia II* stayed on the course testing a new mainsail and four spinnakers in the now steady breeze at 125 degrees.

Race I: *Liberty* by 1.10

The next day there were overcast skies, a true 18 k offshore breeze from the north east and a choppy sea, ideal, the critics said, for the Cup defender. *Australia II*, far from showing herself to be only a light weather machine unable to perform at championship level in a brisk breeze, shocked the Americans by taking charge minutes before the start. She led *Liberty* to the line by 3s, lee-bowed her at the gun, forcing her to tack away for clear air, then out-tacked her on the first beat and led her around the first mark by 8s. *Australia II* added 2s on the first spinnaker reach to lead by 10s. Then, on the second reach, the Australian helmsman Bertrand and his tactician Hugh Treharne seemed to have forgotten one of the basic tenets of match racing on an Olympic style America's Cup course – when leading on reaches, protect your flank from a close rival who will try to climb above your track and get on your wind. After the wing mark gybe that is just what Conner and his shrewd crew did on the second reach. With a staysail set under their spinnaker they got enough to windward to break up the breeze in *Australia II*'s sails, slow her down, then zoom past at 10 k into the lead. The Australians, now too far to leeward to fight back with a similar tactic, were 16s astern when they turned for the second beat. Bertrand said later: 'Dennis [Conner] worked up on our hip on the first reach and he wasn't a threat [*Australia II* gained 2s] and we honestly didn't think he'd be a threat on the next leg.' It was a critical miscalculation that cost *Australia II* 26s.

Conner refused to let the Australians draw him into a tacking duel on the following windward beat. Instead he applied a loose cover, played the wind shifts, picked up two or three that *Australia II* missed, and stretched his lead to 28s when they turned the top mark for the run downwind. Then, for the third time that day the Australians astonished the Americans who, although they acknowledged *Australia II* as a dangerously fast light-weather boat to windward, had from their earlier analysis of her performances come to believe her no faster than themselves running square downwind, especially in a breeze. In fact, *Australia II*'s spinnaker development programme had made her a flyer downwind in all weathers, as Conner and many others were to learn.

Australia II came down on the right hand side of the fifth leg track under a big white spinnaker, overhauling the defender, and 400 m from the mark was within two and a half lengths of her and 70 m to the right of her. With the mark to the right of them both *Australia II* was also nearer to it than *Liberty* and theoretically almost on even terms. Then Conner took the initiative again. With both boats on port tack and *Australia II* to leeward rapidly coming into a position where she could demand that *Liberty*, to windward, not only keep clear but also hold her course, the Americans gybed on to a right-of-way starboard reach. They did it brilliantly, without warning. Instead of having their bowman Scott Vogel climb out of the central cockpit and walk to the bow so that he could stand on the stem outside the forestay and engage the 'lazy' brace as the pole swung across, they had him leap out of a foredeck hatch. In an instant Bertrand and his crew, still on port tack, had *Liberty*, on starboard tack, charging across at them. As the burdened boat on port tack, it was *Australia II*'s obligation to keep clear and even if she, too, were able to make a fast gybe, as windward boat she would need to complete it without hampering *Liberty*. Additionally a gybe by *Australia II* at that stage would have conceded the defender the inside position at the mark and possibly a two length lead when they rounded for the final beat to the finish. So Bertrand attempted to execute a daring manoeuvre as they converged. He put his helm hard up intending, he said later, to shoot across *Liberty*'s stern and immediately to gybe on to starboard so that *Australia II* would have the inside berth and control as they approached the turn.

Then disaster struck. As Bertrand wrenched the helm to port the steering cable slipped off the groove of a guiding sheave, jammed in the case holding it and tore away one of the underdeck welded aluminium brackets supporting the system. The boat was out of control. *Australia II* swooped into a wild broach, her spinnaker pole skied and her spinnaker, cracking like gunfire, collapsed. Somehow Bertrand did manage to get the boat around on to the other gybe, then, steering with the trim tab rudder, around the mark. The crew dumped the spinnaker in the water in the process of lowering it but worked with marvellous speed to recover it and square away the tangle of sheets and braces and hoist their genoa as they came on the wind. Their spinnaker pole was still hoisted well after they had rounded 35s behind *Liberty* which was now too far ahead, considering *Australia II*'s condition, to be threatened.

The defender had stretched her lead out to 1.10 at the finish because of the difficulties the Australians were having. 'We were sailing on the trim tab alone for ten minutes before we got the rudder hooked in again,' said Bertrand. Tactician Hugh Treharne, who crawled into the quarters of the boat under the cockpit and rigged a snatch block and tackle to tension the steering cable, did a remarkable job of seamanship. Navigator Grant Simmer estimated that the mishap overall had cost *Australia II* 2.0—50s more than the winning margin.

That night the maintenance squad in the Australian camp spent four hours re-welding the bracket that had collapsed back on to the inside of the hull and beefing up the others that held the steering cable blocks. Meanwhile Conner and his crew, greatly relieved at beating the feared challenger with the strange keel, had paraded through the spectator fleet. Cannons, sirens and rockets greeted their return to Newport Harbour. Thousands cheered and sang battle songs at the dockside as the victor was hoisted from the water. Conner said soberly: 'Wait until we've got three more on the board.'

Battling at close quarters in 1983, *Australia II* (KA 6), as leeward boat is almost in command position to control the hard-pressed US defender, *Liberty*. (Sally Samins)

Top *Australia II* (KA 6) bursts across the starting line in the opening race of the 1983 drama with defender *Liberty* (US 40) snarling at her heels. Right is judges' launch *Black Knight*. (Paul Darling)

Bottom At the last mark of the 'Race of the Century' in 1983 the Australian challenger is sailing into history while the defender, *Liberty*, still under spinnaker, trails astern. (Paul Darling)

Race 2: *Liberty* by 1.33

Liberty scored her second win the next day when *Australia II*, crippled before the start in a 17 k nor'nor'easter with a broken mainsail headboard, led around the first three marks and then, when the breeze began to fade, was forced to gamble on windshifts that favoured the defender. *Liberty* led around the fourth and fifth marks but was two-thirds up the final leg before her victory was secure. The mark times were *Australia II*: 45s, 31s, 21s; *Liberty*: 48s, 31s, and 1.33 at the finish. But although the Australians lost the race they won honours for resourcefulness, seamanship, and determination to try.

When the top lug of the metal headboard broke away from the hoisting car that normally secured the head of the mainsail to the top of the mast, it seemed for a while that *Australia II* would have to retire from the race before it had begun. It happened while *Australia II* was gybing in a hard gust of wind during the pre-start manoeuvres. The headboard swivelled down pinned only by the lower lug, the sail tore along the bottom of the headboard and the mainsail leech, now depending on a strip of kevlar, sagged down half a metre, converting the after section of the sail into a sloppy sack. The after end of the boom, unsupported by the leech, lay on the deck, then hung down over the topside. Only by bending and tensioning the mast as far forward as they dared and dragging down the luff with the Cunningham Eye tackle could the crew get shape into the sail and get the boom clear of the deck. With this done *Australia II* sailed incredibly well while the wind remained fresh, although she spotted *Liberty* 5s at the start, was leebowed early and forced to tack away to clear her air.

But then, after 8.0 minutes of sailing, at times with her mainsail bucketing and the leech flogging, while her crew worked frantically to adjust the sail, she climbed on a lift in the breeze, sailed proudly across *Liberty*'s bow and cover-tacked upwind of her. They split tacks again, and when next they converged 7.0 later *Australia II* was still in front. Conner, like a prize-fighter concentrating his blows on an opponent's split eye, tacked continuously as they advanced up the track toward the first mark, hoping, he admitted later, to cause a breakdown in the challenger's cobbled-up gear. Bertrand's men, however, by now had adjusted their rig so successfully that so long as the breeze held the mainsail remained in a reasonable shape. They continued to hold off the Americans during one spell of eleven tacks in 4.0. Near the end of the first leg the Australian boat was accelerating out the tacks better and obviously gaining, although still not getting anything like maximum power from her mainsail. Only 400 m from the mark, with *Australia II* on port planted upwind of him, Conner tacked to starboard into a header that forced *Liberty* off course. It lifted *Australia II* high. When next they converged, the Australians had doubled their lead. Bertrand then performed the sailing equivalent of a basketballer's 'slam dunk'. As he crossed he tacked immediately ahead and upwind, bringing his rival directly under his wind shadow and robbing her sails of power. When they tacked again, with *Australia II* in charge, she was able to carry *Liberty* beyond the layline for the mark. Bertrand rounded with 45s to spare, while Conner had to make two tacks to clear.

On the reaches *Australia II*'s mainsheet trimmer Colin Beashel, acknowledged as one of the best men aloft of all the crewmen in Newport for the Cup series, twice went to the masthead 28 m (92 ft) above the water for spells of 10.0 in an effort to lash the broken headboard in place. *Australia II* gybed at the wing

Historic poster advertising Royal Yacht Squadron's special race on 22 August 1851, for the trophy 'The RYS £100 Cup' won by the NYYC's schooner *America*. There have been many arguments about the original English name of the trophy, variously called The Queen's Cup, The Challenge Cup, The 100 Guineas Cup. At last, one hopes, reproduction of this rare notice may settle the issue.

mark with a margin of 31s and was able to cling to her lead by 21s at the next but could not hold off the better rigged American boat on the second beat as the breeze began to ease. *Liberty* caught her half way up the track. In the final stages of the fourth leg the Americans performed a 'slam dunk' which Bertrand protested was illegally close, forcing him to change course to avoid a collision. (He lost the protest the next day because the international jury, after a four-hour hearing, decided that he would not have hit *Liberty* if he had stood on. 'We'd have crushed Dennis Conner in his cockpit,' insisted *Australia II*'s tactician Hugh Treharne, a man never given to over-statement.) They turned for the run with *Liberty* 48s ahead. The faster running challenger gained 17s on the fifth leg and rounded only 31s behind, but her disabled state was apparent when the breeze swung 25 degrees (a new course was set for the final beat) then eased and backed and veered in a series of 20 degree shifts. Half way up the track to the finish *Liberty* was still only 100 m upwind, crawling through fluky patches, when Bertrand made a hopeful tack to the left in search of a new breeze. Instead, *Australia II* sailed into a complete calm that became a header and *Liberty*, lifting in a band of fresher air, gained 1.2 and finished 1.33 ahead.

In the circumstances the challenger had done well but the America's Cup battleground is no place for hard luck stories. *Liberty* had a score of 2–0 and the Australians called a lay day so that their hard-working sailmakers, labouring day and night to restore shape into their huge inventory of sails and to improve them, could check over more basic details, like cracks in headboards.

Race 3: Abandoned on Time Limit

On Saturday, 17 September, *Australia II* came out in a breeze that seemed to be made to order for her—a 10 k sou' sou' easter with a slight sea. Bertrand completely boxed *Liberty* at the start, crossed the line 11s ahead, led around the first mark by 1.15 and then by 2.0, 1.58, 1.46, and by 5.57 at the last mark in a gossamer breeze. But it was an agonising exhibition for Australian barrackers because two hours before the end, when the wind veered and slowly died, it was obvious that the challenger could not finish the 24.3 nm course within the time limit of five and a quarter hours unless there was a sudden weather change. Half way up the final leg, with *Liberty* more than half a mile astern of the challenger, a sou' wester did reach *Australia II* and she began to slice her way to the finish. But she still had 1.5 nm to go when the race was called. The score remained 2–0 in favour of the defender.

Race 3 resailed: *Australia II* by 3.14

Australia II and her crew were in perfect form on Sunday, 18 September, after a delay of an hour and a half, in a true SW breeze that was 7 k at the start, veered only 5 degrees, rose at times to 12 k and was 10 k at the finish. Both helmsmen were eager at the start, but Bertrand had the better of it. *Liberty* was across the starting line 8s before the challenger but the defender was jammed head to wind almost across the committee boat's anchor line and forced to tack to clear it while *Australia II* was romping away further down the line at 7 k in clear air. She was 1.14 ahead at the first mark; 52s at the second; 42s at the third (she sacrificed some time carefully protecting her flanks); 1.15 at the end of the second beat; 2.47 at the end of the run (a gain of 1.32); and 3.14 at the finish. It was the ninth win by a challenger in 103 years, the biggest win by a challenger since 12-metres began to race for the Cup in 1958, and the second biggest win by a challenger since *Livonia* beat *Columbia* by 15.10 over 35 nm off New York in 1871. Ashore in Newport Australian supporters were noisily delighted that at last the challenger had won a race. The Americans were apprehensive.

Conner called a lay day, hoping for heavier winds. Gary Jobson, tactician of the US defence contender *Defender* eliminated by *Liberty*, said: 'Conner and his crew did everything perfectly. They tried to draw Bertrand into mistakes in tacking duels (twenty-nine tacks on the second beat), tried to attack him on the reaches and they gybed seven times to what could have been favourable slants on the run. They were just outclassed by boat speed.' Conner said: 'I tried everything I knew. I'm not against winged keels as such, except that they might make all other 12-metres obsolete. For that reason I'd have to think about my attitude to any move to get the IYRU to ban them. Winged keels might greatly change the performance of many IOR ocean racing boats.' (Two months later, while the IYRU was unequivocally approving winged keels for metre class boats, the International Ocean Racing Council was banning them on ocean racers.)

Race 4: *Liberty* by 43s

It was a sunny day with a light haze and a steady WSW wind of 10–15 k when they lined up for the fourth race on 20 September. In the early stages of the pre-start manoeuvres *Australia II* kept the defender dodging, but with a minute to go Bertrand seemed to misjudge his position in relation to the line. He sailed away from it just long enough to give Conner the initiative. It meant a difference of 6s and a length to windward as they crossed the line with *Liberty* on port tack clear ahead of *Australia II* on starboard tack.

Liberty stood on to the right of the upwind track for 3.0, completely ignoring *Australia II*'s uncovered starboard tack course to the left. The defender got all the lifts that traditionally favour the right hand side in a sou' wester on Rhode Island Sound and the challenger, doggedly keeping left, got all the knocks. It reminded many America's Cup buffs of Sweden's performance in 1977 eliminations against *Australia* when *Sverige* persistently sailed into unfavourable windshifts on the 'wrong' side of the course. When at last they converged, *Liberty* had quadrupled her lead and at the first mark she was 36s ahead. She continued to command the race with leads of 48s, 48s, 46s, 35s and 43s at the finish. Conner ascribed his success to a new mainsail, but close observers noted that for the first time he had departed from his usual copybook tactics — covering upwind and guarding his flank downwind — and for the first time had led all the way. With a 3–1 lead and only one more win necessary to hold the Cup, *Liberty* performed a peacock parade through the admiring spectator fleet. There were few smiles in the Australian camp. Bond said if *Australia II* lost, it was his last challenge. Warren Jones held to his earlier prediction: 'We'll win the Cup 4–3,' he declared.

Left Victoria's *Challenge 12* was bustled out of the contest before the semi-finals without ever developing the potential she had shown in Melbourne trials against *Australia II* and in early American races. (Lou d'Alpuget)

Right Two of *Liberty*'s crewmen working aloft to replace broken jumper strut before start of vital fifth race that could have clinched the Cup for the defenders. But the new strut buckled on the first beat and *Australia II* won. (Bob Ross)

Race 5: *Australia II* by 1.47

Australia II came back from the dead in the fifth race on 21 September in a fresh SxW breeze of 18 k that backed five degrees to the south and was rarely below 16 k. There was a lumpy sea. Bertrand, or at least he and his afterguard, misjudged the start by only a fraction of a second – no more than a metre in distance – after they had herded *Liberty* over the line. But they gave the defender just enough room to duck back behind it before the gun while they remained miserably flat-footed above it. *Liberty*, on port tack, was off and going upwind like a rocket while *Australia II*, still on starboard, was forced to ease away, run back behind the line, gybe and lamely follow her. She had given the defender a colossal start of 37s.

But as it turned out Conner and his crew needed all of that and more. An hour before the start, the stainless steel hydraulic ram that tensioned the port jumper strut and so supported the upper part of the mast had collapsed. Two crewmen, aloft in bo'suns chairs 22 m above the deck, had worked for forty-five punishing minutes to replace the fitting (when a spare was brought by speedboat to the course) and to re-tension the struts. As the vessel had rolled around in the seaway, the crewmen, Tom Rich and Scott Vogel, had been continually battered against the spar and were badly bruised around the shoulders, arms and legs by the time they got back to the deck. But *Liberty's* rig was secure for the pre-start war dance, and, after Bertrand's clanger, she had seemed in good shape, at least for the first 4.0 of the race. It was then, Conner explained later, that the jumper strut tensioning rod collapsed again. 'It certainly made some difference to the boat's pointing ability,' he said.

It was also the reason, Conner said, that he allowed *Australia II* to sail away uncovered to the left hand side of the course on the first upwind beat while he continued to sail *Liberty* to the right. 'We chose not to cover them because we felt that, being crippled, our best chance was to gain distance on a shift,' said Conner. 'We thought the wind might go to the right. Instead, it didn't change and the next time the boats came together they were exactly even.'

Seven minutes later, after *Australia II* got a header, they converged again and the challenger was able to lee-bow her rival, forcing her, after a minute or two, to tack away to clear her wind. They split, converged again and *Australia II* tacked neatly in front of *Liberty*, making the American boat tack to clear again. The next time they converged *Australia II* was able to cross and tack well on top. From that time on she was clear ahead and going away. At the first mark *Liberty* had not only lost her starting 'gift' of 37s but was also 23s astern. *Australia II* continued to lead by 23s, 18s, 1.11, 52s, and 1.47 at the finish. It was the first time a 12-metre challenger had won two races in a series (without being protested out of one of them) and the score stood at 3–2.

Race 6: *Australia II* by 3.25

On Thursday, 22 September, *Australia II* set a number of records. Principally, she became the first challenger in history to square a match three-all and her winning margin of 3.25 was the widest by which a 12-metre challenger had won. She did it in a slight sea that turned lumpy; in a moderate 12 k offshore breeze that turned patchy, dropped to 5 k and freshened to 16–19 k; and over three windward tracks that started nor' nor' west and backed 70 degrees in two colossal switches that forced course changes for the second and final beats. And, although the challenger's helmsman John Bertrand for the third time in succession misjudged the start, he and his crew showed later that they had developed the detection and selection of windshifts into an art form.

At the start, with the course set at 335 degrees, Conner in *Liberty* was clearly in charge, forcing Bertrand to tack away to port before the gun. Conner covered and took *Liberty* across the starting line with full way on 7s ahead and a good two lengths up on the challenger's weather beam. Then *Australia II*, with the defender covering, tacked to starboard and headed left where, in nor' westers, according to local wisdom, the lifts were said to come from, especially when the breeze was forecast to freshen. At first that theory seemed all wrong. There were no lifts. After 14.0, when the challenger tacked to port *Liberty* immediately tacked in front of her, still a clear two lengths ahead. Stifled by the disturbed air from the defender's sails, *Australia II* tacked to starboard, heading again to the left of the windward track, and this time Conner, obviously hoping for lifts where he was, let her go. The breeze was fading. *Australia II* went only 100 m before coming back on to port tack and almost as soon as she did the breeze swung left and she, not *Liberty*, rode it. Soon she was level with the defender's quarter. Then Conner sailed into a soft patch, fell away and *Australia II*, much more responsive in the fluky conditions and still on port tack with the breeze freshening around her, continued to climb. When *Liberty*, now on starboard, came back at her after 10.0 *Australia II* was in charge. She crossed ahead of the defender and then, three lengths directly upwind of her, slammed over to starboard to block her breeze. To escape into clear air, Conner was forced to tack back on to port to the right hand side of the course. In the light conditions, his boat lost speed and direction while the much more nimble *Australia II* was able to spin through her tack and accelerate immediately her sheets were adjusted for the new course.

As *Liberty* sagged on port *Australia II* continued to sail away from her on starboard tack. A few minutes later Bertrand and his crew brought off the manoeuvre that clinched them the race. They had seen a riffle of wind on the water approaching in a narrow band from the left and as it came across to them they tacked to port. The new breeze lifted them at least 15 degrees above their former course, almost straight for the first rounding mark, while *Liberty* floundered in a flat patch more than twenty lengths to leeward. The race was as good as over.

The challenger rounded a crushing 2.29 ahead in 5 k of breeze, now from 295 degrees, almost west nor' west, turning what was intended to be the first of two broad reaches into a very tight one, and the second into a square run. And gradually the strength came back into the breeze until it was a wholesome 12 k. *Australia II* had dropped only 1s of her lead at the wing mark, where her crew performed a stylish gybe-peel to a running spinnaker, and now on their favourite angle of sailing romped away from the slower running *Liberty*. At the bottom turn *Australia II* was 3.46 ahead, having gained 1.18 through sheer boat speed over 3 nm of running. She dropped 24s of her lead on the second beat but persistently headed left, while keeping between *Liberty* and the next mark, and was the first to get another freshening shift, this time 30 degrees to WxS (265 degrees). That put *Australia II* on the layline to the mark from 1.5 nm away. She turned 3.22 clear.

As *Australia II* came down the track on what was intended to be a run but was now, because of the windshift, a beam reach, Conner made a bid to block her. He tacked to starboard and sailed across the course at the challenger, clearly intending, if he could intercept her from leeward, to force her into error or into fouling him as she tried to keep clear as she, the windward boat, would be obliged to do. But the Australians saw him coming, read his intention early, and altered course to clear *Liberty*'s bow by two lengths. Then they ran up a protest flag intending, it was said later, to claim if necessary that Conner had deliberately altered course in breach of Rule 35. That Conner was in breach of the rules was

Australia II (KA 6) minutes ahead under shy spinnaker, sails down track in sixth race while *Liberty* still beats upwind. A minute earlier the US skipper, when on starboard tack, had tried unsuccessfully, and many believed illegally, to block the challenger. (Australian Information Service & Barry Stevens)

the opinion of many indignant eyewitnesses including Sir James Hardy, who, as a director of the Perth syndicate and its sailing adviser, had devoted more than a year to coaching and counselling and standing by to take *Australia II*'s helm in the event of Bertrand's illness or injury. 'I have never seen a more flagrant breach of the rule,' said Sir James. But since Conner could not himself claim any foul there was no need for Bertrand to follow through with a protest after the race.

Australia II rounded the last mark a demoralising 4.08 ahead and although she dropped 43s on the beat to the finish in gusts of 19 k and rising seas she was never in danger of defeat.

There were delirious scenes of joy among Australian supporters on the water and at the dock at Newport. Many Americans also came to cheer the challenger's gallant fight. A chastened Conner tried to explain to a disapproving army of US pressmen why, when clearly in the lead on the first critical beat, he had not clamped a close cover on his rival. To insiders the explanation was simple enough. Conner knew his boat was no match for the challenger in light to moderate air upwind and believed he had to go hunting for favourable windshifts to beat her. He'd gambled on the right hand side of the track and lost.

Alan Bond called for a lay day to prepare for the final Race of the Century.

After a careful maintenance check of all the challenger's equipment Bertrand practised starts against the Irish match-racing expert Harold Cudmore, who steered *Challenge 12*. Conner trimmed 418 kg of lead ballast out of *Liberty* so that he could increase her fore-triangle J measurement from 7.46 m to 7.62 m, gain 2.04 sq m of sail and, hopefully, improve her light-air speed. During much of the summer *Liberty* had sailed under alternative measurement certificates in light, medium, and heavy air modes to suit different wind strengths. There was nothing in the rules specifically to prevent the practice but it infuriated members of rival US defence syndicates when they first learned about it near the end of their elimination series. They claimed that they had been wilfully deceived into trying to tune and improve their boats against a competitor that was not a known quantity. During Conner's final haul out for re-ballasting, Lexcen represented the Australian syndicate as official observer of the defender's re-measurement. 'She's a rough-house kitchen of a boat,' he told friends. 'By comparison *Australia II* looks like a hospital operating theatre.'

Race 7: First attempt—abandoned

History went on to 'hold' on Saturday, 24 September, after an abandoned start and an unavailing one hour, forty minutes wait for the light northerly breeze of 8 k to settle. There was a spectator fleet of 2,000 craft near the start line and spread around the track when officials first set a course of 250 degrees at 11.50 am. But although the committee allowed the starting sequence to begin at noon and continue for 8.0 it was forced to abandon the start 2.0 before the boats were due to cross the line. Dyer Jones, chairman of the NYYC race committee, said the wind had been swinging back and forth in a 55 degree arc. 'To start the race in such conditions would not test the competitors' skill but their luck,' he said. Everyone waited until 1.50 pm, the deadline to hoist more course signals. By then what remained of the breeze had faded and was still variable. So officials were obliged to postpone the race. *Liberty*'s skipper called for a lay day to conduct more experiments on his boat's ballasting. Bertrand practised starts.

Race 7: *Australia II* by 41s

There was another aborted start on Monday, 26 September, when the 8–10 k sou' sou' westerly shifted, and officials called a halt at 12.08 pm after 8.0 of manoeuvring. Then, at 1.05 pm, in a breeze of 205 degrees at 8 k with numerous shifts, the final contest began. *Liberty*, unaltered from her light mode, made an even start. Officially she crossed, on port, 8s ahead of *Australia II* but she had had to dip back at the last instant to keep behind the line at the gun and had little way on. The challenger, on starboard, had crossed with better speed. Conner took *Liberty* to the right, hunting for the windshifts that in a sou' sou' westerly could be expected to come from the right hand side of the course but it was *Australia II*, on the left hand side, that got them. When they changed tacks and began to converge after 6.0 of sailing, *Liberty* tacked back to port clearly indicating that she could not cross ahead of the challenger. With both on port tack, heading right, a series of windshifts from the westerly, left hand side of the course, lifted Bertrand high above Conner's track. When *Liberty* came about to starboard after 20.0 of sailing, *Australia II* was able to cross ahead of her by four lengths. Bertrand tacked to cover, Conner tacked to escape, and when they again tacked and converged, *Liberty* was only two lengths away. Bertrand then astonished many of his supporters by continuing on port tack to the right hand side of the course and failing to cover his rival. He said later that the windshifts were coming in swings of 20 degrees and of varying strengths and that he had believed the next pattern would favour his boat. They sailed on, on opposite tacks for 4.0, then tacked, and after another 4.0 *Liberty* had gained enough to tack on to starboard under *Australia II*'s bow, forcing the challenger to tack on to port, again to the right of the track, to get clear.

The shifts were now clearly favouring *Liberty* on the left and when they again converged, *Australia II* conceded the lead by tacking well below the defender's course. Conner kept Bertrand covered to the mark and rounded 29s ahead. At the worst it was a tactical blunder by the challenger; at the best a lucky gain for the defender, depending on one's point of view. In any case, for the next two and a half hours it seemed likely to keep the Cup safe for America.

Liberty gained 16s to lead by 45s at the wing mark after a 10 degree wind shift had converted the first broad reach into a tight one, but lost 22s of that lead, because what was intended to be a second broad reach became a square run on which *Australia II* was clearly the faster boat. With a lead of 23s on the second beat and the course reset at 195 degrees, Conner sailed in a masterly fashion. For the first 2 nm of the 4.5 nm leg he did not let Bertrand get clear from his cover, and at one stage, with *Liberty* on the inside of two good left hand lifts, appeared to be well over a minute in front. Only in the next mile, when Conner stood on for 2.0 before covering and Bertrand tacked on a header, did the challenger gain any ground. But at the mark *Liberty* was an impressive 57s in front. She had outsailed *Australia II* upwind in a light breeze by 34s. That subdued even the most enthusiastic Australian supporters.

Ben Lexcen, on the syndicate launch tracking the contest, could not bear to watch what he feared was to be another defeat. He said: 'I thought, "Well, at least we won three races, which is more than any other challenger", and I went below and looked through the cabin windows at the NYYC officials on a launch nearby. Their behaviour twenty minutes later brought me up on deck again.' What Lexcen saw was consternation on the American faces. *Australia II* had begun to make the sensational downhill run that was to win her the Cup and *Liberty* was desperately gybing to try to hold her off.

When Conner had rounded the top mark he had gone to the left of the track on a port gybe, angling the breeze across his stern as much as possible to increase his boat's speed, and using whatever shifts there were on that side of the course to her advantage. *Australia II*, almost as fast running dead square as *Liberty* on a quartering run, simply sailed 'deeper' at smaller angles to the mark, and thus had to travel a shorter distance. On the right hand side of the track where his navigator, Grant Simmer, advised Bertrand to take the boat on starboard gybe, she also got a little more breeze. Lexcen admits that he had never considered *Australia II* a fast boat downwind. '*Challenge*, *Azzurra* and *Victory 83* were faster until we developed our spinnakers,' he said. 'The one we used on that final run was a sail that Hughie [Treharne] made and into which Tom [Schnackenberg] put a new middle. It was a lot better shape than *Liberty*'s sail, smaller and it set better. And besides, although they improved *Liberty* upwind for the last race by taking the ballast out of her they made her a slug downwind.'

The challenger made five gybes, three of them tactical, two on to windshifts, that the defender did not get, on that 4.5 nm run. *Liberty* made nine gybes, the seventh in an effort to block the fast-approaching challenger. Conner said later: 'If they wanted to pass, then they would have to sail through us, and that is just what they did. I'd never seen a boat match racing that could sail right up to you and then bear away and sail by, but they did it. Lower and faster!' At the bottom mark, *Australia II* turned 21s ahead. She had gained 1.18.

On the final beat in the 6–8 k breeze, Bertrand did not go looking for lifts either side of the track. He had already had demonstrated to him that *Liberty*, in her latest light-weather trim, although unable to turn or accelerate as quickly as *Australia II*, had just as much boat speed upwind and that the challenger could quickly lose her advantage if the defender got away even for a few minutes into a private windshift. So Bertrand shadowed his rival, carefully keeping between him and the breeze. It paid off handsomely. Over the first 1½ nm when *Liberty* stood on for 3.0 to 4.0 on each stretch before tacking, *Australia II*, holding course above her, three times found herself on the inside of slight windshifts and made gains that good judges agreed put her at least 1.15 ahead. Then Conner and his crew launched a desperate and continuous attack, tacking in all a total of forty-seven times in an effort to break out of their rival's tight cover or at least to force her into error. No helmsman in the history of the Cup more deserves than Conner his reputation for skill and determination to keep fighting. Losing the Cup in no way tarnished it. On three occasions, Conner tried to confuse Bertrand or break his hold with false tacks — pretending to tack his yacht then falling back on to his original course when *Australia II* was beyond head to wind and committed into completing her covering tack; and also initiating a dummy false tack — momentarily pretending to fall back but then completing the tack.

Australia II was caught once by this ruse but she stuck doggedly to the covering task, and, because of Bertrand's cool-headed mastery of her helm and his crew's smooth handling of her gear, she kept clear ahead. It was an exhausting performance for even the fittest athletes. Although Conner won back some of the distance he had lost early on the beat he still needed a tremendous wind shift to win. His final throw was an attempt to lead Bertrand over into the spectator fleet on the starboard side of the lay line where he hoped to tangle him into broken air. Bertrand went to the brink, but then, when he was certain that even with a header he could still make the line, he turned and left Conner sailing away from the mark. All the American could do then was turn and follow. *Australia II* crossed with 41s to spare. And so ended the world's greatest boat race. Pandemonium broke loose, not only in the waters of Rhode Island Sound and in the city of Newport but also across the Australian continent and in many far places of the world.

When *Australia II* came into her crowded dock at Newport, revellers were already chanting, 'The keel, the keel, show us the keel.' So for the first time the boat was hoisted in her slings without her 'modesty skirt' and the keel was revealed. There was awed astonishment at the bizarre shape and at the blue and white painted camouflage pattern, then a riot of enthusiasm. People jumped fully clothed off the docks into the water beside the keel to feel it, kiss it and stroke the wings. The victorious crew who had sailed the boat looked on, bemused.

No sporting team representing Australia at home or abroad in any contest had trained together so long, so hard or with more dedication than the people who had spent two years preparing to race *Australia II*. To give two examples: for more than a year they followed a programme of scientifically and individually

Australia II crosses the finishing line, victorious in the seventh heat with the judges' vessel *Black Knight* firing cannon that signalled first challenger's success in 113 years. (Australian Information Service & Barry Stevens)

designed physical exercises that made them healthier and fitter than they had ever been before in their lives.

They had social and psychological training to strengthen their morale so that they would not break down under pressure of the great occasion. They lived together as a family with a common goal, guided and counselled in group and private sessions by a professional psychologist. The team included, of course, not only the eleven men who were aboard the big boat when she was in competition but also their reserves and replacements and the back-up squad of sailmakers, engineers, technicians and administrators who supported them — a total in all of thirty-five, two of them women. They came from many walks of life. Three were millionaire businessmen, one was a former nuclear physicist, one an army major, one a lawyer, one a school teacher, three were engineers of various kinds and several had university degrees. Most of them had been sailing boats since childhood. Many had won world, national, and State titles in various classes of craft and twelve had previously tried for the America's Cup. There was no aspect of sailboat racing they did not understand, no function of boat handling the men afloat could not perform with expertise stunning to the ordinary yachtsman. That was only basic to their purpose. What they sought to develop for *Australia II* was a coordinated series of flawless techniques that became automatic in every situation. During their final four gruelling months in America they achieved it superbly at every level, in all circumstances, afloat and ashore.

The crew (who sailed the boat in most races) were John Bertrand (skipper), Hugh Treharne (tactician), Grant Simmer (navigator), Colin Beashel (mainsheet), Ken Judge (trimmer), Skip Lissiman (trimmer), Brian Richardson (grinder), John Longley (project manager, grinder), Phil Smidmore (mastman), Peter Costello (pitman, grinder) and Damien Fewster (bowman); with reserves Will Baillieu (grinder), Rob Brown (trimmer) and Scott McAllister (bowman).

The administration and management comprised Alan Bond (syndicate chairman), Warren Jones (managing director), Ben Lexcen (designer), Sir James Hardy (director, sailing adviser, reserve helmsman), Mike Fletcher (sailing coach), Laurie Hayden (sports psychologist), John Fitzhardinge (race committeeman, yacht rigger), Glenn Read (computer technician), Lesleigh Green (public relations) and Alison Baker (secretary).

The team responsible for the sails was made up of Tom Schnackenberg (designer), Ken O'Brien (head sailmaker), Mike Quilter, David Rees and Ted Silbereisen.

Maintenance was the job of Ken Beashel (supervisor), Steve Harrison and Dave Wallace. Manning the tender were Phil Judge (skipper) and Newton Roberts (first mate); and the chase boat, Mark Reid (skipper).

The day after the presentation of the Cup in Newport, Bond, Jones, Lexcen, Bertrand, Treharne, Simmer and Royal Perth Yacht Club commodore Dalziell were whisked to Washington where President Reagan congratulated them on their epic victory. He said: 'Skipper John Bertrand, you and the crew of the *Australia II* have shown us the stuff of which Australians are made. I know that your countrymen are proud of you. And I want you to take this message back, that Americans are proud, too. We're proud to have Australians as our very dear friends. We salute you in your moment of triumph.'

Then they and the other members of the squad who could spare the time were entertained in a series of celebratory parties and parades culminating, when they got back home, with a day-long victory carnival in Perth. Alan Bond had given all the crew $1,000 gold medals to commemorate their win. Some of the afterguard, with their wives, went to Paris for a de luxe holiday as guests of a French admirer. *Australia II*, the remarkable machine that had made it all possible, was put on public exhibition in major Australian cities. When she arrived in Perth the Federal Government announced that it would pay Bond's syndicate $2 million for the boat so that it could be preserved permanently as a national monument. Delivery would not be sought, however, until *Australia II* or her replacement, to be designed by Lexcen, had defended the Cup in the waters of the Indian Ocean, off Fremantle, in January–February 1987.

Soon, in spite of a few early jeremiads, no one had any doubt that the defence of the Cup, efforts by the NYYC to win it back and efforts by those of other American and foreign clubs to take it away from the Royal Perth Yacht Club, would involve Australia in the most colourful and expensive big-boat regatta the world had ever known. Challenges from contending clubs began to pour into Perth. By April 1984 there were twenty-four, each accompanied by its

Australia II's syndicate chief, Alan Bond, triumphantly holds aloft the ancient trophy, symbol of world yachting supremacy. At right is his wife, Eileen Bond. (Australian Information Service & Barry Stevens)

$12,000 cheque of 'serious intent'. Ten challenges came from American clubs and there were four from Italy, three from France, two from Canada and one each from Britain, New Zealand, Sweden, Switzerland and West Germany.

The NYYC announced as its helmsman John Kolius, who had sailed the aged *Courageous* so consistently in the 1983 defence trials until beaten by Dennis Conner in *Liberty*, and a budget of $12 million to back its bid. Conner, challenging on behalf of San Diego Yacht Club, of which he had been elected commodore, indicated that he would aim for a budget of $12 million. Comte Gianfranco Alberini, of Italy's Costa Smeralda Yacht Club, which at its first attempt in 1983 had done so encouragingly with *Azzurra*, did not find it necessary to say how much his club would be prepared to spend. With half a dozen worldwide conglomerates and the Aga Khan as sponsors money was not a consideration.

But it was to some. By late 1985 the field had dwindled to fourteen. Costa Smeralda Yacht Club, appointed by Royal Perth Yacht Club as Challenger of Record (in preference to NYYC) with the responsibility of conducting the eliminations off Gage Roads, Fremantle, between October 1986 and mid-January 1987, had demanded an extra $20,000 a head from each challenging club and Royal Perth Yacht Club wanted guarantees of much more substantial sums to ensure that adequate berthing facilities were booked, some in a new $8 million marina at Fremantle.

The New York Yacht Club's *America II* syndicate acquired from a local deep sea fisherman a dock of its own in the Fremantle fishing boat harbour, at a cost said to be above $750,000. It then rebuilt it inside a security compound and installed a sail loft and an engineering shop on adjoining land so that its challenger, her trial horse, and their tenders could be properly serviced. To accommodate the racing crew and their support troops the NYYC also bought a block of apartments for $1 million or so. Most other foreign syndicates were willing to settle for less permanent but, in some cases, not much less costly premises. An estimated overall total of $200 million was accepted as the likely cost to the final fourteen challenging syndicates and to the four Australian syndicates which nominated candidates for the honour of defending the trophy on behalf of the Royal Perth Yacht Club.

First in the field of these defence syndicates were the 1983 winners, headed by Alan Bond with Warren Jones again as his executive director and Ben Lexcen as designer of the new *Australia III* and of a radical *Australia IV*. When John Bertrand unequivocally announced his retirement from 12-metre sailing there was a choice of four helmsmen—three from Sydney, Hugh Treharne, 1983 tactician; Colin Beashel, 1983 mainsheet hand and mast-climbing hero; and former Olympic dinghy skipper, ocean-racing and 5.5-metre sailor, Carl Ryves; and Gordon Lucas, widely experienced in big and small boats, from Western Australia. The second defence syndicate was headed by Perth retail tycoon Kevin Parry, with former Sydney 18-footer skipper Iain Murray, still smarting after his 1983 mauling in *Advance*, as a helmsman and co-designer with West Australian John Swarbrick of three wing-keeled boats called *Kookaburra*. The third syndicate was led by Sir James Hardy on behalf of a South Australian Government-supported group with a Lexcen-designed, Perth-built and twice altered, wing-keeled *South Australia*. The fourth was a largely Syd Fischer-financed, Sydney-based Eastern Australian syndicate with a well-researched but, some of her supporters feared, under-tuned, wing-keeled boat designed by former sail-maker Peter Cole, who had been one of the pioneers of Australia's bid for the America's Cup.

All Australian designers and some designers of the foreign contenders this time conducted tests on one-third-scale models in the towing tank at Netherlands Ship Model Basin at Wageningen, which had been contracted exclusively for Lexcen's use for the 1983 challenge. Many of the 1984–5–6 designers also used highly advanced computer facilities, at least one of which, in theory, could measure pressure points on the leeward and windward sides of a yacht's hull and keel merely by analysing its taped design. From the outset Lexcen was certain that in *Australia III*, a bigger, heavier, longer boat than *Australia II*, he had created a 12-metre of better all-round potential for Fremantle conditions. Her winged keel was of a different shape, too. The other designers were also sure that the winged keels they had devised were advances on Lexcen's revolutionary 1983 design. Aerospace engineers and scientists of many disciplines were engaged in

Left New York Yacht Club's first challenger since 1851, *America II*, a classy all-rounder, skippered by John Kolius and unlucky to place only third in 1986 world's 12-metre championships.

Right Downwind, *Australia III*, two tonnes heavier than her 1983 predecessor and with a skeg in front of her rudder, was easier to steer in fresh conditions and almost as fast.

research on the challengers. More money and time than ever before was being spent on scientific assessment of yacht design.

From 1985 the Australian Federal Government, the Western Australian State Government, financial corporations and entrepreneurs poured in $80 million in grants and loans to refurbish and modernize the charming nineteenth-century port city of Fremantle, at the entrance of the Swan River, in preparation for the 1987 defence of the Cup. Although Royal Perth Yacht Club, as official defender of the trophy, with its headquarters in the adjoining State capital of Perth, was calling the shots, it was at Fremantle, on the coast, with a complex of three marinas, one only recently built, fixed and mobile hoists, and maintenance berths suitable for 12-metre boats, that the action would be. West Australians in both cities were encouraged not only to create a scene worthy of the occasion but also to expect rich rewards from at least a million visitors from other States and overseas during the four months of elimination races and the final challenge series. Hoteliers and house agents stood by for bookings at prices that seemed outrageous to locals, some of whom had been turned out of rental premises to make way for repairs and the expected new occupants. Fishermen and charterboat proprietors with vessels even vaguely convertible for carrying spectators around the periphery of the racing course, where they might get a distant glimpse of the Cup competitors, were persuaded that they would be able to charge a basic $100 a head a day (double 1983 Newport prices). With more than 100 days listed for racing during the three challenger elimination round robins, the challenger semi-finals and finals, the long period of defence trials and then the best-of-seven challenge series, it seemed like a gold rush with bags of nuggets guaranteed. Some owners on the east coast of Australia planned to steam their vessels 3,000 nm to Fremantle to join the charter boat bonanza. To combine both hotel accommodation and a whiff of salt spray in the vicinity of the 12-metres, shipping companies offered America's Cup galas in cruise liners, to be berthed near Perth by night and anchored at sea during the day. There, with plenty of TV screens, the passengers, while comfortably seated in lounge bars, could watch the action aboard what promised to be only white smudges on the horizon to those less fortunately placed.

Since the courses for the races had to be set within feasible towing distances of Fremantle and as far as possible away from land influences on the wind, officials chose the most obvious area, a circle of 6.5 nm diameter centred on the Fairway Landfall Buoy, 7.5 nm north-west of the harbour entrance. This provided enough room to lay windward and return legs of 3.25 nm with reaching legs of 2.3 nm, whatever the direction of the wind, so that the land would never be nearer than 2 nm. On the eastern side there are the low-lying northern beach suburbs of Fremantle; to the south-west the scrubby 6 nm-long Rottnest Island. To the north, south and west there are thousands of miles of unobstructed ocean.

But there was no question of land masses robbing the Cup contestants of breeze. On summer afternoons the waters off Fremantle are notorious for more wind than yachtsmen need. With rare exceptions, south-westerlies arrive about noon at a brisk velocity of 12–15 knots and build quickly in the next few hours to a steady 20–30 k. After exhausting mornings in light but baking-hot easterly winds from the vast central Australian desert, the people in the coastal cities refer fondly to the cooling afternoon south-westerly from the sea as the life-saving 'Fremantle Doctor'. For yachtsmen, another of the blessings off Fremantle is the wide bed of reefs that begins a little south of Rottnest Island and stretches

New Zealand's *KZ5*, the world's first fibreglass 12-metre, smartly sailed by Chris Dickson and a crew with little experience in the class, finished second in the 1986 world title series.

in an almost unbroken line for 10 nm south east back towards the coast until it joins Garden Island at the northern tip of Cockburn Sound, 12 nm south of Fremantle. The reef breaks up the sweep of the wind-driven seas from the southern Indian Ocean that otherwise would make the near shore area unliveable. There is what amounts to a great bay, 10 nm across behind the reef and island barrier. The water, though, is shallow, generally only 8 to 10 metres deep and in some places almost half that depth. This means that while well-found yachts of up to 2.4 m draft can sail in most of these waters, there is always a punishing chop in moderate winds. When the south-westerly reaches its regular 25–30 k velocity the chop becomes a relentless, pounding, close-packed series of 1.5 m seas, capable of shaking the life out of any vessel not properly built or rigged. On hard reaches especially, it is guaranteed to find the weaknesses in crewmen as well. Those not used to working on wet, bouncing foredecks could be quickly swept overboard. The waters just north of Fremantle, at the open end of the reef-and-island-formed bay, where the America's Cup circle was set, are generally eight metres deeper but the seas are no less boisterous in very hard winds since they have a longer sweep.

In order to make the Cup courses as close as possible to the distance (24.3 nm) used in earlier 12-metre class contests, Royal Perth officials decided on eight legs instead of six — four of 3.25 nm beating to windward, two of 3.25 nm running square downwind, and two of 2.3 nm on shy reaches, a total of 24.1 nm. They began with a beat and a run, then a beat and two reaches around a triangle, gybing usually to port, then a beat, a run, and a beat to the finish. At first cynics were inclined to think the West Australians, confident that they would have faster downwind boats than any of their overseas challengers, had cunningly increased the overall square-running distance from Newport's 4.5 nm to 6.5 nm; and, because US boats in the past had often gained on reaches, that they had reduced the 6.3 nm reaching at Newport to only 4.6 nm. But when representatives of some of the overseas challenging syndicates had inspected the course and tested the conditions they raised no objections. It was believed that some, in fact, after a few afternoons bashing head-on into the Fremantle Doctor, were grateful that they would not have more than a total of 13 nm beating to windward.

Dennis Conner, after a study of the course area in 1984, decided that he would not come to Fremantle until it was absolutely necessary for his final tune-up training before the 1986 eliminations. Instead, he organized all his boat-testing and crew-training in Honolulu. There, without disclosing to potential rivals any of the developments that a team of design scientists had given him in three new boats, all called *Stars and Stripes* and, it was reported, with every phase of their performances linked electronically through a tender by satellite to NASA for computer analysis, he would have constantly hard trade winds and choppy seas similar to the conditions off Fremantle. In Honolulu, Conner was able also to save his syndicate the enormous expense and inconvenience of servicing boats 12,000 nm away from the USA, and keep his team of forty crewmen and technical staff in easy touch with their families and friends.

Kolius and his NYYC squad, on the other hand, set up camp in Fremantle in 1985 with two new boats called *America II* and with container-loads of spare equipment, including three alternative keels that could be secretly swapped inside the syndicate's private shed. The New Yorkers were prepared to ship their boats and gear back home for more training during the northern summer.

Only one other US yacht came to Fremantle for early training. That was the Yale Corinthian Yacht Club's *Courageous IV*, really the basic hull of the defender of 1974 and 1977 refitted for the fourth time and now with a way-out, so-called

Greatest 12-metre regatta: Ten of the fourteen contestants charge the line in this dramatic start of the 1986 world's championship series off Fremantle, WA, on the same course set for the 1987 Cup defence. On the left is *Australia II* (KA6), followed by *South Australia* (partly obscured), *Italia* (I 7), *Australia III* (KA9), *Courageous IV* (X on bow), *French Kiss* (F) and New Zealand's KZ5. (WA Newspapers)

vortex winged-keel designed by engineer Leonard Greene, of New York. In the opinion of many seasoned observers it did nothing to improve the performance of the gallant old boat upwind or down in rough or smooth water except project some developments for the syndicate's proposed *Courageous V.* Three other American challenge syndicates still in the lists in 1986, delayed their arrival in Fremantle. They were St Francis (California) Yacht Club's *Golden Gate* syndicate, Newport (California) Harbour Yacht Club's *Eagle* syndicate, and Chicago Yacht Club's *Heart of America* syndicate. They gave various reasons for preparing their challenge bids near to their home ports — delays in building programmes, alterations due to last-minute breakthroughs in design research, and reorganization in crew-training schedules. They also admitted to an aggravating shortage of funds from sponsors to cover the enormous and constantly growing costs of preparing for competition.

With mainsails of the latest Kevlar design and possibly of the new experimental Spectron 2000 fabric at $24,000 each, and no boat expected to get through the eliminations without wearing out six, as well as twelve genoa jibs ($15,000 each), and twelve spinnakers ($10,000 each), a bankroll of $500,000 just for a wardrobe of sails was conservative.

Canada's Secret Cove Yacht Club, with the rebuilt, now wing-keeled 1983 challenger contender, *Canada I,* frankly gave their reason for not appearing early in Fremantle as lack of money; as did England's Royal Thames Yacht Club with its handsome new heavyweight *Crusader.*

However, by February 1986 there was a roll-up of fourteen boats to sail in a seven-heat regatta for the world's 12-metre championship on the Cup course. They represented seven countries and formed the greatest fleet ever assembled in the long and noble history of the class. The starters were: Bond's 1983 Cup winner *Australia II*, with Gordon Lucas as helmsman and Hugh Treharne in his old position as tactician; the new *Australia III*, with Colin Beashel as helmsman and Carl Ryves as tactician; Gordon Ingate, of Sydney, in his 1970 challenger *Gretel II*, now superseded but spick and span; *South Australia* with Fred Neill as helmsman and Sir James Hardy as tactician; NYYC's *America II* with Kolius as helmsman and a crew not entirely prepared for rough water sailing; Yale Corinthian Yacht Club's *Courageous IV* with Peter Isler; Royal New Zealand Yacht Squadron's brand new *KZ5* and *KZ3*, identical twins of fibreglass, the first 12-metres ever built of that material, designed by a committee consisting of Laurie Davidson, Bruce Farr and Ron Holland and helmed by Chris Dickson and Graham Woodroffe; and from Canada, Nova Scotia Yacht Squadron's powerful *True North* with Hans Fogh, Terry McLaughlin and Jeff Boyd.

The European contenders were, from Italy, Costa Smeralda Yacht Club's new *Azzurra II* with Lorenzo Bortolotti, and the Yacht Club Italiano's *Italia* with Aldo Migliaccio and Flavio Scala, and her trial horse, *Victory 83*, with Tommasco Chieffi, the former British boat that had won the inaugural 12-metre world title series in 1984 off Sardinia with a mixed crew of Italians and Americans; and from France, Société des Régates Rochelaises' high-bowed, full-sterned heavyweight *French Kiss*, helmed by former world FD dinghy champion Marc Pajot. There was also *Challenge 12*, the failed 1983 candidate that never reached her full potential after Bond sold her to Victoria, nor afterwards when sold to Italy. Now she was in the hands of the French Société Nautique de Marseille, but for this series with an Irishman, Harold Cudmore, as helmsman.

The most noticeable absentee, apart from Conner and St Francis Yacht Club's famous match-racing helmsman, Tom Blackaller, was Australian Iain Murray in one of his *Kookaburras*. Although an argument about rating certificates was given as the reason for this failure to compete, it was also suggested that that was only a device to conceal the superior qualities of the Parry-backed boat. In point of fact, what the series of races served to do was confirm the strongly held belief that anyone who beat the superbly organized Bond machine that Warren Jones and team manager John Longley had once again meshed into gear would deserve to win the Cup.

The championships were sailed in unseasonably moderate to light winds, tending westerly, with only two of the seven heats in truly punishing gusts of 25 k. In one, the wind veered to the wèst-nor' west and the seas, not so effectively damped by the reef and island barrier, swept the foredecks of the contestants. During the series two boats lost masts, many tore sails, and six men were washed overboard. Lexcen's *Australia III*, about two tonnes heavier than *Australia II* and with wings on her keel and a skeg ahead of her rudder designed to quell the somewhat skittish motion of her smaller sister in short following seas, made

Left Upwind in medium to heavy air *Australia III* (Colin Beashel), Lexcen's modified wing-keeled development of the 1983 Cup winner, outsailed thirteen rivals to win three of the six races she sailed and the title in the 1986 world title series.

Right *French Kiss*, powerful heavyweight representing Société de Régate Rochelaises and skippered by champion dinghy and ocean racing catamaran sailor Marc Pajot, was outstanding upwind in hard winds and rough seas in the 1986 world title series. She was expected to improve with more crew training.

the opposition look only half-ready for racing. She won three heats, finished second, fourth, and sixth in three others and was so far ahead on points that skipper Beashel did not start her in the last race.

The surprise of the series was the performance of helmsman Chris Dickson's *KZ5*, which finished second on points. With gear hastily assembled and a crew that had sailed the boat only nine times before, they won one race, were placed third four times, once fifth, and once seventh. Kolius' *America II* had a frustrating series, with placings of 2,7,4,2,6,4,2, for third on points. Minor tactical errors, gear failures and a crew whose sail drill still needed polish hampered the boat. *Australia II* came in fourth on points with 3,4,7,1,5,2,6, close behind *America II*, still fastest downwind and clearly superior to all rivals when the wind fell light. The French, who had first entered the America's Cup lists back in 1970, got a tremendous lift with *French Kiss*, a robust boat sponsored by a photographic firm, designed by Philippe Briand with the help of aeronautical engineers and

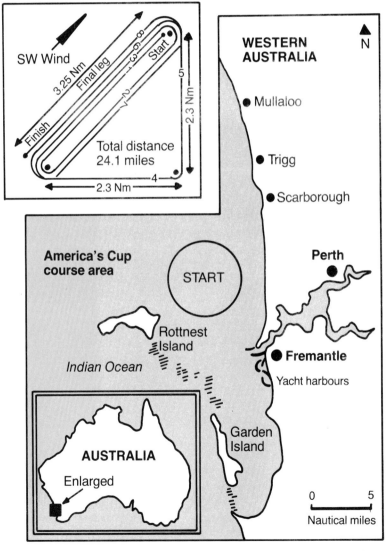

New eight-legged course for America's Cup: First leg to windward.

handled with élan by a confident crew. *French Kiss* won two races and scored 10,6,7,2,6 in the others to finish fifth on points, showing extraordinary pace upwind in heavy air. Canada's *True North,* another big boat, had obvious potential when her crew grew more accustomed to the bouncy Fremantle conditions.

A significant aspect of the racing was that in some heats no more than five minutes covered the first six or seven placings. Because of time lost in packed fleet starts, and through crowding near rounding marks, many boats could have been better placed if engaged only against one rival in a match race.

It was said at the end of the series that Conner, by not competing, had lost valuable experience on the course against potential rivals. His answer was that fleet racing had little relevance to two-boat battles for the America's Cup. He also revealed that his training off Honolulu in his three new boats had been so successful that he had already discarded the 1983 defender *Liberty,* in which he had been so narrowly beaten, because she was too slow to be of any more value as a bench mark. Conner added that he was getting adequate information about Fremantle conditions, including the tangles of floating seaweed that were fouling so many boats' keels and rudders. Warren Jones, although supporting the view that Conner's absence from the world title series could have cost him valuable battle practice on the course, said he still believed that the Californian would win through the eliminations and the San Diego boat would be the ultimate challenger against a Bond-syndicate defender.

Alan Bond, obviously delighted that *Australia III* had outsailed all her rivals in the championships point score, modestly said that he believed Royal Perth Yacht Club had a 50–50 chance of retaining the Cup, whoever was the challenger on January 31, 1987. It seemed, nevertheless, that the ebullient Bond, like a lot of other knowledgeable observers, recognized that there was now little technological difference between at least seven boats and that, while the Australian squad with the resources of fourteen continuous years of 12-metre management, crew-training, and boat-tuning were already sailing at 90 per cent of their potential, the best of the others were only at 75 per cent. With months of dog-fighting ahead of them the challengers had more scope for improvement.

That is the reason, no doubt, why the Bond syndicate, keen to repeat the advantage of *Australia II's* keel three years earlier, sent Lexcen with his specifications for a radical *Australia IV* overseas to consult with Lloyd's London yacht surveyors and Holland's Wageningen test tank operators in March 1986, hopefully to produce another marvel. On the eve of Australia's first defence of the Cup that was what the world was waiting to see.

6

Six Metres:
An Australian-led
Renaissance

IT WAS A BRISK day on Port Phillip Bay with a short, steep sea running over an ebb tide. The 6-metre *Awanui III*, NSW challenger for the Northcote Cup, gybed behind the starting line, slowly climbed to windward and tacked, ready for the gun. Then her rig collapsed clear over the side and she lay crippled, a catastrophic tangle of timber, wire and canvas. The two Victorian defenders of the trophy, *Rip* and *Killara*, rounded up alongside her to check for injuries, found none, then lowered their racing flags and withdrew from the contest.

'It would have been unthinkable to have sailed the course without an opponent', their skippers said.

Noble sentiments! Those were the days when yachtsmen were gentlemen in every sense, when glory could not be earned unless honour were equally served. That 1920 incidence was a sample of the spirit of *noblesse oblige* that had pervaded racing in princely international 6-metre class keelboats since the conception in 1907 of the formula to which they were individually designed and custom built. On occasions, later, in challenge contests for the Northcote Cup, the Australian symbol of supremacy in the 6-metre class since 1908, such standards of behaviour have not always been observed. But they have rarely declined into the bitter dog fights, with winning at all costs the only criterion, that have been accepted as the essence of yacht racing in so many other classes of craft. Perhaps, as we have mentioned elsewhere (see Chapter 16: Level Rating and the Ton Classes) the aristocratic proportions of the 6s, their slim, high-winded elegance and expense and the public expectation of lofty principles among the sportsmen who could afford to race them, contributed to the aura of refinement that they have always enjoyed.

These beautiful wooden sloops, on average about 10.67 m in overall length, reached their highest state of prestige after 1921 when the measurement rules were revised and they were used in international contests for the Scandinavian

184

Gold Cup, the Seawanhaka Cup, the Olympic Games (until 1952) and for the One Ton Cup (until 1962). Until then no one denied that they were worthy of this esteem. They were half-sized replicas, in almost all their linear dimensions, of the 12-metre class racing machines that in 1958 had been chosen (and are still used) for the America's Cup, the apogee of world sailing. Indeed, although it was not then generally recognized by the yachting public, the performance of any individual 6-metre could be closely applied, in theory at least, to that likely from a similarly proportioned 12-metre. Both had to be designed, and still are, under almost the same formula.

But suddenly the 6s fell out of favour and a new breed of boats, mainly 5.5-metres, designed under a completely different formula, came upon the scene. They were lighter, livelier, needed three men instead of five to sail them and, at first, cost less than half the price of a 6-metre to design and build. Although they could not match the 6s in appearance, or in performance to windward, they were not so much slower around a course and were much easier to handle. By the late 1960s it was the fashion to regard 6-metres as vintage curiosities, to be lovingly preserved, perhaps, by yachting purists in a few countries, but hardly to be raced with any degree of seriousness. Then an Australian, John Taylor, a wealthy young vintner and a member of the Royal Prince Alfred Yacht Club, Sydney, gradually brought about their renaissance. Today, because of Taylor's inspiration and persistence during twenty years, the 6-metres are regaining their position as one of the world's premier classes of racing yachts. They compete in an open triennial international challenge series for the Australian–American Cup that closely resembles the America's Cup in concept and organization, and in annual world and European championships, and growing fleets of old and new craft are racing regularly in seven countries. There is even a move in Europe to select a 6-metre of top quality as a mould and to mass produce replicas of it as a strict one-design class. And, of course, the possibility of developing a 12-metre from the lines of a 6, at a cost of about $100,000 for a boat and a season's campaign instead of $4 million, has not been lost on those nations seriously interested in competing for the America's Cup.

But none of this flush of enthusiasm would have occurred if John Taylor had not had his love affair with the 6-metres, and it is probable that he would have never seen such a boat if it had not been for Australia's Northcote Cup. This trophy is a far from tasteful object of brass, not very generously silver plated, standing 62 cm high on an black wooden plinth. It was presented to Victoria by Australia's Governor-General, Lord Northcote, in 1908, as a perpetual interstate challenge prize. Originally it was not intended for racing in 6-metre boats at all but for those that rated 7 metres under the international rule of measurement. When it was revealed to his Lordship that 7-metres were rather a *recherché* class and thin on the ground, or rather, on the water, he agreed that the Cup should be rededicated for 6s. An added concession was that these craft did not have to be sailed interstate in ocean waters on their own bottoms but could be shipped to the race course of the holder's State. The charm of any trophy is not, of course, in its value or its form but in what it represents. In the case of the Northcote Cup it represents seventy-seven years yachting development in Australia, skilful endeavour between rival designers, and between skippers and crews of NSW and Victoria, who sailed their hearts out to win it. The names of most of those men have faded into long forgotten club archives but those of the winning boats and the clubs they represented are enshrined on twenty-three engraved silver shells

185

that encrust the plinth of the trophy and a deep brass collar around its neck. They show that during thirty-one contests, each a best-of-three series of races, Victorian boats have won the cup twenty-two times and NSW boats nine times. Victoria has held the Cup for a total of forty-two years and NSW for thirty-five years.

Stories of Northcote Cup battles abound: of desperate struggles in boats driven beyond the limit in appalling weather; of ill-placed rounding marks that turned certain victory into defeat; of an unchecked starting gun that misfired and blew a hole in the official boat; of stratagems that went sour; of brilliant tactical manoeuvres that saved the day. Some of them may be apocryphal, but there are a few well attested. In the 1920 series, after *Awanui III* lost her rig and her Victorian rivals, *Rip* and *Killara*, had retired, most Victorians approved of their representatives' sporting gesture. Some suggested later, however, that Alex Saxton, owner-skipper of the challenger representing Royal Sydney Yacht Squadron, could have displayed equal generosity in the resailed race by retiring when *Rip*, racing neck and neck with *Awanui III*, fouled a mark and disqualified herself.

In 1918, when there was no interstate challenger and the contest for the Cup was being sailed between the local Victorian boats, *Rip* and *Killara*, representing RYC of Victoria and St Kilda YC, a tornado, claimed to be 200 mph, the strongest wind ever known on Port Phillip Bay, burst on the course. It was accompanied by 'horizontal and blinding rain, dazzling lightning and simultaneous thunder and churned the sea into a cauldron'. Mercifully, it lasted only four minutes. But during that time it killed two people and in Brighton drove two heavy lengths of timber, part of wrecked buildings, high into the air. One baulk crashed down through the roof and ceiling of a building and skewered through the floor between two people without touching either; the other went through the side of a house and impaled a piano. *Killara* suffered only tattered sails and a severe shaking and was towed to her moorings; *Rip* with her gaff broken, her mainsail split, and her boom trailing in the water as a drogue, was blown half a mile off course but later managed to limp home to Williamstown.

In 1930, when NSW had held the Cup for ten years, Victorian William S., Dagg of Royal Brighton Yacht Club, challenged with his *Toogooloowoo* (formerly the Sydney boat *Culwulla II*). She was leading by a good margin on the final downwind leg in the third and deciding race when a dead calm settled on the course. The defending Sydney helmsman, Stan Stevens, in the skinny (1.62 m beam) *Iolaire* (formerly *Awanui III*) then owned by Andrew Wilson and jointly representing RPAYC and RSYS, seemed hopelessly beaten. But Stevens, a peppery little man, was renowned for his tenacity and skill in drifting matches. He ordered his crew to lie still along the yacht's deck and to let go all the leeward rigging so that the boom could be squared ahead of the mast. Then, by-the-lee, he magically oozed up to the challenger and passed her to clinch the match.

In 1947, after Victorian Dagg's *Toogooloowoo II* had won and held the Northcote Cup for eleven years, Jock Carr of RPAYC, Sydney, made a challenge with a brand new boat, *Venger*, designed by Norwegian Bjarne Aas. But Carr withheld notice of his challenge until the last possible minute, believing that this would force the Victorians to defend with their now somewhat out-dated champion and prevent them getting a more modern boat designed and built in time for the match. Dagg was resourceful. He flew to England and persuaded British yachtsman Owen Aisher to sell him his champion 6-metre, *Yeoman*, a beautiful boat of double-diagonal mahogany planking, designed by Charles

Victorian Bill Dagg paid 'a staggering price' for the elegant 6-metre *Yeoman* but it was worth it. She outclassed *Venger*, the challenger, in the Northcote Cup series. (RSYS Archives)

Nicholson to gain all advantages under the measurement formula. *Yeoman* was also superbly outfitted. Aisher had stored her in Scotland during World War II and had intended to campaign her for the London Olympics of 1948. To persuade him to part with the boat and to get her shipped immediately to Melbourne, Dagg was reported to have paid 'a staggering price'. To such an enthusiast and his fellow Victorians, who were highly protective of the Cup that they had held so long, the effort was worth it. *Yeoman*, with Jock Sturrock at the helm, outclassed Carr's Sydney challenger. And *Yeoman* continued to outsail all rivals during six more challenges. By 1956 everyone agreed that with a good skipper and crew in her she was unbeatable.

In 1959 *Yeoman* had been stored out of the water, on a special cradle under covers, at the Royal Yacht Club of Victoria for three years. Although Dagg, now an old man, had no one to race he maintained the boat in perfect order. Her hull outside, from the bottom of her lead keel to her deck edge, was sealed under gleaming white enamel; she had a broad British Racing Green boot-topping at the waterline and inside was varnished from keel to deckhead, from stem to stern. The king plank of her scrubbed teak deck was varnished, too. *Yeoman* had a dozen bags of American-made racing sails, all carefully packed and preserved like the rest of her equipment, just in case some sassy New South Welshman with ambitions arrived. But none did, until John Taylor, a complete innocent in the field of high-powered yacht racing, approached Dagg; and Taylor did not want to challenge *Yeoman*, he wanted to buy her. Dagg's first reaction was indignant refusal. But he warmed to Taylor's ecstatic admiration of the boat and his obvious intention to pamper her, and finally agreed to consider his proposal.

Taylor's sailing experience at that stage had been limited to a few years cruising about, learning the ropes in an amateur-built 8.53 m sloop with the windward qualities of a wardrobe. He was telling Jack Kydd, the secretary of The Alfreds, of his boat's limitations when the shrewd old yachtsman told him that if he really wanted to go sailing seriously he should buy a boat of better design, take a place in its crew and get a really good yachtsman to helm her for him in races. Kydd suggested Len Esdaile, one of Taylor's fellow members of The Alfreds, as the ideal helmsman and tutor. Kydd added that his personal preference would be a 6-metre class boat because they were the most highly refined under the international metre formula and, in his opinion, capable under the arbitrary time allowance scale (81s a mile) of beating an 8-metre in light weather. 'Even *Saskia*?' asked Taylor, who had read of Bill Northam's 8-metre victory in the Australian Sayonara Cup series. 'Yes, if you can persuade Bill Dagg to part with *Yeoman* and get Esdaile and a good crew to sail with you,' said Kydd. Taylor had never heard of *Yeoman* but he wrote to Dagg in Melbourne, then visited him and his infatuation with 6s began.

'I was lost from the moment they folded back the covers and I saw how graceful *Yeoman* was,' he recalls. 'From what I'd been told about her hard racing career I had expected to see an old boat, a bit battered, but she was absolutely beautiful, as good as brand new. The dear old chap eventually agreed to sell her to me because I promised to look after her and never to fish out of her! There were tears in his eyes as we hauled her out on a road trailer.'

So Taylor brought *Yeoman* to Sydney and for the next four years left the Northcote Cup field to lesser Victorian craft which raced for the trophy between themselves on Port Phillip Bay. He spent his time learning to handle his boat, mostly in the crew, with Esdaile on the helm. Taylor, then a massively heavy man, stripped off stones in weight to make himself fit enough to move smartly around the cockpit and he studied racing tactics and everything that had been written about the history of the 6-metre class. Soon he had an encyclopaedic knowledge of the boats and was corresponding with buffs overseas. *Yeoman* raced every weekend, alternating between RSYS and The Alfreds point scores in which she was one of the Division 1 scratch markers; and Taylor got his chance to test Kydd's theory that a good 6-metre, with a time allowance of 81s a mile, would outsail an 8-metre in smooth water. He put up the *Saskia-Yeoman* Metre Yacht Trophy for a 20 nm challenge match in light weather off Sydney Heads and *Yeoman* beat *Saskia*, then owned by Reg Jeffreys and skippered by Bill Solomons, by a handsome margin. (In later races for the trophy in fresher winds and sloppy offshore seas, *Saskia* twice beat *Yeoman*, and the 12-metre *Vim* — *Gretel's* 1962 America's Cup trial horse — conceding big margins, once beat them both.)

In 1965, after Dagg's death, Taylor and Esdaile took *Yeoman* to Melbourne to challenge for the Northcote Cup. It was often said that a condition of *Yeoman's* sale to Taylor had been that she must not challenge for the trophy during Dagg's lifetime. But that is not true. 'In fact, I think if the old man had been alive it would have delighted him to see her in action again,' says Taylor. In any case, the series was little more than a formality. *Yeoman* waltzed over the Victorian defender, *Venger*, and brought the Cup to Sydney for the first time in thirty-four years. It has remained there, among the many other trophies in The Alfreds' collection. Taylor has twice successfully defended it; once with *Yeoman* and when it was last contested in 1969, with *Toogooloowoo IV*, one of his later string of new 6-metres that were to revitalize the class worldwide.

Taylor adopted the strange name of *Toogooloowoo* (which contrary to popular opinion has no true Aboriginal connotation and is believed to have been coined by the Australian writer C. J. Dennis) when he sponsored a new 5.5-metre class yacht, *Toogooloowoo III* for the Australian 1964 Olympic trials. As mentioned earlier, it had been the name William Dagg had given one of his early Northcote Cup champions and Taylor, ever courteous, had formally asked Dagg's widow for permission to borrow it. The 6-metre *Toogooloowoo IV* was, therefore, a natural progression. Although Taylor still owned *Yeoman* (and was to keep her until 1978) he had *Toogooloowoo IV* built in 1968 because by then he was completely hooked on 6s. Another fancier with whom he corresponded was American Olin Stephens, then unchallenged as the world's leading yacht designer and creator of most of the 12-metres that defended the America's Cup. Stephens casually mentioned to Taylor in a letter that he had developed the design of Harold 'Mike' Vanderbilt's 12-metre *Vim* (one of the most celebrated of the America's Cup defence contenders) directly from the lines of *Goose*, a former Olympic champion 6-metre, that was still sailing on Puget Sound, Seattle, with a fleet of old 6-metres in the Corinthian Yacht Club. Taylor asked Stephens if it was possible to work backwards and design a 6-metre from the lines of a 12-metre and, if so, how a modern boat taken, say from the lines of the 12-metre *Intrepid* (which Stephens had last designed to defend the America's Cup) would compare with the old *Goose*. 'No trouble', said Stephens, the lines could be taken almost directly from the tank-tested models of the 12-metre and he thought such a modern 6-metre would have to be able to beat *Goose*, if they were equally well sailed. 'Well, I'm waiting for the design', was Taylor's reply.

When *Toogooloowoo IV* was launched in Sydney she soon proved that in fresh conditions, with a little slop in the sea, she was certainly superior to Taylor's other 6-metre *Yeoman*. With the standard time allowance she also beat the 8-metre *Saskia*. Stephens, intrigued, asked Taylor's permission to mention his new boat in a retrospective article about 6s in the American magazine *Yachting*. Three months later Taylor had an international challenge on his hands.

Eustace 'Sonny' Vynne, of Seattle's Corinthian Yacht Club (and later to manage the 'Knock on Wood' syndicate that supported *Intrepid* as The People's Boat in her gallant fight against *Courageous* for the right to defend the America's Cup), came to Sydney in 1969 to see Taylor and organize a 6-metre match between *Toogooloowoo IV* and *Goose*, owned and skippered by Brian Wertheimer. They decided on neutral ground and chose the bouncy tide-swept waters of San Francisco Bay, with officials of the exclusive St Francis Yacht Club in charge. It meant a 7,000 nm sea voyage in a freighter for the Sydney boat and a 1,800 km road haul for the Seattle boat. Taylor, sailing as mainsheet hand, took Esdaile as helmsman, Jack Gale and Jim Gannon as for'ard hands and sailmaker Rob Antill as winchman. The Alfreds obligingly let them carry the club flag on the understanding that Taylor carried all the expenses. They put up a willing battle in bewildering conditions that none of them had ever faced before – shallow waters, in places only 30 cm deeper than their keel, and 5 k tidal rips. 'At times it was like sailing up a stormwater drain,' says Gale. 'If Hank Easom [one of San Francisco's champion helmsmen] hadn't given us some coaching we'd have been slaughtered.' *Toogooloowoo IV* went down 3–4 in the best-of-seven series, scoring one of her wins on a protest when the Seattle crew called for shore room, then failed to tack. But she greatly impressed the San Franciscans. One of them, Bill Stewart, of St Francis Yacht Club said, 'Why don't we buy your boat and establish a regular international challenge series, like the America's Cup, for 6-metres? It would save you the cost of shipping your boat home and then you would have enough money from the deal to build a new one in Australia.' So the matches for the American–Australian Six Metre Challenge Cup, an antique piece of sterling silverware unearthed from the vault of a Sydney jeweller, began.

One of the conditions is that it must always be contested under the joint control of representatives of St Francis Yacht Club, San Francisco, and Royal Prince Alfred Yacht Club, Sydney. Another is that it must be sailed alternatively on San Francisco Bay and on a course off Broken Bay, Sydney, regardless of who holds the trophy. But it is still open to challenges from boats representing any yacht club in the world provided that they comply with the international 6-metre rules of measurement approved by the IYRU.

The inaugural match for the American–Australian Cup was sailed in 1970 off Sydney's Broken Bay between St Francis Yacht Club's *St Francis IV* (the renamed *Toogooloowoo IV*) that the Americans had substantially re-rigged and re-decked on the advice of West Coast yacht designer Gary Mull, and Taylor's new *Toogooloowoo V*, which Olin Stephens had designed from the lines of his latest (and unsuccessful) 12-metre America's Cup defence contender, *Valiant*. It was an expensive disaster for Taylor and a great disappointment for RPAYC members. *St Francis IV* won 4–0 in a tame mismatch in light to moderate weather. Former Olympic and Sayonara Cup helmsman, and reserve helmsman for *Gretel* in the America's Cup, Bill Solomons, skippered the Australian 6-metre for The Alfreds. He was roundly criticized for his failure to do better. But in fairness it must be said that Solomons was hampered by a quite ridiculous steering system that had been adopted for the boat — three wheels of varying sizes mounted one behind the other on a pedestal in the cockpit. One wheel operated the main steering rudder, another the trim-tab rudder and the third engaged both or disengaged them so that they could be used in tandem or individually. It was a valid though questionable system for a big yacht, and just possible in a vessel the size of a 12-metre, with a spare crewman available to help the helmsman, but altogether unsuitable for the cramped cockpit of a 6-metre, with one man trying to operate everything and, at the same time, to concentrate on a close-quarters tactical battle. 'I was like the engine driver of an old-fashioned steam-roller, winding and unwinding wheels and I could never settle down,' said Solomons bitterly. 'Anyway, *Toogooloowoo V*, like her big sister, *Valiant* , was a clunker, one of Olin Stephens' few failures, as history has proved.' Solomons was also unfortunate to have as his rival helmsman one of America's toughest marine gladiators — Tom Blackaller, world Star class skipper and a master of match race tactics, backed by a brilliant crew. Blackaller steered *St Francis IV* with a tiller. He had discarded the steering wheel that the boat had originally carried. He chuckled at predictions that he would not be able to handle the ocean swells off the Sydney coast and, to demonstrate his superiority in the conditions, in one race literally sailed rings around the floundering *Toogooloowoo V*.

The Americans took the trophy home and Taylor and The Alfreds, with their blood now properly up, planned a three-year campaign to recover it in 1973 with a new boat.

This time Olin Stephens provided the design of *Pacemaker*, a half-sized version of the 12-metre *Courageous* and, against his better judgement but under pressure from Taylor and his advisers, gave her a keel without a trim-tab rudder behind it. Australia's Olympic Star class helmsman David Forbes, fresh from his gold medal win at Munich, took her to San Francisco. He had four of Australia's outstanding crewmen with him: Olympic helmsman and future America's Cup skipper John Bertrand, Rick Le Plastrier, John Hebden and Rob Antill. Between them they had won almost a hundred international, national and State sailing titles in a variety of boats. Taylor and Gale managed the crew and a Jumbo Jet load of Alfreds members went to cheer them. But they met Blackaller on his home waters, the Berkeley Circle of San Francisco Bay, in *St Francis V*, a new superlight 6-metre designed by Gary Mull, and went down 4–0. The match was not, however, as much a one-sided wipe-off as the bald record book may suggest. *Pacemaker* finished first in one race but was disqualified after a protest by Blackaller that left the usually placid Forbes and the other Australians blazing with anger. *St Francis V* won by only 62s, 39s and 58s and finished 74s behind *Pacemaker* in the race she was awarded on a protest. The Australian crew was somewhat hampered in tacking duels by a futuristic deck layout, rudely described as a 'family three-holer', that split them into groups and gave one crew man for'ard too little to do, two aft too much and forced the fourth, in the middle, to do the winch grinding alone. No one could slither under the low deck in time to back up his mates.

But the critical weakness that cost *Pacemaker* much time to windward was the Australian boat's headsails. The Americans told them (after the series) that they had closely studied headsails suitable for high-winded racing machines, from 6-metres to 12-metres, and that *Pacemaker*'s were definitely cut too flat in the lower sections and too full in the higher sections. (Four years later, during the 1977 challenge for the America's Cup, quite a radical difference between the headsails of *Australia* and the superlative defender *Courageous* was clear for all to see. *Australia*'s co-designer, Ben Lexcen, named it the main cause of the challenger's defeat.) Positive proof of the flaw in *Pacemaker*'s sails in the American–Australian races, was given a fortnight later in Seattle, during the first Six Metre World Cup series organized by Puget Sound Six Metre Association with twenty-one boats, representing six nations competing, and Taylor, who had created so much interest in the class, as a special guest of honour. An ace Seattle sailmaker, Scott Rohrer, persuaded Taylor to let him make the Australian boat a new headsail on the basis that if it did not improve her performance he would not accept payment for it. *Pacemaker*, her original crew suddenly reduced to Forbes and Antill by business commitments and injuries, and filled with three middle-aged substitutes — Taylor, Gale and Rick Corben — until then had trailed *St Francis V* in two races of the World Cup series. Under the new headsail she immediately won two races and was well ahead in the third and deciding race until a windshift gave *St Francis V* a winning break. The swashbuckling Blackaller was in an almost conciliatory mood when he came ashore. 'You guys are beginning to learn,' he said.

So the Australian boat in the end was far from disgraced. Taylor, who had now suffered three successive defeats with good grace and, in the process, had spent a considerable private fortune on his boats, was acclaimed an admirable loser and compared with Sir Thomas Lipton, the Irish tea millionaire who had made five unsuccessful challenges for the America's Cup. Taylor agreed to sell *Pacemaker* in America at a loss 'further to strengthen the 6-metre class'. St Francis Yacht Club entertained the large contingent of Alfreds members with typical American generosity; reciprocal honorary membership was arranged between both clubs, and many friendships made.

The stage was thus well set for a pleasant American–Australian challenge series in friendly rivalry off Broken Bay, Sydney, in 1976. The Americans again sent Blackaller with a good crew in another Mull design, *St Francis VI*, a purposeful machine of fibreglass-balsawood sandwich construction. Sweden, challenging for the first time, sent *May Be X*, a new wooden boat that a few months earlier had won the world 6-metre series in Sweden against a classy international fleet of old and new boats. Some members of the Swedish squad were also associated with the preparations of Royal Gothenburg Yacht Club's 12-metre *Sverige*, which a year later was to challenge for the America's Cup. The Alfreds, for the first time taking the full expense of the club's challenge from Taylor's shoulders, raised $40,000 among a syndicate of 180 members to build their boat. She was *Prince Alfred*, one of the most radical monohull sailing yachts ever built. Speculation about the boat's shape spread in many countries when it was hinted that she would be sensational and that secret tank tests had shown that she would sail 10 per cent faster downwind than any 6-metre ever launched and would be fast upwind, too. That over-used word 'breakthrough' was widely circulated. *Prince Alfred* was the concept of 'The Great Dane' Paul Elvstrom, the world's most successful single-handed dinghy sailor, who had won four Olympic gold medals and nineteen international titles in other boats, centreboard and keel, and his assistant, Jan Kjaerulff.

The Australian boat, in fact, was a half-sized replica of a 12-metre design that Elvstrom had conceived for Baron Marcel Bich's 1977 America's Cup challenger but which was not built when those two strong-minded men quarrelled. The secret of *Prince Alfred* was kept for months while Sydney shipwright Bill Barnett built her, of wood, behind the locked doors of his Berry's Bay shed. When it was ultimately revealed there was no sense of anti-climax. *Prince Alfred* was certainly sensational. Under her overhanging bow and just below the waterline there extended a half metre long bullet-shaped snout of reinforced fibreglass, 25.4 cm in diameter and similar but much bigger and longer in proportion to the bulbous underwater bow extensions of modern supertankers and large ocean-going ships. If such bulbs eased the hydrodynamic resistance around the bows and shoulders of big power-driven ships, Elvstrom had reasoned, why could they not be adapted for smaller craft driven by sail? His tests on models for Bich's proposed 12-metre had proved his theories, Evlstrom claimed. 'Prince Alfred should be the most successful 6-metre ever built,' he said.

And although controversy raged about the Battle of the Bulb, Elvstrom was almost right. *Prince Alfred* was incredibly fast downwind for a heavily ballasted craft of her class; she also went through the water fast, pointing high, on beats to windward. But her fatal defect was that upwind she also slid sideways, robbing her of all the advantages she had gained. In scaling down his 12-metre design, Elvstrom had given the 6-metre the same proportion of fin keel as the much deeper, heavier boat. *Prince Alfred* made leeway mainly because she lacked lateral plane. But Elvstrom, who sailed as tactician and relieving helmsman in the boat, with Dave Forbes as the main helmsman, refused at first to accept that. *Prince*

At *Prince Alfred*'s launching her underwater snout aroused snorts of disapproval. Few commented, though, on the tiny keel, her real weakness. Builder Bill Barnett's smile is restrained. (*SMH*)

Alfred's noticeable sideslip was at one stage ascribed to a mysterious quality in her 'form stability', then to her rig. Major surgery was performed on her deck and cockpit layout so that her mast could be moved 30 cm aft of its designed position and so that her crew could shift their weight towards the stern of the boat. The changes made little difference to *Prince Alfred*'s windward performance.

Only an incomparable series of tactical races sailed by Forbes and Elvstrom and their crew, Olympic gold medallist Peter 'Pod' O'Donnell, Rob Antill and Geoff Gale (son of Jack Gale), enabled them to beat Sweden's *May Be X* 4–1 in the elimination contest. *Prince Alfred* scrambled in with only 2s to spare in one race and had a margin of 51s in another. But against *St Francis VI*, with her almost contemptuously confident Blackaller and his experienced crew, she went down in four races straight. Heavy rain, fresh winds and lumpy seas in three races added to the Australian supporters' misery. Forbes was convinced after two of these final races that *Prince Alfred*'s keel was too small. He passed the helm over to Elvstrom to try to persuade him that that was the trouble. The Dane was not entirely satisfied, especially when he was able to squeeze a little better performance out of the boat than Forbes. Nevertheless he ascribed the improvement when he got within 1m 7s of Blackaller in the final race not to *Prince Albert*'s inherent qualities or to his own skill but to a better cut, flatter mainsail.

During postmortems after the races some critics of distinguished ignorance condemned Elvstrom and his bulb bow, trumpeting that Baron Bich had acted wisely in rejecting such a boat for his America's Cup challenge and that The Alfreds would have spent their money better if they had raced an orthodox boat designed by Olin Stephens. The acute Jack Gale took a different view.

193

If *Prince Alfred* had been given a bigger keel when she showed her sideslip in early tuning, I think she just might have been good enough to beat *St Francis VI*. Elvstrom would then have been hailed as a genius and every 6-metre and every America's Cup 12-metre thereafter would have had a bulb. Eventually I think bulb bows will prove their worth, especially in the international metre boat classes because this is an area in their measurement formula where, unlike ocean racers, they take no penalties. Now it will be many years before we know.

The Alfreds lost a chance to experiment with a new keel on *Prince Alfred* when an unexpected engineering bill for $13,000 for work done on the yacht's specially geared steering mechanism, forced the American–Australian Syndicate (a registered company) into liquidation. In 1977 the yacht that had cost a total of $53,000 only a year earlier was sold with all her gear for $9,000 to Denmark, where Prince Henrik, husband of Queen Margrethe II, sailed her under her new name, *Dania*.

In 1978 a new Alfreds syndicate was formed so that the club could have at least a token representative in the 1979 American–Australian Challenge Cup series on San Francisco Bay. But after the *Prince Alfred* debacle, money was hard to raise. The best the club could do was to charter the former Australian challenger *Pacemaker* from Seattle and to send a good skipper and crew to sail her. 'Pod' O'Donnell, by then national champion helmsman in 9.14 m Etchells class keelboats and runner-up in the Etchells 1978 world title series (which he won in 1980), was chosen to helm *Pacemaker*. In his crew were Richard Coxon, Lee Killingworth, Dick Lawson and Taylor's son, Graeme Taylor. They faced an almost impossible task.

Six metres had become so popular and so highly competitive that *Pacemaker*, although extensively refitted and now with a trim tab, was outdated. She did not get past Sweden's latest challenger, *May Be XII*, skippered by Patric Fredell, who had eliminated two other Swedish contenders. O'Donnell and his crew handled their boat with style and all the races were close but *May Be XII* was much higher winded and could squeeze up from leeward to escape from seemingly impossible positions. She won 4–0, once on a protest that many experts believed should have gone against her.

The US defender was the new *St Francis VII*, designed by Gary Mull and skippered by Tom Blackaller, representing St Francis Yacht Club. She won that right after a ferocious elimination series against *Ranger*, a near sistership, representing Fort Worth Boat Club, Texas, and sailed by America's Cup helmsman Ted Turner. Two other American defence contenders, both new boats, had earlier been swept aside. Then Blackaller walked over Fredell 4–0 in the challenge final, not so much because of superior boat speed but because of masterly match-race tactics and superlative crew-work.

The victory was somewhat over-shadowed, however, by Blackaller's second placing, in *St Francis VII*, in the Six Metre Championships, sailed on Puget Sound, near Seattle, three weeks earlier. The winner there was *Irene*, a new boat designed and helmed by Pelle Petterson, the Swedish America's Cup skipper, whose commitments to his 12-metre *Sverige* prevented him competing in the American–Australian Six Metre Challenge Cup series. It was significant that jutting forward under *Irene*'s bow there was a little bulge, nothing compared with the bulb on the ill-fated *Prince Alfred*, but unquestionably a development from it.

In 1982 many members of the Alfreds had developed almost a love-hate attitude to the 6-metres. Some, interested mainly in semi-social club handicap racing, felt the 6s were too highly refined and a waste of time, money, and effort; others, in the pursuit of excellence in class boat racing, still saw them as the ultimate of achievement, the equivalent, for their size, of the 12-metres that raced for the America's Cup but at a miniscule fraction of the costs now involved in challenge campaigns in such vessels. And there remained also for the traditionalists in the proud old club the unfinished business of four consecutive defeats without a win in the competition for the American–Australian trophy that the Alfreds had initiated. This had inspired the enthusiasts to build three new Australian boats in 1981–82 to find a worthy challenger. The Americans shipped two boats to Sydney to sail off for the right to defend.

The challenger elimination series was a spirited if one-sided affair that went to *Arunga VI*, skippered by former world 5.5-metre and Etchells 22 class champion Frank Tolhurst who, in partnership with John Taylor and Neil Wyld, had the boat designed and built in Sweden by Pelle Petterson. *Arunga VI* defeated *Prince Alfred II*, a Gary Mull-designed boat partly built in Victoria and later purchased by a club syndicate with Ken Hudson and Don Oastler at its head. The third Alfreds contender was *Pacific Highway*, an English, Ed Dubois design for skipper Graham Jones. This boat had been beautifully built in foam fibreglass by Lloyd North, of Mona Vale, Sydney, but under the measurement rules was found to need substantial reconstruction to enable her to carry what was considered an effectively sized mainsail. She was then barely tuned and no match for Tolhurst and his smart crew: Hugh Treharne, Norm Hyett, Colin Beashel, and Mark Tolhurst. The American defender was St Francis Yacht Club's *St Francis VII* helmed by John Bertrand, a former world Laser and Finn dinghy champion (no relation to the Australian Olympian and America's Cup skipper) and a young crew of mainly dinghy sailors, who beat off Fort Worth (Texas) Yacht Club's contender *Ranger*, helmed by Andy Rose. The match between *Arunga VI* and *St Francis VII* off Palm Beach, Sydney, was the closest and most vigorously contested since the competition had begun twelve years earlier. Although the Americans won 4–1 and, indeed, finished ahead in the race they lost in the protest room, there was rarely more than a couple of hundred metres between them upwind and down. In the first race, sailed in a fluky 8 k breeze that died and revived to 5 k, the margin in time was 3.43 but only 200 m in distance. The other races were sailed in wholesome winds from 12 k to 20 k, with 35 k gusts in one. *Arunga VI* was well in the lead in two races and seemed certain to win until wind shifts helped the US boat. Still, *St Francis VII*'s final margins in those four were 1.30, 15s, 59s, and 1.15, on average she gained 4.78s a mile, and the Americans went home victors for the fifth time.

Tolhurst and his partners, somewhat disillusioned by what they saw as half-hearted support from some influential members of their club, decided to cut their 6-metre losses. They shipped *Arunga VI* to America for sale. In 1983 the St Francis Yacht Club syndicate, which had sold its *St Francis VII*, chartered *Arunga VI*, renamed her *St Francis VIII* and used her as a defender against Graham Jones' *Pacific Highway*, which her owner-skipper had been persuaded had now been greatly improved by re-rigging and re-tuning. The story of the sixth challenge, this time on the tricky Berkeley Circle course in San Francisco harbour, was much the same as the earlier ones. Although the Australian boat and crew showed form, they lacked the class of the Americans, who won 4–1.

The 6-metres continued their growth in popularity, especially in Europe and in America. In 1985 a fleet of thirty-nine boats competed in the world title series in Cannes, France. Seven new boats were built especially for the event; some had slight bulges under the bows, and three, whose designers had been inspired by Australia's sensational America's Cup winner in 1983, carried winged keels. Unhappily, in the dead light air of the series, none of these were successful.

Nor, indeed, was the wing-keeled Australian contender, *Pacific Highway*, successful in the 1986 competition for the American–Australian Cup, sailed in the more robust waters of Sydney's Palm Beach circle. Members and sponsors of Royal Prince Alfred Yacht Club, ever hopeful, had been persuaded by an enthusiastic committee to contribute $60,000 to rebuild and campaign *Pacific Highway* for her third tilt at the trophy which the Americans had won six times.

Ben Lexcen was engaged, some believed against his better judgement since the boat lacked beam, to redesign *Pacific Highway*'s underbody and to replace her orthodox keel with a winged keel, said to be an advance on that which he had created for the victorious *Australia II* in the 1983 America's Cup. *Pacific Highway* was also rerigged with new sails of the latest kevlar, dacron, and mylar fabrics. With the yacht's part-owner Graham Jones as helmsman, and a smart crew (co-owner Richard Hudson, Peter Antill, Kendall Barry Cotter, Paul Carfrae and Peter Isaacs, one as a reserve) *Pacific Highway* spent two months training against the club's other 6-metre, *Prince Alfred II*, on Pittwater and in the open Tasman Sea, two miles off Palm Beach. Officials were convinced that *Pacific Highway* was much improved by the changes, especially on runs downwind. Disturbingly though, in some training sorties she was able to gain little on her old trial horse. And against Sweden's orthodox keeled *Irene* (on which a winged keel had been tried but discarded) in the best-of-seven elimination series for the right to challenge the orthodox-keeled American defender, *St Francis IX*, the Australian boat's weakness was soon revealed. Upwind, in moderate air, 8–17 k, she was definitely off the pace of her rival, designed and skippered by former world champion Pelle Petterson. Only in very light air and in fresh to strong winds of 18–25 k was *Pacific Highway* truly competitive to windward. Downwind, though, in all conditions she generally had an edge on the Swedish boat.

But Jones and his crew made a magnificent fight of it. They lost the first three races, over 12.5 nm, five-legged, windward-and-return courses, by margins of 1.35, 1.52, and 40s in slight seas and winds of 10–16 k. Then, in the next race, after a bitter struggle in rough seas and winds above 25 k, *Pacific Highway* gained a lead of 1.25 on a wild, downwind run, increased it to 1.55 on the next windward beat and to 4.08 on the following run when *Irene* retired with damage to her rigging. *Pacific Highway* finished 34s behind in the next race in an 18 k breeze but won on a port and starboard protest; then dramatically she squared the match 3–all when she led at every mark and finished 1.24 ahead in a shifty breeze that backed 200 degrees and never got above 8 k. But Petterson clinched the series 4–3 when he sailed *Irene* home 1.27 ahead after leading all the way in a 5–15 k breeze.

Match race enthusiasts gathered eagerly for the final between the Swedish boat and St Francis Yacht Club's *St Francis IX*, also designed by Petterson, helmed by the redoubtable Tom Blackaller, and crewed by some of his squad preparing for the 1987 America's Cup challenge. Although the boats were almost identical, except for a slight deepening in the American skeg just ahead of the rudder, there was no comparison in their performance. In breezes ranging from 5–12 k (gales

A rebuilt, wing-keeled *Pacific Highway* (No 13), well-sailed by Graham Jones, made a real fight of the Am–Aus Six Metre elimination series but went down 4–3 to Sweden's *Irene* (Pelle Petterson), here well clear to windward. USA's *St Francis IX* won challenge final 4–0. (Jim Booth)

and rough seas caused two postponements) Blackaller led around fourteen of the sixteen marks they turned — Petterson lost a 1.31 lead when he failed to cover in the third race — won by margins of 3.17, 1.30, 1.59, and 2.08 and took the match 4–0. So, for the seventh time the Cup remained with the Americans and members of the Royal Prince Alfred Yacht Club wondered what they had to do to win it.

7

Eighteen Footers: Unique Racing Machines

THE WHIMSICAL GHOST of Sir Francis Chichester must have chuckled with delight over Plymouth Sound during the English summer of 1978. There, on the old boy's own stamping ground, was at last the contest about which he had dreamed for half his lifetime — a true international championship, with Britain competing, between Australian 18-footers — the world's fastest and most exciting single-hulled boats.

'I have admired and marvelled at Australia's unique 18-footers and the skill with which you people sail them since I first saw them race in Sydney as a young man,' he wrote to author Lou d'Alpuget in 1962. 'Let us try to encourage someone to sponsor a challenge contest in them between our two countries. When the public of Europe see those boats in action they will never again think sailing races are dull, academic affairs.'

Chichester's and d'Alpuget's efforts to promote such an 18-footer series in the early 1960s foundered on the rocks of British conservatism; a small group of 'hidebound satraps', Chichester scornfully called them, fearful of professionalism and disdainful of the taint of commercialism that the Australian boats might bring to a sport that they then believed reserved for gentleman amateurs. The British sang a different tune a few years later, and with extravagant enthusiasm embraced commercial sponsorship of all forms of yachting. But by then Chichester was a round-the-world sailor, and d'Alpuget had other kites to fly.

Commercial sponsorship of boats and crews has for more than twenty years been the life blood of 18-footer sailing, and colourful behaviour by their crews, like the signs on their sails, has set them apart since the foundation of the class in Sydney in 1895. The boats of the Sydney Flying Squadron in those early days were heavy-weight centreboard craft made with 12 mm cedar planks, full-bodied and strongly timbered, with incredible spreads of sail and up to sixteen men triple-banked on the gunwales to balance them. They were a development of the undecked, gaff-rigged 22-footers adopted by the Sydney Flying Squadron when it was formed in 1891. Those 6.7 m long, 2.89 m wide, 914 mm deep vessels had evolved from commercial rowing skiffs widely used in the port for ferrying people and small packages. They carried mainsails and jibs totalling 93 sq m when racing in light weather; up to 279 sq m downwind, set on massive spars, and up to twenty men crammed on to each other's laps. At least one unfortunate crew member, usually chosen for his lighter weight, was continuously engaged in bailing out the water that slopped over the raised canvas leecloths, propped with cane posts along the leeward side, and over the 'booby', a canvas spray dodger across the bows from gunwale to gunwale. The most vigorous of the bailer boys were highly prized but at the end of a race some, bruised and trampled, were in such a state of exhaustion that they had to be lifted out of the boats. Strong, skilful men were needed, too, to manhandle the maze of sheets, halyards and tackles that controlled the set of the sails. The work, and therefore a great deal of the success or failure of a boat, invariably fell upon three key for'ard hands and a brawny mainsheet hauler, although the rest of the crew, the swingers, had to be well organized, too, especially on beats to windward, so that they transferred their weight evenly from side to side as the craft tacked. Four men were needed to raise the 2.44 m deep, 10 mm thick steel centreboard in its case for runs downwind. A capsize was a major disaster. The boats could not be righted, since they had no reserve buoyancy tanks, and it could take an hour of floundering in the water to unrig the gear before the craft could be towed to safety.

Preposterous spread of canvas on Norman Abrahams' three-man 6-footer (of 6 ft beam) *Emily* sailing on Sydney Harbour in 1898. (Norman Abrahams)

The much more refined 18-footers, which gradually replaced the 22-footers in the late 1890s, were still monstrous by today's standards. In light weather they set a total of 79.5 sq m of sail on beats to windward, on booms 8.84 m long, gaffs of 5.49 m, and bowsprits jutting 6.1 m from their stems, and carried ballooners of 43.7 sq m from the masthead and spinnakers of 80.4 sq m rigged to ferruled poles of 12.19 m overall length. They had topsails, too, and some added 37.2 sq m ringtails down the leeches of their mainsails for square runs, and watersails under their booms. The overall width of such a manifestation, from the end of the spinnaker pole to the end of the ringtail spar, was 21.64 m, as wide as Sydney's George Street at the GPO, with the spoon-shaped boat, 2.6 m wide, insignificant beneath it. Many of the 18-footers were skippered and crewed by wildheaded waterfront characters — wharf labourers, out-of-season footballers, slaughtermen, fishermen, professional boatsmen — with a natural talent for bravado, little consideration for the niceties of maritime etiquette and an unquenchable thirst for outrage and beer. The brawls between some of them were notorious; they fouled, boarded, punched, kicked and capsized each other and used language that turned the Harbour bluer than the summer skies. Spectators, delighted at these donnybrooks and the tremendous sailing skills displayed, crowded on to following ferry boats and on to Harbour vantage points (the best spot was Bradley's Head, known as Scotchman's Hill because there one saw the race without paying the price of a ferry ticket) and laid bets on the outcome. Referees, not time-keepers, were required to name the winners. There were less rowdy and even gentle-mannered skippers and crews among the 18-footer sailors, too, and some prominent businessmen, including bank managers, engineers and solicitors, and at least one academic. Their club founder, commodore and, later, life patron, was a wealthy and assertive draper, Mark Foy. It was he who first thought of carrying coloured symbols on the mainsails instead of identifying numbers. Foy could quell the rowdiest club meeting, arguing the rights and wrongs of a collision merely by rising to his feet. 'Quiet, you ignorants,' someone would shout, 'The Boss is going to give a ruling.' In his younger days Foy had rebelled against the yachting establishment and, by threatening to run rival functions (he held one in 1892), had bludgeoned the committee of Sydney's Anniversary Regatta into accepting the entries of his Squadron's boats, in spite of the outlandish coloured signs on their sails. Foy was also not averse to some sea lawyering on his own behalf. When his entry of the catamaran, *Flying Fish*, was rejected from an early club race on the grounds that its length exceeded the maximum allowed, he hurried to Double Bay, roused the boatbuilder Billy Messenger from his bed, and instructed him to lop off the stern of both hulls and to rebuild them before the weekend so that Foy could qualify. Foy won the race, too, but later helped to rewrite the rules that defined an eligible contestant for SFS races as a boat of one hull, not two.

Foy's permanent memorial at the club he founded is a particularly hideous trophy, the Anglo-Australian Shield. He acquired it for the SFS in peculiar circumstances. Foy was in England on a business trip in 1898, boasting freely about the speed of Australian boats in the club of which he was then commodore, when, almost as if in answer to the silent prayers of his audiences, his nemesis arrived in the hold of a ship. She was the former champion Sydney 22-footer *Irex*, sent as a gift, with all her equipment, by Foy's friend, James Macken, who had bought her from a man who had won her in a raffle. Foy was inordinately proud of the boat and ignored the fact that *Irex* was badly strained, leaked like

Illuminated memorial celebrating Mark Foy's famous challenge in 1898 with the 22-footer *Irex* for the Anglo–Australian Shield. (*SMH*)

Sydney Flying Squadron founder Mark Foy (standing centre) with his twelve-man crew of *Irex* which raced Britain's *Maid of Kent* in 1898. Author's uncle, Albert d'Alpuget, wearing fine moustache, is sixth from left. (Mrs M. McCahey)

a basket, had sails that were stretched out of shape, and was of a hull form that had long been superseded. He challenged the British to put up a boat for a match race against *Irex*, with the only proviso that the defender should not exceed 16.3 m when its overall length was added to its waterline length and to its beam — a scale of measurement with which *Irex*'s plumb stem and stern of 6.7 m and beam of 2.9 m complied. Foy did not care what rig, size of sails or crew his rival carried or whether it was of fixed keel or centreboard, was decked-in or completely open, like *Irex*.

The English needed considerable urging but ultimately agreed to sail three races over twelve-mile courses on the River Medway, and nominated a beautifullyproportioned 7.32 m, centreboard yacht *Maid of Kent*, a sloop designed by Linton Hope, one of Europe's leading naval architects. She was 6.7 m on the waterline, 2.29 m beam, completely decked, carried 56 sq m of sail on a standing lug rig, and was less than half the weight of the Australian boat. She also needed a crew of only six, as against *Irex*'s minimum of twelve and, as Foy was to learn later, few craft anywhere near *Maid of Kent*'s size in England could match her for speed, upwind or down. When the English announced that Mrs Maud Wyllie, wife of the head of the syndicate that owned *Maid of Kent*, would skipper the yacht, Foy gallantly replied that he would normally hesitate to defeat a lady, but, since a challenge was a challenge, he must not let chivalry stand in the way. If the poor deluded fellow had made a few inquiries he would have learned that there was no need for pretty speeches. Maud Wyllie was not only one of the best helmswomen in Europe; few men were her equal on the tricky tidal waters of the Medway. She gave Foy and his crew of live ballast, who were recruited largely from Australians living in England, with little sailing experience, a dreadful drubbing. *Maid of Kent* won by 10m 53s, by 3m 25s, and by 22m. *Irex* blundered around the courses. Only in the second race, on one windward leg, when she led at one rounding mark, did she show any promise.

Foy took his defeat well and made no complaint at the celebratory banquet for the crews, but then he began to brood about it, and asked for a re-match. As he and his supporters warmed to that idea, Foy claimed that the River Medway was really no place to race and that honour could be satisfied only with races on clear, open waters, such as the Solent, off the south coast of England. The English replied that *Irex* would still be no match wherever they sailed. So Foy returned to Sydney, had built a decked yacht similar in shape to *Maid of Kent*, which he called *Southerly Buster*, and shipped her to England, this time demanding a match 'for any side wager the British cared to nominate'. He got a series of polite but firm refusals. It was rumoured that English yachtsmen feared he would bring over a crew of Australian professionals to man his boat, and also that certain Australian yachting officials had written to the Royal Yacht Squadron advising that the aggressive draper was not challenging with their approval. Foy was furious. He petitioned English clubs, made statements to newspapers about his treatment, and his enthusiasm did not wane until, after five years, the English — it was said under pressure by King Edward VII — sent him the Anglo-Australian Shield that had been made for the first challenge and had been won by Mrs Wyllie. Foy maintained until his dying day, at the age of eighty-five in 1950, that under reasonable conditions *Southerly Buster* would have beaten the English, and that he had rightly won the trophy by default. Over the years a series of baseless legends had grown about Foy's efforts: that the English cheated in the races between *Irex* and *Maid of Kent*; that they had to race over sandbanks that favoured the shallow-drafted English boat; that *Irex* was nobbled and was fouled by spectator craft. Foy used to deny these stories but the roots of them sank deep and a tree of lies stood where once only a twig of truth had grown. Some of the leaves of this arboreal fiction still rustle when old timers, standing before the historic trophy in the Squadron's harbourside clubhouse, relate the stories their fathers told them about its acquisition. It is perhaps no wonder that the English, with long memories for contumacious behaviour, in subsequent years were reluctant to engage in challenge contests, whoever proposed them, against Australian modern 18-footers, and why, until a few years ago, they had never seen such electrifying craft in action on their home waters.

But in Australia the class has always prospered. Queenslanders, in Brisbane, Cairns and Townsville, and, for many years, West Australians, in Perth, who won national titles in 1907, 1912 and 1922, adopted them. (WA interest declined and died in 1938 but was resurrected in 1978 with a fleet of six boats, two of which competed unsuccessfully in Sydney for the world series in January 1979.) Constant support for the 18s has always centred on Sydney Harbour, where the class began, and races have been held weekly for six months through spring and summer for eighty-nine years. On only five occasions have SFS races been cancelled — as a mark of respect after the death of King Edward VII in 1911; in mourning for the victims of the *Greycliffe* ferry disaster on Sydney Harbour in 1927; and, in recent times, when 60 k storms swept the course. 'Few sailing classes in the world can boast such a record,' says Bob Lundie, formerly for twenty-five years president of Sydney Flying Squadron, who began sailing with the club in 1928 and did not miss a race, either as a competitor or as a spectator, in fifty years. In the early 1900s the now-defunct Sydney Sailing Club held races for the 18s, but they amalgamated with the Squadron fleet. In 1980 a few former Sydney 18s of modern construction were sailing on Lake Burley Griffin, in Canberra, and at St George's Basin, on the south coast of NSW.

The 'troopships', as the early boats are now derogatorily called because of their big crews, continued with few changes except refinements in rig and bigger peakhead spinnakers until the early 1930s. Then, in 1933, a sensational Queensland boat called *Aberdare*, skippered by Vic Vaughan, of Brisbane, arrived on the scene. She was only 2.13 m in maximum beam, inside her 50 mm gunwales, and so was at least 150 mm narrower and a little shallower than most of her rivals; was incorrectly called a 'skiff type' because she had no built-in heel or skeg under her transom (she nevertheless carried leecloths and a small foredeck across her bows, which qualified her as a dinghy); had slightly smaller sails than usual; and had a crew of only seven. Upwind, despite *Aberdare*'s alleged lack of directional stability and grip of the water that a heel was supposed to give a boat, she outpointed the heavyweights, and downwind she left them standing. With a gale behind her she was once credited with a speed of 23 k during a quarter-mile burst. In Brisbane her supporters called her 'The Galloping Ghost'. Apart from winning the national title in Brisbane in 1934, a two-State affair between NSW and Queensland, *Aberdare* turned the class topsy-turvy. She was condemned by Sydney's traditionalists as a narrow-gutted mistake that would destroy the spectacle of boats racing under big sails with big crews, and would therefore drive supporters away. Progressive elements disagreed. Bob Cuneo, a Sydney-based bond-store manager and a member of the Brisbane sailing family who were later to produce one of our great Olympic and America's Cup helmsmen, John Cuneo, defiantly built one of the northern 18-footers and called her *The Mistake* to emphasize the point. The boat had a huge black and white sail symbol that showed the figure '2' added to '2' and gave '5' as the answer. *The Mistake* in unofficial trials mowed down the locals and was banned from racing unless she carried ten men as a penalty handicap. Besides the hard-driving skipper Cuneo, her crew was led by Stan Higgins, a for'ard hand renowned for the speed and daring of his spinnaker sets, and who later, as a sailing administrator, for many years guided the development of the 18s. Arguments raged for a year until the SFS, although it then had no definite limitation on minimum beam, rejected all boats of 2.13 m and narrower beam and withdrew from interstate racing against the rebel Queenslanders. For two years, between 1935 and 1937, the SFS staged national title series between orthodox boats representing NSW and Queensland's Brisbane Flying Squadron. Then the latter club disbanded and these events lapsed.

Meanwhile the field was left open to a breakaway club. The NSW 18 Footers' League (later renamed the NSW 18 Footers Sailing Club) was formed in 1935. The new club's founder, secretary and organizer was James J. Giltinan, a veteran sporting entrepreneur, who twenty-nine years earlier had encouraged and engineered a similar breakaway in football, the Rugby League code from Rugby

Top left In light weather in the early 1930s the 18-footer *Britannia* (right) spread her 55.7 sq m mainsail on a boom of 9.45 m, a gaff of 7.01 m, and hoisted it 6.4 m up her mast. Her jib measured 22.3 sq m. It took fourteen men to balance the rig. To leeward is the much more conservatively rigged *Miranda*. *(SMH)*

Top right Famous Robinson family of East Balmain Sydney, with 'Wee Georgie' Robinson on the helm and Bob Lundie for'ard hand, drive *Britannia* before a north-easterly gale on Sydney Harbour in 1930. (Bob Lundie)

Bottom Men and boys, triple-banked in places, on the windward gunwale as Australian champion 18-footer *Arawatta*, skippered by Charlie Hayes, ploughs down Sydney Harbour. (Barry Clarke)

Union. Under Giltinan's genius for promotion, and with the help of the lively committee he enlisted, the NSW 18 Footers' League, racing on Sunday afternoons (when no other organized sporting events were held) instead of Saturdays like the SFS, was an instant success. Soon a fleet of seven large ferries packed with up to 7,000 spectators, with bookmakers calling the odds, was following the light, narrow-beamed boats. The League also welcomed old-style craft, carefully awarding time-at-the-start handicaps to give all-comers a chance at the £12 first prize. Even appearance money was promised for all starters in subsequent seasons. Sydney's Monday morning semi-tabloid newspaper, the *Daily Telegraph*, devoted most of its back page to stories and pictures of each Sunday race, and detailed the performances of the runners and their prices like horse races. Sailing races had never previously been covered in such a manner. It increased the 18-footers' popularity tremendously. The amounts of money bet on the ferries were not large — the biggest single wager recorded on one boat was £500 but the NSW State Government, prodded by opponents of all forms of gambling, ultimately declared public ferries on the Harbour in the same category as streets, and conducted raids on the bookmakers who, until then, had openly displayed betting boards and had altered the odds in running as the pattern of a race developed. The public bitterly resented the official interference with their weekend flutters on the boats and so, of course, did the bookmakers. One of the latter leapt overboard to avoid arrest, leaving punters with winning bets angrier than the police he had eluded. He was widely known as Dick the Diver, and it was said that he would leap overboard to avoid paying debts more readily than to escape the Law. Generally the bookmakers were straight dealers but some did retain advisers with good sailing knowledge to help them keep their books 'round' if not profitable. This practice was one of the arguments raised against betting on the sailing races. Dark stories abounded, too, of crews bribed to lose races. The bookmakers, hounded and sometimes arrested on the League's ferries, hired private launches for their clientele, to elude police raids. The League displayed notices on its official ferries warning that betting was illegal and urged, instead, the purchase of tickets in club sweeps at two shillings each, in order to sustain patrons' interest. But clandestine betting continued, and still does, although with so many rival sporting attractions now held on Sundays, crowds following the 18-footers have dwindled.

During the pre-World War II period, to encourage the spread of the class, the League bent its own liberal rules to allow a group of NZ 18 ft sloops — highly refined, bermudan-rigged, half-decked centreboard yachts, really — to race in 1938 for what was called a world title series on Sydney Harbour. The Sydney boat, *Taree*, skippered by Bert Swinbourne, of Botany, and a superbly drilled crew, won the championship after a dramatic battle. In one of the races a 60 k southerly buster spread-eagled the fleet from one end of the Harbour to the other but the men aboard proved they were seamen of a high order and although one New Zealander capsized, most boats survived to regroup in the ensuing calm for a drift to the finish. The New Zealanders won world honours a year later with *Manu*, skippered by George Chamberlain, in a series sailed at Auckland, and so ensured a continuation of interdominion interest in the class.

Many years later, in the 1960s and early 1970s, long after the New Zealanders had adopted Australian-style boats, and the Aucklanders Don Lidgard and Bruce Farr had developed them, NZ designs were to dominate the class on both sides of the Tasman. By then the boats were not built, as they had traditionally been, merely by scaling-up a hand-carved block of wood that looked right to the eye. Science had entered the field, and the effect of the spring in the keel, the depth of a U-section behind a fine entrance, the flatness of a run aft, and the angle at which an arced bottom disappeared in a chined topside, were calculated on plans as detailed as those of any deep-keeled racing yacht.

But the evolution was slow. After World War II, when the previously recalcitrant SFS accepted the new style of lighter, narrower boats, designs began to change and some experiments in rigs and construction were encouraged. By 1946–47 crews had started to sail boats of 1.83 m beam and only 533 mm in depth amidships. Six men, and five in light weather, if they were smart enough, could race them around a course. For a while it was the NSW 18 Footers' League's turn to complain about freaks, but there was no stopping progress now. The League wisely accepted the 1.83 m-beamers after a phasing-out period for the wider boats. But both the League and the SFS called a halt when a 1.67 m-beamed boat, that persistently capsized on shy spinnaker runs and catapulted its crew into the water, was tried. Then in the early 1950s trapeze harnesses, rigged on wires high up on the mast, began to appear on the boats. (NZ's Peter Mander, world 18-footer title winner and Olympic champion in 12 sq metre Sharpies, is credited with this innovation on an 18-footer, although trapezes were already becoming popular on smaller centreboarders.) The trapezes in following seasons allowed one man, then two, three and four, and finally the skipper, operating the rudder with a 2.44 m tiller extension rod, to hang parallel with the water, feet braced on the gunwale. It gave crews tremendous leverage against the weight of the wind, although in fresh conditions they were constantly drenched with spray. To race this way crews needed a lifetime of sailing experience (most had started in small boats as infants, anyway), a high degree of physical fitness, and automatic reflexes to trim into and out of the boat in response to changes in the strength of the breeze, and they had to develop techniques and special ready-release equipment to handle the sheets and to transfer from side to side on windward beats. By 1954 featherweight hulls of plywood were gaining popularity, and five men could handle the 18s. With the lighter boats and smaller crews less area of sail was needed, and efficient fully battened, bermudan mainsails quickly replaced the old gaff and gunter rigs. Previously, bermudan rig had never been popular on 18-footers because of the difficulty of rigging a spar tall enough to carry sails big enough to power the old-style heavy boats, although boatbuilder Charlie Hayes, with a beautifully crafted hollow wooden spar (13.1 m high) had achieved it for James J. Watt's *Arawatta* in the season of 1930–31 and had won the national title in her.

In the late 1950s came sails of man-made terylene and US dacron fabric and strong but gossamer-thin spinnakers of nylon. When later they were rigged on aluminium alloy masts they reduced weight aloft and improved windward speed by a knot or more. Upwind the new lightly rigged 18s easily averaged 8 k, and average speeds downwind were 12 k, with bursts of 20 k common. 'At that stage no deep-keeled yacht three times the length could pace it with an 18-footer around a course in enclosed water,' says Bill Miller (in 1985 the League's commodore for the previous twenty-four years), who, from 1946 to 1974 had skippered a string of eight boats called *Donnelly*, five of his own design and construction. In the 1960s, four-man teams and occasionally three, on trapezes, were sailing 18-footers in all weathers, and the boats, relieved of unnecessary crew weight, were travelling faster than ever before. Two of them, *Taipan* and *Venom* radically built chiners, of thin sheets of plywood and precursors of later NZ creations, came from Brisbane. They were designed, built and skippered by the dashing young Bob Miller (now called Ben Lexcen), later to become internationally famous as the designer of champion ocean racers and the sensational America's Cup winner *Australia II*. With only two crewmen, comparatively small sails and go-fast equipment of his own concept, Miller dazzled his rivals in *Venom* and won the 1961 world title series. His boats infuriated some die-hard officials who tried hard to find technicalities in the rules to ban them. Miller contemptuously abandoned the class, predicting that in the future 18-footers would be much more daring in shape and construction, lighter and faster. 'You'll have to change your rules to suit the boats that will follow these and change your techniques of sailing, too,' he told one senior administrator. How right he was.

Sydney boatbuilder, Ken Beashel, twice world champion skipper in boats of his own design, *Schemer* and *Daily Telegraph*, who started sailing in the 18s at the age of 10 in 1946, and is the son of the late Alf Beashel (one of the founders of the League) and a grandson of Dick 'Rocko' Beashel (a champion skipper of the class in 1908), says,

> You needed more than sailing skill on the new style of boats; you had to be an acrobat and as fit as a gymnast to work any part of them. Setting a spinnaker needed perfect judgement and coordination between all aboard. The slightest mis-timing could pickle you. But by the 1960s the 18s went so fast you could get round the old nine-mile courses we used to sail in a bit over an hour. The club twice had to extend the courses, finally to fifteen miles to give the spectators a show.

By 1961 18-footers' sails had been reduced in size and crews had dwindled to five, with three on trapezes. But few boats, even under storm rig, could handle such seas as this in a 60 k blow on Sydney Harbour. *Jan*, with Jim Frazer as skipper, pictured here, capsized soon afterwards. (*SMH*)

Hobie 14, world's most popular cat-rigged catamaran class, with 75,000 sailing in 100 countries. It was designed originally by American Hobie Alter for casual single-handed surf sailing, with asymmetrical banana-shaped hulls and no centreboards, but has become a boat for racing in smooth water. (Coast Catamaran Corp).

Superlative control by Iain Murray and crewman, Andrew Buckland and Don Buckley, brings world and Australian champion 18-footer *Color* 7 onto the plane. (ATN Channel 7)

By the late 1960s chine construction was general and, with built-in buoyancy tanks that allowed a boat to be righted after a capsize, transformed the boats once again.

By the mid 1970s most boats were racing with only two crewmen and a helmsman, and the further decreases in weight brought even higher speeds and consequently greater demands on fitness and skill. Twenty-six such boats were racing with the NSW 18 Footers' League and twenty with the SFS. The newspaper, radio, and finally television coverage that these spectacular dinghies attracted, the advertising potential of the signs on the sails, and the constant repetition of their names in the news media, brought commercial sponsorship to its peak. Great coloured advertising plasters were built into their sails, and there was rarely room on the boats' transoms for their names — the lettering spread, instead, halfway and more along their topsides. But the sponsors provided money for experiment, for better boats and equipment, and subsidized their representatives on interstate and overseas trips for championship regattas. A top skipper and crew could expect their sponsor to provide a new hull, moulded of paper-thin timber veneers, every season, and three complete suits of sails and spars to match different weights of wind, with spares in case of breakages, so that no boat remained in the shed, under repair, on race days. Carefully made cradles fitted inside trailers for transport to launching sites were essential, too.

By 1980 the cost of such a new craft and a season's campaign, racing on Saturdays with the SFS and on Sundays with the club, could total $50,000. A bare hull without fittings cost $8,000. Even allowing for inflation, it was a far cry from the days when the old-style wooden-planked boats could be built for a standard £3 a foot. Today's most successful boats are moulded of thin skins of fibreglass, with kevlar or carbon-fibre, sandwiching honeycombs of klegecell foam or nomex nylon paper. Their hull weights, including fittings and paint, are only 67 kg and the hulls do not last more than a season or two under the prodigious strains of hard racing. Even for that period they need constant repair and, on the average, twenty-five hours of maintenance each week for the few hours they spend on the water. (Some of the old wooden boats, lovingly tended, lasted for twenty years of racing and then, with a few structural alterations to enable engines to be fitted, were still giving service as launches in the 1970s. In 1985, 'Wee Georgie' Robinson's powerful *Britannia*, launched in 1919 and a flyer downwind in her day, had been restored to her former glory for display in Sydney's maritime museum, and Robinson, a member of a long-lived Balmain family of champion 18-footer sailors, at the age of 92 had supervised the work.) As the hulls have got lighter their speeds have again increased. According to club records, in the early 1930s a good 18 might average 6.45 k around a nine-mile course. A modern boat averages 10.73 k around a fifteen-mile course — much faster than a 65 ft America's Cup 12-metre class yacht — with bursts of 20–30 k common on shy spinnaker reaches in fresh winds.

Magnificent trophies are provided by some sponsors and some subsidize the cash prizes paid by the clubs. By comparison with the meagre prize-money the old-timers got — £1 for a win from sweepstakes to which each boat-owner contributed — the 1986 rewards seem high. But the cash prizes that the modern boats can win are still trifles compared with the value of public exposure a consistent boat can earn its sponsor or the worth of effort and skill a crew brings to the sport. In 1985 a total of $500 was being split between the first eight place-getters (with $120 for the winner) in each of the club's weekly handicap races in the average fleet of sixteen starters. All boats got $15 for starting. The SFS split $260 between the first three boats ($100 to the winner). In special championships and point scores the winners have a chance for higher prizes. ($5,000 was total prize money for the Sydney-held 1979 world championships), but an outstanding crew cannot hope to win much more than $15,000 in cash prizes over a full season, racing twice each weekend for six months in both SFS and club events, and in title races for which the clubs now combine. By 1985 some sponsors had begun to find places on their firms' payrolls for the most successful skippers and were agreeing completely to subsidise the cost on new boats — then close to $100,000 with three rigs for different conditions — and to pay all the expense of maintenance of the boats and out-of-pocket expenses of the crews. Even so, there is no comparison with the rewards available to Sydney's Rugby League footballers and professional golfers of a comparable athletic prowess and technique. The attraction, as always, is still the challenge of sailing an extraordinary boat, poised on the edge of seemingly impossible performance.

The latest 18-footers, no longer needing the clouds of sail under which the old-timers staggered, are almost stemhead-rigged (bowsprits are now no more than a metre long from the stems), nor do they need long overhanging booms, although there are still no restrictions on the rigs or sail areas they may carry. Mainsails today average about 24 sq m; jibs, 14 sq m; and light-weather spinnakers 100 sq m. Only spinnaker halyards are carried. Mainsails and jibs are locked into their hoisted positions before a race and cannot be lowered with the boat upright. Jib luffs can be adjusted with tack downhauls, and mainsail shapes controlled by flexing the masts. Rigging tensions are pre-set and sustained with small hydraulic jacks. These can be operated underway to bend back the upper section of the mast and so flatten the head of the mainsail to de-power the rig as the wind increases. The only restrictions are on hull sizes — not less than 5.41 m or more than 5.4863 m in length; minimum beam 1.82 m — although moulded gunwale 'wings' outside this beam, sometimes extending 25 cm and more from either topside, are allowed, which make the boats 2.54 m wide overall; minimum depth 508 mm. Buoyancy compartments fore and aft are limited to 60 per cent of the volume of the hull. Many modern boats have chines moulded into the hulls and self-bailing venturi devices fitted in their bottoms with water discharge 'clappers' in their transoms. With these aids, in moderate conditions an expert crew can right its boat in half a minute after a capsize, but races are usually so hotly contested that this loss of time can often mean the difference between winning and missing a place. In 1985 all competitive boats were carrying tubular aluminium wing frames over their side decks with the outer edges extending a maximum of 3.4 m from the centreline of the hull, thereby allowing crews to trapeze further outboard and carry big sails in fresh conditions. At first sight the spectacle of three men dangling on wires so far away from the craft they are operating suggests that it is a circus performance, not to be taken seriously as a sporting competition. On the contrary, so skilled are the skippers at using 6 m tiller extension rods to steer their boats and the crews at working the equipment that the craft are rarely out of control. By 1985 self-tacking jibs were fitted, so reducing the work of the for'ard hands on beats to windward, and very few 18s carried orthodox spinnaker poles. Instead, most were built with extraordinary nose poles, of light but strong carbon fibreglass or aluminium tubes, jutting almost 5 m out from their stems. Some were half telescopic. On these long, unstayed and semi-stayed types of bowsprit a new style of

Top By 1971 four men, all on trapezes, were sailing 18-footers with the skipper (here Brian Zemanek in *Century Battery*) operating a 2.43 m tiller rod. But most boats still had conventional transoms and topsides. By 1980 they also carried tubular swing-frames for trapezing. (*SMH*)

Bottom Space-age version of the 18-footer. Widely flared topsides, extended wing decks, enabled gymnastic teams of three, like these on Iain Murray's champion *Color 7*, to hike 3 m outboard from the centreline of the boats and to drive the featherweight machines to windward with extraordinary efficiency. (*SMH*)

Modern 18s carry much less sail than earlier boats but, with only 64 kg hull weight and three men to carry, regularly plane downwind at speeds of 25 k, like Dave Porter's former world champion *KB*, pictured here. (*SMH*)

'balloonaker', a cross between a ballooner and a spinnaker, was set for runs and reaches. The theory behind their use was that, since the boats easily reached enough speed to pull the apparent wind well forward, one did not effectively run square downwind. It was therefore better to carry the breeze a little abaft the beam in a sail that was flatter cut than the usual parachute spinnaker and fasten the tack of the sail well forward in a set position. Without a movable spinnaker pole and its braces and foreguy to handle, gybing one of the new type of downwind sails was quick and easy. Over 3 nm, a series of so-called tacks downwind could save minutes compared with times taken when using orthodox running gear. Some supporters of the 18s saw the development of this new style of Formula One racing machine as a natural application of technical knowledge and skill. Others, appalled at the sight of the featherweight structures that could no longer be expected to weather a blow or a really choppy sea and that were constantly prone to gear failure and to thousands of dollars of damage if they came into collision with each other, pronounced the boats ungainly freaks and races between them no longer tactical endeavours but merely skid tests in floating billboards to amuse spectators.

If one accepts the time-honoured Australian definition of a sailing skiff (compared with a dinghy) as a completely open boat without side decks or foredeck, a booby and leecloths, then the modern 18s cannot be called skiffs, as they are so often described. They have no leecloths or booby but with their extended wing decks, enclosed foredecks over buoyancy compartments, they should strictly be called dinghies. In any case, no one would recognize the early 18s as the forerunners of the latest Grand Prix performers, or could accurately compare the gunwale swingers of the old days with the lithe young athletes who sail the boats of today. But veteran fans still talk with awe of the great natural sailing ability of the phlegmatic Chris Webb, who was credited with seven national championships between 1907 and 1927 (four officially, after the conditions of those title events were standardized) and who was still able to steer a boat until his eyesight began to fail at eighty years of age. In following era Lance Watts, of Brisbane (still living in 1985, aged ninety-six) and, in later styles of boats, Len Heffernan, of Sydney, won five national titles. Vic Vaughan, of Brisbane, won four national titles in succession between 1933 and 1937, in *Aberdare*. Norm Wright, of Brisbane, and Bill Barnett, of Sydney, both famous for their skill as shipwrights who also skippered keel yachts (Wright won a national Dragon class title) each won four national 18-footer titles. But an achievement that stood on the record books for many years was that of Bob Holmes, a small man, highly intelligent and extremely polite afloat and ashore, and equally brilliant at the helm of the biggest ocean racer and the smallest dinghy. In the 18-footer *Travelodge*, Holmes won four national titles and five world titles between 1965 and 1973. That record was ultimately eclipsed by the massive young sailor Iain Murray, of Sydney, a designer-builder-skipper who, between 1977 and 1982, won five consecutive national titles and six consecutive world titles in his scarlet-hulled boats called *Color 7*, sponsored by the television Station ATN7 (to be strictly correct, the first boat to win the world championship was called *7 Color*). In most races, Murray sailed with Andrew Buckland as his mainsheet hand and Don Buckley as for'ard hand. They all worked together

World champion 18-footer in 1984–85 *Bradmill*, skippered by America's Cup squad crewman Rob Brown, planes at 20 k with all hands trapezing on hiking frames. In 1986 Brown successfully defended his title in Auckland, NZ, in a new boat, *Entrad*.

with bewildering efficiency. At twenty-five years of age Murray retired from the 18s undefeated to sail keelboats in round-the-buoys races inshore and offshore in major ocean races. He won a world title in the 9.14 m Etchells 22 class and became helmsman of America's Cup contenders.

For two years after Murray's retirement his friend and close rival, skipper Peter Sorensen, a gymnastic Sydney solicitor, won the world title in boats called *Tia Maria* designed by Murray and built (of carbon fibre and nomex honeycomb then baked in an autoclave) by Sorensen's quite remarkable wife Marilyn, herself a highly competent boatswoman. Sorensen's crew were David Stephens and Andrew Buckland. Pressing them hard were Trevor Barnabas in *Chesty Bond*, Rob Brown in *Bradmill*, and Tony Scali in *Nick Scali Furniture*. Then, in season 1984–85, Rob Brown, fresh from Newport, Rhode Island, where he had been a member of the victorious *Australia II* America's Cup squad, put together a dynamic series of wins in the NSW, national and world championships in a new boat of his own design called *Bradmill*. His assistant in the design was Dr Peter van Oossanen, director of the Netherlands Ship Model Basin where Ben Lexcen had designed *Australia II* for the America's Cup. Brown's boat did not have a winged keel but a hollow area in her afterbody designed to concentrate air pressure and make her plane. *Bradmill* was a great success but she had fierce competition. Brown won the NSW title, with Barnabas second on points, in a last-heat, last minute tactical duel, against the skinny two-handed boat, *Prime Computers*, when he cut corners in a fading easterly and got the gun by nine seconds. He overwhelmed his rivals in the national championship with three straight wins, then a fourth, third, and second. He could not be beaten on points and did not need to start in the last race but tried to do so as a duty to his sponsors. On the way to the start on Sydney Harbour, *Bradmill* collided with a yacht and Brown was catapulted overboard on to his rudder and broke it.

In the world titles on Waterloo Bay, Brisbane, Brown won a most contentious series in which he placed 3, dsq 2, 3, 1, 2, 1. He was disqualified for tacking in a rival's path and twice had appeals disallowed by higher authorities. Hot favourite *Chesty Bond* twice snapped off her centreboard and in a collision (with *Bradmill*) was severely holed; and title holder, *Tia Maria*, clear points leader in the last race and needing to finish only fourth, broke her nosepole and retired.

In a subsequent 25 nm Ocean Classic Championship from Pittwater, north of Sydney, to the Opera House in Sydney Harbour — the first in which 18-footers had raced outside sheltered waters — Brown, in *Bradmill*, was more than half a mile in front when the rudder of his boat snapped off and he had to be towed home by his shadowing tender. Barnabas, in *Chesty Bond*, and Sorensen, in *Tia Maria*, then took the lead and scudded, almost side by side, before the fresh, following north-east breeze for the next 9 nm. Barnabas and his crew Adam South and Phil Barnett snatched the lead at the finish to win by one second with Englishman Jeremy Sharp, sailing a two-man boat, *Control Data*, in third place, They averaged almost 15 k for the course. Between Barranjoey Headland and North Head, at the entrance to Sydney Harbour, a distance of 15.6 nm, they averaged 20 k.

At the end of the season Brown had acquired an impressive shelf-full of trophies and $3,000 prizemoney, and Barnabas, victor in the 'money races', had won a record $15,000 in prize money. Both were smiling and so were their sponsors who backed them for new boats of even more adventuresome high tech development in the 1986 season.

8

Sixteen and Twelve Foot Skiffs: Speed and Gymnastics

SIXTEEN FOOTERS

'ANYONE who can sail a 16 ft skiff can sail anything', said the late Stan Stevens, a champion Sydney helmsman in yachts of many classes and a member of one of Australia's pioneer sailing families. 'In fresh breezes they are the crankiest, the most unforgiving and the fastest boats their length in this country or any other.' As Stevens knew the 16s — and from 1901 to 1946 he had seen forty years of sailing in these so-called Port Jackson Skiffs — he was right. They were narrow, shallow centreboarders, completely open from stem to stern with no decking at all. They had no leecloths like the 18-footers, and the only barrier to a quick swim over the leeward side, just lipping the water, was a 50 mm gunwale around the top plank with a 25 mm saxboard inside it. On the windward side, over these narrow, thigh-grinding pieces of timber, the three-man crews, or four in hard weather, and often the skipper as well, hooked their legs into straps and hiked out to balance the weight of wind in the sails. Nothing kept a 16 afloat in a gusty breeze on choppy water except lightning reflexes by the man on the helm and the sheet trimmers spilling wind from the sails, and a frantic bailer-boy flailing non-stop with a scoop on a handle. Once capsized there was no way of righting the boat. It had to be unrigged and towed to shallow water before it could be emptied. Devotees of the class — in NSW, Queensland and Western Australia, where the 16s spread and are still popular — were justly proud of their skill in staying afloat, regardless of where they finished in races. The class has recently been re-introduced into Victoria, and Frankston Yacht Club, Port Phillip, was chosen as the venue for the 1985–86 national title series.

The 16s are Australian originals, like the 18-footers and 12-footers, and have remained completely open, true skiffs, governed by strict rules and limitations, since the foundation of the class in 1901. (With winged sidedecks and flush

215

foredecks from gunwale to gunwale, enclosing buoyancy tanks, 18s, by strictest definition, come into the category of dinghies.)

But although the threat of a capsize is constant it is no longer the end of the race for a 16 as it was in former years. Since 1958, when buoyancy tanks were permitted, a good crew has been able to get a boat up inside a minute and sail on. The boats now also have self-bailing devices in their underbodies and are allowed a 4,000 sq mm drain hole in their transoms. However, the rules governing the buoyancy tanks – at the most, no further than 1,830 mm from the stem or 915 mm from the stern, and all at least 100 mm below the gunwales – ensure that they cannot be used to prevent water entering the boat, and therefore the premium on good handling is preserved. In hull concepts, weight and rig, though, the 16s have experienced a metamorphosis. They are no longer the round-bilged, 155 kg, 8 mm cedar-planked and seambattened boats, with 38 mm by 10 mm timbers that were *de rigeur* until the mid-1950s. First came the chiners, built of sheet plywood, later of moulded veneers. Then they sported trapeze wires from which two members of the crew were allowed to swing at any one time. Concurrently they gained lightweight sails of terylene and nylon on bermudan-rigged alloy masts. The boats are now much easier to control, much less demanding physically on crews than in previous years, and this has contributed greatly to their continued popularity, especially with mature men who are still active and enjoy the excitement of speed sailing but who no longer have the agility and endurance of their youth. And the 16-footers today, although they are easier to sail than they used to be, travel faster, upwind and down, than at any time in their long history. They readily plane to windward in fresh breezes, and on a close reach in hard weather are not much slower than most modern 18-footers. Bursts of 20 k under a shy spinnaker are common. The 16s are no match for the 18s on other points of sailing or in light weather because the bigger boats have no limit on sail sizes and rarely carry more than three men, including the helmsman. In match races conducted occasionally, modern 18s concede 16s starts of about ten minutes around a 15 nm course.

Administrators of the 16s have retained strict limitations on sail sizes and by modern standards the boats are under-rigged for light weather, and over-crewed. There is no doubt that they would travel faster and would probably become popular overseas if the class rules allowed a skipper and two crewmen to sail them. But no fewer than four people, including a skipper, are permitted to race the boats and, to prevent lightweight infants being used to make up the number, no crewman under the age of twelve years is allowed to sail. A fifth person may be carried if required but only two persons can be on the trapezes at any one time. The Australian 16 Ft Skiff Association has successfully resisted many attempts to reduce crew numbers. It maintains that this would cause a decline in the strong club interest and support the class enjoys. But in 1985 it was under strong pressure to change its mind and in some clubs' races, three-man boats were accepted. By mid-1986 a general change seemed imminent.

Although concepts of hull shapes have changed radically, the measurement limits, except for a 76.2 mm increase to 1.22 m in transom width, have changed only 2 mm since they were laid down in 1901. In 1980, on the eve of the Association's conversion to approximately equivalent metric measurements, except for the name of the class which remained 16 ft skiff, the limits were: minimum length, approximately 4,800 mm; maximum length, 4,880 mm; minimum beam, 1,524 mm; maximum beam, 1,680 mm; minimum depth,

Left With minimum crews of four, minimum weight limits on hulls, and restricted sail sizes, 16 ft skiffs need fresh winds to bring them to high speeds. But then they plane. (*SMH*)

Right This crew in the 1974-75 national champion 16 ft skiff *Viggers Shondell* from Belmont, NSW, pile to windward to keep their boat on her feet in a snorting southerly blow. (*SMH*)

480 mm; maximum depth, 560 mm. Total area of mainsail and jib was 20.5 sq m; maximum area of spinnaker 13 sq m; maximum area of ballooner 13 sq m. In 1982, spinnaker areas were increased to 30 sq m and, with modified rigging, could be set from the masthead. It greatly increased the boats' speed, especially in light weather. No restrictions are placed on materials that may be used in construction but the minimum hull weight allowed for many years was 68 kg, increased in late 1979 to 70 kg, and since this is easily achieved with glue-moulded wooden laminates that are tremendously strong and, more important, fairly durable, there was little incentive to use exotic and more expensive materials to reduce weight. But by 1986, completely water-resistant moulded hulls of fibreglass-foam sandwich construction were most popular.

Still, a modern, fully-equipped 16, with a reasonable wardrobe of sails, can cost $20,000, so many crews combine into syndicates and share the costs and labour of maintaining their boats. Others have turned to commercial sponsors for support and provide them in return with boats named after their products that get news media publicity when they perform well and, like the 18-footers and 12-footers, carry advertising symbols, instead of distinguishing numbers, on their mainsails. But the sponsorship of the 16s, unlike that of the modern 18s, most of which are fully supported, rarely covers more than part of the purchase and outfitting of a boat. It usually pays only for replacement of gear and maintenance. About two-thirds of the best boats in NSW and Queensland get some commercial sponsorship but three in the NSW team of twelve that represented the State in the 1979 Australian championship in Perth were individually owned and not sponsored. By 1985, all the team of twelve NSW boats, nine of the WA boats, two of the Queensland boats and two of the four Victorian boats were sponsored. NSW and Queensland had for many years placed no restriction on commercial sponsorship but the WA Yachting Association, with which the local 16 ft skiff club is affiliated, had until 1980 refused to permit it. This, the club claimed, was seriously hampering the growth of the class in Perth. WA nevertheless had a good record of successes in national title races, having won eleven championships. The Perth skipper, Jack Cassidy, won six national titles between 1954 and 1964 — more than any other 16 ft skiff sailor in any State.

Probably more important than the sponsorship of boats are the valuable trophies and generous cash prizes that commercial firms provide for important races. Prize money for the 1979 NSW championship series totalled $5,000, with $150 for the winner of each of the four heats. Prize money for the 1979 national titles totalled $2,800. An outstanding champion boat, like *Buckle Toyota*, sponsored by a car dealer and formerly skippered by Trevor Barnabas, of Manly (Sydney) club, who in 1979 was national champion helmsman for the third consecutive time, may win $2,000 in cash prizes in a season, as well as valuable and useful trophies. One of Barnabas' trophies was a colour television set. Dennis Tanko, of St George (Sydney) Club, in his dual national champion *Allen Burwood Calendars*, in 1984 and 1985 probably won at least as much in cash and trophies. A prize that has eluded Barnabas, and Tanko, and thousands of other champion helmsmen who have sailed for it, is the Dumaresq Cup, a handsome silver trophy given to the 16 Ft Skiff Association in 1922 by John Saumarez Dumaresq, our first Australian-born Navy admiral and a keen open-boat sailor, for an annual interclub handicap and fiercely contested every year since. Apart from commercial sponsors' support, the great strength of the 16 ft skiff movement, which officials jealously guard, is the wealthy NSW clubs that they have developed. These clubs, enriched by poker machine profits, give cash prizes for weekly handicaps, interclub and zone championships and State and national title regattas. One NSW skiff club, at Belmont on Lake Macquarie, in 1986 had 9,000 members, by far the greatest number in any yachting or sailing club in Australia. Belmont strongly supports the 212 members sailing the 28 skiffs on its register, encourages yachtsmen in other classes, and provides excellent facilities for them and its thousands of social members in its $4 million clubhouse. In 1984, Belmont race secretary Colin Dingle headed a committee that organized an Hawaiian tour of ten Australian 16s and a party of 110 skippers and crews and their families for a series of demonstration races in Pearl Harbour and over Waikiki Yacht Club's near offshore courses. It was so successful, that at the time of writing he was planning a similar tour for twenty boats with a party of 200 for 1986.

Other NSW 16 ft skiff clubs, with fine clubhouses and big memberships are: Drummoyne, 4,000 senior members and 34 boats; Georges River, 3,500 – 20; Illawarra, 3,000 – 14; St George 3,000 – 30; Yarra Bay, 1,500 – 13; In 1986 there were ten 16 ft skiff clubs in NSW, with a total membership of 30,000 and 200 boats registered for racing. In Queensland, clubs in Brisbane, Cairns, Townsville, Bowen and Maryborough had 40 boats registered for racing, and in WA one club at Perth had 14 boats registered. More than 1,600 helmsmen and crewmen race the boats every weekend throughout Australia's spring and summer. Most of the NSW clubs also organize races in other types of sailboats — lively little dinghies for youngsters who might later qualify for the faster skiffs, and less demanding craft for former skiff sailors who have grown too heavy — 13½ stone (86 kg) is generally considered the maximum weight for any crewman or skipper in a competitive 16. Drummoyne club in 1986 had a fleet of 32 trailer-sailers on its register, and junior divisions of Flying 11, and Sabot dinghy classes. It also had an annual financial turnover of more than $1,190,000, made sales of more than $524,000 on liquor and tobacco, and took $621,000 on its poker machines, paid licence fees and taxes of $160,000, and cleared a profit of $56,000. Many senior yacht club officials, struggling to balance their budgets, look with envy on the booming successes of the skiff organizations.

On another issue, however, the attitude of the hierarchy of yachting associations in NSW and Queensland towards the club and State 16 ft skiff organizations is not wishful thinking but disapproval. This is the refusal of these skiff bodies fully to adopt the International Yacht Racing Union's racing rules. These rules govern races in all other classes of sailing craft, from the biggest deep keel yachts to the smallest dinghies including, in recent years, 18-footers and 12-footers. But administrators of the 16 ft skiff class refuse to accept the rules as entirely applicable to their races, and, although they have adopted most of them, they insist on retaining umpires (except since 1982 in national championships) at starting lines and at strategic places around the courses, to control the boats. These umpires have the right to disqualify competitors and order them off the course at any stage of a race. Disqualified boats may, however, sail on under protest. Under the IYRU system, interpretation of the racing rules is left to individual helmsmen, who are expected to behave honourably and withdraw if they commit a gross breach, even accidentally, and who are encouraged to protest against each other with flag signals for technical breaches during races, and in writing after races. Some 16 ft clubs and associations also allow written protests by individual helmsmen against each other after races and written appeals against umpires' rulings. They contend, nevertheless, that the chance of an immediate warning off the course keeps racing clean. The Yachting Association's view is that the honour system, with protests if necessary after races, is preferable, that it is impossible for umpires to police all breaches of the rules that may occur around a course, and that many 16 ft skiff sailors ignore the rules if they think the umpire is not watching them. They cite instances of rule breaches at mass starts of 100 boats that no yachtsmen racing under the IYRU system would dare commit. Indeed, some officials have been known to declare vehemently that the 16s' races appear to be conducted under rules devised on the spur of the moment by Patrick Rafferty himself. Skiff administrators, on the other hand, present cases of IYRU sailors failing to protest against breaches that would earn instant disqualification by the 16s umpires. Ken Beashel, of Sydney, former NSW and Australian champion helmsman in 16 ft skiffs, twice world champion in 18-footers and an outstanding helmsman in a variety of yachts, says,

> I've raced for many years under both the 16s' and the IYRU systems and I'm not sure which I'd prefer. In my wild youth I once wanted to job a 16-footer umpire who I thought had disqualified me unfairly, and I suppose at that time I thought the system was bad. But in the top bracket of 16 ft skiff sailors you don't get any more deliberate or silly breaches of the rules than in some of the important keel yacht races I've sailed. The umpires in the 16s might dispense rough justice and miss a lot but their presence usually keeps everyone on his toes. I sometimes think an umpire or two might help to keep some keelboat sailors honest.

So the 16-footer men generally are happy with their rules, and they insist that their races are sailed in the best spirit of understanding camaraderie. Many of their champion helmsmen and crews remain faithful to the class throughout their sailing lives, and hundreds, delighted with the speed and excitement that the boats provide, compete well past middle age. Many of their sons and grandsons follow them into the class. The five Price brothers, Harry (skipper), Ted, Ern, Jim and Alf, of Port Jackson club, raced together in various 16s for more than twenty years. One of their boats, *Valete*, built in 1911, was still sailing competitively until 1930. Among their Port Jackson club rivals were the Rodrick brothers, Arthur (skipper), Ernie, Dave and Bill, in *Arlene* and other skiffs. They were cousins of Horace Rodrick, first national champion in 1909–10. William 'Billo' Hayward, twice national champion in 16s, national and world champion in 18s, and widely regarded by all open boat sailors as one of Australia's greatest helmsmen, tacticians and seamen, usually sailed with his sons, Jack and Tom, in his crews. As a young man Hayward, in his 16-footer, *St George*, was the only skipper still afloat and racing after a 60 k storm wrecked the big fleet in the inaugural 1922 Dumaresq Cup handicap on Botany Bay. Officials abandoned the event but Hayward won the resail.

In 1980, NSW 16 Ft Skiff Association treasurer, Frank Bonnitcha, fifty-six years of age, and his life-long friend, Max Boyle, fifty-five, commodore of Drummoyne club, had sailed together, either as for'ard hand or helmsman, for thirty-six years and had raced in ten boats called *Action*. They retired from the 16s after forty years in the class in 1983, but sailed together in a more sedate Hartley TS16 class centreboarder, which they jocularly named *Jerryaction*. In 1985 Bonnitcha's son, David, then thirty-six, who began sailing as his father's bailer-boy, was commodore of Drummoyne club and skipper of the champion boat *Red Nymph*. And in 1985 St George Club's famous former president Hamilton (Pat) Collis, seventy-six years of age and patron of the NSW Association, was preparing for his sixtieth year of skippering 16 ft skiffs. This was in *Verity* one of the twenty-four with a name starting with a 'V' he had owned during his long career and in which he had won every title except the national. Collis' two middle-aged sons, Brian and Laurie, who began sailing with him at the age of twelve, in 1985 raced together in their own boat 'so dad could train some youngsters'.

The late Jack Tier, editor of the Sydney afternoon newspaper *The Sun*, although he rated himself as only a 'poor hand', actively crewed in 16s until his mid-fifties and founded the Sydney Harbour Marathon Handicap, a combined 20 nm race for 18s, 16s, 14s and 12s with $5,400 in cash prizes, including $800 for each class. Tier would obliquely 'put the acid' on the principals of large firms for sponsorship of the race prizes by inviting them to lunch and diverting the conversation from newspaper campaigns to the importance of healthy outdoor sport and the excellent public image that commercial supporters of sailing enjoyed. The Sydney Harbour Marathon is a perpetual reminder of his enthusiasm. Tier owned two 16s at the same time and, like scores of others faithful to the class, scorned the idea of racing seriously in other types of craft. He grew impatient when keel boats, in which he sometimes cruised, failed to reach anything like the speed of the skiffs. 'I'm prejudiced,' he would say, 'but all I want to do in any other boat is read a book.'

TWELVE FOOTERS

While modern developments, under rigid controls, have made 16 ft skiffs easier to handle, the 12 ft skiff, another Australian original, has become, like the 18-footer, much more difficult — and a great deal faster. The 12, a two-man trapeze craft, once a heavyweight four-handed boat, is now strictly for agile super-sailors. It is an extraordinary little vessel, with no limits on sail size and a minimum hull weight of 40 kg and therefore has a potential ratio of power to displacement that is unsurpassed by any other single-hulled racing machine in the world. On average, the most successful unrigged hulls with fittings, weigh only 41 kg and in light weather carry 19 sq m of working sail and 51 sq m spinnakers — almost as much as some 8 m, 1.5 tonne keel yachts. For their length, which must be between 3.675 m and 3.7 m and maximum beam of 1.53 m — there is no minimum — the 12s are also probably the fastest single-hulled craft in the world. They plane to windward at about 9 k in fresh winds and downwind touch 18 k in bursts.

Originally, when Unrestricted 12s were formally recognized as a class in the early 1920s (developed from Sydney's now-extinct spoon-shaped 6, 8, and 10-footers, craft that carried hilarious clouds of sail), they were strongly cedar-planked and timbered boats like the 18s and 16s of the period, and carried huge gaff-rigged sails. They had bowsprits that protruded 2.4 m over their stems, booms extending 2 m over their transoms, and up to five in their crews. Ringtails of 18.6 sq m were often carried down the leeches of their mainsails in light, following winds. But, like the 18s and 16s, the 12s have become unrecognizably different from their forebears. They first carried trapezes in 1956, about six years after these aids to stability were rigged on 18s. This allowed reduction in crew weight, and smaller sails on 8 m bermudan-rigged masts, and by 1959 lightweight, two-man boats had become the vogue. Although there is still no maximum limit on the number of crew that may be carried, few 12s today have more than the minimum two — a skipper and an extremely busy for'ard hand. In moderate breezes both operate almost entirely in trapeze harnesses, dangling on wires at leg length over the side.

By 1986 most 12 ft skiffs could get around a course only 100s-a-mile slower than an 18, and 50s-a-mile slower than a 16. Like both other classes, the 12s are allowed buoyancy tanks fore and aft so that they may be righted after a capsize and, like the 16s, these tanks must be carried well below the gunwhales, which are restricted to a maximum width of 65 mm outside the edge of the top planking and 25 mm inside (a total of 90 mm); and since they may have 'no decking, leecloths, collapsible sides, splash boards, shelves or other contrivances' (and no outside 'wings' like the 18s) there it nothing to stop water slopping over their bows, shoulders and sides and filling them. They have self-bailing venturi drains in their shallow underbellies and are allowed 80 sq cm of drain tubes through their broad transoms, but these, of course, do not prevent them from capsizing. A moment's failure by either the skipper or the crew to keep a 12 on her feet in a fresh wind and choppy water ensures a quick swim. 'It is quite remarkable when even a champion crew gets around a course without one capsize,' says former NSW 12 Ft Skiff Association secretary Bruce Taylor. So only the most skilful aquatic athletes can compete successfully in 12s. Often they use not only their hands but also their toes, teeth and armpits to hold and trim the gear in the boats.

High-tech featherweight construction, big rigs, remarkable acceleration upwind and down, make 12 ft skiffs like former national champion *Freshwater Sails* among the hardest boats to handle. (Bob Ross)

One almost incredible exception to the belief that all 12 ft skiff sailors must have a pair of tremendously 'fast' hands was the Lane Cove (Sydney) skipper, Peter Cowie, who lost his right arm at the shoulder in a tram accident as a boy. Until he was forty-eight years of age, Cowie, with his crewman, Ross Gardner, raced for eleven years in 12s and five times represented NSW in championships against Queensland and New Zealand in his boats *Lisa Jane* and *Cowie Engineering*, which he built himself. In 1985, at the age of fifty-two, he was racing in the crew of a keel yacht. Cowie, however, is an instinctive sailor, with phenomenal anticipation, who began skippering dinghies at the age of six. He is a third generation member of a famous Sydney family of yachtsman. His father, Peter Cowie snr, was national 12 ft skiff champion in 1934–35.

Twelve foot skiff skippers and crews graduate to 18-footers with only a few hours of training to get used to the roomier boats, although, since side trapezing wing-frames were fitted to the 18s in the early 1980s, special techniques are needed to manage them, 'If you took all the former 12 ft skiff sailors out of today's 18s there'd hardly be anyone left to sail them,' says John Bennett, former president of the NSW 12 Ft Skiff Association, a senior official of the Sydney Flying Squadron's 18-footer club and, with his brother, Bruce Bennett, organizer of that body's 12-footer fleet.

A few 12 ft skiff skippers and crewmen who remain physically fit enough stay with the class until middle age, but most are in their mid-twenties or late teens and have learned their skills in smaller rigged high-performance dinghies, principally the Cherub and Flying 11 classes.

In 1986 there were seventy 12s registered with six Sydney clubs, six boats at Gosford, on the NSW central coast, and twelve in one club in Brisbane. (The class has never prospered in other States although Victoria sailed a few of the heavyweights up to 1957.) They compete weekly throughout the spring and summer in club and interclub handicap and scratch races, and in annual interdominion championships against New Zealand. For some years the NZ boats were dominant. In 1959 they won the title with a catamaran when a loophole in the rules (quickly closed) was found that did not specifically bar twin-hulled boats. But from 1970 to 1985 while the New Zealanders were permitted to compete with boats that were not true 12 ft skiffs by Australian standards, but craft known as Q class, with unlimited buoyancy and winged decks, Australia's representatives consistently won the interdominion championships. Then, in 1985, with three Australian-designed boats of proven performance, the NZ teams made a serious assault on the interdominion championship sailed over seven heats on Waterloo Bay near Brisbane. One of the NZ boats, *Dimension Sailcloth*, skippered by Tim Bartlett and crewed by Malcolm Dawson, overwhelmed her twelve NSW, five Queensland and three NZ rivals. She placed 3, 2, 1, 1, 1, 4 in light, medium, and heavy (35 k) winds and did not start in the seventh race because on points she could not be beaten.

With few exceptions the Australian boats are of double-chine shape although there was a trend to return to completely curved shapes in the mid 1980s. Most of the top boats are moulded of fibreglass skins sandwiching sheets of plastic foam. The NZ champion, *Dimension Sailcloth*, was of edge-grained Balsawood sandwiched between fibreglass skins. One building method is to fit the sandwiched shell, weighing about 12.2 kg, inside an aluminium tubular frame that in one piece forms the external gunwales and incorporates a short bowsprit and transom bar and bracket from which the rudder is hung. A standard joke is that a modern 12 is the only boat with its rudder connected to its bowsprit. Tubular struts and brackets welded to the gunwales also support the boat's centreboard case and form the mast-step. This metal assembly gives the boat tremendous overall rigidity and strength.

A fully equipped 12 of this kind, with the best of gear, professionally built, can cost up to $10,000 and the average costs $7,000. About half the boats are sponsored by commercial firms but some of the leading skippers, who get good publicity in the news media, are paid up to $5,000 for naming new boats after various firms and so advertising their products. By comparison with the 18s and 16s, however, the 12s race for modest cash prizes. An interdominion title is rarely worth more than $100 to the winner unless the series is generously sponsored by a commercial firm. But there is a special cachet about sailing a boat that few others can hope to manage.

9

Multihulls and the C Class Waterspiders

IN THE MOST ELEMENTARY TERMS, sailing speed depends on the ratio of power to resistance, so slender, modern multihulls — catamarans and trimarans (no one has yet developed a successful quadmaran) — are the fastest practical wind-driven craft afloat. They lose their hydrodynamic and aerodynamic advantages over orthodox monohull craft running square downwind in very light air, but on all other points of sailing nothing with the same sail area can match them around a course. And their rate of acceleration is prodigious. In a steady 15 k breeze in smooth water an international B class cat, like the 6.10 m Olympic Tornado, with a limit of 20.9 sq m of sail, can at least pace an 18-footer, the world's fastest monohull dinghy, carrying almost double the working sail area and, with a spinnaker set, five times the area. As the strength of the breeze increases so does the Tornado's chance of out-pacing the 18-footer. In a 20 k to 30 k beam breeze a scientifically designed ocean-going trimaran, like Britain's 18.28 m *Apricot*, would sail the 24.08 m world champion offshore keel boat, *Boomerang*, out of sight in a few hours. And while a single-hulled ocean racer, hard driven into fresh winds, may heel to an angle of 30 degrees, with seas sweeping the edge of her leeward deck, a properly proportioned multihull, skilfully handled, remains almost horizontal, comfortably depending not on ballast in her keel for stability but on the upward thrust of the leeward hull, counter-balanced by her centralized weight.

Even crude South Sea Island trimarans and catamarans, fashioned from dugout logs (*kattumaran* means 'tied wood', in Tamil) and overburdened with deck houses and people and rigged with primitive matting sails, astonished early European seafarers with their speed. But they remained a curiosity during more than a century of yachting because even refined Western versions of these 'native outrigger canoes', lightly planked and with centreboards and yacht rigs, were awkward to manoeuvre in confined waters, slow to tack in very light weather, and difficult to right when completely capsized. They still are.

Top With Trevor Barnabas as owner-skipper, the Sydney 16 ft skiff *Buckle Toyota* had a remarkable career against strong opposition, winning almost every scratch race in which she competed and the national championship. (Bob Ross)

Bottom Only instinctive sailors of rare skill like Greg Hyde and crewman Rick Murray can handle 12 ft skiffs. (Ron Hyde)

Top Tacking duel: *Courageous* (left, on port) crosses clear of *Australia*'s bows. On beats to windward the US defender always had an edge on the challenger in their 1977 match for the America's Cup. (Warren Clarke)

Left Ted Turner, champion of champions, in dinghies, small keel yachts, ocean racers and, his ultimate achievement, skipper of *Courageous* in the America's Cup. (Warren Clarke)

Australia had one remarkably successful catamaran as early as 1880 — William Cope's 6.1 m *Gemini* — 'built like a single boat split in halves lengthways and bridged over in the centre' which 'won by a street' in Sydney Amateur Sailing Club's 6.1 m-and-over class at the national Anniversary Regatta of 1881. Her appearance and speed affronted many rival yachtsmen, however, and a protest against her was upheld — because she did not carry a suitable distinguishing flag. Reasons were also found to condemn other catamarans over the years, and it was not until the early 1950s that the worldwide explosion of popularity that these craft today enjoy really began.

Australia first took to catamarans as class-racing boats when Victorian shipwright-designer Charlie Cunningham and his talented engineer son, Lindsay, created the 6.1 m two-man box-sectioned Yvonne class, in the early 1950s. It was sloop-rigged, stable, fast, carried a spinnaker which helped put it on level terms with monohulls on square runs in light weather, and could be easily built by amateurs with the new wonder material, plywood. For the first time beginners found they could quickly learn to manage a high speed craft without years of graduation through dinghy classes. Scores of Yvonnes were launched within a few seasons, and although they have been superseded by dozens of lighter, faster, better shaped boats of moulded plywood and fibreglass, they established the multihull movement in Australia and in many other countries as a viable form of sailing.

The one-man 4.88 m Quickcat, the next of a string of Cunningham multihulls, had even greater success. The criss-crossing of its joining frame made it look somewhat like a Bailey bridge, but it was even simpler than the Yvonne for a handyman to build, cost about £150 complete with its single 11.7 sq m sail, and an agile youth perched on the end of its sliding swing-plank could control it in half a gale. It was strong, too. In a southerly buster one of them, with national champion Max Press clinging to it, cartwheeled four times like a blown-away umbrella across Sydney Harbour and needed only a day of repair. The Quickcats were recognized as ideal for hard winds and bouncy, enclosed waters like Port Phillip Bay, where they became enormously popular. They were built by the hundreds in all States but in 1986, under seige from many other types, there were only eleven Quickcats registered in Victoria.

Other designers in Australia, New Zealand, America and Britain provided countless variations of the multihull theme. The most successful of those intended for amateur construction was the NZ-designed Paper Tiger, a fast, stable, one-man plywood 4.27 m boat (it is now also available in fibreglass) that spread to Australia, Britain, Sweden, and the USA. In Victoria, in 1986, twenty clubs, some with fleets of forty, raced Paper Tigers, and the national total of the class registered for racing and unregistered was estimated to be 2,000. Trapezes that allowed crewmen to swing horizontally from the windward hull, as in monohull dinghy classes, added stability to lightweight structures (usually aluminium tubing and fabric trampolines), further increasing sail-carrying capacity and speed. Yachting associations, even the IYRU, began to wonder if the newfangled multihulls that pulled the apparent wind ahead of them as they gathered speed and thus seemed to be permanently close-hauled, weren't really boats after all. Some officials were daring enough to suggest that world recognition might be given to approved types. Catamaran enthusiasts proposed that races for twin-hulled boats should be included in the Olympic Games. By 1976 they had achieved that ambition.

225

Left Stingray is a high-performance 5.48 m class raced in three Australian States. It was originally designed in Sydney by a committee of four. But it is no boat for beginners and accelerates so fast that tyros on the trapeze can find themselves dangling astern. (*SMH*)

Right Quickcats look awkward by standards of modern design but they are remarkably strong and helped to establish the catamaran movement in Australia. (John Carnemolla)

By 1986 there were 3,854 smooth-water catamarans of thirty-four different classes officially registered for handicap and championship fleet racing with yachting associations in all States of Australia, all sailing in their own individual club, State, and, in most cases, in national titles. This large number of catamaran classes, as in the case of Australia's sixty-eight registered monohull dinghy classes, greatly dilutes the talent available to sail the boats against other countries in high-performing, internationally recognized types. But, as in all other forms of sailing in Australia, no more than 10 per cent of catamaran yachtsmen aspire to national or international championship honours or are willing to make the effort that might fit them for such aspirations. The rest are content with moderate successes, proud of their individual positions in hundreds of small clubs, but applauding, nevertheless, the achievements of the champions whom they feel represent them all. In Australia in 1986 there were also at least 6,000 unregistered multihulls of many types that did not race at all, even in modest club events, and were sailed casually as fun boats, some of them in the surf; and more than

200 much larger catamarans and trimarans, ranging up to 18.3 m, designed for offshore racing and cruising, some with luxurious accommodation.

Lock Crowther, of Sydney, who is one of the world's foremost designers and sailors of catamarans and trimarans and a senior official of the AYF, representing all classes of multihulls, and who has spent twenty-five years promoting their cause, is obsessed with the need for safety in sea-going craft. In the face of strong opposition from conservative monohull yachtsmen, he insists that there is no more inherent danger in sailing multihull craft offshore than in orthodox keel-ballasted monohull yachts, provided that the multihulls are of properly engineered design and construction and sensibly handled. Crowther ascribes the loss of most multihull craft offshore to the normal hazards of the sea and, in defence, lists many disasters that well-found orthodox yachts have suffered and dozens of successful ocean passages in multihulls, in races and on cruises, some of them around the world. Nevertheless, in the 1960s offshore multihulls got a bad public image, especially in Australia, when there were seventeen well-publicized drownings from them. Some of these craft were suspect in design and construction and were sailed by inexperienced beginners, but they also included boats sailed by the seasoned Brisbane multihull designer-sailor Hedley Nicol and the American designer Arthur Piver. And one of the craft was a well-found 10 m racing trimaran, *Bandersnatch*, designed by Crowther himself, from which four men were lost, including his 21-year-old brother Bruce Crowther. *Bandersnatch* was wrecked at sea off the Victorian east coast in 1967 when she presumably ran into a whale or a heavy floating object in a storm, on a voyage from Melbourne to Sydney. The central hull of the vessel, with one float torn off, was found still afloat near Wilson's Promontory a week after her crew failed to report, and the missing float was later found at sea, 400 nm north of the wreck. 'I suffered deeply through the loss of my brother and my friends, and additionally when a great outcry was made about the unseaworthiness of multihulls in general,' says Crowther.

> The fact that *Bandersnatch* was still afloat after a 70 k mid-winter storm and that no crew of any yacht of any type has much chance of survival after a collision in those conditions was brushed aside. I don't claim that sea-going multihulls, properly handled, are any safer than monohulls, but they are faster, more comfortable and more easily managed than many orthodox yachts and hundreds have sailed the world's oceans through the roughest weather. A popular and misguided theory is that multihulls tip over easily in a beam sea because one hull lifts and the other dips. In truth, both hulls skid sideways in heavy beam seas and stay more upright than keel yachts, unless they are stupidly overdriven under too much sail.

Crowther doesn t sit safely behind a drawing board voicing these opinions. He has cruised and raced and continues to do so across most of the world's oceans as skipper or navigator in multihulls of his own design, and many of them hold course records. (In 1974 one covered 240 nm in 14h at an average speed of 17 k.) In 1986, a total of 2,000 multihull craft designed by Crowther were sailing or under construction overseas and in Australia. Because of opposition from officials of orthodox ocean racing yacht clubs, especially from Sydney's Cruising Yacht Club, only one Sydney–Hobart race, in 1966 — and that without official recognition — has been sailed in multihulls. The race was won by John Hitch in his illfated *Bandersnatch* (lost six months later but without Hitch aboard) from

Ken Berkeley in *Viva*, another 10 m trimaran. Two other trimarans started, but one disqualified herself when her crew went ashore to stretch their legs, and the other withdrew when her crew got bored with the light winds. *Bandersnatch* sailed the course in the slow time of 5d 4h 53m 36s and was beaten across the finishing line in Hobart by only two of the forty-four monohulls in the official Sydney–Hobart race – the 18.6 m NZ sloop *Fidelis*, line-honours winner, and the 14 m Admiral's Cup representative *Balandra*.

Offshore multihull races have been sailed regularly between Brisbane and Gladstone, since 1964 (see Chapter 13: Queensland Ocean Racing) and, since 1977, occasionally from Melbourne across Bass Strait to Tasmania. But the fleets have been small. Crowther, who recently helped overseas officials to lay down new international safety codes and a handicapping system, expects a strong development of offshore multihull racing in Australia in the late 1980s.

But the great strength of the multihull movement in Australia remains in those boats designed for sailing in sheltered waters. Their numbers and classes are proliferating every year, as in many other countries. Between 1969 and 1986 international commercial exploitation of moulded fibreglass 'pop out' construction was fully organized and more than 200,000 mass-produced catamarans between 3.66 m and 5.49 m were sold in America, Europe and Australia. By 1979 the US-based Hobie Cat organization (Coast Catamaran Corporation) alone, by cleverly marketing a strong boat – without the worry of centreboards that anyone could sail in a few feet of water or in a light surf – had sold more than 75,000 of its 4.27 m so-called Hobie 14 class worldwide (5,500 in Australia). World figures for sloop-rigged Hobie 16s totalled 100,000 (Australia, 2,500) and for centreboard Hobie 18s 20,000 (Australia, 500).

The popularity of these banana-shaped, multi-coloured fun boats, held together with aluminium frames and, in the case of the 14s, with no pretensions to high performance, outstripped even the wildest dreams of success of the boat's original designer Hobie Alter, a middle-aged Californian. The 14 could be easily trailed or taken apart and stacked on the roof of a car. The Hobie 16s and 18s are higher performance craft in which Australians have excelled internationally. Since 1981 skippers Brett Dryland, of NSW, and Gary Metcalfe, of Queensland, have won world titles in both classes, and Ian Bashford, of NSW, won the world Hobie 18 title. In 1981 Dryland and Bashford with Rod Waterhouse, of NSW, relieving each of them, also won the USA's Hobie 16 East Coast 1,000 nm non-stop endurance race in seven days. In 1983, when the format was changed to allow overnight stops, Dryland and Waterhouse won again.

The Hobie movement encourages its devotees to register with it and with clubs for ordinary racing, and is now so strong that it does not need to seek the imprimatur (and thereby comply with all the strictures) of the International Yacht Racing Union for its world championship regattas. It rotates these carnivals, in the form of gala holiday festivals, with associated novelty events, at some of the world's most exotic seaside tourist centres. Even the losers and their friends who flock to the Hobie fiestas are assured of fun. Other popular mass-produced fun catamaran classes are following this trend.

But a rising tide of less frolicsome sailors who seek to promote the status of catamarans as craft for serious club racing under the aegis of State and national yachting associations and of the IYRU, deplore the attitudes of some of the unregistered newcomers. They claim that there is an element of unruly incompetence among those who know nothing about the nautical rules of the road, ignore the normal courtesies of the sea and, increasingly, are causing mayhem on the waters. Lock Crowther, while enthusiastically supporting the idea of fun afloat, fears that compulsory government registration of all boats may ultimately be necessary to restrain nautical hooliganism. 'Sailing should be for pleasure and no one wants it under bureaucratic control, but too many people are behaving badly in some high-speed catamarans,' he warns. 'Anyone without the slightest qualification for handling a boat of any kind can now buy an off-the-hook cat that is a lethal weapon in high winds in inexpert hands and can wreak havoc in a few seconds. A motorist would be gaoled if he drove an unregistered car in the manner of some of these irresponsibles on the water.'

Australia's position as one of the world's most serious catamaran racing nations was established in 1963 when the Victorian boat *Quest* challenged Britain for the International Catamaran Challenge Trophy, a match race competition founded by New York's Sea Cliff Yacht Club in 1961. The trophy is a surrealist fantasy in silver which someone once described as an exploding pepper grinder, and it was given the pretentious nickname 'Little America's Cup' for no better reason than that it, like the real America's Cup, was to be awarded to the winner of a best-of-seven series of races between a club challenger of any one nation and a club defender from another. The type of craft to be used over a 20 nm course was designated C, with the only restrictions being 7.62 m of overall hull length, 4.27 m extreme beam from the outside of each hull, and 28 sq m of sail with half the total surface of the mast measured as part of this area—an extraordinarily loose set of definitions later dignified by the IYRU with the classification International C. With no limitations on hull shapes, depths, widths, buoyancy or weight, materials or rigs, the C class could be truly described as developmental, open to the wildest extremes of experimentation. The only criterion was speed, which the C class certainly has (22.5 k in an 18 k breeze has been officially recorded, and short bursts of 30 k in hard winds claimed) and this hatched a queer brood of waterspiders, as frail and as cranky as 1910 aeroplanes, and quite unsuitable as fleet-racing class boats. They have come to cost almost as much as small, modern aeroplanes, too. On the credit side, the invention and development of superbly engineered equipment for C class cats and of the hollow rotating aerofoil mast, first with only a narrow wing of sail fabric behind it and ultimately of the rigid-surfaced elliptical, wing-mast-sail with no trailing fabric at all and instead controllable, articulated flaps down the after edge, have had many side benefits for lesser craft, both multihull and monohull, and have considerably advanced the science of low-speed aerodynamics.

Australia's first bid for the C class trophy against Britain—whose boats had won it immediately when the Americans first offered it for challenge competition and had successfully defended it against America—was a disaster. The Australians built five craft fitting the C class category and, after round-robin trials on Port Phillip Bay, sent two to England for final trials. The Cunningham-designed *Quest*, 'tank tested' in an irrigation ditch, with sealed sailcloth hull skins, a sloop rig on an orthodox yacht mast, and sailed by John Munns and Graeme Anderson, of Victoria, went down in four straight races to *Hellcat III*, a much more sophisticated boat with a lofty rig and experienced cat sailors Reg White and Rod MacAlpine-Downie in charge.

The Cunninghams did much better with *Quest II* in 1965. The hulls of this one had plywood sides moulded into fibreglass underwater and a tall, streamlined aerofoil mast of plywood and aluminium, with a well-battened fabric sail behind it. The mast was the first of its kind used in the event and was a development of a spar that Lindsay Cunningham had seen in America. It measured 381 mm fore-and-aft and was 100 mm thick, tapering to a narrow tip, and it took up almost an eighth of the 28 sq m of measured sail area. But the spar was primitive compared with the great aerofoil masts and articulated wings that were to follow. *Quest II* was unquestionably a faster boat, especially in fresh conditions, than the British defender *Emma Hamilton*, also sloop-rigged and again skippered by Reg White, this time with John Osborn as crew. The English sailors, however, handled their boat much better than the Australians and were at home on the tricky tidal waters around the mud banks of Thorpe Bay (Essex) where the races were held. The British lost the first race, won the next three to lead 3-1, then dropped two more and scrambled home 4-3 when *Quest II* nose-dived, capsized and cartwheeled in a 38 k squall while well to windward of her rival and leading by a minute with 3 nm to go.

Lindsay Cunningham, who skippered the Australian boat with John Buzaglo as crew, claimed that the English race committee should have cancelled the event when the wind reached more than 30 k which, he insisted, was the agreed limit for racing in such craft. The English, whose crew had weathered the blow by easing their sheets momentarily, bucketing the wind out of their sails, then bearing away, brushed the objections aside. The rules, they said, stated that only when the wind was above 30 k at the start should a race be cancelled. White blandly remarked that Cunningham had been caught running square above the rounding mark in too much wind for his rig and had nothing left to ease when the squall hit him—a situation that many catamaran sailors in other classes were to learn was fraught with danger. The technique to avoid a nose-diving capsize, they found, was to have enough sheet to ease and enough room to bear off. Unlike monohulls, catamarans cannot be suddenly rounded up to spill wind in hard squalls when they are over-canvassed because they accelerate so quickly as the wind comes across their quarters, making a nose-dive almost inevitable.

Australia's next challenge was in *Quest III*, in 1967—the British still held the trophy, having again beaten off the Americans—and it ended in a convincing 4-1 defeat for the challenger, a badly tuned Cunningham boat with Victorians Peter Bolton and Lindsay Rees as skipper and crew. *Quest III* was una (cat) rigged and had an elongated sleeve-luff in her sail that went all the way down her thin, orthodox alloy mast. The sleeve extended back 610 mm from the mast, and the Cunninghams' theory was that it would streamline the airflow just as effectively as a wide aerofoil spar, reduce weight aloft and increase stability. In fact, the rig did not help the boat at all. The sleeve rarely took up the desired shape, and *Quest III* just could not point with the British defender *Lady Helmsman* (named after the paint company that had sponsored her), skippered by Pete Schneidau with Bob Fisher as crew, and constantly sagged below her on works to windward. *Lady Helmsman* won the first race in light weather with 20m to spare inside the time limit of four hours. *Quest III* was almost half an hour astern at the last mark and failed by 10m to finish in time. The British took the second race by 6m in fresher winds, and the third in hard weather and choppy seas by 1m 49s. They lost the fourth in another hard breeze when the centreboard case in their starboard hull split and the jammed board threatened to tear the boat in two. *Lady Helmsman* was forced to retire with one hull submerged. Round-the-clock repairs by a team of shipwrights put her back on the course in two days and she won the fifth and deciding race in light weather by 11m 30s. During the middle stages of this finale, the boom momentarily jammed on the curved mainsheet horse, then swung free, hit the British skipper and knocked him unconscious. He lay inert for three minutes on the trampoline between the two hulls while crewman Fisher, still wearing his trapeze harness, managed both helm and mainsheet. It was six minutes before Schneidau was able to steer the boat.

In 1968, the Americans lost to Britain for the fifth time. But they went close. Their *Yankee Flyer* broke up in heavy seas, was rebuilt in two days and went down only 3–4 to *Lady Helmsman*. With eight consecutive matches won, the British seemed unbeatable on their home course, and when Denmark challenged in 1969 with *Opus III*, they mounted what many considered an inferior defence with *Ocelot*, an old boat designed and skippered by Reg White, with John Osborn as crew.

With the match squared three-all and *Ocelot* trailing by a leg of the course in the deciding light-weather race, White infuriated the Danes and other yachtsmen with what they considered unsporting tactics. The British skipper cut out two marks and sailed across the course in an attempt to intercept the challenger and blanket her so that she could not finish within the time limit. There was nothing in the rules that specifically stated that he had no right to do so, and White defended his last-ditch effort to nullify that race and so get another chance. But the Danes escaped, finished the course within the time limit, and Britain for the first time lost the trophy — under a cloud of criticism. When Britain challenged the Danes for a match in 1970, they were rebuffed, and a tentative bid from Australia was accepted.

Australia nominated a rebuilt *Quest III* with a new, superbly engineered aerofoil mast, exhaustively tested in a private wind tunnel. It was elliptical, 12.5 m high, 1.07 m fore-and-aft, 30.5 cm thick at its widest part, and streamlined to a fine edge, into which the luff of its narrow sail fitted. The mast was made of light plywood with timber and urethane foam formers and had a 12 mm foam skin covered with sealed fabric, and a surface of glass-smooth plastic. It had struts and wires attached to full length battens so that the shape of the sail could be adjusted to achieve the best aerodynamic flow; and backstays leading to trolleys on a semicircular mainsheet track to keep the rig in correct tension as the mast rotated on its base plate. At that stage no yacht mast had been built to compare with it and to ordinary yachtsmen it seemed a complicated nightmare. In point of fact, when it was set up it was comparatively easy to control — if one had skill, a cool head, and the Cunninghams as technical advisers. It was costly, too, but commercial sponsors, headed by Dunlop (Australia) supported the challenge generously. Trials on Port Phillip Bay had been expected to prove *Quest III* vastly superior in speed to her Australian rivals, but these tests were inconclusive, disrupted by bad weather and mishaps to other challenge contenders. One of the latter sank, one fell apart, one was smashed in a storm when left on a beach overnight and, to cap it all, *Quest III* and her main rival, *Red Roo*, designed and sailed by Bill Hollier, of Sydney, barely beat a much smaller, simply rigged B class cat they had been expected to annihilate.

Still, *Quest III*, with Bruce Proctor as helmsman and Graham Candy as crew, won all seven final trials and was sent to Denmark with *Red Roo* for tuning. America's Cup skipper, Jock Sturrock, went as team manager and Lindsay Cunningham as technical adviser. The two Australian boats duelled for a week on the race course at Oresund (near Copenhagen) until *Quest III* was confirmed as challenger against the Danish defender *Sleipner*, a development of *Opus III* by Wagner Smitt, who skippered her with Klaus Anton Neilson as crew. The Danish boat had a rig similar but much lower than the challenger's, and was well suited to the hard weather which was forecast. Instead, *Sleipner* got light conditions for the first three races and lost them. She took the fourth in a 20 k breeze and the fifth by default when *Quest III*'s mainsheet traveller jammed and she failed to reach the starting line. The Danes jogged around the 20 nm course alone in 2h 15m at an average speed of just under 9 k and only once went into overdrive, when they skated over a reaching leg at 16 k. They squared the match three-all in the sixth race in a 15 k wind but it was slightly lighter in the seventh and *Quest III* led narrowly all the way (in the middle stages by only 5s) and finished 59s ahead.

So, at last, after seven years of trying, the Cup was brought in triumph to Sorrento Sailing Club on the shores of Port Phillip Bay, and Victorians, with justifiable pride — since they had initiated and organized all the Australian challenges and raised most of the sponsorship money to make them possible — saw it as a monument to their superiority as multihull sailors. It was a tribute, too, to the magnificent efforts of Charlie and Lindsay Cunningham who, more than anyone else, had devoted a considerable slice of their lives and income to its pursuit. On the way home from Denmark, Proctor and Candy visited Newport, Rhode Island, to watch the battle between Australia's *Gretel II* and *Intrepid* for the real America's Cup, and took some solace that they had not been involved in such an imbroglio of protests and ill feeling as had surrounded that contest.

In 1972 *Quest III*, with adjustments to her rig (her sail battens were now articulated) and again skippered by Proctor, this time with Graeme Ainslie as crew, beat off half a dozen defence candidates, including Sydney's *Helios*, similarly rigged, designed by Lock Crowther and jointly owned by John Haynes and Bill Hollier. Then *Quest III* made short work of America's challenge with *Weathercock*, sailed by Chuck Millican and Jack Evans. The US boat went down 4–0 in a tame mismatch. The rig on *Weathercock*, although designed by George Patterson, whose early aerofoil masts had inspired Lindsay Cunningham, looked old-fashioned alongside *Quest III*'s scientically designed spar.

But even more advances were on the way. The most successful of *Quest III*'s defence rivals in 1972 had been *Miss Nylex*, heavily subsidized by the Nylex Corporation and rigged with a hollow spar that carried no sail fabric behind it at all and stood naked like a vertical aeroplane wing. To many it appeared to carry the principles of aerodynamic power to the ultimate conclusion. The rigid aerofoil flaps on the trailing edge were operated by a system of wires that led to a central console of levers at deck level and could be used to control the wind power. It made the craft closer winded than any catamaran ever previously devised. On a beat to windward in a 20 k breeze *Miss Nylex* could reach 16 k and completely outpoint any C class rival; but on downwind runs in heavy seas she was almost uncontrollable and in very light air downwind she was comparatively slow. It was clear that more research was needed on the rig. By 1974, the Melbourne engineer Roy Martin, who had designed *Miss Nylex*'s mast, had developed it further. It made her the fastest smooth-water sailing craft then afloat in Australia in winds of 15 k and above. With Proctor and Ainslie aboard her in a series of defence trials, against a new Crowther-designed, Haynes-

 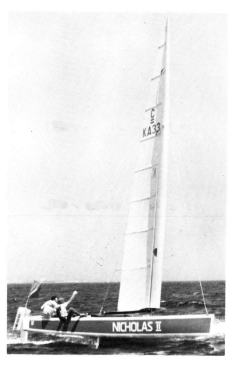 

Left With rigid wing sail *Miss Nylex* hit 16 k to windward in 20 k breeze. (Nylex Corp.)

Centre 1977 challenger *Nicholas II* had soft sail, was well beaten. (Nicholas P/L)

Right The Other Cup: In 1985 on Long Island Sound, NY, Victoria's superbly engineered C Class catamaran *Victoria 150,* sailed by Olympians Chris Cairns and Scott Anderson, broke the US nine-year grip on The Little America's Cup. In a 1986 match race on Sydney Harbour, the big cat again demonstrated her speed by outpacing the fastest 18-footers by more than 10 minutes around a 15 nm course.

skippered *Helios* (carrying a similar but less mechanically developed wing) and against *Quest III*, *Miss Nylex* seemed to be the last word in C class catamarans, never likely to be beaten. She no longer ran wild downwind and she went on to overwhelm a NZ challenger, *Miss Stars*, in four straight races.

But in 1976, to the consternation of those who were confidently predicting rigid wing-mast-sails for all high performance cats of the future, *Miss Nylex*, again with Proctor and Ainslie as skipper and crew, went down 2–4 against a completely orthodox American featherweight, *Aquarius V*, of Cabrillo Beach Yacht Club, California, skippered by the youngster Robbie Harvey and crewed by a white-bearded 52-year-old trapeze artist Alex Kozloff, the boat's owner. The winds were predominantly light. *Aquarius V*'s secret was in the construction of her kevlar and carbon fibre re-inforced hulls that made her just strong enough for racing but reduced her total weight to only 209 kg compared with *Miss Nylex*'s 309 kg. The American boat, with a simple, pencil-slim alloy mast and a big, well-battened fabric sail, could move in the faintest air and was faster than *Miss Nylex* on all points of sailing in winds below 8 k. She was also faster on broad reaches in moderate conditions. It was only above 14 k that the Flying Wing could beat her. Australian catamaran aficionados changed their views quickly. Within a month of *Miss Nylex*'s defeat, the received opinion was that rigid wing-mast-sails were suitable only for fresh to strong winds, and that for the full range of conditions in which races had to be sailed, a better rig was a broad, aerofoil mast backed by a well-battened fabric sail. The Cunninghams agreed, and designed a new boat according to those principles. She was *Nicholas II*, backed by an Australian pharmaceutical firm and representing McCrae Yacht Club, Port Phillip Bay.

In 1977, the Americans, in their first defence of the International Catamaran Challenge Trophy, proved the latest Australian theories wrong on all counts. They fielded *Patient Lady III*, a craft of 338 kg overall in weight — 129 kg heavier than the super-lightweight *Aquarius V* and 29.5 kg heavier than *Miss Nylex* — but rigged with a rigid wing-mast-sail of wonderful efficiency. The trailing aerofoil flaps of it were framed with light aluminium ribs sheathed in tensioned sailcloth. They could be adjusted to almost any angle to control wind power and also flexed to induce twist, with wires led to the deck through struts inside the hollow for'ard section to which they were attached. *Patient Lady III*'s rig was designed by Reg Hubbard, and her hulls by Skip Banks. Her owner, Tony Di Mauro, of Roton Point Yacht Club, Connecticut, had spent fifteen years developing the craft. She was helmed by Duncan MacLane and crewed by Skip Banks, who handled her with nonchalant ease. They beat off eleven US rivals for the right to defend the trophy and then, on the waters of San Pedro, California, proceeded to whip Australia's challenger, *Nicholas II*, skippered by Lindsay Cunningham and crewed by Candy, in four straight races. Actually the American boat won five races straight (the first a walkover when *Nicholas II* sprang a leak and retired) in winds that ranged between 9 k and 16 k; but the third race was discarded when the race committee upheld an Australian protest that the start had been inordinately delayed and that the course was longer than the 20 nm specified under the rules. *Nicholas II* had led by 4m 27s with three legs to go, but had lost time when her crew had been forced to jury rig her aerofoil mast with a trapeze wire after her starboard headstay broke. She had struggled home 1m 35s behind the US defender. In another race, when the wind was never above 9 k, the lead changed five times and the US defender won by only a minute.

Before the Australians left the US they talked of another challenge soon, as did enthusiasts from England, Germany, Italy, and Sweden. But by mid-1978 only Italy remained in the lists. Di Mauro's new *Patient Lady IV*, said to have cost $125,000, won the right to defend. She weighed only 250 kg, had an even more refined rigid wing-mast-sail than her predecessor, and the same two superbly conditioned men aboard — Duncan MacLane as skipper and Skip Banks as crew. They beat the Italian boat *Miss L* (for Lancia, the car company that sponsored her) in four straight races on Long Island Sound, New York. *Miss L*'s mast was a tall, tapering, enclosed D shape, with a doubled-sided fabric sail, stiffened by battens extending from each corner of the flat after side of the D to smooth the airflow. Surprisingly, to some aerodynamicists, the Italian boat outpaced the defender on a wind; but she could not hold her off on reaches. The races excited little interest except among the most dedicated buffs. The C class had become machines beyond the ambition and understanding of ordinary sailors. The boats were too expensive to design and build; too delicate to withstand the slightest misuse; they needed special waterfront sheds and hangars for their great wingsails and pit crews to attend them when they were brought out for racing.

By 1979 an air of disenchantment had settled on the once-euphoric International Catamaran Challenge Trophy scene. And the general public and the news media, who still got so excited about other international yachting challenges, seemed indifferent to it. This attitude irritated many of the catamaran hierarchy, who pointed out that the C class boats were the world's most scientifically developed craft and that in the right conditions of wind and sea they could sail rings around the heavy 12-metre keelboats that commanded TV and radio audiences of millions and pages of newspaper coverage when they raced for the 'Big' America's Cup. But the Italians came back for two more tries, in 1980 and 1982, with boats called *Signor G*. Both sported highly refined versions of *Miss L*'s rig and, hearteningly, both had the edge on the Americans upwind. Unfortunately, both also suffered constantly from crippling breakages of equipment, and, even when they did not, *Patient Lady IV* and *V* ran away from them downwind. The Americans won both matches 4–0. So Di Mauro and his helmsman MacLane, crewman Banks and designer Hubbard, had between them amassed a score of sixteen straight wins and a reputation of being miles ahead of the rest of the world in practical technology.

That, nevertheless, did not stop Lindsay Cunningham and his remarkable father Charles, now in his eighties, from trying, theoretically at least, to beat them. For seven years after *Nicholas II*'s defeat they experimented in their own private wind tunnel until they believed that at last they had got it right. The soft-sail concept was abandoned. They, too, had now designed a rigid, articulated, aerofoil-shaped wing. It was 10.97 m high, rotating at the base so that its leading edge could be given any angle of attack to the wind. It was divided vertically into three sections and lopped square, top and bottom. The for'ard section was about a metre wide fore and aft at the bottom, angling off, half way up, to half a metre at the top. The centre section, hinged on an arc down the back of the for'ard section, was 300 mm fore and aft all the way from bottom to top and divided horizontally in the middle. Then, similarly hinged behind the centre section, were two leech flaps, divided horizontally, and each 5.48 m high. The bottom leech flap, in profile, was an oblong about a metre wide. The top leech flap was in the shape of a trapezium, a metre wide where it separated horizontally from the bottom section, and half a metre wide at the top. Both leech flaps tapered away to a fine edge. The centre sections of the wing and the leech flaps could be manipulated on their hinges and control wires led down to the crew to give camber to the wing. The upper leech flap could also be operated individually to de-power the rig if it developed too much power for the boat.

But the great secret of the design was the wind-slotting effect through the two narrow gaps between the five vertically hinged, aerofoil-shaped sections and over the leeward sides of these sections. According to the degree of camber chosen and the angle of attack set to the wind by the mainsheet, this slotting effect could enormously increase the inherent power of the wing's shape and therefore give a pair of well-designed, lightweight hulls terrific speed. The Cunninghams said 13 k in a 10 k breeze could be expected. And they were proved right.

The hulls eventually built were carbon fibre and plywood designed by catamaran expert Tony Love. They were U-shaped underneath, slab-sided above the water, knife-bowed and had sloping transom sterns. Each weighed only 41 kg. They were joined for'ard by a main beam of alloy tube and aft by a carbon fibre I-beam inside an oval of moulded plywood. This machine, called *Victoria 150* to celebrate her State's sesqui-centenary, did 15 k in a 12 k breeze in early trials. Meanwhile, McCrae Yacht Club, having issued a challenge for a match in America for September 1985, set about getting sponsors. They aimed at a modest total of $150,000 to cover the cost of a spare wing; transport of the boat and all its equipment, crew, and a small support team; accommodation in the USA; and minor exigencies. The Federal Government gave $5,000 and the Victorian Department of Sport and Recreation $17,500. A dozen other contributors, from airlines to insurance companies, brought the total to about $53,000 in money, goods, and services — about $37,000 short of what challenge organiser and team manager, Barry Scott, a former AYF president, had agreed, without a spare wing, was absolutely the basic minimum. The greatest contribution remained the 2,500 hours of voluntary labour put in by the builders Barry Marmion and Andrew Mason, the Cunninghams, and hull designer Love.

The wing alone was a work of art. It was built of marine ply webs, rigid cellular foam sections, carbon fibre tubing frames with a sheathing of heat-shrunk cloth, the same as used on model aeroplanes. With its controls the total assembly weighed only 90 kg.

Although the scientists and the McCrae Yacht Club enthusiasts finally realised the futility of seeking financial support for such a high tech development from people who didn't know the difference between a cosine and a cuscus, it didn't destroy their confidence. They also brought off a remarkable coup in persuading some parochially minded Victorians that two Sydneysiders should skipper and crew the southern State's boat. These were Chris Cairns and Scott Anderson, and there was no doubt that they were the best catamaran sailors in Australia. They had won the bronze medal in the Tornado class at the 1984 Olympics and for two years had been holders of the world Tornado championship. It did not matter that they had had no experience in C class catamarans. Very few other people with competitive sailing skills had any either.

When the boat was launched in April, 1985, Cairns and Anderson had only a few weeks to spare for trials before they were due overseas to defend their world Tornado title off Travemunde, West Germany. They were fascinated by *Victoria 150*'s potential and easily outpaced her old trial horse, *Nicholas II*, sailed by Graeme Fraser and Simon McKeon. 'We still needed to get used to *Victoria 150*, but she was like a rocket downwind, and she sucked the apparent wind around at least 60 degrees,' said Anderson. 'Compared with a Tornado there was little to do. On the boats we normally raced, we had to worry about batten poundage, mast bend, mast rotation, luff downhaul, slot width, mainsail foot outhaul, mainsheet trim and working the jib sheets, apart from steering and trapezing. On the C class cat, all the real work had been done by the designers ashore. The slot control alone, accelerating the air over the leeward side of the wing, was a masterpiece of engineering. Apart from steering and trapezing, all we had to do was decide the camber and set it and work the mainsheet to control the angle of attack.'

Cairns and Anderson were somewhat frustrated when they arrived at Roton Point Yacht Club, near Norwalk, in Long Island Sound, in mid-August to join their team-mates and *Victoria 150*. They had won a week-long international Tornado contest at Travemunde in a hired boat against sixty-five rivals, but had finished only eighth in the following world championship regatta in the same boat, on the same course, in a series of fluky winds that ranged from 0–25 k, with shifts of 30–180 degrees. But the tough competition had brought them to a high pitch of aggression for the C class battle. They gave *Patient Lady VI*, another Hubbard creation, with carbon fibre-foam sandwich hulls and a newly developed four-part rigid wing, (but with only two slots) a sensational 4–0 drubbing. The winds varied from 5 k to 18 k and the surface conditions from smooth to rough. It was the first time the American helmsman MacLane and crewman Banks had been beaten in eight years. The courses were set over eleven legs totalling 19 nm, starting with a right-angled triangle of 1.5 nm to windward along the base, a 90 degree left turn for a beam reach of 2 nm up the perpendicular and a free reach of 2.5 nm down the hypotenuse, back to the starting line. Then there followed another windward leg of 1.5 nm and a return square run, another triangle, another windward and return, and a final windward beat.

Cairns and Anderson, mindful of the difficulty of manoeuvring catamarans in light airs, made no really serious attack on their rivals in the first race, in a SW wind of 8–10 k and a short, low chop. They just herded *Patient Lady VI* away from the line before the start, then turned at the critical time and crossed at 12 k with the defender 9s, in distance about 55 m, astern. The challenger could add only 2s to that margin at the first mark, where she led by 11s. But on the following reach (although the true breeze was on the beam the cats drew the apparent wind so far ahead they looked to be hard on a wind) *Victoria 150* streaked away from the American defender. She won by a demoralizing margin of 3.47, in distance about three-quarters of a mile, sailing the course which, with the extra distance covered on the five beats, totalled 25 nm, in exactly 2h, at an average speed of 12.5 k.

In the second race, in flatter water with a WSW breeze of 5–10 k *Patient Lady VI* did much better. The Australians won the start by 3s but the lead changed five times around the course, with the defender usually gaining, on average, about 10s on each of the five working legs and the challenger gaining about 25s on each of the six reaches and runs. At the last mark, *Victoria 150* had a lead of 1.20. Then, with only half a mile of the final beat to go, a roller inside her wing broke, and Cairns and Anderson were unable to put any camber into it. They limped home only 38s ahead.

The seas were still flat for the third race with the wind again WSW at 10–12 k. *Patient Lady VI* won the start clearly and led by 25s, in distance about 150 m, at the first mark. But once again *Victoria 150* ran her down on the reaches and at the end of the first square downwind run led by 1.22. The breeze eased, then freshened on the following upwind leg and the Americans, apparently misjudging the angles, tacked away from the new breeze while the Australians tacked on to it. They rounded the next mark 2.30 ahead. On the following reach *Patient Lady VI*'s leeward bow began to split and she was forced to retire, leaving *Victoria 150* to complete the course alone. Two lay days allowed the US defender's works team to repair the damage before they lined up for the fourth race.

This time there was a fresh easterly breeze blowing into Long Island Sound from the Atlantic Ocean, averaging 15 k with gusts of 18 k. The hard, outrunning tide against the wind lifted a short, punishing sea, more than a metre high — almost survival conditions for such lightly built, high-speed machines. When they burst through the waves at 15 k upwind, they were almost airborne and the strain on their gear as they crash-landed was prodigious. They had an even start, with *Patient Lady VI* pointing a fraction higher than the Australian challenger. At the first mark, the Americans led by 11s, but once again *Victoria 150* outsailed them downwind. She was 30s ahead at the end of the first triangle, but lost 10s of this on the next beat and gained another 30s on the next run. At the end of the second square run, the Australians had built their lead to 1.30 and, with only 1.5 nm to beat to the finish, the long-coveted trophy was almost theirs. But for more than five minutes Cairns and Anderson had been hearing 'funny noises' inside their boat's hulls, sounds, they learned later, of longitudinal construction stringers breaking loose from the fastenings as the hulls pounded through the seas. So they gybed as carefully as they could at the bottom mark and nursed their craft home. She finished 54s ahead and thus won the best-of-seven match. Apart from Cairns' and Anderson's superb sailing, it was a special triumph for Cunningham and a great achievement for Scott, Love, Marmion, Mason, Fraser, and McKeon who had come to America to tend the boat they had built, sail the trial horse *Nicholas II* and live on a shoe-string budget, three to a motel room, pouring money out of their own pockets to cover the extra costs.

No drums were beaten when the news of the victory reached Australia, no politicians declared public holidays, there were no street parades, although, in a way, the performance of the Australian boat had been no less a scientific breakthrough than that of the radically keeled *Australia II* in the real America's Cup two years earlier.

But then there was no social glitter in the Little America's Cup, not many millionaires, nobody called anyone a liar or a cheat or a scoundrel, and they all parted good friends, promising to meet again with rivals from Italy and Britain on Port Phillip for the next series in 1987.

10

Ocean Racing: The Beginning and the Sydney–Hobart Classic

OCEAN RACING is many things. It is overwhelming tiredness, a constant physical pounding, a struggle against seasickness and obstinate sailcloth, as often as not in near-total darkness, when only a lifeline stands between safety and a lonely, miserable end. Ocean racing is a test of balance, experience and ingenuity brought to bear on taking a sextant sight on a diffused horizon, from a slanting, swooping deck. Ocean racing is being roused from an uneasy sleep to clamber up for a sail change, or for two hours' concentration at the helm while water bursts aboard in barrelsful. Ocean racing is wedging into a cubicle over a sloping chart so as to plot courses that can bring victory, or wreck the hopes of a year's ambition. Ocean racing is a spell at a stove bouncing from its gimbals and defying every effort to prepare a hot meal for shipmates. Ocean racing is the exhilaration of swooping downhill hour after hour with the spray flying in a hard, following wind; or the delight of gliding effortlessly under sunny skies with the clean sea air setting the spirits as free as the seabirds overhead. Ocean racing is lying becalmed with the sails flapping, the boat rolling to a swell, drifting uncontrollably as the crew broods on the private breeze that is driving the rest of the fleet forward over the horizon. Ocean racing in small yachts needs and breeds sailors of a special type. They must be able to live nose-to-nose in uncomfortable quarters for a week on end, and not only must they have all the skills of those who wage short tactical battles around harbour buoys, but also have the stamina and determination to sustain their efforts beyond the point of normal endurance.

Organized ocean racing, on truly offshore courses, began in Australia in 1864 when Charles Parbury's *Xarifa* thrashed the daylights out of William Walker's *Chance* in a southerly gale over 140 nm from Sydney to Newcastle and back. It was a two-boat challenge match arranged to test the qualities of *Xarifa*, a Sydney-designed-and-built, wooden-hulled cutter of 30 tonnes, against *Chance*, an English-designed-and-built, iron-hulled schooner of 71 tonnes. The rival owners were

239

Charles Parbury's *Xarifa*, topmast carried away, fights her way back to Sydney in a southerly gale to win Australia's first long distance ocean race. (From a painting in RSYS Archives)

wealthy foundation members of Royal Sydney Yacht Squadron, formed eighteen months earlier, and the prize was vainglory and a purse of 250 gold sovereigns, (today worth $31,000). Walker, because of the greater potential speed and allegedly proven design of his vessel, laid odds of six to four (150 to 100). There were many side bets, too. But, *Chance*, a poor performer to windward and with a mainly professional crew distinguished by over-confidence and bad judgement, finished four hours behind her smaller rival. *Chance*'s failure so depressed Walker, a man accustomed to success, that he sold her immediately as a Pacific Islands trader. *Xarifa* continued triumphant as 'Cock of Sydney Harbour' for six years.

That first race, and a few short informal bursts 'outside', some minor offshore handicaps, and occasional challenges to sail across the Tasman Sea and Bass Strait — which were recorded as epics of daring — seemed in the next eighty-two years to satisfy most of Australian amateur yachtsmen's blue-water racing ambitions. Even those who went on extended coastal cruises were considered dashing and Harold Nossiter and his sons, of Sydney, the first Australians to sail around the world in their 16.15 m schooner *Sirius* during 1935–37, were regarded with respectful awe.

Since 1898, there had been Tasmania's annual Bruny Island race, down Storm Bay, that although sometimes hazardous, could not rightly be called an ocean race at all, since most of it was sailed in sheltered waters; and there was one promising passage race in 1907 over 190 nm across Bass Strait from Queenscliff (Victoria) to Georgetown, in the mouth of the River Tamar (Tasmania). In the latter, four yachts, ranging from 11.58 m to 15.54 m, competed for an American trophy which was offered to inspire Australians to sail regularly in the open sea. Two of the skippers took their wives along as members of their crews and although one lady, after a tumultuous voyage, reached port with a wholesome distaste for the sea, the other, Mrs Edgar Newlands, who sailed aboard her husband's winning vessel *Thistle*, a 14.63 m yawl, enjoyed the experience so much that she

240

Edgar Newlands's 14.63 m Victorian yawl *Thistle*, winner of the Bass Strait race for the Rudder Cup in 1907. (RBYC Archives)

announced she would sail to England if invited. She and her husband treasured the elegant silver trophy, the Rudder Cup, that they had won, and it remained with the Newlands family for sixty-one years until it was re-dedicated for ocean racing in 1968 (detailed elsewhere). However, immediately after that first Bass Strait race, which started with a hard downwind run and finished in a full-scale southerly gale, most people supported the opinion that neither gentlemen yachtsmen nor their wives should be encouraged in such dangerous adventures, and it was twenty-two years before another similar contest could be organized. Even so, only three of the six entrants completed the second Bass Strait course, and the event lapsed until 1934, after which there was another spell of twelve years before it was sailed again.

During the 1930s there were also two dramatic Trans-Tasman races, one of 1,281 nm, the other 1,630 nm (described below). But it was not until 1945 — when

British Royal Navy captain John Illingworth persuaded a group of Sydney sailors to turn what had been planned as a 630 nm cruise to Hobart into a race — that regular long-distance ocean racing events were organized in Australian waters. The competitors were members of the Cruising Yacht Club of Australia (a body formed during World War II to provide occasional competition for those who could not race their boats because all established clubs had suspended operations) and one Tasmanian boat and crew. The salty Illingworth, an engineer in Sydney on duty with the British fleet, showed them how to handicap the boats according to the British Royal Ocean Racing Club's rating formula and himself agreed to compete in his newly acquired 10.67 m cutter *Rani*. The course, direct to Hobart, was down the NSW coast, across Bass Strait, down the east side of Tasmania, up Storm Bay and into the Derwent River.

Although few knew it, they were really in high class boating company. The tall, softly spoken Englishman, behind the gold braid and the diffident manner, was one of the toughest off-shore buckoes who had ever driven a yacht through a seaway, greatly respected in America (where regular long distance competition in small vessels had started in1906) and in England (where the first Fastnet Cup Race had been sailed in 1925). So, with a carefree spirit, the crews in nine craft, *Rani* among them, lined up for the event on Boxing Day and sailed out of Sydney Heads in a sparkling nor'easter for the run south. Before they had gone 80 nm, a lot of them began to learn about ocean racing. As the seas built up, untested gear began to carry away; poorly trained hands began to make those horrible sounds that indicate that they would sooner die than eat; decks and hulls, under unaccustomed strains, began to behave like badly constructed colanders. To top off this unhappy situation there came a bouncing southerly gale. A few not-so-stout hearts ran for brief shelter, others hove-to, and Captain Illingworth put on his oilskins and sniffed the air appreciatively. For the next two days Illingworth gave *Rani* and his crew all they could take on deck and below. When the garboards opened and water rose over the floor boards, Illingworth announced that bailing had always been more efficient than pumping; when the water tanks ran salt instead of fresh, he handed around a drinking ration in bottles; when the boys muttered unphilosophically about saturated bunks, he advised them to wait a bit and they would be able to wring them out. In fact, when the southerly eased and a nice westerly arrived to replace it, *Rani* was so far in front of the seven other craft still racing, that air searchers, despatched to look for survivors, failed to fly far enough south to sight her. It is sometimes said that most of those pioneer competitors, amazed at their own intrepidity, would not have wanted to repeat the experience had it not been for that air search and the astonishing publicity that attended the affair.

Newspaper editors, weary of four years of war news, saw in the ocean race all the elements of escapist adventure, ideally timed during the Christmas holiday period. The late Brian Penton, editor of the Sydney *Daily Telegraph*, and himself a yachtsman, led the way by encouraging his yachting reporter, Lou d'Alpuget, to boost the story to front-page treatment. The rest of the Press followed. Illingworth's awesome 'disappearance' at sea in *Rani* and reappearance after six days off Tasman Island, at the entrance of Storm Bay, 50 nm from the finishing line, paralyzed his rivals. *Rani* was first home in 6 days, 14 hours, 22 minutes — seventeen hours before the second boat home, Tasmania's 15.9 m *Winston Churchill* — and won the race on corrected time by thirty hours. The Englishman politely attributed his success to his crew and to luck. Apart from the race prizes,

Former Tasmanian 15.9 m *Winston Churchill* finished second when skippered by her Hobart owner-builder in the first Sydney–Hobart race and later competed for many years in major offshore events under the ownership of Victorian Sir Arthur Warner and his son Graham. *(SMH)*

he collected a wager of twenty-five guineas he had made with the then doyen of Sydney yachtsmen, James March Hardie, later commodore of Royal Sydney Yacht Squadron, who, although not competing, had bet Illingworth he would not get *Rani* to Hobart in under a week. The two men blew the stakes and a lot more on a memorable banquet for *Rani*'s complement and Hardie's harbour racing crew of *Windward II*.

Some of the members of the Cruising Yacht Club remained indignant at the highly coloured bravura ascribed by the newspapers to the men 'fighting for their lives in the raging seas'. But the more sophisticated welcomed the publicity knowing that no sailing race in history, apart from the America's Cup, had been brought to such public notice. Earl Le Brun, foundation secretary of the Cruising Yacht Club, shrewdly said, 'The more stories the better; this will make the yacht race to Hobart, and will give all forms of sailing a new dimension in the eyes of Australians.' And so it proved. The Sydney–Hobart handicap, which has started out of Sydney Harbour every Boxing Day (26 December) in unbroken sequence since 1945 (except in 1948 when it was delayed for a day 'so as not to desecrate the Sabbath') with the record 1985 fleet totalling 178, is now one of the major sporting events of Australia's year and one of the principal sailing races in the world. Ocean races over short, medium and marathon distances have become so popular that yacht clubs in every State of the Commonwealth hold them regularly. Illingworth saw that the development of ocean racing in Australia was assured after all the first-race brouhaha, and he congratulated the Press on an amazing coverage they had given to such an 'uneventful and routine performance'. 'You have elevated us to the stature of heroes,' he said.

Publicity has remained the keynote of the Sydney–Hobart race's success. At its Rushcutter Bay, Sydney, headquarters, the CYC mans an efficient Press centre eighteen hours a day from the time the race starts until it finishes and all competitors are safely in or nearing port. In Hobart the Royal Yacht Club of Tasmania, joint organizer of the race, operates an ancillary Press unit. Since 1957 every yacht, to qualify for entry, has had to carry an efficient radio transceiver and to report its position at least twice a day so that its progressive placing for line honours and possibly on handicap can be passed on to every branch of the news media. Since 1967 the progressive placings have been assessed by computer. A powerful, motor-driven radio relay vessel escorts the fleet, monitors all messages, issues weather forecasts and is on stand-by for distress calls. It is the CYC's boast that no yacht has ever been lost while racing to Hobart, nor any crew that sought help ever denied it since the event began. And up to and including the 1985 contest, when 2,614 yachts, manned by an estimated total of 20,744 men and boys and 132 women and girls had taken part in the races, only three men had died (two from heart attacks). Crewmen have, of course, suffered many minor and some serious injuries, as one would expect in the course of such a vigorous and sometimes violent sport, but none has been permanently incapacitated.

The enormous success of the compulsory radio-relay system in publicizing the Sydney–Hobart race and keeping it safe, and in stimulating public interest in all forms of yachting, ultimately persuaded overseas yacht clubs, who were resistant at first to what they regarded as regimentation of their sport, to adopt modified versions of it. Many have also followed the CYC's lead in imposing safety inspections of hulls and equipment and in modification of handicapping systems to give yachts of various types and sizes an equitable chance against each other. But in publicizing their races their efforts have remained a pale imitation of the Australian organization. Overseas movie coverage of yacht racing, with the exception of the America's Cup and, on a few occasions, the Royal Ocean Racing Club's Admiral's Cup world ocean racing championship series, cannot compare with the superb documentary feature films fostered by the CYC of the Sydney–Hobart race, photographed by daring cameramen from aeroplanes and helicopters hovering almost at masthead height in heavy weather and from aboard the competing yachts. Australia has also been among world leaders in attracting substantial commercial sponsorship for yachting, so much so that in 1976 the

Up to 1985 a total of 132 women and girls had sailed in the Sydney–Hobart race. Eight of them were in this all-woman crew of *Barbarian* in 1975. (L to R) Lesley Brydon, Ruth Rynehart, Narelle Cox, Nancy Shaw, Pam Brinsmead, Sheila Beach, Helen Neville and Vicki Willman (TAA sweater), the skipper. They placed 92nd in the fleet of 99. *(Hobart Mercury)*

CYC officially re-named the event the Hitachi Sydney–Hobart race and up to 1983 annually extracted a six-figure sum of money from a Japanese firm to cover expenses until Amalgamated Wireless Australia took over sponsorship and the race title in 1984.

Crowds of up to 200,000 now line the foreshores and headlands of Sydney Harbour and pack aboard a huge spectator fleet to watch the annual start on Boxing Day, and a million television viewers follow the progress of the race from the traditional starting line between Bradley's Head and Steel Point down the Harbour for two miles until the fleet turns south into the open sea. The crowding by unruly spectator craft, some manned by people with little regard for the basic rules of the nautical road and less for the safety and convenience of the racing boats negotiating this obstacle course down the Harbour, year after year used to turn the early stages of the race into chaos. Only the vigilance and skill of the crews in the sailing yachts averted serious collisions and loss of life. It appeared at one stage in the mid-1970s that the Harbour start would have to be abandoned in favour of a line set in clear water in the open sea off Sydney Heads, in order to avoid the riotous rubberneck fleet. But finally, with the help of patrol craft of the Maritime Services Board of NSW, water police and the Royal Volunteer Coastal Patrol, the spectators were herded clear from officially prohibited areas to give competitors a better chance of clear sailing.

The worldwide recognition of the Sydney–Hobart race as a worthy challenge to any sailor has induced ocean-racing enthusiasts from all Australian States and from many foreign countries to sail or ship their craft to Sydney to compete.

Confusion and curses: At the start of the 1967 Sydney–Hobart race, two-thirds of the fleet of 67 chased the drifting rounding mark at Sydney Heads, but the rest turned out to sea at the spot where the buoy should have been. Officials, exercising the wisdom of Solomon, decided that in a race of 630 nm no one was unduly prejudiced by having to sail an extra few hundred yards. *(SMH)*

Some wanted to enter multihulled craft — catamarans and trimarans — which they believed fit enough for the open sea. Their owners were keen to race against the accepted monohulls or to compete in a separate division but the Cruising Yacht Club vehemently rejected these downwind flyers on the grounds that they were unsafe, especially in heavy weather. The race has remained exclusively for monohulls.

At first the foreign competitors were round-the-world cruising vessels, refitting in Sydney, with owners who hopefully believed that their proven seagoing craft might make a showing. But the standard of competition improved so rapidly and these days is so high that only yachts designed and outfitted specifically for ocean racing within the modern handicapping rules, with specialized crews, can be seriously expected to have a chance. Modern ocean racing yachts, to qualify for the Sydney–Hobart race range, under the internationally accepted system, from the 20.5 ft rating (there is no metric equivalent in this system) to 70 ft rating and, on 1986 prices, are worth between $A80,000 and $A3 million. These yachts, on average, according to their size, cost their owners between $A8,000 and $A250,000 a year to campaign and maintain in ocean racing condition. A new spinnaker alone for a maximum rating yacht on 1986 prices costs $A15,000 and some would wear out three of these sails in a full season. As well, for the half year, the giants, among their crews of sixteen to twenty men, often carry four professionals whose wages, food, and air transport home may total $A130,000.

Because of the quality of their crews, the big vessels are usually driven to the limit of their potential performance. But even against moderately well-handled fleets of modern ocean racing yachts, Illingworth's performance in *Rani* would not place her within a day and a half of craft of comparable size and rating, sailing in the same conditions as those of that inaugural race of 1945.

The major overseas competitors in the Sydney-Hobart race have come from New Zealand, the USA, England, France, Japan, Germany, Hong Kong, South Africa, Ireland, Italy, Holland, Canada, and New Caledonia. Among them have been many of the world's outstanding offshore champions. Two of them, S. A. ('Huey') Long's 17.37 m yawl *Ondine* (in 1962) and Jim Kilroy's $A1.5 million 24.1 m ketch *Kialoa* (in 1975) have set first-home records for the course. *Kialoa's* mark, established in a series of favourably hard gales, was 62h 36m 56s for the 630 nm and was still standing in 1986. On handicap these visiting craft have performed well, too. Ted Turner's 21.9 m long, converted 12-metre class *American Eagle* (1972) and Kilroy's *Kialoa* (1977), both representing the USA, NZ Round The World Committee's *New Zealand* (1980), joined Illingworth's *Rani* (1945) as dual handicap and line honours winners. *Rainbow II* (Chris Bouzaid), of New Zealand, in 1967; *Morning Cloud* (Edward Heath), of England, in 1969; and *Pathfinder* (Brin Wilson), of New Zealand, in 1971, have taken handicap honours.

But in the forty-one races sailed up to 1985, thirty of the handicap winners have been yachts owned, built and crewed by Australians, and twenty have been Australian designed. The proudest record of any one vessel belongs to the sturdy 11.9 m double-ended *Freya*, built and jointly skippered by the Norwegian-born Sydney brothers Trygve (the designer) and Magnus Halvorsen, respected for the quality of yachts and power craft their family firms have built during two generations, for their ability as seamen and for their meticulous attention to detail. (By 1985 Magnus Halvorsen had sailed in thirty Sydney-Hobart races — five wins, six seconds, two thirds and two line honours.) Every part of the hull and item of equipment aboard the Halvorsens' craft, from masthead to keel, from stem to stern, down to spare shackles and rigging cotter pins, was double-checked and tested before the brothers put to sea. *Freya* won the main, overall handicap Sydney-Hobart prizes (the magnificent Tattersall's Cup, RORC, Government of Tasmania, CYCA and navigator's trophies — there are a dozen others for placegetters and for different categories) three times in succession, in 1963-64-65 in a variety of weather patterns and on each occasion came to her victor's berth in Constitution Dock, on the waterfront at Hobart, in immaculate condition, with her crew fresh and lively. Only one other yacht in the history of the world's major ocean races has equalled *Freya's* feat — American Carlton Mitchell's 11.6 m centreboard yawl *Finnisterre*, which won the overall handicap prize in the USA's biennial Newport-Bermuda race of 653 nm in 1956-58-60. In 1979, the Victorian One Ton Cup class yacht *Hot Prospect*, owned and twice skippered by Jim Searle, of Melbourne and then skippered by his son Neil, won the 480 nm West Coaster handicap from Port Phillip to Hobart for the third consecutive time. But neither the length of that race nor the quality of the opposition had yet put it in the same major category of the Sydney-Hobart or the Newport-Bermuda contests.

The Halvorsens also won the Sydney-Hobart handicap race in other yachts of their own design and construction — *Solveig*, 10.9 m (in 1954), and *Anitra V*, 11.6 m (in 1957), although in the former event, when the brothers were unable to sail because of illness, the yacht was skippered by their regular navigator, Captain Stanley Darling. With *Saga*, 10.5 m (1946); *Solveig* (1953); and *Anitra V* (1956-58-59), the Halvorsens took second placings. They were third in *Peer Gynt*, 10.9 m, in 1947. *Anitra V* would have won the 1956 race if she had been sailing on her correct rating but a mistake by the measurer cost her the margin of twelve minutes of corrected time by which she was beaten into second place.

Left Champion of Champions: The Halvorsen brothers' superb 11.9 m double-ended *Freya*, winner three times in succession, in 1963–64–65, of the Sydney–Hobart handicap and in a variety of weather patterns. *(Hobart Mercury)*

Right Happy crew: *Freya's* 1964 team after the yacht's second successive win in the Sydney–Hobart race. (L to R) Keith Brown, Trygve Halvorsen, Trevor Gowland, Magnus Halvorsen, Stan Darling, Barry Gowland and Stan McRae. *(Hobart Mercury)*

Up to 1985 only four yachts had won the race twice. These were the rugged Tasmanian-designed, built and owned 12.5 m cutter *Westward* (1947–48) skippered by George Gibson with Jock Muir as sailing master; Graham Newland's Sydney sloop *Siandra*, an English-designed Lion class of 10.7 m (1958–60); Vic Meyer's 17.4 m steel, Sydney sloop, *Solo*, designed by Alan Payne (1956–62); and Peter Kurts' American-designed 14.3 m sloop *Love and War* (1974–78). *Solo* was later famous as the round-the-world cruiser and, in 1978, as an Antarctic exploratory vessel. (*Solo* was not the first steel yacht to win the race — that honour went to Merv Davey's 13.1 m self-designed *Trade Winds* in 1949.) A score of yachts have come close to winning and each year produces its crop of hard luck stories . . . of those with the race within their grasp becalmed by freak changes of wind or current or foul tides while rivals, beaten earlier in wholesome breezes, have sneaked up into the lead on slants of wind that should not have been there; of crewmen who threw away critical hours by failing to report wind changes while their navigators were sleeping; of skippers who played it safe when they should have taken risks; of agonizing drifts in dead air over the final stages, across Tasmania's notoriously fickle Storm Bay and up the Derwent River to the finishing line, that have taken thirty hours instead of ten and have gnawed winning margins down to minor places.

In the forty-one Sydney–Hobart races sailed up to 1985 the thousands of crew men and women aboard the yachts have experienced almost every phase of emotion in scenes that ranged from high drama to slapstick comedy. There have been punch-ups before, during and after races, love affairs, irreparable quarrels, religious conversions, accusations of cowardice and dishonesty (including a claim that a yacht's auxiliary engine had been deliberately run and the seal replaced later) and the foundations laid for friendships that have endured unshaken for more than half a lifetime. A few crews have come ashore swearing they would never again sail with such a swine of a skipper or such an incompetently stupid watchmate as they had suffered during the race, but by far the greater number, having shared the hazards and efforts of four to eight days of close confinement in a common effort, have learned tolerance and respect for their shipmates.

One man who earned the admiration of his companions for fortitude and the title 'Stiff Upper Lip' was a handsome young Englishman Andrew Forbes, a marine scientist sailing aboard Sir Robert Crichton-Brown's burgundy-hulled, aluminium 16.5 m *Pacha*, in 1975. Forbes, working on the foredeck, had the top joint of his second finger of his right hand crushed off between the wire spinnaker pole toppin' lift and the mast when *Pacha* rolled during a gybe, walked calmly aft and said to Sir Robert, 'I'm afraid I won't be able to finish my watch, sir. I've cut off one of my fingers.' A crewmate found the piece of finger and packed it in dry ice but no micro-surgical junction was possible when Forbes reached Hobart six hours later. His only complaint was that he had been rushed ashore to hospital unnecessarily by a radioed launch and had missed sailing in *Pacha*

Gigantic organ pipes: Remarkable columns of dolerite, a coarse-grained basaltic rock, rise almost 305 m from the sea along parts of the Tasmanian peninsula. Tasman Island, final landfall for yachts in the Sydney–Hobart race, is crowned by a lighthouse. (Don Stephens)

across the finishing line.

The post race celebrations some crews conducted became legendary. The seriously minded, most efficient crews contented themselves with modest parties but for a period during the 1950s and 1960s it was traditional for the less inhibited to get drunk. Some remained in that condition for days. One crew on its first day ashore is said to have ordered 1,000 glasses of Tasmania's renowned Cascade beer and, with friends, to have continued to drink until they slid senseless alongside the hotel bar. A few incidents of wild horseplay and some acts of vandalism strained relations with the tolerant and hospitable Tasmanians who annually turned the town over to the yachtsmen. Ultimately the state of riot that had sometimes pervaded the Constitution Dockside for the first few days after the yachts had berthed subsided into reasonable forms of celebrations, socializing and renewal of friendships.

There are still, nevertheless, some spontaneous acts of *joie de vivre* that leave spectators in a state of shock. Few will forget or want to see repeated the terrifying gymnastic feat performed by *Ragamuffin*'s for'ard hand, Jack Christoffersen, in Constitution Dock in 1970. It was accepted as a gesture of defiance and frustration on behalf of the crew who sailed with owner-skipper Syd Fischer in *Ragamuffin*, then an Australian ocean racing champion that could win everything, it seemed, except the overall handicap prize in the Sydney–Hobart race. In the boisterous 1970 race *Ragamuffin* had been beaten into the second place by Sir Robert Crichton-Brown's *Pacha* by the narrow margin of 5m 41s. Christoffersen, a yacht engineer (and in 1977 an America's Cup challenge crewman and equipment trouble-shooter in *Gretel II*), renowned for his skill and agility aloft and for his strength for body weight — he stands 1.7 m and weighs 76 kg — swarmed hand-over-hand to the top of *Ragamuffin*'s 19.8 m mast, then almost incredibly, at first with both arms outstretched, stood upright on the cup-sized truck on one foot while he opened and drank a can of beer. The merrymaking crowd of some hundreds below gaped up at him, awed into silence until Christoffersen bowed, reached down, grasped the yacht's forestay and slid safely to the deck. Then the spectators' roar of relief, and some said disbelief at what they had seen, echoed from one end of the waterfront to the other. A special notice appeared on a wall at Constitution Dock next morning: 'Warning to birdmen and monkeys. All refreshments must be taken at deck level. By order, Race Committee.' In more recent times an increasing number of regular crewmen have dodged Hobart parties and have flown out immediately after the prize-giving formalities, leaving picnic crews to sail the yachts on holiday cruises along Tasmania's picturesque east coast back to their home ports.

Many of the crews, like those who sailed with the Halvorsen brothers, have found heroes to worship. In Hobart, old salts still talk of the intrepid Mrs Jane Tait, the middle-aged wife of the owner-skipper of the 15.5 m *Active*, and the first woman to sail the race, who, in 1946 during a 60 k sou'westerly nursed her injured husband, bailed with the crew when the pump jammed, took four-hour spells on the helm, and did the cooking for six days. Those who sailed aboard Phil Bullock's skinny 15.2 m gaff-rigged, converted international 8-metre class sloop *Defiance*, in 1947, remember the courage and determination of their skipper, Jack Tiernan, who ran the boat out of a 65 k storm into partial shelter behind Maria Island on the Tasmanian coast, climbed hand over hand up the 19.8 m mast and cut away the topsail that was jammed between the gaff and topmast so that the torn mainsail could be lowered and a stormsail set. *Defiance*

Syd Fischer's *Ragamuffin* No. 3, hard driven under spinnaker, blooper, tallboy and main, surges south to Hobart through a sparkling sea. Although Fischer, in six boats of the same name, had won almost every important offshore handicap sailed from Sydney up to 1985, he had missed the main Sydney-Hobart prize. But he was second twice. *(SMH)*

fought on to finish fifth across the line to the late Sir Claude Plowman's 19.8 m cutter *Morna*, establishing the first of her three consecutive line-honours victories. (Later, renamed *Kurrewa IV*, under the ownership of the South Australian grazier brothers Frank and John Livingston, she was four more times first across the line in Hobart.)

Defiance had led *Morna* most of the way and had sailed a splendid race, but two days after she finished was disqualified, on a technicality. She had been involved, blamelessly as it seemed, with *Morna* and the previous year's winner

Elderly South Australian millionaire grazier brothers, the late John (left) and the late Frank Livingston, owners of ocean racers *Kurrewa III* and *Kurrewa IV* (formerly *Morna*) always had a new gadget and lent colour to the sailing scene. *(SMH)*

Christina, in a mêlée at the start five days earlier. *Defiance* had been jammed up at the windward end of the line into collision with the starter's boat. This incident led to *Christina*'s disqualification (in spite of her crew's protestations of victimization) because officials judged her guilty of failing to give *Morna* right of way as the boats manoeuvred before the gun. *Defiance* was disqualified because neither Bullock, her owner, nor Tiernan, her skipper, had reported their boat's part in the incident in writing within twenty-four hours of having crossed the finishing line. At the time it seemed a raw decision and many yachtsmen who saw the incident believed the real culprit had been *Morna*, barging down at the windward end of the line with doubtful rights.

The same year the crew of Hal Evans's 10.4 m yawl *Moonbi*, second on handicap (and later to establish a record over four races of a win, two seconds and a fourth) came ashore communicating mysteriously between themselves with peculiar cooing sounds. They had good reason. In those early years, until radio position reports became routine in 1951 (compulsory from 1957 onward), no individual ship-to-shore communication was encouraged. Indeed one of the CYC's flag officers had so bitterly opposed such a 'heresy' that his committee rejected the idea when Lou d'Alpuget, then navigator of the 14.3 m *Josephine*, first proposed it. Evans decided to thwart the verandah admirals. So *Moonbi*'s team, encouraged by her watch captain, the young newspaper reporter Frank McNulty (later a crewman in *Gretel*'s 1962 America's Cup challenge and in *Ragamuffin* in the Admiral's Cup) took aboard two baskets of carrier pigeons. McNulty's plan was to get exclusive eye-witness reports of the race back to his newspaper by loosing the pigeons daily with rice paper messages fastened in capsules on their legs. He got one report through in this way, but the pigeons generally were a disaster. Some were seasick and refused to fly off when the weather was bad.

One did a tight circuit of the yacht then swooped back down the main hatch on to its basket. Worst of all, the birds kept everyone awake with their incessant cooing, spilt pigeon peas from one end of the yacht to the other and made the cabin stink like a fowlyard. The crew wanted to make them into a pie, but this McNulty refused to allow. He was rewarded when one of the birds laid an egg on his pillow.

The Halvorsens, too, had bird trouble, in a later race, but these were sea birds, allegedly gifted with a sixth sense of direction but on this occasion in a thick Tasmanian fog blundering about everywhere. They repeatedly flew into *Freya's* sails and perched like hens in her rigging. Then a great Southern Albatross, as big as a turkey, banged head-on into the mainsail and tobogganed down on to helmsman Magnus Halvorsen's head and shoulders. It clung to him with its enormous talons, squawking wildly and snapping with its dangerous hooked beak as he tried to dislodge it. Finally crewman Trevor Gowland, wearing gloves, grabbed the bird by its legs and slung it overboard.

Stories of encounters with sea monsters and other creatures of the deep are common among the Sydney–Hobart race crews. There have been constant near-misses with whales and some collisions with them and with sunfish and submerged logs, resulting in varying degrees of damage. In 1953, a giant whale surfaced alongside Norman Howard's immaculate, blue-hulled South Australian sloop *Southern Myth* off the Tasmanian coast and blew so hard that the jet of water and air from its head burst the yacht's straining spinnaker. In 1955, a pack of sharks off the Tasmanian coast swarmed around John Colquhoun's 10.7 m *Lass o'Luss*, Rus Slade's 11.6 m *Janzoon* and John Palmer's 16.5 m *Even* and one shark, biting at the spinning rotator of *Even's* log, followed it right up to the stern of the yacht as the line was being hauled in. The shark, 4.26 m long, surged clear out of the water at deck height, snapped at a sheet block and, after sliding back, seized the rudder in its jaws and shook it violently. The hardwood rudder blade, heavily scored from the shark's teeth, was an object of considerable interest when *Even* reached port.

In 1954, *Solveig*, scoring the Halvorsen's first race win, bent her 45 mm stainless steel rudder stock when she ran into a two ton sunfish basking just under the surface. A killer whale, all of 9.14 m long, haunted *Anitra V* for almost a day in 1956, at times lifting its massive head clear of the water as it eyed crewmen working astern. On a dark night in 1960 John Colquhoun's *Lass o'Luss* ran right up on the back of a sleeping whale and was flipped off as the startled creature sounded. The slap of its 6 m wide tail missed the yacht but sent half a barrelful of water down the open main hatch into the cabin.

In a less spectacular encounter with wildlife in the 1960 race, Jack Earl's crew of *Maris*, oozing along in a light following wind wide off the Tasmanian coast, fed sausages to a family of friendly seals who had been sheltering, apparently from the midday sun, in the shade of huge fronds of floating kelp. Such experiences with sea creatures have become so commonplace during the forty-one Sydney–Hobart races sailed up to 1985, in which the fleets have logged a combined total of 1.9 million man-hours across Bass Strait, that these days they need some special twist for crewmen even to mention them.

Personal quirks of behaviour, like that of the for'ard hand who ate nothing but raw carrots and cheese for five days, and the girl who announced her engagement to a shipmate after one race because he was the only crewman who cleaned his teeth every day ('I had to marry one of them,' she quipped) still qualify

Spinnakers set in a fresh southerly and a nightmare ahead of crews trying to keep clear of the unruly spectator fleet on the run down Sydney Harbour on the way to Hobart. (*SMH*)

for the folklore of the event. The behaviour of some skippers has earned them esoteric nicknames, some so explicit as to be unprintable. One skipper was widely known as Chaos because of his inability to organize anything, and another, in the early days, had the unenviable title Starvation. He provisioned his yacht with a carton of tinned stores, a bucket of potatoes, ten loaves of bread and a hunk of cheese, to feed his crew for six days. They finished the race eating sardines on slices of the fruit cake that the navigator's wife had given them just before they sailed. Such gastronomic nightmares are not so uncommon as one may think, but most properly run ocean racers are well provisioned and the meals are carefully balanced. All yachts usually carry emergency rations to feed everyone aboard for at least a fortnight. Racing menus may include grilled steaks, roast beef, ham salads, mushroom omelettes, with a wide choice in between according to the capacity and inspiration of the cook. Much of the food is pre-cooked, or pre-prepared, frozen, labelled and stacked in ice boxes in order of intended use. In most ocean racers two or three people are rostered as cooks, with others deputed to clear up after them. A few of the really big visiting yachts, with sixteen to twenty men in their crews, have carried professional cooks, who spend eighteen hours a day serving three separate sittings for the different watches, with occasional snacks. Some of these highly prized and well-paid sea cooks have been women, permanently employed by the millionaire owners of the vessels and flown regularly half way across the world to race starts.

The dangers of sailing offshore in small craft that are properly designed and built for the open sea and handled by seasoned crews are statistically fewer than the dangers of driving motor cars on a wet road. Smooth-water sailors, though, unused to the ocean's occasional roar and the looming, foam-topped masses of water that offshore sailors accept as part of the scene, regularly sound off about the need for extra safety controls. No one denies the need for restrictions on the foolhardy and reckless, but the timid and fearful often imagine hazards where none exist. The American Thomas Fleming Day, father of modern ocean racing and celebrated for his colourful polemic in defence of the sport in the US magazine, *Rudder*, which he edited with panache, once delivered himself of a broadside against the croakers and their published opinions:

> Newspaper men ought to know better than to consult a lot of grey-headed, rum-soaked piazza scows about such racing. What do those miserable old hulks, who spend their days swigging booze on the front stoop of a clubhouse, know about the dangers of the deep? If they ever make a voyage from Larchmont to Cow Bay in a ten-knot breeze it is the event of their lives, an experience they never forget and never want to repeat. What does the average yachtsman know about sea sailing? Absolutely nothing! Then let him hold his tongue.

But occasional alarms, when proven offshore racing yachts suffer unexpected damage, are badly managed or fail to report their position after storms, resulting in expensive sea and air searches, do bring official disapproval on the sport in general — and incite the 'piazza scows' to another chorus of calamity howling. While there have been some near-disasters, no yacht had sunk while competing in the Sydney–Hobart race up to 1985. John Farren-Price's disabled 10.4 m *Lolita* came close to it in 1963 and was saved only when an Australian Navy submarine answered her radioed SOS call and towed her to safety. It was a near thing, too, for Graham Shields' 11 m *Thunderbolt* in 1970 until a weather research ship took her in tow. Also in 1970, fishermen plucked Vince Walsh's crippled *Boambillie* off the notorious St Helen's bar, on the north-east coast of Tasmania, after she had alerted the nearby town with rockets. Veteran Peter Green, one of the true shellbacks of Australian ocean racing who by 1984 had sailed for Hobart thirty-three times, tells of a near disaster with a happy ending:

> In 1954 I skippered the *Gipsy Queen* for Charlie Eden and our rudder head snapped off in heavy weather 200 miles from the finish. We were crippled. Then the wind fell light and came astern, and we managed to steer the boat by careful sail trimming all down the Tasmanian coast and into Storm Bay and Derwent River, during a series of extraordinary wind changes. In the last 20 m, just as we were about to cross the finishing line for second place on handicap (only 43m 14s behind the Halvorsens' *Solveig* in the fleet of seventeen) an official boat forced us off course and we bumped the finishing buoy. We were disqualified for that but after an appeal direct to the IYRU we were given the prize.

Many men have fallen, slipped or been washed overboard. All but one have clambered back, been hauled aboard by shipmates or saved by lifelines attached to safety harnesses. In the wild race of 1984, a seventy-year-old crewman, Wal Russell, of Lake Macquarie, sailing his sixteenth time to Hobart, was swept overboard at night 20 nm of the NSW coast into heavy seas from John Elgar's 11.58 m *Yahoo II*. In spite of desperate efforts at rescue by his shipmates they were unable to reach him. He was last seen, apparently unconscious, floating face down, and an intense search of the area for two days by Sea Safety aircraft failed to find his body. It was the first drowning in the history of the race. In 1973, a young man, John Sarney, died of a heart attack on the NZ yacht *Inca* (see Chapter 15: Southern Cross Cup); and, in 1975, Harry Vallance, crewman of the Sydney boat, *Zilvergeest*, died of a heart attack when the yacht ran aground not far from the finishing line. A near drowning had occurred on 30 December 1965 when, off the Tasmanian coast at dawn, Lieut Franco Barbalonga, navigator of the Italian Navy's 19.81 m ketch *Corsaro II* was flicked over the side by a wire spinnaker brace. The yacht's gear was in such a tangle that *Corsaro's* crew of naval cadets could not sail back to him, and their emergency engine would not start. But they had the good sense to fire distress rockets, and radioed an alarm. Half an hour later, Lieut Barbalonga was two miles astern of his yacht, chilled through and just afloat, when Gordon Marshall, sailing master in the sloop *Corroboree* (and later a senior flag officer of the CYC), spotted him and altered course for the rescue. *Corroboree* took him to Hobart. The Italian community there hired the city's Town Hall for a thanksgiving party to *Corroboree's* crew and the Italian Government made them all life members of their Navy's yachting association. Marshall still keeps as a memento the one item of clothing Lieut Barbalonga was wearing when *Corroboree* rescued him — a white sock.

The element of danger, no matter how minor compared with other boisterous sports, adds spice to the public interest in the Sydney–Hobart race. Inevitably, too, any one event in which more than 1,000 people from all walks of life, from millionaires to milkmen, from doctors to dustmen, are engaged at the same time, using machines worth a total of $A20 million, is hardly likely to be ignored. Nevertheless, since very few people ashore see anything of the event after the start, there is little doubt that the race would soon lapse into a semi-private contest between the participants without the tremendously efficient information service now behind it. On the other hand, the non-yachting public persistently fails to understand that the real race is not the battle to be first across the finishing line but is a handicap for an overall prize and for a growing number of divisions of craft of comparable size.

The overall handicap winner is the yacht with the lowest corrected time after all elapsed times for the course have been multiplied by a Time Correction Factor. This TCF is a four-figure decimal fraction (one plus the decimals for very big, high-rating vessels). Each yacht has its own TCF based on a scientifically devised international formula of ratings, intended, theoretically, at least, to give every vessel, whatever its size or rig and whatever the weather conditions, an equal chance against every other vessel. So no Sydney–Hobart race winner can be named until most of the small, low-rating craft have finished the course. This may be a day or more after the big, fast, front-runners have finished. To try to stimulate public interest in the true handicap race the CYC's Press Centre issues a computer-assessed handicap placing along with details of the line-honours placings. Since these assessments can be based only on each boat's last radioed latitude and longitude and no realistic projection of its progress over the rest of the course can be given, even the time it would take to reach the leader's position (if the race were to end there), placings by computer are far from accurate. It is rare, indeed, for any computerized handicap leader, right up to the last day of the race, eventually to prove the winner. So news media writers, well aware of the weakness of pre-finish handicap forecasts, whatever way they may be assessed, and often suspicious that lime-lighters, to attract attention, may have advanced their radioed latitudes and longitudes, dodge the handicap handouts and concentrate their stories on the front runners. These big yachts usually have the best navigators and their positions can be more accurately

Sydney's colourful Jack Rooklyn and his crews sailed the 22.3 m *Ballyhoo* with verve and determination and added line honours in the Sydney–Hobart race to their many international victories. *(SMH)*

checked. The main public interest therefore continues to focus on the first-home, line-honours battle. Yachtsmen know, of course, that the biggest boat, if it is well designed, rigged and sailed, is theoretically the fastest and therefore must be the first in. So the experienced sailors try to take educated guesses about the best performed smaller craft in relation to each other.

There has been genuine interest in line-honours battles, however, in recent years when a number of big vessels of comparable speed have competed. Those races in which the American maxi-ketches *Windward Passage*, owned and skippered by Fritz Johnson, *Kialoa* (Jim Kilroy), the Australian sloop *Ballyhoo* (Jack Rooklyn), and *Buccaneer* (Tom Clark) of New Zealand competed, were truly exciting. In 1975 *Kialoa*, driven to the limit of her speed in fresh reaching winds, finished first in the record time (still standing in 1986) of 62h 36m and 56s, at an average speed of better than 10 k. *Kialoa* was 22m 4s ahead of *Windward Passage* at the line with *Ballyhoo* 1h 41m 13s further back. In that race those three, and six other much smaller yachts, bettered the earlier record 73h 32m 9s that the Sydney-owned, ferro-cement 22 m *Helsal* (Dr Tony Fisher) had set in 1973. But the closest contest was sailed in 1982 when, in light weather near the finish, Bob Bell's visiting 23.46 m *Condor of Bermuda* beat Jack Rooklyn's 21.94 m *Apollo* by 7s, a distance of one metre in the drifting conditions. Some members of the Australian boat's crew and some spectators were certain that the luff of *Apollo*'s spinnaker was just ahead as they crossed the line, that officials in the judge's box had been unsighted and had declared Bell's boat the winner because her stem head was clear. In any case, each skipper and each crew congratulated the other for a wonderful performance. *Apollo*'s senior watchkeeper, Sandy Schofield, a 1967 America's Cup crewman who had been aboard eight earlier first-home boats and had raced in big vessels across the North Pacific, the Atlantic and in the Bermuda race said: 'You'd sail a lifetime and not be in such a finish. I thought the forty men aboard the two boats were going to explode with excitement.'

Until then the closest contest had been in 1962 when, also in light weather, near the finish, 'Huey' Long's 17.37 m American yawl *Ondine* overhauled Victorian Peter Warner's 22.25 m schooner *Astor* (formerly *Ada*) which had led throughout, at one stage by 40 nm, in hard reaching conditions, and beat her to the gun by exactly 60s. Yachtsmen thought that the aluminium-hulled *Ondine*'s then record time, 75h 46m 16s, was the ultimate in speed for a vessel of her size over the 630 nm course. They could not foresee the next sixteen years of scientific development in yacht design, application of sophisticated engineering principles to hull construction, the use of strong new lightweight materials and improvement in equipment, especially of electronic aids to navigation, that would bring *Ondine*'s performance within the scope of craft four metres shorter, when they got conditions to suit them.

By 1977 some of the developments in design, especially of yachts qualified for internationally recognized level rating class championships (in which those of the same rating race against each other off the mark, without handicaps) were sensationally radical by previous standards. Many designers rejected hull forms that had once seemed ideal for the open sea and produced, instead, tortured shapes that beat the rules on which ratings were based, thus giving them a built-in advantage when time-correction factors were applied to elapsed times to establish handicap winners. To reduce the drag of wetted surface, ballast keels had been shortened to such a degree that some yachts had little directional stability, even with stern rudders mounted on skegs, and demanded extreme concentration from the most skilful helmsmen to keep them on course. On reaches in fresh winds many of the new short-keeled yachts would broach (round up) violently with consequent strain on crews, rigging and sails. Some designers, depending on a minimum of inside ballast and on crew weight for stability and on retractable centreboards for lateral plane, had discarded ballast keels altogether. With their boards lifted their yachts had the ability to plane downwind like smooth-water dinghies.

Worst of all, or so it seemed to the die-hard purists, designers regarded weight of construction that had been synonymous with strength as a dirty word. Scantlings of decks, topsides and strengthening framework had been reduced to such minimums to save weight that from the waterline up some hulls were a quarter of the weight of fine racing craft of the same volume that had proved themselves in all conditions offshore. Many yachts were so frail throughout that

Joy and frustration: Roaring downwind at 16 k in hard following easterlies in 1962, the massive Sydney schooner *Astor* led the US boat *Ondine* to Tasman Island by 40 nm. But around the corner, caught under the lee of Cape Raoul, *Astor* lies becalmed, losing the time that was later to cost her line honours to *Ondine* by exactly 60s. (*SMH* and *Hobart Mercury*)

their ballast keels, precariously attached to hulls with thin bolts, threatened to split away from their hull joints when they bounced off a moderate sea. Some had decks that flexed like trampolines.

Nevertheless, despite their frailty, the new breed of lightweights and ultra-lightweights were fast, a delight to sail in moderate conditions, and, because their designers had exploited the measurement rules, their ratings were so low that older craft of more conventional design and construction needed special age allowances to be able to compete reasonably against them. There remained on the debit side, though, the inescapable fact that the newcomers were useless except for racing, were so skinned out of equipment that they had no proper accommodation for cruising, and were so capricious in hard winds that only a crew of experts could manage them.

By late 1977, administrators of the ORC who had observed this worldwide trend to what conservative yachtsmen called ultra-lightweight freaks, were beginning to realize that some form of restriction was needed, either by imposition of minimum scantlings (and therefore strength) for various materials or by penalties on rating. Some officials, while privately deploring potentially dangerous boats, had previously sought to justify their public tolerance of them by claiming that owners, driven by a fierce competitive spirit, wanted them that way, and had spent millions of dollars in the process, and that ocean racing must be a 'development sport' open to experiment, using new methods and materials. Most people would agree that there was nothing inherently wrong with lightweight

Stan Edwards' *Margaret Rintoul II* (formerly *Ragamuffin* No 1) proved, in 1978, that she was still a grand boat when hard driven by a seasoned crew. She placed second in the Sydney–Hobart race. But here, under storm rig in 1977 she, like many others, was forced to retire. *(SMH)*

construction provided that the materials and the engineering systems had enough strength to withstand the rigours of use, as had been achieved in the aircraft industry. An easy solution to the problem of weight for yachts, it seemed, would be for science magically to produce a material with the specific gravity of polystyrene foam and the tensile and impact strength of mild steel. But as things stood, how could the administrators continue to recognize scientific advances in building materials and methods, at the same time identify types of craft suitable for all conditions of the open sea — which had been the original concept of yachts that were to take part in ocean racing — make pragmatic decisions and yet be ready to change them without inconveniencing everyone?

That was the position in 1977 when a record number of 131 yachts, many of them conspicuous for their development in design and in lightweight and ultra-lightweight construction, started in the Sydney–Hobart race. The fleet included seventy-six craft with hulls constructed from various forms of glass-reinforced plastic or what is popularly known in Australia as fibreglass (the first such vessel to race to Hobart, and indeed the first fibreglass yacht in Australia, had been Russell Slade's 12.7 m *Janzoon II* in 1961), many with lightweight cores of foam and other materials; thirty-four from timber, of conventional planks or of plywood (cold-moulded laminates and sheet); sixteen from welded aluminium plate; three from welded steel plate and two from ferro-cement.

The race was sailed in generally moderate to light conditions with forty hours of intervening gales, averaging 30 k but in gusts reaching 50 k, and punishing head seas that revealed many weaknesses in the yachts, their rigging and crews, and forced fifty-eight retirements. Unfortunately, as reports of the retirements mounted, a bulletin issued by a CYC official from race headquarters hoping, no doubt, to explain the embarrassing number of failures, stated that the conditions were the roughest in the history of the race and that the seas were mountainous. This was far from true: many races had been sailed in consistently harder winds and rougher seas. But, considered in conjunction with a mayday call from one yacht and with complete radio silence from some yachts (unknown to officials they were still racing but their radio transmitters had broken down), fears were felt for their safety and help was sought from the Commonwealth Marine Operations Centre's rescue organization. Immediately, extensive air and sea alerts began, involving the Royal Australian Air Force, commercial aircraft and shipping, police and fishermen. The cost in time, effort and public money was high. And it was not necessary, although no one was to know that until some days later.

It turned out that no yachts, even those that had been dismasted through rigging failure, had been in desperate straits. Nearly all those that had retired had made their own way to port under jury rig or, after breaking propeller locks on emergency engines, under power, without any help whatever, and there had been no need to push the panic button so hard. Still, there remained the question of fifty-eight retirements, 44 per cent of the total of 130 boats that had been racing until they met the first of the heavy weather. The 131st competitor, the massive ferro-cement *Helsal*, had retired in the first fifteen minutes because of severe hull damage suffered in a pre-start collision with a State Government-owned spectator ferry. It might have been reasonable to expect a heavy crop of withdrawals in the early days of Australian ocean racing when small yachts were rarely designed for merciless driving in the open sea and few crewmen had even extended cruising experience offshore. But after thirty-three years of development and regular, year-round competition over a variety of courses surely one could expect better than this. So a great deal of soul-searching began.

Of the drop-outs, thirty-two had been built of fibreglass, eighteen of timber, six of aluminium and two of steel; there was, therefore, no positive clue that any one type of material was necessarily preferable to another for hull construction. Size did not prove seaworthiness, either, since Division A yachts, the biggest, had a 31 per cent retirement rate; Division B, 48 per cent; Division C, 52 per cent; and Division D, 39 per cent (including three visiting ultra-lightweight Half Ton Cup class boats but only 30 per cent if those were excluded).

A detailed analysis of the reasons given by the skippers and crews for their retirements was most revealing. The weather was plainly too rough for 24.5 per cent and another 24.5 per cent suffered rigging failure; hull failures represented 19.7 per cent and seasickness another 17 per cent; 4.7 per cent suffered sail damage; 3.8 per cent battery failures (no communications or navigation lights); 2 per cent had men hurt and another 3.8 per cent gave a variety of unclassified reasons. It appeared, therefore, that at least twenty-four of the vessels that had started, that is, those who found the conditions too rough and those who suffered too much seasickness, had no business taking part in the race, and that at least eleven others had had hulls unequal to the task. Officials went deeper than this in their analysis, concluding that ultra-lightweight yachts, especially those with centreboards, were the least suitable craft for storm conditions. Of the seven of ultra-lightweight construction – six of them with centreboards – all but one had retired, hull damage being given as the reason in five of the six cases. The seventh reached the finishing line but had suffered structural damage to the hull. While ultra-lightweight boats constituted only 5 per cent of the fleet they made up 50 per cent of the hull failure retirements.

'A means has to be found to identify these yachts adequately so that such a high retirement rate can be avoided in the future,' said Gordon Marshall, CYC rear commodore and chairman of the sailing committee, who prepared the analysis. 'Although the International Offshore Racing Council has already made clear its intention to re-rate these types of yachts to reduce their rating-to-speed advantage under the present rules, we have to face up to the safety hazards of those already built and also those which may be constructed notwithstanding the new rules.'

Marshall was also critical of that nursery of ultra-lightweight type of yachts: level rating competitions in which craft compete off the mark, without handicaps, for State, national and world championships. The 1977 Sydney–Hobart race had immediately followed national and world championships for Half Ton and One Ton level rating classes off the NSW coast and in New Zealand, and the ultra-lightweight yachts had emerged tried and tested from these contests. 'If this is the type of yacht which proves best for level rating, then it is time we all recognized that ocean racing, as typified by the Sydney–Hobart race, is an altogether different league,' added Marshall.

Such a broadside from one of Australia's most senior and respected officials could not be ignored. By December 1978, on the eve of the thirty-fourth Sydney–Hobart race, the Australian Yachting Federation and the world Offshore Racing Council had imposed worldwide penalties on light displacement yachts by introducing a basic displacement to length factor which meant that boats that were light and long suffered an increase in rating. Officials also took away the rating advantage that lightweight boats could previously obtain when artificially immersed at the bow for measurement. Penalties were imposed on any rigging which was below 25 per cent of the distance between the deck and the top of the forestay. Adjustment of the fore and aft position of the masthead was limited. Although centreboarders were not specifically penalized for the 1978 Sydney–Hobart race, their owners were forewarned that in future a penalty of 1.5 per cent increase to their ratings would be imposed if they chose not to lock their boards down. These measures assuaged those owners of the more traditional yachts who saw their vessels outrated and obsolete. Although officials had not banned the lightweights, as some yachtsmen had hoped they might, the new rules sought more equitably to handicap them. The owners of the so-called freaks railed against the rule-makers but they took heart when their yachts continued to win major and minor placings in short, middle and long-distance events in light, moderate and fresh conditions. 'Light is fast,' they intoned defiantly. 'If you are good enough to sail our boats, they are easier to handle all-round than traditional old heavyweights and better seaboats.' Conservative sailors, on the other hand, pointed to the spartan living conditions on the new machines, to the chances of being swept overboard and to their awkward habit of flicking their masts over the side. They applauded the officials.

Starters in the thirty-fourth Sydney–Hobart race were down to ninety-seven from the record of 131 of the previous year. But it was still a record entry for a slack year because many overseas and some interstate yachtsmen who normally came on odd-numbered years to compete in the biennial Australian-controlled Southern Cross Cup series of four races, of which the Sydney–Hobart is one, had not nominated.

Only a few half-hearted skippers and crews, mindful of the dusting they had taken a year earlier, had lost their stomach for the adventure. Officials felt reassured that the race had lost none of its charisma. An excited spectator fleet followed the racing yachts out of Sydney Harbour in a fresh north-easter and a million television viewers saw them beat their way to the Heads and peel away for the run southwards. But then there was a series of dreadful anticlimaxes. First, Alan Bond's highly fancied 14 m *Apollo IV* (the former USA and world Two Ton Cup class champion *Williwaw*), imported only a week earlier and sailing her first race in Australia, broke her carbon-fibre-reinforced rudder stock and had to retire only 15 nm south of Sydney. On the second day, Syd Fischer's chartered 14 m *Superstar* (the former Victorian Admiral's Cup representative, considered by many a certainty for a major placing) suffered rigging failure and withdrew. Then the fresh following breeze that was carrying the eight front-runners—led by Tony Fisher's *Helsal*, Jack Rooklyn's 17.7 m *Apollo*, Josca Grubic's giant South Australian ketch *Anaconda II* and Ken Page's and George Mottle's *Casablanca*—at a fast clip down the NSW coast, faded and left the main body of the fleet stranded 50 nm behind them in a completely different weather pattern. When the leaders reached the northern Tasmanian coast, after an easy Bass Strait fetch in a light westerly, they were 80 nm clear of the boats at the head of the next group and 150 nm ahead of scores that had been forced to claw to windward in fickle winds. Many of these yachts had handicaps that would have given them good chances in consistent winds but they were now so far behind that they had no hope. The race was virtually over for them before they had sailed halfway.

The line-honours race was a special triumph for Rooklyn's *Apollo*, designed ten years earlier by Bob Miller (Ben Lexcen). She had reached Sydney from Honolulu only ten hours before the start and a maintenance gang waiting at the dockside had joined her tired delivery crew to get her ready. *Apollo* finally outpaced *Helsal* by 38 m on the beat up Storm Bay and Derwent River in light winds in the slow time of 4d 2h 23m 40s. A wry Rooklyn, who had been first home in his 22.3 m superboat *Ballyhoo* in 1976, said, 'You don't need to spend a million bucks to get here first.' But the ultimate honour, the handicap, went to Peter Kurts' 14.3 m *Love and War* (the 1974 winner), shrewdly sailed by a well-balanced team who benefited from the boat's age allowance, new sails, a bigger mainsail and re-ballasting.

But neither Rooklyn nor Kurts would have had so much joy if officials had recognized West Australian Rolly Tasker's 22.9 m aluminium sloop *Siska* as a starter. They were under much pressure from the public to do so because Tasker, a former world dinghy champion and Olympic silver medallist, had designed

In 1983, Victorian Lou Abrahams in *Challenge*, after years of consistent trying, read the tricky windshifts right and outsailed a fleet of 172 to win the Sydney–Hobart handicap. (Bob Ross)

and built the big red-hulled boat himself and, with his wife, had sailed her to Sydney only three days before the race, believing, he claimed, that *Siska*'s entry had been formally accepted. But the yacht rated 4 ft above the maximum IOR limit of 70 ft, and Tasker failed, through a series of errors and misunderstandings, it seems, to make changes in spinnaker and spinnaker pole sizes that would have enabled him to present a valid certificate (of 68.5 ft) in time to qualify. Tasker criticized officials when they declared his boat a non-starter, and, with a protest flag flying, sailed *Siska* across the starting line five minutes ahead of the gun and set out for Hobart. At the end of the first day *Siska* was 30 nm clear of the race leaders and continued to gain on them, proving herself by far the fastest yacht in Australia. Unofficially she crossed the finishing line in Hobart after three days and a few hours of sailing, almost 23h ahead of *Apollo*. If Tasker had complied with the rules and had qualified for a rating certificate, *Siska* would have won not only line honours but also the handicap, joining *Rani*, *American Eagle* and *Kialoa* as a double victor. There was consolation nevertheless for Tasker in Victoria's Great Circle race of 810 nm two weeks later (see Chapter 13). As an epilogue to the 1978 Sydney–Hobart race, the light fickle winds that wrecked so many handicap chances and completely confused the theories of rating adjustments that officials had hoped would be defined, finally turned to savage gales on the Tasmanian coast. The Brisbane 7.9 m *Klinger*, a former champion Half Tonner of lightweight NZ design and the smallest boat ever to sail in the race, finished last after a desperate struggle of 8d 4h 48m 42s. On the seventh day, off the Tasman Peninsula, she capsized in a storm and rolled completely over before she righted herself. All her crew survived. '*Klinger* proved one thing about lightweight ocean racers,' said one grim CYC official. 'They need crews that are tough — and bloody lucky.'

The thirty-fifth race, in 1979, produced a crop of new records: a fleet of 147 starters; 142 finishers; the fastest time for the slowest boat to finish reduced to 4d 9h 34m 51s; and Tasmania's third win, with the smallest boat ever to take the handicap prize. She was *Screw Loose*, a 9 m Half Ton Cup class sloop owned and skippered by Bob Cumming, a Burnie butcher from Mersey Yacht Club, Devonport, and crewed by five friends who had not given themselves much chance before the start. But they drove *Screw Loose* hard in an unusual pattern of free-sheet winds that greatly favoured the small backmarkers and that freshened for them in the final stages after the bigger front-runners had lost time groping their way through fogs and calms. Indeed, a squad of small boats, all in D and C divisions, filled the first fourteen handicap places. *Screw Loose*'s winning margin was only 3m 11s from the Sydney Half Tonner *Wheel Barrow*, with another 2m 38s to the Tasmanian Half Tonner *Apalie*, in third place. The best of the bigger craft was John Kahlbetzer's 23.2 m aluminium sloop *Bumblebee 4* (fifteenth on handicap), with a superb crew of twenty-one aboard who convincingly outsailed Bob Bell's visiting 23.5 m maxiboat *Condor of Bermuda* (103rd on handicap) by 6h 17m 6s. Rolly Tasker's *Siska* (104th on handicap) and Tony Fisher's new 20.1 m *Helsal II* (113th), third and fourth across the line, were 53m 55s and 1h 53m 18s behind *Condor of Bermuda*. *Bumblebee*'s line honours time of 73h 45m 52s was 11h 8m 56s outside *Kialoa*'s race record of 62h 36m 56s.

Officials, mindful of the disastrous loss of life in the 1979 Fastnet Cup race five months earlier (see Chapter 14), imposed even stricter safety precautions than usual, and three powerful sea-going motor vessels were stationed on the course ready for emergencies. There was none, although tension remained until all boats were safely in port. Two weeks before the race, the 11.3 m Tasmanian One Ton Cup class yacht *Charleston*, owned and skippered by Charles Davies, of Hobart, had disappeared at sea and presumably foundered with all hands in heavy weather off the northern Tasmanian coast on her way to Sydney for the start. Aboard with Davies were Lawrence Corkhill and his son Geoff, of Bentleigh (Victoria) and Hobart; Ian McIndoe, of Hobart, and David Symes, of Melbourne. Extensive air and sea searches found no trace of the men or the yacht.

A tragic epilogue to the Sydney–Hobart race was the disappearance also of the 37 ft NZ One Tonner *Smackwater Jack*, a former champion of her class, which had placed thirty-eighth on handicap. She is believed to have foundered in mid-Tasman during a seven-boat race from Hobart to Auckland. Her owner-designer-skipper Paul Whiting, his wife Alison, and John Sugden, all of Auckland, and Scott Coombs, an American, were aboard the boat. Whiting's last radio report, six days after the start of the race to Auckland, said that his yacht was lying ahull in a cyclone. *Charleston*, designed by former New Zealander Ron Holland (who also designed the Sydney–Hobart race winner *Screw Loose*), and *Smackwater Jack* were of modern concept and of comparatively lightweight construction.

But what many saw as the ultimate test for ocean racers of all kinds of construction and design and also of the men sailing them, came in the Sydney–Hobart race of 1984.

A fleet of 152 boats started and only forty-six finished.

In spite of dismastings and severe damage, crew injury and illness, all managed to struggle into port unaided. One boat had her mast torn off when she rolled through 360 degrees and was flooded. Her crew, like many others, bailed for their lives. As detailed earlier, one man was drowned when swept overboard by a succession of heavy seas. At least four men were thrown into the sea when their boats were knocked down but were saved. A few suffered crushed and broken bones and there were numerous lesser injuries. Gale force headwinds from the SSW, building from 35 k on the first night to 50 k on the second, with steep (up to 7.6 m) seas, battered the fleet for two days. There were forty-three retirements in the first twenty-four hours and a flood of others in the next twenty-four hours. Jauntily turned out racing machines were reduced to disabled, jury-rigged shells, fighting for survival. Many crews who had swaggered out to sea were brought to their knees, weakened by fatigue, seasickness and anxiety.

The unusually vicious sea conditions were created by hard winds blowing diagonally and constantly against the south-setting East Australian Current, and the intensity of the gale was sustained by a deep, almost stationary, low pressure cell on the south-east corner of the continent. In addition, immediately to the west of the low, was a high-pressure system that combined to accelerate the winds up from the eastern end of Bass Strait onto the NSW coast. Crews determined to hold as near as possible to the rhumb-line track of 185 degrees to the Tasman Island turn into Storm Bay were forced, therefore, to fight their way close-hauled into massive square-fronted seas with breaking tops. Many of the smaller craft were swept sideways in a welter of foam as they attempted to climb, hour-after-hour, through these advancing mountains of water. All took a pounding. Even the powerful 24 m maxiboats, although able to handle the weight of the wind, often found the seas more than they had bargained for and were dumped bodily into 6 m 'holes' as they burst through into the troughs. Bob Bell's *Condor*, the early leader, tore a steering cable sheave bracket off the side of her hull and retired on the first day. Syd Fischer's *Ragamuffin* (former *Bumblebee 4*) was forced out when she tore her mainsail and split her boom at the gooseneck and had veteran helmsman Boy Messenger (the only man in the fleet who had sailed in the first race forty years earlier) painfully hurt when a big sea hit the rudder and flicked him over the wheel. His elbow was broken. Jack Rooklyn's *Apollo*, with rigging and sail damage, retired when two helmsmen were hurt in a similar accident at the helm. Sandy Schofield suffered concussion and Duncan van Woerden injured his leg when the wheel 'kicked' and flung them down. But other maxis, the 23.77 m *New Zealand*, sailing her first race as a shakedown for the following 27,000 nm Whitbread Round-the-World marathon, Bernard Lewis's 23.46 m *Vengeance* and Bill Ferris's 20.11 m *Bewinched*, with some nursing, stood up well to the conditions. *New Zealand*, robustly built and equipped for the Roaring Forties, was unscathed. Her experienced twenty-five man crew suffered some sea-sickness but all continued to work. When they had established a 60 nm lead over the nearest boat in the fleet, their skipper Peter Blake eased the pressure a little to avoid being dropped as they broke through the seas. Then, after two days of beating, when the wind in their area hauled to the SE, they were able to go bowling down the Tasmanian east coast under full sail. *New Zealand* reached the finishing line in 3d 11h 31m 21s, more than 90 nm ahead of *Vengeance* but 20h 54m 25s behind *Kialoa*'s course record of 1975.

The crews of most of the successful smaller boats from the outset had eased their way over the seas under stormsails to save themselves punishment. They were carried well to the east of the rhumb-line track but when the wind finally shifted to the SE and lost strength they were in many cases able to sail under free sheets for Tasman Island.

That was the strategy used by the handicap winner, *Indian Pacific*, a NZ-designed Bruce Farr 40 of the One Ton Cup class owned by John Eyles of Sydney (who sailed aboard), but chartered for the race by her builder, Gunter Heuchmer. The seasoned crew of ten needed all their expertise from the outset when a rival yacht ran into their starboard quarter at the crowded starting line and tore a metre long gash through *Indian Pacific*'s outer skin and her inner foam core. Fortunately, the inner kevlar skin held and two crewmen hanging over the side during the passage down Sydney Harbour to the sea were able to patch over the hole with adhesive fabric. Only men of great certainty in their technical ability to repair the damage would have taken the boat to sea in such condition. But *Indian Pacific*'s gang had more than that. They were imbued with magnificent courage, confidence in their skill and knowledge of the sea, and a burning desire to win. The first night out, the cabin was converted into a greasy shambles that could not be properly cleaned for days when a huge sea, estimated to be 12 metres high, broke over the boat and bounced a large pot of hot stew out of its fiddles on the galley stove. The next morning foredeck man John Vale refused to be subdued when a wave swept him along the deck and he broke three ribs.

As the wind increased *Indian Pacific*'s crew rigged down to a storm trisail and storm jib, just enough to drive them on over the ferocious seas while they headed 45 degrees away from the most desired course. They were more than 100 nm to the east of Gabo Island on the far south coast of NSW on the morning of 28 December when the wind finally hauled to the south east. Then, after twenty-six hours on starboard tack, *Indian Pacific* was able to hitch onto port tack and lay a course almost direct to Tasman Island. By the next morning, as the wind eased, she was under full mainsail and spinnaker and the only boat in the fleet ahead of her was the giant *New Zealand*, more than 60 nm inshore. *Indian Pacific* eventually finished fourth across the line when the maxis *Vengeance* and *Bewinched* overtook her in the final stages but she won the handicap by 49m 57s from Victorian Rob Green's gallant little Half Tonner, *Lawless*, which lost all of that time and more when the breeze died and she lay becalmed in the Derwent River near the finish. She, too, had gone 'wide' but not quite as far offshore as *Indian Pacific*.

Third on handicap was the famous Western Australian 10.36 m sloop *Perie Banou*, in which her owner-skipper Jon Sanders had circumnavigated the world single-handed, non-stop, on one occasion once round, and on another twice. This time *Perie Banou* carried a crew of four and, like the winner, she too was eased over the seas on a long starboard tack and was wide off the coast when the wind swung to the SE. 'Fundamental tactics,' said Sanders. He added that, although he had faced much bigger seas in other oceans, the hard winds against the current had created dangerous conditions similar to those between Patagonia and the Falkland Islands. Sanders thought, too, that those skippers and crews who had retired from the race, although their boats were not severely damaged, were wise. 'It's good seamanship to retire if you are not confident in your boat, crew or rig,' he said.

Officials who later analysed the reasons for the high retirement rate agreed with Sanders, although some prominent yachtsmen shortly after the race had criticized the construction and design of modern ocean racing craft and erroneously blamed these alleged weaknesses for most of the retirements. On the other hand, some ascribed the high failure rate to poor boat handling and a light-minded picnic atmosphere aboard too many of the competitors. It was significant, said one critic, that twelve of the forty-six boats that sailed the course came from Tasmania where yachtsmen were taught a proper respect for the sea. Nine of the twenty-one Tasmanian boats in the race had retired nevertheless.

A careful survey of all the reasons given by representatives of the boats for their withdrawal only partially justified some criticism of modern design and construction. Gordon Marshall, CYCA rear commodore and chairman of the sub-committee appointed to conduct the inquiry into the race, reported that rig failure accounted for 25 per cent (twenty-six boats) of all retirements, with thirteen of those totally dismasted. Prudence, the decision that it would be unsafe to continue, covered 17 per cent of those crews who retired, another 13 per cent had crews who were too seasick to continue, 3 per cent had injured crewmen and 2 per cent had people suffering severe fatigue. Damage to sails forced out 12 per cent and electrical failure, so that there was a loss of communication and navigational equipment, covered 8 per cent more.

But surprisingly to many critics, especially of the so-called 'modern light-weight flimsies', only 15 per cent of boats were forced to retire through hull damage. However, since 37 per cent of those that withdrew for this reason were built of exotic laminated materials, more than twice as many as those of laminated fibreglass (17 per cent) and more than five times as many as those built of ordinary homogeneous fibreglass (5 per cent), it would appear that designers and builders ought to have a better understanding of the loads imposed on such structures.

'Apart from design aspects, building techniques need to keep pace with the new technologies as they develop, bearing in mind that the search for lighter construction within the hull leaves less margin for safety which might otherwise compensate for errors in construction,' said the report.

It had earlier commented: 'A singular case of ridiculous weight-saving on one new yacht involved the connection of a fundamental rig stay to the deck instead of through onto the hull. When the deck peeled open in the heavy conditions it created an extremely dangerous situation which could have been avoided completely if the design had used a meagre few extra pounds of structure. If designers repeat this type of thinking (and if builders are short-sighted enough to build to such designs) then we are headed for troubles in the future. (This is the second time in successive races that a gaping deck hole has been created in one of the yachts by the rig).

The analysis also showed that of the boats that retired through hull damage 39 per cent had been built in 1984, and 5 per cent before 1974. There was also less rigging failure among the older boats.

The committee's report overall made no trenchant criticisms. Nor did it propose any dramatic reforms. The facts were stated for owners, crewmen, designers, builders, riggers and sailmakers to study so that they might form their own opinions and accept individual and collective responsibility for the future. How well they had done so and their judgement that the Sydney–Hobart was still the best race to be sailed was stated clearly enough when entries for 1985 closed in late November.

A huge fleet of 196 yachts, ranging from 24 m to 9 m in length, had been nominated. This number had shrunk to the still-record 178 on the day of the race but it was too many for the traditional 1,100 m Sydney Harbour starting line.

There were collisions, 'contacts', wilful and unavoidable breaches of the steering rules, and at least ten boats ahead of the line when the gun went. Officials, peering through a blanketing wall of sails, were able to identify only six premature starters and order them to return and recross. Three obeyed and avoided penalties. Officials penalized the other three by adding a number (fifty-three) equal to 30 per cent of the number of starters to their finish places. Others who broke the start officially undetected escaped scot-free. In itself that was enough to mar the event.

But another incident, a minor technical 'contact' between two boats, of which few members of either crew were even aware, and its distasteful aftermath, left the race in limbo. The incident occurred a minute before the start when Syd Fischer's massive 24 m maxiboat *Ragamuffin* approached the line with her bow slightly overlapping Peter Kurts 13 m *Drake's Prayer*. According to statements made later, just as Kurts, at the helm, luffed his boat, as he was entitled to do while *Ragamuffin*'s bows were looming overhead, David Forbes, a member of the afterguard behind the helmsman in *Drake's Prayer* involuntarily raised his hand. It was said that his fingers momentarily touched the rail of *Ragamuffin*'s pulpit before she tacked away. With both boats still anxiously manoeuvring for the start, crew members who had noticed the touch thought nothing more of it.

But four days later after a comparatively run-of-the-mill race to Hobart — a squally north-easter and a fresh southerly that hit the fleet the first night and blew for a couple of days, found weaknesses that forced thirty-three to retire — Kurts and Fischer were hauled before an international jury of yachting boffins.

By then *Drake's Prayer*, superbly sailed, had crossed the finishing line in 99h 29m 03s and, with a corrected time of 76h 17m 14s, had been provisionally declared the winner, having just managed to beat Gary Appleby's 13 m *Sagacious* (the former Tasmanian sloop *Huon Spirit*) into second place by 17m 23s. It was hailed as another triumph for Kurts, a veteran of twenty-one Sydney–Hobart races, twice aboard his own handicap winner, and a leader of Australian teams in the Admiral's Cup and other international contests. On the other hand, it was a bitter disappointment for Appleby's crew, who, with less than 30 nm to go had lain becalmed for three agonizing hours in Storm Bay until the breeze filled and they were able to reach the finish. After some soul-searching a member of *Sagacious*'s crew who had noticed the contact between *Drake's Prayer* and *Ragamuffin* before the start and had learned that neither boat had reported the incident to the race committee, entered a protest.

The international jury of five already handing out judgements on other less traumatic aspects of the event, approached the *Sagacious* protest with what many yachtsmen believed to be reluctance. But as four of them were registered international IYRU judges and one was the celebrated English authority, Mary Pera (chairwoman of the Royal Yachting Association's Racing Rules committee and a member of the IYRU Racing Rules Committee), there was no question about their ability to interpret the rules strictly according to the book and the evidence available.

Fischer could not help the jury. He said he had not seen any contact. Kurts said there was no contact between the hulls and the only contact, which he had been told about much later, was when a member of his crew had raised an arm in an involuntary reflex action. The jury was therefore bound to find that *Ragamuffin* and *Drake's Prayer* had 'made contact' in contravention of rule 33.2 of the International Yacht Racing Rules and that they both must be penalized. The prescribed penalty was the loss of the number of placings (thirty-six) equal to 20 per cent of the number of starters.

That relegated *Drake's Prayer* from first on corrected time to 37th and *Ragamuffin* from 75th to 111th. It also dropped *Ragamuffin* from third place on line honours to fortieth.

Then officials of the Cruising Yacht Club of Australia, the race organizers, fired a broadside. As they interpreted the rules of the race, they said, when a boat lost places for a rules breach the next boat in sequence could not be elevated to a higher position. Therefore *Sagacious*, which had been second to *Drake's Prayer*, could not be moved to first place. No boat would be shown as first and *Drake's Prayer* would be shown as having the lowest corrected time but placed thirty-seventh. Then, at the Hobart prize-giving ceremony, astonishingly Appleby was given the prizes that are normally awarded to the boat with the lowest corrected time and in first place. It was a sorry affair, with little satisfaction to anyone.

Many critics blamed race organizers for contributing to the early chaos by providing the traditional mass start for too many boats across a restricted line. This, they claimed, was devised as a TV spectacular mainly to attact a huge crowd to please sponsors contributing at least $150,000 in cash, goods and services to the CYC. A simultaneous start between divisions of boats across three well-separated lines over a much larger area of the Harbour, or time-separated starts between divisions, would be needed in future, they said. The only alternative was an offshore start away from the crowded Harbour, the spectator fleet and the public relations hoopla.

Of course, there were joyful aspects to the race, apart from the grim fight for the main handicap prize. One of the truly happy people in Hobart was Jack Rooklyn, veteran owner of the maxiboat *Apollo*. With the assistance of a crack crew (including the renowned yacht organizer Graeme Freeman) Rooklyn's only son, Warwick, had skippered the big green family sloop to a magnificent line-honours victory in the Sydney–Hobart race. Contrary to all expectations *Apollo* had outsailed the highly fancied *Windward Passage*, at the start, upwind and down for 630 nm miles and had led her in by almost three hours, with *Ragamuffin* more than another hour behind and a squad of other big boats over the horizon. 'Nobody got near enough to Warwick to protest about anything,' said Rooklyn senior proudly. After the race, the crowds still massed at Hobart's Battery Point finishing line to welcome the seafarers; the celebrations and parties were just as vigorous, and the legends grew.

No major ocean race anywhere in the world had been sailed so many times. Britain's biennial (odd years) Fastnet Cup race, first held in 1925, had long since been outnumbered, and so had the USA's biennial (even years) Bermuda race, which had lapsed between 1910 and 1923 and between 1938 and 1946 when sailors were in different sorts of battles or were recovering from them. The Australian race that had begun as an extended picnic and had frightened the pants off half the first participants, that became for a few years an excuse for a wild booze-up between bravos who wanted to prove that it had been hell out there, had now established itself as one of the most important sporting contests in the world – a true classic.

And so it will remain.

11

New South Wales Ocean Racing

MONTAGU ISLAND RACE

THE IMPETUS given to offshore sailing by the early Sydney–Hobart races was immediate. Soon everyone wanted to be in the act. Amateur sailors who had previously spoken derisively of 'ocean wallopers' now saw virtue in escaping from the tedium of constricted inshore courses and enjoying the freedom of adventure on the tall water. Many developed a swagger to suit their new-found intrepidity.

Royal Prince Alfred Yacht Club, the second most senior sailing organization in NSW (founded in 1867), noted for the spirited camaraderie of its members in their round-the-buoys racing on Sydney Harbour (and in later years, on Pittwater) and their occasional short dashes offshore between Port Jackson and Broken Bay and, more daringly, forty-five miles south of Sydney to Wollongong and back, in 1947 inaugurated their annual 250 nm Montagu Island race. The course the committee chose was inspired — from the Harbour 175 nm down the south coast of NSW to Montagu Island, five miles off the coast near Narooma, and back to Sydney. The plan was to start always in the late afternoon of the Friday before the traditional long Labour Day holiday weekend in early October. This offered contestants either an alternative to the long passage race to Hobart and its time-consuming return journey or, for some, an opportunity to practise for that more strenuous event. By driving the yachts hard during three days of concentrated effort over the Montagu course there seemed a near-certainty of getting back to work by the following Tuesday without loss of business or wages. That was the theory, anyway, although it did not always work that way in practice. Some crews in some of the early races took a week and more to sail the course and came ashore declaring the Montagu one of the most exhausting experiences anyone could devise. Another theory that often took a shaking was

272

that the navigation to the Island and back was comparatively simple, even for beginners, because of the well-defined coastal features of NSW, a good range of distinguishable minor mountains not far inland and nearly as many lights along the shore as in a well-lit street. The trouble was that at that period of the year, close to the southern hemisphere's vernal equinox, the weather could be almost guaranteed to be variable, often with rain that obscured landmarks completely. The track also seemed to be bedevilled with gales interspersed with leaden calms, and more often than not there was a swingeing sou'sou'easterly current right on the nose for most of the journey from the Island back home. If a north-easterly wind imposed a windward beat up the coast to the finish,

Brian Penton and his harbour racing crew in *Josephine* drove her through a widely varying pattern of winds to win the first Montagu Island ocean race in 1947. (RPAYC Archives)

the only way to avoid the worst of the set — which sometimes reached two knots, with short head seas, only two miles out — was to work short tacks close to the coast. This put a premium on alert helmsmanship and tireless crew work.

The first race seemed deceptively easy for those who kept their wits — a feather-light south-westerly inshore, a fickle nor'westerly a few miles off the coast, then a nor'easter that swung south-west, and finally a sizzling west-nor'westerly that averaged 25 k for much of the reach home and swung westerly for a two-mile windward thrash up the Harbour to the finish. Brian Penton, the newspaper editor who had inspired the dramatic front-page stories about the Sydney–Hobart race twenty-one months earlier, won that first 1947 Montagu Island race in fifty-one hours in his 14.3 m *Josephine*, a Scottish, William Fife-designed, Australian-built aristocrat that he and his smart Harbour racing crew drove like demons. That win and fine performances in other races, including a fiercely contested Sydney Harbour handicap for the Albert Gold Cup, won Penton a complete new wardrobe of sails from his admiring employer, newspaper tycoon Sir Frank Packer. Penton treasured those sailing successes beyond many of his other achievements. When he lay dying from cancer in 1951, at the age of forty-eight, he held a miniature of the Albert Gold Cup in his hands.

The second race, in 1948, set the real tone of the Montagu — a day of light winds from almost every point of the compass, then a north-wester that veered north-east to south-west and, on the third day, when most of the fleet were around the Island, a howling 55 k southerly. Only seven of the sixteen starters sailed the course, with a victory for Merv Davey's 13.1 m steel cutter, *Trade Winds*. The front runners, *Mavis*, 13.7 m, skippered by Archie Robertson, *Kyeema*, 16.5 m (Colin Galbraith) and Penton's *Josephine* ran wild, by the lee, in a daring triangular match race over the last 80 nm.

Unpredictable equinoctial gales and calms continued to plague the fleet year after year. In 1958, Rus Slade's 12.2 m *Janzoon* ran past Sydney in a southerly gale with heavy rain, made her landfall 50 nm north of the finishing line and had to fight her way back. In 1959, the three biggest competitors, *Kurrewa IV*, 19.8 m; *Solo*, 17.4 m and *Even*, 16.5 m, sailed the course in light to moderate winds which swung into a south-west gale and brought the back-markers flying home before it. Sid Moray's 11.6 m *Sylvena* flew 60 nm too far and suffered what was officially described as a 'harrowing experience' off Newcastle harbour. The sloop *Lass o'Luss*, 10.7 m, was dismasted, and *Archina*, a 15.9 m ketch, lost her mizzen. Further south, off Ulladulla, Phil Rudder's beautifully appointed 13.7 m *Blue Waters* (formerly *Janet M*), crewed by youngsters from Avalon (Pittwater) Sailing Club, ran aground on a reef and was pounded to pieces when the southerly hit her. All the crew was saved. In 1960, a southerly caught the fleet early, and quickly reduced the eighteen starters to two — the cutter *Solo* and Ron Hobson's 10.7 m *Joanne Brodie*. The smaller boat lost little to her powerful rival and on the Royal Ocean Racing Club handicaps under which they competed won by more than two hours. Old-timers shook their heads at all the retirements, observed that boats and crews were getting soft and added that there was nothing like a good wholesome blow to separate the men from the boys. But the Montagu fleets continued to grow, and although a few yachts shed their masts and others ducked for shelter, the good ones proved they could take whatever blew up or down the track, and the best of them went on to take major placings in the Sydney–Hobart race and in international contests. Course record times for the Montagu were regularly sliced. In 1974, Tony Fisher's 22 m

Helsal rocketed around the 350 nm with her sheets sprung in 36h 49m and 30s, a record that was to last seven years.

Then, in 1975, came the biggest ever fleet or forty-four starters, many with crews prepared more for a frolic than a battle against the sea. Maybe the official last-minute weather forecast put them in the wrong frame of mind — 'SW to SE winds, 10–15 k moderating, with seas slight to moderate and a swell rising to moderate'. What they got within an hour of the start were 25–35 k SSE squalls with steep, punishing seas that gave them no respite throughout the night and most of the next day. Within thirteen hours nineteen crews had cried quits; after twenty hours only fifteen were still racing, and, even after the wind fell light, three more retired. The last to give up was the all-woman crew led by Vicki Willman, in the 1961 Sydney–Hobart race winner, *Rival*, an 11.3 m sloop. But this was on the seventh day, after the women had beaten the bad weather, fought their way around the Island in light airs and struggled back against the current to within 90 nm of the finish. Among those forced out early were Sydney poker-machine czar Jack Rooklyn and his all-star crew of the 22.3 m aluminium *Ballyhoo*, the international champion maxi-boat that had campaigned around the world in all weathers but in this race had lost her 30.5 m mast. Half a dozen other boats with reputations previously unblemished in scores of tough races had to retire. The winner, after four days, was Peter Hill's 11 m *Ruthless*, an international One Ton Cup class sloop that had held a respectable place against the proven rough-water performers in the early blow and had outclassed them in the following light winds. And not only did the racing yachts take a battering. The Alfred's stout, twin-diesel-driven official launch, *Greg Cutler*, which had ventured eight miles down the coast in the wake of the fleet, was almost swamped by the head seas and staggered back to port with much of her deckhouse swept away and several of the complement badly bruised. 'Some yachtsmen have been inclined to take the Montagu Island race lightly, as a sporting gallop, but I don't think anyone who was involved in 1975 would describe it as that', commented The Alfred's highly experienced race secretary-manager, Jack Gale, in the understatement of the season.

In 1984 all of the 200 yachtsmen who manned the twenty-five starters in the thirty-eighth race were embellishing Gale's views. They began in a light east-south-easterly and reached gaily down the Harbour under spinnakers. Within twenty-three hours, however, all had retired. During the night a southerly gale of 50 k, with higher gusts, roared up the coast and, with the strongly setting southerly current against it, raised tumultous seas. The yachts took a dreadful pounding, but only one needed assistance to get back to port. Two men were washed overboard from one boat but crewmates quickly rescued them. A full scale air–sea search was organized for anthropologist Dr Peter Hinton and his crew in the stout little 9 m *Saltpeta* when they had failed to answer radio calls for thirty-six hours, but they sailed back to Sydney unharmed shortly afterwards, cursing their broken transmitter and damaged batteries. It was the first time no one had sailed the course.

In 1985 the race was sailed in pleasant following winds of 15–18 k until the fleet of twenty-two had rounded the Island. When the leaders had battled a quarter of the way back in fresh headwinds there was a sudden calm, then, after two hours, a beam breeze from the west followed by a brisk southerly that sent them all romping back towards the finish. But as a further demonstration of equinoxial frolics, the wind dropped when only half the fleet were home, leaving the rest to wallow in fluky calms. The well-handicapped, hard-driven Farr 37 (11.27 m) *Groundsfor*, skippered by Brad and Neville Hines, of Lake Macquarie, sailing her first major race, won the handicap. Arthur Bloore's Adams-designed 20.11 m *The Office* was first home in 41h 42m 48s — 8h 49m 48s slower than the course record of 32h 53m set in 1981 by *Helsal II* with her sheets sprung in fresh winds most of the way.

Although the Cruising Yacht Club has remained Australia's premier ocean racing club and has gradually developed a weekly programme of eight months of offshore events for many classes of approved yachts over distances up to 180 nm, with only a short break during the winter (when its fleet sails on Sydney Harbour), it and all other NSW sailing organizations recognize the Montagu as one of the great outside contests and the opening race of the spring season. They adjust their fixtures so as not to clash with it. The Montagu, like most other major inshore and offshore events, is open to entries from suitable yachts on the registers of all clubs, ensuring a high standard of competition. It has also become a test bench for new designs and for aspiring crewmen and women.

SOUTH SOLITARY ISLAND RACE AND COFFS HARBOUR RACES

As the standard of competition in the Montagu Island race and the Sydney–Hobart race grew keener it became increasingly clear that only highly tuned yachts, designed for the latest changes in the international offshore rating rules, expensively equipped and sailed by truly expert crews, could be expected to fill the major placings. Capricious weather might occasionally give a few outsiders a lucky break and lift them half a dozen rungs up the ladder, but overall, two-thirds of the starters in either event virtually had no chance. Most of them recognized this and were there only for the ride.

This left dozens of frustrated NSW owner-skippers with moderately efficient boats whose allowances for age of design just could not bring them to the first rank, and many enthusiastic crewmen, still thirsting for long-distance racing. There were others, too, who could not afford the time to sail to Hobart and the minimum of a week it took to cruise back home, even in the most favourable conditions. Some also clung to the old-fashioned idea that the period immediately after the Christmas holidays was a time for restful family cruising, away from the gung-ho atmosphere that pervaded serious ocean racing. It was the combination of all those factors that persuaded The Alfreds in 1972, in collaboration with Middle Harbour Yacht Club, Sydney, to found the annual 460 nm South Solitary Island handicap.

The starting time for the first race was set for the mid-afternoon on 26 December, a few hours after the Sydney–Hobart race. The course from off The Spit, in Middle Harbour, around South Solitary Island, on the NSW north coast, near Coffs Harbour, and back to Pittwater (16 nm north of Sydney), was designed to be sailed in four days and get the yachts across the line and near enough to home berths on New Year's Eve for their owner's families and friends to join them in holiday cruises on the inland waterway of Broken Bay. Another attraction was that points scored in the event, together with those from the Montagu Island race and Middle Harbour Club's 480 nm Sydney–Brisbane race, went towards deciding the winner of the Tasman Sea Trophy, sponsored by the oil company,

Ampol. In addition, until 1977, there was a special Solitary Island race prize for those yachts that competed under handicaps allotted arbitrarily on a basis of the known performance and the estimated potential of each yacht, skipper and crew, rather than on straight International Offshore Racing rule handicaps, which inevitably would favour craft of the most advanced designs. (After 1977, when all competitors were IOR assessed, the arbitrary handicap division was dropped.)

So the Solitary Island race served multiple purposes, especially when the weather was moderate. A few of the races, however, provided skippers and crews with more than they had bargained for — punches to windward against fresh north-easters and southerly-setting currents and rollicking, sometimes gear-busting, downwind gallops back home to the finish with the current under them. At other times, there were tedious crawls both ways that extended the spell at sea for some yachts to six days. Indeed, a few competitors have reached the finishing line declaring that what they then needed was not a holiday cruise but three days in bed to recover.

Middle Harbour yachts dominated the IOR section in the first eight races, to 1979, with Tig Thomas' stout Half Tonner, *Plum Crazy*, winning the first two, and Geoff Foster's superbly handled 9.7 m *Harmony*, three of the other five in which she sailed. In the races Foster did not win, he was placed second, either in *Harmony* or his earlier yacht *Senyah*. In 1977, *Harmony* clawed her way for the first 60 nm close into the coast against a light nor'easter and head current, then was hit by a southerly that, as it built up to 50 k in gusts, blasted her spinnaker to ribbons and forced her to run bare-headed for six hours with her mainsail double-reefed. She went round South Solitary Island in a welter of foam in company with the much bigger *Stormy Petrel*, a former world champion One Ton Cup class yacht, owned and skippered by Arthur Palmer. On the dead muzzler back home, Foster and his crew stood wide out to get the best of the current and came in three hours ahead of all of the ten yachts, out of the fleet of eighteen, that had not retired. *Harmony* won on handicap, too, clinching points that were later to win Foster the Tasman Sea Trophy for the fourth time.

By 1980, however, the vicissitudes of the weather on the one hand and the disinclination for holidays afloat after what too often had been a harrowing time at sea on the other, seem to have destroyed interest in the Solitary Island race. Only eight boats started in 1980 and Graham Jones' highly tuned Half Tonner *Beach Inspector* outclassed the others. In 1981 too few owners wanted to race, so by mutual agreement officials of The Alfreds and Middle Harbour decided to let the event lapse. But by 1982, The Alfreds, in collaboration with the burgeoning Coffs Harbour Yacht Club and with the generous sponsorship of the radio station 2MC later conjoined by Atlantica Insurance, then sponsors of the Montagu Island Race, had devised a brand new competition to be sailed over the same waters at approximately the same time of year. This was the 210 nm Pittwater to Coffs Harbour race, starting at 11.30 am on 27 December, with excellent shelter at the finish in the new yacht marina in the home club's north coast headquarters, and the promise of an enthusiastic welcome by the local organizing committee. Along the way, too, apart from ordinary radio schedules with the organizing clubs, there was the continuing guarantee of radio contact in emergencies with those highly efficient volunteer guardians of the NSW coast, Derek and Jeanine Barnard, who manned Penta Base at Gosford seven days a week. And following the main race there was a regatta, endowed locally with prizes, of three short races off Coffs Harbour with entertainments ashore for crews and their families and friends who could easily drive up the coast from Sydney in a few hours. The event was an immediate success. A fleet of forty-eight started in the inaugural regatta; there were fifty-six starters in the second and forty-nine in the third.

SYDNEY–BRISBANE (MOOLOOLABA) RACE

The Middle Harbour sloop *Harmony* was close-hauled in a sparkling early morning north-easter off Port Macquarie, on the NSW north coast, when veteran owner-skipper, Geoff Foster, and his watch captain, Frank Likely, saw a sea turtle a few hundred yards ahead of them. It seemed to be heading slowly north, just as they were. As the yacht approached, the turtle accelerated and swam further ahead but still remained in view. Foster responded to the challenge, trimmed his headsail sheet, adjusted the mainsheet traveller, and concentrated on every lift of the breeze and the shape of every sea in an effort to catch up. It took him and his crew more than an hour, and when they drew alongside they found to their astonishment that what they had thought to be a turtle was, in fact, a battered oil drum used to buoy an anchored fish trap. It had remained stationary, while the yacht had been carried stern-first at three and a half knots on the southerly setting current.

That almost sums up Middle Harbour Yacht Club's annual 480 nm Sydney to Brisbane race — a fight most of the way against a current that can test the windward ability of every competitor to the limit and can put a premium on accurate navigation. Even when there is a moderate following southerly wind it pays to keep in close to the coast, rock-hopping around the headlands, to avoid the current. But sometimes it may swirl in a great semi-circular eddy, run erratically to the north instead of to the south and help the boats.

Middle Harbour Yacht Club founded the Sydney-Brisbane race, then over 500 nm, in 1964, mainly as a 'feeder' for Queensland's 308 nm Brisbane to Gladstone Easter holiday event and as an opportunity, for those who wanted a winter cruise to the Great Barrier Reef, to cover much of the ground in company. Statistically, the weather conditions up the NSW central and north coast rarely had head winds above 15 k. Mainly there were light following southerlies. It seemed to the organizers an easy way to round off a hard season of serious racing and to begin a cruise into a bland climate before the onset of Sydney's winter. What the organizers had not reckoned on was the unpredictable current, that some years could run up to 4 k to the sou'sou'east, from 1–40 nm offshore. There was another hazard, too, for the first eight years, when the finishing line was laid off Sandgate in Brisbane's Moreton Bay. The state of the tide that ebbed and flowed across the Bay could add or slice hours off winning and losing times. A late arrival that had been outclassed at sea could catch the right tide across Moreton Bay and gain a great advantage. So in 1973 the finishing line was moved to Mooloolaba, north-west of Moreton Bay, cutting 20 nm off the course but making the race a much fairer contest for all.

Nevertheless the calms and currents remained as hazards, and some years the southerlies were far from light. The race, instead of being a pre-holiday shake-down, became a test for the best of yachts and their crews. The softest calms were in 1968. That year the crew of the line-honours winner, the 13.7 m *Sundowner*, owned by Ron Swanson and Jack Parker, which took 125h 31m 15s to sail the course, anchored off Point Lookout, at the northern end of Stradbroke Island, rather than drift backwards in the current and the ship's company jumped overboard for a swim. The hardest southerlies were in 1966, when the race started in 30 k of wind that at times gusted to 50 k for twenty-four hours before easing; and in 1976, when the fleet of thirty-six had an average of 25 k of wind, with gusts of 50 k, all the way, and Tony Fisher's 22 m *Helsal* set the course record that still stands of 45h 27s, at an average speed of 10.6 k.

There have been the usual crop of dramas that yachtsmen have grown to expect in offshore racing — crewmen swept overboard (and rescued), minor injuries and dis-mastings — and two incidents that could certainly have ended in disaster. In 1971 Peter Hill's powerful 13.1 m fibreglass-foam sandwich sloop, *Boomerang VII*, was swept ashore near Wooli Head when her navigator, Peter Kurts, ventured too close to the coast in the dark in an effort to avoid the current; and in 1977 when Joel Mace's beautifully appointed 13.1 m wooden sloop, *The Rajah* (formerly *Moonya*), caught fire off Hungry Head, near Coffs Harbour, and her crew were forced to abandon the ship in their rubber life-raft. *Boomerang VII's* crew suffered abrasions only, and the vessel was later salvaged with comparatively minor damage to her hull. *The Rajah* burned below deck, filled and sank beyond recovery. Her crew, with skipper Mace so badly burnt that he had to spend some months in hospital, were rescued by water police from Nambucca Heads and jet boat volunteers, after shore watchers had reported the fire at sea.

Two yachts have established enviable records in the Sydney–Brisbane race. The 9.1 m double-ended sloop *Cadence* (designed and built in Sydney by Ron Swanson), an outstanding champion in any company and magnificently skippered by her owner, Jim (H.S.) Mason, took the 1964 and 1965 events on handicap. Then, in 1974, after Mason had sold *Cadence* and bought her back, she won again. It rounded off a remarkable career for the yacht that had won the Montagu Island race in 1965 and the Sydney–Hobart race in 1966. Jack Rooklyn's downwind flyer, the 17.7 m *Apollo*, designed by Ben Lexcen (formerly Bob Miller) twice won both line honours and handicap in the Sydney–Brisbane race, in 1973 and 1977. Middle Harbour commodore Alan Sweeney in his One Ton Cup class *Diamond Cutter* has twice won the race on handicap, in 1978 and 1980, and in 1983 Ray Johnston in his *Scallywag* brought off a rare double — the preceding Sydney–Hobart race then the Sydney–Mooloolaba race on handicap. With Marine Hull insurance company backing the race, its popularity has grown steadily from thirty-five starters in 1979 to the record fleet of seventy-five in 1985. That race had a dramatic start when Simon Green's *Thirlmere* ran on to the Sow and Pigs Reef in the middle of Sydney Harbour, drove her keel up through her hull and sank. It ended in some confusion, too, when crewmen at night could not distinguish between two closely placed finishing-line buoys and had to re-cross. The winner, Albert Hoggett's *Flying Circus*, had to survive a protest against 'outside assistance' because officials had told the crew they had not finished when they first sailed past one of the buoys. It seems certain that in future there will be enough boats entered in the race to Mooloolaba for a realistic competition between teams representing NSW and Queensland clubs.

A delight to handle, able in a seaway and fast too, *Cadence,* the 9 metre yacht in which Jim Mason won the Sydney–Brisbane race three times, the Sydney–Hobart, and the Montagu Island races. (*SMH*)

HOLIDAY RACES

In recent years NSW yacht clubs have established four long-distance passage races, three of them to foreign countries, that offer tropical island holidays to participating crews. The races are open to all approved seaworthy vessels, competing on both IOR and arbitrary handicaps, and also include divisions for cruisers, using auxiliary power besides sails, that are awarded points for standards of tidiness, navigation, radio communication, and culinary achievement.

The races are: Broken Bay, at the mouth of Pittwater, to Lord Howe Island, off the NSW coast, 420 nm, held annually, starting at the end of October and organized by the Gosford Aquatic Club; Sydney to Noumea, New Caledonia, 1,100 nm, biennially (odd years) in June, organized by the Cruising Yacht Club of Australia conjointly with the *Cercle Nautique Caledonien*; Sydney to Suva, Fiji, 1,735 nm, biennially (even years) in June, organized by the Middle Harbour Yacht Club conjointly with Royal Suva Yacht Club; and Sydney to Vila (Vanuatu), 1,620 nm, first held in 1984, organized by the Cruising Yacht Club of Australia.

The Gosford–Lord Howe Island race was founded in 1974 largely through the enthusiastic efforts of Sydney and Gosford yachtsman Peter Rysdyk. Although the event is not of a highly competitive character it has provided some crews who approached it too light-heartedly with anxieties they did not foresee. As a result, the dangerous rounding of unlit Ball's Pyramid, south of the Island, in the final stages — a severe test for any navigator at night, especially in heavy weather — was taken out of the course in 1978, reducing the distance to 405 nm. Tony Fisher's *Helsal* holds the course record of 47h 52m 42s, which she set in the first race.

The first Sydney–Noumea race, in 1953, was a triumph for Harry Hughes' home-built 12.5 m schooner, *Irene*, of Lake Macquarie Yacht Club. She outran four well-tried rivals to finish only five minutes behind George Brenac's line-honours winner, *White Cloud*, a 14.6 m cutter, and won on handicap by 10h 25m 26s. That race was also remarkable for the fact that the brothers Trygve and Magnus Halvorsen for the only time in their offshore careers failed to make a last-minute, pre-race rigging check of the yacht they were racing, in this case the handicap favourite, *Solveig*, which had finished second in the preceding Sydney–Hobart race and was destined to win it at her next attempt. But three days out in the 1953 race to Noumea, in mild weather, a rigging cotter pin worked loose, one of *Solveig's* cap shrouds dropped to the deck, and seconds later her mast fell over the side. The Halvorsens grimly radioed the incident to the escorting Navy vessel, declined a tow, and sailed *Solveig* home under jury rig.

A race to Noumea in 1957 attracted seven starters, only two of which finished, and a proposed race in 1966 was cancelled because only three yachts entered. There were thirteen starters when the race was next held in 1974 (to celebrate Captain Cook's discovery of the island 200 years earlier), and eleven sailed the course in a series of gales and calms ahead and astern of them. Former America's Cup crewman Mick York won it in his 10.7 m steel yawl, *Tui Manu*. The casualties were the big front-runners *Helsal*, which cracked her ferro-concrete hull, and *Apollo*, which lost control of her mast when a cap shroud chainplate was uprooted from its fastenings. *Apollo's* owner, Jack Rooklyn, made some uncomplimentary remarks about the shipwrights who, only a fortnight earlier, had been entrusted with the job of refitting the yacht, including the chainplates. But almost everyone who reached Noumea had a delightful holiday in the carefree atmosphere of the place and around the adjoining islands. They also fascinated their hosts with feats of eating and drinking, and convulsed them to the point of hysteria with their French. There was no doubt about the future success of the event.

In 1977, the fleet totalled thirty-three and included Josca Grubic's 25 m South Australian ketch, *Anaconda II*, and *Helsal*, her wounds healed, having another try. There were eighteen in Group A, racing off IOR handicaps; seven in Group B, off arbitrary handicaps, and eight in the cruising division. Many crews bargained on a balmy passage once they got clear of the wintry Australian coast into the tropical south-east trades that the travel books said 'rarely blow more than 25 k'. Instead, they found themselves punching into a 40 k north-east wind, with heavy rain. *Helsal*, clear of the worst head winds, carried a following breeze most of the way, shouldered aside the head slop when it came, and sailed the 1,100 nm in the excellent time of 7d 1h 43m 11s. This set a record for the course twenty-eight hours better than that previously held by Victorian John Jarrett's powerful steel sloop, *Banjo Patterson*, which had led in the 1974 fleet. Although *Anaconda II* came in two hours after *Helsal* she won a prize for popularity during a subsequent picnic when she took ninety guests for a sail. The IOR handicap race went to Ron Langman's One Ton Cup class sloop, *Mark Twain*, and Brian James and his crew won the arbitrary handicap in his 12.8 m *Swifty*.

It was a punch to windward nearly all the way in 1979. The fleet of fifty-one were close hauled for almost seven days, sometimes in 40 k of wind and more. This took a heavy toll of the cruising boats, seven of which retired. One Melbourne boat, *Clair de Lune*, was dismasted and struggled to Lord Howe Island under jury rig. Yves Garioud, a crewman in the Noumean sloop *Gelinotte*, was knocked overboard by the boom in the dark and saved only when the end of his unclipped lifeline tangled around a cabin top fitting. It held long enough for crewmates to haul him back aboard. There were other scares — flooded bilges, broken steering, radio breakdowns and some severe cases of seasickness. Tasmanian Hedley Calvert's former One Ton Cup champion, *Huon Chief*, seemed to have the IOR handicap won 50 nm from the finish but the wind suddenly died. She covered only 15 nm in the next twenty-four hours. The main handicap prize went to Marshall Phillips' US designed and built Two Tonner, *Sweet Caroline*. Airline pilot John Brooks' 11.6 m *Quadrille* won the arbitrary division and David Beer's *Mandalay II* was awarded most points for cruisers. A festival of feasting and entertainments left many sailors weak, but there were enough, together with wives and girlfriends who had flown over to join them, to man a fleet of twenty-five boats in an inaugural 300 nm encore from Noumea to Vila. This was a downwind idyll in close company won on corrected time by veteran Tasmanian skipper Frank Hickman in his 12.2 m *Antagonist*. Three of the first four boats, in fact, were Tasmanians in search of the sun. And then the tropical frolics, including a Bastille Day ball, began anew. In 1981 the winds were all that the original organizers of the race to Noumea could have hoped for — two days of hard work, then fresh, following conditions easing towards the finish. Ron Walters' 19.2 m powerful Peter Cole-designed centreboard schooner, *Anitra May*, on the first leg of a long Pacific cruise, set a new course record of 6d 54m 31s, and New Zealander John Lidgard's self-designed 12.8 m racing cruiser, *Regardless*, romped away with the handicap prize. At the same time a fleet of sixteen yachts, starting from Brisbane, sailed a 780 nm course to Noumea. Doug Jewry's *Siska II*, skippered by Jeff Smith, got in first in 4d 17h 30m 24s and Mal Hewitt's 12.8 m *Envy* won on handicap. In 1985 political turmoil in the French colony persuaded officials that Noumea was no place for a carefree holiday, and the race was suspended. They hoped it might be possible to sail there again in 1987.

Middle Harbour Yacht Club's inaugural Sydney–Suva race in 1976 lived up more to the promise of a brisk downhill ride once the fleet of eight got clear of the Australian coast. Peter Kurts' 14.3 m *Love and War*, 1974 (and 1978) Sydney–Hobart winner and a former Australian representative in the Admiral's Cup, outclassed her seven rivals for almost 1,400 nm then, when her mast cracked badly below deck, sailed another 290 nm under a restricted rig until she was forced to quit in head winds 45 nm from the finish. Alby Burgin, of Lake

Macquarie, in his 12.8 m foam-fibreglass *Boomerang of Belmont*, finally led the fleet into Suva Harbour, on the island of Viti Levu, after a run of 9d 22h 35m 9s, at an overall average of 7.2 k. But the main handicap prize went to Victorian Lou Abrahams in his 12.8 m *Vittoria*. Another Victorian yacht, the Peter Cole-designed 13.1 m sloop *Bacardi*, prototype of her class, sailed by Bill Rockliffe, beat *Vittoria* in a neck-stretching duel to the line by 52s, but because she rated slightly higher than Abrahams' boat, lost to her by 25m 23s.

After celebrations in Suva, some of the race crews spent two months cruising the Fiji Islands and others visited Noumea. Their travellers' tales inspired an entry of fourteen yachts for the 1978 Suva race. One of these was Syd Fischer's Australian champion, *Ragamuffin*, using the race as a stepping stone on her passage to Honolulu for the Waikiki Yacht Club's first international Pan Am Clipper Cup series of five races, in which she was a member of the winning Australian team (as described elsewhere). *Ragamuffin* won the 1978 Suva race on IOR handicap by 5h 33m 52s from Lou Abrahams' Victorian sloop *Vittoria*, with another Victorian, Bill Rockliffe's *Jisuma*, a further 49m 44s behind. Kanga Birtles' *Callala* took the arbitrary handicap prize. The race was unremarkable except that David Beer's 13.1 m *Mandalay II* was struck by lightning, which wrecked her radio and electrical gear, forcing her to retire; and Tom Seccombe's *Rival* had to put into Lord Howe Island to land a sick crew member. *Rival* then sailed on to a creditable eleventh on IOR.

The 1980 and 1982 weather for the Sydney–Suva race was far from favourable — on the nose for most of the way and at times a lot harder than the sixteen starters bargained for. The fastest boat in 1980, *Mary Muffin* (formerly *Ragamuffin*), took almost thirteen days to sail the long course, and, in 1982, Victorian Lou Abrahams' *Challenge*, dual line honours and handicap winner, took 11d 5h 32m 57s. Generally the skippers and crews felt that the race took too long, was too hard and that modern yachts designed for high performance under the IOR rule were too uncomfortable for such sustained efforts at sea. There were no takers in 1984 and no sponsors, either, so officials put the event 'on suspense' and endorsed the Cruising Yacht Club of Australia's new race of 1,620 nm from Sydney, around Norfolk Island as a mark of the course, to Vila, the capital of Vanuatu (formerly the New Hebrides). That 1984 event had twenty starters from Sydney with three setting out from Brisbane for the same destination. Tony Fisher's 19.8 m *Helsal II*, with Dick Bearman as skipper and chartered for the occasion under the name *Spirit of Vanuatu* by Port Vila Yacht Club, walked away with both line honours and handicap in 8d 6h 22m, two days ahead of Ken Berkeley's 15.24 m *Kamber*, the next boat in. Crews enjoyed their reception at the end of the race, but persuaded officials to set more benign courses for May, 1986 — directly to the southern end of New Caledonia from starting lines in Sydney, Brisbane, and Hobart, with a sort of fifteen hour offshore 'pit stop' near Amedee Island while they all motored or sailed to the other end of the New Caledonian lagoon, then re-started for the final 300 nm to Vila. By this means they hoped to avoid some of the more tedious stretches that they had experienced in earlier sorties into the Pacific that so often belied its name when sailors sought to sail east.

12

Trans-Tasman Epics

THE SURFACE of the hurricane-driven ocean 300 miles east of Sydney was swirling with foam like the smoke of a bushfire. The air, supercharged with spray, was almost unbreathable and the roar of the wind was so loud that only by yelling could the men aboard the yacht communicate with each other.

It was 9 o'clock in the morning of 31 January 1948, and they had been scudding before the 80 k easterly for twenty hours with only a storm staysail set. Then a great wave, 18 m high, rose up, towering above the truck of *Peer Gynt's* 17.7 m mast. It sucked the 20 tonne cutter bodily into its arch and hurled her down sideways, on to her beam ends, with her mast in the water, ploughing her, deck-first, with tremendous force against the sea. On her deck, dinghies, lifebuoys, ventilators, heavily bronze-bolted fittings, were torn away; below, in the cabin, batteries, ballast, the wireless transmitter, stove, equipment of all kinds, burst from their fastenings. Three of the seven men below were flung on top of each other against the deckhead; some coins from a shelf were embedded into paintwork. And then, miraculously, after what seemed a lifetime to her crew but was probably less than half a minute, *Peer Gynt* staggered upright again, her stout wooden mast and rigging intact and her storm staysail still set. She reeled on to score a glorious victory, three days later.

That was only part of the story of the epic 1948 Trans-Tasman ocean race, from Auckland (NZ) to Sydney, the roughest, wildest and most dramatic event ever sailed in Australian waters. Ten nautical miles away to the westward that same day, a similar wave broke over the 17.7 m Victorian ketch *Kurrewa III* (jointly skippered by the SA grazier brothers, Frank and John Livingston), causing much damage and injuring two of her crew—one of whom was thrown through a plate-glass partition. And two nights earlier, 120 miles to the north-east, another wave, believed to be 24 m high, picked up, smashed down and crippled the 11.6 m gaff-rigged NZ cutter, *Rangi,* leading to one of the most intense air and sea searches in Australia's maritime history.

Right Few ocean racing yachts in modern times have been so solidly built as the Halvorsen brothers' 20 tonne, 11 m cutter *Peer Gynt*. Her strength saved her and her crew when a huge comber sucked her bodily into its arch and hurled her down sideways in the 1948 Trans Tasman race. (Warren Clarke)

New Zealand gaff cutter, *Rangi*, 11.6 m, was shattered and swamped and almost sunk by tremendous seas in mid-Trans Tasman hurricane but her crew bailed for their lives and reached the Australian coast, where they were towed to port fourteen days later. (*SMH*)

Crew of *Rangi* after rescue from the disabled cutter. (L to R) Peter Cosgrave, Jack Keen, Mark Anthony (owner-skipper), Henry Podmore, Arthur Anthony. Keen was swept 50 metres off the yacht in the hurricane but another wave carried him back aboard. (Lou d'Alpuget)

285

'Modern, lightly-built ocean racing yachts could not live through such knock-downs,' says Trygve Halvorsen, co-designer with his brother, Magnus, builder and joint owner-skipper of *Peer Gynt*.

> They would be stove-in completely, ripped apart if thrown down and driven sideways as *Peer Gynt* was by that enormous wave. I believe that even she, massively constructed with heavy deck beams and frames as she was, with eight tonnes of ballast, might not have survived if the staysail we had set and her big wooden mast had not prevented her from rolling upside down and filling. We know now that we, and probably *Kurrewa III* and *Rangi*, passed over pinnacles of an undersea mountain range that stretches southward for hundreds of miles, parallel with the NSW coast, from Elizabeth Reef, north of Lord Howe Island in the Tasman Sea. Oceanographic surveyors have confirmed that in places there is only about 16 fathoms (29 m) depth of water over these peaks although the surrounding ocean may be up to a mile deep. In very heavy weather such as the hurricane we experienced in 1948 (at Lord Howe Island wind gusts of 112 mph [90 k] were recorded before the anemometer needle went off the graph) the general body of wind-driven water banks up over the undersea peaks, creating giant combers. I am satisfied that these rare waves in the Tasman Sea have been responsible for many unexplained shipwrecks in the past.

The shattered *Rangi*'s survival, with her half-dazed crew bailing frantically and continuously for twenty-four hours to keep her afloat — at one stage she had a metre of water inside her — and her appearance off the south coast of NSW twelve days later, after eighteen days at sea, when hope for her and her crew had almost been abandoned, has more the elements of a Hollywood drama than the usual realities of a rough sea passage. *Rangi* got the worst of it because her crew had set a course much further northward than the others, and she had been caught right in the track of the hurricane. One crewman, Jack Keen, of Auckland, had been swept fifty metres from the yacht's deck by the wave that had engulfed her but had swum and been drawn in the backwash aboard again. Everything inside the yacht — food, blankets, clothes, charts, navigation, wireless and cooking equipment — had been mashed into a soggy pulp. Half of it looked as if it had been churned through a concrete mixer. All of *Rangi*'s deck beams, including those of her coach-house, had been fractured or dislodged and her deck from bow to stern was sprung. Her deck rail was broken but somehow her short mast, and gaff, boom and sails that had been lashed down to the rail, were usable. After riding to primitive, improvised sea anchors for three days she struggled on. The wind had then subsided to a moderate, following breeze.

Mark Anthony, *Rangi*'s owner-skipper, and his exhausted crew actually got the yacht to within 15 nm of Sydney at midnight on 8 February, only five days behind the line-honours winner *Kurrewa III*, while officials of the co-organizing Royal Prince Alfred Yacht Club and officers of the RAAF were arranging a search for her. But Anthony mistook the Harbour lights for those of Newcastle, 60 nm north, and he headed south. Lincoln bombers, Catalina flying boats, private aircraft, ships, and fishermen scoured 20,000 sq nm of ocean around the hurricane's track north and south of Lord Howe Island, 420 nm away, for five days. Meanwhile *Rangi* tried to claw back to Sydney against the current and light north-east head winds. Her crew could not drive the vessel hard to windward for fear of splitting her in two and, with their wireless wrecked, they had no means of communication. They had no auxiliary engine. Anthony said later that, because he and his crew believed all the other seven vessels that had started in the race must have suffered similar damage in the hurricane, they had been determined to finish the course if they could. The mid-ocean air search had been abandoned as hopeless when sketchy reports of sightings off the NSW south coast of a yacht 'something like *Rangi*' came from the pilot of a small private plane and from shore watchers. Finally, on 13 February, the Sydney *Daily Telegraph* newspaper's twin-engined Avro Anson plane, despatched by editor Brian Penton, with author Olaf Ruhen as co-pilot to Jack Hacking, yachting writer Lou d'Alpuget and photographer Gordon Balmer aboard, found *Rangi* 18 nm off Kiama and 56 nm south of Sydney. As the plane banked 122 m above the yacht for photographs, the enthusiastic Balmer, leaning through the open doorway with both hands around his camera, almost fell out on top of her, dragging d'Alpuget, who was clinging to Balmer's belt, with him. Ruhen obligingly banked the other way, tumbling the pair of them back into the plane. The *Daily Telegraph*, with hot scoop interviews in the bag, arranged for a trawler to take its news team to sea and to tow *Rangi* to port. So the ocean race to end all ocean races was over and once again, as after the inaugural Sydney–Hobart race, many members of the non-sailing public, suitably appalled at the dangers and scandalized at the cost of rationed petrol used by the searching aircraft (it was estimated to have totalled £11,000, worth about $250,000 in today's currency), declared that sailing out of sight of land with no shelter nearby should be banned. The authorities said that the RAAF would have used the petrol anyway, on exercises, and that the search, although fruitless, was good practice. Yachtsmen also pointed out that all eight of the vessels that had started in the race, although they had taken a terrible battering, had crossed the Tasman Sea in weather equal to the worst in history; that seven yachts had sailed the course; that more people died in motorcar accidents each month than had lost their lives in pleasure sailing accidents in all the hundred years since the sport had begun. Mark Anthony handed *Rangi* over to the Halvorsen yacht yard for rebuilding, so that four months later he could sail her back to New Zealand.

Then everyone settled down to analyze the race and the Halvorsen's remarkable performance in sailing their 11 m boat 1,281 nm in 10d 4h 44m, only 5h 2m slower than the 17.7 m *Kurrewa III.* The Halvorsens' passage did seem a stunning record for a yacht of *Peer Gynt's* size at that time, although, as in other long-distance ocean races, days were to be sliced off the Trans-Tasman in the later years by other yachtsmen and by the Halvorsens themselves, as the design of offshore craft developed and their equipment became more sophisticated. The Trans-Tasman race, nevertheless, especially the midsummer passage between Auckland and Sydney, with its general pattern of strong westerly head winds, storms and fluky calms, remains one of the world's great challenges to offshore sailors. It is probably the fairest race to all craft built for the open sea because, once clear of the NZ coast and for more than 1,000 nm until the yachts close the Australian coast, land masses and local knowledge have little influence.

The first Trans-Tasman race was sailed in March 1931 when the Victorian yachtsman, Frank 'Doc' Bennell, of Royal St Kilda Yacht Club, Melbourne, on a NZ cruise in his 12.8 m, 15 tonne Tasmanian-built auxiliary ketch *Oimara*, formerly called *Maude* and then *Gwen*, of which he was inordinately proud (she had won a Bass Strait Race in a full southerly gale), challenged anyone who cared to race him back to Australia, calling first at Sydney for twenty-four hours, then sailing on to Melbourne. Most NZ yachtsmen, especially of Royal Akarana

Yacht Club, who agreed to organize the race, were justly proud, too, of their seamanship and the quality of their craft, but in those years at the start of the world economic depression, few could afford the time and money for such a long contest and the passage back home. It seemed that Bennell would get no takers, until the Norwegian journalist, Erling Tambs, who was in Auckland on a protracted world honeymoon cruise with his wife, Julie, and their infant son, Tony (born on the way in the Canary Islands) in their famous double-ended *Teddy*, said he was willing to represent the people of New Zealand who had been so kind to him. A public subscription was raised to help outfit *Teddy*, a 35-year-old, 12.2 m former North Sea pilot vessel, for racing, and four smart Auckland yachtsmen were chosen for her crew. Because *Teddy*, heavily built of oak, was considered a slow, cumbersome cruising boat, Bennell gladly agreed to give her a time allowance of ninety-six hours. Bennell spotted time, too, to a last-minute entry, *Rangi* (the same 11.6 m gaff cutter that was later to survive the 1948 hurricane) originally a fishing vessel, whose owner at that time, Alan Leonard, had just arrived back in Auckland from a cruise. *Rangi* crossed the starting line in Waitemata Habour forty-five minutes late, well behind the other pair, and in the mixed bag of wind they encountered, mainly fresh and following, she surprisingly continued to drop astern, completing the voyage with a navigational clanger that took her 240 nm south of Sydney and cost her at least three days. But the shock of the race was the Norwegian cutter, *Teddy*. Bennell's ketch, *Oimara*, reached Sydney in 11d 20h with *Teddy*, hard driven by the NZ crew who had replaced Tambs' pregnant wife and young son, only 49h behind the Victorian boat, in 13d 21h. With her time allowance of 96h, *Teddy* won by 47h. *Rangi* took 19d 16h for the course. The proposed second leg of the race, from Sydney to Melbourne, was abandoned by mutual consent.

It was three years before another Trans-Tasman race could be organized, and then only two contenders started on a 1,630 nm course from Auckland to Melbourne — German-born sea wanderer, George Dibbern, in his 10.1 m yawl, *Te Rapunga*, and the young New Zealander, John Wray, in his backyard-built 10.4 m hard chine cutter, *Ngataki*. It took Dibbern nineteen days and Wray twenty-two days in moderate, mainly following winds. Wray got his worst dusting over the last few miles to the finish in Port Phillip, and his 17h time allowance was little help to him.

Two Auckland craft lined up for the third race in 1938 — the 12.2 m schooner, *Aurora Star*, and the 11 m cutter, *Wayfarer*, bound for Hobart, 1,570 nm away. A southerly gale hit them almost as soon as they cleared New Zealand's North Cape, and *Wayfarer* limped back with a damaged rudder and a bilge full of water. *Aurora Star* battled on until forced to heave-to for three days 400 nm north of her course. Then she abandoned the race and headed for Sydney, where her owners sold her.

Much more serious maritime conflicts engaged yachtsmen shortly afterwards, and it was not until 1948, when *Peer Gynt* triumphed in the hurricane, that the Trans-Tasman race was sailed again. After that 1948 blockbuster, the New Zealanders found it hard to believe that the four yachts they had nominated against *Peer Gynt* and the two other Australians, *Kurrewa III* and *Wayfarer* (Peter Luke), had been so completely outclassed. It must also have been luck, some thought, that even the homely 7.9 m American cruising cutter *Pagan* (representing Valparaiso Yacht Club, Chile, because that was the only club to which her owner, Bill Weld, had ever belonged), had beaten the best NZ yacht by fifteen hours. So in 1949 three NZ boats — *Te Hongi*, a 13.1 m schooner, and *Seawind*, a 10.4 m cutter (both of which had competed in 1948) and *Ghost*, an 8.5 m sloop, sailed to Sydney to challenge *Peer Gynt* for a race back to Auckland. The Halvorsens, still with their ace navigator Captain Stan Darling (RNR) and the core of their original crew aboard, obliged. This time the winds were light and mainly from the east. *Peer Gynt* did not wet her deck but she made the crossing in 14d 9h 56m 20s, easily winning line honours by more than a day and the handicap by 13h from the low-handicapping *Ghost*. The NZ sailors were foiled again. Next year the Halvorsens shipped *Peer Gynt* to America, sold her there, and built a beautifully proportioned 11 m sloop, which they appropriately named *Solveig*, after Peer Gynt's girlfriend in the Norwegian Ibsen's dramatic poem.

They sailed *Solveig* to Auckland in January 1951 directly after competing with her in the Sydney–Hobart race in which she placed sixth on handicap (it was her maiden race after a launching only three weeks earlier). In New Zealand, she lined up against a fleet of eight for the challenge contest back to Sydney. It was the same story. *Solveig* won on handicap and beat the best performed NZ boat, the 10.1 m *White Squall*, by almost 6h on corrected time. So the Halvorsens still held the Trans-Tasman Cup. But there was some consolation for the New Zealanders. The superbly outfitted 16.5 m lightweight Auckland cutter, *Leda*, designed by Sweden's Knud Reimers, and owned, built and skippered by the brothers Dooley and Sandy Wilson, with their wives, Kit and Erica aboard, won line honours in sparkling moderate weather, with only one short-lived blow, in 11d 6h 54m. They were in radio communication all the way with Auckland, and Tasman Airways flying-boats air-dropped them newspapers almost daily — and on one occasion also tin openers, to replace one that had been broken. *Leda* had aboard, as navigator-wireless operator, a brilliant young New Zealander, Terry Hammond, at twenty-three already a veteran offshore sailor, who had skippered and navigated the 8.5 m *Ghost* against the Halvorsens' *Peer Gynt* in 1949. Hammond was later to distinguish himself as navigator of Australia's first America's Cup challenger, *Gretel*, in 1962. There was another minor achievement for New Zealand, too, when Mark Anthony, in the rebuilt *Rangi*, placed eighth in the nine-boat fleet. But, on the debit side, *Solveig* had finished fourth across the line, only 13h behind the much bigger *Leda*, with *Southern Maid*, of Sydney, and *Tara* (sporting a bipod mast), of Auckland, both 16.5 m, between them. *Leda* placed only fifth on handicap. Later that year the Tasman at last claimed the venerable *Rangi*. She was wrecked when she broke adrift from her anchorage on a cruise to Norfolk Island, while her crew were ashore. (There is also a sad footnote to *Leda*'s Trans-Tasman race and to the delightful, light-hearted people who owned and sailed her. In 1952 the Wilsons, with their wives, took *Leda* to America and Sandy temporarily joined the crew of a Californian yacht for a race to Mexico. A freighter ran down that yacht and all aboard were drowned.)

After 1951, no one seemed especially interested in organizing another demonstration of the Halvorsen brothers' skill as ocean racing designers, builders and sailors, and serious Trans-Tasman competition between top class craft and crews lapsed for ten years. In 1952 an Auckland yacht, *Ladybird*, skippered by W. J. Woollacot, won a two-boat contest from Hobart to Auckland, and in 1954 another New Zealander, *Taihoa* (N.Arrow), crossed from Auckland to Hobart with Ken Furley's 10.4 m ketch, *Bounty*, trailing weeks behind her with a broken mainmast. It took *Bounty* an agonizing thirty days to sail the course.

But by 1961 members of Royal Akarana Yacht Club felt the sap rising high enough to stage a real race, in collaboration with Royal Prince Alfred Yacht Club, in Sydney, and they issued the necessary entry forms for what was called the eighth Trans-Tasman Cup Challenge from Auckland to Sydney. Six Australian boats accepted and crossed the Tasman to the starting line: *Astor* (formerly *Ada*), a magnificient 22.3 m teak schooner built in Scotland in 1924 but little used; Vic Meyer's redoubtable 17.4 m steel cutter, *Solo*; *Archina*, a 15.8 m ketch, a veteran of the first Sydney–Hobart race whose inexperienced crew in those days had cried quits when the short-lived southerly had hit them; *Kintail*, a 12.2 m cutter; *Southerly*, a 10.7 m sloop; and the Halvorsens' latest creation, *Norla*, launched only six weeks earlier. The name *Norla* was a break from the Norwegian-born Halvorsens' traditional Ibsen allusions— *Saga*, *Peer Gynt*, *Solveig* and *Anitra*—and was formed from a combination of syllables from the names of Trygve's wife, Noreen, and Magnus' wife, Paula. She was an 11.6 m cutter and at first glance she looked more like a beautifully appointed cruising boat, comfortable and sea-kindly, with a generous transom stern, than a racing yacht designed for hard competition offshore. But out of the water it was obvious that she had some unusual features for those days—fine U-shaped lines for'ard with a long flat run in her afterbody, a moderate fin keel and a deep spade rudder. The Halvorsens already knew that she was an able boat upwind and a flyer with the sheets eased, and they had equipped her with the best of go-fast gear. Also, since they set so much store by pin-point navigation, they had aboard, besides their regular, highly skilled navigator, Stan Darling, another of the world's great small-boat pilots, the 32-year-old former New Zealander, Terry Hammond, now a Queensland engineer, who had navigated *Leda* so superbly in the 1951 race and had cruised the world and crossed the Tasman a dozen times both ways.

Royal Akarana Yacht Club had at first expected at least nineteen starters in the race but four Auckland yachts withdrew at the last moment leaving *Fitheach Ban*, a 25.3 m schooner; *Kestrel*, a 12.2 m yawl; *Ceciline*, a 12.2 m cutter; *Jeanette*, a 10.4 m cutter; *Bounty*, a 10.4 m ketch; *Fandago*, a 10.4 m cutter; *Shiralee*, an 8.5 m ketch; *Maroro*, an 8.5 m ketch representing New Zealand; and *Awahnee*, a 15.8 m cutter from San Francisco—a total fleet, with the six Australians, of fifteen. With *Fitheach Ban*'s overall length of 25.3 m it might have been supposed that she would have a chance for line honours. But she was, in fact, more a cruising houseboat than a racing yacht. She had been built thirty years earlier in Southampton (England), was square rigged on the foremast, and, although comfortable, was a lumbering beast by comparison with the others.

The race started on 28 January in light following winds that freshened, sagged for a day then came away hard and developed into a gale. The fleet galloped before it, with the schooner *Astor* and *Solo* at times logging 15 k and *Norla* skating hot on their heels. They carried the wind for almost 900 nm, until, on the seventh day, they were closing the NSW coast. Then, after a patchy calm, they picked up a coastal north-easter that took them to the finish. *Astor* lost line honours through a navigational error in the final stages, but Peter Fletcher, *Solo*'s navigator, hit Sydney right on the button and crossed the line in the new course record time of 7d 21h 12m. *Astor* came in 36m behind her, with *Norla* only 10h 50m further back. On handicap, *Norla*, which had sailed the course in 8d 8h 39m, at an average speed of 6.3 k, won by 6h 50m 59s from *Solo*, then considered one of the world's best ocean racers (she had won the Sydney–Hobart handicap in 1956, and in 1962 was to outsail the American Champion, *Ondine*, to score in that race again).

But the most crushing defeat for the New Zealanders was that all six Australian yachts had finished ahead of them over the line and on handicap, and even *Awahnee*, heavily weighted with world-cruising gear, had beaten four of them out of a place on handicap. The New Zealanders were good-natured about it though, and, like everyone else, they honoured the Halvorsens as the greatest of all Australasian blue-water sailors. But some of them said privately that they would never again try to race them across the Tasman between Sydney and Auckland, or in the reverse direction, until NZ yachts could be brought up to the excellence of design and equipment of Australian craft. That time, of course, has long passed. Since 1961 NZ ocean racers and their crews, especially of the One Ton Cup class, have distinguished themselves in international championships and have regularly outsailed the best Australians, three times winning the Sydney–Hobart handicap and, in 1971, filling the first three places in that classic.

But up to 1986 the Trans-Tasman, between Sydney and Auckland or vice versa, the course originally chosen as the ultimate challenge to the cream of yachts and crews, had not been sailed again. A number of Trans-Tasmans have been staged from Hobart to Auckland between yachts heading back to New Zealand or to the northern Pacific after Sydney–Hobart races. The classiest fleet ever to sail the 1,570 nm Hobart-Auckland course raced in 1972. It included the US superstars, *Kialoa II*, a 22.3 m yawl, and the sloop, *American Eagle*; New Zealand's *Pathfinder*, *Runaway*, and *Wai-Aniwa*, fresh from their Sydney–Hobart and concurrent Southern Cross Cup triumphs; other boats, *Buccaneer*, *Cassandra*, *Satanita II*, *Skinflint*, and *Whispers II*; Sydney's *Ragamuffin*; Perth's *Siska*; Holland's *Stormy*, and Japan's *Vago II*. *Kialoa II*, with Magnus Halvorsen as skipper-nagivator in the absence of Jim Kilroy, took line honours and the handicap in consistently fresh reaching weather (with final calms) in the course record time of 8d 2h 10m 28s, which was 15m 14s inside the previous record set by New Zealand's slender 18.9 m *Fidelis* a year earlier. *American Eagle*'s second place on handicap to *Kialoa II* gave her the world ocean-racing championship, a US-sponsored points competition decided over seven approved races, one of which was that Tasman crossing. In subsequent Hobart–Auckland races many boats were not fully manned by their best crews and in recent years some of these contests have developed into farces.

To 1985 there had also been four single-handed endurance tests from Auckland to Mooloolaba (Queensland) in a variety of craft but serious offshore-racing yachtsmen, while admitting the daring and fortitude of the competitors, regard such contests as circus acts not worthy of the name of races, because no man, alone, whatever self-steering device he may use, whatever aids to navigation are incorporated in his equipment, can sail a yacht offshore over a long distance at maximum efficiency.

13

Ocean Racing in Victoria and Other States

VICTORIAN OCEAN RACING

Iᴛ ᴡᴏᴜʟᴅ ʙᴇ ʀᴇᴀsᴏɴᴀʙʟᴇ to expect Victorians to be dominant in ocean racing, since it was they who started offshore fleet sailing in Australia, with their Bass Strait event of 1907 for the Rudder Cup (detailed earlier). A Victorian also instigated the first Trans-Tasman marathon, in 1931. But, as noted elsewhere, the Bass Strait race lapsed for twenty-two years after the first contest, and it gained little support when pre-World War II attempts were made to revive it. Moreover, the first Trans-Tasman race did little to inspire Victorians when their contender, *Oimara*, was so soundly beaten by *Teddy*, an aged cruising boat. However, in 1946 public interest in blue-water battles — the uproar about the CYC's first Sydney–Hobart race having filtered south, even through the sedate portals of the Royal Yacht Club of Victoria and to Royal St Kilda Yacht Club — nerved Victorians to try again across their notorious Bass Strait. Nevertheless, when the RYCV organized the first postwar Bass Strait race of 200 nm from Queenscliff, in Port Phillip, to Devonport, Tasmania, for a trophy given by Frank Bennell to honour his father, 'Doc' Bennell, there were six entries only and their efforts went almost unnoticed except by the contestants themselves. Other Victorian yachtsmen, well satisfied with what they considered, with some justification, to be their national pre-eminence in tactical battles around buoys, and in dealing with the rigours offered by bouncy Port Phillip Bay, were also inclined to regard deliberate ventures into Bass Strait as the height of folly. For one thing, unless one were lucky enough to have a berth at Geelong it took a tedious six hours to traverse Port Phillip from one's moorings on the north and eastern sides of the Bay before a yacht could get near the open sea, and then one had to wait for the critical 'slack water ebb' before attempting the exit through The Rip. No one in his right mind would try this 4–6 k mill race at the wrong tide, especially through overfalls driven by a southerly wind. Over the years it had been the scene of a score or so of maritime disasters.

Even after the better publicized next Bass Strait contest in 1947, when the popular young shipwright-skipper, Jack Savage, fought his way to victory across the Strait in a gale in the 10.7 m sloop *Lorraine*, which he had recently designed and built (for £650 complete) for owners Max Glover and Bill Loftus, a prominent Victorian yacht club official, when questioned about the possibility of growing interest in offshore sailing, said with some hauteur, 'The best yachting people do not go in for that sort of thing.' In spite of this attitude in some quarters, there was still a core of enthusiasts thirsting for deep sea adventures, and the race to Devonport was included in the yachting calendar as an annual event. It has been sailed ever since, with only two cancellations (in 1956-57) when interest temporarily waned. (From 1949 the Bass Strait race has been controlled by the Cruising Yacht Club of Victoria, a body formed that year, which changed its name to the Ocean Racing Club of Victoria in 1974. Under its aegis, a growing number of major and minor offshore events is also contested. In 1986 the annual ORCV programme listed seven ocean races from 33–480 nm between September and June.)

The Bass Strait race to Devonport gained tremendous impetus in 1963 when for the first time craft of only 18 ft rating were allowed to compete, provided they met strict safety rules and were of approved seaworthy design and construction. A fleet of thirty-two yachts started in 1963, and by 1985 the average number of competitors was fifty. The race had at last got some of the recognition it deserved as one of Australia's most sporting maritime contests. Bass Strait can be bland, sparkling and pleasantly frolicsome, with tricky runs of tide and current in moderate, following winds. But few stretches of sea in the world can provide such concentrated violence as this strait in south-westerly blows that, with little warning, come howling unimpeded straight up from the Antarctic. (The race to Devonport is now also part of the Bass Strait Circuit series, which includes a short 'Top of the Island' event along the Tasmanian north coast, sailed in collaboration with Tasmanian yachts from Mersey, Port Dalrymple, and Circular Head [Stanley] Clubs.)

Still, in late December, when the race to Devonport is sailed, skippers and crews of many of the best Victorian blue-water yachts continue to be attracted more by the Sydney–Hobart race and the chance it gives them to prove themselves against interstate and overseas craft. In 1956, as a shakedown for those vessels determined to race to Hobart, the CYCV inaugurated the annual Queenscliff to Sydney course of 600 nm for mid-December. The Queenscliff–Sydney event has the potential of a tough uphill fight against the NSW coastal current and north-east head winds, with the possibility of a following southerly gale thrown in, but from the outset it failed to raise much blood pressure. Some crews drove their yachts to the limit and arrived in Sydney bedraggled and in need of minor refits, but mostly, since their target was the Sydney–Hobart race shortly afterwards, the yachts were nursed to preserve their sails and equipment for that later effort. One crew who made the grand gesture was with owner-skipper Graham Warner in the former Tasmanian yawl, *Winston Churchill*, in 1960. They flogged that noble old war horse all the way to Sydney in a series of following gales to sail the 600 nm in 71h 34m 30s and defeat three rivals on handicap. In 1979 that record still stood, when owners and crews decided to abandon the event because it was too punishing and reduced their chances in

Sir Arthur Warner's *Winston Churchill*, a Sydney–Hobart pioneer driven ashore in heavy weather on the Victorian south coast in 1959, was salvaged, refitted and raced on for many years. (*SMH*)

the immediately following Sydney–Hobart race. (Unfortunately, for all their efforts up to 1985, only one Victorian yacht had won the Sydney–Hobart race, although in recent years their quality and crew work had greatly improved.)

In November 1960, rather than sail races to 'foreign' ports, the Victorians laid down their own home-waters course — from Queenscliff, out through Port Phillip's rip, westward around the tide-swept Cape Otway to Portland. With only 163 nm to be covered, it looked deceptively easy, an ideal annual pipe-opener in those days for the offshore season that could be traversed in a day and a half, with enough time left to cruise back to Melbourne inside a long holiday weekend. A group of Portland yachtsmen, after some nudging, had offered to put up £400 prize money for the race, although this 'professionalism' was at first considered by some to be outrageous. The promise of £150 first prize, ranging down to £80 for fourth, eventually persuaded several who had earlier opposed the contest to start in it. The place-getters earned their money. The weather off the south-western Victorian coast is far from settled in November, and that first race set a salutary pattern for some that were to follow. Only four of the eleven starters finished the course, in boisterous conditions, and three of the seven that had to retire could not even round Cape Otway. The race to Portland in head winds has remained a stiff challenge for even the most able of modern yachts, although in following winds they have made little of it. In 1978, Dick Thurston's *Apollo II* scored her third consecutive line-honours win with a record run of 20h 10m 19s. In 1985 Gary Graham's 18.3 m aluminium sloop *Quasimodo* sailed a new 200 nm Melbourne–Geelong–Portland course in 20h 45m 30s and covered the 163 nm Queenscliff–Portland leg in less than 15h.

Still, in the developing years the Victorians were not easily discouraged, and on 27 December 1964, urged by South Australians, they tried a much more demanding race — 550 bitter miles from Queenscliff westward around Cape Otway, past Portland and Cape Dombey, through the hazardous Backstairs Passage behind Kangaroo Island, across Gulf St Vincent and Spencer Gulf, with its islands and reefs, to Port Lincoln, South Australia. It is a course that requires extreme hardihood from crews, a high degree of excellence from navigators and a stoutness of construction in yachts. Near-freezing west-south-westerly gales can make it a dead muzzler half the way, with an inhospitable lee shore close by; seas can be steep and irregular; and currents over some sections of the Backstairs Passage can run up to a bewildering 5 k.

The first Queenscliff–Port Lincoln race was a ripper in more ways than one. Four South Australian yachts and eight Victorians set out on 27 December, and five finished. They had two days of moderate head winds, then a howling sou'wester with heavy seas and rain, and after four days the leaders had covered only 300 nm. It was not until the wind backed a little and they were able to ease the sheets for the north-westerly section that they began to make reasonable progress. *Winston Churchill* then came home like a train to take line honours, covering the final 201 nm in twenty-four hours. Josca Grubic, of Royal South Australian Yacht Squadron, won on handicap in his *Marina*, starting a sequence of four handicap victories over that course for the yachts of his club. The races of 1965-66-67 were sailed in less gruelling conditions, but many yachtsmen were still dissatisfied because the savage currents and rips behind Kangaroo Island could favour those who arrived at the right time to ride them, and could wreck the chances of those who had to stem them; and somehow the South Australians, who perversely relished this stretch of vicious water, always seemed to win. Perhaps it was desperation to get back home that drove them to such extravagant and successful efforts. In any case, after four tries the Victorians had had enough, and the race to Port Lincoln was abandoned 'through lack of interest'.

Enthusiasm for offshore sailing, however, had by no means waned, and the quality of Victorian yachts and crews strengthened as they raced over other courses along the Victorian coast, east and west of Port Phillip Bay, and across Bass Strait. And then, in 1968, the celebrated Rudder Cup, which had been in the possession of the Newlands family for sixty-one years, ever since *Thistle* had won the first Bass Strait race to Georgetown in 1907, dramatically reappeared — a glistening, solid silver phoenix, half a metre high and now valued at $1,800, arisen from the salty ashes. At the age of sixty-nine, Edgar D. 'Felix' Newlands, who as a boy of eight had accompanied his mother and his sister, Minnie, aged nineteen, as members of *Thistle's* crew of ten on that historic race, had agreed to surrender the trophy. Officials of the CYCV (now ORCV), led by commodore Graham Warner, tactfully negotiated for, then formally accepted, the gift of the cup, and agreed to the conditions imposed in a deed of gift by the Newlands family. These conditions were that the Rudder Cup must become a perpetual trophy (as, indeed, some had believed it was originally intended to be), that it must now be offered regularly as the main prize for a Bass Strait ocean race (with the winners' names recorded on silver plates around the ornate polished wooden plinth of the trophy), and that, if no race were held, then the trophy must be handed to the Victorian Yachting Council for another competition.

The CYCV's success in establishing itself as custodian of the Rudder Cup was a coup that later irritated some members of Royal Geelong Yacht Club, who claimed that because their former commodore, Thomas A. Dickson, had arranged the original endowment of the trophy by the American Thomas Fleming Day, editor of *The Rudder* yachting magazine; because the then Geelong Yacht Club had organized the first race; and because the name of the club was prominently embossed on the trophy, it should rightfully be under its control. This suggestion was rejected by the CYCV and by 'Felix' Newlands. But the ocean racing club members (once known as 'The Cuckoos' since they had no clubhouse of their own and met in the premises of other clubs) continued their skilled diplomatic manoeuvres. They arranged for the cup to be displayed at Royal Geelong Yacht Club, together with the racing flag that *Thistle* had worn, and they set up alongside these two items a framed copy of the deed of gift positively stating that the ORCV (formerly the CYCV) was officially in charge of the trophy. 'Some Geelong members still pretend to fester about the Rudder Cup, though,' ORCV official Warwick Hoban said. 'At a presentation night a few years ago a couple of them tried to "steal" the Cup and smuggle it out of the hall under someone's coat. They were caught in the act. It was very funny.'

In 1969 it would have been fitting to make the Rudder Cup the main prize for the now well-established Bass Strait race to Devonport, but in the intervening sixty-two years, that contest had been endowed with a great many other trophies. Another would have been an embarrassment. So the CYCV adroitly founded another race, to be sailed 165 nm across the Strait on the Labour Day weekend holiday every March to Stanley, on the north-west coast of Tasmania. The friendly boatsmen at Stanley agreed to accommodate all the visiting yachts in their harbour, nestled behind the remarkable 142 m headland called The Nut, and the local Apex Club organized an annual garden party and barbecue at the nearby town of Smithton for skippers and crews, with special buses to transport them to and fro. For ten years, this rollicking function and others in the area were among the most popular of the Victorian yachting season, and the Stanley race was well supported. In the inaugural race of 1969 a fleet of modern craft competed, and the winner on handicap was Stan Gibson's *Four Winds II.* This time there were no ladies in any of the yacht's crews likely to discourage future competition, as had happened in the founding race for the Rudder Cup (as told elsewhere). The course record, set by John Gould's *Bacardi*, 13.1 m, stands at 20h 29m 53s. Many Victorian yachtsmen, rather than attempt to sail back to Port Phillip Bay immediately after the heady pleasure of the Stanley–Smithton parties, left their yachts snugly berthed in the care of Stanley boatsmen, and flew home, returning on following weekends for leisurely cruises. Some sailed the northern coast of Tasmania, visiting Mersey Yacht Club, in the excellent deep-water port of Devonport, sixty miles to the eastward of Stanley, or went on another twenty-five miles to Port Dalrymple Yacht Club at the mouth of the Tamar River—reversing the route that *Thistle* took when she cruised home after her victory so long ago. But by 1979 interest in the Stanley race had waned, and when it appeared that only nine yachts would be entered for the event officials agreed to let it lapse in favour of a shorter, more suitable course of 110 nm to King Island. The Rudder Cup was then transferred to the Devonport race as had been originally intended.

In 1972, with ocean racing increasingly popular in their home waters, the Victorians decided that the time was ripe for a long-distance course that would provide a local alternative to the Sydney–Hobart race, which continued to draw away their best yachts. They wanted a true, tough test of offshore sailing; one that would satisfy all interstate critics that there were no advantages in local knowledge of tricky tides or currents; and, as well, would attract outside entrants of quality. So they founded their 480 nm West Coaster, with generous sponsorship from Swan Insurance Co., Ansett Airlines, and other commercial firms, and from the Victorian Government. The course was from Queenscliff across Bass Strait; past the Hunter Islands with their attendant reefs on the north-west corner of Tasmania; down the westward, and usually windward, side of the State's rugged coast; around the fearful South West and South East Capes; and up Storm Bay to Hobart. In heavy sou'westerly and southerly winds, with the pounding seas from the Southern Ocean that accompanied them, no race course anywhere in the world could be more potentially dangerous or so cruel on men, yachts and equipment. And the Ocean Racing Club of Victoria defiantly listed the start of this annual event for 26 December, in opposition to the CYC's Sydney–Hobart race start – at first ruffling a few NSW feathers. Some well-experienced sailors pronounced the Victorians out of their heads to put on such a race, with a 40 per cent chance of battling nearly all the way to windward across Bass Strait down the western side of Tasmania, which offered so few places to hide in an emergency, except Macquarie Harbour and Port Davey. 'It would certainly be an honour to win such a race,' admitted one CYC official, 'but who wants wound stripes? They'll need to be very selective about the boats they let start in it, and they'll get the walloping of their lives. There'll be boats lost, and crews, too, mark my words.'

Well, up to 1985, in spite of such predictions, Victorians had succeeded in running the West Coaster fourteen times without disasters or tragedies. They had the normal dramas of ocean racing – a few dismastings, minor injuries, and more salt water in the bilges of some yachts than fresh in the tanks, but in each of the races the weather was much less ferocious than had been expected, although there had been gusts of 70 k from astern in 1972 and 30–40 k on the nose in 1977. Some starters had to quit, and a few crews arrived in port wide-eyed from their experiences, though overall they had taken no more of a pounding than many who had sailed the Sydney–Hobart course, 200 nm to the eastward, down the allegedly easier east coast of Tasmania. The West Coaster fleet totalled twenty-four in 1976 (and again in 1978), when the 22 m concrete cutter, *Helsal*, owned and skippered by Tony Fisher, of Sydney, set the course record of 56h 18m 51s in hard westerlies that allowed her to reach most of the way. She did it mainly under headsails – a yankee jib and a stays'l – when her main halyard broke ten minutes after the start in a 20 k breeze and it was considered too dangerous in the building wind to send a man aloft to replace it. Off the north-west corner of Tasmania a sou'westerly came in at 60 k, forcing *Helsal* to claw off the coast under stays'l only. But the wind eased, swung to the west and allowed her to average 10 k under number three genoa all the way to South West Cape. Once around the corner in light winds Fisher was able to jury rig his mainsail with a spinnaker halyard and a toppin' lift. *The Flying Footpath* then came in with only 13.0 to spare from the hard-driven *Imogene*, a 13.4 m sloop that had skated down the big seas under spinnaker with her crew counting their broaches and their blessings when their mast remained standing. On handicap the race went to the 12.5 m *Monsoon*, skippered by Ian Cameron.

In 1978 Jim Searle skippered his NZ-designed skimmer, *Hot Prospect*, to her second successive handicap win, in moderate to fresh reaching breezes. Three front runners finished within 18m and line honours went to the ketch *Sandra*, a thirty-year-old converted 8-metre class boat skippered by veteran Jack Behrens and owned by Federal Labor Party president Neil Batt, a member of the celebrated Tasmanian sailing family. The next year Neil Searle replaced his father as skipper in *Hot Prospect* and brought off the handicap hat trick. In 1980 he won again, this time in *Relentless*. The biggest fleet was thirty-five in 1982, when Tasmanian Craig Escott won in his father's *Solandra*, a nimble 10 m wooden sloop, in which a year earlier he had placed an admirable second in the Sydney–Hobart race. A year after her Melbourne–Hobart win, *Solandra* was wrecked on her way to Sydney when she hit a reef off Flinders Island. All her crew were saved. In 1984 Victorian Ocean Racing Club commodore, Alan Collins, won the West Coaster in his *Eastern Morning* after almost drifting down much of the 'dangerous' west coast of Tasmania in a series of calms. At the same time hard winds and steep seas on the NSW coast were bringing the Sydney–Hobart fleet to its knees and forcing 149 boats to retire. In recent years a joint start has been arranged for both the West Coaster and the Devonport race across the same line at Portsea, on the Mornington Peninsula, on 27 December. The start is carefully timed to

Left Victorian cutter *Mary Blair* is carrying full main but needs no spinnaker in these savage squalls in the final stages of the race from Melbourne to Hobart. (Brian Curtis, Hobart)

Right *Helsal* on her way to line honours in the 1976 West Coaster. A broken halyard forced her to sail much of the race under headsail alone. (Hobart Mercury)

suit the most favourable daylight tide so that the fleets for both races can get safely across The Rip at the entrance to Port Phillip and out to sea. On 26 December a well-promoted 20 nm Cock of The Bay carnival race from St Kilda to Mornington, and open to all comers in different divisions, brings a large spectator fleet and thousands of holiday makers watching from the shore.

However, the West Coaster still lacked the charisma of the Sydney–Hobart race, and in spite of the handsome trophies offered, it had failed to draw many entrants away from the classic. The hottest Victorian competitors continued to set themselves for the Sydney-controlled race, especially on those odd-numbered years when NSW clubs, with the endorsement of the Australian Yachting Federation, ran the Southern Cross Cup ocean racing championship, of which the Sydney–Hobart on 26 December was the main race of four, with teams of three yachts competing from all Australian States and from several foreign countries.

So, for 7 January 1979, the Victorians organized the most ambitious ocean race ever sailed in Australian coastal waters, and one of the most richly endowed in the world—the $40,000 Golden Fleece (Oil Co.) Great Circle handicap, of 810 nm, with prizes worth $10,000 to both line-honours and handicap winners. The course, non-stop, was from Portsea, inside Port Phillip, across Bass Strait to the eastward, through the north-eastern Tasmanian islands, down the east coast of Tasmania, around the south coast, up the west coast, and across Bass Strait to finish off Flinders in Western Port Bay. Here, at last, it was felt was a race challenging enough to make every tall-water sailor in the world sit up and take notice. The Victorian Government conjoined with the oil company and other commercial firms as financial sponsors. Invitations to compete were sent to a score of foreign yacht clubs and to individual owners of champion offshore yachts in a dozen countries.

The response from overseas was lukewarm. No one was willing to ship or sail his yacht all the way to Australia to compete in only one race. Even if one aimed also for the Sydney–Hobart handicap, starting thirteen days earlier, there would be little time at the end of it to reach Melbourne and to prepare for the start of the longer event, especially if repairs and replacement of equipment were necessary. The closeness of the two races also forced Australian owners to make a choice, and only three of the ten yachts that entered for both events were able to start in them. But twenty-one, mostly Victorians, competed, and although the weather was light and variable for half of the way, they got a dusting across the bottom of Tasmania that their crews will not forget in a long time. The event was a double triumph, on line honours and handicap, for West Australian Rolly Tasker in his new self-designed, 22.9 m aluminium cutter *Siska*, competing in her maiden race. *Siska* had earlier sailed 3,000 nm from Perth to Sydney to race to Hobart but had been debarred from that contest because the rating she then carried exceeded the 70 ft limit. The publicity that surrounded Tasker's rebellious private race over the Sydney–Hobart course and *Siska*'s runaway from the CYC's fleet made the big red-hulled boat the glamour contestant of the Great Circle marathon.

A spectator fleet of some 850 craft and thousands of people on shore saw the start off Portsea in Port Phillip. *Siska* took the lead shortly after the start, streaked away in light following winds across Bass Strait and down the Tasmanian east coast, beat her way quickly through the early stages of a 40 k blow off Maatsuyker Island, in the Southern Ocean, until she was able to turn north, then came home hard on a wind, and finally with her sheets sprung, in a fresh nor'westerly. She crossed the finishing line 23h 45m (and 200 nm) ahead of her nearest rival, Josca Grubic's 25 m ketch *Anaconda II*. *Siska's* elapsed time for the 810 nm course was 4d 19h 32m 32s at an average of only 7 k, but she took three days of it to cover the first half when the weather was light. *Siska* won the handicap by 31m 29s from Dick and Ian Thurston's aluminium-hulled 13.7 m *Apollo II*, formerly Alan Bond's Admiral's Cup representative, with Jock Sturrock's new Two Ton Cup class sloop, *Fiona*, the Division II winner, 3h 3m 8s further back. *Apollo II* had an excellent handicap chance until the final stages when the wind dropped and she took 1h 30m to sail the last three miles.

In the middle stages, many of the smaller competitors up to 100 nm behind *Siska* had to battle for almost two days through the south-west blow. Sturrock said he made good only ten metres to windward in one night of sailing against 50 k gusts and a vicious current.

Two yachts were forced to retire — *Ariadne* when she fell off a huge sea and cracked her hull, and *Jindivik* when she broke her tiller. All the rest sailed the course and many said they would line up again when the race was next held.

Nevertheless the 1980 race, which started 13 January, attracted only eleven starters, five of which had sailed in the Sydney–Hobart nineteen days earlier. This times seven fought their way around the same Great Circle course in a series of gales that at stages reached 60 k in gusts, with soft patches in between. Tasker, in *Siska*, again won line honours — in 4d 18h 53m 1s — faster by 39m 31s than a year earlier. Tasker said that the weather between Maria Island, on the Tasmanian east coast, and Maatsuyker Island was at times so thick 'you could have cut it with a screw driver'. Second across the line, only 19h 6m 8s behind the much bigger *Siska*, and winner of the race on handicap was Victorian Lou Abrahams in his *Challenge*, a handsome new American-designed 14 m sloop that had placed only ninety-fourth in the Sydney–Hobart fleet, although she had top-scored for Victoria in the just completed Southern Cross Cup series. Other Victorians — Keith Farfor in his 13.7 m *Superstar*, and Bruce Edmunds and John Aitken in their 10.4 m *Aquila* — placed second and third; *Siska* was fourth on handicap.

Some of the crews in the four yachts that failed to sail the course said they found the conditions even tougher than they had expected and retired for a variety of reasons — stress of weather, broken gear and illness. Peter Sleigh, chairman and chief executive officer of the major sponsors, gave a special trophy for fortitude and determination to Alan Collins, skipper of the 11 m *Eastern Morning*, who with his five-man crew, took 11d 3h 5m to sail the course. They were forced to shelter twice during their epic struggle, once for twenty-four hours while they rebuilt sails torn apart in heavy winds. The crew of *Dorado*, forced out of the race when dismasted off the north-eastern Tasmanian coast, organized a tow into Hobart where their skipper Jim Lake sold the boat. In 1981, when the race was again proposed, yachtsmen decided the course was more a test of endurance than sailing skill; there were few entries and the contest lapsed.

QUEENSLAND OCEAN RACING

Admiral Sir Francis Beaufort, the renowned British cartographer and marine scientist, said of a hurricane, 'Waves rise so high that ships within sight are hidden in troughs, the sea is covered with streaky foam, the air is filled with spray.'

Although the Queensland cyclone Emily did not occur until 1972, some 115 years after Beaufort's death at the valiant old age of eighty-three, there is no doubt that he, observer of 1,000 storms, would have endorsed it as a full-scale, genuine hurricane. Emily reached a top official velocity of 96 k, from the east-south-east, and brought up seas so high that they blotted out not only ships, but also the sky, and filled the air with spray driven so hard that it stripped paint, varnish and even galvanizing off vessels that encountered the full force of it. Six yachts fought their way for twelve hours through Emily and a seventh was doing so, too, until she was dismasted, in the wildest Brisbane to Gladstone ocean race since the 307 nm annual event was first staged in 1949. Peter Hopwood, in the 9.8 m *Harmony*, won the handicap honours and Rob George took line honours in the 11.6 m *Kintama*. But there were honours for everyone when they got ashore after that blow — and officials of the organizing Queensland Cruising Yacht Club began to sigh with relief that all crews for which they felt responsibility had survived, and that the eighteen yachts that had dived for shelter in the early stages, after a radioed warning of the hurricane's approach, were safely in port.

There had been some near misses. When the 11.6 m NSW sloop *Rival* was bowled right over by a tremendous beam sea and dismasted, her owner-skipper, Alby Burgin, found himself in the water well clear of his yacht. He was still wearing his safety harness but the cleat to which his lifeline was attached had broken. Burgin swam back to the wallowing yacht and, as he was struggling aboard, the crew comedian yelled out to him, 'What do you want?' *Kintama*, fighting her way around Bustard Head, 33 nm from the finish, was lifted bodily by a sea and hurled sideways to within a few lengths of the rocks at the base of the headland. Then the backwash sucked her out and her desperate crew managed to sail her into clear water. A wave broke clean over the top of Neville Gosson's 13.7 m steel *Makaretu*, tore away the life-raft that had been lashed down on her deck, but failed to dislodge the man clinging to her wheel. *Makaretu*'s wind gauge had earlier jammed at its maximum reading — 80 k. Yachtsmen learned a lot about survival procedures in that race, and passed on their knowledge in reports and seminars. They also learned why the organizers of the Brisbane–Gladstone race, so often advertised as one of the most richly endowed with useful trophies for an Easter Holiday downhill slide, gnaw their fingernails year after year on a hurricane watch. The prevailing winds generally can be expected to be moderate from the south-east, giving the yachts free-sheet-sailing most of the way, with only occasional blasts from the east-north-east. But there can be constant head winds and seas and regularly, during the weeks before Easter, there are cyclonic systems brewing in the northern Coral Sea with hurricane force winds (above 65 k on Admiral Beaufort's scale) that may come tearing down the Queensland coast.

Even so, up to 1986, only one Brisbane–Gladstone race, the 1964 event, had to be postponed and then only for twenty-four hours, until the edge of a cyclone moved away and the south-easterly squalls eased to 30 k. *Ilina*, the 18 m ketch owned and skippered by the newspaper proprietor, Rupert Murdoch, romped home in 33h 23m 54s — a time that stood as a course record until Tony Fisher's 22 m *Helsal* reduced it to 31h 29m 25s, in 1976. To disprove the popular theory that the Brisbane–Gladstone race always has some free-sheet sailing, the wind in 1978 blew consistently from ahead, varying in direction between north-west, north, and north-east. Many of the highly fancied 'downhillers' in the fleet of thirty-four did not like this but it was a joy at least to *Gretel II*'s America's Cup challenge skipper, Jim Hardy, in his aluminium-hulled 12.5 m *Nyamba*, which won on handicap. It was, in fact, the first race *Nyamba* had won after a year-long campaign in which, under the name *Runaway*, she had scored enough minor placings to earn the right to represent Australia in the Admiral's Cup world ocean racing championship. The 1978 race was also the twenty-sixth in which the handsome 14.6 m cruising ketch *Laurabada* had competed (her best placing was third in 1954) and the thirtieth in which her owner-skipper-designer-builder Ivan Holm, a former commodore of the QCYC, and his first mate, Doug Kemp, had sailed. By 1985 they had brought their score to thirty-three in *Laurabada* (in addition to four races each in other boats), had led the fleet home once, and had placed second in the arbitrary handicap division. In 1985, Holm's son, Peter Holm, was the QCYC commodore, and his son, Peter junr, was a member of the sailing committee. In 1985, there was another rare race into headwinds, won by Richard Hudson's Sydney Half Tonner, *Public Nuisance.*

The year of the postponed race in 1964 was notable also because the QCYC for the first time held a race over the same course for multihull yachts — catamarans and trimarans — starting them fifteen minutes earlier than the main fleet of monohulls. The multihulls, controlled and organized after 1964 by the Queensland Multihull Yacht Club (because as a policy, most ocean racing clubs consider such craft suitable only for protected waters) have raced ever since, starting fifteen minutes after the monohulls and with some spectacular results. In 1976 Cliff Fraser, in the Lex Nicol-designed 11.3 m aluminium-framed trimaran *Devil 3*, with its fibreglass-foam sandwich hull, rocketed to the finish in 27h 45m, leaving the fastest monohull *Helsal* (setting the then course record of 31h 29m 25s) to follow her in later. And Fraser's time for the race is not the fastest ever recorded. In 1982 Adrian Rogers in his 18.28 m Lock Crowther-designed catamaran *Shotover* sailed the course in 21h 21m at an average speed of 14.33 k.

Crowther, of Sydney, world-renowned as a multihull designer, skipper and navigator, who has sailed in fifteen Brisbane–Gladstone multihull races and in scores of much longer offshore events overseas, was sailing master in Brian Willey's 12.2 m *Captain Bligh* in the 1972 hurricane, Emily. They sailed the course in 33h 30m — more than 21h faster than the first-home monohull, *Kintama.* 'We probably got in before the worst of it,' says Crowther. 'At times we ran at speeds above 30 k. That was the figure at which the needle in our sum log speedo fell out. We carried some sail at all times and at no stage were out of control.' But one of the other two trimarans in the race could not handle the conditions and retired. The third, *Australian Maid*, skippered by Bob Brown, capsized when skirting the surf near Bustard Head and two of her crew were drowned. *Australian Maid* was driven 1.5 nm inland from the normal shoreline by the heavy seas sweeping into the coast but was later righted, refloated and repaired. A fleet of nine trimarans and a catamaran started in the 1979 Brisbane–Gladstone multihull race in a 10 k east-south-east breeze that freshened to 30 k and Sid Luxford, in his 12.8 m tri, *Assassin*, skated over the 308 nm in 28h 1m 21s, for line honours. That was more than 5h faster than Jack Rooklyn's 17.7 m *Apollo*, first monohull across the line.

By 1985, Sydney's Rooklyns — Jack or his son, Warwick — in their two boats called *Apollo*, 17.67 m overall and 23.16 m, and in their 22.25 m *Ballyhoo*, all designed by Ben Lexcen, had been first home nine times in the Gladstone race. In 1980, the smaller *Apollo*, again leading, ran on to Lady Elliott Island reef in darkness and was totally wrecked. In 1982, the larger *Apollo* set a new course record of 29h 46m 56s, but lost time when she stood by to assist a catamaran in distress and later when she had to retrace her course after missing a fairway buoy on her way into Gladstone for the finish. In 1986, *Windward Passage*, then Australian-owned by Rod Muir, reduced the record to 28h 57m 6s. After a total of thirty-eight races had been sailed in 1986, the boat with the best handicap record in the Brisbane–Gladstone event was the 21-year-old *Wistari*, a near flat-bottomed 10.66 m downwind flyer, designed and built of plywood by Port Curtis (Gladstone) Sailing Club's much-honoured Noel Patrick. When the weather had been fresh and behind him, Patrick had won four times and been placed second, fourth and fifth, outsailing some of the hottest IOR performers in Australia. In the gale-torn 1982 race, *Wistari* won after her crew had taken part in two gallant rescues of multihulls. She held in tow one that had capsized while another yacht, Tom Melville's steel-hulled 13.1 m *Jacqui*, took aboard its crew, and she towed another to shelter, then sailed on. *Wistari* was granted 5h 30m allowance for the time taken on the rescues (Patrick and his crew had kept a detailed log of the incidents) but her win was not confirmed until a rival's protest against the time allowance had been overturned on appeal. Later Patrick and Melville were awarded the Queensland CYC's special seamanship award. In 1985, another downwind flyer, the superbly sailed Sydney Half Tonner *Public Nuisance*, jointly owned by Richard Hudson, Graham Jones, and Robert Cole won the main prize, capping her win a year earlier in the Sydney–Mooloolaba race. *Public Nuisance* is a near sistership, but with a slightly finer stern, of *Beach Inspector*, winner of the Brisbane–Gladstone race and the Sydney–Mooloolaba race in 1981, when owned by Jones and Hudson.

Although ocean-racing multihulls are still regarded as ratbag boats by many conventional offshore yachtsmen, the generous-hearted citizens of Gladstone equally welcome skippers and crews of both types of craft after their races, and scores of the men from the monos and multis intermingle on cruises north to the Great Barrier Reef during the winter.

Queensland's longest race up to 1979 was the triennial Gladstone to Cairns handicap of 600 nm. The seventeen contestants in the inaugural race in 1976 took an unexpected dusting when an intense low pressure system, which fortunately did not develop into a full cyclone, wandered onto the track. The race went to Noel Patrick's Gladstone sloop *Wistari*.

Another Queensland snorter, this time with 45 k from the south-east and higher gusts, blasted the fleet of thirteen in Capricornia Cruising Yacht Club's inaugural Yeppoon to Mackay handicap of 180 nm, in 1975. The Sydney sloop, *Willi Willi*, skippered by John Hawley, of Middle Harbour Yacht Club, was first in after an exciting run of 19h 54m. At times her speedo touched 22 k as she zoomed down the face of the steep following seas. The 16.2 m Mackay ketch *Heemskerk*, skippered by John Donkin, equally hard-driven, came in exactly 60s behind *Willi Willi*. Six yachts retired. Two of them were dismasted; one, a 9.1 m boat, dived through the top of a wave then dropped so violently into a trough that she bent her rudder level with her bottom, and another hit a reef and was wrecked. Her crew spent a day and a half in a rubber life-raft until they were rescued by ship and seaplane. A 5.9 m Mackay sloop, *Gilden*, skippered by Peter Rule, prudently sailed the course under storm jib. Officials, with a dazzling talent for understatement, agreed that one of the trials of the 'exhilarating event', which skirted many islands, was the mechanical blackout of the lighthouse on High Peak Island, 'a circumstance which, in the heavy rain squalls, made this rounding mark impossible to see'.

Queensland's offshore calendar for 1985–86 season included, among seven major races, the 304 nm Gladstone–Hamilton Island handicap (first held in 1984) jointly organized by Port Curtis Sailing Club and the newly formed Hamilton Island Yacht Club, at that luxurious Barrier Reef tourist resort. A fleet of fifty boats, many from Sydney, sailed in the inaugural event, and in the following Hamilton Island race week series, with a testing contest for navigators and watch-keepers in the 170 nm Coral Sea race. For those skippers and crews whose competitive spirit had survived the festivities before and after that carnival, there remained the Hamilton Island to Cairns contest of 300 nm organized by Cairns Cruising Yacht Squadron; and then Royal Papua Yacht Club's 455 nm derby through the reefs to Port Moresby (Papua New Guinea). In 1979, Cairns CYS and RPYC first held the race in a 35 k easterly with steep seas that surprised officials and weather forecasters who had expected moderate head winds. The easterly provided a free-sheet romp for Jack Rooklyn's well-crewed 17.7 m Sydney sloop, *Apollo*, which sailed the course in a few minutes under two days at an average of 9.5 k and won both line honours and handicap. The performance established a unique record for the boat — five successive line-honours wins in major distance events in the same season. The others were: Sydney–Hobart, Sydney–Brisbane, Brisbane–Gladstone and Gladstone–Cairns.

In 1985 on the first night of the race to Moresby, Queenslander Arthur Bloore, in his 20 m *The Office*, was leading the fleet of twelve by 6 nm in a following south-easterly gale when the steering gear collapsed, forcing the boat to return to port. That left Warwick Rooklyn in the 23.16 m *Apollo* well in front and, it seemed, certain to break the course record set by his father six years earlier. But the breeze died 20 nm from the finish and it took *Apollo* six hours to get to the line, two hours outside the record. She placed second on handicap to Bill Sykes' well-campaigned 12.5 m *Di Hard* from Port Moresby, which did well in a series of vicious tropical NW rain squalls after the long period of calm. Before the race, the 11.4 m *Altair*, on her way from Port Moresby to Cairns for the start, hit a submerged log and sank. Her crew of eight took to a life-raft, were rescued by a freighter and landed at Thursday Island. Still keen to sail, they made their way to Cairns where most got crew places aboard other competitors. As a grand finale *Starbuck II* hurdled a reef into a lagoon 38 nm, from Port Moresby, and, after a 'Mayday' radio drama, was towed home in time for the post-race party.

Other Queensland ocean racing events over shorter distances are organized by clubs at Mackay, Townsville, Cairns, and Hamilton Island, but the main competitions are held off the southern coast. The annual Northern Ocean Racing Championship (NORC) is conjointly conducted during February–March–April by Mooloolaba Yacht Club and Queensland Cruising Yacht Club. This consists of three races up to 130 nm between Moreton Bay and Mooloolaba. The annual Sunshine Coast Ocean Racing (SCOR) series, off Mooloolaba in July–August, consists of five races, up to 158 nm, for yachts on both International Offshore Rating and arbitrary handicaps. JOG boats sail shorter courses. After three foundation years, starting in 1975, the SCOR ultimately attracted a record fleet of thirty-nine yachts from four States in 1977. The lightweight NZ-designed Quarter Ton Cup class boat, *Waikikamukau* (Hugh Treharne and Rob Mundle), of Sydney, then holder of the national level rating title in her class, dominated the first two regattas, and the Queensland and national champion Quarter

Tonner, *Locomotion* (Frank Hurd) took the third series. The winner in 1978 was *Seaply,* a NZ-designed Sydney Quarter Tonner, skippered by Hugh Treharne and launched only a fortnight earlier. Two months later *Seaply,* renamed *Seaflyer,* placed third in the world Quarter Ton championship in Japan. By 1985, some of the best IOR boats in the southern States were making the SCOR series one of the features of their annual racing campaigns.

WESTERN AUSTRALIAN OCEAN RACING

One of the treasured memories of Western Australian yachting is of skipper Lennie Darlot arriving at the start of an ocean race in the early 1900s in his sloop *Berringarra* holding a black umbrella over his balding head. Though no doubt comforting to him, it was thought to spoil the effect of his impeccable dress and that of his crew, all of whom wore white shirts, black ties, long white duck trousers, white socks and white canvas shoes.

Few of WA's offshore yachtsmen have been seen afloat with black umbrellas lately or, for that matter, with black ties, but then the whole scene has changed quite a deal. In 1902 West Australian Yacht Club and the Bunbury Rowing and Sailing Club arranged WA's first recorded offshore contest, a somewhat casual affair for three yachts over 50 nm from Mandurah to Bunbury, both south of Fremantle. In 1985 more than eighty yachts of various types and classes competed in sixty-eight WA ocean races over courses totalling 3,747 nm. Fleets of thirty, in different divisions, sailed distance races over courses ranging from 20 to 325 nm, and a few of them sailed 3,000 nm to Sydney to race 630 nm to Hobart and then sailed 3,000 nm back to their home ports. Jonathan Sanders in 1984 made the trip to Sydney single-handed in his 10.4 m *Perie Banou,* a feat he was able to dismiss with some aplomb since he had earlier sailed the same boat three times around the world. Two of those circumnavigations were continuous with two short rendezvous at sea for re-provisioning. In 1981, Fremantle Sailing Club held its inaugural 1,510 nm race from Fremantle to Bali for a fleet of forty-eight yachts, with three short races on the way back — to Dampier, Geraldton, and Fremantle. At the time of writing the club was planning a similar passage-race regatta for 1986. It was through a tradition of intrepid seafaring of such quality that WA clubs were inspired to challenge four times for the America's Cup (see Chapter 5) and to organize the Parmelia Race, an 11,650 nm one-stop marathon from Plymouth (England) to Cape Town and then to Fremantle, in which an international fleet competed to celebrate the State's sesqui-centenary in 1979.

The 19.8 m WA ketch *Independent Endeavour* won both major IOR handicap legs, from Plymouth to Cape Town and from Cape Town to Fremantle. She was skippered by the young American Skip Novak for owner, the late Peter Wright, a WA newspaper proprietor. The 10.4 *Bluebell,* owned and skippered by Max Shean, of Fremantle, won the overall open handicap division from Sanders' *Perie Banou.* The 22.9 m Perth sloop *Siska,* skippered by her owner, Rolly Tasker, sailed the first 6,650 nm leg of the race in 37d 14h 28m 15s — a record passage for a yacht from Plymouth to Cape Town — and the second 5,000 nm leg in 19d 23h 14m at an average speed of 10.4 k, giving her the fastest overall time (the starting times were staggered) of 57d 13h 42m 15s.

WA's ocean racing developed in the face of difficulties that would have discouraged less enthusiastic sailors. They have a wild coastline, hard onshore winds and, once outside the Fremantle–Rottnest Island area, no shelter except for Cockburn Sound, for hundreds of miles. For years, to reach the open sea, yachts have had to travel from the broad inner sanctuary of Melville Water down the long connecting neck of the Swan River, under three low-level bridges, then out through Fremantle Harbour, where they are not allowed to delay since it is totally reserved for commercial shipping. To pass under the bridges along the Swan each yacht has had to carry its mast in a tabernacle on deck so that it could be temporarily lowered, then smartly raised. Certainly these manoeuvres have developed an expertise in the art of rigging and setting-up spars rarely seen among amateur yachtsmen, although it is a time-consuming exercise many feel they could do without. But relief came in 1979 with the opening of Fremantle Sailing Club's magnificent $10 million Success Yacht Harbour, a huge, man-made basin outside Fremantle, with protected berthing pens for 750 craft and lift-out slipway facilities for those up to 65 tonnes. The lease rights to the pens were each sold for $3,250 upwards, plus an annual rental charge, and an even greater surge of offshore sailing was assured.

Although regular, organized ocean racing did not properly begin until 1948 (interest in early events was sporadic and discouraged because of a number of tragedies) it has grown in popularity at an astonishing pace. Eight clubs, spanning the coast between Geraldton, 235 nm north of Perth, to Albany, 620 nm around the south-west corner, then another 212 nm east to Esperance on the southern shores, coordinate their efforts under the Yachting Association of WA's Offshore Racing Committee. Races start in mid-September and are held at least fortnightly for seven months until mid-April. 'Our protected waterways on the Swan River are so crowded with small craft [massed fleets of more than 800 regularly sail on Melville Water] that outside is the only way to go,' says Offshore treasurer and president of YAWA, Bruce Campbell. In 1985 WA's eight main ocean races were: Fremantle to Geraldton, 220 nm; Geraldton to Fremantle, 220 nm; Mandurah, starting and finishing off Fremantle, 101 nm; Cape Naturaliste (and return), Fremantle to Fremantle, 200 nm; Fremantle to Albany, 325; Albany to Fremantle, 325 nm; Bunbury, Fremantle to Fremantle, 180 nm; Port to Port, Fremantle to Fremantle, 130 nm. Many of the races had divisions for yachts of different sizes, classes and IOR categories, and all were linked with point score competitions.

Since WA began to prepare for its 1983 campaign to win the America's Cup (see Chapter 5) and then to defend it, a classic form of short, offshore match racing had developed off Fremantle. This is the annual Australia Cup series contested between ten helmsmen, Australian and foreign, who are invited to compete because of their internationally recognised status. Like America's Congressional Cup match-racing series, the contest is sailed over a series of nine short races in identically rigged class yachts, with every helmsman racing against each of his nine rivals. The winner is the helmsman with most wins. The vessels chosen for the WA competition are of the Viking class, robust 9.24 m sloops designed by Ben Lexcen. Winners, all aspiring America's Cup 12-metre helmsmen at the time of their competition, have been: 1982, John Bertrand (Australia); 1983, Mario Pelaschier (Italy); 1984, Harold Cudmore (Ireland); 1985, Colin Beashel (Australia).

Those WA sailors who make the mid-season voyage east for the Sydney–Hobart race have a lot to live up to. Peter Packer's 12.2 m *Rampage*, from Perth, won the Sydney–Hobart handicap in 1975, after placing third in 1973, and a score of others have competed with distinction since 1963, when Alan Williams' *Narani* was the first yacht from the West to sail in the race. Packer, with two sons, Ron and Chris Packer, in his crew, won in a series of hard following winds with gusts well above 40 k, and covered the course in 76h 43m 3s, a remarkable 8.2 k average for a yacht of her size. But the weight of the wind did not bother them at all. West Australians are at their best in robust conditions and their seamanship is always of a high order. It needs to be. Their prevailing summer breeze is a stiff south-westerly piping in from the Indian Ocean at up to 25 k by mid-afternoon, and bringing with it lumpy seas that sweep unimpeded along a vast, almost unprotected lee shore. Perth city dwellers call this cooling wind the 'Fremantle Doctor' because it brings relief from the baking heat of easterlies from the Australian Central Desert. But once outside Fremantle Harbour, with few places to hide, a consultation with the 'Doctor' can be a salutary experience for those boats and crews in poor health. And his locum, 'The Roarer', from the north-west with gusts of ferocious intensity — whose arrival, fortunately, is usually well heralded — can be a fearsome creature.

In the 1974 Albany race — 325 nm from Fremantle to Albany — the 'Doctor' was in a violent mood and gusted up to 40 k. There were heavy head seas. Three of the ten starters retired, two with broken masts. The Albany sloop *Mistress* lost her mast twenty miles south of Cape Leeuwin, a place long-dreaded by mariners in the biggest ships, and after much travail was towed to safety. The powerful *Apollo II*, with John Fitzhardinge as skipper, won the race in 65h, good time considering the conditions but 25h slower than that of the inaugural event of 1968, when Fitzhardinge set the course record in his 12.8 m plywood yawl, *Theanna*. Only five yachts started in that race in a hard breeze that veered north-west behind them and quickly increased to 50 k. One participant remarked that any spinnakers which had not been dropped by 3 am on the second day blew out. John Farmer, in Peter Packer's *Corsair*, reported that as they approached the dangerous lee shore cliffs of Hamelin Bay with the fragments of their storm kite streaming from the yacht's masthead like a flag, the land was 'coming up far too fast'. Then, during a momentary lull, it was possible to let go the halyard, run over the sail and drag it aboard.

'Later that same morning, the lighthouse keeper at Leeuwin registered the wind speed at 75 k, and reported that the seas had become mountainous', wrote Farmer in *Offshore*, the Cruising Yacht Club of Australia's official bulletin.

Corsair, which was rounding the Cape, fell off the largest sea any of us had ever seen — it blotted out a wintry sun and loomed higher than our spreaders with an ugly white curling top. *Corsair* fell on her beam ends and I was tossed like a piece of jetsam over the furled boom into a boiling sea. As she shook herself like a wet terrier, I managed to grab a trailing jib sheet and only just scraped back on board; that was a moment, that was. The south coast was a scene of wild magnificence as the wind settled down to a steady 45 k, with occasional gusts of 55 k from the west-north-west. As night fell on the second day we approached the white-topped rocks — two huge chunks of granite towering some 43 m out of the ocean with large seas breaking at their base and shooting great plumes of water right over their tops, an awe-inspiring sight which none of us will ever forget. *Theanna* recorded speeds over 20 k during the trip from Cape d'Entrecasteaux to Albany and she subsequently set a record elapsed time of 40h for the 325 nautical miles.

But the winds in the West are not always gale force, and ocean racing is not all of such Captains Courageous quality. In recent years, only three yachts have been lost in organized races. One was Jon Sanders' 12.8 m Sabre class *Theadora*, which sank when her keel bolts worked loose. Her seven-man crew, who took to a life raft, were picked up within a few minutes. Jack Cassidy lost his 12.8 m *Evelyn* when she ran full bore on to a reef and was shattered beyond repair. Her crew walked ashore. In the 1981 race to Bali, Ray Parker's 13.7 m ferro-cement *Tahara 'a*, was 'torpedoed' amidships, 700 nm from Fremantle, by a suicidal whale, and sank within two minutes. Her eight-man crew were rescued from their raft when night fell by a fellow competitor, *Lois III*, whose watch-keepers saw their distress flares.

SOUTH AUSTRALIAN OCEAN RACING

Most South Australians might well be considered to be taking part in a modified form of ocean racing every time that they venture beyond Adelaide's constricted outer harbour. Unlike yachtsmen of the eastern States, they have few protected waterways for craft of any size near large areas of urban settlement. The finest harbour in South Australia is Port Lincoln with adjoining Boston Bay, on the western shores of Spencer Gulf, a superlative 50 sq nm of well-sheltered deep water ideal for all forms of sailing. But it has a population of only about 10,700 and is 724 kilometres by road and 254 kilometres by air from the State's capital, Adelaide (pop. approx 979,000). On the other hand, the shallow waters of Gulf St Vincent, adjacent to Adelaide, on which the main body of keel boats and dinghies are forced to sail, are renowned for short, punishing seas and fresh onshore sou'westerly winds. It is no place for the foolhardy or the incompetent. These conditions, and only two artificial harbours, near Adelaide, the larger built in 1980, in which yachts can safely shelter have greatly restricted the growth of big class yachting in SA, in spite of its 2,500 kilometres of coastline.

At the same time, however, this State has produced amateur sailors with a degree of skill and seamanship often lacking among those blessed with softer conditions. SA yachts have distinguished themselves in many interstate offshore championships, and two of them, *Nerida*, then owned and skippered by Colin Haselgrove, and *Ingrid* (Jim Taylor) won the Sydney–Hobart race, in 1950 and 1952. Both yachts, their skippers and crews, were well seasoned in tough Gulf races. *Nerida*, 13.7 m and rigged as a bermudan yawl (she has since been restored in Sydney by the wine-making Hardy family, her original owners, to her former gaff cutter rig) won in a series of southerly gales that had the leaders hard on a wind for four of the five days it took them to sail the 630 nm Sydney–Hobart course. *Nerida's* crew came ashore saying, 'It was just like home'. *Ingrid's* win, two years later, in a series of fickle calms, astonished her crew, who said they had hoped for Gulf weather and couldn't believe their luck in doing so well in light conditions. By 1967, South Australian Norman Howard had made the 3,200 nm round trip from Adelaide to Sydney, then to Hobart and back to Adelaide, twelve times in his elegant blue-hulled *Southern Myth* in order to compete in the Sydney–Hobart race. Only once was he able to overcome the heavy handicap penalties his yacht suffered under the rating rules. This was in 1958, when *Southern Myth* placed third, in a series of fickle breezes ahead and astern of the fleet. Since 1969, SA, with admirable persistence but little success, has fielded teams in the biennial Southern Cross Cup series (see Chapter 15). Bob Francis, chairman of the State's keelboat committee, says wryly: 'We regularly come tenth out of twelve, but it has broadened our viewpoint of international racing.' In 1983 Jamie Cowell, in his 10.36 m *Morning Hustler*, and in 1984 Jim Howell, in his 13.10 m *Bacardi*, both of Adelaide, have won the Victorian Sovereign Cup, a points score competition sailed over three races — from Melbourne to Portsea (Cock of the Bay), 20 nm; from Portsea to Hobart (West Coaster), 480 nm; and the King of the Derwent handicap, 16 nm.

In 1964-65-66-67 SA yachts dominated the rough race from Melbourne to Port Lincoln (see p. 295 Victorian Ocean Racing), again revelling in the heavy conditions. But, of course, it does not always blow in the Gulf St Vincent and the seas are not always bumpy; it happens only half of the time.

SA has a regular fortnightly programme of short offshore races in its summer season, with fleets in different divisions sometimes totalling eighty. The main races over longer distances, all jointly conducted by the State's senior club, Royal South Australian Yacht Squadron and the Cruising Yacht Club of South Australia are: 250 nm, Adelaide to Neptune Island, off Spencer Gulf, and back through reef-strewn passages that test the skill of the best of navigators; 200 nm, Adelaide to Haystack Island in the Althorpe group, to Kangaroo Island and back; 160 nm, Adelaide to Port Lincoln in Spencer Gulf (jointly held with Port Lincoln Yacht Club and with a five day short-race regatta following); 154 nm, Adelaide to Kangaroo Island and back; 102 nm, Adelaide across Gulf St Vincent to MacDonnell Sound and back. Other regular Gulf races in summer range between 32 nm and 80 nm and by 1985 there was growing interest in short winter events with fifty starters every fortnight.

TASMANIAN OCEAN RACING

Tasmanians have a natural affinity with the sea. It is their heritage, their main lifeline with the rest of Australia, and a source of much of the wealth of their beautiful island State. No coastline in the world is more varied and majestic than that which surrounds Tasmania; no harbour-gulf is bolder than Hobart's huge Storm Bay; and no ocean is less forgiving than the vast southern stretches that sweep up from the Antarctic to its doorstep. Tasmanians have used sailing boats casually, as an obvious means of local transport around their shores, since early settlement. Their eye for hull shape, their knowledge of construction, and their high standards of seamanship have developed from generations of experience. It is a rare Tasmanian who cannot handle a boat. And they have been blessed with stands of superb timber, especially, until recent times, with honey-coloured Huon Pine, the finest softwood for boat planking in the world. It is straight-grained, easily worked, resinous and durable. Many craft built of Huon Pine have lasted a century, and some, well into their eightieth year, are still sailing.

But, although Tasmanians have cruised and raced extensively for 140 years, they have originated few long distances races of their own. They say whimsically that they have hardly needed to do so. One of the world's richest ocean races, the Great Circle of 810 nm, from Melbourne, inaugurated in 1979, used to girdle their island; two of Australia's longest races, from Sydney and Melbourne, finish in Hobart; and a Bass Strait classic, from Port Phillip, finishes in the northern Tasmanian port of Devonport. As well, officials in Sydney and Melbourne consult Tasmanian yachting authorities about the organization of all those events, and the Royal Yacht Club of Tasmania has conjointly controlled the Sydney–Hobart race with the Sydney-based Cruising Yacht Club of Australia since the event was first held in 1945. Once the Sydney–Hobart leaders are across Bass Strait, the Royal Yacht Club of Tasmania largely directs the radio monitoring of yachts' positions, records their finishing times, announces the winners, and arranges the prize giving. Officials of RYCT, when necessary, also provide protest committees and search-and-rescue craft for yachts in distress.

'Tasmanians are usually so busy competing in other people's ocean races, and helping to organize them, that they don't have overmuch time for their own,' said the late Graham Blackwood, a senior Tasmanian official and, in 1979, President of the Australian Yachting Federation.

By 1985 a total of 184 Tasmanian yachts and crews had sailed in Sydney–Hobart races. They had won the handicap three times, scored a second, a third, three fourths, two fifths, five sixths and six divisional wins. In 1979 there were nineteen Tasmanian entries, and in 1984 and 1985 a record twenty-one. The oldest Tasmanian, and indeed the oldest person to compete in the Sydney–Hobart race, was 'Pop' Spaulding who, at the age of ninety, skippered *Kalua* in 1946; the youngest was Colin Philp, who was twelve in 1947 when he crewed aboard his father's *Southern Maid*. (The youngest group of persons ever to sail in the Sydney-Hobart race were the Brooker children of Sydney – Peter, aged 13; Jacqueline, 10; Kathrin, 8; and Donald 6, who, with their parents, shipwright Doug Brooker and his wife, Val, were aboard the family's handsome 13.1 m sloop *Touchwood* in 1978. All the children had been taken regularly on ocean races since infancy and the elder two stood watches in the Sydney–Hobart race.)

Tasmanian Frank Hickman skippered his first Sydney–Hobart racer, *Nell Gwyn*, in 1948 and competed for the twelfth time in his *Antagonist* in 1978. The veteran Massey brothers, of Launceston, when in their seventies competed eight times in their foresail schooner *Wanderer*, between 1947 and 1954. Duncan McCrae, a World War I veteran, paralyzed from the waist down by a bullet in the spine at Gallipoli but with great strength in his arms and shoulders that enabled him to work on deck, skippered his raised-decker *Kintail* to two fourths, a fifth and a sixth in four races in the late 1940s and early 1950s. Hedley Calvert, a Huon Valley orchardist and a third generation member of a family of famous Tasmanian yachtsmen, skippered his beautifully built wooden *Huon Chief* to a divisional win in the Sydney–Hobart race in 1974 and went on to win the national One Ton Cup class title in that yacht in 1975. Tasmanians so admired the boat and the man that they raised $30,000 the same year to send *Huon Chief* to Newport, RI, USA, for the world title series. In light weather against a fleet of rule-beaters in that 'numbers game' *Huon Chief* finished only fourteenth; but she won unstinted admiration all round for her wholesome construction and seaworthiness. Tasmanians, like yachtsmen in other Australian States in recent years, have been forced to adopt lightweight craft to remain competitive, but they still respect traditionally built yachts of wood, and speak of them with genuine affection, more as living creatures than as machines.

Up to 1985 the only completely Tasmanian-controlled races of any distance sailed regularly out of Hobart were the Derwent Sailing Squadron's 200 nm handicap to Schouten Island and back, and Royal Yacht Club of Tasmania's 178 nm handicap to Maria Island and back. The shorter of these was first held as a challenge match in 1935 between *Yeulba* (Angus Cumming), which won, and *Landfall* (Charles Davies and Guy Rex). Since 1947, the race has been open to all comers that qualify under the offshore rules. The average number of starters is twelve, but they are always of high quality. They need to be. The course runs south down the appropriately named Storm Bay into the south Tasman Sea, outside the spectacular cliffs of Tasman Island and the 272 m Cape Pillar, and north for forty-five miles up the east coast to Maria Island, around it, and back again. Sea fogs and hard currents sometimes make navigation difficult; in prevailing summer south-easterly winds the race can be a windward beat for almost half the distance; in heavy southerly weather, with colds winds and wild seas, it can be a bitter slog on the way home until contestants clear Tasman Island and enter Storm Bay. No one starts ill-prepared in the Maria Island race, and it has been a proving ground for some of Tasmania's most able offshore craft. George Gibsons' powerful 12.5 m cutter, *Westward,* won the first Maria Island handicap in 1947, and no Tasmanian was surprised when she also won the Sydney–Hobart race that year and the next. Graham Blackwood's *Bindaree,* driven throughout like a harbour racer around buoys, won the Maria Island race three times in 1964-65-66, and Hedley Calvert's *Huon Lass* won it twice. In a gale in 1967 *Huon Lass* was the only finisher out of six. Among her classy rivals, *Norla* was in danger of losing her mast when she carried away her crosstrees; *Nell Gwyn* blew out all of her headsails, and *Carousel* opened up some planks when she crashed through heavy seas. The record for the course is 25h 34m 3s, set in 1983 by Roger Jackman's 14.8 m *Margaret Rintoul II* (formerly *Ragamuffin*).

In 1985, Don Calvert's outstanding One Ton Cup class boat, *Intrigue,* Australia's best performer in the 1985 Admiral's Cup, won the Maria Island race. The event finished on 24 November, coinciding with Tasmania Day to celebrate Abel Tasman's discovery of the Island in 1642, and Calvert crossed the line heartened by the news that he had just been awarded the title 'Tasmanian of the Year'. The Schouten Island race takes the fleet over much of the same east coast course, but allows contestants to pass either side of Maria Island on their way to the Freycinet Peninsula. Rounding of Schouten Island requires accurate navigation to avoid a tricky bed of reefs on the north-western corner.

In 1956 the Royal Yacht Club of Tasmania tried one of the most daring and hazardous ocean races in the world—a 170 nm handicap from Hobart out of Storm Bay, south-west to Mewstone Rock, an isolated 134 m pinnacle in the Southern Ocean on latitude 43 degrees 44m S, around it and back. The Rock is an albatross rookery and its rugged sides are often swept by freezing gales. The prospect of fighting any vessel to windward against the prevailing westerlies of those Roaring Forties, with heavy, breaking seas and a strong current, was enough to daunt the most intrepid. But Tasmanians started the race seven times until 1968, when it was abandoned because too few competitors were able to get to the rounding mark. In 1966, Hedley Calvert was leading in a full gale in his recently launched *Huon Lass* but ran for shelter when an apprehensive crew member reported that he could see cracks in the hull just for'ard of the base of the mast. In calm water, later, it was found that the 'cracks' were pencil lines drawn by the builder Max Creese, to mark the positions for special floors where it was intended to install a hydraulic-drive engine. 'The seas were fearsome but we might just have got around and won that race if we'd continued,' says Calvert.

By 1968, when the race was abandoned because of its difficulties, Calvert had competed in six of the seven attempts to sail the course. He had won four races outright. Three wins were in his 10 m *Turua,* in 1960 (only boat to finish), 1961, and 1963; one in his *Huon Lass* in 1967.

In 1984, when Tasmanians decided to revive the Mewstone, Calvert sailed again, this time aboard Roger Jackman's *Margaret Rintoul II.* For once it was a soft race. The seven starters got around the island in light winds and it was only when they were in Storm Bay, on the way back, that the westerly bullets started to fly. John Cole-Cook's *Natelle II,* expertly navigated by co-owner John Solomon, won both line honours and handicap. She repeated the performance in 1985, this time in an unforecast 45–50 k sou'westerly gale that came howling at them halfway to the dreadful rock. *Natelle II* fought her way round in mounting seas, was first home 30.0 ahead of Brian Woods' bigger *Parmelia,* and took the handicap from Don Calvert's classy One Tonner *Intrigue* by 18.0. Hedley Calvert, this time racing his new *Huon Spirit* (subsequently sold, renamed *Sagacious* and centre of the 1985 Sydney–Hobart controversy), suffered damage to his mainsail ('kevlar is awful stuff to reef') and retired. After reconsidering the hazards, Hobart officials decided once again to drop the event from the racing calendar.

Tasmanians would like to be able to describe their historic Bruny Island handicap as a true ocean race, since the 95 nm course takes competitors through turbulent seas near the Friar Rocks at the southern end of the island, but much of the race is sailed in enclosed waters. The Bruny Island handicap was first sailed in 1898 by the Derwent Yacht Club (later the Royal Yacht Club of Tasmania) and, except for a break between 1916 and 1926, has been held annually ever since. The main difficulty of the course, according to one Hobart authority, lies in the 'lofty cliffs (on Bruny Island) south of Adventure Bay, 245 m in height, which in fine weather mean light baffling airs and doldrums, and in hard offshore winds, fierce whirlwinds'. Less hearty sailors have found other difficulties. Percy Douglas won the inaugural race with his half-decked centreboarder *Sunbeam* 'in a sinking condition' which, it was laconically reported, 'finished her career as a yacht'; and in 1902 George Cheverton's 8.5 m waterline *Mabel* was wrecked when her crew, fighting their way across Cloudy Bay, on the bottom of South Bruny, in a southerly gale, were forced to beach her under South Bruny lighthouse to save themselves from drowning. No lives were lost but poor *Mabel* was pounded to pieces.

The race got its first interstate flavour in 1899 when Victorian Ernest McCaughan sailed his *Lahloo* down from Melbourne to compete and was beaten by Hobart's *Clytie,* skippered by George Clarke. In 1910 Walter Marks's superb 10-metre class racing machine *Culwulla III* (later called *Eunamara*), from Sydney, first cruised to Hobart on her way to Melbourne for the Sayonara Cup interstate challenge championship (which she won), and, to sharpen her crew, competed in the Bruny Island race. Very light weather, in which it was impossible to handicap her, enabled *Culwulla III* to outclass the Hobart fleet on their home course. In 1913, five of Hobart's 6.4 m waterline One Design class yachts filled the first five places in the Bruny Island race. The winner, *Pandora,* was still racing in club events on the Derwent in 1985. Another yacht of the 6.4 m One Design class, *Weene,* won the Bruny Island handicap in 1914, starting the Batt brothers' family tradition of winning almost every sailing contest to which they set their minds. After the ten-year break between 1916 and 1926, the Bruny race was recognized as part of Tasmania's yachting history that has to be preserved, and although in some subsequent years fleets were small, it is now a popular annual fixture, sailed usually at the end of January, especially for IOR Half Ton Cup and bigger classes.

The three major clubs, Royal Yacht Club of Tasmania, Derwent Sailing Squadron, and Bellerive Yacht Club, cooperate to conduct ten short races for three divisions of offshore boats — Junior Offshore Group, Half Ton Class, and above Half Ton Class — over courses between 40 nm and 60 nm in Storm Bay, down the D'Entrecasteaux Canal and into Frederick Henry Bay. In early January, Derwent Sailing Squadron runs an exclusive and popular 16 nm race for the title 'King of the Derwent'. Only those yachts that have sailed in the recently completed Sydney–Hobart, Melbourne–Hobart and Melbourne–Devonport races may enter. Fleets of seventy usually compete in the event, the only truly interstate, smooth-water, round-the-buoys contest for ocean racers in Australia.

Along the northern coast of Tasmania, free of the long ocean swells of the Tasman Sea on the east, and of those of the Southern Ocean on the west, and somewhat sheltered by the curving 1,220 m high land mass of Tasmania which stretches in a 322 km crescent to the south, there is one of Australia's least used cruising grounds and an excellent spread of water for ocean racing. The seas nevertheless can be boisterous, the currents treacherous and the weather at times cold to those not acclimatized to it, but there are snug harbours and safe anchorages for careful navigators with local knowledge. Mersey (Devonport), Port Dalrymple and George Town (mouth of River Tamar) and Tamar (Launceston) Yacht Clubs jointly conduct a regular and growing number of short races and two of medium length, up to 140 nm, along the coast and to nearby islands on the southern end of Bass Strait, and back. Yachts of the northern Tasmanian clubs are also welcome competitors among Victorian fleets in the major Bass Strait events.

14

Challenges for the Admiral's Cup and the Honolulu Races

BY 1965, the individual prowess of Australian yachtsmen in various types of boats was widely known. Overseas, Australians were no longer regarded, as once they had been with some justification, as maverick roisterers, stimulated by gallons of beer, battering their way around harbour courses in weird, over-canvassed, spoon-shaped dinghies, with little knowledge of or concern for the refinements of racing rules.

Victorian Jock Sturrock had won a race in the international Star class at the London Olympics in 1948 and had taken a bronze medal in the sophisticated 5.5-metre class at the Melbourne Games; West Australian Rolly Tasker had been politicked by the French out of the 12 sq metre Sharpie gold medal in 1956 but had taken the silver, then two years later in Austria had won the FD world title and in the 1962 series had been runner-up; South Australians Brian Farren-Price and Chris Hough in 1963 had won the world 505 dinghy title in the USA, and a year afterwards in Ireland another Adelaide helmsman, John Parrington, with Hough as crew, had scored again; the wise-cracking Sydney grandpa, Bill (later Sir William) Northam had won the Olympic gold medal at Tokyo in the bitterly contested 5.5 series. And, to cap it all, the Australians, off Newport, RI, USA, had astonished everyone, especially members of the New York Yacht Club, when their 1962 America's Cup challenger, *Gretel*, had won one race and had finished only 120 metres, twenty-six seconds in time, behind the USA's defender, *Weatherly*, in another, providing one of the closest finishes in the history of that prestigious trophy.

Nevertheless, in 1965, when Australia shipped its first team of three Sydney yachts to England to compete in the biennial Admiral's Cup contest, they were received with what seemed to be some degree of condescension. At a pre-race cocktail party, a well-known English yachtsman said lightly, 'Jolly sporting of you fellows to bring your old-fashioned boats all the way over here.' The

314

Australians did not take offence, nor was any meant, but in the light of later events, the remark was recalled with some relish. At first many of the Australian contingent of thirty crewmen and officials, some of whose wives had accompanied them, were starry-eyed about the venue of the races. Here they were in historic, not to say sacred, Cowes; on the beautiful Isle of Wight, mecca of sailing, where the British (with some encouragement from the Dutch, who had given Charles II one of their yachts) had started the noble pastime. The Australians were awed by the Royal Yacht Squadron's stone castle (built by Henry VIII), whose officials, with those of the Royal Ocean Racing Club, would control the Cup races, and charmed by the twisted, cobble-stoned streets, and they hardly noticed that much of the town along the waterfront was scruffy, insanitary and in an advanced stage of decay. They viewed the tide-swept, dirty waters of the Solent — a long, boomerang-shaped, two-miles-wide stretch between the Isle of Wight and the mainland — with reverence. Even the mudbanks had famous names.

The British, of course, took it all in their stride. They might be weak on plumbing and pollution but they were strong on play. And Cowes, for a century and a half, had been a place to play. They had started the Admiral's Cup point-score team races there in 1957 as a continuing duel, always held over the same courses, between British and American offshore yachts, and had later opened the contest to other nations. The English were amused that the series had now been given the dubious status of the world's ocean racing championship, but they kept a straight face about it. They knew that over the four races — the first 225 nm across the English Channel to France and back (counting double points for placings); two of 30 nm each around a maze of buoys up and down the Solent (single points); and the final, 605 nm to the Fastnet Rock, off the South Coast of Ireland and back to Plymouth (triple points) — they had the tremendous advantage of local knowledge, gained during 500 years and more of commercial seafaring in the area, and, during the previous century, in small pleasure craft. The English yachtsmen could read the weather better than professional meteorologists, and they knew every gutter along the shorelines where one could escape into slack water to avoid the tidal rips in midstream.

Plan of Admiral's Cup courses. Single points are scored for Solent races, double points for Channel race, and triple for the Fastnet. (*SMH*)

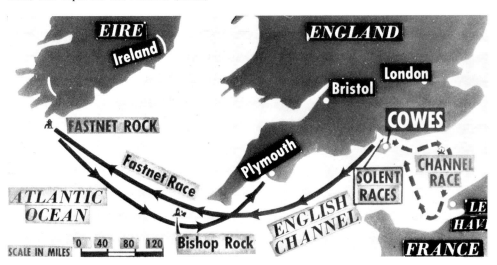

The English also had a good eye for a boat to suit these tricky local conditions of flat water, light, fluky winds, and occasional gales.

Most of their modern racing yachts were rigged tall, with fine lines to get them smartly to windward. Their crews depended on seamanship to get these boats through heavy weather. So if the expert English had been asked seriously to assess the Australian yachts in 1965 they probably would have endorsed their colleague's opinion that the boats from Down Under were old-fashioned, or at least out of their league.

Two of the Australian boats, *Freya*, 11.6 m, jointly owned and skippered by Trygve and Magnus Halvorsen, and *Camille*, 11 m, owned and skippered by Ron Swanson, (both of Sydney) were stout double-enders, strongly built for true, deep-sea, rough-water sailing, with sloop rigs that tended to be squat by comparison with the loftier European racing craft, and of a hull form designed ideally for hard, downwind running and for punishing beats to windward in heavy seas — the sort of conditions so often experienced off the NSW coast and in Bass Strait in the Sydney–Hobart race. *Freya* had already won that race twice in succession and she was to take it for the third time later that year. *Camille* had finished second in the 1964 Sydney–Hobart race. The third member of the Australian Admiral's Cup team, *Caprice of Huon*, a 13.7 m sloop, was deceptive until you saw her out of the water. She had been built thirteen years earlier in Tasmania, to a 1938 design of Englishman Robert Clark, and she was owned and skippered by Gordon Ingate, a former dinghy and 5.5 metre boat skipper.

Ingate, of Sydney, had bought the boat from Olympic champion Bill Northam. Although under Northam the yacht had been successful in harbour racing and had placed fourth in the Sydney-Hobart race, she had not been taken very seriously as an offshore competitor until Ingate had unburdened her of a massive wooden mast, and had outfitted her with an aluminium spar 101 kg lighter and also with well-cut masthead genoas and spinnakers. What Ingate and his crew immediately recognized at Cowes in early trials, but what his Cup rivals from Britain, the USA, France, Germany, Holland, Ireland and Sweden failed to notice was that *Caprice of Huon's* under-water shape was ideal for European conditions. Although she was heavily built in the Australian tradition, she had fine, almost 'metre boat' lines, a reasonable spread of sail, and a rating under the then current RORC measurement rules that gave her an advantage over many much more modern craft her size. *Caprice of Huon's* rivals were not prepared, either, for the highly volatile, competitive spirit of Ingate, sharpened by a thousand dogfights in class boat racing, nor for his intimate knowledge of the racing rules that enabled him to exploit every legitimate advantage and to force unwary helmsmen into errors. He was also backed by a crew experienced in round-the-buoys racing, and a superb navigator-tactician, Bill Fesq, then captain of Royal Sydney Yacht Squadron and a former champion Dragon class helmsman.

While the less manoeuvrable *Camille* and *Freya* were often disadvantaged by the scrambling confusion of racing on the Solent, especially in light winds, walled-in by hundreds of non-Admiral's Cup boats picnic-racing around the same courses as the Cup yachts in the concurrent Cowes Week regatta, and by blundering tourist launches, mudbanks, shoals and three-knot tidal eddies, *Caprice of Huon*, Ingate and his crew were in their element. They outclassed twenty Cup rivals to win the first event, the 225 nm Channel race to France and back, and outwitted them in the two 33-mile rough-and-tumbles around the Solent for the Britannia Cup and the New York Yacht Club Cup — three incredible wins in a row. Within

Caprice of Huon, with volatile Gordon Ingate as owner-skipper, and a highly competitive crew, won three Admiral's Cup races when the Australian team first went to Cowes in 1965. *(SMH)*

a week *Caprice of Huon* and Ingate and his crew were lionized. They began airfreighting trophies back to Sydney. No longer was there any shadow of patronage towards the Australian team, even though *Freya* and *Camille* had performed without distinction. In one of the 33 nm races, *Freya* had lost half an hour and many placings when her navigator had unaccountably mistaken the course. And *Camille's* crew had finished last after missing a rounding buoy and sailing 20 nm that had had to be retraced.

Still, *Camille* had gained six valuable points for doggedly trying, and the Australians started in the final event, the 605 nm Fastnet Cup, notorious for its gales and calms, only seventeen points behind the English. If the weather had blown consistently hard, as had been forecast for the Fastnet (which carried triple points), or even it if had come from the direction that the official meteorologists had predicted, Australia would certainly have won the Admiral's Cup series at the first attempt. As it was — even in the variable moderate to

317

fresh to occasionally gale force winds that prevailed over different sections of the course on the way to the Fastnet Rock, the turning point off the southern coast of Ireland — the Australians were well placed. Then, on the way back, the English team, cleverly ignoring the forecast of a northerly windshift, headed south into the Channel, caught a south-east breeze, and came home to the finishing line off Plymouth with sheets free. Their placings were first, third and eleventh. The Australians, believing the forecast, went north and were caught in fog and bewildering patterns of gales and calms that forced them to claw to windward over some sections against a hard running tide. *Camille* did well to finish fifth on corrected time; *Caprice of Huon* came home seventh, and *Freya* was twelfth. England, who had won the Admiral's Cup in 1957, 1959 and 1963 (having lost it once only, to the USA, in 1961), had scored its fourth victory, but narrowly. The Australians were forty-four points behind them in the final tally and had beaten Holland, the USA, France, Sweden, Ireland and Germany. The English, used to winning, were relaxed about it, but they were delighted with the Australians and encouraged them to come again.

There was no question after that about the standing of all Australian yachtsmen in any part of the world. They had done exceedingly well as a team in spite of two boats unsuited to the conditions in which they had raced, and it was clear that, with the right ones, they would almost certainly have won. That knowledge led to a revolution in the philosophy of Australian ocean racing. Powerful deep-sea boats with conservative rigs might be ideal for rough waters, but to be truly competitive in comparatively smooth water and light airs and in tactical battles around buoys, one must have craft of a different kind. Ideally the yachts should have outstanding windward performance, be almost as manoeuvrable as dinghies, have smart crews who were also seamen, and should rate well for handicap allowances. With those principles in mind, officials of the Cruising Yacht Club of Australia and of the Australian Admiral's Cup challenge committee at once began to plan a campaign for 1967.

They were doubly fortunate right then to have the support of two keen owner-skippers, Bob (later Sir Robert) Crichton-Brown, and Ted Kaufman. Crichton-Brown, prominent in commerce and later to become CYC commodore, had already built the 14 m *Balandra*, to an English design from which *Quiver IV*, England's top Admiral's Cup performer in 1965, had been copied. Although *Balandra* was a difficult boat to control downwind in hard weather, she was at that time probably the closest winded offshore yacht in Australia, and in spite of teething troubles, she had sailed fourth in the Sydney–Hobart race in her first attempt, in conditions that did not suit her.

Kaufman, industrialist, grazier, and a graduate engineer, a former Star boat skipper who had already designed and built a moderately-performed steel ocean racer, chose to develop his own theories in collaboration with the rising star of naval architecture in Australia, sailmaker-helmsman Bob Miller (Ben Lexcen) already famous for his successes with dinghies and small yachts. Between them they created a radical ocean racer for those days, 12.2 m overall, built in Sydney by Cecil Quilkey, from thin, cold-moulded, glued and stapled laminations of Oregon timber. Kaufman called her *Mercedes III*. The yacht was strong, light, especially in the ends, comparatively shallow-bodied, and had such a hard turn in the area of her garboards that her lead keel became almost a fin. To find precisely the right place for the keel, Kaufman and Miller, apart from making calculations, had physically weighed the hull then set it, fore and aft, across a heavy steel beam to establish its point of balance. They had bolted the keel with its centre of gravity directly below the centre of balance. The result was a remarkably easy boat in a seaway with none of the hobbyhorsing vices of many offshore craft of those days. *Mercedes III* would rise boldly to a head sea, maintaining an almost level position without losing speed, and she was a delight to steer, upwind or down, in any weather. Her concept anticipated by years the designs of overseas naval architects who were not too proud to acclaim it and to develop it.

From the time of her launching, *Mercedes III* was a champion. In her first fourteen races she won nine times, was once second, twice third and once fourth. In 1967, the Australian Admiral's Cup Challenge committee, with generous backing from commercial sponsors and private donations, shipped *Balandra*, *Caprice of Huon* and *Mercedes III* to Cowes and flew over their twenty-eight crewmen with a strong support team of officials and advisers. They had planned to arrive a clear three weeks before their international rivals (this time, apart from the British team, Finland, France, Germany, Holland, Ireland, the USA and Spain) and to continue the intense training that they had started in Sydney six months earlier. But there was a sudden and alarming hitch. When the yachts, deck cargo on a freighter, were in the middle of the Indian Ocean, halfway to their destination, the Israeli–Egyptian war broke out, and the Suez Canal through which they were due to pass was closed. The freighter was diverted to South Africa and the yachts were offloaded. For a week it seemed there would be no hope of getting them to England. Influential CYC officials Norman Rydge junr, Ted Kaufman and Ron Adair flew to Cape Town and, with a skill worthy of international statesmen, negotiated the yachts aboard a passenger ship that took them direct to Southampton. They arrived ten days before the Channel race, right in the middle of a dock strike. But nothing could stop that Australian team. The waiting crewmen, with some help from the ship's officers, manned the derricks themselves and unloaded the yachts straight over the side into Southampton harbour, rigged them and sailed them across the Solent to Cowes. Although they had lost eleven vital days of training they concentrated their efforts, day and night, upon the time remaining. They were up early every day for roadwork and exercises, and on the water for ten hours a day tuning their rigs, practising starts, match racing each other, studying the courses. At night they were in huddles planning tactics. No one in English yachting had seen anything like it before.

Ingate was not involved (he'd spent his summer seeking a place as *Gretel's* skipper in her unsuccessful America's Cup trials with the ultimate 1967 challenger, *Dame Pattie*) but he had chartered *Caprice of Huon* to Gordon Reynolds, his first mate in the 1965 Admiral's Cup effort, who, at considerable expense, had completely refitted the yacht above and below water, and had chosen an excellent crew. The previous watch captain, Graham Newland, was with him and so was Bill Fesq, the navigator. The crews aboard *Balandra* and *Mercedes III* were of top quality, too, and so were their navigator-tacticians, Stan Darling and Richard Hammond. In an effort to match the English tacticians' local knowledge, the three Australian navigators spent hours every day before the races at Southampton University, half an hour's speedboat ride from Cowes, studying the Solent tides on a huge working model of the waterway that belonged to the School of Engineering.

But the final strength of the Australian effort was the crews' determination to sail their boats as a team, rather than as individuals, as so many of the yachts of other nations seemed to do, and also deliberately to 'tag' the British yachts they knew would be their main rivals. *Balandra's* mark was to be Ron Clarke's *Quiver IV*, again in the British team; *Caprice of Huon* was to mark Ron Amey's *Noryema*; and *Mercedes III* was set for Dennis Miller's *Firebrand*. The Australians also conducted private lectures and discussions on the finer points of the racing rules and on emergency procedures to avoid collisions with the hundreds of picnic sailboats jamming the Solent and with the non-Admiral's Cup craft that were still allowed to compete as independent entries in all the races.

It was just as well that they were properly prepared. After a fine beginning in fresh winds in the Channel race, in which *Mercedes III* was placed third, *Balandra* fourth and *Caprice of Huon* seventh, they lined up with a good points lead from Britain for the Britannia Cup in the Solent and were at once involved in a typical Cowes Week imbroglio, from which they were lucky to escape undamaged.

Reynolds, in *Caprice of Huon*, had shrewdly judged the foul tide, and at the gun had got his yacht fourth across the line in the fleet of seventy-four, when one of the forty-seven non-Admiral's Cup boats, the 18.3 m *Bloodhound*, with the Duke of Edinburgh at the helm, came at her on a port tack, then slowly tacked to starboard, forcing Reynolds to tack from right-of-way starboard to port to avoid a collision. After five minutes against the tide, *Caprice of Huon* was swept back into fortieth place, and Reynolds tacked again on to starboard in an attempt to get close inshore into slack water. This time Baron Rothschild's 27.4 m *Gitana*, another non-Admiral's Cup contender in the race, came at him on port tack, and Reynolds was forced once more to tack out into the tide. In eight minutes of sailing he had dropped from fourth to seventy-fourth. Reynolds did not protest either yacht, although he had every right to do so, reasoning that since neither was an Admiral's Cup contender, their disqualification, if his protest were upheld, would in no way profit his team. Moreover, he had been told that it was an unwritten law at Cowes that one gave royalty right of way, in any circumstances. But some of his foredeck crew had addressed the helmsmen of both the offending yachts in tones that were unmistakably hostile. At a party aboard the Royal Yacht *Britannia* that night, Reynolds began to apologize to the Duke for the indignant antipodean yells that had come from *Caprice of Huon* and, instead, got an apology himself. 'I was completely in the wrong in thinking that *Bloodhound* would turn quickly enough,' said the Duke. 'I've been on her helm only once in the last year and I'm very rusty. I hope I didn't hamper you too much?'

As it was, *Caprice of Huon* had fought her way through the fleet and had finished fifth. *Mercedes III* had come third and *Balandra* ninth, and the Australians were still leading all the Cup teams on points. There was also an unexpected windfall in store. During the race the strong French team, led by Eric Tabarly in his 16.2 m black-hulled, clipper-bowed schooner, *Pen Duick III*, had noted that American Dick Carter, who had finished second in his yacht *Rabbit*, had failed to go around a special gate buoy. The French protested against this breach of the sailing instructions and in so doing set the stage for an international comedy of errors that almost resulted in a riot. At first, harassed officials, trying to sort out the finishing times of hundreds of non-Admiral's Cup yachts that were competing in scores of Cowes Week races, set the time for the protest hearing at 8 o'clock in the morning. In the absence of any formal written instructions in the matter, the French rejected this barbarous hour and took it to mean 8 pm. So they did not attend to give evidence, their protest lapsed, and Carter's second placing in the race was confirmed. The French then tried to protest the protest committee, claiming that the Royal Yacht Squadron and the Royal Ocean Racing Club had victimized them and had cunningly contrived with the Americans to dodge the issue. A crowd of indignant supporters gathered with the French team outside the Squadron Castle, waving the Tricolour and singing the Marseillaise. A French yachting writer declared passionately that no French craft would ever again sully its keel in the foul waters of the Solent or be associated with perfidious Albion. *Les Anglaises*, he cried, were not fit to run a hen race or, for that matter, a public urinal which, in his opinion, was what the Cup headquarters were most suited for, anyway. He then went on to use the lawn in the way he thought appropriate. British race officials, aghast at the uproar, anxious to see fair play, and realizing that perhaps the French had a genuine grievance about the time set for the protest meeting, agreed to re-open the matter. The French attended and called witnesses whose evidence Carter and his US colleagues refuted. There were some language difficulties but enough French and English was spoken on both sides at last to get to the core of the trouble. The British, however, believed the Americans and dismissed the protest, confirming *Rabbit's* placing for the second time. The French left the meeting again enraged. Then, in the corridor outside the protest room, Carter suddenly stopped, thunderstruck. He rushed back to where officials were tidying their papers, snatched up his written declaration form, which swore that *Rabbit* had sailed according to the rules, tore it up, and said, 'I want to be able to sleep at night'. It had not been until that moment that Carter had understood the significance of one of the buoys on the course, and had recalled that he had indeed sailed the wrong side of it, just as the French were claiming.

Officials, now in confusion, sent messengers to recall the French to tell them that their protest, although officially dismissed, had been justified after all; Carter had withdrawn from the race. Two French boats would therefore be elevated to better placings. To bring the unfortunate matter to a close, all that now needed to be done was official endorsement of the French race declaration forms. These had been due before the noon deadline the previous day. But no French declaration forms had in fact been handed in. In their anxiety to prepare their protest against the Americans, none of the French team had remembered this detail. Automatically, therefore, since the time limit for making the declarations had long since passed, all three of the French yachts must officially be considered as non-finishers! And so the Australian boat, *Mercedes III*, originally third in the race, was now the winner, since *Rabbit* and *Pen Duick III* had disqualified themselves. And *Caprice of Huon* and *Balandra* would be promoted two placings, to third and seventh. For some hours afterwards it was dangerous to be on the streets of Cowes, especially near the French docks.

In the second Solent race, for the New York Yacht Club Cup, sailed in moderate winds, *Mercedes III* was placed third, with *Caprice of Huon* fourth and *Balandra* fifth, further increasing the Australians' points lead. They came through well again in the Fastnet, an exciting contest, with gales and calms ahead and astern, fogs, moderate breezes and foul tides that at some stage forced many yachts to anchor to hold their positions, or for fear of drifting ashore. Peter Green, the burly red-headed mate in *Balandra*, well on his way to establishing his reputation as one of Australia's most experienced blue-water sailors (by 1985 he had sailed his thirty-third Sydney–Hobart race, and had covered 255,000 nm offshore), spent five hours with crewman Bruce Gould jammed under the cockpit of the yacht in a blow while they repaired her broken steering cables. *Balandra* placed fourth.

With *Mercedes III* third and *Caprice of Huon* seventh, the team registered the paralyzing total of 495, a record winning margin of 104 ahead of their main rival, Britain. *Mercedes III's* score, highest of all Cup contenders, made her the world's number one ocean racing yacht. The jubilation in Plymouth, where the Fastnet finished, lasted for a week. Yachtsmen and designers from many countries quizzed the Australians about their methods of crew training, navigation, deck layout, and equipment. Unique, Australian-designed fittings on the yachts were photographed and sketched for reference and for manufacture overseas. It was plain that, in future, anyone who wished seriously to challenge for the Admiral's Cup must also copy the Australians' methods, especially their deliberate match racing of dangerous rivals, and must also seek the commercial sponsorship they had arranged to cover their expenses.

'We don't really like your grim attitude; it takes the jollity out of sailing,' Ron Amey, owner-skipper of *Noryema*, told Reynolds, 'but there's no doubt it works.' Thereafter, the British and others adopted almost exactly the same methods.

Australia challenged for the Admiral's Cup in 1969, 1971, 1973, 1975, 1977, 1979, 1981, 1983 and 1985, but none of those efforts reached the heights of glory of the 1967 series.

In 1969, sailing against many new boats from ten nations, Australia was represented by the beautifully refined American-designed, 14.6 m *Ragamuffin*, owned and skippered by Syd Fischer; by *Mercedes III*; and by a slightly larger version of *Mercedes III*, *Koomooloo*, the 1968 Sydney#Hobart race winner. Fischer, fiercely competitive, was a former Sydney surf-boat rower and house carpenter who had built himself an empire of development companies through enterprise and effort. *Koomooloo's* owner, Denis O'Neil, was a wealthy young businessman new to competitive sailing but learning so quickly, that he was later twice to represent Australia at the Olympic Games. *Ragamuffin* won the Channel race, and her placings in the Solent scrambles — seventh and third — together with *Koomooloo's* sixth and fourth and *Mercedes III's* thirteenth and third, had earned the team a small points lead when they lined up for the final race.

Two-thirds of the way through the Fastnet, after light winds early, then two days of fresh weather, Australia seemed to have it won. *Ragamuffin* was near the leaders and *Koomooloo* and *Mercedes III* were well placed. Then the wind gradually dropped out completely. *Ragamuffin* got enough of the dying breeze to finish in second place, but the other pair took an overall total of 145 hours to complete the course. At times during two days of drifting they made a few miles, until the tide changed and swept them back again. More than twenty of their foreign rivals caught catspaws and passed them, and they spent half a day at anchor. The British team suffered badly in the calms, too, but the Americans came out of it well and squeezed the Australians into second place by a margin of fourteen points.

Gordon Reynolds, who had so efficiently crewed in *Caprice of Huon* in the 1965 series, and skippered her in 1967, distinguished himself in that frustrating 1969 contest as Australia's trainer-manager, a role he was to repeat in the challenges of 1971, 1973 and 1977. 'In light, moderate or hard breezes, the 1969 team would have won hands down,' he said. 'But the drifting match in the Fastnet turned the series into a farce. Our boys were disillusioned about all the courses as a fair test of sailing on which to base the world's ocean racing championship.'

There were more disappointments for Australia in 1971 when *Ragamuffin*; her near-sister-ship, Arthur Byrne's *Salacia II*; and *Koomooloo* (then owned by CYC commodore, Norman Rydge junr, with ace helmsmen Jock Sturrock and Mick Morris in his crew) carried the flag to Cowes. This time, after bad starts and uninspiring places in light airs in the first two races (*Salacia II*, fourth and twenty-first; *Ragamuffin*, thirteenth and seventh; and *Koomooloo*, nineteenth and ninth), the Australians got fresh winds in the second Solent thirty-miler. *Salacia II* placed second, *Ragamuffin*, third; and *Koomooloo*, fourth. Half their forty-eight opponents from sixteen nations could not handle the vicious gusts and tide-churned waters, and on the spinnaker reaches they careered wildly out of control. At the start of the Fastnet, Australia had pulled up into second place on points behind the British team, led by Prime Minister Ted Heath in his new *Morning Cloud*, a beautiful-looking 12.5 m sloop with gleaming mahogany topsides. The other two British boats were Bob Watson's white-hulled, 12.2 m *Cervantes IV* and the royal blue 13.7 m *Prospect of Whitby*, owned and ably skippered by one-legged Arthur Slater, who steered from an ingenious swivelling armchair built into the cockpit. All three British boats had been designed by the American firm of Sparkman and Stephens, a circumstance that in the light of Britain's desperate promotion of home products, caused questions in Parliament. But the yachts were ideal all-rounders for Channel and Solent conditions, as they had proved during a long series of selection trials, and had continued to do under pressure in the Cup races.

At the start of the Fastnet they had a lead of 22 points over Australia, despite the disqualification of *Cervantes IV* for fouling *Koomooloo* in an early race. In the opening stages of the Fastnet, with thirty hours of light winds, the British seemed to be in control. Then the wind came away hard from the westward and rose to gale force — and suddenly the Australians were in command. Soon after the Fastnet Rock turn, *Ragamuffin* was clear leader, with *Koomooloo* third and *Salacia II* fourth. All they had to do was run home across the Irish Sea. *Ragamuffin* came roaring back in the gale with her crew surfing her down the seas. At times she hurtled clear through the back of the wave ahead of her and rode down the front of it. She blew out two spinnakers, one in a terrifying all-standing gybe in pitch darkness. But they drove her on mercilessly. *Ragamuffin* won, not only the Admiral's Cup section of the Fastnet race, but also the open handicap against more than 200 outside competitors. *Salacia II* had some steering difficulties but came in eighth. It remained for *Koomooloo* to finish within the first twelve for Australia to take the Cup for the second time.

With 141 nm to go, *Koomooloo* was easily holding third place. In the next mile, with no warning, her rudder blade broke right off. Stainless steel tie-rods, embedded inside the laminated blade, all fractured where they joined the rudder stock. *Koomooloo*, crippled, radioed for help, an exercise that was to involve her owner in considerable expense and to reflect small credit on those ashore who might have organized it better, and on the attitude taken by some commercial ship masters to craft in distress. With no score from *Koomooloo* in the Fastnet, Australia dropped into third place behind Britain and the USA in the final points tally.

The Australian crews returned home far from entranced with the RORC's organization of the Admiral's Cup series. The difficulties of competing in the tricky Solent against other Admiral's Cup boats were real enough, but increasingly the casual British Cowes Week sailors, racing between themselves or socializing on the water, were behaving with a vacuity that was almost criminal. Hundreds obviously knew little about their responsibilities afloat, and many were wilfully determined to create situations that put visiting boats into hazard and cost them time. 'Hanging on to starboard tack, well off course, in order to catch a Cup boat on port tack and force her to concede right of way has become a popular game,' said Australian team manager Reynolds.

The Australians also had a message for their own racing yacht measurers. 'Overseas measurers, who determine how a yacht rates and consequently the basis of her handicap allowance, go out of their way to help owners, often granting liberal interpretations of the measurement formula,' added Reynolds. 'Australian measurers go rigidly by the book, and often we find ourselves giving away half a foot of rating to yachts that should at least be on the same mark as we.'

It was also obvious that organizing, planning and controlling the Admiral's Cup, arranging facilities for berthing, slipping and repairs for the growing fleets of visiting craft, checking rating certificates and measurements and issuing race instructions, was getting beyond the resources of officials in charge. The rickety marina at Cowes, where scores of yachts were jammed rail-to-rail, was a nightmare. The British, without summoning an army of professional helpers, were staying cool, nevertheless, and trying valiantly. They asked some of the foreign clubs and associations how improvements might be made, and promised changes when possible, especially in the courses and starting times, so as to separate the Cup contests from the Cowes Week gala. But the improvements were slow in coming.

However, in 1973, unprompted by anyone outside Britain, the RORC introduced a new system of handicapping. It was to replace the old Basic Speed Factor allowances in short races and the direct Time-on-Time Correction Factors in longer races. For years it had been shown that in slow, light-wind races the old handicapping system had favoured small yachts, and in fast, heavy-weather races had favoured big yachts. It was now argued that the new scale of Performance Factor handicaps, with a built-in component for distance to be sailed and the time each yacht took to do it (this latter provision somewhat like that used in the USA) would bring beneficial changes in the results of both fast and slow races. A number of foreign experts on the handicap systems vehemently disagreed. Any changes that the new system brought, they claimed, would be so disproportionate that big yachts would be favoured in slow races and small yachts would be favoured in fast races. Those that would suffer, all round, they said, would be yachts of medium size. As it turned out, the 1973 series produced some very peculiar results, which were blamed on the Performance Factor scale. This view, on later analysis, was not entirely justified, but the outcry was so great that the British, with their talent for diplomacy, dropped the system and replaced it with a less complicated Time Multiplication Factor method.

In the meantime, *Ragamuffin*, firmly established as Australia's blue-water champion, was again in the national team for the 1973 challenge. She had as partners two 13.7 m near-sister-ships, designed by Bob Miller (Ben Lexcen). They were *Ginkgo*, built of wood and owned by Gary Bogard, a Sydney commercial entrepreneur; and *Apollo II*, built of aluminium and owned by WA land and property developer, Alan Bond. Both owners sailed aboard with outstanding helmsmen and crews, who, apart from ocean racing experience, had won scores of national and international championships in class boats and had represented Australia in the America's Cup and the Olympic Games. They included Jim Hardy, Dave Forbes, John Bertrand, Peter O'Donnell, Dick Sargeant, Carl Ryves, John Anderson, and Bob Miller. But they had problems even before they got to the starting lines. British officials questioned the ratings of *Apollo II* and *Ginkgo*, and it was only through the protestations of team manager Reynolds that the 228 mm planing boards extending from the yacht's transoms were not penalized. As a counter-measure to the official moves, an assessment by Reynolds and the young Australian yacht designer, Scott Kaufman, son of *Mercedes'* owner, Ted Kaufman, suggested that some foreign yachts had been given concessions that Australia's strict measurers would never have allowed. One boat that seemed especially favoured was the German-owned *Saudade*, a 14 m steel sloop with a red hull. This American-designed boat was skippered by Berend Beilken. She was to prove the star of the 1973 series. (Speculation about *Saudade's* Admiral's Cup rating was revived when she was sold to an American who, on submitting her to US officials for a national measurement certificate, was given a figure much higher than that which the yacht had previously carried. The new owner claimed that he had made no alterations that could have affected the rating.)

In the Cup contests, *Saudade* raced off the rating of 34.1 ft that the German measurers had given her and that the British had accepted, and was granted time by many craft of the same size and sail area and by some that were smaller. Two of them were Australia's *Ginkgo*, rating 36.3 ft, and *Apollo II*, rating 36.4 ft. As well, *Ragamuffin*, rating 38.1, and about the same size and rig as Germany's *Rubin*, was required to concede that yacht 1.7 ft of rating. The third member of Germany's team, *Carina III*, 13.1 m, skippered by former world One Ton Cup class helmsman, Hans Beilken, came in with a rating of 33.2 ft.

It was clear that the Germans had made a thorough examination of the rating rules and had cleverly exploited every loophole. It also seemed that the ocean racing numbers game would probably become so intense that yacht designers would no longer be able to consider the inherent speed and seaworthiness of a hull form without a computer analysis of every measurement. Purists began to complain that this and, indeed, the race to beat the ratings, together with schemes to prune hull and equipment weights to a minimum, were inevitably going to lead to unhealthy boats and to a chaotic state of the sport. (And, indeed, this was what happened, forcing world ocean racing administrators by 1978 to make drastic changes to the rules.) But in the 1973 Admiral's Cup the performances of the rule-beaters were complicated, on the surface at least, by the strange new British system of applying the Performance Factor scale to ratings to establish each yacht's handicap.

It seemed to turn the results of the first event, the 225 nm Channel race, topsy-turvy. There were fresh following winds most of the way, and, under the old Time-on-Time system this, it was claimed, would have given the higher rating boats a distinct advantage. Instead, the clear winner on handicap under the new system was the little French dinghy-style *Revolution*, with Britain's smallest contender, *Frigate*, noted not for hard, downwind runs but for her prowess in light works to windward, in second place. Third was *Lightnin'*, USA's beefed-up One Tonner, just within the 29 ft to 45 ft rating limits that then applied to

Ploughing through the Solent obstacle course, Australia's *Ginkgo* (KA252) leads USA's much bigger *Charisma,* carrying the world's first kevlar mainsail (it split) in the 1973 Admiral's Cup. (Bob Ross)

the series. She was another upwind specialist, owned and skippered by the dynamic young millionaire, Ted Turner, who was guaranteed to electrify almost any social gathering with his drolleries and who was affectionately known in America as 'The Mouth of the South'.

Yachting experts from a dozen countries analysed the results of the Channel race to compare them with those that would have been given if the previously-used Time-on-Time system had been applied. Australian Bob Miller voiced a widely held opinion when he walked away from the scoreboard muttering, 'The Brits have gone bonkers.' Others were not so sure. They realized that in the Channel race the strong tidal flow off the French coast, concurrent with a temporary lull and a shift in the wind, had hampered the big yachts, which were forced to stem the tide, while the small yachts, much further back, were not so badly affected. Also, once round the final mark the little yachts had been helped when the wind had come in hard, behind them. And so the controversy raged on.

Still, *Ginkgo* had placed fifth on corrected time, with *Apollo II* twelfth, and *Ragamuffin* twenty-fourth, and the Australians had amassed 212 points, only twenty fewer than the leaders, Germany, whose *Saudade* had finished fourth, with team-mates *Rubin* thirteenth and *Carina III* fourteenth. The Dutch, with three smallish boats, placed sixth, ninth and twentieth, were between Germany and Australia.

There had been the usual scrambling start, with the ebullient Turner in *Lightnin'* through the line early and, it seemed, seriously in breach of the rules against Britain's *Morning Cloud,* whose skipper, Ted Heath, had had to alter course to avoid a collision. *Morning Cloud* had carried a red protest flag throughout the race but the British protest committee averted what might have become an international slanging match by advising their Prime Minister that he should have hoisted the flag immediately after the incident, instead of delaying for five minutes while his crew extracted *Morning Cloud* from the mêlée. But other topics and events also enlivened the scene. The talk of the town, which was swarming with even more visitors than usual, was the continuing tension between the Germans and the Australians, whose *Ginkgo* and *Apollo II* had been tipped to sweep aside all opposition — until the Germans had produced their rating certificates.

Another source of gossip and speculation was a queer new super-strong, stretchless fabric called kevlar, woven from beta fibre, that the chemical wizards of Du Pont had invented to strengthen motor car tyres, and which now made its first appearance at Cowes. It was predicted that kevlar would revolutionize sailmaking when someone learned how to stop it splitting. The world's first experimental kevlar mainsail, carried on the US yacht *Charisma* in the Channel race, had split from leech to luff when a running backstay had accidentally rubbed across it, wrecking the vessel's chances.

Dockside critics continued to tell one another with satisfaction that the British had ruined their own Cup team's chances by introducing the new handicapping system. Local residents hurried indoors when the exuberant Brazilian crew from the silver-hulled *Wa Wa Too III* performed in public for the first time on shriek whistles and bongo drums, and the rhythm of the jungle throbbed through the town. Visitors complained once again about Cowes' ghastly food; the flat, tepid beer; the tattered accommodation; and the surrealist plumbing.

But, in spite of all these diversions, interest in the races was at a high pitch because, for the first time in years, the winds were holding. They continued to blow fresh to strong for the two Solent races, and *Saudade* continued to overpower all opposition. She won both races by handy margins and, although *Rubin*, with a tenth and a sixth, and *Carina III*, with a thirteenth and a twenty-first, did not sail up to expectations, the team scored enough points to maintain Germany's lead. The Australian crews aboard *Ginkgo* and *Apollo II* at times sailed brilliantly and at others made elementary mistakes. *Ginkgo* lost vital places through bad choice of headsails for some legs of the courses, and *Apollo II* suffered when she returned unnecessarily to re-cross the starting line and again when she ran aground on a mudbank. But they were always close to the leaders in both races. *Apollo II* placed fourth and fifth; *Ginkgo*, seventh and eighth; and *Ragamuffin*, fifth and tenth in the forty-eight yacht Cup fleet.

When the Fastnet race started in a 10 k to 14 k easterly the Australian team was well established in second place and had gnawed down the Germans' lead to 7 points. Britain was third, 24 points behind Australia, followed well back by the Dutch, the Americans and the Italians. Short of miracles, it seemed, no one else had much chance. As the race extended into the second day, still with moderate following winds, the Australians, unquestionably superior downwind, were better placed overall than the Germans. When they rounded the Fastnet Rock, after the 345 nm outward leg, for the beat back to Plymouth, the Australians needed only to hold their relative positions to win. The next day the curse of the Irish Sea descended once again — a glassy calm, with occasional zephyrs, that lasted four agonizing days. The forty-eight Admiral's Cup boats and the 220 independent Fastnet Cup contestants drifted hopelessly back and forth as the tide ebbed and flowed. Some, near enough to shallow water to anchor, remained stationary for twelve hours a day.

Light, fluky draughts of air carried forward a few of the biggest boats, led by the 10.7 m American *Charisma* and the Brazilian 17.4 m *Saga* (both of which had made great progress in the early breeze), and gradually they crawled to the finishing line. But as a test of sailing skill and offshore seamanship it was no contest. Luck and good guesswork played the greatest part, and the Germans' luck held. After rounding the Fastnet Rock in a fair wind, *Saudade* and *Carina III* had headed south into the Atlantic and then into the Channel towards the coast of Brittany, hoping that way they would hold the wind. The third German yacht, *Rubin*, stayed close inshore. It seemed a crazy gamble by the other two, involving many extra miles of sailing, and the shrewd, weather-wise English did not attempt it. The safest tactic, they and most of the others (Australia among them) decided, was to sit secure on the rhumb-line track until the wind pattern swung north or north-west. But the two Germans got a band of south-easterly breeze forty miles south of the armada of becalmed yachts, and sailed a wide arc around them. It was not until the Germans were approaching the finish that the same breeze as they had carried reached the other yachts that had chosen the shorter course and theoretically had been far ahead of them. One of those skippers who had remained for almost a day off Rame Head, 17 nm from the finish, was Britain's Prime Minister, Ted Heath, in *Morning Cloud*. When the breeze got to many yachts, they outsailed the Germans but they could not beat them on team points. *Saudade* placed seventh, *Carina III* tenth and *Rubin* eleventh, bringing the German tally to 831. At first, officials placed *Carina III* twenty-first, penalizing her 5 per cent of her time for breaking the start, until skipper Beilken proved to them that he had been securely anchored and could not have started prematurely. It would have made no difference to the final result. Even with *Carina III* placed twenty-first, Germany would still have had the top score, with 798 points. Australia, with *Gingko* twelfth, *Apollo II* fifteenth, and *Ragamuffin* sixteenth, took second place with a total of 779. The British totalled 752 for third, and the Americans 738 for fourth.

Once again the Australian team had an excuse for its sponsors and supporters who had raised $80,000 to send the yachts and crews away. Anyway, second place in the world against the concentrated efforts of 500 yachtsmen from fifteen countries was a worthy perch from which to crow.

So in 1975 Australia, although faced with costs inflated to $125,000 to ship and service its yachts and to fly and accommodate its crews, tried again for the Admiral's Cup. Later on, the team, its members all from Sydney, was unkindly called the Three K's Vaudeville Act because of the initial letters of each owner-skipper's surname — Kurts (Peter), Kaufman (Ted), and Kalbetzer (John). But there was nothing funny about those three earnest men. Their yachts — *Love and War*, 14.3 m (1974 Sydney–Hobart race winner and winner again in 1978); *Mercedes IV*, 12.5 m; and *Bumblebee*, 16.2 m, seemed equal to any in the world. The crews they had aboard were polished and confident. The only criticism possible, perhaps, was that they were a shade too sure of themselves. But they did not remain that way for long. They met competition fiercer than anyone had known before in this arena.

The Admiral's Cup — mainly as a result of the Australians' own game of hard training, intense tactical match racing and heavy commercial sponsorship, and the German example of scientifically pruning decimal points off the ratings of the best designed yachts — was no longer the jolly midsummer sporting adventure it had started out to be. Even in earlier days when two or three teams were seriously trying, the others had not cared overmuch if they won or lost, so long as they enjoyed good fellowship afloat and the frolics ashore. Now everyone was bitterly contesting every point, and no quarter was given or expected. In the ten years since Australia had made its first challenge, ocean racing had grown from an esoteric pastime practised by an enthusiastic few to a worldwide sport with thousands of yachts of all sizes competing regularly in scores of countries. Few big racing yachts were now built for any other purpose.

For yacht designers, builders, mast and sailmakers, ship chandlers, clothing manufacturers, it brought business worth millions. Works teams of outstanding helmsmen, and crewmen, employed directly or indirectly by these firms, promoted the latter's products by sailing yachts for owners willing to buy those products. Olympic and America's Cup champions were wooed aboard to lend further prestige to already distinguished crews. The Admiral's Cup scene was now not only the finest showroom in the world for the latest in winning boats and equipment of every kind; it was also a theatre of war. In 1975, in Europe alone, dozens of new yachts, each costing on an average of $250,000 and all refined like aeroplanes, had been built for the Cup trials, and those that had won through for the right to represent their countries were formidable indeed. The Australian effort, good as it was, fell apart under the strain of this competition.

In preliminary tune-up training races across the Channel, sailed in moderate to fresh breezes before the best foreign boats arrived at Cowes, *Bumblebee*, with Mike Fletcher (Australia's Olympic coach and a national champion helmsman in a variety of craft) as her sailing master, had showed fine form. In the first Cup race across the Channel and back in the same sort of weather conditions but now pitted against the full force of the fifty-four other competitors from eighteen nations, she finished only tenth, with *Love and War* ninth and *Mercedes IV* fourteenth. There was some excuse for *Mercedes IV*. She got her rudder tangled in a long rope from a lobster pot and tore off the underwater heads of her electronic navigation aids. England's new *Noryema* won the race from Ireland's *Irish Mist*, with the Americans, *Robin* and the new *Charisma*, next, and two new German yachts close up, straddling craft from Holland and Sweden.

The first Solent race put Australia further back. *Bumblebee* came in twelfth, *Love and War* fifteenth, and *Mercedes IV* was disqualified when she broke the starting line and failed to return. The English, with *Yeoman XX* second, *Noryema* sixth and *Battlecry* seventh, established a clear points lead. Australia's ultimate disaster came in the second Solent race, which started in a lively breeze but dropped to a fluky, tide-torn calm. Fletcher got a brilliant start in *Bumblebee* and, after 20 nm of the 30 nm course, had the race well won. *Bumblebee* was judged to be fourteen minutes ahead on handicap when she ran into a band of airless water and a foul tide, 8 nm from the finish. Opponents that had been left miles astern carried the breeze up to her, gaining handicap time every metre. Then they, too, fell into the calm that was now broken by occasional flickers of breeze. A tangled mass of boats clawed against the tide. We learned cuss words in fourteen languages,' said Fletcher.

Ultimately, a few hundred yards from the finish, at the port hand Prince Consort mark, a massive black steel buoy with a light on the top, *Bumblebee* seemed to have just enough room and headway when she bore away to clear the mark. But a tidal eddy caught her and swept her against it, denting her aluminium topsides and automatically disqualifying her from the race. Hours later *Mercedes IV* and *Love and War* limped in thirty-ninth and forty-sixth. But the race was another triumph for the British, and they deserved it. Robin Aisher and his crew in *Yeoman XX*, who had spent their lives racing in the Solent, gave a demonstration of the value of local knowledge as they approached the tidal swirls streaming past the Prince Consort mark that had wrecked *Bumblebee's* chances. They headed *Yeoman XX* away from it, right inshore to Cowes Harbour and into the mouth of the River Medina, until its ebbing tide, running in the opposite direction from the main stream, picked them up and carried them well along the shore into slack water. Then they eased out, riding the main Solent tide to the Prince Consort mark until they just had enough room to clear it, and worked inshore again for another ride in the opposite direction on the river tide until they could sneak along the shore in slack water to the finish.

The Australian team, outpaced, out-manoeuvred, and out in the cold on points after the first three races, went to the start of the Fastnet final without hope. The breeze was fresh early but dribbled away on the home leg into another seemingly interminable calm. It was anybody's race except Australia's. *Mercedes IV* finished twenty-sixth, *Bumblebee* fortieth and *Love and War* forty-first. The Dutch got two yachts home first and third, the Spaniards took second place, and Hong Kong fourth. Britain, with *Noryema* fifth, *Yeoman XX* eleventh, and *Battlecry* twelfth, had a massive points lead. Germany was next, from the USA, Holland, New Zealand, Spain, and Ireland. Australia scored ninth, her worst ever, ahead of Switzerland, France, Argentina, South Africa, Sweden, Brazil, Norway, Italy, Canada, and Belgium.

Australian team manager Alan Brown, who had worked tirelessly for months to make the challenge viable, reported the failure realistically. 'It was in no way due to bad luck,' he said.

For more than a year after that, ocean racing officials in Australia argued about the sense or otherwise of trying to raise the $180,000, from sponsorship and other contributions, that it would cost to send a team to England for the 1977 series to race against a brand new crop of yachts designed and built for the Cup conditions. Finally, after a series of trials up and down the Sydney coast, they hopefully despatched three new aluminium sloops — Syd Fischer's new *Ragamuffin*, 14.3 m, Victorian Keith Farfor's 14.6 m *Superstar*; and Jim Hardy's 12.5 m *Runaway*. The Royal Australian Navy saved a decent slice of the fund-raising committee's costs by transporting the yachts in between-decks hangars of the aircraft carrier, *Melbourne*, on her way to England for Queen Elizabeth's Jubilee celebrations. Nevertheless, each yacht owner had to contribute $4,000 on top of the normal refitting and maintenance charges, and each of the thirty crewmen had to pay $600 towards accommodation, plus extras. The able Gordon Reynolds was persuaded to take the unenviable job of official team trainer, manager and worrier. He had plenty to worry him.

The winds off Cowes were strong and consistent in mid-July but by the end of the month when the serious racing was due to start they sickened and died. A fortnight of sepulchral calm settled on the place. Only rarely did any gust of wind get much above 15 k, and three of the five races (an extra Solent event had been added) were sailed in winds between 6 k and 10 k, with long spells when there was no wind at all. One race was abandoned when the wind dropped completely — with Australia's *Superstar* stuck firmly on a mudbank. The only consistent disturbance to the surface of the sea was the tides that regularly reached 4 k. By no stretch of imagination could it be called ocean racing. 'It was more like sailing in an underground reservoir with the plug half out,' said one disgruntled Australian crewman.

The Australian yachts were well-prepared and well-equipped, and were probably handled better than they had been at home, but once again in the flat water and light winds they could not match the best of the foreigners that had been designed and rigged for those conditions. On the final points tally, Australia scored seventh place behind Britain, (winners for the seventh time), the USA, Hong Kong, Germany, Italy and France. There were twelve teams behind the Australians. In the fleet of fifty-seven yachts, *Ragamuffin's* placings, starting with the new Solent race, then the Channel race and ending with the Fastnet, were 22, 25, 21, 10, 16. *Runaway* was disqualified for a port and starboard breach in her first race, then placed 8, 30 30, 31; *Superstar* placed 20, 26, 9, 4, 48.

It was hard for many to admit it, but Australia, after so much success before the ground rules had been changed, had finally been out-classed. Few CYC members had the heart to suggest that the minimum $150,000 now needed should be raised by public subscription to send Australian yachts to the 1979 Admiral's Cup. Some, however, still yearning for past glories, were determined to go even at their own expense with new yachts, and others talked of chartering European craft to sustain an unbroken run of challenges.

Gradually, however, during 1978, as the memories of the recent horrors at Cowes began to fade, a new mood of confidence spread among a group of owners, especially those who had commissioned new boats, about the chance of challenging once again for the Admiral's Cup, in the series to start in August 1979. This time they agreed that only those craft that had been designed and built to the latest concepts of the rating rules and with especially good performance in light weather should be considered. With the approval of the AYF and the support of the Ocean Racing Club of Australia, now firmly established as the policy-making and fund-raising arm of Australia's international offshore efforts, a series of eight short and medium-distance selection trials was arranged — to be sailed in March 1979 around Victoria's almost landlocked Port Phillip Bay, with a 300 nm final in Bass Strait. Port Phillip was chosen for three reasons: the comparatively smooth water (and, hopefully, light winds) would be similar to conditions in the Solent; ocean racing was booming in Victoria, enjoying strong commercial sponsorship, and yachtsmen in that State who had suffered little exposure to the realities of overseas offshore competition were enthusiastic; many members of Sydney's CYC who had worked hard to raise funds for all seven previous Admiral's Cup challenges were disillusioned after the failures of 1975 and 1977 and opposed to further efforts.

Nine yachts, six of them brand new, competed in the trials. Four were from NSW, two from Victoria, two from WA and one from Queensland. Fortunately, in view of what was to happen later, neither the seas in Port Phillip nor the winds cooperated. Most of the trial races were sailed in bouncy, fresh conditions, three of them in gales. After adjustments to some rigs, the yachts stood up well. Although of the latest overseas designs, the majority were strongly built and complied with standards of stability on which Australian officials had insisted in the face of some international opposition, especially from Britain. The sensation of the series was the WA sloop *Police Car*, broad-sterned, reasonably lightweight, three-quarter-rigged, 12.8 m, owned and skippered by Peter Cantwell and designed by a young English naval architect, Ed Dubois. She performed especially well in fresh winds and held her own on the few occasions when they were light. On points over the ORCA series, *Police Car* tied with John Crisp's and Graeme Lambert's NSW 12.5 m *Impetuous*, designed by former New Zealander Ron

Holland. Syd Fischer's new *Ragamuffin* (the fourth he had owned of that name) a 13.9 m Doug Peterson design, was next. Those three, all of aluminium, were named as Australia's Cup team for 1979 and each owner agreed to contribute $10,000 towards expenses. Victorian Lou Abrahams was chosen as team manager. All that remained was for ORCA to raise another $80,000 through sponsorship and an art union and for the thirty crewmen to chip in $500 each to cover their own costs. Guarantees were signed, overdrafts arranged, the yachts shipped and the crews flown to England in late July, for the Cup series starting 1 August.

The Australians had no illusions about the quality of the opposition when they arrived in Cowes. Fifty of the fifty-seven boats, in teams of three from nineteen nations, were less than a year old. They had been designed to gain every advantage under the rating rules and they were stacked with crews of superstars, some renowned as ocean bravos, some as Olympic champions and some openly professional, engaged as part of works teams to display their companies' products. Still, as Australian team manager, Lou Abrahams, observed, our crews were equal to any in skill and expertise around the buoys or in the open ocean. They included America's Cup helmsman Jim Hardy and his former tactician Hugh Treharne, both masters of smooth and rough water, with ace 18-footer hands Rob Brown and Richard Chapman, sailing in *Impetuous*; former world champion 18-footer skipper and big boat steerer Bob Holmes in *Ragamuffin*; NZ world One Ton Cup champion, Fastnet Cup and Sydney–Hobart race winner Chris Bouzaid, West Australian Chris Packer and former Australian Three-quarter Ton Cup champion Jim Robson-Scott in *Police Car*. The navigators, Richard Hammond in *Ragamuffin*, Ron Packer in *Police Car* and Phil Eadie in *Impetuous* were unquestionably among the best, too. And the technological gaps had closed. Because of free interchange of information and international marketing systems, no boat had equipment much better than any other. The stage was set for a true test of sailing ability, of boat and handling, helmsmanship and navigation, provided the winds were honest and fluky calms did not turn it all into a lottery.

Such fears were quickly dispelled. For once the weathermen made confident forecasts. There would always be wind, they said, some light, but mainly moderate to fresh, day after day. And they were right. Their only error was to under-rate, to some extent, a catastrophic twenty-four hour storm — with near hurricane-force gusts and steep, punishing seas — that was to turn the Fastnet race, the last of the five-race series, into a tragic shambles, the worst disaster in the history of yachting, for the 249 outsiders which were allowed to compete in it alongside the Admiral's Cup competitors. The storm wrecked the chances of many Admiral's Cup boats too, but it provided a victory for the Australians that will remain a permanent monument to their good seamanship, courage and skill.

However, they began the series shakily, in spite of the honest winds from the outset. On the eve of the first race, 29.5 nm around the Solent buoys, the three Australian skippers and their crews planned safe starts. They were determined to avoid *mêlées* with other boats that could bring disqualification or penalties for technical breaches and thus loss of points. Few of the other competitors had such conservative ideas. The wind was a steady 10 k from the west at the start (and later to freshen to 25 k from the south-west) and more than forty boats charged like a stampeding herd of cattle, ignoring the risks. There was little room for tactical manoeuvres; the starting line was laid so that the course was a 2.5 nm fetch to the first mark. The Australian boats that had hung back, clear of the ruck, were soon buried in foul air under the wind shadows of the yachts to windward and ahead of them. It took *Police Car* and *Ragamuffin* half way down the next leg to fight their way out of it and they did well to finish seventh and thirteenth on corrected time. *Impetuous* could not get clear whatever Jim Hardy, her helmsman, tried. She placed thirtieth. Their total point score was thus 124, based on a point for starting and one for every boat each one of them beat in the fleet of fifty-seven. That put them in fifth place overall. Hong Kong, with its boats third, fourth and fifth for 162 points, was the leader. Britain was next with a first, eighth and fourteenth, on 151 points, only one point ahead of the USA with second, tenth and twelfth placings, followed by Italy, with three good boats, that had placed eleventh, sixteenth and seventeenth to score 130 points.

The Australian team conference that night decided that they would have to take more initiative at the starts but still avoid the chance of collisions. Our boats had the speed and their crews the skill to win but so did a lot of others. It was obvious that they would never get the chance unless they got through the pack early and sailed to advantage throughout. The next day, in a 28.6 miler around the Solent, with a sou'wester rarely below 20 k and at times gusting to 30 k, the Australians got away well and came in third with *Police Car*, fourth with *Impetuous* — in spite of time lost when she sailed off course and then grounded for half a minute on a mudbank — and ninth with *Ragamuffin* for a score of 158 points. It was the best of any team that day and gave them an overall total of 282. That lifted them to third place on the international table. Hong Kong, with fifth, tenth and nineteenth, was still leader on 302 points; USA, with sixth, twelfth and fourteenth was next on 292. British boats, seventh, twenty-first and forty-second, were now back in fourth place on 255 and Ireland, with first, second and fifty-fourth, were fifth with 236. Officials took no action when advised that the American 14 m *Aries* had probably sailed illegally through the starting line on the first circuit of the course (in the same manner as Dick Carter's *Rabbit* back in 1967) and could be penalized. Race stewards blandly explained that none of them had seen the alleged incident. Maybe some of them could remember the turmoil that had occurred when the French made a similar complaint against the Americans twelve years earlier.

The 217 nm Channel race to France and back, rating double points, was next, and, although it started in a 25 k westerly, the breeze eased and for much of the time was lighter than the Australians would have liked. It was also a soldier's course, with little windward work, favouring the smaller boats with lower ratings. The tidal changes helped them, too, and hampered the higher rating boats ahead of them. *Police Car* came in eighth; *Impetuous*, well up early, was caught in a 30 degree windshift that cost her at least seven places and scrambled in nineteenth; and *Ragamuffin*, although she sailed excellently, outpacing the US champion *Williwaw*, her near-sister-ship, placed only thirty-first.

The Australians' score of 232 points for the race gave them an overall total of 514. Still, when the tallies were examined it was not such a bad result because many of their main rivals with big boats in their teams had crashed. Hong Kong's boats placed twenty-sixth, twenty-eighth and forty-fifth for a score of 150 and a total of 452. The Americans got fourth, thirty-fifth and fortieth for 190 and a total of 482; and Britain, third, fifty-third and dnf (when Ted Heath's *Morning Cloud* broke her carbon fibre reinforced rudder and was forced to retire) for 124 points, had a total of 379. Ireland's medium-sized boats did best with first, ninth and seventeenth for 294 points and an overall score of 530. That put them in the lead by 16 points from Australia (514), with America (452) third, another 62 points back.

Safety was again the Australian watchword for the fourth race, another switchback around the Solent, this time of 32.4 nm. 'Now we are within striking distance of them, let's keep out of trouble' was the advice of team captain Syd Fischer, a Solent veteran. The day dawned with poor visibility, 15 k to 25 k of wind, and squalls of rain, and for much of the time stayed that way. And trouble came thick and fast, even before the start. First there was a general recall when more than half the fleet barged the favoured end of the line and burst through before the gun. Then, as they manoeuvred for another try, they encountered part of the massed fleet competing in Royal Cowes Week regatta, a scramble of 800 craft of all shapes and sizes handled with varying degrees of expertise and ineptitude. Soon it was a football scrum of boats, with the Admiral's Cup crews dodging to keep clear and handy to their starting line as they waited for a new warning signal. Two of them, *Police Car*, reaching on port tack, and the foam-fibreglass Brazilian 14 m *Indigo*, on starboard tack, converged. The Australians prepared to harden up. 'Hold your course,' they yelled to the young American Gary Weisman, on the helm of *Indigo*. But the Brazilian lookout man on the bow either confused the call or Weisman mistook it. He put his helm hard down and crashed his bow into *Police Car's* starboard side. The impact of many tonnes knocked down some of *Police Car's* life rail stanchions and ripped through her aluminium plating, cutting a wedge half a metre down her topsides and 20 cm horizontally across her deck. It also tore a zigzag hole like a shark's half-open mouth in the Brazilian's stem. The hulls slewed side by side.

But that was the least of it. *Indigo's* bow caught Australian crewman John Mooney, of Victoria, on *Police Car's* leeward deck as he scrambled to get clear and flung him between the two grinding topsides. In the few seconds before he fell into the water Mooney's left arm was broken, his right leg crushed, and he suffered many cuts and abrasions. If the yachts had not swung apart he would almost certainly have been killed or drowned. WA navigator Ron Packer, heavily clothed with wet weather gear and seaboots, immediately leaped over the side to save him, and so did one of *Indigo's* crewmen. Mooney was semi-conscious by the time Packer had towed him back alongside *Police Car* and the Australian crew, hanging outboard, had begun to lift him to the deck. Then an outboard-driven rubber duck, manned by photographers, dashed up in answer to yells for help. But first, instead of taking Mooney aboard, they plucked Packer out of the water. It took him some minutes to convince them that he did not want to be rescued but that they must rush Mooney ashore for medical attention. This they did. (Mooney spent several days in hospital and although still in considerable pain, heavily bandaged and walking with difficulty, was later able to join the Australian team at Plymouth after the Fastnet race.)

Meanwhile *Indigo*, with water sloshing through her smashed bow, was limping to port for repair, and *Police Car*, with Packer back aboard, Peter Long, a crewman transferred from *Impetuous* to replace Mooney, and the split in her topsides jammed with towelling and sailbags to stop leaks, lined up again for the race. Since the incident had happened when she was not in the starter's hands there was no obligation for her to withdraw, whatever the rights or wrongs of the case.

The crew were distressed about the injuries to Mooney, but they rallied. Starting helmsman Chris Packer, younger brother of *Police Car's* navigator, got the boat away in the middle of the fleet. She revelled in the hard squalls and soon was on level terms with most other boats her size. But there were more horrors to come. At the end of the third leg, a run, Packer, conceding buoy room to the Japanese boat *Koteru Teru II*, took a safe leeward berth and prepared to gybe as soon as she had rounded ahead of him. He stepped across the cockpit to what was to become the windward side, slipped, landed on his back under the tiller, lost control, and *Police Car* rounded up with a wild swoop. She slammed into the starboard quarter of the Japanese boat. When they had bumped clear the Japanese were already flying a red protest flag. *Police Car*, leaking from a gash in her bow, hoisted code flag 1 to acknowledge that she had committed a breach, and both sailed on.

Down below in the Australian boat, sewing back the headboard of the number three genoa, torn out earlier, joint helmsman Chris Bouzaid, master sailmaker of the international firm of Hood Sails, said, 'I seem to be missing some of the excitement of this race. What's next on the programme?' He might well have asked.

At the second last mark *Police Car*, with Britain's *Morning Cloud* a couple of lengths astern, rounded in what seemed a safe position and was instantly protested by Ted Heath, claiming she had forced him to give her buoy room. There seemed little justification for Heath's view, and the Australians rejected any illegality in their sailing. Nevertheless it was an apprehensive crew that came ashore that evening. *Police Car* on corrected time had placed a good sixth but she faced three protests. The first, from *Indigo*, was merely a formality to clinch the legality of the Brazilian boat's insurance claim for damage. Since neither boat had been under the control of the starter the question of fault would not affect the result of the race. The second breach, protested by the Japanese, was indefensible and openly admitted, except that it had been accidental. The third protest, from *Morning Cloud*, had scant substance. The international jury saw it that way, too. *Indigo's* injury was noted and no action was taken; *Police Car* was penalized eleven placings, relegating her to seventeenth, for clobbering *Koteru Teru II*, and *Morning Cloud's* protest was dismissed. With *Ragamuffin* twenty-second and *Impetuous* twenty-third (she'd had an accidental pre-start rigging brush with the Swedish 15.2 m *Midnight Sun* that had broken the wind indicator on the top of her mast) in that fourth race there was no reason for joy. But the team had scored 112 points and when the other totals were checked Australia was in third position. Ireland, with twelfth, thirteenth and thirtieth, had scored 119 points for a total of 649, to lead overall, and America, with first, second and eighteenth, were next with 635. The Australians arranged a roster to visit Mooney in hospital, organized repairs to *Police Car's* topsides, and set themselves for the clincher of the series, the 605 nm Fastnet, carrying triple points and to start in four days time.

The weather outlook remained good — moderate to fresh winds. From the general pattern of the isobars, there seemed little chance of the calms that had turned the Fastnets of 1975 and 1977 into high farce. Some experienced yachtsmen, and the Southampton Meteorological Office, with which the Australians kept in close touch, thought there were possibilities of really hard weather if intense cyclonic disturbances across the Atlantic, near Newfoundland, and especially north, near Iceland, developed.

But the race started off Cowes, at 2 pm, Saturday 11 August, in light to moderate westerlies and sparkling sunshine, ideal sailing weather that gave little hint of the catastrophic violence that was to follow fifty-six hours later. The little Half Tonners among the armada of 249 non-Admiral's Cup competitors in the race relished the conditions. Although the westerlies would give them a dead beat all along the south coast of England to Land's End, until they could veer north-west across the Irish Sea, they had the help of three to four knots of spring tide under them for the first five hours. The shrewd ones stood well offshore, ready to avoid the worst of the contrary sweep off Portland Bill when the tide turned. A hundred or more that did not were clawing against it when the long twilight ended and darkness fell. Before dawn they were riding the tide again in freshening winds when the first swirls of a thick sea fog descended. It rolled around them like a clammy, grey blanket. Even ten hours later, by mid afternoon, Sunday, visibility in much of the Channel was down to 200 m. Commercial ships of vast size loomed through the murk, the thud of their engines drowning the puny bleats of the yachts' foghorns.

Only the great front-runners of the Fastnet fleet, Bob Bell's *Condor of Bermuda*, Jim Kilroy's *Kialoa* (USA) and Rolly Tasker's *Siska* (Australia), all rating near 70 ft and too big to compete in the Admiral's Cup (restricted to ratings between 30 ft and 40 ft) were clear of the fog. They were already nosing into the Irish Sea, making good an average of 10 k with their sheets sprung. And not far behind them was America's Cup skipper Ted Turner in his 18.6 m *Tenacious*, another independent entry. At 6 pm on Sunday, the BBC shipping and weather forecast announced: 'A low in the western Atlantic, 1,000 millibars, moving rapidly east; expected 998 millibars noon Monday, 350 miles southwest Valencia [an island on the extreme west coast of Ireland]'. At 3 am the next morning, Valencia reported that it had a barometric pressure of 984 millibars. Jim Hardy, aboard *Impetuous*, remarked upon the big rolling swells moving in from the west. 'Seems like a blow coming,' he told co-helmsman Hugh Treharne and Graeme Lambert. That was the opinion, too, of Ron Packer, navigator in *Police Car*. 'We look like having a snorter for the run home to Plymouth,' he advised skipper Cantwell and the rest of the crew. 'Well,' they said, 'that's just what we need.' But the essence of the official forecast, for the immediate future at least, was 13 k to 18 k of wind from the south-west to the north-west. At 9 am Monday, *Police Car* was in the Irish Sea, running under spinnaker in a 10 k south-easter. Packer listened carefully for the official forecast at 2 pm. It had been issued at 7 am that morning and was for SW winds Force 5 (15 k to 20 k) increasing to Force 7 (26 k to 33 k) for a time and veering to the west later. 'They're on the ball now,' he told Chris Bouzaid and co-helmsman Jim Robson Scott. At 6 pm *Police Car* was shooting down the front of seas in a constantly increasing south-westerly, her speedo at times touching 18 k. 'Winds of Force 8 (40 k) later', said the forecast. By 10 pm, *Police Car* had 35 k. A few minutes afterwards a 50 k gust hit her and she drove down the face of a wave and plunged at full power into the back of the one ahead of her. Solid water welled over her bow and swept aft down her decks. There was a heart-stopping shudder through the rig as she staggered, then, mercifully, the spinnaker brace parted and the pole whipped for'ard, relieving the load. 'There was no panic,' says Robson-Scott. 'The seas were lumpy, the sail was flogging and the wind was starting to howl, but that crew knew their business. They smothered the kite, dropped it smartly and had it stowed below in a few minutes. It was obvious, though, that we were in for a full-scale storm. The question was how long it would last. We ran for a while under full main, then treble reefed it to a quarter of its normal size and reached downwind to the island bald-headed. And that's all we needed.' The wind was 55 k and getting stronger when *Police Car* tacked to clear the lighthouse-capped rock at 1.45 am Tuesday. She got around about an hour and a half behind *Ragamuffin* and an hour before *Impetuous*, which earlier had been only a mile behind her.

Aboard *Ragamuffin*, the vastly experienced navigator Richard Hammond, who had sailed in four earlier Fastnets, had anticipated the blow early and had advised Fischer to prepare to drop the big spinnaker they had been carrying as soon as the wind began to veer from SW to WSW. 'This is eventually going to come away really hard,' said Hammond. 'Those that peel off too far to keep their kites full could find themselves fighting up to the island close hauled.' Hammond set a course so that *Ragamuffin* could maintain a fast reaching angle to the Fastnet Rock. As the wind increased, *Ragamuffin's* crew gradually reduced sail, first to one reef in the main, then two, ultimately, three. To balance the rig they changed down their headsail, too, and still averaged 10 k. Ten miles short of the port hand turn it was a number four jib. They tacked to clear the rock with half a mile to spare (*Impetuous* shaved it by less than 200 metres two and a half hours later) and eased away with a full gale on their beam for the return passage. 'The wind was getting harder, about 60 k, and we changed to a storm jib with the treble-reefed main,' says Hammond.

> The seas were 10 m high, but with the sheets eased we were flying. Half an hour after the turn we carried away a connecting shackle on one of the running backstays, near the deck. The spar took the extra load well but we breathed easier after we'd fixed it. A little later a big comber broke right over our stern. It filled the cockpit and forced open the after hatch and we got a bit of water down below. But it still wasn't too bad. Then, at 3.30 am, a great cross sea came out of the dark and hurled *Ragamuffin* down onto her side. Four things happened in quick succession. The boom vang parted, thus saving the boom, the headboard fitting on the mainsail let go, Bobby Holmes was tossed out of his bunk and Hugo von Kroetchmar, who was steering, was smashed against the wheel, twisting the frame and making it difficult to turn. But no one was hurt.
>
> We lowered the mainsail, lashed the boom and the sail to the deck and straightened the rim of the steering wheel. We got the storm trysail ready but did not set it until daylight. Syd Fischer, who had stayed on deck all night, either steering or helping the helmsman, did not want to endanger a man working down to leeward in the dark to fit the trysail tackles. So we carried on for two hours under storm jib alone. And we still logged 8 k all the time. The wind gusts then were about 70 k. Many of us had been in conditions as bad in Australian races. One Montagu Island race I sailed aboard Rus Slade's *Janzoon* was much the same, hurricane force winds with big breaking seas. But the wind this time began to ease at daylight and haul to the westward. By the time we got to the Scilly Islands it was only a gale and it continued to fall. We were under full sail with a spinnaker up by the early evening and for a while during the night it fell calm. We had a light breeze behind us to the finish at 11.32 am next day.

Police Car had the wind at 70 k from the WSW an hour after her Fastnet turn. Her crew also dropped the main and reached along the return track with only the number four jib set, and still logged 8 k. *Impetuous*, with Hugh Treharne relieving Hardy on the helm, made the turn under treble-reefed mainsail and storm jib in 55 k, but dropped the headsail later and carried on for a few hours under mainsail alone when they, too, judged the gusts at 70 k. By 8 am on Tuesday, they were adding sail.

Jim Robson-Scott, chairman of the Australian Yachting Federation's Offshore Committee, and whose voice as Australasian councillor is heard with respect at the Offshore Racing Council's international conferences, says, 'From aboard *Police Car*, the seaway at its worst was one of the most vicious I've seen but no more punishing than some of the big blows in the Sydney–Hobart race, and about the same as the hurricane in the 1972 Brisbane–Gladstone race, when some wind gusts were more than 100 k.'

Most of the Australians said afterwards that they had been concerned during the storm for some of the smaller non-Admiral's Cup boats that had started in the Fastnet, particularly those with inexperienced crews. But none of them was prepared for the reports of loss of life from so many boats when they got to port. Nor, indeed, had been the officials. It was a full six hours after the first of the gale hit the fleet that the shore party of the Royal Ocean Racing Club, the organizers of the Fastnet, had even any inkling that some boats might be in difficulty. First, at midnight, Monday, came a report to the makeshift race centre at Millbay Docks, Plymouth, that *Accanito*, a member of the French Admiral's Cup team, had lost her rudder and was making for Cork, Ireland. *Scaldis*, an independent entry from Holland, radioed that she was similarly disabled. The incidents were formally recorded, ready for issue to the Press. Then, gradually, and finally in a flood, came reports of Mayday calls for help from yachts sinking, yachts being driven towards the rocks of the Scilly Isles, yachts about to be abandoned with crews swept overboard into tumultuous seas; and of distress flares and rockets fired from life-rafts. Royal Navy helicopters, a Dutch frigate, English and Irish coastguard lifeboats, fishing trawlers, were out there rescuing people.

Officials, alarmed initially, were now horrified. No one had even contemplated the possibility of the disaster that was unfolding. In the first fifteen hours, the RAF and the Royal Navy had plucked seventy-four men, alive and dead, from the sea. Brave helicopter pilots, rushing back from leave, had flown in relays over the devastated fleet. They had hovered just clear of the tops of the churning seas so that winchmen could be lowered to strap harnesses on those struggling for their lives in the water. And the search and rescue went on for three ghastly days.

The RORC could not immediately give the Navy a definite total of the number of yachts and the crews that had to be accounted for. A fleet of 333 yachts had officially entered. It was decided that 303 of them had started, but it was thought that there were probably some that had set out to cruise the course just for the adventure. (One such craft was a trimaran, later found to have been lost with all four people aboard her.)

Of the yachtsmen officially racing, fifteen lost their lives. Another 136 men and women were rescued from yachts, life-rafts and from the sea by surface vessels and by aircraft. A total of twenty-four yachts, from 8.5 m to 11.3 m, were abandoned or lost, believed sunk. Of the 303 starters, including fifty-four Admiral's Cup contenders, 218 failed to sail the course because they were abandoned or sunk, or ran for shelter, or retired. A total of eighty-five sailed the course. Eight yachts were reported to have lost their rudders, and ten were believed to have been dismasted. Of the fifty-four Admiral's Cup boats that started in the Fastnet race, forty-one sailed the course and thirteen retired, mainly through damage. No Admiral's Cup crewman lost his life.

Australia's *Impetuous*, third on corrected time, *Police Car* (fourth) and

Ragamuffin (thirteenth) scored 462 points in the race to bring their overall winning total in the five-race series to 1,088. America, with fifth, fifteenth and twenty-eighth, placed second with a total of 1,013. Hong Kong, with ninth, eighteenth and twenty-fourth, totalled 944 and tied for third place with Italy, whose yachts finished tenth, twelfth and seventeenth in the Fastnet.

Two of Ireland's fancied performers, *Golden Apple of the Sun* and *Regardless*, lost their rudders and failed to sail the course. *Golden Apple's* crew abandoned her in the Irish Sea when offered rescue by a helicopter but some of them rejoined her the next day when the weather had eased. But even if those Irish boats had finished first and second among the Admiral's Cup contenders in the Fastnet race, Australia would still have won the series because the third Irish boat finished thirty-fourth.

Many lessons, of course, were learned from the race. Serious-minded administrators of ocean racing believe that, in time, restrictions on the type of craft, the type of construction, the type of safety equipment and especially the type of people aboard the yachts will eventually quell much of the exuberant holiday atmosphere that has pervaded the Fastnet in recent years. They hope that it and other races will be much more tightly organized and controlled, with regulations similar to those considered basic for Australian offshore races.

But the mid-1980 report made by the British committee appointed to inquire into the 1979 Fastnet disaster left a lot of yachtsmen wondering how long they would have to wait for strictures on the ignorant and foolhardy. The committee found no reason to castigate any officials for inept organization or lack of control of the event, for inadequate radio communication between competitors and the shore-based squad at race headquarters, or for equivocal weather reports and the absence of early storm warnings. The report did suggest stronger and better fixed washboards in hatchways (to stop cabins flooding so easily), more attention to the design and operation of safety harnesses and life rafts, and that there should be at least two people aboard each vessel who had adequate offshore experience. It was a pallid document compared with what many people had expected and alongside other published opinions of what was necessary to ensure reasonable safety standards. 'Of course,' said one senior Australian official, 'the Brits, behind their bland exteriors, can be pretty bloody-minded. I've got no doubt that some feel that everyone should know the dangers of going to sea unprepared and that those who don't should take their chances. Compared with other vigorous sports, ocean racing is safe when you consider the thousands of miles so many people sail each year. Still, officials can't dodge some responsibility. They've got to lay down definite guidelines.'

Australia continued to send teams to the Admiral's Cup, with each depending heavily on sponsorship organized by the Ocean Racing Club of Australia and other fund-raising schemes to help cover the ever-increasing costs of shipping the boats to England and back and air transport for their thirty or so crewmen. By 1985, apart from sponsorship, owners of those yachts chosen to represent could each expect to pay a minimum of $25,000 in extra fees besides the expense of outfitting their vessels for selection trials. Costly additional equipment was needed in the English races. Few crewmen could expect to spend less than $2,000 on accommodation, meals, and incidentals.

But our best boats and sailors were only occasionally able to outshine the brilliant performers that the rest of the world sent to the contest. On team total points we placed equal seventh with Italy against fourteen other nations in 1981;

fourth out of a total of fifteen in 1983; and fourth out of eighteen in 1985. The three Australian boats in 1981, *Hitchhiker* (Noel Robins helmsman for owner Peter Briggs) of WA, *Apollo V* (John Bertrand for Alan Bond), WA, and *Ragamuffin* (Syd Fischer), NSW, were new and highly fancied after ten closely fought selection trials against nine rivals on Port Phillip. They were especially good in light conditions and this time the English weather showed none of the ferocity of two years earlier. Races around the boomerang-shaped Solent were sailed over the usual tide-riven courses in winds that ranged from fluky catspaws to calms to moderate and occasionally fresh breezes. On one of the triangular legs of the 217 nm Channel race the wind, after calms and swirling currents, got up to a lively 25 knots. Those that were not fighting against the wind and a foul tide, to get around marks, came home at a gallop.

Hitchhiker, a low-rating (31.2 ft) Frers-designed sloop of 12.49 m overall length, with the Irish match-racing wizard Harold Cudmore aboard as tactician to help skipper Robins, was expected to match all comers in the light to moderate air races. However, in the first race — a farce that should have been over 22 nm but had to be shortened to 9 nm because officials stubbornly started it in 2–3 k of wind that never rose above 7 k — *Hitchhiker* began a series of disasters. She was caught in the hard-running tide at the start, involved in a chain reaction of collisions, forced over the line and lost 2.20 struggling to return. She finally sailed the truncated course twenty-ninth out of forty-five. (*Apollo V* was twelfth and *Ragamuffin* twenty-first). That night, protest officials penalized *Hitchhiker* twenty-four placings in spite of Robins' arguments that he had not caused the collisions but had been clobbered by overtaking boats. *Hitchhiker* took another pounding in the second inshore race when she tried to pinch around a mark,

On occasions ashore and afloat, Syd Fischer (left) and Alan Bond have not seen eye to eye but here, in 1981, they conjoin as team-mates in an effort to retain the Admiral's Cup that Australia won in the tragic 1979 Fastnet storm.

this time in a steady 12–15 k breeze, misjudged the tide, thumped into the mark, then fell back on port tack and fouled the Spanish boat *Bribon III*. Robins suffered fourteen more penalty points and so earned only six points from his thirty-first placing. *Apollo V* was tenth and *Ragamuffin* fourteenth.

Star of that race was the new English Dubois-designed *Victory*, 13.41 m (44 ft) overall, campaigned by Peter de Savary as crew-training for his forthcoming 1983 America's Cup bid, and skippered by 12-metre helmsman Phil Crebbin. *Victory*, a powerful boat with a big rig, sailed under an official but surprisingly low rating of 33 ft, that five months later in America was discovered to be 1.4 ft less than it should have been and became the subject of an international scandal that the most sophisticated arguments could not satisfactorily explain. But since *Victory's* false rating had not been revealed at the Admiral's Cup, she continued to sail under it, and — with placings of seventh in the Channel race, second in the third short inshore race, and fifteenth in the Fastnet — helped her team-mates *Yeoman XXIII* and *Dragon* to a comfortable win from the USA and Germany, with Ireland fourth, New Zealand fifth, and Canada sixth.

Ragamuffin did best of the Australian boats in the Channel race with sixth to *Hitchhiker's* twenty-first and *Apollo V's* twenty-fourth. In the third inshore race *Apollo V* was fifth, *Hitchhiker* twelfth, and *Ragamuffin* nineteenth. That put them in equal second place with Italy, only 78 points behind Britain at the start of the Fastnet. As in so many previous years, that race was a light-wind lottery. A total fleet of 244, including the forty-eight Admiral's Cup yachts, competed in light to moderate to light breezes that died to patchy calms. After the leaders had re-crossed the Irish Sea, with 90 miles to go to the finish in Plymouth, the whole flotilla bunched together and all the advantages won and lost over the preceding 516 nm were nullified. Only 20 nm separated the first and last of the Admiral's Cup boats. At one stage, the Australians were theoretically in positions that could have given them second place. But other boats that hugged closer to the coast got a private breeze out of the bays and *Hitchhiker* came in twenty-eighth, *Ragamuffin* twenty-ninth, and *Apollo V* thirty-eighth. Syd Fischer, who captained the Australian team, summed up: 'It's a hell of a place to hold a boat race, but it's all they've got.' On *Hitchhiker's* way home from the series, she atoned somewhat for her indifferent performances at Cowes by winning the world Two Ton Cup class series off Sardinia.

In 1983, Australia, ever hopeful, again sent *Hitchhiker* and Robins, this time with the boat's near-sister-ship, *Bondi Tram*, NSW (Bernie Case skipper for Denis O'Neil); and the Dubois-designed 12.19 m (40 ft) *Once More Dear Friends*, skippered by her owner, Peter Kurts, who also captained the team. Tony de Young was manager. They placed fourth on points behind the carefully chosen, scientifically built and lowest handicapping West German team. Italy was second and the USA third.

Hitchhiker began brilliantly with a win in the first inshore race then sagged to twenty-third, fifteenth, (Channel), eighteenth, and twenty-ninth (Fastnet). *Bondi Tram* scored 18, 32, 17, 32, 12 and *Once More Dear Friends* 41, 18, 11, 23, 23. Once again, better luck in the triple point-scoring Fastnet (there were 188 starters besides the forty-five Admiral's Cup boats) could have elevated the Australian team's final placing. The team went into that last race in third place on points but fluky stop-go winds — at one stage above 28 k before a period of calms — turned predictions upside down. Certainly local knowledge did not help; title holder Britain came in eighth. The essence of success was consistent boat speed for rating, and that was certainly something that the Australians lacked alongside the winners. The Americans tried to protest the 32.7 ft rating of the biggest German boat *Pinta* (the other Germans, *Outsider* and *Sabina*, were 30 ft minimum raters) but the international jury rejected the protest because it was lodged too late. The Germans nevertheless explained *Pinta's* rating and their analysis of the rating rule for all willing to listen. They also pointed out that their boats were built stronger than most and, unlike some rivals, complied with the American Bureau of Shipping's constructions standards.

For once the dreaded Solent courses were reasonably fair to all, with good proportions of wind-ward work, reaching and running. Race one was sailed in a 8–10 k breeze that faded to 3–5 k. For race two, there was a steady 12–20 k. In the Channel race, the wind was never more than 12 k, and so mixed with calms and switches of direction that the fleet bunched and the event restarted three times. *Hitchhiker* took 40.0 to drift the final 40 m to the line.

An example of other hazards: Early in the race, off Portsmouth in the Solent, *Diva*, the outstandingly fast French boat, got her keel caught for 10.0 on a steel mooring cable attached to a sewerage pipe. Her crew lowered her sails, then two of them jumped over the side, and, with one man standing on the other's shoulders, sprung the wire free of their boat with their feet. They sailed on to place eighth. Conditions favoured the bigger, higher handicapping boats in the fourth race, over a 30 nm Olympic style course in Christchurch Bay, the first time an inshore Cup race had been sailed outside the Solent. The breeze started at 10 k and rose at times to 22 k with lulls between thunderstorms. The shifts on the five 3 nm windward legs allowed the bigger boats almost to lay the marks on one stretch, while the small ones had to beat. The Australian team at no time seemed able to get into phase with the wind changes. Their unhappy performances in that race and then in the Fastnet were generally discounted back home by a populace inflamed by the concurrent sensations at Newport, Rhode Island, where *Australia II* was overwhelming all opposition in the America's Cup eliminations and 'keelgate' was raging.

Australia again finished in fourth place in 1985, but this time team manager Tony de Young said firmly: 'We lost the Cup at home before coming here.' He was referring partly to the failure of a fitting in the rig of Lou Abraham's new Victorian yacht *Challenge III* which caused her dismasting and, of course, her retirement early in the boisterous (30-15-20-14-40 k winds) Channel race. Team captain Peter Kurts' *Drake's Prayer* (NSW), once well placed in the same race, also suffered partial rig failure and limped home under jury rig in thirtieth place. Excellent seamanship by her crew and hazardous repair work 15 m above the deck in 40 k wind gusts by the boat's tactician Grant Simmer (*Australia II's* 1983 America's Cup navigator) saved the spar. The third boat in the team, Tasmanian Don Calvert's *Intrigue*, placed ninth in the Channel race. Manager de Young blamed bad workmanship for the rupture of the diagonal stay in *Challenge III's* rig which cost her the mast and her kevlar mainsail when the tangle was chopped free. 'It's a case of space-age technology without space-age technologists,' he said.

De Young and team captain Kurts were generally disappointed with the form of all three Australian boats after the first four races when the three had been pushed down into eighth place behind West Germany, Britain, New Zealand, Denmark, Austria, the USA and Singapore. Although the Australian crews were skilful and experienced, their boats had, at times, been well off the pace of the German and British boats. 'Australia has really got to try and improve its efforts.

Tasmanian-owned One Ton cupper *Intrigue* (Don Calvert), best of Australia's 1985 Admiral's Cup team, placed tenth overall on individual points in the international fleet of fifty-four. She was later sixth best point scorer in the Southern Cross Cup fleet. (Bob Ross)

We've got to have tougher selection trials in Melbourne and put more effort into them,' said de Young. Olympic and America's Cup coach Mike Fletcher said: 'We've got the men to sail the boats, but we've got to have low rating competitors at the venue for the Admiral's Cup to train more than they've been able to do. It will cost a lot more money. We need more sponsorship.'

Ultimately, only the consistently hard winds in the 605 nm Fastnet race saved Australia's face, enabling the boats to recover enough points to put them into fourth place. *Intrigue* placed thirteenth, *Challenge III* fourteenth (she had brought a spare mast, and Hood loft sailmaker Col Anderson in twenty-four hours made a new kevlar mainsail to replace the one lost in the dismasting), and *Drake's Prayer* sixteenth. *Drake's Prayer* had lost 1h 40m shortly after the start, when her main halyard broke and she was forced to return to Cowes for repairs before restarting. After the Fastnet race de Young's earlier criticism of Australia's lack of space-age technologists might well have been directed also at other nations with similarly built and rigged boats. A total of twenty-two of the Admiral's Cup fleet of fifty-two — fifty-four in eighteen teams of three but with two non-starters — retired from the Fastnet race and seven were dismasted. The winds were unrelentingly hard, above 20 k most of the three and a half days it took the leaders to sail the course, but they blew at 40 k for only one spell of six hours. And the lumpy seas, though punishing, were not comparable with heavy-weather Australian conditions or with the storm-driven waves of the 1979 race. Nevertheless only the winning West Germans, the Irish and the Australians got full teams of three around the course and across the finishing line. That lifted Australia's points tally to 1,429 behind West Germany's 1,906, Britain's 1,626 and New Zealand's 1,487. Although the British lost *Jade* (dismasted), one of their top performers, in the Fastnet their *Panda* finished first and *Phoenix* was fourth.

Unlike so many previous series, the three inshore races were sailed in fresh to moderate to only occasionally calm and shifty conditions, with breezes ranging from 17–21 k in the first race; 8–10–15 k (with calms and windshifts) in the second; and 10–15 k (with windshifts) in the third. For the record the Australian team placed as follows: *Intrigue* (Don Calvert) Tasmania, 11, 28, 9 (Channel), 20, 13 (Fastnet), making her tenth in the overall international point score; *Drake's Prayer* (Peter Kurts) NSW, 7, 19, 30 (Channel), 17, 16 (Fastnet), fourteenth overall; *Challenge III* (Lou Abrahams) Victoria, 22, 46, retired (Channel), 19, 14 (Fastnet), twenty-second overall. The winning German team, with two very low rating boats, *Outsider* (Tilmar Hansen) and *Rubin VIII* (Hans Otto Schumann) and *Diva G* (Jorn Bock), were placed second, fifth and eighth in the Fastnet. All three, like thirty-three other boats in the Admiral's Cup fleet (including the Australians', *Drake's Prayer* and *Intrigue*) carried complete wardrobes of sails designed and made in Norths' worldwide lofts, an indication of the enormous success of this US-founded company.

A total fleet of 222, including fifty-two of the fifty-four Admiral's Cup contestants still on their feet, started in the Fastnet race, and 149 withdrew, mainly because the boats and crews could not handle the tough conditions. Many, fearful of a repeat of the 1979 disaster, showed admirable discretion. But American Marvin Green's 24.7 m (81 ft) maxiboat *Nirvana* revelled in the hard winds and freesheet sailing, and covered the course in the record time of 2d 12h 41m 15s, eclipsing the time of Bob Bell's *Condor*, set in 1983, by 10h 20m 55s.

CLIPPER CUP — HONOLULU

As early as 1978 owners, crewmen and officials had foreseen increasing difficulties for Australians hoping to compete successfully in future Admiral's Cup world championships. European and American teams were now designed, crewed and tuned especially for the series. Australia's problems, apart from huge increases in costs, were that trials to select the best boats had to be held in Australia no later than March so that those chosen could be refitted during April, cradled and packed ready for shipping in May in order to be available in England in July for a minimum two weeks' re-tuning before the series. This meant that after the selection trials the crews who won selection were generally without their boats for a full three months and were denied the constant training to sharpen their handling of their boats so critical for high performance. Even if a crew were able to borrow another vessel of similar size and type and sail together in it until they flew to England to unload and rig their own boat, simulated training was no substitute for the real thing.

In the southern hemisphere, though, and in the more accessible northern Pacific to which yachts could sail on their own bottoms, saving $50,000 each way in shipping freights, Australia's future in international offshore competition remained bright.

An inaugural Pan Am Clipper series of five races off the Hawaiian Islands, originally proposed by CYC official Alan Brown, with one well-established around-the-state event of 775 nm, was first sailed in August 1978. Many yachtsmen hoped it could be developed into a worthwhile alternative to the Admiral's Cup. In June 1978 the Ocean Racing Club of Australia, formed to promote offshore competition on a national basis and, later, after some argument about autonomy, given the blessing of the Australian Yachting Federation, hastily assembled two teams. The No 1 team was: *Ragamuffin* (Syd Fischer), *Magic Pudding* (formerly the Australian national One Ton Cup champion *B195*, owned by Victorian John Karrasch but still skippered by Tom Stephenson), and the US-built *Big Schott* (a sister-ship to the former American and world Two Ton Cup champion *Williwaw*, skippered by Marshall Phillips of Sydney). The No 2 team was: *Geronimo* (of Sydney, under charter from owner Geoff Lee to Victorian Dick Thurston); *Nyamba*, formerly *Runaway* (Jim Hardy); and *Apollo* (Jack Rooklyn). All sailed 4,000 nm to the start on their own bottoms from Sydney, except *Big Schott*, which came from the USA, and *Magic Pudding*, which was shipped from Melbourne. They met fifteen yachts in teams of three from New Zealand (two teams), the USA (two teams) and Japan. Another twenty-two local yachts sailed as individual entries, with representatives from France (Tahiti) and Taiwan. In fresh trade winds averaging 18–25 k — apart from massive lees under the wind shadows of the mountainous islands — *Ragamuffin* (with placings 9, 3, 2, 1, 3), *Magic Pudding* (3, 8, 6, 13, 1) and *Big Schott* (7, 10, 9, 14, 6) scored a dramatic victory with 2,583 points from New Zealand's A team, 2,529; NZ (B team), 2,514; the USA (Red), 2,450; the USA (Blue), 2,411; Australia (B), 2,279; and Japan, 2,230.

The standard of competition among the first ten yachts in every race was in world class, although the helming and handling of many of the tail-enders left much room for improvement. New Zealand's A team just overshadowed Australia's No 1 team in the first four races, over 100 nm, and three of 27 nm, and the New Zealanders went into the final of 775 nm with a two point lead. But in that event, accurate navigation and shrewd tactics (to avoid the sixty mile wind shadows of the islands) devised by *Ragamuffin's* navigator, Richard Hammond, who had been around the course three times before, earned the Australians the winning points. Australia's No 2 team suffered a series of disasters. Damaged and unserviceable sails forced *Geronimo* out of two races and she was disqualified from another. *Apollo* lost the services of her skipper, Jack Rooklyn, in one race when he was thrown from his bunk in a heavy sea and broke two ribs; and she was forced to retire from another race when crewmen Paul Netherby (broken ribs) and Mike Bourke (broken hand) were injured by the spinning handles of a broken pedestal winch. *Apollo* missed another race while waiting for spare parts for the winch to be flown from America. *Nyamba* was the best of the trio, but she was forced to withdraw from one race after fouling *Big Schott* in a starting-line collision.

In the divisional scores, *Ragamuffin* won every race in A Division but she could not quite match the individual overall score of the Division B winner, New Zealand's Two Tonner *Monique*, which took home the handsome Pan Am Clipper Gold Cup.

One of the great spectacles of the series was the off-the-stick needle match between the US 24.1 m *Ondine* (Huey Long), re-rigged from a ketch to a sloop, and the ketch *Kialoa* (Jim Kilroy). Their multimillionaire owners and semi-professional crews drove them to the limit, and, when *Ondine* brought her score to 3-2, Long, wearing the victor's garland and lei as he helped his crew drink celebratory maitai rum cocktails out of a garbage can, remarked, 'I imagine Kilroy is thinking about giving up his split rig and changing *Kialoa* to a sloop'.

Overall, the most critical observers were much satisfied with the wholesome breezes they enjoyed in the Pan Am Clipper series, in contrast with the soggy Admiral's Cup calms, and they were full of praise for Waikiki Yacht Club's high standard of organization. The hospitality ashore on the pullulating tropical island, after the scruffy boredom of Cowes, was also something to be remembered with pleasure. ORCA officials forecast three Australian teams of high quality at the next Pan Am Clipper Cup in 1980, and possibly a dozen teams from other nations.

Although there was no European support and little interest from the east coast of America, possibly because of the preoccupation at Newport with elimination trials for the America's Cup, the 1980 Clipper Cup series was another great success. Australia did send three teams of three boats as promised. There were also three US teams, two from New Zealand, and one from Japan, Canada, and Hawaii. The trade winds still blew steadily, from moderate to fresh, the hospitality remained generous to a fault and Waikiki Yacht Club's organization was a model of enthusiastic efficiency. There was special satisfaction, too, for ORCA officials when Australia's No 1 team clearly beat the other ten competing teams and Australia's No 1 boat, *Ragamuffin*, the latest in a string of the same name owned and skippered by Syd Fischer, was the outstanding individual performer in the overall point score against all comers.

Ragamuffin, Peterson-designed 13.71 m (45 ft), rating 35.2 ft, placed tenth in the 100 nm Oahu race then fourth each time in the three round-the-buoys events and, with skilful sailing and shrewd navigation, was a brilliant first in the quadruple-point-scoring 775 nm Round the Islands race. Her team-mates *Challenge* (Lou Abrahams), Sparkman and Stephens design, 14.02 m (46 ft), rating 34.5 ft, placed 4, 3, 17, 3, 9; and *Sweet Caroline* (Marshall Phillips), Laurie Davidson, 12.49 m (41 ft), rating 31.0 ft, placed 7, 16, 8, 9, 4. That put them on a total of 2,886 points, ahead of the USA Red team (*Carrie Ann V*, *Tomahawk* and *Shenandoah*), second on 2,664 with Australia's No 2 *Impetuous* (Graeme Lambert), *Moonshadow* (John Taylor), and *Satin Sheets* (Andrew Strachan) on 2,615. New Zealand's No 1 team was fourth; New Zealand's No 2, fifth; Australia's No 3, sixth; Canada, seventh; Hawaii, eighth; Japan, ninth; the USA White, tenth; and the USA Blue, eleventh. There was consolation for the Americans when Fritz Johnson's mighty *Windward Passage* 21.94 m (72 ft), revitalized under her 29.87 m (98 ft) sloop rig and beautifully refitted, not only took line honours in most races, but also won handicap places of 3, 1, 1, 2, and 12 − a remarkable achievement for a big vessel giving so much time away in such a mixture of conditions. It must be noted, however, that the US system of time-on-distance handicapping does favour larger vessels more than the European and Australian system of time-on-time allowances.

The third Pan Am Clipper Cup competition in 1982 dispelled any previous conception of the regatta as a carefree, shirts-off affair. A tropical hurricane passing south of the Hawaiian island chain funnelled a series of hard winds and gales with occasional rain on to the courses for the first four of the five races and overturned many strategies planned for the 775 nm grand finale. There were short, vicious seas. No race started in a breeze much below 25 k and in one the gusts were 40 k and more. There were many casualties among the seventy-eight boats that competed in the international teams series, in the races between clubs and as individual entries. Seven lost masts, nine broke booms, eight blew out mainsails, twenty blew out spinnakers and a large number did major and minor damage to hulls and deck fittings. Among the personal injuries there were two broken legs, one severed finger, nine cases of concussion and an uncounted number of strained tendons, muscles, cuts, bruises and contusions.

For the first time the Americans sent teams of some of their best west-coast boats with proven champion offshore helmsmen and crews aboard. They stood up slightly better to the rough conditions than did the carefully chosen Australian team, and won the point score series. There were three US teams (named Red, White and Blue), three Japanese teams (Red, White and Blue), two from New Zealand (Red and Green), Australia's sponsored team, and one each from Victoria and Queensland. This time, races one, two, and four were set over Olympic style triangular courses of about 27 nm; race three was a windward and return course of 148 nm (double points) up and down the hazardous Molokai Channel, and race five the usual triple-point scoring Round the Islands classic.

The winning American Blue team included Jim Kilroy's Holland-designed 24.38m (80 ft) *Kialoa*, sporting a single 32.91 m (108 ft) mast and rating 69.6 ft (which placed 4, 32, 14, 1, 1); Dave Fenix's Peterson-designed 16.76 m (55 ft) *Bull Frog*, skippered by Tom Blackaller, rating 44.7 ft (2, 2, 7, 3, 37); and Clay Bernard's Davidson-designed 15.24 m (50 ft) *Great Fun*, rating 40.8 ft (8, 3, 1, 7, 17). They scored a total of 2,249 points against the 2,181 scored by the second-placed Australian team: Stan Edwards' Frers-designed 15.45 m (51 ft) *Margaret Rintoul III*, skippered by Graeme Freeman, rating 41.2 ft (3, 1, 10,

American maxi ketch *Kialoa* (left), hailed as world champion after Southern Cross Cup triumphs, but three times outsailed by Jack Rooklyn's *Ballyhoo* (right) in Sydney and US challenges. *Kialoa* was later rerigged as sloop in Clipper Cup series. (Bob Ross)

10, 20); Jeremy Whitty's and Greg Halls' Davidson-designed 11.88 m (39 ft) *Szechwan*, rating 29.5 ft (24, 25, 24, 13, 3); and Peter Briggs' Frers-designed 12.49 m (41 ft) *Hitchhiker*, skippered by Noel Robins, rating 31.4, (14, dnf (dismasted), 16, 25, 12). Next, third on 2,171 points, was the US White team. Then came Victoria, 2,045; Japan Blue, 2,042; New Zealand Red, 2,035; US Red, 2,030; Japan Red, 1,924; New Zealand Green, 1,888; Japan White, 1,825 and Queensland, 1,650.

Kialoa had a most spectacular series. After her impressive fourth in the first race, she was the focus of attention in the second, sailed in winds that were rarely below 30 k and regularly 35 k. She went upwind at a withering speed and came roaring downwind at well above 20 k, on the way performing a number of uncontrollable and awe-inspiring broaches which helped her to blow out two $10,000 spinnakers. In the savage Molokai race, *Kialoa* broached again on the long home run, broke her boom, stripped the gears in a winch, and burst another spinnaker, the flogging shreds of which tore the wind instruments off the top of her mast. Crewmen estimated the damage at $85,000 but owner Kilroy ordered repairs done within twenty-four hours so that 'the boat can be fit to win the next two races' — which she did.

Although there was never more than 25 k of wind in the triple-point-scoring final race, which eased to light and patchy at times before it freshened back to 20–25 k, there were none of the usual mountain-induced inshore calms. Meteorologists ascribed this to the influence of the passing hurricane. Vessels that cut the corners around the islands, instead of standing wide offshore always had breeze. *Kialoa* came through to set a new course record of 3d 23h 49m 46s for the 775 nm. Until that race, *Kialoa* had also been engaged in a tense, three-sided heavyweight contest against Bob Bell's Holland-designed 24.38 m (80 ft) *Condor* and the fourteen-year-old *Windward Passage*. Now owned by William Johnson of Florida, *Windward Passage* sailed under a new 29.87 m (98 ft) mast with a new keel and a new featherweight titanium rudder, which was said to have cost $25,000 of a $500,000 refit; these additions certainly gave the handsome 21.94 m (72 ft) former ketch a new lease of life. *Windward Passage* was well able to hold the bigger boats upwind and was a shade faster in surfing conditions downwind. With handicap placings of 5, 13, 3, and 8 she went into the Round the Islands race two points ahead of *Condor*, with *Kialoa* another point behind. Australian Jack Rooklyn's Ben Lexcen-designed 21.94 m (72ft) *Apollo* (also a candidate for maxi honours but at that stage underpowered even in the hard conditions), was sedately following in their wake. A third of the way around the course, *Windward Passage* was leading the fleet, with *Kialoa* next a quarter of a mile astern. Then a rigging spreader collapsed and the top of *Windward Passage*'s mast came tumbling down. Her crew disconsolately motored back to port. Australia's *Hitchhiker*, a proven all-rounder, had an unhappy series. She was well placed until dismasted on the downwind run in the rough second race when she dived, bows-under, into the back of a green sea and performed a terrifying gybe-broach with her spinnaker pole in the water. Then, repaired for the Molakai race, a demolition derby for many, *Hitchhiker* split her kevlar main sail and lost half an hour while her crew replaced it with a dacron sail. In race four she broke the start and lost 3.0 when recalled. The American boat *Great Fun* had astonishing speed downwind. For her win in the Molokai race, she surfed constantly at speeds of 22 k and finished 36.0 ahead of Australia's similarly sized *Margaret Rintoul III*. The American *Bull Frog* was of extraordinary construction.

Left Western Australia's *Hitchhiker* (Peter Briggs and Noel Robins) suffered a series of disasters, including a dismasting, in the 1982 Clipper Cup series. Her best placing was twelfth but other fancied competitors did worse. (Lou d'Alpuget)

Right *Szechwan*, Jeremy Whitty's lively 11.9 m sloop did not relish the wild winds in some races of the 1982 Clipper Cup series, but her third in the triple-scoring 775 nm finale lifted the Australian team into second place on points behind the US. (Bob Ross)

To save weight, her hull above the waterline was made of only 3 mm sheets of aluminium glued on to T-shaped alloy frames with a deck of nomex honeycomb between two thin alloy sheets. She had a conventionally plated hull below the waterline, fastened to strong frames. Her deck fittings were also extremely lightweight and included a titanium steering wheel weighing only 2.75 kg. The boat was reputed to have cost $650,000 to build and outfit. Members of her crew said they had constant worries with her small-section, triple-spreader rigged mast which was of an alloy that could not be welded and had an internal, mechanically fastened spinnaker pole track that kept coming loose. But *Bull Frog*, with world champion helmsman Tom Blackaller and a team of renowned 'heavies' aboard, seemed certain to take out the individual point score after her early placings of 2, 2, 7, and 3. Then they placed only thirty-seventh in the high-scoring final race when they deliberately went very wide offshore of the islands of Hawaii and Maui to avoid expected cushions of calm that this time were not there. Top individual point scorer was the fast-running Japanese 11.88 m (39 ft) *Tobiume*, designed by Osamu Takai, who sailed in the crew. She was a development of his successful smaller craft — shallow, wide, with low freeboard, little bow overhang, and fine forward seconds. *Tobiume* placed 9, 14, 2, 9, and 6. A protest against illegal hollows in the hull was dismissed by the international jury after the boat was hauled out for remeasurement. The jury conceded that the original measurer should not have proceeded with the measurement until the hollows that did exist were removed, but said that 'the evidence before this jury was that the effect on the boat's rating would not have been significant'.

The Americans won again in 1984 with sound performances from three well prepared and expertly crewed boats. One was the Frers 51 *Tomahawk* (owned by John Arens), formerly Australian Stan Edwards' *Margaret Rintoul III*, that had not fully realized her potential in 1982. Another was the Peterson 55 *Checkmate*, formerly *Bull Frog* in 1982, now owned by Monte Livingston and rigged with a spar in which her crew had more confidence than previously. The third boat was *Camouflage*, a Frers 44, owned by Al Schultz. These three, called the US White team, on 2,211 points, outscored the NZ A team of *Shockwave* (Neville Crichton), a Frers 43, *Sundance* (Delvin Hogg), and *Exador* (Tom McCall), both Farr 40s, by the narrow margin of 12 points. The New Zealanders scored 2,199. Third was the US Red team, *Artemis*, *General Hospital*, and *Sidewinder*, only 6 points behind, on 2,193 points. Next, fourth, on 2,133 points, was Australia's Dunhill sponsored squad: *Bondi Tram*, a 12.5 m Frers 41, rating 31.6 ft, owned by Denis O'Neil and skippered by Iain Murray; *Indian Gibber*, a 12.29 m Farr 40, rating 30.4 ft, owned by John Eyles and under charter to Bill Ferris; and *Once More Dear Friends*, a 12 m Dubois 39, rating 30.2 ft, owned and skippered by Peter Kurts. Then, fifth, were NSW (*Ragamuffin*, Syd Fischer; *Freight Train*, Bob Williams; and *Sweet Caroline*, Marshall Phillips) with 2,048; Japan West, 1,970; New Zealand B, 1,905; Japan East, 1,887; US Blue, 1,866; Victoria (*Challenge*, Lou Abrahams; *Seaulater* Peter Gourlay; and *Seaquesta*, Alf Neate), 1,861; and Hong Kong 1,852.

The races were sailed in generally wholesome breezes. The first two, over 27–30 nm triangular courses, never had less than 20 k with gear-busting squalls of 35 k to 38 k. Seas in the Molokai race were softer than usual with winds ranging from 20 k down to 12 k and up to 22 k at the finish. And although there was rarely much more than 18 k of breeze and some calms in the 775 Round the Islands race, American George Coumantaros' new Frers 24.68 m (81 ft) *Boomerang* got around the course in the astonishing new record time of 3d 22h 34m 55s.

The performances of the Australian team were much below expectations. Although *Bondi Tram* did win every race in her Division D against rivals of the same class, she placed only 7, 7, 10, 11, 3 against her Clipper Cup opponents and sixth overall. *Indian Gibber* did reasonably well in Division E with 2, 4, 4, 4, 4, but in the Clipper Cup was only 11, 11, 10, 20, 7 for sixteenth overall. *Once More Dear Friends* was 7, 9, 8, 6, 9, against Division E boats, and in the Clipper Cup had placings of 18, 19, 17, 21, 22 for thirty-first overall. The New Zealanders, however, sailed brilliantly throughout. Only the dismasting of *Exador*, a Farr 40, in extraordinary circumstances in the final series of the last race, cost them the series. Helmsman Ray Haslar, one of New Zealand's most experienced offshore sailors, had carefully set his course through calm water showing a minimum depth of 9 m (30 ft) over a small reef, working close inshore of the big island of Hawaii, when suddenly, without any warning, a towering wave rose ahead of the boat. Although Haslar tried to swing his boat away to ride with the sea the boat plunged through, fell heavily into the trough and her rig collapsed. Then another similar wave broke over the boat and almost swamped her. The eventual race winner, American Charles Short's *Sidewinder*, which was 300 m astern of *Exador* when the incident occurred, gamely came almost alongside the floundering New Zealanders and hove to until assured that they did not need help. *Sidewinder* was later awarded a time allowance of 5.15 for her trouble. Haslar said: 'The two waves that broke on *Exador* were truly "rogues", the only ones we encountered in the area all the time we were cleaning up the mess.' Until then *Exador's* Clipper Cup placings had been 3, 2, 1, 5. She had been in a winning position in the last race, but even if she had finished only in the middle of the fleet, her team's point score would have put them well ahead. In retrospect, the series had another lesson for Australia: As in other international offshore series, the competition was getting tougher all the time.

15

Southern Cross Cup Internationals

BY 1978, Australia's offshore racing yachtsmen were facing the hard economic facts of international competition – the enormously inflated costs of shipping vessels overseas and, after two salutary Admiral's Cup defeats, a marked reticence among financial backers who had been willing to support the challengers when they seemed to have a chance of winning. Some yachtsmen of lesser leagues had also shown little sympathy for the Admiral's Cup aspirants. They had had the temerity to suggest that, since most owners of big vessels were wealthy, the latter should not expect public support but should be willing to pay their own costs and their crews', too. This was to ignore the fact that to campaign a top class 13.7 m yacht in racing condition annually cost an owner on average $100,000 in pre-tax income, apart from the loss of interest on the respectable slice of capital tied up in the design, building and outfitting of such a vessel. The prospect of a personal payout of another $50,000 nett every second year was enough to dampen the competitive ardour of even the keenest potential representative of Australia.

One group of heretics when approached for support for the Cup fund brutally replied that since the yachts were ocean racers they should be sailed to England on their own bottoms as were most European, US and South American contestants. This, of course, did not allow for the tyranny of distance from which Australia has historically suffered in commercial as well as sporting endeavours. While it is true that, theoretically, our contenders in the Admiral's Cup were capable of sailing to England and back, the time involved in each of two such 12,000 nm journeys, and the cost of refits at either end to restore the yachts to thoroughbred racing condition after the wear and tear of four months at sea, would have been prohibitive – and at least equal to the shipping charges.

So, in 1978 the yachtsmen, looking closer to home for international competition, gave their support for the inaugural Pan Am Clipper series in Hawaii

Flight of *Bumblebee 4:* John Kahlbetzer's 23.2 m alumimium sloop soars out of Sydney Harbour to outpace visiting maxiboats in 40 nm challenge in 1979. A fortnight later she led a then record fleet of 147 to Hobart, then set out for an overseas campaign. In 1986 Syd Fischer raced her, lengthened, as *Ragamuffin* (No 6). (Lou d'Alpuget)

Right Rolly Tasker's WA superboat *Siska*, fastest overall in 11,650 nm Parmelia race from Plymouth to Fremantle. Later, as *Vengeance*, she performed well for Bernard Lewis of Sydney. (Photomarine, Perth)

Bottom Not so balmy trade winds: Australia's *Ragamuffin* gives her crew a lively time in the Pan Am Clipper Cup series off Waikiki Beach. (Adrian Herbert)

(see Chapter 14), only 4,000 nm away, to which yachts could be sailed in about four weeks without the need for expensive refits when they got there. Fortunately, there was also, ready to hand, a local contest which had the potential to be built up into an event increasingly attractive to overseas competitors. This was the Southern Cross Cup, founded in 1967 by the Cruising Yacht Club of Australia virtually as Australia's own version of the Admiral's Cup. The trophy is contested in four (since 1983, five) races down the south-east coast of Australia. The series includes the Sydney–Hobart race.No age allowances are given.

One special attraction of this series was that the net for entries was spread much wider than that of the Admiral's Cup, which was by now restricted to craft of between 30 ft and 40 ft international rating. The Southern Cross Cup conditions allowed much smaller and less expensive yachts of 21.5 ft rating (under Half Ton Cup) to compete with those ranging up to the limit of 70 ft rating, maxi-giants whose multimillionaire owners were not so concerned about costs, and big enough to make fast international passages with the professional delivery crews employed to maintain them. The other attraction about the Southern Cross Cup that Australian organizers were not too modest to mention to potential visitors was that the races were at least as well organized as similar events overseas; that they were sailed in honest winds, with no bonuses for local knowledge of tides or currents; and that the courses were better all-round. It had to be admitted, of course, that the final scramble across Storm Bay and up the Derwent River in the main event, the Sydney–Hobart race, was a lucky dip, but this, even so, was equally unfair to everyone.

Like its British counterpart, the Southern Cross Cup is held biennially (in December of the same odd-numbered years as the Admiral's Cup) and the series carries double points for placings in a race of medium distance (usually 180 nm); single points for two (since 1983, three) short races (each 30–35 nm), triple points for the 630 nm Sydney–Hobart race. Other Sydney clubs, Royal Prince Alfred Yacht Club, Royal Sydney Yacht Squadron, and Middle Harbour Yacht Club, conjoin with the CYC in organizing the races and they give trophies.

The Cup races had started as a modest contest between Australian and NZ teams after the flush of the CYC's early successes in the Admiral's Cup, and as a means of attracting interstate and, hopefully, foreign entries to the Sydney–Hobart event. It was an instant success locally and, by 1977, all States were competing against each other and against New Zealand. There was also a regular trickle of teams coming from further abroad. By that time not only had the British and Americans as well been prominent in the Cup contest, but also Japan, Hong Kong, and the European Economic Community (representing France, Germany, and Ireland) had competed.

Although no one has sought seriously to give the series the status of the Admiral's Cup or America's east coast Onion Patch and Southern Ocean Racing Conference contest, which can draw high quality teams from large centres of population in Europe and South America, the Southern Cross Cup nevertheless is a worthy challenge to those with the zest for racing at sea. It offers northern-hemisphere owners and crews the temptation to try themselves and their yachts in the boisterous midsummer seas and fresh winds of the Australian east coast and to experience the widely publicized sleigh ride to Hobart which only occasionally turns into a desperate battle against head winds and seas.

Britain sent the first of a string of teams in 1969 – the 12.5 m Admiral's Cup sloop *Prospect of Whitby*, owned and ably skippered by one-legged Arthur Slater;

Sir Max Aitken's 18.9 m cutter *Crusade;* and Rodney Hill's 10.4 m sloop *Morning After. Prospect of Whitby* scored second place in the Sydney–Hobart race, but on total points the British team finished well behind NSW's No 1 team: *Ragamuffin* (Syd Fischer), *Mercedes III* (Ted Kaufman), and *Boambillee* (Vince Walsh), with the New Zealanders, *Rebel* (Brin Wilson), *Renegade* (John Lidgard, with his wife Heather, as navigator), and *Outrage* (Clyde and Victor Colson) third. But there was a consolation for the British for having come so far. Their reserve yacht, *Morning Cloud,* skippered by Ted Heath, who became their Prime Minister the following year, won the Sydney–Hobart race. In some Australian eyes, the one event seemed a natural consequence of the other. Heath's navigator, Anthony Churchill, was quick to point out that here was a double event never likely to be repeated.

The British sent their champion American-designed Admiral's Cup team in 1971 – Arthur Slater's new 13.7 m aluminium *Prospect of Whitby;* Bob Watson's wooden 12.2 m *Cervantes IV;* the Prime Minister's new wooden 12.5 m *Morning Cloud,* this time skippered by first mate Sammy Sampson, since affairs of state demanded that her owner remain at the helm of No. 10 Downing Street. *Morning Cloud* had aboard the first single sideband radio transmitter fitted to a racing yacht in Australia, so that messages could be relayed through a special channel direct to her owner, chafing on the other side of the world. But the British team and all others – including the American squad of giants: Ted Turner's *American Eagle* (the former 12-metre class America's Cup contender), *Kialoa* No. 2 (Jim Kilroy) and *Ondine II* (Huey Long), both 22.3 m – met the pride of New Zealand, three brilliantly designed and sailed One Ton Cup class yachts. They were *Pathfinder* (Brin Wilson), *Runaway* (John Lidgard) and *Wai-Aniwa* (owner Ray Walker, skipper Chris Bouzaid, the latter the winner of the Sydney–Hobart race in 1967 and the world's One Ton Cup in 1969 with his *Rainbow II*). The New Zealanders had trained for months in their home waters, carefully tuning their yachts, and had sailed across the Tasman in company, determined to win.

They began badly, nevertheless. In the first race there was a furore when *Wai-Aniwa* carried the world's first blooper (known now also as a shooter), a full-cut stays'l flown for'ard in combination with a spinnaker on square runs. The British protested, claiming that the yacht should be disqualified for carrying an illegal sail 'in that the stays'l had been carried upside down to gain an unfair

Sea-going wife of rare skill: Heather Lidgard, navigator of her husband's New Zealand sloop *Renegade* in the 1969 Southern Cross Cup series. (SMH)

advantage'. The New Zealanders furiously resisted the charge, insisting that the blooper had been carried the right way up and that the loosely hoisted manner in which they had set it was thoroughly legal. Photographic evidence confirmed their claim and the British protest was dismissed. (An International Ocean Racing Council inquiry later endorsed the Australian ruling, and bloopers are now used universally.) The New Zealanders ran into more trouble, this time with no escape, in the second short race when *Pathfinder*'s crew put her aground in Sydney Harbour at Bradley's Head (on to a rock ledge that every local child learns to identify in his first season afloat), started their motor to get clear, and were disqualified. But then the disconsolate New Zealanders placed first *Pathfinder*, second *Runaway*, and third *Wai-Aniwa* in the Sydney–Hobart race and gained such a bag of points that their anxieties turned to glee. In the final tally they beat Britain, the early leaders, into second place, with NSW third.

The British came back in 1973 with a new 14.3 m *Prospect of Whitby* (Arthur Slater), *Superstar*, 13.4 m (owner Alan Graham, skipper Dave Johnson), and *Quailo III*, 16.8 m (Don Parr), and this time they won narrowly from another hot NZ team: *Inca*, 13.7 m (owner Evan Julian, co-skipper Roy Dickson), *Quicksilver*, 12.5 m (Brin Wilson), and *Barnacle Bill*, 12.8 m (Doug Johnstone). Third placegetters were Hong Kong, fielding *Ceil III*, 12.2 m (owner Bill Turnbull, skipper Craig Whitworth, of Sydney), and two chartered Australian yachts, the Sydney 17.7 m *Apollo* (Peter Jolly), and *Aquila*, 10.4 m (Bill Park), of Victoria. NSW's team was well beaten into fourth place, with WA fifth, Victoria sixth, the USA seventh, SA eighth, and Tasmania ninth.

The final race to Hobart was a rollicking downwind run all the way, won for Hong Kong by *Ceil III*, designed by Whitworth's then business partner, Bob Miller (later known as Ben Lexcen), beautifully built by Doug Brooker, a master-craftsman, of Sydney, and fearlessly driven by a gang of champion Sydney round-the-buoys and offshore sailors with owner Turnbull, a Hong Kong lawyer, urging them on. *Prospect of Whitby* was second in the Sydney–Hobart race and that, after a shaky start, ensured the British of their Cup win. The New Zealanders had seemed to have a safe lead after the first three races but did not do so well in the fresh running conditions in the final. They would certainly have been closer to the British on points if *Inca* had not had a young crewman (John Sarney) die of a heart attack during the first night of the Sydney–Hobart race. *Inca*'s crew, to honour what they considered a national obligation, sailed on after they had lost seven hours transferring their dead companion's body, and their distraught skipper, Julian, to a rescue vessel; but they had little spirit left for racing. *Inca* finished twenty-third in the Cup fleet, sixty-third overall in the general Sydney–Hobart fleet, well below yachts she normally would have beaten.

However, the New Zealanders were in full fig in 1975, with a team that included a revolutionary new concept in ocean racers — Noel Angus's skiff-type plywood sloop of the One Ton class, called *Prospect of Ponsonby*. She was the first of a line of three-quarter rigged craft of various sizes, semi-lightweight, wide-sterned, and stripped out, created by Auckland's Bruce Farr, a brilliant young open-boat designer. *Prospect of Ponsonby* had a fine entrance and a broad, planing afterbody set on a narrow fin keel; an extremely flexible rig that needed skilled handling; and a tendency to bury her head upwind unless her crew packed to windward on her weather quarter. But she was fast on all points of sailing, and downwind in a fresh breeze she got near to planing. *Prospect of Ponsonby* was well supported in the NZ team by two modern, more conventional craft — *Tempo*

Windward Passage (7099), Fritz Johnson, and *Kialoa* (13751), Jim Kilroy, staged a match race battle throughout the 1977 Southern Cross Cup series and, in one race, came into heavy collision forcing both boats to miss the 180 nm event while round-the-clock repairs were made. *Kialoa* won the contest when she took Sydney–Hobart line honours and the handicap double. In 1986 both were rigged as sloops and *Windward Passage* was Australian-owned by Rod Muir. (*SMH*)

(Cliff Johnson–Norm Vitali), an 11.6 m One Tonner; and *Quicksilver*, 12.5 m (Richard Wilson). But the new yacht dominated the series. *Prospect of Ponsonby* won the first 30 nm race and finished second in the next, won the double-points-scoring 180 nm race, and finished third of the Cup boats in the fastest Sydney–Hobart ever sailed. With *Quicksilver*'s placings of 8, 2, 4 and 18, and *Tempo*'s 14, 12, 11, 12, New Zealand won the series from the powerful NSW team of *Love and War, Mercedes IV,* and *Patrice III*.

The British, with their best Admiral's Cup performer *Noryema* and two chartered Australian boats, *Meltemi* and *Apollo III*, finished third. Fourth was WA, whose team included that year's Sydney–Hobart race winner, (*Rampage*), a sister-ship to *Ceil III* (which had won in 1973), but with a taller rig; Rolly Tasker's skinny 16.2 m *Siska*; and Guy Fornaro's 11.3 m *Brutta Faccia*. Fifth were the Americans with their yellow-hulled world champion One Ton Cup boat, *Pied Piper* (Ted Turner), a flimsy aluminium featherweight, some of whose apprehensive crew prayed for following weather on the Bass Strait crossing to Hobart, and got it; Jim Kilroy's new 24.1 m superboat, the third *Kialoa* (which averaged better than 10 k all the way to Hobart and reduced the course record to 62h 36m 56s); and the 11.9 m *Anduril*. Sixth was Victoria, then came Tasmania, SA, Japan, Queensland, and Papua New Guinea.

There was some grumbling, among those yachtsmen who sensibly went to sea hoping for the best but prepared for the worst, about boats built as lightly as *Pied Piper* and about the trend the New Zealanders were setting with craft of *Prospect of Ponsonby*'s type. On the other hand, scores of Australian owners saw Farr as the new messiah of ocean racing design and his as the critical path to follow if one were to have a chance of winning. So stock yachts in fibreglass of the One Ton class similar to *Prospect of Ponsonby* became a rage. They seemed entirely justified when one of them, *Piccolo*, skippered by John Pickles of Lake Macquarie, 73 kilometres north of Sydney, with a tough, seasoned crew, won the 1976 Sydney–Hobart race (a non-Southern Cross Cup year) after a close haul in 35–40 k of wind across Bass Strait. Then the rating rule makers started nibbling at the advantages Farr had designed into the boats, imposing penalties that greatly increased their handicap allowances. Most yachts went up almost a foot in rating.

The resourceful New Zealanders, however, had another surprise in store for the Southern Cross Cup authorities. In 1977 they sent two teams, one of conventional yachts, the other composed of three featherweight centreboarders, all designed by Farr, that enraged the owners of many of their rivals. Critics described these new boats as 'flatwater dinghies with lids on' and claimed that they lacked stability, were contrary to the spirit of offshore racing, and should not be allowed to compete against real seagoing yachts. They sought to have the centreboarders banned. The new NZ breed were: *Swuzzlebubble* (Ian Gibbs), a Half Tonner; and *Jenny H* (Ray Haslar) and *Smir Noff Agen* (Don Lidgard), both One Tonners. Officials were in a quandary. *Swuzzlebubble* had succeeded in sailing fifth in the world's Half Ton Cup level rating championship in New Zealand just before coming to Australia. Ultimately, in spite of official misgivings, an exchange of cables between Australia and the London-based International Offshore Racing Council, and consultations with the Australian Yachting Federation, all the centreboarders (three more were included in other teams) were allowed to start. The final line-up of Cup teams was: New Zealand (two); the USA (two); Britain, EEC, Papua New Guinea, WA, SA, Victoria, Tasmania, Queensland, and NSW.

After the first three races, in light to moderate conditions, the decision to let the centreboarders in seemed justified. *Jenny H* won the first two and finished fourth in the third race. *Smir Noff Agen* placed second twice and then won, and *Swuzzlebubble* came in ninth, fourth, and second. The New Zealanders started in the final race to Hobart with a lead of 130 points from Britain's team of *Knockout* (owner Sir Max Aitken, skipper Bobby Lowen), *Winsome 77* (David May), and *Xaviera* (A.B. Lang and R. A. J. Woodbridge); with NSW's *Ragamuffin* (Syd Fischer), *Nyamba* (Jim Hardy), and *Mercedes V* (Harry Janes) 10 points further back. The EEC squad was next. Victoria had slid from second to fifth after losing 111 points because her well-performed Two Tonner, *Nitro*, had sailed under an incorrect rating and had been forced to withdraw from all three races.

All the earlier doubts about the unsuitability of the lightweight centreboarders were revived in a tidal wave of criticism when New Zealand's main team collapsed in the wild 1977 Sydney–Hobart race (see Chapter 10), although they were not the only ones who failed to stand up to the conditions. *Smir Noff Agen* scuttled into Bermagui, on the NSW south coast, with smashed hull frames after her first encounter with the southerly gale that raked the fleet. *Swuzzlebubble's* crew got further south, then, after two men were washed overboard (their lifelines held and they were dragged back aboard), decided that Bass Strait was no place for mock heroics and joined the scores of other retired yachtsmen from craft of all kinds who by then were licking their wounds in mainland ports. *Jenny H's* crew, although the yacht had suffered some hull damage, gamely nursed her through two days of gales and, when the weather eased to calms, ghosted the final 200 nm to Hobart to finish fifth of the twenty-two (out of thirty-eight) Cup yachts that completed the course. *Jenny H* also placed twelfth among the total Sydney–Hobart fleet of seventy (out of 131 starters) that reached the finishing line.

The effort by Haslar and his crew earned New Zealand 96 points for a final winning total of 507. Second placegetters were NSW (456), with Britain (433) third. So the recalcitrant New Zealanders, with their weird yachts, had won the Southern Cross Cup for the third time, and the ocean racing world was in turmoil, with talks of prohibitions, penalties and rigid limitations on construction for future contests. The received opinion was that offshore racing yachts must become wholesome, with cruising capability. One could almost hear snorts of approval from the crypt of Thomas Fleming Day, the USA's late founding father of ocean racing, who had said just that, three-quarters of a century earlier. No one, however, could deny that the Aucklanders were magnificent seamen and fine competitors, whatever they sailed. Australian officials just wished they would use less alarming craft. Many felt that, if 'the NZ disease' were allowed to spread, it would inevitably cause tragedies (what, they asked, would have happened if the 1977 gales had caught the 'flimsies' when they were in the middle of Bass Strait, with no handy place to hide?); discourage foreign teams from competing; and jeopardize the whole future of the Southern Cross Cup. When Farr announced early in 1978 that he was retiring from the hassles of designing radical ocean racers and would concentrate more on cruising-type yachts, there were sighs of relief. (The ultra-lightweight centreboarder controversy, however, did not die down, and argument continued until late 1978, when it was partially resolved by the International Offshore Racing Council, as discussed in Chapter 10 – and Farr was not long away from racing machines.)

Overall, the twenty Southern Cross Cup races sailed in the eight years to 1977 provided Australian sailors from all States with an intensity of competition they would never have gained in domestic club events, helped them to improve designs of hulls, rigs and equipment, and to develop maturity of skill and judgement. The races also eliminated a previously widespread cockiness among Australian yachtsmen – a conviction that in big rolling seas and heavy winds they were men apart. The Cup results table shows that the British, mostly sailing their own boats, designed and rigged for smoother European seas and lighter winds, scored two second placings (1969 and 1971), a win (1973), and two thirds 1975 and 1977), and were therefore on a par with Australia's strongest teams (from NSW), who scored a win (1969), a third (1971), a fourth (1973), and second placings in 1975 and 1977. Balanced against the results of Admiral's Cup events during the same period, it was clear that British helmsmen and crews were much more adaptable than Australians.

The Southern Cross Cup races also brought a new dimension to line-honours racing in Australia. The US west coast giants, *Kialoa*, 24.1 m, and *Windward*

The Southern Cross Cup races brought a new dimension to line-honours racing in Australia. US west coast giant *Kialoa*, 24.1 m, roaring downwind to set the Sydney-Hobart race record of 2d 14h 36m 56s in 1975. Her Sydney navigator, Magnus Halvorsen, recorded that she held off repeated challenges from her closest rival, *Windward Passage*. (*Hobart Mercury*)

Passage (Fritz Johnson), 22.3 m, set the pace against the local maxis, *Helsal*, 22 m; *Ballyhoo*, 22 m; and *Anaconda II*, 25.3 m; and New Zealand's *Buccaneer*, 22.3 m. The big American ketches carried on in Australian waters a sporting feud that had developed in Trans-Pacific and Atlantic races. *Kialoa* twice beat *Windward Passage* in neck-and-neck races to Hobart (in 1975 setting the course record) and narrowly outpaced her in all but two shorter events.

The duel reached a climax in a special 1975 race, a non-Cup event, but one of the finest and most dramatic offshore contests ever sailed off Sydney's coast — a specially arranged Battle of the Giants over 40 nm. Other starters were round-the-world competitors *Great Britain II*, 22 m (in Sydney refitting after the second stage of that 30,000 nm event) and South Australia's *Anaconda II* (Josca Grubic); Sydney's sloop *Ballyhoo* (Jack Rooklyn), Tony Fisher's 22 m *Helsal* and the former America's Cup Challenger *Gretel*, 20.4 m (Jock Sturrock). Although *Kialoa* (second) finished ahead of *Windward Passage* (third) in that race, *Ballyhoo*, with the former world champion 18-footer skipper, Bob Holmes, as Rooklyn's main helmsman, beat the American boats by 4m 23s and 9m 38s. *Gretel* was sixth, 34m astern of the winner. Holmes and a crew culled from the best of Australia's big boat sailors, with Stan Darling as navigator and Hugh Treharne as tactician, in the closing stages of the race first worked windshifts on a ten-mile leg to windward. Then, having established a clear lead, *Ballyhoo* held off *Kialoa* on a close reach (on which at times both yachts touched speeds of 14 k) and a square spinnaker run up Sydney Harbour to the finish. *Kialoa* and *Windward Passage* carried 930 sq m of sail on the final run, flying spinnakers on both masts, and bloopers each the size of a 9 m yacht's total wardrobe of sails. A huge fleet of spectator craft, and some 50,000 people lining the foreshores, watched the race and its finish.

Rooklyn's success inspired him to take *Ballyhoo* on a worldwide ocean racing campaign, and among his successes in the following year were two more victories over *Kialoa* and *Windward Passage*, establishing *Ballyhoo* as one of the world's fastest yachts and certainly the best to windward. Both American owners spent large sums of money to improve their yachts for the 1977 Southern Cross Cup races. They rigged them with taller masts, and Kilroy had *Kialoa's* after underbody rebuilt, her rudder moved and a new keel fitted. (*Ballyhoo* by this stage was no longer a potential rival, as Rooklyn had sold her overseas.)

The clash between the American pair literally came in the first 30 nm Cup race off Sydney Heads — there was a collision at a rounding mark that left Kilroy's ketch with a hole through her starboard quarter, and Johnson's heavily framed bowsprit assembly pointing at right angles to her deck. Sydney navigator, Dave Kilponen, and John Kilroy, son of *Kialoa's* owner, were thrown out of the yacht's cockpit by the impact, but neither was seriously hurt and both were soon rescued. The yachts retired hurt and after some hard words the race committee that heard their protests disqualified *Windward Passage* for trying to force a passage. Teams of engineers and shipwrights, hired regardless of cost, worked in relays for two days to repair the damage to the big boats. They missed the next Cup race over 180 nm, but were ready for the second 30-miler. *Windward Passage* was on the attack from the start, vigorously squeezing *Kialoa* from a safe leeward berth, gassing her with foul air until she was well astern, and winning by two minutes. But Kilroy got his revenge in the Sydney–Hobart race when the hard southerly, with squalls up to 45 k, hit the pair on the second day out while they were still battling within sight of each other in light following winds. Both crews were caught badly unprepared for the sudden wind change, but *Kialoa's* team stripped her rig down more quickly for the ensuing bash to windward, and held the lead for the next forty-five hours to cross the finishing line 2h 24m 57s ahead of *Windward Passage*.

'We out-sailed them and out-thought them,' said Kilroy in a terse summary. That race provided the ultimate triumph for Kilroy's yacht — not only her line-honours defeat of *Windward Passage* but also the Sydney–Hobart handicap double. When *Kialoa* had finished, the wind began to fade so that the speed of the lower handicapped yachts that were within striking distance to beat her (if the wind held) dropped to a crawl. As these rivals bled slowly to a mathematical death along the Tasmanian coast and in Storm Bay, excitement aboard the big white $A1.5-million ketch moored in Constitution Dock, Hobart, was not shown in undignified emotion but by icy calm. 'Real-life tycoons know how to keep their cool,' remarked one fascinated observer. Kilroy remained calm even when his crew reminded him that *Kialoa's* handicap win, although it could not shake New Zealand's Cup success, had clinched for him, as the culmination of his three-year international campaign, the official world's ocean racing championship. This title, set up by the American magazine *Yachting*, covers seven of the world's major events, including the Southern Cross final. But even though Kilroy raised no cheer at having reached this highest pinnacle of ocean racing success, there was no doubt that he was pleased. He broke into a broad grin. 'Let's drink to that,' he said.

In 1979 the free-sheet conditions that favoured the small boats in the Sydney–Hobart race (see Chapter 10) also enabled NSW's team to win the Southern Cross Cup. But they did it with nothing to spare. Until that final triple-points-scoring event in the four-race series, Britain's team seemed certain of victory. The British boat *Marionette* (Chris Dunning), 13.9 m, had placed fourth in the first 30 nm race; third in the 180 nm race and second in the following 30 nm race. Her team-mates *Yeoman XXI* (John Wooderson), 14 m, and *Blizzard* (Edward Juer), 15.6 m, had placed 9, 4, 10 and 2, 6, 5. With a points total of 350 they were 42 points ahead of Victoria and 63 points ahead of NSW, then in third place. The NSW team were all One Ton Cup class boats, all 11.3 m long and of modern concept: *Deception* (John Bleakley), with placings of 1, 11, 11; *Relentless* (Peter Hankin), 6, 9, 4, and *Diamond Cutter* (Alan Sweeney), 20, 15, 9. Victoria's team was bigger: *Sunburst* (Ron Young), 12.2 m, with placings of 10, 16, 14; *Moonshadow* (John Taylor), 12.7 m, with 8, 5, 8; and *Challenge* (Lou Abrahams), 14 m, with 3, 7, 1.

Some Sydney yachtsmen, disregarding the results of earlier trials that had clearly indicated the good form of the chosen One Tonners, gratuitously offered the NSW team selectors some advice. Selectors had been foolish, said the critics, to overlook proven bigger boats that would have balanced the NSW team and so matched the performances of the British in the medium and fresh winds of the first three races. The selectors replied with some asperity that NSW had been represented by so-called balanced teams of yachts to cover all weather conditions in four previous Southern Cross Cup contests, and all of those teams had been beaten. Their opinion this time, the selectors added, was that the three One Tonners would at least sail up to their ratings and not disgrace the NSW side whatever the conditions. And if in the Sydney–Hobart race they got moderate winds that would favour small to medium-sized craft, their placings would not be so scattered as those of a balanced team of big and smallish boats. And so it proved.

In the Sydney–Hobart race, *Relentless* placed first among the Cup boats; *Deception* was third, and *Diamond Cutter* eighth, giving the NSW team 270 more points for an overall total of 557. Britain's *Marionette* came in sixth among the Cup boats; *Yeoman XXI* was ninth and *Blizzard*, suffering like many other heavy boats in light and fluky wind patterns as she neared the finish, struggled in twentieth. The British score for the race was 201 for an overall total of 551. That put them in second place, six points behind NSW. Victoria's *Sunburst* placed eleventh, Challenge sixteenth, and *Moonshadow* failed to score when she was dismasted in Bass Strait. Victoria's overall total of 431 put that State in third place. Other points totals were WA, 391; New Zealand (Nth), 377; Ireland, 309; New Zealand (Sth), 306; Tasmania, 290; the USA, 265; SA, 237; Queensland, 202. So for the first time since 1969 the Southern Cross Cup was back in Australia and ocean racing officials, determined to keep it there, were talking about nominating, not only State teams for the next series in 1981, but also a national team chosen, as are our Admiral's Cup teams, from eligible yachts in all States.

Before the Southern Cross Cup series a 40 nm maxiboat challenge scratch race, ambitiously labelled Cock of the World (although many big American champions were not competing) was sailed off the Sydney coast. John Kahlbetzer's new and then untuned 23.2 m *Bumblebee 4* convincingly outpaced Bob Bell's visiting 23.5 m *Condor of Bermuda* by 5.38. It was a prelude to the caning *Bumblebee 4* 4 later gave the handsome mahogany giant and all other line-honours candidates in the Sydney–Hobart race. The maxi race was held in a hot 15 k to 12 k nor'westerly wind over a course laid close offshore to give spectators a view. After the first half hour, when it was obvious that Kahlbetzer, his sailing master Graeme Freeman and their big crew were increasingly confident of *Bumblebee 4*'s new 32.3 m mast (she had dropped her first spar of a similar size but with less strengthening, four months earlier), they began to drive the boat really hard and the race turned into a procession. Rolly Tasker's 22.9 m *Siska* finished 10.45 behind *Bumblebee 4*. Tony Fisher's new 20.1 m *Helsal II* was fourth over the line, followed by Bernard Lewis's converted 12-metre class *Gretel*, Josca Grubic's *Anaconda II*, and American Jake Wood's *Sorcery*. A handicap in conjunction went to *Gretel*, delighting her current owner who had spent a great deal of time and trouble restoring and refitting the yacht that in the America's Cup races of 1962 had fascinated millions with her performances.

In 1981, the slowest Sydney–Hobart race in twenty-nine years upset the calculations of many offshore enthusiasts. Only five of the 143 finishers in the then record fleet of 158 sailed the course in less than five days. Most took half a day more and a few, six days. On the Australian system of time-on-time handicapping this meant that the smallest, lowest rating boats, which had amassed generous time allowances, merely needed reasonably favourable winds in the final stage to take the major prizes. These they got, a rollicking northerly that swept them down the Tasmanian east coast, while the bigger boats ahead of them were struggling home in fluky calms, then a snorting sou'westerly change behind them up Storm Bay to the Derwent River finish.

So the NSW team of comparatively small boats which placed second, third and fourth among the Southern Cross Cup fleet of thirty-three (eleven teams of three) in the Sydney–Hobart race, after counting their triple points, amassed a total of 537 to Britain's 527 and Australia's 522. Next were Victoria, 507; Hong Kong, 401; New Zealand, 308; Tasmania, 260; WA, 242; SA, 210; Papua New Guinea, 205; Queensland, 172. After the first three races, two 30 nm Olympic style and 180 nm offshore, the NSW team — *Beach Inspector* (Graham Jones) 9.4 m, rating 22.5 ft, Half Ton class; *Smuggler* (Trevor Simpson, Bob Fraser skipper), 11.1 m, rating 27.4 ft, One Ton class; *Szechwan* (Jeremy Whitty) 11.9 m, rating 29.1 ft — had been in fourth place on 258 points, behind Australia on 333, from Britain, 314, and Victoria, 309. The Australian team — *Apollo V* (Alan Bond, John Bertrand skipper) 13.1 m, rating 32.9 ft; *Hitchhiker* (Peter Briggs, Noel Robins skipper) 12.3 m, rating 31.4 ft; *Ragamuffin* (Syd Fischer) 13.0 m, rating 33 ft — had only just returned from Britain as national representatives in the Admiral's Cup. Although they had not shone in that competition (equal seventh with Italy), their overall performances in the first three events of the Southern Cross Cup series appeared to have justified the opinions of those who had argued that the Admiral's Cup team should automatically go into the local equivalent of the British regatta. On the other hand, there were also many critics who had strongly argued against the choice of the little *Beach Inspector* for the

NSW team. But the chancy Sydney–Hobart race had once again demonstrated why it is so popular with those who believe in marine miracles. And the race also provided a double deal of ironic satisfaction to Sydney engineer Jim Dunstan, chairman of the selection panel that had chosen the NSW team. He had the pleasure of sailing his own little boat *Zeus II*, another half-tonner but not a Southern Cross Cup team contender, to an outright handicap win in the Sydney–Hobart race. It was only the second time in thirty-seven years that such a small boat (*Screw Loose* was the first in 1979) had won the event.

Most of the fifteen boats that failed to sail the course were early casualties who took a beating the first night out when light head winds turned into 40 k squalls. Out of the race even before it blew hard was Jack Rooklyn's Ben Lexcen-designed maxiboat *Apollo* which broke her boom in the first hour. Among the other retirees were Sir James Hardy's doughty *Police Car*, with a broken rigging spreader, and Jack Violet's *Ultra Violet*, with a navigator suffering from appendicitis. The biggest boats remaining — Bob Bell's *Condor of Bermuda*, Bernard Lewis's *Vengeance* (the former *Siska*), and *Helsal II* (renamed under charter to Fred Williams, *Of Our Town, Newcastle*) — duelled throughout the heavy weather and also during the light head winds and reaches that followed. *Vengeance* eventually outpaced them in the final stages by more than four hours.

Of course, the lottery-like end of the series did not particularly amuse British, NZ and Hong Kong visitors. The British, especially, argued that the range of ratings in the Southern Cross Cup was much too wide. It was ridiculous to allow vessels of up to 70 ft rating to compete against those down to 20.5 ft in a serious teams event, they said. The yachts could be on different parts of the course in completely different weather patterns from the rest of the fleet. The British themselves, in recognition of such inequalities, had narrowed the competition for the Admiral's Cup down to boats rating between 30 ft and 40 ft. If Australia wanted the Southern Cross Cup series to be accepted as an international grand prix regatta it should do the same. Australian officials, always mindful of chances to improve standards, agreed to consider the matter well before the next series. After all, when big boats did want to come, special events could be organized for them. For the record, the placings of the major teams in the four races of the series were as follows: NSW, *Beach Inspector* placed 13 over 30 nm, 18 over 30 nm, 29 over 180 nm and 2 over 630 nm; *Smuggler*, 2, 1, 10, 4, and *Szechwan*, 11, 3, 12, 3; for Britain, *Mayhem* (David May) 12.2 m, rating 30.2 ft, placed 9, 6, 14, 9; *Wee Willie Winkie* (Seamus Gallagher, Harold Cudmore skipper) 12.5 m, rating 30.3 ft, placed 10, 4, 5, 7 and *Yeoman XXIII* (Robin Aisher) 13.8 m, rating 33.8 ft, placed 3, 20, 2, 15; for Australia, *Apollo V* placed 8, 9, 3, 14; *Hitchhiker*, 5, 12, 1, 6; and *Ragamuffin*, 10, 15, 4, 19.

For 1983, the Australian organizers restricted the Southern Cross Cup competition to those boats rating between 30 ft and 40 ft under the International Offshore rules. To make the series even more like the Admiral's Cup, a third 30 nm race was also included, and all three round-the-buoys courses had offshore starts and finishes. In addition, for the first time no individual entrants were permitted in the short events. The changes provided high class tactical racing for nine teams, each of three yachts, and an impressive return to international form by New Zealand. Its squad of near identical Farr 40s, all rating One Ton Cup size under the new measurement rules, outclassed all rivals. New Zealand won with 531 points from NSW's 430, Hong Kong's 388, Papua New Guinea's 353, Australia's 350, Britain's 342, Victoria's 291, Tasmania's 191 and SA's 141.

The NZ boats and their placings were *Pacific Sundance* (Del Hogg, Bruce Morris owners, Peter Walker skipper), rating 30.5 ft, placed 3, 4, 1 (180 nm) 1, 1 (630 nm); *Geronimo* (Owen Champtaloup owner, Stu Brentnall skipper) rating 30.3 ft, placed 7, 9, 2, 13, 3; and *Exador* (Tom McCall owner, Ray Haslar skipper) 30.5 ft, placed 14, 19, 8, 22, 5. The NSW team and placings were *Bondi Tram* (Denis O'Neil owner, Iain Murray skipper) rating 31.6 ft, placed 6, 24, 7, 5, 8; *Hitchhiker* (Peter Briggs owner, Noel Robins skipper) rating 31.6 ft, placed 5, 3, 24, 9, 10; and *Indian Pacific* (Jack Eyles owner, Bob Fraser skipper) rating 30.3 ft, placed 11, 7, 15, 20, 2. The Hong Kong team and placings were: *The Frumious Bandersnatch* (Alan Burge) rating 33.2 ft, placed 24, 8, 9, 14, 16; *Bandido Bandido* (Andy Soriano and Peter Jolly owners, Tony Parsons skipper) rating 33.9 ft, placed 2, 21, 3, 2, 14; and *Highland Fling II* (Irvine Laidlaw owner, Harold Cudmore skipper) rating 30.9 ft, placed 16, 6, 20, 4, 11.

The first four races were sailed in slight seas with light east to east-north-east breezes that ranged from only 5 k to 12 k with rare draughts to 15 k. Even the Sydney–Hobart race, after a benign, free-sheet start in an easterly, the highest gusts reached only 30 k and those subsided for most of the fleet during the first thirty-six hours, giving way to moderate head winds and then following breezes and slow beats and drifts in Storm Bay. The conditions throughout the series generally suited the expertly crewed NZ One Tonners. Overall, they dominated the record Sydney–Hobart fleet of 173 starters (thirteen retired) in the early windward beats, although during some of the later stages they suffered in the light following airs and sloppy seas. Apart from their high triple-point-scoring places in the Southern Cross Cup squad they also placed with remarkable consistency in the overall fleet. *Pacific Sundance*, first in the Southern Cross competition, was fourth in the Sydney–Hobart race; *Geronimo* third (sixth), *Exador* fifth (seventh). The British team lost 48 points and dropped from third in team positions to sixth when *Panda* (13.1 m, rating 33.1 ft) was disqualified from the Sydney–Hobart race, in which she had finished thirteenth, for a port and starboard collision with Hong Kong's *The Frumious Bandersnatch* beating out of Sydney Heads shortly after the start. With her British team-mates *Jade* (12.12 m, rating 30.3 ft) and *Indulgence* (12.8 m rating 32.6 ft), *Panda* had sailed well in the round-the-buoys events. But they were all unhappy in the final race. *Jade* did a fruitless 10 nm losing tack to sea looking for a shift that never came and finished twenty-fourth (placing 104 in the overall fleet). In the late stages, *Indulgence* broke two spinnaker poles and poked a hole in her mainsail in a squall, and in one knockdown remained pinned on her side for two minutes. She recovered well to place twelfth (twenty-second). Highest point scorer for the Australian team was Peter Kurts' *Once More Dear Friends*, fourth among the Cup competitors in the Sydney–Hobart race and, with her age allowance, second overall. Cup results are based on straight IOR ratings with no age allowances.

The surprise and popular outright winner of the Sydney–Hobart race was Lou Abrahams' shrewdly sailed 14 m *Challenge* (rating 34 ft), a powerful American-designed and aluminium-hulled sloop and the first Victorian to take the main prize in the thirty-nine years' history of the event. She sailed right up to her proven form in the fresh windward conditions early and then, on three occasions – off Gabo Island before entering Bass Strait, off Eddystone Point on the Tasmanian north-east corner, and in the Derwent River on the way to the finish – got wind changes that suited her.

Left New Zealand's *Geronimo* (Owen Chamtaloup and Stu Brentnall), one of three almost identical Bruce Farr—designed One Tonners that outclassed the 1983 Southern Cross Cup field. (Shirley Cherry)

Right Bob Bell's magnificent maxi *Condor of Bermuda* soaring down the coast in 1982 to Hobart where she won the closest line honours finish (by 7s from Jack Rooklyn's 21.94 m *Apollo*) in the history of the ocean classic. (Australian Consolidated Press)

The sensation of the Sydney–Hobart race, though, was the incredibly close duel between the 24.38 m giants *Condor* (Bob Bell), from Bermuda, and American Marvin Green's *Nirvana*. They had earlier fought out four races of a specially arranged South Pacific Maxiboat Championship with two wins each but favouring *Nirvana*, because she came in first in the double-scoring 180-miler. The climax came in the last stages of the Sydney–Hobart race with *Nirvana's* disqualification. She had earlier been 3 nm astern of *Condor*, but had caught her in Storm Bay. They fought head-to-head all the way up the Derwent River towards the finish. In Opossum Bay, 6 nm from the line, they were still in combat, tack for tack. Then, with both on starboard tack, with sheets sprung, *Condor's* crew, to windward, 20 m off the beach and overlapping ahead, called for water. *Nirvana* was slow to respond, and, when she did swing away into deeper water, her radio antenna, secured to her pulpit on the starboard side, hit *Condor's* boom and broke. At the same time *Condor* ran aground on a submerged rock and stopped dead. The impact threw her helmsman Ted Turner, the famous America's Cup skipper, to the deck. *Condor's* crew of twenty swarmed into action. They immediately gybed the boat's mainsail on to the shore side, three men climbed out on to the end of the boom to pin it down and to try to make the boat heel, another gang set a spinnaker and others shoved with a spare spinnaker pole over the side against the rock. They got her off within 5.0 and sailed on, to cross the finishing line in 3d 00h 50m 29s, only 2.16 behind *Nirvana*. The next day in the protest room Turner, with the aid of video tapes of the incident, presented *Condor's* case. The jury disqualified *Nirvana* for failing to give *Condor* enough shore room under Rules 42-1a, 42-3a, 42-3f. It all made fine theatre and somewhat overshadowed the Southern Cross Cup news but, apart from the New Zealanders, that was something a lot of the contestants were anxious to forget.

The hazardous, scrambling start of the 1985 Sydney–Hobart race across a line much too short for the 178 yachts (detailed elsewhere), convinced many Southern Cross Cup sailors that in future they should compete separately from the rest of the mob.

Although many of the thirty-six boats racing in twelve teams of three in the international competition were hampered by the crush, only two, both in the Australian team, suffered unduly. The crew of Nick Girdis's *Marloo II*, unaware until she had sailed seven miles and was off Bondi that they had been recalled for breaking the start, lost three hours returning to recross. It made no difference to *Marloo II's* point score since she subsequently retired from the race. But Peter Kurts' *Drake's Prayer*, as explained earlier, severely penalized for her 'contact' a minute before the start, had her overall placing in the Sydney–Hobart handicap dropped from first to thirty-seventh. In the Southern Cross Cup, she went from first to eighth and the 269 points she lost cost the Australian team fourth place behind the British, New Zealand B, and NSW teams. This was because the rules of the Southern Cross Cup competition, unlike those for the Sydney–Hobart race, provided for boats to be elevated or relegated to placings in order to replace those lost by penalized boats. So, although *Sagacious* remained in her original second place in the Sydney–Hobart handicap, she was lifted to first place in the Southern Cross Cup competition and gained points for her NSW team when *Drake's Prayer* was relegated.

The final points scored, under a brand new system that some found unnecessarily complicated, were: UK 2, 210.93, NZ B team 1, 913.74, NSW 1, 907.28, NZ A team 1, 730.57, Australia 1, 518.08, Victoria 1, 498.07, WA 1, 403.30, Tasmania 1, 212.63, SA 888.98, Hong Kong 876.37, Queensland 808.18, Papua New Guinea 793.64.

The British team of three smart, superbly handled One Tonners deserved their win. They had a series of consistently good placings throughout, except for one clanger in the first short race and one forced retirement (through severe hull damage) in the Sydney–Hobart finale. They had established a tremendous points advantage with a magnificent first, second and third in the 170 nm treble-scoring race, sailed off the NSW coast in a series of 10 k breezes, mainly from the north-west, and slight seas. The British boats and their placings (race distances bracketed) were: *Highland Fling* (Irvine Laidlaw — Harold Cudmore skipper) 32 (24 nm race), 7 (24 nm), 1 (170 nm), 3 (24 nm), 7 (630 nm); *Cifraline III* (Chris Griffiths) 6, 3, 3, 8, 10; *Panda* (Peter Whipp) 8, 4, 2, 21, retired. New Zealand B team was: *Mad Max* (Chris Beckett) 1, 1, 6, 1, 11; *Thunderbird* (Don St Clair Brown) 2, 9, 12, 2, 16; *Barn Storm* (John Hall) 25, 15, 27, 29, 27. NSW Team was: *Sagacious* (Gary Appleby) 7, 21, 8, 12, 1; *Another Concubine* (John Parker — Bob Fraser skipper) 21, 13, 7, 13, 9; *Paladin* (Col Franklin) 16, 28, 24, 10, 6.

As can be seen from an examination of those placings, the NZ B team was badly let down by the consistently dreadful performances of *Barn Storm*, a Peterson-designed 42, rating 32.3, that her crew never seemed to be able to get to her feet. But the team was sustained by the dazzling form of *Mad Max*, a new syndicate-owned Davidson One Tonner that romped up and down the tracks in all weathers and outscored every other boat in the competition. A refreshing overview of the series came from a statement by Irvine Laidlaw, the British owner of *Highland Fling*, which got to the line in Hobart cracked in a number of places and shored up with pieces of her floorboards and cut-up sections of a spinnaker pole. Like many others in the fleet she had fallen through some hollow-backed waves and had come out much the worse for wear. 'These boats are great to sail,' said Laidlaw, 'but they are inshore boats, not offshore boats. They're in the forefront of technology where one always has problems. It's only by having problems that designers and builders will learn. The next generation of boats won't have these problems.' No doubt other owners and skippers aboard the thirty-three boats in the Sydney–Hobart race that were forced to cry quits in the 40 k southerly, found comfort in that philosophy. Sir James Hardy, chief helmsman in Nick Girdis's *Marloo II*, a wholesome scorer for the Australian team until she dropped through a void and broke three main frames for'ard of the mast, took a more personal view. Sir James said: 'This is the third of four Hobarts I've had to pull out of. Maybe God is trying to tell me something.'

In retrospect, there were a few grizzles that the new point-scoring system must be flawed if it allowed the Brits to win when one of its boats failed to finish in the high-scoring (quintuple points) Sydney–Hobart race. In fact, use of any of the scoring systems, old or new, Australian, British or American, would still have given them the trophy.

16

Level Rating and the Ton Classes

OCEAN RACING, traditionally between yachts of varying rig and size, is rightly called a numbers game. No matter how well a yacht is sailed, two factors govern its success or failure. One is its rating, established according to length, breadth, depth, displacement, sail area, and type, within a complicated formula. The other is the system of handicapping that is applied to the rating in order theoretically to give each vessel as near as possible an equitable chance against all comers of achieving the lowest (and therefore winning) corrected time.

Rating is therefore a challenge to the ingenuity of designers, who try to improve a yacht's performance by taking advantage of loopholes within the now-internationally accepted, though often altered, measurement rules. Handicapping is a desperate exercise of judgement (after research into performances of a variety of craft) by which officials try to catch up with the rule-beaters and give each yacht a pre-determined time allowance to suit all conditions of wind and sea in races of varying distances.

No rating or handicapping system has yet been found that is entirely satisfactory, although some of the world's best mathematicians, recently using computers, have applied themselves to the problems for half a century. Under the original, but since modified, European (Royal Ocean Racing Club) system of straight-out Time-on-Time Correction Factor — based on a formula that incorporates rating, by the time it took that yacht to sail the course, regardless of distance — big yachts were favoured in fast, usually heavy-weather races (because they sailed at top hull speed and gave away less time) and small yachts were favoured in slow, usually light-weather races (because they did not sail so much slower than big yachts in such conditions, and the longer the race lasted the more time they gained).

Under the Cruising Club of America's original but now modified Time-on-Distance system — pre-race multiplication of each yacht's special Distance

Top To France and back again: Australia's *Impetuous* bursts free from the Solent in the Channel race for the 1979 Admiral's Cup. (Adrian Herbert)

Bottom *Police Car*'s downwind speed on the Solent left many rivals standing and lifted Australia's score in the 1979 Admiral's Cup. (Adrian Herbert)

Top Kite shy and 14 k on the clock. Jack Rooklyn's *Ballyhoo* winning the 1975 Battle of the Giants off Sydney Heads. (Ian Cherry)

Bottom Australia's Quarter Ton Cup champion *Seaflyer*, finished third in a rough world title series in; Japan. After changes in the rating rules she became a JOG racer. (Soehata-Cemac)

Correction Factor against the number of nautical miles to be sailed in a particular race — big vessels usually did better in slow to medium-speed races, in light to moderate conditions of wind and sea; and small ones did better in fast races. This situation seemed to arise mainly because most American races of reasonable distance were sailed over courses in which the prevailing winds were abeam or astern, whereas European (and Australian) courses had a fair mixture of head winds.

Gradually, because of the weakness of handicapping systems, the emphasis worldwide came to be placed less on finding an overall winner of a race between big, medium and small yachts, and more on winners of different divisions between yachts of approximately the same rating, and it has continued that way. In some major races these days no overall winner is announced, although inescapably comparisons are made between the corrected finishing times of craft of different divisions.

Introduction in 1969 of a universal International Offshore Rule of rating was at first believed likely to restore the balance between the performances of yachts of different sizes (ratings), and to close many of the loopholes that designers had previously exploited. It was a vain hope. In spite of a patch-work of

The enormous (600 mm wide) but elegant One Ton Cup was originally nick-named for a class of boat but eventually had a class of boat named after it. (Bob Rice)

369

amendments (in 1977, IOR Mark III (a) ratings were in operation, and the rule book had grown from a pamphlet in the early RORC and CCA days to a sizeable volume) the system has been denounced in many quarters — unfairly, say the hardworking administrators — as a signal failure. Not only have designers still found margins within the limitations by which they can gain advantage, but also they have exploited it by using new lightweight materials and styles of construction that give yachts greater sail areas for displacement and therefore greater potential performance.

With straight faces, designers, naturally demanding high fees for their esoteric labours, have announced that no one should stand in the face of progress, and that offshore racing by its very nature is a development sport. Some of the yachts they have created have been a delight to sail, exciting upwind and down, others have been brutes of boats, hard to handle, uncomfortable, often dangerous, and not necessarily faster than their predecessors — but they have rated low and won the prizes.

Unsatisfactory, too, have been some attempts to devise handicaps to suit the new rating rules. Scales, based on time and distance and whether a race was sailed fast, slow, or at a medium pace, with factors for what was considered theoretically the potential performance of a given yacht according to its rating, were applied and rejected. Australian clubs, led by our premier ocean racing body, the Cruising Yacht Club of Australia, pioneered special allowances for age of design in earnest attempts to help owners of yachts disadvantaged by constantly changing rating systems and those whose boats were slower by comparison with stripped-out machines that had slipped under the rule makers' guard. Age allowances have helped, but they have not been entirely sufficient, with a few notable exceptions, to make older yachts, no matter how modern their equipment, or how well handled, thoroughly competitive against the newcomers. So year after year the Offshore Racing Council solemnly meets in international congress, announces its intention of encouraging ocean racing in true seagoing, cruising-type yachts (as the founders of the sport so positively intended), and sews on a few more patches — and the designers try to shoot holes through them, and the handicappers despair.

Of course, it is obvious that the only solution for completely equitable ocean racing is to eliminate handicaps altogether, and to have all yachts (in different categories) of the same rigid one-design classes, restricted to the same rigs, sails and equipment, just as are many smooth-water, round-the-buoys keel boats and dinghies. Then, theoretically, competition between such groups of ocean racers would be a test solely of the skill of the men aboard, and not of the machines. But that would mean that yachts of even slightly differing rig, construction, and rating could no longer compete together, and that would destroy the traditional concept of matching different types against each other. It would also make obsolete for racing all the thousands of fine craft, with many years of life remaining to them, that have cost billions of dollars. This would be a disaster indeed that their owners would not tolerate.

So the only rational solution is to continue to darn up the elbows of the present rating system, and for handicappers to puzzle over methods of applying checks and balances to give all who want to race a tolerable chance. For those who don't want handicaps there are always level rating races, if they are willing to change their boats, like their clothes, when they become unfashionable. Until yachtsmen lost their innocence about the ability of the IOR rule makers to work out equitable, foolproof ratings that designers could not blast apart, level rating was for a few years hailed as the acme of competitive sailing offshore. It started in 1965, with the One Ton Cup class.

The name of this modern class of ocean racing yacht and its offshoots (Two Ton, Three-quarter Ton, Half Ton, Quarter Ton, and Mini Ton) are misleading. The basic name was inherited in 1965 along with the historic trophy called the One Ton Cup, which the French that year re-dedicated for world championship racing in offshore vessels that rated 22 ft under the then extant Royal Ocean Racing Club's rules of measurement. These sloops at that time were about 11 m in overall length, and nearer to seven tons than one ton in displacement. But confusion caused by the name seems worthwhile, considering the trophy. It is a magnificent object, as big as a baby's bath-tub, and an elaborate Art Nouveau creation by the nineteenth century goldsmith, Linzeler. He moulded and carved it with overlaid patterns of water-lilies from a 10 kg block of silver. It is correctly called the *Coup Internationale du Cercle de la Voile de Paris*. In 1898, the group of French yachting enthusiasts who had commissioned Linzeler to make the trophy had presented it to the *Cercle de la Voile de Paris* as the perpetual prize for annual international challenge races between craft then considered the *dernier cri* of sailing elegance — the slim, smooth-water sloops that conformed to what was called the One Ton rule. Soon, instead of calling the trophy by its proper French name, English yachtsmen nicknamed it the One Ton Cup. Such a barbarity at first scandalized the French, normally resistant to Anglicizing anything Gallic, but in time they came to think of it as chic, and called it the One Ton Cup themselves. The first six contests were sailed off Meulan, at the mouth of the River Seine, France, and off Cowes, England, and the social activities that went with the sailing began to rate among the most exclusive events of the sporting season.

Then, in 1907, with the introduction of the daring new International Metre Rules of yacht measurement, the French decided to change the One Ton Cup to a trophy for racing in the prestigious 6-metre class. These yachts were at that stage toys for princes, fast, high-winded sloops, averaging 11 m overall, beautifully built and equipped, half-sized replicas of the powerful racing machines of the 12-metre class today used for the America's Cup contests. The One Ton Cup remained the top trophy for international 6-metre challenge races for fifty-five years. Seven nations held it at different times and fiercely defended it on their home courses. Sweden won thirteen times; Britain, twelve; France, nine; Norway, five; Germany, four; Switzerland, four; Holland, twice; and the USA, twice.

But by 1962, democracy had invaded the waterways, and many of the *arrivistes*, conscious of the social status that had traditionally surrounded the 6s, found reason to resent them. They were seen as yachting anachronisms, too expensive in comparison with craft of the same size and speed, and soon they were on the wane. (Six Metres have since enjoyed a renaissance, largely because of the efforts of an Australian yachting enthusiast, John Taylor, of Sydney. See Chapter 6.) For three years until 1965, racing for the One Ton Cup lapsed. Then the *Cercle de la Voile de Paris* (one of whose members had won the trophy in 1960 and had successfully defended it at Cannes in 1961 and Palma de Mallorca in 1962) graciously offered it as the symbol of world supremacy in a new breed of 22 ft rating offshore racing-cruisers that was growing in popularity. This time, instead of calling the trophy after the type of yacht that was to race for it, everyone happily reversed the process and called the yacht after the trophy — the One Ton Cup class.

The first world title races for the One Ton Cup in the new One Ton Cup class yachts were held in France in 1965 and attracted a jet-set fleet. The yachts seemed reasonably well matched; none was of extremely different design or rig, and the results were believed to reflect more the ability of helmsmen and crews over the series of five races in which the championships were contested than any inherent speed in the craft themselves. Yacht owners in a dozen countries, Australia included, with a thirst for even competition without handicaps, commissioned new One Tonners, and soon they were racing off the mark in special divisions in club, State and national events. There were noticeable developments in shapes and styles in the next four years as rival designers sought advantage, but these were as nothing compared with those that followed the introduction of the brand-new IOR Rules in 1969. These new measurement rules established the One Ton Cup class at the 27.5 ft rating. At first the yachts built to suit the rating were of approximately the same size overall, as previously, but before long designers saw that they now had great freedom of choice in the balance between hull form, displacement, rig, and construction, and they exploited these concessions to the limit. One Tonners became the top development class, a platform for experiment in engineering principles, for refinement of equipment, and a bonanza for those who could devise craft to suit special conditions, no matter how demanding the finished products might be on the men who had to sail them. In eight years, One Tonners changed from the RORC originals that had been robust craft of wood, steel, aluminium, and fibreglass construction, into flimsy throwaways — and their costs soared. So did those of the Three-quarter Ton Cup class, with a rating of 24.5 ft; Half Ton, 21.7 ft; Quarter Ton, 18 ft; and, to a lesser extent, Two Ton, 32 ft.

But offshore yachtsmen, dazzled by the idea of level rating, accepted the changes and the price increases, encouraged the designers to go to the wildest extremes, and discarded yachts that had become uncompetitive against the newcomers. Only those who could not afford new yachts clung to their faith in the Offshore Racing Council's ability to close the gaps in the rules. Australian and NZ yachtsmen fitted into both categories, and inevitably most were disillusioned. They have sunk millions of dollars into Two, One, Three-quarter, Half, and Quarter Ton fleets for level rating races in club, State, and national championships, but, by the late 1970s, few of their yachts remained competitive by international standards against the latest of the same classes. Worse still, because of rule changes, many of these costly boats could no longer even rate in the classes for which they were designed unless they underwent radical alterations or reductions in sail area that would have further reduced their competitive capacity.

Of course, there are some owners with enough ambition, money, or commercial sponsorship who can still afford to reach for the stars with brand-new boats, but not many. One of the most significant reactions to level rating came from the Cruising Yacht Club of Australia, which had done more than any other organization in the country to foster that branch of the sport, and which, in 1974 and 1975, held the world's first combined national championship regattas for five of the Ton classes — Two, One, Three-quarter, Half, and Quarter types before passing them over to other States. 'Our interest in level rating development as it stands at present is minimal,' said CYC Rear Commodore Gordon Marshall, who is also one of the Australian Yachting Federation's senior national offshore measurers. 'Level rating design has led to some craft so frail and of such types that we do not consider them suitable for true offshore competition. We have declined to organize championship regattas for such yachts.' That opinion, like so many others on ocean racing that have originated in Australia, by late 1979 was being echoed in many countries. Still it had been fun while it lasted.

To 1985, Australia had scored world championships in Two Ton, One Ton, Half Ton and Quarter Ton classes and worthy placings in other international level rating series, although our record cannot now compare with that of New Zealand, with three world titles in One Tonners, three in the Half Ton class and two in the Quarter Ton class. New Zealand brought the One Ton Cup to the Southern Hemisphere in 1969 when the vigorous Auckland sailmaker, Chris Bouzaid, and a superbly drilled young crew, sailing *Rainbow II*, defeated twelve yachts from eight nations at Heligoland (Germany). A year earlier *Rainbow II* had been runner-up to Germany's *Optimist* and had beaten eighteen other One Tonners from eleven countries. New Zealand's first defence of the Cup was in 1971, when Australian skipper Syd Fischer sailed the 11.3 m *Stormy Petrel* across the Tasman as our main challenger. He had with him Graham Newland, Hugh Treharne, Peter O'Donnell, Ian Treharne, and Butch Dalrymple-Smith, the first three champion helmsmen in their own right, and the others outstanding deckhands of vast experience. They stunned the New Zealanders (who had built a fleet of new yachts), and challenging helmsmen from Germany, Hong Kong, Italy, Sweden, Switzerland, Canada, and Great Britain, and Australia's two other contenders, *Maria* (Des Cooper) of Hobart and *Warri* (Bill Hart) of Sydney, by decisively winning the five-race point score series. Three races were sailed over 27.5 nm, near Auckland, and one each over 150 and 270 nm into the fringe of the Pacific Ocean. *Stormy Petrel* had not seemed impressive when first launched for another owner earlier that season, but Newland, an engineer and a professional yacht doctor adept at operations that gained advantages under the rating rules, had persuaded Fischer to charter her. At Newland's suggestion, they increased her ballast and her rig and fitted her with new sails that Treharne had designed and made for NZ conditions.

Stormy Petrel remained, according to Fischer and his crew, 'a bitch of a boat' to steer, but her extra weight and taller, more powerful rig carried her through the light to moderate winds and lumpy seas in which most of the races were sailed. The over-confident New Zealanders — they fielded three boats — also indulged in some savage in-fighting among themselves instead of covering their rivals, resulting in the disqualification of Bouzaid's new *Wai-Aniwa* for a technical breach. This made Fischer's job easier. NZ newspapers, describing the regatta as the golden era of that country's sporting history, went yacht crazy, before and during the series, bewildering many of their non-sailing readers with tack-for-tack descriptions of the preliminary defence trials and the championship races. By the time Bouzaid was disqualified and a photograph of a papier mâché model was published depicting one of Bouzaid's former crewmen from *Rainbow II*, by then a rival skipper, poking him in the eye while Fischer stood grinning in the background, it seemed that even lubbers might have begun to understand what yacht fighting is all about.

Australia was called on to defend the One Ton Cup off Sydney in 1972 against nine countries, and almost succeeded in the closest series sailed until then, or

Australia's *Stormy Petrel*, world champion in the One Ton Cup class but 'a bitch of a boat to steer' according to skipper Syd Fischer and his crew. (SMH)

since. In the fifth and final race of 27 nm, four yachts had a chance with Graham Evans's *Pilgrim*, of Sydney, helmed by Jim Burke, narrow points leader. *Pilgrim* needed only to finish sixth, but Burke made the mistake of failing to cover a rival (the USA's *Bushwhacker*) in a dying breeze over the last two miles, and crossed in seventh place. Bouzaid's *Wai-Aniwa*, which crept in fourth in that race, scored a total of 74.5 points to *Pilgrim's* 73.87, and the Kiwis had the Cup again. The bad luck story of that series belonged to Germany's *Ydra* (steered by Hans Beilken, a dual cup winner in 1967-68), an almost flat-bottomed, aluminium fin-keeler. *Ydra* had to get only tenth place in the longest, 270 nm race to clinch the series. But she carried away a forestay rigging crew, was forced to retire, and finished a close fourth overall.

That 1972 series marked the beginning of a new era in One Ton Cup racing, indeed in level rating races of all classes. The pleasure of sailing a moderate boat well was scorned: winning was everything. Designers responded to demands (and in many cases created them) for faster boats within the rating rules; officials tried to close the gaps with other rules; designers, with the resources of a vastly increased technology, out-thought the rule-makers; and officials tried again. Owners, caught in these continuing thaws and freezes, leapt from crisis to crisis like penguins on an ice floe, their tattered cheque books flapping.

At first, Australian helmsmen and crews, fancying that they had a chance with new yachts built to suit recent rule changes, went overseas for world titles with high hopes. Regularly they came back chastened. Their main rivals seemed always one jump ahead of them in design and equipment, with yachts produced to suit the particular venue of the championship regatta, crewed by expert works teams willing to wring the last ounce out of throwaway boats in order to advertise the skills of their backers. Bruce Cameron and later Peter Hill, of Sydney, with *Wathara* and *Maria Van Dieman*, had learned that lesson early; so did Hedley Calvert, of Tasmania, with his handsome One Tonner, *Huon Chief*. Sydney's grimly competitive Syd Fischer tried a different tack by chartering a European boat, allegedly of the latest design, but found that he was outmatched. Australian sailors were not the only ones to suffer. Ninety per cent of all competitors in the One Ton title races had no chance against the crack boats. They were like amateur drivers of rally cars trying to race against Formula One machines, with aces behind the wheel, backed by pit crews and unlimited resources.

In 1977, Victorian Tom Stephenson seemed to have a chance of beating the game when he took the US-designed, lightweight, laminated timber *B195*, a centreboarder seemingly the last word in sophistication, to New Zealand for the One Ton Cup championship. *B195* got her enigmatic name (after her sail number) when officials of the Cruising Yacht Club rejected her chosen title, *Pioneer Sound* because it directly advertised the commercial firm that had sponsored her. NZ officials were not so squeamish about the names of three of the radical featherweight centreboarders (all creations by Auckland's *enfant terrible* of yacht design, Bruce Farr) that sailed for their country. They were called *The Red lion, Mr Jumpa*, and *Smir Noff Agen*. No one suffered too much intellectual strain identifying them as representing a brewery, a knitwear manufacturer, and a brand of vodka. Farr had taken these boats to the limit of the rules, knowing that they would just qualify for the title series before impending changes in the rating system. Their construction was so light that they seemed to some traditionalists in imminent danger of falling apart. But they were extraordinarily fast upwind and down, and were crewed by fearless sailors who drove them in gales and calms to fill all the major places in the series. In heavy weather, with their centreboards up, they out-planed *B195*, herself rocketing along at 19 knots. The Australian boat came in fourth behind the three weirdos, condemned to obsolescence as soon as the IOR officials caught up with them. But they served their purpose — the One Ton Cup was back in Auckland.

In the Two Ton Cup class world championships of 1981, then for yachts rating 32 ft, Australia had a heartening success with West Australian Peter Briggs' *Hitchhiker*, skippered by Noel Robins. The series was sailed off Porto Cervo, Sardinia, headquarters of Italy's luxurious Costa Smeralda Yacht Club. The win encouraged a number of owners to consider building similar boats, until the

Left High speed lightweight flyer *B195* won the Australian One Ton Cup with Tom Stephenson as skipper but was unable to plane downhill with Kiwi centreboarders in the 1977 world series. (Bob Ross)

Right Irishman Harold Cudmore's unlucky *Silver Shamrock* seemed set to win the world's Half Ton title off Sydney in 1977 until her mast collapsed near the finish of a vital race. She lost by one point. (Bob Ross)

international rule makers decided the Two Ton Cup class was no longer viable and also that the rating for the One Ton Cup class needed another boost. So they dropped the Two Ton Cup class altogether and changed the rating for the One Ton Cup class from 27.5 ft to 30.5 ft. At one stroke they had rendered all previous One Tonners and Two Tonners obsolete as international level rating class competitors. A compelling argument in favour of the new 30.5 ft rating for the One Ton Cup class was that, apart from level rating competitions, it was within the 30–40 ft rating range allowed in most of the world's major international offshore competitions, including the Admiral's Cup. That certainly inspired many owners to build new One Tonners to suit the new rating rule. Generally they were lightweight machines, engineered to the most advanced technology and designed to screw the last decimal point out of the current interpretations of the measurement rules. Most had pencil-thin spars and the latest in hydraulics and deck hardware. They also needed helmsmen of a high order of excellence to keep them moving at their best upwind and downwind, and squads of skilled and dedicated crewmen to handle them. The new boats dominated the world One Ton Cup class title series of 1985, held around Olympic triangles and offshore at Poole, England. And although some lost their rigs and suffered other breakdowns when the weather was heavy, they also dominated the following Admiral's Cup series off the south coast of England. Australia's newest One Ton Cup class boat, *Intrigue*, skippered by her owner, Don Calvert, of Tasmania, was an excellent all-rounder. But in soft conditions she was a little too robust to hold some of the lightly rigged, highly tuned opposition in the One Ton Cup series, and her crew, at the start of the series, also lacked experience at such a keen level of competition. *Intrigue* was placed twenty-seventh in the fleet of thirty-eight, having missed the triple-point-scoring long race in order to make alterations. These helped her to place tenth against all comers in the Admiral's Cup the following week. Peter Briggs' new *Hitchhiker II* placed twenty-second in the One Ton Cup series. Another Australian-owned boat, *Sudpack*, a good two-year-old German design, skippered by Leslie Green, could do no better than thirty-third.

New Zealand first clinched the Half Ton Cup, in late 1977, with a centreboarder of Farr's design — *Gunboat Rangariri*, owned and skippered by Peter Wilcox, an Auckland medical practitioner with a zest for high competition — after a controversial series sailed off Sydney. Officials had imposed stiff tests of stability, pinpoint examination of the rules and physical and computer checks of all the yachts' measurement certificates before the racing. Australia had earned the right to conduct the Half Ton championship largely because the Victorian Tom Stephenson (skipper of the Melbourne One Tonner *B195*) with Sydney's Hugh Treharne as co-helmsman-tactician, and with an excellent Melbourne crew, had won the title in the chartered US boat, *Foxy Lady*, in Chicago in 1975. Stephenson and Treharne, as reigning champions, had also competed in 1976 off Trieste (Italy) with almost the same crew as before, and had finished fifth, using another chartered boat. The winner that year had been Irishman Harold Cudmore, a whimsical young man with a wild mop of Cupid curls and a quiverful of tricks to match. Cudmore had sailed *Silver Shamrock*, an exact sister-ship in hull design by USA's Doug Peterson to Stephenson's boat. But the Irishman, knowing how light the winds would be off Trieste (they rarely got to 12 k and were usually 6 k with a mirror-smooth sea), had taken 150 kg of lead out of his boat's ballast keel just before the series and slightly increased her rig. It gave him just enough advantage in speed to outsail a big fleet, and provided another demonstration, if any were now needed, that only by squeezing the last ounce out of the rules could anyone hope to win. Earlier, Australians who had gone overseas with our best Half Tonners — fine, well-sailed, robust boats like Tig Thomas's *Plum Crazy*, from Sydney, and Alan Nicol's much lighter *Bodega*, from Perth — had been convincingly outclassed. So, by 1977, everyone was aware of the need for lightweights in the Sydney Half Ton series, and a fleet of new yachts was built and tuned for the races. Crews drilled for months beforehand. The locals were hoping for honest winds, typical of Sydney, at least one heavy blow, and good testing seas. They got nothing above 20 k in gusts, mostly gentle draughts of 8–10 k, and a preponderance of flat water. Those who had guessed that centreboarders would do best were right. It was the first time such vessels had sailed for the Half Ton Cup title, but in the fleet of twenty-two all the winners, of all five races, all the major place-getters, and all the final top six point-scorers were centreboarders. Cudmore's new *Silver Shamrock*, of US design, seemed the best of them until her fragile mast fell down on the final run a quarter of a mile from the finish of a vital race, and she drifted across the line. Her resourceful crew held out the sails to catch enough breeze for steerage way, and so she lost only one place. But that place was lost to *Gunboat Rangariri* and this was enough to give that NZ boat the one point by which she took the title. Cudmore also suffered through queer windshifts and by a decision of race officials who rejected his protest that they had prejudiced his chances by incorrectly moving a rounding mark.

The Irishman took his defeat philosophically, which was more than many of his rivals could bring themselves to do. Moreover, one owner, who had spent $40,000 on a new Half Tonner and now found that it was to lose its rating when another spate of rule changes came into effect before the next title series, expressed an opinion later voiced by many in the same predicament, 'If this damn boat were strong enough I'd fit accommodation into it for holiday camping and rig it for cruising,' he said. 'But it isn't, so I'll sell it for half its price if I can find someone who wants a club handicapper. To hell with level rating!'

Still, sponsors had not completely deserted the stage, and in October–November 1978 skipper Hugh Treharne and a smart Sydney crew sailed *Seaflyer* (first called *Seaply* to advertise the plywood manufacturing firm that financed her, but threatened with disqualification unless the name were changed) as Australia's first contender for the world Quarter Ton Cup championship in a heavy weather five-race series off Yokosuka, Japan. *Seaflyer* finished a close third to two Japanese boats in a strong fleet that included representatives from New Zealand, England, West Germany, and Hong Kong. A third of the fleet, with crews gambling on light conditions, fell apart in the boisterous seas, two capsized and one sank. They raced under measurement rules then in force in the northern hemisphere at the time of their entry, allowing them to rate within the Quarter Ton Cup class limit of 18 ft. Immediately after the contest, the latest IOR rule changes brought the ratings of most of the fleet to 19 ft or more, therefore making them obsolete as class boats. They got little relief when the Quarter Ton limit was raised from 18 ft to 18.5 ft rating along with an increase from 21.7 ft to 22 ft for Half Tonners. Mini Tonners were established at 16.5 ft rating.

In 1982 the world's Quarter Ton Cup class championship was allocated to Australia, to be run by the Royal Yacht Club of Victoria on Port Phillip. But this aroused so little enthusiasm among overseas sailors that no one came to contest the title. Versatile Sydney helmsman, Graham Jones, equally at home around-the-buoys in smooth water as offshore, took his English-designed downwind flyer, *Quartermaster*, and a smart crew to Melbourne and won a somewhat lopsided contest against a small fleet of local boats.

In 1985 an Australian crew sailing the French-designed *Comte de Flandre*, with Ross Lloyd, of Melbourne, as skipper had scored placings of 1, 2, 1, 2 in the Quarter Ton championship off Ajaccio, Corsica, and seemed certain to take the series. They were leading in the final race in a 45 k gale when they were dismasted and lost enough points to place them fourth. The series went to South African Geoff Meek, who gained the winning points when he protested the committee for failing to have a mark of the course laid in time for him to round it. In Australian eyes that result seemed a fitting comment on the Level Rating circus.

17

JOG:
An Alternative

By 1979, an alternative to the overall ocean rating tangle that had robbed many fine yachts of their internationally competitive status or had converted them into mere club handicappers was emerging, at least for the small fry. Why not put a brave face on it and accept, as truly important, a branch of ocean racing that for years had struggled for proper recognition in some Australian States — Junior Offshore Group sailing? All one had to do was ignore the connotation of 'Junior' as something less than equal to the best and regard the acronym JOG as an accolade for worthy competition in tough little seagoing ships. The English had done it successfully since the late 1950s.

The great benefit of such competition was that the existing JOG rules ignored the limitations of rating (although the boats were handicapped under modified IOR rules of measurement) and allowed craft with waterline lengths between 5.5 m and 7.3 m to qualify for races offshore. This meant that most Quarter and Half Tonners, even those that still 'measured' under the level rating rules, were eligible and, more significantly, that it included also many of the stock boats of various designs that had flooded the market. All these had to do was to pass formal stability tests and conform with the Ocean Racing Council's generally accepted formula for seaworthiness and safety equipment. And provided that they raced on outside courses that took them no further than 25 nm from the starting lines and kept them reasonably close to shore, they did not need to be loaded with inconvenient and expensive life-rafts and two-way radios. The longest distance of any race would be 90 nm, which the fleet could normally cover within twenty-four to thirty hours. Crews of only three were required to man each boat and, with current allowances for the age of a design, even an old boat could have a reasonable chance, provided she was well equipped and competently handled. With careful administration by State and national bodies it seemed an ideal way to sustain interest and to preserve a spirit of

Few keel yachts in recent years have enjoyed the worldwide popularity of the US-designed J24 class, 7.31 m, a speedy racer-cruiser, decked and with the lively responses of a dinghy. John Lockeridge of Sydney won the national JOG title in a J24 in 1982 and was runner-up in 1983 but new stability rules forced the boats to carry extra ballast. (The Sailing Centre, The Spit, Sydney)

competition so essential to the future of the sport.

Still, there were some problems, as officials in Victoria and Queensland, where JOG racing was firmly established, and to a lesser extent in NSW, had already had demonstrated to them. The inaugural JOG national title series in 1978, sailed off Mooloolaba, Queensland, had underscored problem number one: How did one deal with an inherently fast class of stock boat that, more by accident than design, rated extraordinarily well under the JOG measurement rules? Problem number two: What scale should be applied to a very good old boat that gained an inordinate time bonus for the age of its design? Both of these nemeses had appeared in the shape of *Longshot*, an Olympic Soling class smooth-water racing machine. She had been cleverly converted for outside racing, with raised topsides, an enclosed cabin and a watertight cockpit, and re-rigged to conform with the offshore rules. Before she went to Queensland, *Longshot*, with her Victorian owner-skipper-rebuilder, Ken Wilson, and a smart crew, had made mincemeat of all comers in JOG title races in her home State. She proceeded to do the same in the national series. *Longshot* clearly won four of the five races over distances between 20 nm and 50 nm in light, medium and heavy winds, and was certain of at least second place in the main race of 80 nm, until that event ended in confusion and was abandoned when no one could find a critical rounding mark.

Among the thirty-four boats *Longshot* outclassed were the former national Quarter Ton champion *Locomotion*, of Brisbane, that for two years had dominated JOG racing in Queensland; a new US-designed Quarter Tonner in the charge of former world Half Ton champion skipper Tom Stephenson, of Victoria; and many highly fancied craft of proven design representing NSW, Queensland and Tasmania. A protest that claimed the alterations to *Longshot*'s superstructure should have disqualified her for the design-age allowance of twelve years that had been conceded to her was upheld in principle but not applied to the results of the series and was set aside for consideration by the Australian JOG Association.

By early 1979 officials thought that they had closed the gaps on the extent to which alterations should be allowed to influence design-age allowances, and confidently called for entries in the national JOG championships set down for Port Phillip, Victoria. This time there was a fleet of forty-one boats. They included the Australian Quarter Ton champion *Seaflyer*; a new US-designed J24 and a dozen other different types of stock boats – Endeavour 24s and 26s, Holland 25s, Waarships, Seaway 25s, Farr 727s, Admiral 21s, Cole 23s, Boomerang 20s, Supersonic 26s and Bonbridge 215s. In addition there were rated Half Tonners and other one-off designs. The rake in the grass that rose to smack them all across the chops was an ancient plywood 'boxy' design, a Thunderbird class 7.9 m boat. She was called *Royalist* and had been designed in the late 1940s and converted by her Victorian owner-skipper Frank Joel with a modified cockpit and an Etchells 22 mast to suit the ocean racing rules.

Royalist didn't win any of the races in the series of five, but she placed consistently high in a variety of winds and conditions of what passes for a seaway on Port Phillip, and clinched the title on points. And that elusive Soling, *Longshot*, still a go-boat, although pruned of some of her age allowance, finished second. Some of the races were astonishingly close, considering the broad range of craft that differed so much in size, design, construction and age. In one race only a minute separated the first eighteen boats on corrected time. Officials might justifiably have felt that the JOG system of handicapping had provided racing close enough to satisfy anyone. But there were grumbles from those who felt ill served and, like the gurus of the IOR council, the JOG administrators were asked to do better.

By mid-1979 they had come up with revisions in the measurement rules, developed mainly by Victorian Hilton Hergt that, it was believed, would give a more realistic assessment of a boat's displacement by applying a new hull-depth measurement and eliminating a previous factor that had arbitrarily judged the ratio of beam to length. One of the results of the changes would be to push the rating of the pesky Soling, *Longshot*, from 18.9 to 20.8 and to lop some of the advantage that the Thunderbird, *Royalist*, had enjoyed. The new rules would also allow yachts of only 4.9 m waterline length to race and would still include those that rated up to Half Ton under the IOR rules.

'We hope with the new measurement rules to satisfy everyone', said the then NSW JOG secretary Captain Hedley Watson.

> Our aim in this State is to end the fragmentation of racing of more than 100 potential JOG class boats that at present compete only in small fleets in separate club point score events. Without destroying their club identities we plan to encourage them to compete in combined JOG races and give them the best of both worlds. It is only a matter of cooperation. We believe we have now a good set of measurement rules. If we do find some craft are getting under the wire because of peculiarities of design or that designers find loopholes to exploit we will, of course, consider changes in the rules.

It was an admirable philosophy and it worked well, even in championship racing, until shrewd designers realized it was still possible to produce between the minimum waterline length of 4.87 m and the maximum overall length of 9.44 m almost flat-bottomed planing hulls that could zoom past more conventional boats. This new breed of light, high-tech machine, broad-beamed with fine 'U' sections for'ard, nearly plumb stem and a reverse transom stern, could also, under the rules, carry enough sail upwind in all conditions to outpace heavier vessels. Even when national measurer Hergt, NSW measurer Ian Findlay and other State measurers devised new hull angle penalties that encouraged the building of a 'V'd section into the bottoms of boats, designers still succeeded in keeping them flat where it mattered. With fine, flexible, fractional rigs they maintained their Formula One performance. Indeed, some of these JOG boats — like Mal Jones' *2 Desperados*, formerly of Brisbane, then Sydney, national champion in 1983–84–85 — were capable in certain conditions of out-sailing good IOR performers rating 2 m higher. (All JOG craft are now rated in metrics as distinct from the IOR retention of imperial measurements.)

The imposition of a most rigorous self-righting index that required all JOG craft to be especially stable and able to recover quickly after a knockdown did not stop them either, although it eliminated some boats that were not so inherently stiff or forced owners to add shoes of lead to their ballast keels. A long inquiry by senior yachting administrators (after the loss of four lives when two boats, *Waikikamukau* and *Montego Bay*, filled and sank during a night race in rough weather off Sydney in 1983) had recommended that all JOG boats should come under the same self-righting category as larger IOR craft in much longer races. Officials point out, nevertheless, that the two vessels that sank during the race off Sydney not only passed the then existing stability rules but also would have passed the new, stricter ones, and that other causes contributed to the sinkings and the subsequent loss of life. Although the 25 nm limit range from the starting line has been abandoned, other safety rules require efficient radios to be aboard all boats, and for clubs conducting night races for JOG boats to maintain a constant radio–listening watch until all competitors have returned to port. Boats must also carry other safety equipment, including harnesses fitted with belts that have ready-release hooks either end so that a person swept overboard can get free from his or her harness if it becomes absolutely necessary and does not remain

Lightweight NZ-designed *Waikikamukau* won the Australian Quarter Ton title and later performed well in the JOG fleet until lost in a tragic sinking off the Sydney coast in 1983. (Bob Ross)

attached to the boat (where the other end of the belt is secured).

These strict controls have not discouraged JOG enthusiasts. Nor has the domination of championship events by the new rule-exploiting 'flying ironing boards' (as designer Ben Lexcen called them after the 7.31 m *Dunc An Co*, owned by a syndicate with John Lockeridge as its leader, scudded past his much larger, conventionally hulled, wing-keeled, Half Ton Cup class sloop, *King George V.*) At least, officials were able to point out to Lexcen, JOG rules, unlike IOR rules, did not ban his winged keel. By late 1985, there were 330 JOG boats registered for racing in Australia – 100 in NSW, eighty in Victoria, seventy in Tasmania, fifty in Queensland, thirty in SA – only about 150 fewer than the nation-wide

Ben Lexcen called the 1986 breed of JOG racers, like this one, *Dunc An Co*, sailed by John Lockeridge and Frank Martin, 'Flying Ironing Boards', as the beamy, almost flat-bottomed little boats scudded past much bigger vessels. (Frank Martin)

total of much larger ocean racing vessels registered for competition under the IOR measurement formula. Perhaps this success is because JOG officials have found an excellent method to encourage everyone, even those with old conventional-style heavyweight boats whose age allowances have been severely pruned under the new regulations. In NSW, well-sponsored, club-controlled regattas are held monthly and, in some places, fortnightly, for combined JOG fleets in three divisions. Equal emphasis is placed on success in the division for conventional craft fitted out with relatively comfortable accommodation between decks as in that for high performance skaters that have no room inside to swing a mouse, let alone a cat. Point scores and teams events with sprinklings of craft from each division in each team are regular features of the racing. Even in State and national championship events, all divisions can still race together because there are separate prizes and, of course, just as in IOR events, when the breeze becomes fluky or there is an unexpected change in the weather pattern there is also the chance of the turtles with luck beating the tearaways.

Appendix

Appendix

The following tables of Australian sailing champions in national and international classes, of Australia's Olympic representatives and of place-getters in the Sydney–Hobart races, have been compiled with the generous assistance of Jack Pollard, publisher of the *Ampol Book of Records*.

AUSTRALIAN CHAMPIONS

Centreboard Classes

CHERUB

1963–64	*Cupid III*	G. Wright (WA)		1975–76	*Kai*	M. McAlary (NSW
1964–65	*Ace*	G. Lucas (WA)		1976–77	*High Voltage*	G. Hyde (NSW)
1965–66	*Ace*	G. Lucas (WA)		1977–78	*Stardust*	A. Pearson (NSW)
1966–67	*Pepper*	G. Adams (NSW)		1978–79	*Stairway to*	I. Boyle (NSW)
1967–68	*Ace*	G. Lucas (WA)			*Heaven*	
1968–69	*Dia-Jo*	J. Cerutty (Tas)		1979–80	*Black Friday*	S. Morphett (ACT
1969–70	*Jennifer Julian*	R. Bowler (NSW)		1980–81	*WOP*	P. Smith (NSW)
1970–71	*Checkmate*	K. Baddiley (Qld)		1981–82	*Colour Me*	B. Lehmann (NSW
1971–72	*Vitamin C*	K. Baddiley (Qld)			*Too*	
1972–73	*Hush Power*	I. Murray (NSW)		1982–83	*Colour Fast*	B. Lehmann (NSW
1973–74	*Slithy Tove*	N. Bethwaite (NSW)		1983–84	*Colour Fast*	M. Lehmann (NSW
1974–75	*Slithy Tove*	N. Bethwaite (NSW)		1984–85	*Foreign Affair*	B. Hartnett (NSW)

CONTENDER

1970				1977–78	*Lady Madonna*	M. Baker (NSW)
March	*Toenail*	M. Alsop (NSW)		1978–79	*Lady Madonna*	M. Baker (NSW)
December	*Helter Skelter*	K. Tickle (Qld)		1979–80	*Savoir Faire*	K. McCarthy (Qld)
1971–72	*Helter Skelter*	K. Tickle (Qld)				
1972–73	*Toenail*	M. Alsop (NSW)		1980–81	*Lady Madonna*	M. Baker (NSW)
1973–74	*Bon Vivant*	P. Hollis (Qld)		1981–82	*Wind Dancer*	P. Randall (Vic)
1974–75	*Excaliber*	R. Hawthorne (NSW)		1982–83	*Wind Dancer*	P. Randall (Vic)
1975–76	*Lady Madonna*	M. Baker (NSW)		1983–84	*Cowpat Shadow*	B. Watson (NSW)
1976–77	*Lady Madonna*	M. Baker (NSW)		1984–85	*Cowpat Shadow*	B. Watson (NSW)

FINN

1956–57	C.S. Ryrie	1966–67	R. Jenyns	1976–77	C. Proctor
1957–58	C.S. Ryrie	1967–68	R. Jenyns	1977–78	C. Proctor
1958–59	R. Jenyns	1968–69	A. James	1978–79	G. Davidson
1959–60	R. Jenyns	1969–70	R. Jenyns	1979–80	G. Davidson
1960–61	R. Jenyns	1970–71	P. Burford	1980–81	G. Davidson
1961–62	R. Jenyns	1971–72	J. Bertrand	1981–82	G. Davidson
1962–63	R. Jenyns	1972–73	S. Kiely	1982–83	C. Pratt
1963–64	R. Jenyns	1973–74	A. James	1983–84	L. Kleist
1964–65	C.S. Ryrie	1974–75	A. James	1984–85	C. Pratt
1965–66	R. Jenyns	1975–76	J. Bertrand		

FIREBALL

1965–66	Sydney	*Vulcan III*	G. Vick
1966–67	Frankston	*Innuendo*	P. Moore
1967–68	Sandy Bay	*Warutjara*	E. Nichol
1968–69	Sydney	*Zara*	J. Hardie
1969–70	Geelong	*Cheetah*	C. Scott
1970–71	Hobart	*Prani IV*	K. Olver
1971–72	Adelaide	*Skedaddle*	B. Inns
1972–73	Lake Macquarie	*James II*	J. Wilmot
1973–74	Spencer Gulf	*Screwdriver*	G. Lucas
1974–75	Frankston	*Ome-n-'osed*	J. Cassidy
1975–76	Melville Waters, WA	*Screwdriver*	G. Lucas
1976–77	Lake Cootharaba, Qld	*Fascination*	C. Tillett
1977–78	Derwent River, Tas	*Naked Kneecaps*	G. Lucas
1978–79	Belmont, NSW	*Fascination*	C. Tillett
1979–80	Glenelg, SA	*Fascination*	C. Tillett
1980–81	Perth	*Naked Kneecaps*	G. Lucas
1981–82	Frankston	*Fascination*	C. Tillett
1982–83	Lake Cootharaba, Qld	*Bed Rock Fundamentals*	S. Hamilton
1983–84	Hobart	*Average White Boat*	G. Smith
1984–85	Brighton, Vic	*Superfeat*	N. Abbott

505

1958	Vic	*Tempest*	J. Bagshaw (SA)
1959	NSW	*Naiad*	D. Brooker (NSW)
1960	SA	*Ya-Hoo*	F. Neill (SA)
1961	Vic	*Aeolian*	J. Bagshaw (SA)
1962	SA	*Ya-Hoo*	F. Neill (SA)
1963	Vic	*Aeolian*	B. Price (SA)
1964	NSW	*Yani*	B. Barnes (Vic)
1965	SA	*Daring-Kestrel*	J. Cuneo (Qld)
1966	ACT	*Topique*	R. Dalgleish (ACT)
1967	SA	*Taylor Maid*	R. Lanyon (SA)
1968	Vic	*Tornado*	J. Schramm (SA)
1969	NSW	*Brumby*	P. Harvey (ACT)
1970	SA	*Classique*	R. Dalgleish (ACT)
1971	NSW	*Brumby II*	P. Harvey (ACT)
1972	Vic	*Torrente*	M. Bethwaite (Vic)
1973*	SA	*Fof*	R. Dalgleish (ACT)
		Kooringa	G. Mellody (Vic)
1974	ACT	*Liberator*	V. Hyles (NSW)
1975–76	SA	*Lindy Lou*	T. Kyrwood (NSW)
1976–77	NSW	*Lindy Lou*	T. Kyrwood (NSW)
1977–78	Vic	*Lindy Lou*	T. Kyrwood (NSW)
1978–79	SA	*Go Boat*	G. Kyrwood (NSW)

387

1979–80	NSW	*Lindy Lou*	T. Kyrwood (NSW)
1980–81	SA	*Sublime*	T. Kyrwood (NSW)
1981–82	ACT	*Planning Platypus*	N. Harrison (SA)
1982–83	SA	*Swingshot*	N. Harrison (SA)
1983–84	NSW	*Dees Nerf*	D. Porter (NSW)
1984–85	NSW	*OD*	P. Hewson (NSW)

*Equal first

FLYING DUTCHMAN

1957–58	R.L. Tasker	1967–68	C. Ryves	1976–77	G. Stanway
1958–59	N. Brooke	1968–69	C. Whitworth	1977–78	G. Stanway
1959–60	R.L. Tasker	1969–70	C. Whitworth	1978–79	C. Ryves
1960–61	J.A. Muston	1970–71	M. Bethwaite	1979–80	M. Peelgrane
1961–62	C. Whitworth	1971–72	M. Bethwaite	1980–81	A. Allsep
1962–63	R.L. Tasker	1972–73	D. Lawrence	1981–82	A. Allsep
1963–64	J.G. Hardy	1973–74	M. Bethwaite	1982–83	M. Peelgrane
1964–65	A.I. Twentyman	1974–75	J. Wilmot	1983–84	J. Wilmot
1965–66	C. Whitworth	1975–76	J. Wilmot	1984–85	I. McCrossin
1966–67	C. Whitworth				

420

1968–69	*La Mouette*	J. Gilder (SA)	1979–80	*Shellgrit*	C. Ferris (NSW)
1969–70	*La Mouette*	J. Gilder (SA)	1980–81	*Lime Flash*	I. Simpson (WA)
1970–71	*Nereus*	J. Gilder (SA)			
1971–72	*Nereus*	J. Gilder (SA)	1981–82	*52 Girls*	G. Backshall (WA)
1972–73	*Nereus*	J. Gilder (SA)			
1973–74	*Tooloona*	D. Young (SA)	1982–83	*Menace*	D. Jones (WA)
1974–75	*SCD*	C. Arnold (SA)	1983–84	*Malpractice*	M. Higgins (SA)
1975–76	*Fair Dinkum*	C. Arnold (SA)	1984–85	*Taking Liberty*	B. Young (SA)
1976–77	*Fair Dinkum*	C. Arnold (SA)			
1977–78	*Soumetar*	A. Wangel (SA)			
1978–79	*If it won't come when you call it why name it*	G. Backshall (WA)			

470

(First Australian 470 championship staged by Brighton Yacht Club, Vic, in 1975 and the Class first competed in an Olympic Games at Montreal in 1976)

1974–75	*Pyrotechnics*	G. Gietz (NSW)	1981–82	*Hocus Pocus*	P. Holmes (NSW)
1975–76	*Hocus Pocus*	I. Browne (NSW)	1982–83	*Superbickies*	R. Beurteaux (WA)
1976–77	*Super Vision*	J. Golding (NSW)			
1977–78	*Jack's Union*	A. Day (NSW)	1983–84	*Curleys Quest*	D. Jones (WA)
1978–79	*Pyrophoric*	G. Gietz (NSW)	1984–85	*Deckchair*	N. Abbott (Vic)
1979–80	*Pyrotechnics*	G. Gietz (NSW)			
1980–81	*Dynamic Duo*	C. Sutherland (NSW)			

14 FT DINGHY

1920	Perth	*John Nimmo*	H.C. Brooke (Vic)
1921	Melbourne	*John Nimmo*	H.C. Brooke (Vic)
1922	Adelaide	*John Nimmo*	H.C. Brooke (Vic)
1923	Perth	*Schemer*	A. Rose (Vic)
1924	Sydney	*White Cloud*	A. O'Grady (WA)
1925	Melbourne	*John Nimmo*	H.C. Brooke (Vic)
1926	Adelaide	*John Nimmo*	H.C. Brooke (Vic)
1927	Perth	*Scandal*	E. Kelly (Vic)
1928	Sydney	*Aussie*	H.C. Brooke (Vic)
1929	Melbourne	*Scandal*	E. Kelly (Vic)
1930	Adelaide	*Sunny South*	P. O'Grady (SA)
1931	Perth	*White Cloud*	A. O'Grady (SA)

1932	Melbourne	*Triad*	W. Osborne (Vic)
1933	Adelaide	*Triad*	W. Osborne (Vic)
1934	Perth	*Triad*	W. Osborne (Vic)
1935	Melbourne	*Triad*	W. Osborne (Vic)
1936	Perth	*Triad*	W. Osborne (Vic)
1937	Adelaide	*Triad*	W. Osborne (Vic)
1938	Hobart	*Vamp*	W. Rogers (NZ)
1939	Melbourne	*Maringa*	R. Lang (SA)
1940–45 No contests because of war			
1946	Perth	*Scamp*	L. Tomlinson (WA)
1947	Adelaide	*Triad*	W. Osborne (Vic)
1948	Melbourne	*Scamp*	L. Tomlinson (WA)
1949	Perth	*Quest*	W. Osborne (Vic)
1950	Adelaide	*Quest*	W. Osborne (Vic)
1951	Sydney	*Quest*	W. Osborne (Vic)
1952	Melbourne	*Scamp II*	L. Tomlinson (WA)
1953	Perth	*Delta*	R. McCallum (Vic)
1954	Adelaide	*Charles Marshall*	N. Brooke (Vic)
1955	Melbourne	*Restless*	A. Rann (NSW)
1956	Brisbane	*Daring*	K. Keeley (Vic)
1957	Sydney	*Darkie*	S. Corser (WA)
1958	Perth	*Darkie*	S. Corser (WA)
1959	Adelaide	*Darkie*	S. Corser (WA)
1960	Melbourne	*Comet*	D. Devine (WA)
1961	Brisbane	*Ripple*	I. Sutcliffe (Vic)
1962	Sydney	*Ripple*	I. Sutcliffe (Vic)
1963	Perth	*Teal*	T. Betts (WA)
1964	Adelaide	*Teal*	T. Betts (WA)
1965	Melbourne	*Leanne V*	B. Burke (WA)
1966	Brisbane	*Rampage*	K. Buhr (Qld)
1967	Sydney	*Confusion*	L. Abbott (NSW)
1968	Perth	*Ballerina*	P. Nevard (WA)
1969	Adelaide	*Leanne VI*	B. Burke (WA)
1970	Melbourne	*Ballerina*	P. Nevard (WA)
1971	Sydney	*Valiant III*	D. Anderson (WA)
1972	Perth	*Valiant III*	D. Anderson (WA)
1973	Brisbane	*Valiant III*	D. Anderson (WA)
1974	Adelaide	*Valiant III*	D. Anderson (WA)
1975	Melbourne	*Redwing IV*	I. Blanckensee (WA)
1976	Sydney	*Target*	R. Hancock (WA)
1977–78	Perth	*Target*	R. Hancock (WA)
1978–79	Brisbane	*Target*	R. Hancock (WA)
1979–80	Adelaide	*Target*	R. Hancock (WA)
1980–81	Melbourne	*Valiant VI*	D. Anderson (WA)
1981–82	Sydney	*Valiant VII*	D. Anderson (WA)
1982–83	Perth	*Red Ned*	C. Burton (WA)
1983–84	Brisbane	*Red Ned*	C. Burton (WA)
1984–85	Adelaide	*Dangermouse*	G. Coutts (Vic)

18-FOOTERS

1894–95	Sydney	*Ariel*	G. Ellis (NSW)
1895–96	Brisbane	*Britannia*	A. Earl (Qld)
1896–97	Sydney	*Thalia*	W. Read (NSW)
1897–98	Brisbane	*Stella II*	G. Ellis (NSW)
1898–99	Sydney	*Stella II*	F. Doran (NSW)
1903–04	Sydney	*Amy*	A. Farr (NSW)
1906–07	Perth	*Aeolus*	E. Tomlinson (WA)
1907–08	Sydney	*Australian*	C. Webb (NSW)
1908–09	Perth	*Australian*	C. Webb (NSW)
1909–10	Sydney	*Australian*	C. Webb (NSW)
1910–11	Brisbane	*Pastime*	C. Crouch (Qld)
1911–12	Perth	*Westana*	C. Garland (WA)

1912–13	Sydney	*Kismet*	W. Dunn (NSW)
1913–14	Perth	*Australian*	C. Webb (NSW)
1917–18	Brisbane	*Britannia*	C. Clark (Qld)
1918–19	Sydney	*Mavis*	F.W. Moppett (NSW)
1920–21	Sydney	*Vision*	C. Clark (Qld)
1921–22	Perth	*Mele Bilo*	C. Garland (WA)
1922–23	Brisbane	*Vision*	C. Clark (Qld)
1923–24	Sydney	*H.C. Press*	C. Webb (NSW)
1924–25	Perth	*H.C. Press*	C. Webb (NSW)
1925–26	Brisbane	*Queenslander*	J. Crouch (Qld)
1926–27	Sydney	*H.C. Press*	C. Webb (NSW)
1929–30	Brisbane	*Waratah*	H. Crouch (Qld)
1930–31	Sydney	*Arawatta*	C. Hayes (NSW)
1931–32	Brisbane	*Tangalooma*	L. Watts (Qld)
1932–33	Sydney	*Arawatta*	C. Hayes (NSW)
1933–34	Brisbane	*Aberdare*	V. Vaughan (Qld)
1934–35	Sydney	*Aberdare*	V. Vaughan (Qld)
1935–36	Brisbane	*Aberdare*	V. Vaughan (Qld)
1936–37*	Sydney	*Aberdare*	V. Vaughan (Qld)
(dead heat)		*Lightning*	B. Swinbourne (NSW)
1937–38	Brisbane	*Malvina*	W. Hayward (NSW)
1938–39	Sydney	*Victor*	V. Lucas (Qld)
1939–40	Brisbane	*Marjorie*	L. Watts (Qld)
1940–41	Sydney	*Marjorie*	L. Watts (Qld)
1942–45	Not held		

(In 1946 new streamlined 18-footer introduced. Minimum beam reduced to 6 ft and depth 21 ins.)

1946–47	Sydney	*Australia*	W. Stanley (Qld)
1947–48	Brisbane	*Culex II*	L. Watts (Qld)
1948–49	Sydney	*Myra*	W. Barnett (NSW)
1949–50	Brisbane	*Culex III*	L. Watts (Qld)
1950–51	Sydney	*Myra Too*	W. Barnett (NSW)
1951–52	Brisbane	*Jenny IV*	N. Wright (Qld)
1952–53	Sydney	*Jenny V*	N. Wright (Qld)
1953–54	Brisbane	*Jan*	W. Barnett (NSW)
1954–55	Sydney	*Myra*	W. Barnett (NSW)
1955–56	Brisbane	*Jenny VI*	N. Wright (Qld)
1956–57	Sydney	*Ajax*	D. Barnett (NSW)
1957–58	Brisbane	*Jenny VI*	N. Wright (Qld)
1958–59	Sydney	*Jantzen Girl*	L. Heffernan (NSW)
1959–60	Brisbane	*Jantzen Girl*	L. Heffernan (NSW)
1960–61	Sydney	*The Fox*	V. Robinson (NSW)
1961–62	Cairns	*Crystal Lad*	L. Heffernan (NSW)
1962–63	Sydney	*Aberdare*	L. Heffernan (NSW)
1963–64	Brisbane	*Aberdare*	L. Heffernan (NSW)
1964–65	Sydney	*Schemer*	R. Holmes (NSW)
1965–66	Brisbane	*Travelodge*	R. Holmes (NSW)
1966–67	Sydney	*Assoc Motor Club*	D. Barnett (NSW)
1967–68	Brisbane	*Kaiser Bill*	D. Lehany (NSW)
1968–69	Sydney	*Travelodge*	R. Holmes (NSW)
1969–70	Brisbane	*Willie B*	R. Zemanek (NSW)
1970–71	Sydney	*Travelodge*	R. Holmes (NSW)
1971–72	Brisbane	*Nock and Kirby*	D. Lehany (NSW)
1972–73	Sydney	*Travelodge*	R. Holmes (NSW)
1973–74	Brisbane	*KB*	D. Porter (NSW)
1974–75	Sydney	*KB*	D. Porter (NSW)
1975–76	Brisbane	*Miles Furniture*	S. Kulmar (NSW)
1976–77	Sydney	*KB*	D. Porter (NSW)
1977–78	Brisbane	*7 Color*	I. Murray (NSW)
1978–79	Sydney	*Color 7*	I. Murray (NSW)
1979–80	Perth	*Color 7*	I. Murray (NSW)
1980–81	Sydney	*Color 7*	I. Murray (NSW)

1981–82	Brisbane	*Color 7*	I. Murray (NSW)
1982–83	Perth	*Tia Maria*	P. Sorensen (NSW)
1983–84	Adelaide	*Tia Maria*	P. Sorensen (NSW)
1984–85	Sydney	*Bradmill*	R. Brown (NSW)

Note: in 1936 objections to the *Aberdare* type of boat caused certain factions to stage Australian championship races between a newly formed Brisbane Flying Squadron and Sydney Flying Squadron. So two national championships were held. After two years the 'rebels' gave up staging rival national titles and the Brisbane Flying Squadron ceased to function. The two 'rival' Australian championships resulted: 1935–36 in Sydney – *Tangalooma*, W. Duncan, NSW; 1936–37, Brisbane, *Tangalooma*, R. Phythian, Qld.

*No sail-off. *Aberdare* retained title.

16 FT SKIFF

1909–10	*Minoru*	H. Rodrick (NSW)
1918–19	*Vaucluse*	F. Newton (NSW)
1919–20	*Valmae*	C. Clark (Qld)
1920–21	*Agnes*	T. Deane (Qld)
1921–22	*C.M.*	A. Whereat (Qld)
1922–23	*Furore*	R. Fennell (NSW)
1923–24	*Ajax*	A. Whereat (Qld)
1924–25	*Furious*	T. Deane (Qld)
1925–26	*Victor*	V. Lucas (Qld)
1926–27	*Ajax III*	A. Whereat (Qld)
1927–28	*Memory*	C. Cadman (Qld)
1928–29	*Verona*	J. Norris (WA)
1929–30	*Ajax*	A. Whereat (Qld)
1930–31	*Ajax*	A. Whereat (Qld)
1931–32	*Victor II*	V. Lucas (Qld)
1932–33	*Marjorie*	J. Mitchell (WA)
1933–34	*Victor III*	V. Lucas (Qld)
1934–35	*Ace*	C. Boulton (NSW)
1935–36	*Aeolian*	J. Mitchell (WA)
1936–37	*Imp*	R. Hendry (Qld)
1937–38	*Imp*	R. Hendry (Qld)
1938–39	*Imp*	R. Hendry (Qld)
1939–40	*Imp*	R. Hendry (Qld)
1940–41	*U-Dear*	J. Lyons (NSW)
1946–47	*Joy*	R. Wright (Qld)
1947–48	*Vi VI*	V. Lucas (Qld)
1948–49	*O'Johnny*	W. Hayward (NSW)
1949–50	*O'Johnny*	W. Hayward (NSW)
1950–51	*Romp*	F. Hudson (WA)
1951–52	*Joy VI*	R. Wright (Qld)
1952–53	*Return*	J. O'Rourke (NSW)
1953–54	*Evelyn IV*	J. Cassidy (WA)
1954–55	*Evelyn IV*	J. Cassidy (WA)
1955–56	*Evelyn V*	J. Cassidy (WA)
1956–57	*James H*	R. Schroeder (NSW)
1957–58	*Elva II*	R. Gray (NSW)
1958–59	*Evelyn VII*	J. Cassidy (WA)
1959–60	*Joan IX*	K. Minter (NSW)
1960–61	*Evelyn IX*	J. Cassidy (WA)
1961–62	*Seaforth*	K. Beashel (NSW)
1962–63	*Joan*	K. Minter (NSW)
1963–64	*Evelyn XII*	J. Cassidy (WA)
1964–65	*Joan*	K. Minter (NSW)
1965–66	*Joan*	K. Minter (NSW)
1966–67	*Julie Ann*	N. Buckley (Qld)
1967–68	*Pamm Paints*	N. Buckley (Qld)
1968–69	*Gazeaway*	D. Reid (NSW)
1969–70	*Minx*	T. Beardsmore (NSW)
1970–71	*Minx*	T. Beardsmore (NSW)

1971–72	*Gazeaway*	D. Reid (NSW)
1972–73	*Gazeaway Too*	D. Reid (NSW)
1973–74	*McKellar Sails*	G. McKellar (NSW)
1974–75	*Viggers Shondell*	G. Bruniges (NSW)
1975–76	*Matana*	W. McMahon (NSW)
1976–77	*Manta*	T. Barnabas (NSW)
1977–78	*Manta Marine*	T. Barnadas (NSW)
1978–79	*Buckle Toyota*	T. Barnabas (NSW)
1979–80	*Merlin*	P. Riley (NSW)
1980–81	*McKellar Sails*	G. McKellar (NSW)
1981–82	*International Yacht Paints*	D. McKay (NSW)
1982–83	*Otis*	A. Gray (NSW)
1983–84	*Burwood Calendars*	D. Tanko (NSW)
1984–85	*Burwood Calendars*	D. Tanko (NSW)

12 FT SKIFF

From 1925 to 1962 restricted to teams of six boats chosen to represent NSW and Qld

1925–26	*Defiance*	A. Whereat (Qld)
1926–27	*Schemer*	B. Roff (NSW)
1927–28	*Dove*	J. McLeer (Qld)
1928–29	*C C II*	J. Crouch (Qld)
1929–30	*Schemer*	B. Roff (NSW)
1930–31	*Schemer*	B. Roff (NSW)
1931–32	*Dove*	J. McLeer (Qld)
1932–33	*Schemer*	B. Roff (NSW)
1933–34	*Viking*	J. Muston (NSW)
1934–35	*Jean*	P. Cowie (NSW)
1935–36	*Dove*	J. Thomas (Qld)
1936–37	*Nina*	S. Elms (Qld)
1937–38	*Old Bill*	H. Spring (Qld)
1938–39	*Scandal*	J. Briggs (NSW)
1939–40	*Resolve*	R. Hawgood (Qld)
1940–41	*Ariki*	R. Brown (NSW)
1941–42	*Beryl*	W. Munce (NSW)
1945–46	*Nina*	B. Sinclair (Qld)
1946–47	*Dynamic*	R. Hawgood (Qld)
1947–48	*Dove*	L. Johnston (Qld)
1948–49	*Query*	C. Ryrie (NSW)
	Toogara (dead heat)	C. Monkhouse (NSW)
1949–50	*Resolve*	W. Vaughan (Qld)
1950–51	*Desire*	R. Hawgood (Qld)
1951–52	*Estrillita*	H. Ware (Qld)
1952–53	*Ajax*	D. Barnett (NSW)
1953–54	*Estrillita*	H. Ware (Qld)
1954–55	*Yandoo*	J. Winning (NSW)
1955–56	*Yandoo*	J. Winning (NSW)
1956–57	*Yandoo*	J. Winning (NSW)
1957–58	*Escapade*	G. Colless (NSW)
1958–59	*Yandoo*	J. Winning (NSW)
1959–60	*Syntax*	R. Phillips (NSW)
1960–61	*Syntax*	R. Phillips (NSW)
1961–62	*Sayonara*	D. McGoogan (NSW)

1969–70	*Venture*	D. Morgan (NSW)
1970–71	*Pol*	M. Chapman (NSW)
1971–72	*Yandoo*	J. Winning (NSW)
1972–73	*Viking*	A. Griffith (NSW)
1973–74	*Vagabond*	S. Kulmar (NSW)
1974–75	*Freshwater Sails*	B. Hewish (NSW)
1975–76	*Miles Furniture*	P. Gardner (NSW)
1976–77	*Contract Engineering*	M. Coxon (NSW)
1977–78	*Contract Engineering*	M. Coxon (NSW)
1978–79	*Buckle Toyota*	K. Wadham (NSW)
1979–80	*Summer Formula*	D. Adams (NSW)
1980–81	*Caroline*	A. White (NSW)
1981–82	*Hunters Hill Realty*	D. Adams (NSW)
1982–83	*Steve Jarvins Motors*	A. White (NSW)
1983–84	*S.O.S. Marine*	M. Walsh (NSW)
1984–85	*Nature's Gate Herbal Cosmetics*	G. Colless (NSW)

No further national title series were held until the 1969 season because the 12 ft skiff movement had declined in Queensland and no representatives were available from that State. From 1969 the championships were resumed on the basis of open competition for any number of competitors from any State and the ACT, provided all boats complied with current rules of measurement.

GWEN 12

1953	*Jill III*	D. Langlands (Vic)	1970	*Jepi*	I. Whitton (NSW)	
1954	*Gee Wiz*	R. Sedgman (Vic)	1971	*Seaweed*	R. Shortridge (NSW)	
1955	*Storm*	M. Fletcher (Vic)				
1956	*Typhoon*	B. Bennet (Vic)	1972	*Illusion*	G. Smith (NSW)	
1957	*Storm II*	M. Fletcher (Vic)	1973	*Moonraker*	G. Atkinson (NSW)	
1958	*Storm II*	M. Fletcher (Vic)	1974	*Concorde*	P. Hughes (Vic)	
1959	*Villain II*	T. Gaunt (WA)	1975	*Concorde*	P. Hughes (Vic)	
1960	*Villain II*	T. Gaunt (WA)	1976–77	*Apocalypse*	R. Dunbar (NSW)	
1961	*Top Secret*	K. Jenyns (Qld)	1977–78	*Flying Circus*	P. Dollin (NSW)	
1962	*Clementine*	I. Outhred (NSW)	1978–79	*Adios*	K. Colwell (SA)	
1963	*Nimble*	R. Crooke (Qld)	1979–80	*Turtle*	D. Tanko (NSW)	
1964	*Mary Jane*	I. Outhred (NSW)	1980–81	*Spun Out*	P. Dollin (NSW)	
1965	*Kestrel III*	A. Morrison (Vic)	1981–82	*Turtle*	D. Tanko (NSW)	
1966	*Kestrel III*	A. Morrison (Vic)	1982–83	*Spaced Out*	P. Dollin (NSW)	
1967	*Jill*	J. Hooper (Vic)	1983–84	*Apocalypse*	D. Ashton (NSW)	
1968	*Kestrel V*	A. Morrison (Vic)	1984–85	*True Blue*	K. & C. Colwell (SA)	
1969	*Jill II*	J. Hooper (Vic)				

HERON

1960	*Saranga*	F. Jones	1974	*Chainvalley Bay*	I. Cull
1961	*Theron*	K.W. Payne			
1962	*Theron*	B. Mortlock	1975	*Chainvalley Bay*	I. Cull
1963	*Windoo*	S. Dearnley			
1964	*Bluejacket*	J. Muston	1976	*Deft*	A. Imlay
1965	*Seaforth*	E. Quarford	1977	*Outcast*	J. Armitage
1966	*W.A.P.*	P. Hopkins	1978	*Eigen Vector*	A. Payne
1967	*The Saint*	J. Weddell	1979	*Outcast*	J. Armitage
1968	*Kumale*	P.V. Sievewright	1980	*Abracadabara*	D. Jamieson
1969	*Nook*	M. Fletcher	1981	*Outcast*	J. Armitage
1970	*Aquatic*	R. Rowe	1982	*Eigen Vector*	C. McPhee
1971	*Sobraon*	A. Payne	1983	*Eigen Vector*	C. McPhee
1972	*Lady G*	P. Carnall	1984	*Eigen Vector*	C. McPhee
1973	*Wiwirri*	A. Payne	1985	*Outcast*	J. Armitage

LASER

1975–76	Holdfast Bay, SA	P. Burford (SA)	1980–81	Pittwater	C. Beashel
1976–77	Black Rock, Vic	P. Burford (SA)	1981–82	Blairgowrie, Vic	A. Roy (Canada)
1977–78	Manly, Qld	A. York (NSW)	1982–83	Hobart	A. Hodder (Vic)
1978–79	Perth, WA	P. Conde (Qld)	1983–84	Hervey Bay, Qld	D. Cummins (NSW)
1979–80	Port Lincoln, SA	C. Beashel (NSW)	1984–85	Busselton, WA	A. McLure (Vic)

NATIONAL E

1966–67	*Fury IV*	D. Clark (Vic)	1976–77	*Lady Jo II*	M. Syme (Vic)
1967–68	*Tanjel*	J. Lawler (Vic)	1977–78	*Pyewacket*	P. Miller (SA)
1968–69	*Lady Jo II*	J. Davies (Vic)	1978–79	*Toothache*	A. Handley (Vic)
1969–70	*Tammy*	R. Pollock (NSW)	1979–80	*Nonsuch*	D. Taylor (Vic)
1970–71	*Tango*	A. Hollins (Vic)	1980–81	*Toothache*	I. Walker (Vic)
1971–72	*Tango*	A. Hollins (Vic)	1981–82	*Santoy*	P. Seal (Vic)
1972–73	*Xellanon*	R. Dix (SA)	1982–83	*Cheeky*	D. Wise (SA)
1973–74	*Xellanon*	R. Dix (SA)	1983–84	*Cheeky*	D. Wise (SA)
1974–75	*Tartan Maid*	R. James (WA)	1984–85	*Cheeky*	D. Wise (SA)
1975–76	*Xellanon*	R. Dix (SA)			

LIGHTWEIGHT SHARPIE

1960	Adelaide	*Kestrel IV*	A.J. Barclay
1961	Hobart	*Daring II*	J.C. Cuneo
1962	Melbourne	*Daring II*	J.C. Cuneo
1963	Brisbane	*Futura*	G. White
1964	Perth	*Daring III*	J.C. Cuneo
1965	Adelaide	*Daring III*	J.C. Cuneo
1966	Sydney	*New Statesman*	P. Hosking
1967	Hobart	*Crescendo VII*	R. Thompson
1968	Melbourne	*Triad*	J. Bertrand
1969	Port Moresby	*Firefly*	K. Arcus
1970	Brisbane	*US III*	M. Bethwaite
1971	Perth	*Eleanor Rigby*	M. Peelgrane
1972	Adelaide	*Eleanor Rigby*	M. Peelgrane
1973	Sydney	*Eleanor Rigby*	M. Peelgrane
1974	Hobart	*Roeboat*	E. Roe
1975	Melbourne	*The Flasher*	A. Dey
1976	Brisbane	*Ostara*	E. Roe
1977	Perth	*Ship of Fools*	G. Simmer
1978	Largs Bay, SA	*Dynamo Hum*	A. Hunn
1979	Sydney	*Ship of Fools*	G. Simmer
1980	Hobart	*Coronation Rag*	S. Deussen
1980	Hobart	*Coronation Rag*	S. Deussen
1981	Port Melbourne, Vic	*True Colours*	M. Soulsby
1982	Keppel Bay, Qld	*Meadow Lark Lemon*	W. Henderson
1983	Perth	*Phantom XVI*	R. Beurteaux
1984	Adelaide	*Natural Gas*	R. Dussen
1985	Lake Macquarie, NSW	*Natural Gas*	R. Dussen

MOTH

1953–54	*Mark II*	B. Morris (Vic)		1968–69	*Imperium*	D. McKay (NSW)
1954–55	*Wonga II*	M. Fletcher (Vic)		1969–70	*Twora*	P. Holmes (NSW)
1955–56	*Fram II*	E. Quarford (NSW)		1970–71	*Imperium*	D. McKay (NSW)
				1971–72	*Ocelot*	R. Pitt (Qld)
1956–57	*Mistrel*	L. Andersson (NSW)		1972–73	*Cavalier*	J. Stapley (NSW)
1957–58	*Fram II*	E. Quarford (NSW)		1973–74	*Gidget*	R. O'Sullivan (WA)
1958–59	*Nil Desperandum*	J. Henderson (NSW)		1974–75	*Snubby*	P. Moor (NSW)
				1975–76	*Snubby*	P. Moor (NSW)
				1976–77	*Red Ned*	C. Burton (WA)
1959–60	*Fram III*	E. Quarford (NSW)		1977–78	*Gidget*	R. O'Sullivan (WA)
1960–61	*Gizelle*	A. Holt (NSW)		1978–79	*Bunyip*	G. Hilton (WA)
1961–62	*Vamoose*	R. Coxon (NSW)		1979–80	*Red Ned*	C. Burton (WA)
1962–63	*Vamoose*	R. Coxon (NSW)		1980–81	*Bunyip*	G. Hilton (WA)
1963–64	*Chaloupe*	G. Marshall (NSW)		1981–82	*Stunned Mullet*	P. Lamb (Vic)
1964–65	*Intrigue*	R. Le Plastrier (NSW)		1982–83	*Wombat*	A. McDougall (Vic)
1965–66	*Tango*	J. Hebden (NSW)		1983–84	*Wombat*	A. McDougall (Vic)
1966–67	*Mystique*	D. Bowen (NSW)				
1967–68	*Red Wings*	D. Pearce (WA)		1984–85	*In The Pink*	V. Tidy (WA)

OK

1962–63	Melbourne	*Pandora*	J. Powell (NSW)
1963–64	Sydney	*Pandora*	J. Powell (NSW)
1964–65	Hobart	*Gremlin*	J. Hardie (NSW)
1965–66	Cairns	*Aurora*	D. Blundell (NSW)
1966–67	Adelaide	*Tempest*	N. Beale (Qld)
1967–68	Brisbane	*Tempest*	N. Beale (Qld)
1968–69	Melbourne	*Comanche VIII*	N. Clarke (Qld)
1969–70	Sydney	*Comanche VIII*	N. Clarke (Qld)
1970–71	Hobart	*The Red Queen*	J. Firth (Vic)
1971–72	Mackay	*Comanche X*	N. Clarke (Qld)
1972–73	Adelaide	*Comanche X*	N. Clarke (Qld)
1973–74	Adelaide	*Esbe*	J. Smallwood (NSW)
1974–75	Brisbane	*Villian*	W. Bell (Vic)
1975–76	Melbourne	*Villian*	W. Bell (Vic)
1976–77	Sydney	*Villian*	W. Bell (Vic)
1977–78	Hobart	*Inca*	B. Ashton (Vic)
1978–79	Adelaide	*Inca*	B. Ashton (Vic)
1979–80	Brisbane	*Mug's Game*	P. Gale (Vic)
1980–81	Batemans Bay	*Cookie Monster*	P. Tackle (Vic)
1981–82	Melbourne	*Cookie Monster*	P. Tackle (Vic)
1982–83	Hobart	*Floozie*	G. Collings (Vic)
1983–84	Adelaide	*Floozie*	G. Collings (Vic)
1984–85	Lake Macquarie	*Floozie*	G. Collings (Vic)

Keel Classes

DIAMOND

1966	Perth	*Aries II*	K. Sullivan (WA)
1967	Sydney	*Spyder*	J. Dempster (NSW)
1968	Melbourne	*Taworri II*	N. Robins (WA)
1969	Hobart	*Mistress Kate*	H. House (NSW)
1970	Perth	*Taworri II*	N. Robins (WA)
1971	Lake Macquarie	*Rebecca*	A. Allsep (Vic)
1972	Moreton Bay	*Classic II*	A. Edwards (WA)
1973	Melbourne	*Rebecca*	A. Allsep (Vic)
1974	Hobart	*Lahloo*	R. Batt (Tas)
1975	Perth	*Jenise*	C. Doig (WA)
1976	Belmont Bay, NSW	*Teraki*	A. Perkins (Tas)
1977	St Kilda, Vic	*Wy-ar-gine*	W. Wardle (NSW)
1978	Hobart	*Teraki*	A. Perkins (Tas)
1979	Perth	*Classic II*	A. Edwards (WA)
1980	Sydney	*Wy-ar-gine*	W. Wardle (NSW)
1981	Melbourne	*Wy-ar-gine*	W. Wardle (NSW)
1982	Hobart	*Corsair III*	R. Hick (Vic)
1983	Perth	*Osprey*	R. Lucas (WA)
1984	Lake Macquarie	*Iona V*	K. Waller (WA)
1985	Williamstown, Vic	*Hot Stuff*	P. Miller (Vic)

DRAGON—Prince Philip Cup

1953–54	A.S. Sturrock	1965–66	N.G. Booth	1976–77	M. Purdon
1954–55	A.S. Sturrock	1966–67	F.A. Manford	1977–78	D. Calvert
1955–56	F.A. Manford	1967–68	J. Cuneo	1978–79	E.F. Albert
1956–57	W.L. Fesq	1968–69	J. Cuneo	1979–80	E.F. Albert
1957–58	A.S. Sturrock	1969–70	F.A. Manford	1980–81	R. Donohue
1958–59	W.E.H. Strain	1970–71	N.G. Booth	1981–82	S. Shield
1959–60	A. Jarman	1971–72	W.E.H. Strain	1982–83	J. Wilmot
1960–61	H.C. Brooke	1972–73	R. Watson	1983–84	R.B. Lynn
1962–63	J. Linacre	1973–74	S. Parker	1984–85	P. Bowman
1963–64	F.A. Manford	1974–75	N. Wright		
1964–65	F.A. Manford	1975–76	N. Longworth		

ETCHELLS 22

1975–76	*Jan IV*	B. Ritchie (NSW)	1980–81	*Footloose*	J. Byrne (Vic)
1976–77	*Jan IV*	B. Ritchie (NSW)	1981–82	*Cobra*	G. Sheard (Vic)
1977–78	*Rattler*	N. Brooke (Vic)	1982–83	*The Empire Strikes Back*	D. Forbes (NSW)
1978–79	*Impala*	P. O'Donnell (NSW)	1983–84	*Force Nine*	J. Savage (Vic)
1979–80	*Gull II*	J. Savage (NSW)	1984–85	*Force Nine*	J. Savage (Vic)

5.5-METRE

1955–56	Pt Phillip, Vic	*Buraddoo*	A.S. Sturrock (Vic)
1956–57	Pt Phillip, Vic	*Buraddoo*	A.S. Sturrock (Vic)
1957–58	Pt Phillip, Vic	*Buraddoo*	A.S. Sturrock (Vic)
1958–59	Sydney Harbour	*Buraddoo*	A.S. Sturrock (Vic)
1959–69	Pt Phillip, Vic	*Buraddoo*	A.S. Sturrock (Vic)
1960–61	Pittwater, NSW	*Kirribilli*	G.W. Ingate (NSW)
1961–62	Pittwater, NSW	*Kirribilli*	G.W. Ingate (NSW)
1962–63	Pittwater, NSW	*Southern Cross*	N.G. Booth (NSW)
1963–64	Lake Macquarie, NSW	*Barranjoey*	W.H. Northam (NSW)
1964–65	Pittwater, NSW	*Southern Cross II*	N.G. Booth (NSW)
1965–66	Pittwater, NSW	*Pam*	G.W. Ingate (NSW)
1966–67	Botany Bay, NSW	*Crest*	C. Halvorsen (NSW)
1967–68	Botany Bay, NSW	*Altair*	A.B. Carr (NSW)
1968–69	Palm Beach, NSW	*Pam*	G.W. Ingate (NSW)
1969–70	Palm Beach, NSW	*Pam*	G.W. Ingate (NSW)
1970–71	Palm Beach, NSW	*Carabella*	D.J. Forbes (NSW)
1971–72	Palm Beach, NSW	*Southern Cross III*	F.H. Tolhurst (NSW)
1972–73	Palm Beach, NSW	*Baragoola*	W.R. Slade (NSW)
1973–74	Palm Beach, NSW	*Baragoola*	W.R. Slade (NSW)
1974–75	Palm Beach, NSW	*Arunga*	F.H. Tolhurst (NSW(
1975–76	Palm Beach, NSW	*Arunga*	F.H. Tolhurst (NSW)
1976–77	Palm Beach, NSW	*Antares II*	H. Vaughan (NSW)
1977–78	Palm Beach, NSW	*Antares II*	H. Vaughan (NSW)
1978–79	Palm Beach, NSW	*Southern Cross III*	F.H. Tolhurst (NSW)
1979–80	Palm Beach, NSW	*Arunga III*	F.H. Tolhurst (NSW)
1980–81	Palm Beach, NSW	*Arunga IV*	F.H. Tolhurst (NSW)
1981–82	Palm Beach, NSW	*Skagerak*	C. Halvorsen (NSW)

1982–83	Not Held		
1983–84	Not Held		
1984–85	Palm Beach, NSW	*Southern Five*	C. Ryan (NSW)

SOLING

1968–69	*Solong*	C. Ryves	1977–78	*Aphrodite*	A. Manford
1969–70	*Kono*	R. Pattison	1978–79	*Odds 'n Ends*	J. Bertrand
1970–71	*Caliph*	R. Miller	1979–80	*Odds 'n Ends*	J. Bertrand
1971–72	*Alexia*	R. Miller	1980–81	*Verve*	M. Bethwaite
1972–73	*Alexia*	J. Bertrand	1981–82	*Verve*	M. Bethwaite
1973–74	*Wringer*	J. Coggan (USA)	1982–83	*Verve*	M. Bethwaite
1974–75	*Terror*	J. Hardy	1983–84	*Golden Swan*	P. Gilmour
1975–76	*Pocohontas*	D. Forbes	1984–85	*Kookaburra*	P. Gilmour
1976–77	*Darkie*	S. Corser			

STAR

1935–36	*Virginia*	J.A. Sturrock (Vic)	1959–60	*Ishkoodah*	R. Smith (NSW)
			1960–61	*Ishkoodah*	R. Smith (NSW)
1936–37	*Virginia*	J.A. Sturrock (Vic)	1961–62	*Pakaria*	R. Smith (NSW)
			1962–63	*Arakoola*	M. Visser (NSW)
1937–38	*Virginia*	J.A. Sturrock (Vic)	1963–64	*Maryke*	M. Visser (NSW)
			1964–65	*Tempo II*	D. Forbes (NSW)
1938–39	*Virginia*	J.A. Sturrock (Vic)	1965–66	*Tempo II*	D. Forbes (NSW)
			1966–67	*Ginger*	D. Forbes (NSW)
1939–40	*Moorina*	J.A. Sturrock (Vic)	1967–68	*Ginger*	D. Forbes (NSW)
			1968–69	*Ginger*	D. Forbes (NSW)
1944–45	*Moorina*	J.A. Sturrock (Vic)	1969–70	*Maryke*	W. Hock (NSW)
			1970–71	*Maryke*	W. Hock (NSW)
1945–46	*Moorina*	J.A. Sturrock (Vic)	1971–72	*Scallywag*	D. Forbes (NSW)
			1972–73	*Scallywag*	R. Corben (NSW)
1946–47	*Moorina*	J.A. Sturrock (Vic)	1973–74	*Scallywag*	Mrs J. Forbes (NSW)*
1947–48	*Leander*	R. Franklin (Vic)	1974–75	*Hush*	W. Toft (NSW)
1948–49	*Hornet*	B. Harvey (Vic)	1975–76	*Scallywag*	R. O'Connor (NSW)
1949–50	*Hornet*	B. Harvey (Vic)			
1950–51	*Hornet*	B. Harvey (Vic)	1976–77	*Scherezade*	W. Toft (NSW)
1951–52	*Tranquil*	K. Whalley (NSW)	1977–78	*Oxometry*	P. Hollis (Qld)
			1978–79	*Ingrid*	D. Forbes (NSW)
1952–53	*Hornet*	B. Harvey (Vic)	1979–80	*Impala 2*	P. O'Donnell (NSW)
1953–54	*Naiad*	R. French (Vic)			
1954–55	*Cheetah*	B. Harvey (Vic)	1980–81	*Quickstep II*	C. Bate (NSW)
1955–56	*Mercedes*	H. Kaufman (NSW)	1981–82	*Coho*	I. Ford (NSW)
			1982–83	*Woomera II*	C. Bate (NSW)
1956–57	Replaced by Games Trials		1983–84	*Impala 2*	C. Beashel (NSW)
1957–58	*Maryke*	M. Visser (NSW)	1984–85	*Twinkle*	P. Gale (Vic)
1958–59	*Tempo II*	M. Anderson (Vic)			

*Wife of 1972 Olympic gold medallist David Forbes

Catamarans

A CLASS

1967	*A. Cat*	G. Johnston (NSW)	1973	*Rhapsody*	H. Stevenson (NSW)
1968	*Ann*	J. Goodier (NSW)			
1969	*Talahessee II*	A. Wright (Vic)	1974	*Catel VII*	P. White (Vic)
1970	*Goldvita*	A. Glanville (NSW)	1975	*Rage*	B. Thomas (Vic)
1971	*Spellbound*	B. Leverton (NSW)	1976	*Rhapsody*	H. Stevenson (NSW)
1972	*Nine Lives*	B. Leverton (NSW)			

1977	*Rage*	B. Thomas (Vic)	1982*	*Good as Gold*	G. Goodall (Vic)
1978	*Beerik II*	K. Austin (Qld)		*Ramrod*	B. Hooper (Qld)
1979	*Rhapsody*	H. Stevenson (NSW)	1983	*Ramrod*	B. Hooper (Qld)
			1984	*Ramrod*	B. Hooper (Qld)
1980	*Zodiac*	B. Hooper (Qld)	1985	*Speculator*	S. Anderson (NSW)
1981	*Crusader*	K. Holmes (Qld)			

*Joint Winners.

PAPER TIGER

1971	*Tigeros*	W. Thomas (NSW)	1980	*Artful Dodger*	R. Cann (Vic)
1972	*Artful Dodger*	R. Cann (Vic)	1981	*Bobscat*	R. Ramsay (Vic)
1973	*Jumbo*	B. Litttle (NZ)	1982	*Williwarrior*	M. Williamson (Vic)
1974	*Y-For*	P. Anderson (Vic)			
1975	*Drifter*	J. Goy (Vic)	1983	*Williwarrior*	M. Williamson (Vic)
1976	*Paper Brick*	P. Anderson (Vic)			
1977	*Courageous*	M. Carey (Vic)	1984	*Characin*	G. Williams (NSW)
1978	*Paper Brick*	P. Anderson (Vic)	1985	*Characin*	G. Williams (NSW)
1979	*Hart-A-Tack*	D. Hart (Vic)			

TORNADO

1968	*Windsong*	M. Davies (NSW)	1977	*Daring*	B. Lewis (WA)
1969	*Windsong*	M. Davies (NSW)	1978	*Daring East*	B. Lewis (WA)
1970	*Windsong*	M. Davies (NSW)	1979	*Daring East*	B. Lewis (WA)
1971	*Windsong*	M. Davies (NSW)	1980	*Daring North*	B. Lewis (WA)
1972	*Windsong*	M. Davies (NSW)	1981	*Daring North*	B. Lewis (WA)
1973	*Akuna III*	J. Dachtler (WA)	1982	*Daring*	B. Lewis (WA)
1974	*Akuna III*	J. Dachtler (WA)	1983	$E = Mc^2$	C. Cairns (NSW)
1975	*Akuna III*	J. Dachtler (WA)	1984	*Daring*	B. Lewis (WA)
1976	*Daring*	B. Lewis (WA)	1985	*Daring*	B. Lewis (WA)

AUSTRALIAN OLYMPIC REPRESENTATIVES

		Class	Helmsman	Crew	Medals
1948	London (off Torbay)	Firefly	R. French		
		Star	A.S. Sturrock	L. Fenton, junr	
1952	Helsinki (Gulf of Finland)	Dragon	A.S. Sturrock	D. Buxton, B. Worcester	
		Star	B. Harvey	K. Wilson	
		Finn	P. Attrill		
1956	Melbourne (Port Phillip)	5.5 metre	A. Sturrock	D. Mytton, D. Buxton	Bronze (Buraddoo)
		Dragon	G.H. Drane	B. Carolan, J. Carolane.	
		Star	R. French	J. Downey	
		12 m Sharpie	R. Tasker	H. Scott	Silver (Falcon IV)
		Finn	C. Ryrie		
1960	Rome (Bay of (Naples)	5.5 metre	A. Sturrock	E. Wagstaff, D. Bingham	
		Dragon	H.C. Brooke	A. Cain, J. Coon	
		Star	R. French	J. Downey	
		Flying Dutchman	R. Tasker	I. Palmer	
		Finn	R. Jenyns		
1964	Tokyo (Sagami Bay)	5.5 metre	W. Northam	P. O'Donnell, R. Sargeant	Gold (Barranjoey)
		Dragon	G. Drane	J. Coon, I. Quartermain	
		Star	M. Visser	T. Owens	
		Flying Dutchman	J. Dawe	I. Winter	
		Finn	C. Ryrie		
1968	Mexico (off Acapulco)	5.5 metre	W. Solomons	S. Kaufman, J. Hardy	
		Dragon	J. Cuneo	J. Ferguson, T. Anderson	
		Flying Dutchman	C. Ryves	R. Sargeant	
		Finn	R. Jenyns		
		Star	D. Forbes	R. Williamson	
1972	Munich (off Kiel)	Dragon	J. Cuneo	T. Anderson, J. Shaw	Gold (Wyuna)
		Star	D. Forbes	J. Anderson	Gold (Simba V)
		Flying Dutchman	M. Bethwaite	T. Alexander	
		Finn	J. Bertrand		
		Soling	R. Miller	K. Berkeley, D. O'Neil	
		Tempest	G. Ingate	R. Thornton	
1976	Montreal (off Kingston, Lake Ontario)	Soling	D. Forbes	J. Anderson, D. O'Neil	
		Finn	J. Bertrand		Bronze (Pop Two)
		Flying Dutchman	M. Bethwaite	T. Alexander	
		Tempest	J. Hellner	J. Byrne	
		470	I. Brown	I. Ruff	Bronze (Hocus Pocus)
		Tornado	B. Lewis	W. Rock	
1980	Moscow (off Tallinn Gulf of Finland)	AYF withdrew yachting team			

AUSTRALIAN OLYMPIC REPRESENTATIVES

		Class	Helmsman	Crew	Medals
1984	Los Angeles (off Long Beach)	Star	C. Beashel R. Coxon		
		Soling	G. Sheard D. Gordon T. Dorning		
		Finn	C. Pratt		
		Flying Dutchman	J. Wilmot J. Cook		
		470	C. Tillett R. Lumb		
		Tornado	C. Cairns S. Anderson		Bronze $(E = Mc^2)$
		Windglider	G. Hyde		

SYDNEY TO HOBART RACE PLACE-GETTERS

(Times are in days, hours, minutes and seconds)

P1	Yacht	Owner	Elapsed Time	TCF	Corrected Time

1945 (9 starters)

1	*Rani*	Capt J. Illingworth, RN	6 – 14 – 22	.6670	4 – 09 – 38
2	*Ambermerle*	J. Colquhoun, C. Kiel	8 – 08 – 19	.6722	5 – 14 – 39
3	*Winston Churchill*	P. Coverdale	7 – 07 – 38	.7706	5 – 15 – 20

Fastest time: *Rani* 6 – 14 – 22 (timed to nearest minute)

1946 (19 starters)

1	*Christina*	J.R. Bull	6 – 18 – 51 – 15	.6625	4 – 11 – 53 – 27
2	*Saga*	B.J. Halvorsen	6 – 09 – 52 – 00	.7161	4 – 14 – 11 – 02
3	*Morna*	C. Plowman	5 – 02 – 53 – 33	.9104	4 – 15 – 52 – 53

Fastest time: *Morna* 5 – 2 – 53 – 33

1947 (28 starters)

1	*Westward*	G.D. Gibson	5 – 13 – 19 – 04	.7232	4 – 00 – 24 – 56
2	*Moonbi*	H.S. Evans	5 – 22 – 46 – 02	.6807	4 – 01 – 10 – 54
3	*Peer Gynt*	T. & M. Halvorsen	6 – 01 – 18 – 15	.6853	4 – 03 – 34 – 37

Fastest time: *Morna* 5 – 3 – 3 – 54 Dsq: *Christina, Defiance*

1948 (18 starters)

1	*Westward*	G.D. Gibson	4 – 14 – 17 – 32	.7232	3 – 07 – 45 – 48
2	*Seevogel*	W. Harris	4 – 14 – 24 – 03	.7597	3 – 11 – 52 – 17
3	*Archina*	P.G. Goldstein	4 – 11 – 28 – 10	.7900	3 – 12 – 54 – 03

Fastest time: *Morna* 4 – 5 – 1 – 21

1949 (15 starters)

1	*Trade Winds*	M.E. Davey	5 – 11 – 15 – 34	.7288	3 – 23 – 39 – 43
2	*Waltzing Matilda*	P. Davenport	5 – 10 – 33 – 10	.7406	4 – 00 – 41 – 15
3	*Ellida*	J. Halliday	6 – 05 – 26 – 10	.6603	4 – 02 – 40 – 22

Fastest time: *Waltzing Matilda* 5 – 10 – 33 – 10

1950 (16 starters)

1	*Nerida*	C.P. Haselgrove	5 – 06 – 15 – 49	.7597	3 – 20 – 17 – 13
2	*Margaret Rintoul*	A.W. Edwards	5 – 05 – 28 – 35	.7606	3 – 23 – 26 – 14
3	*Mistral V*	G.W. Rex	5 – 05 – 47 – 01	.7704	4 – 01 – 21 – 23

Fastest time: *Margaret Rintoul* 5 – 5 – 28 – 35

1951 (14 starters)

1	*Struen Marie*	T. Williamson	4 – 03 – 38 – 35	.6805	2 – 19 – 48 – 26
2	*Lahara*	D. Ashton	4 – 07 – 24 – 59	.6652	2 – 20 – 47 – 33
3	*Lass o'Luss*	J. Colquhoun	4 – 03 – 12 – 05	.7059	2 – 22 – 01 – 35

Fastest time: *Margaret Rintoul* 4 – 2 – 29 – 1

1952 (17 starters)

1	*Ingrid*	J.S. Taylor	6 – 17 – 07 – 22	.6576	4 – 09 – 56 – 18
2	*Moonbi*	H.S. Evans	6 – 17 – 10 – 23	.6654	4 – 11 – 14 – 40
3	*Nocturne*	J.R. Bull	6 – 02 – 34 – 47	.7337	4 – 11 – 32 – 44

Fastest time: *Nocturne* 6 – 2 – 34 – 47

1953 (23 starters)

1	*Ripple*	R.C. Hobson	5 – 12 – 58 – 36	.6633	3 – 16 – 12 – 12
2	*Solveig*	T. & M. Halvorsen	5 – 07 – 12 – 50	.7048	3 – 17 – 39 – 37
3	*Horizon*	S. Berg	5 – 10 – 41 – 46	.7016	3 – 19 – 41 – 47

Fastest time: *Solveig* 5 – 7 – 12 – 50 Dsq: *Wild Wave*

1954 (17 starters)

1	*Solveig*	T. & M. Halvorsen	5 – 07 – 38 – 56	.7048	3 – 17 – 58 – 01
2	*Gipsy Queen*	A.C. Eden	5 – 09 – 26 – 33	.7006	3 – 18 – 41 – 15
3	*Carol J*	J. Halliday	5 – 07 – 37 – 37	.7112	3 – 18 – 46 – 06

Fastest time: *Kurrewa IV* (formerly *Morna*) 5 – 6 – 9 – 47

SYDNEY TO HOBART RACE PLACE-GETTERS

(Times are in days, hours, minutes and seconds)

Pl	Yacht	Owner	Elapsed Time	TCF	Corrected Time
1955	**(17 starters)**				
1	*Moonbi*	H.S. Evans	5 − 01 − 28 − 24	.6697	3 − 09 − 21 − 05
2	*Cooroyba*	C. Haselgrove	5 − 00 − 14 − 52	.6782	3 − 09 − 33 − 01
3	*Janzoon*	W.R. Slade	5 − 02 − 41 − 21	.6939	3 − 13 − 08 − 02
Fastest time: *Even* 4 − 18 − 13 − 14					
1956	**(28 starters)**				
1	*Solo*	V. Meyer	4 − 05 − 03 − 33	.7927	3 − 08 − 33 − 52
2	*Anitra V*	T. & M. Halvorsen	4 − 16 − 43 − 34	.7164	3 − 08 − 45 − 25
3	*Carol J*	J. Halliday	4 − 20 − 31 − 58	.7069	3 − 10 − 22 − 37
Fastest time: *Kurrewa IV* 4 − 4 − 31 − 14					
1957	**(20 starters)**				
1	*Anitra V*	T. & M. Halvorsen	4 − 06 − 38 − 30	.7105	3 − 00 − 55 − 37
2	*Solo*	V. Meyer	3 − 20 − 19 − 16	.7973	3 − 01 − 36 − 37
3	*Catriona*	D.M. Brown	4 − 07 − 42 − 45	.7596	3 − 06 − 46 − 48
Fastest time: *Kurrewa IV* 3 − 18 − 30 − 39					
1958	**(22 starters)**				
1	*Siandra*	G.P. Newland	5 − 10 − 02 − 37	.6596	3 − 13 − 46 − 35
2	*Anitra V*	T. & M. Halvorsen	5 − 04 − 08 − 57	.7037	3 − 15 − 21 − 50
3	*Southern Myth*	N.C. Howard	5 − 04 − 00 − 06	.7250	3 − 17 − 54 − 04
Fastest time: *Solo* 5 − 2 − 32 − 52					
1959	**(30 starters)**				
1	*Cherana*	R.T. Williams	5 − 02 − 13 − 53	.6590	3 − 08 − 33 − 02
2	*Anitra V*	T. & M. Halvorsen	4 − 18 − 01 − 47	.7094	3 − 08 − 53 − 34
3	*Southerly*	D.E. Mickleborough	5 − 03 − 59 − 11	.6612	3 − 09 − 58 − 47
Fastest time: *Solo* 4 − 13 − 33 − 12					
1960	**(32 starters)**				
1	*Siandra*	G.P. Newland	5 − 00 − 59 − 03	.6596	3 − 07 − 48 − 04
2	*Kaleena*	H.E. Godden	5 − 01 − 59 − 03	.6565	3 − 08 − 04 − 57
3	*Malohi*	N.H. McEnally	5 − 01 − 58 − 04	.6609	3 − 08 − 37 − 19
Fastest time: *Kurrewa IV* 4 − 8 − 11 − 15					
1961	**(35 starters)**				
1	*Rival*	A. Burgin & N. Rundle	4 − 17 − 28 − 21	.6694	3 − 03 − 57 − 31
2	*Janzoon II*	W.R. Slade	4 − 16 − 25 − 35	.6803	3 − 04 − 29 − 01
3	*Joanne Brodie*	R.C. Hobson	5 − 00 − 05 − 39	.6501	3 − 06 − 04 − 24
Fastest time: *Astor* 4 − 4 − 42 − 11					
1962	**(42 starters)**				
1	*Solo*	V. Meyer	3 − 04 − 29 − 15	.7943	2 − 12 − 45 − 14
2	*Ondine*	S.A. Long	3 − 03 − 46 − 16	.8105	2 − 13 − 24 − 45
3	*Galatea M*	N.W. Kestel	4 − 03 − 53 − 00	.6323	2 − 15 − 09 − 22
Fastest time: *Ondine* 3 − 3 − 46 − 16					
1963	**(44 starters)**				
1	*Freya*	T. & M. Halvorsen	4 − 15 − 17 − 03	.7014	3 − 06 − 03 − 17
2	*Cavalier*	I.E. McDonnell	5 − 04 − 36 − 12	.6428	3 − 08 − 05 − 22
3	*Lorita Maria*	N.B. Rydge, junr	4 − 22 − 36 − 21	.6855	3 − 09 − 18 − 15
Fastest time: *Astor* 4 − 10 − 53 − 00					
1964	**(38 starters)**				
1	*Freya*	T. & M. Halvorsen	4 − 01 − 17 − 35	.8014	3 − 05 − 58 − 14
2	*Camille*	R. Swanson	4 − 04 − 09 − 22	.7901	3 − 07 − 08 − 00
3	*Janzoon II*	W.R. Slade	4 − 05 − 13 − 34	.7823	3 − 07 − 11 − 21
Fastest time: *Astor* 3 − 20 − 5 − 5					

SYDNEY TO HOBART RACE PLACE-GETTERS

(Times are in days, hours, minutes and seconds)

P1	Yacht	Owner	Elapsed Time	TCF	Corrected Time
1965	**(52 starters)**				
1	*Freya*	T. & M. Halvorsen	4 − 06 − 23 − 32	.8014	3 − 10 − 03 − 26
2	*Camelot*	J.G. Borrow	4 − 10 − 07 − 31	.7943	3 − 12 − 17 − 43
3	*Cadence*	H.S. Mason	4 − 20 − 37 − 32	.7372	3 − 13 − 58 − 34
Fastest time: *Stormvogel* 3 − 20 − 30 − 9					
1966	**(46 starters)**				
1	*Cadence*	H.S. Mason	5 − 13 − 25 − 24	.7403	4 − 02 − 46 − 24
2	*Salome*	R. Swanson	5 − 11 − 47 − 19	.7589	4 − 04 − 00 − 53
3	*Tamboo*	R.J. Green	5 − 12 − 16 − 22	.7566	4 − 04 − 04 − 40
Fastest time: *Fidelis* 4 − 8 − 39 − 43					
1967	**(67 starters)**				
1	*Rainbow II*	C. Bouzaid	4 − 19 − 59 − 38	.7653	3 − 16 − 39 − 15
2	*Pen-Duick III*	E. Tabarly	4 − 04 − 10 − 31	.8946	3 − 17 − 37 − 00
3	*Matika*	N. Long	4 − 22 − 04 − 33	.7722	3 − 19 − 10 − 40
Fastest time: *Pen-Duick III* 4 − 4 − 10 − 31					
1968	**(67 starters)**				
1	*Koomooloo*	D. O'Neil	4 − 10 − 26 − 52	.8046	3 − 13 − 38 − 52
2	*Boomerang VII*	J. Baker	4 − 07 − 34 − 58	.8375	3 − 14 − 45 − 02
3	*Ragamuffin*	S. Fischer	4 − 05 − 01 − 35	.8596	3 − 14 − 50 − 32
Fastest time: *Ondine II* 4 − 3 − 20 − 2					
1969	**(79 starters)**				
1	*Morning Cloud*	E. Heath	4 − 05 − 57 − 53	.7496	3 − 04 − 25 − 57
2	*Prospect of Whitby*	A. Slater	4 − 00 − 19 − 19	.8024	3 − 05 − 17 − 19
3	*Salacia II*	A. Byrne	4 − 02 − 40 − 57	.7945	3 − 06 − 24 − 11
Fastest time: *Crusade* 3 − 15 − 7 − 40					
1970	**(61 starters)**				
1	*Pacha*	R. Crichton-Brown	3 − 17 − 41 − 18	.9157	3 − 10 − 07 − 39
2	*Ragamuffin*	S. Fischer	3 − 20 − 42 − 28	.8869	3 − 10 − 13 − 20
3	*Salacia II*	A. Byrne	3 − 22 − 09 − 23	.8893	3 − 11 − 43 − 59
Fastest time: *Buccaneer* 3 − 14 − 6 − 12					
1971	**(79 starters)**				
1	*Pathfinder*	B. Wilson	4 − 00 − 02 − 04	.7835	3 − 03 − 14 − 34
2	*Runaway*	J. Lidgard	4 − 01 − 00 − 50	.7844	3 − 04 − 05 − 51
3	*Wai-aniwa*	R.H. Walker	4 − 01 − 15 − 07	.7844	3 − 04 − 17 − 03
Fastest time: *Kialoa II* 3 − 12 − 46 − 21					
1972	**(79 starters)**				
1	*American Eagle*	R. Turner	3 − 04 − 42 − 39	.9681	3 − 02 − 15 − 49
2	*Caprice of Huon*	G. Ingate	4 − 00 − 31 − 29	.7730	3 − 02 − 36 − 49
3	*Ginkgo*	G. Bogard	3 − 15 − 16 − 35	.8621	3 − 03 − 14 − 27
Fastest time: *American Eagle* 3 − 4 − 42 − 39					
1973	**(92 starters)**				
1	*Ceil III*	W. Turnbull	3 − 12 − 05 − 34	.7786	2 − 17 − 28 − 28
2	*Prospect of Whitby*	A. Slater	3 − 07 − 49 − 47	.8471	2 − 19 − 29 − 48
3	*Rampage*	P. Packer	3 − 12 − 44 − 57	.8031	2 − 20 − 03 − 43
Fastest time: *Helsal* 3 − 1 − 32 − 9 Dsq: *Alcheringa, Ruthean*					
1974	**(63 starters)**				
1	*Love and War*	P. Kurts	4 − 04 − 27 − 19	.8503	3 − 13 − 25 − 02
2	*Bumblebee III*	J. Kahlbetzer	4 − 01 − 03 − 51	.9044	3 − 15 − 47 − 05
3	*Granny Smith*	W. Anderson	5 − 06 − 47 − 59	.7016	3 − 16 − 57 − 45
Fastest time: *Ondine* 3 − 13 − 51 − 56					
1975	**(102 starters)**				
1	*Rampage*	P. Packer	3 − 04 − 43 − 03	.7968	2 − 13 − 16 − 56
2	*Fair Dinkum*	J. Robson-Scott	3 − 10 − 35 − 23	.7442	2 − 13 − 27 − 47
3	*Superstar*	K. Farfor	3 − 03 − 13 − 00	.8228	2 − 13 − 53 − 18
Fastest time: *Kialoa* 2 − 14 − 36 − 56 (Race Record)					

SYDNEY TO HOBART RACE PLACE-GETTERS

(Times are in days, hours, minutes and seconds)

Pl	Yacht	Owner	Elapsed Time	TCF	Corrected Time
1976	**(85 starters)**				
1	*Piccolo*	J. Pickles	4 − 05 − 30 − 15	.7857	3 − 07 − 45 − 07
2	*Rockie*	P. Kinston	4 − 07 − 30 − 12	.7774	3 − 07 − 27 − 49
3	*Ragamuffin*	S. Fischer	3 − 21 − 49 − 58	.8638	3 − 09 − 03 − 10

Fastest time: *Ballyhoo* 3 − 7 − 59 − 26

Pl	Yacht	Owner	Elapsed Time	TCF	Corrected Time
1977	**(131 starters)**				
1	*Kialoa*	J.B. Kilroy	3 − 10 − 14 − 09	1.0454	3 − 13 − 58 − 10
2	*Ragamuffin*	S. Fischer	4 − 06 − 29 − 42	.8596	3 − 16 − 06 − 17
3	*Windward Passage*	Fritz Johnson	3 − 12 − 39 − 00	1.0435	3 − 16 − 19 − 56

Fastest time: *Kialoa* 3 − 10 − 14 − 9 Dsq: *Cordon Bleu, Vanessa*

Pl	Yacht	Owner	Elapsed Time	TCF	Corrected Time
1978	**(97 starters)**				
1	*Love and War*	P. Kurts	4 − 04 − 45 − 43	.8358	3 − 12 − 13 − 0
2	*Margaret Rintoul II*	S.R. Edwards	4 − 03 − 34 − 39	.8499	3 − 12 − 37 − 51
3	*Constellation*	J.W. Garner	4 − 04 − 8 − 25	.8613	3 − 14 − 14 − 54

Fastest time: *Apollo* 4 − 2 − 23 − 40

Pl	Yacht	Owner	Elapsed Time	TCF	Corrected Time
1979	**(147 starters)**				
1	*Screw Loose*	R. Cumming	4 − 12 − 54 − 38	.6934	3 − 3 − 31 − 06
2	*Wheel Barrow*	I. Tringham	4 − 12 − 59 − 13	.6934	3 − 3 − 34 − 17
3	*Apalie*	Syndicate (J. Hansen, N. Cook, P. Moore, F. Chatterton)	4 − 13 − 05 − 51	.6931	3 − 3 − 36 − 55

Fastest time: *Bumblebee 4* 3 − 1 − 45 − 52

Pl	Yacht	Owner	Elapsed Time	TCF	Corrected Time
1980	**(102 starters)**				
1	*New Zealand*	NZ Round the World Committee	2 − 18 − 45 − 41	1.0369	2 − 21 − 13 − 29
2	*Gretel*	B. Lewis	3 − 02 − 03 − 55	.9380	2 − 21 − 28 − 23
3	*Challenge*	L. Abrahams	3 − 10 − 31 − 21	.8434	2 − 21 − 35 − 58

Fastest time: *New Zealand* 2 − 18 − 45 − 68

Pl	Yacht	Owner	Elapsed Time	TCF	Corrected Time
1981	**(158 starters)**				
1	*Zeus II*	J.R. Dunstan	5 − 13 − 48 − 41	.6833	3 − 19 − 25 − 59
2	*Salandra*	J.W. Escott	5 − 13 − 48 − 46	.6913	3 − 20 − 30 − 17
3	*Scallywag*	R.J. Winton	5 − 19 − 13 − 53	.6766	3 − 22 − 12 − 14

Fastest time: *Vengeance* 3 − 22 − 30 − 00

Pl	Yacht	Owner	Elapsed Time	TCF	Corrected Time
1982	**(118 starters)**				
1	*Scallywag*	R.E. Johnston	3 − 13 − 56 − 44	.7833	2 − 19 − 19 − 16
2	*Audacity*	N.W. Marr	3 − 18 − 13 − 14	.7465	2 − 19 − 20 − 59
3	*Police Car*	Sir James Hardy	3 − 11 − 14 − 52	.8147	2 − 19 − 49 − 19

Fastest time: *Condor of Bermuda* 3 − 00 − 59 − 17

Pl	Yacht	Owner	Elapsed Time	TCF	Corrected Time
1983	**(173 starters)**				
1	*Challenge*	L. Abrahams	3 − 13 − 37 − 28	.8307	2 − 23 − 07 − 42
2	*Once More Dear Friends*	P. Kurts	3 − 18 − 09 − 20	.8015	3 − 00 − 15 − 35
3	*Szechwan*	J.S. Whitty	3 − 19 − 12 − 18	.7931	3 − 00 − 20 − 05

Fastest time: *Condor* 3 − 00 − 50 − 29

Pl	Yacht	Owner	Elapsed Time	TCF	Corrected Time
1984	**(152 starters)**				
1	*Indian Pacific*	J. Eyles & G. Heuchmer	4 − 04 − 03 − 49	.7970	3 − 07 − 45 − 03
2	*Lawless*	R. Green	4 − 18 − 39 − 38	.7028	3 − 08 − 35 − 00
3	*Perie Banou*	J. Sanders	4 − 19 − 39 − 09	.7165	3 − 10 − 51 − 54

Fastest time: *New Zealand* 3 − 11 − 31 − 21

Pl	Yacht	Owner	Elapsed Time	TCF	Corrected Time
1985	**(178 starters; no first placing − see Chapter 10)**				
2	*Sagacious*	G. Appleby	4 − 00 − 19 − 23	.7950	3 − 04 − 34 − 37
3	*Hummingbird*	E. Blackadder	4 − 02 − 59 − 09	.7752	3 − 04 − 44 − 02
4	*Silver Minx*	G. Player	4 − 03 − 33 − 01	.7732	3 − 04 − 58 − 20

Fastest time: *Apollo* 3 − 4 − 32 − 28

AMPOL-AUSTRALIAN YACHTSMAN OF THE YEAR AWARD

Ampol Petroleum Limited and *Modern Boating Magazine* introduced the Ampol Yachtsman of The Year Award in 1963 after Ampol's participation with Australian Consolidated Press Ltd in the sponsorship of the 1962 Australian Challenge in *Gretel* for the America's Cup. The inaugural award in 1963 went to Jock Sturrock, who skippered *Gretel* in the America's Cup Challenge. Awards since then have been:

1964   Brian Farren-Price of Adelaide, for his world 505 title win in 1963.

1965   Bill Northam of Sydney, yachting gold medallist at 1964 Olympics.

1966   Trygve and Magnus Halvorsen, of Sydney, three times winners of the Sydney–Hobart race.

1967   Bob Miller and Craig Whitworth of Sydney, Flying Dutchman champions, noted sailmakers.

1968   John Cuneo, of Brisbane, Australian Dragon class representative at 1968 Olympics.

1969   Carl Ryves, of Sydney, outstanding performances in NSW, national titles, Olympic trials & at Olympic Games in Flying Dutchman class; and in national Soling keel boat class.

1970   David McKay, of Sydney, world champion in Moth class, subsequently successful defender of title.

1971   Syd Fischer, skipper and owner of noted ocean racer *Ragamuffin*.

1972   John Gilder, winner of the first Australian championship in 420 dinghies and of two world championships in this world renowned class.

1973   David Forbes, Olympic gold medallist, America's Cup crewman, winner of numerous Australian championships.

1974   Peter Hollis, twice world International Contender champion.

1975   Kevin McCann, chairman of the Olympic planning committee of the Australian Yachting Federation, for his outstanding efforts in obtaining unprecedented financial support and sponsorship for Australian yachtsmen to travel overseas to compete in world championships and international regattas.

1976   Tom Stephenson, of Melbourne, winner of the 1975 world Half Ton Championships in the US.

1977   John Bertrand, Olympic bronze medallist, winner of Australian championships in Finn, VJ and Lightweight Sharpie classes and tactician-helmsman of *Superstar*, an Australian representative in the 1977 Admiral's Cup ocean racing series at Cowes, England.

1978   Brian Lewis, the first catamaran sailor and the first West Australian to win the award, runner-up for the second time in the world Tornado championship and winner of the Australian Tornado championship three times in a row.

1979   Mike Fletcher, Olympic Coach from 1972 to 1979, who virtually introduced the concept of personalized coaching of yachtsmen into Australia, including the successful AYF Youthsail, where, for the first two years, he was on-the-water coach and senior lecturer.

1980   Peter O'Donnell, for an outstanding year's racing performance and a continuing record of competitive sailing: World Etchells 22 class champion; Australian champion and Olympic trials winner in Star Class.

1981   Sir James Hardy, sailed in three America's Cups.

1982   Mark Bethwaite, winner 1982 World Championship in J24 and Soling classes.

1983   Ben Lexcen, John Bertrand and Alan Bond, *Australia II*.

1984   Chris Cairns and Scott Anderson, winners of the Tornado bronze medal 1984 Olympic Games, 1983 and 1984 World Champions.

1985   Iain Murray, winner of world E22 championship held off Sydney December, 1984.

Index

This index comprises the names of people and yachts only. Yacht names are printed in *Italics*. Page numbers in **BOLD** type refer to illustrations.

421

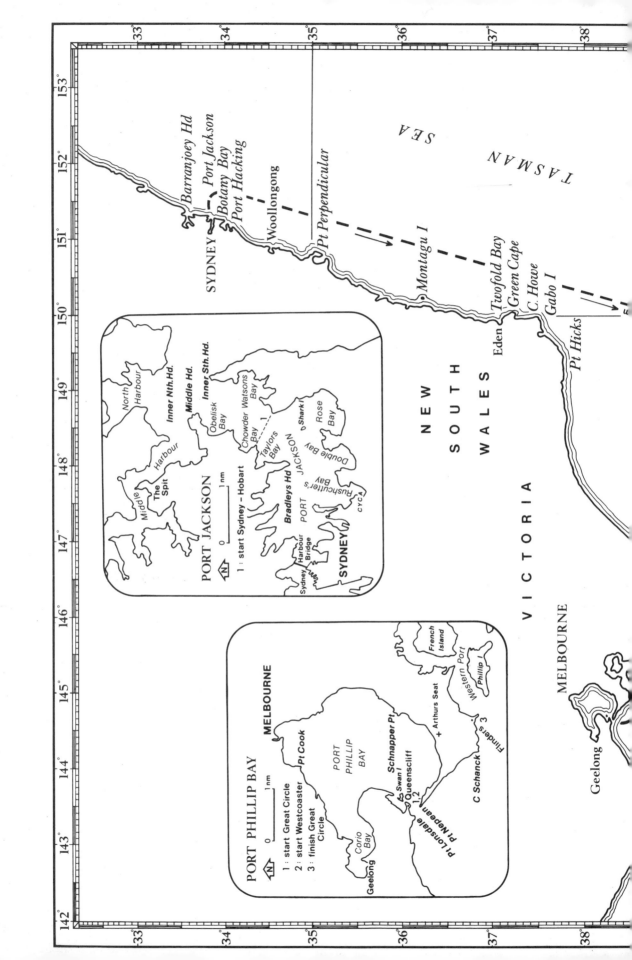